# ADVANCES
## IN
# INFANCY RESEARCH

VOLUME 7

# CONTRIBUTORS TO THIS VOLUME

Israel Abramov
Jill Y. Bargones
Jacquelyn Bertrand
Kayreen A. Burns
William J. Burns
Norman A. Constantine
James S. Gyurke
Louise Hainline
Claes von Hofsten
Kathy E. Johnson
Robert I. Kabacoff
Philip J. Kellman
Lynn Lagasse
Dana LeTendre
Lewis P. Lipsitt
Susan J. Lynch
Carolyn B. Mervis
Cynthia A. Mervis
Hanuš Papoušek
Jerry W. Rudy
David T. Scott
Linda Siegel
Donna Spiker
Benjamin R. Stephens
Lynne A. Werner

# ADVANCES IN INFANCY RESEARCH

## VOLUME 7

**Co-editors**

## Carolyn Rovee-Collier
Department of Psychology
Rutgers University
New Brunswick, New Jersey

## Lewis P. Lipsitt
Department of Psychology
and Child Study Center
Brown University
Providence, Rhode Island

ABLEX Publishing Corporation
Norwood, New Jersey 07648

ISBN: 0-89391-666-8
ISSN: 0732-9598

ABLEX Publishing Corporation
355 Chestnut Street
Norwood, New Jersey 07648

# CONTENTS

*List of Contributors* .............................................. xi
*Preface* ........................................................... xii
*Dedication* ....................................................... xv

*Experimental Studies of Appetitional Behavior in Human Newborns
and Infants* ...................................................... xix
Hanuš Papoušek

*Uses of Linear Systems Models of Infant Pattern Vision* ............. 1
Benjamin R. Stephens
   I. INTRODUCTION ........................................ 1
  II. PATTERN DETECTION AND CSF-BASED MODELS ........ 3
     A. Adult Pattern Detection .............................. 3
     B. Infant Pattern Detection ............................. 5
 III. SUPRATHRESHOLD PATTERN VISION ................... 7
     A. Apparent Contrast .................................. 7
       1. Adult apparent contrast .......................... 7
       2. Infant apparent contrast ......................... 9
     B. Contrast Discrimination ............................ 12
       1. Adult contrast discrimination ..................... 12
       2. Infant contrast discrimination .................... 14
     C. Implications for Adult Models ...................... 18
  IV. APPLICATIONS: FACE PREFERENCE
      AND SELF-PERCEPTION ............................... 27
   V. CONCLUSIONS ...................................... 33
  VI. REFERENCES ....................................... 34

*Assessing Visual Development: Is Infant Vision Good Enough* ........ 39
Louise Hainline and Israel Abramov
   I. INTRODUCTION ..................................... 40
     A. A Context for Assessing Infant Vision ................ 41
     B. The Need for Assessment of Infant Vision ............ 42
  II. DEVELOPMENT OF VISUAL STRUCTURES .............. 43
     A. Infant Retina ...................................... 44

III.  DEVELOPMENT OF SPATIAL VISION ..................... 47
      A.  Spatial Contrast Sensitivity ............................. 47
      B.  Infant Spatial CSF ..................................... 49
      C.  Spatiotemporal Interactions ............................. 54
      D.  Functional Consequences of the Infant CSF .............. 58
IV.  DEVELOPMENT OF ACCOMMODATION
      AND VERGENCE ........................................ 62
      A.  Accommodation ....................................... 62
      B.  Vergence ............................................. 63
      C.  Measures of Accommodation and Vergence .............. 64
      D.  Developmental Studies of Accommodation and Vergence .... 67
          1.  Accommodation ................................... 67
          2.  Vergence ........................................ 69
          3.  Simultaneous measures of accommodation and vergence .. 69
V.  OCULOMOTOR DEVELOPMENT ......................... 71
      A.  Measuring Infants' Eye Movements ...................... 73
          1.  Observation ...................................... 73
          2.  Electro-oculogram (EOG) .......................... 74
          3.  Corneal reflection eye trackers .................... 75
      B.  Pointing the Fovea: Saccades and Fixations ............. 78
          1.  Infants' saccades ................................ 78
          2.  Infants' fixations ................................ 82
      C.  Stabilizing Moving Images: Smooth Pursuit, Optokinetic
          Nystagmus, and the Vestibulo-ocular Reflex ............. 85
          1.  Smooth pursuit (SP) ............................. 85
          2.  Optokinetic nystagmus (OKN) and vestibulo-ocular
              reflex (VOR) .................................... 87
VI.  CLINICAL APPLICATIONS OF INFANT
      VISION RESEARCH ..................................... 91
VII.  CONCLUSION ......................................... 94
VIII.  REFERENCES ......................................... 95

*Psychoacoustic Development of Human Infants* ..................... 103
*Lynne A. Werner and Jill Y. Bargones*
      I.  INTRODUCTION ...................................... 103
          A.  Auditory Systems Development ...................... 105
          B.  Infant Psychoacoustics: Methods and Limitations .......... 106
      II.  ABSOLUTE SENSITIVITY ............................. 111
      III.  DIFFERENTIAL SENSITIVITY .......................... 123
      IV.  FREQUENCY RESOLUTION .......................... 125
      V.  TEMPORAL RESOLUTION ............................ 131
      VI.  CONCLUSIONS ...................................... 135
      VII.  REFERENCES ....................................... 137

**The World of the Moving Infant: Perception of Motion,
Stability, and Space** ............................................ 147
*Philip J. Kellman and Claes von Hofsten*
   I.  INTRODUCTION ......................................... 148
  II.  DEVELOPMENT OF SENSITIVITY
       TO OPTICAL MOTION .................................. 149
       A. Attention to Motion ................................ 149
       B. Sensitivity to Motion ............................... 149
       C. Thresholds vs. Preferences .......................... 151
 III.  INFORMATION FOR MOTION AND STABILITY
       DURING OBSERVER MOTION .......................... 152
       A. Object Motion and Observer Motion .................... 152
       B. Analyses of Optic Flow .............................. 154
          1. Rigidity vs. nonrigidity ........................... 154
          2. Specification of self-motion ........................ 155
          3. Limitations of optic flow information ................. 155
  IV.  OPTICAL CHANGE, MOTION, AND DISTANCE ........... 156
   V.  THE DEVELOPMENT OF MOTION PERCEPTION
       AND POSITION CONSTANCY DURING OBSERVER
       MOTION ............................................... 158
       A. The Kellman, Gleitman, and Spelke (1987) Experiment ..... 159
       B. The Object-Observer Motion Paradigm .................. 163
  VI.  DEVELOPMENT OF DEPTH PERCEPTION
       FROM MOTION ........................................ 177
 VII.  CONCLUSION .......................................... 181
VIII.  REFERENCES ........................................... 182


**A Symposium on the Bayley Scales of Infant Development:
Issues of Prediction and Outcome Revisited** ...................... 185


INTRODUCTION ............................................. 185
*James S. Gyurke*

ESTABLISHING THE "CEILING" ON THE BAYLEY SCALES
OF INFANT DEVELOPMENT AT 25 MONTHS ................ 187
*Dana LeTendre, Donna Spiker, David T. Scott,
and Norman A. Constantine*

ITEM AND FACTOR ANALYSES OF THE BAYLEY SCALES
OF INFANT DEVELOPMENT ................................ 199
*William J. Burns, Kayreen A. Burns, and Robert I. Kabacoff*

SPEEDED ITEMS: WHAT DO THEY TELL US ABOUT
AN INFANT'S PERFORMANCE? . . . . . . . . . . . . . . . . . . . . . . . . . . . . . 215
*James S. Gyurke, Susan J. Lynch, Lynn Lagasse,
and Lewis P. Lipsitt*

INFANT MOTOR, COGNITIVE, AND LANGUAGE BEHAVIORS
AS PREDICTORS OF ACHIEVEMENT AT SCHOOL AGE . . . . . . . . 227
*Linda S. Siegel*

DISCUSSION: THE BAYLEY SCALES OF INFANT
DEVELOPMENT: ISSUES OF PREDICTION
AND OUTCOME REVISITED . . . . . . . . . . . . . . . . . . . . . . . . . . . . 239
*Lewis P. Lipsitt*

***Development of Learning: From Elemental
to Configural Associative Networks*** . . . . . . . . . . . . . . . . . . . . . . . . 247
*Jerry W. Rudy*
  I. INTRODUCTION . . . . . . . . . . . . . . . . . . . . . . . . . . . . . . . . . . . 248
 II. SOME CONCEPTUAL AND METHODOLOGICAL ISSUES . . . 249
      A. Organism X Task Analysis . . . . . . . . . . . . . . . . . . . . . . . . . 250
      B. Dissociations . . . . . . . . . . . . . . . . . . . . . . . . . . . . . . . . . 250
III. DEVELOPMENT OF ELEMENTAL
      ASSOCIATIVE SYSTEMS . . . . . . . . . . . . . . . . . . . . . . . . . . . . 251
      A. Associative Learning . . . . . . . . . . . . . . . . . . . . . . . . . . . . 252
      B. Learning in the Neonate . . . . . . . . . . . . . . . . . . . . . . . . . 252
      C. Learning about Gustatory Stimuli . . . . . . . . . . . . . . . . . . . 253
      D. Learning about Auditory Stimuli . . . . . . . . . . . . . . . . . . . . 256
          1. Simple conditioning . . . . . . . . . . . . . . . . . . . . . . . . . 256
          2. Differential conditioning . . . . . . . . . . . . . . . . . . . . . . 259
      E. Learning about Visual Stimuli . . . . . . . . . . . . . . . . . . . . . 262
      F. A Generalization and Some Speculation . . . . . . . . . . . . . . 263
      G. Stimulus Coding Changes During Early Infancy . . . . . . . . . . 264
      H. Temporal Constraints: The Emergence of Short-Term
          Associative Memory . . . . . . . . . . . . . . . . . . . . . . . . . . . 265
 IV. ELEMENTAL ASSOCIATIVE SYSTEMS: SUMMARY . . . . . . . 267
  V. DEVELOPMENT OF THE CONFIGURAL
      ASSOCIATION SYSTEM . . . . . . . . . . . . . . . . . . . . . . . . . . . . 268
      A. Functional Properties of Elemental and Configural Systems . . 269
      B. The Hippocampal Formation and Configural Associations . . . . 271
      C. Access to the Configural System Occurs Late
          in Development . . . . . . . . . . . . . . . . . . . . . . . . . . . . . . . 272
          1. Place learning . . . . . . . . . . . . . . . . . . . . . . . . . . . . . 272
          2. Conditional delayed alternation . . . . . . . . . . . . . . . . . 275
          3. The role of context in conditioning . . . . . . . . . . . . . . . 275
      D. Summary . . . . . . . . . . . . . . . . . . . . . . . . . . . . . . . . . . . 278
      E. The Emergence of Relational Systems in Primates . . . . . . . . 280

VI.  DISCUSSION .......................................... 281
     A.  A Jacksonian Perspective ............................ 283
     B.  Conclusion ........................................ 284
VIII. REFERENCES .......................................... 284

***Studying Early Lexical Development: The Value***
***of the Systematic Diary Method*** ............................... 291
*Carolyn B. Mervis, Cynthia A. Mervis, Kathy E. Johnson,*
*and Jacquelyn Bertrand*
   I.  INTRODUCTION ...................................... 292
     A.  Value of Case Study Methodology for the Study
         of Language Development ............................ 293
     B.  Characteristics of a Systematic Diary Study
         of Early Language Development ....................... 293
  II.  GENERAL METHODOLOGY ............................ 295
     A.  Subject ............................................ 295
     B.  Procedure ......................................... 295
     C.  Data Reduction and Coding .......................... 298
 III.  THE NATURE OF EARLY WORDS ...................... 305
     A.  Introduction ....................................... 305
     B.  Method ........................................... 307
     C.  Results ............................................ 308
     D.  Discussion ........................................ 311
  IV.  ANALYSIS OF A CATEGORY: THE INITIAL EXTENSION
       AND SUBSEQUENT EVOLUTION OF *DUCK* .............. 314
     A.  Introduction ....................................... 314
     B.  Method ........................................... 318
     C.  Results ............................................ 319
     D.  Discussion ........................................ 325
   V.  PROPORTION OF OBJECT WORDS OVEREXTENDED
       DURING EARLY LEXICAL DEVELOPMENT .............. 330
     A.  Introduction ....................................... 330
     B.  Method ........................................... 331
     C.  Results ............................................ 332
     D.  Discussion ........................................ 335
  VI.  ACQUISITION OF AN ATTRIBUTE DOMAIN: COLOR ...... 336
     A.  Introduction ....................................... 336
     B.  Method ........................................... 337
     C.  Results ............................................ 339
     D.  Discussion ........................................ 344
 VII.  ACQUISITION OF THE PLURAL MORPHEME ............. 346
     A.  Introduction ....................................... 346
     B.  Method ........................................... 348
     C.  Results ............................................ 349
     D.  Discussion ........................................ 356

VIII.  GENERAL DISCUSSION  ............................... 360
       A.  The Systematic Diary Method: A Response to Previous
           Methodological Issues  ............................... 360
       B.  Unique Contributions of the Systematic Diary Study  ........ 364
       C.  Further Uses of the Diary Corpus ....................... 368
       D.  Conclusion .......................................... 269
  IX.  REFERENCES .......................................... 370
   X.  APPENDIX: TWO EXAMPLES OF DIARY
       RECORD CARDS ....................................... 375
AUTHOR INDEX  ............................................ 379
SUBJECT INDEX  ........................................... 390

# LIST OF CONTRIBUTORS

(Numbers in parentheses indicate the pages in which the author's contributions begin.)

*Israel Abramov:* Infant Study Center, Department of Psychology, Brooklyn College of the City University of New York, Brooklyn NY (39)

*Jill Y. Bargones:* Department of Speech and Hearing Sciences, Department of Otolaryngology, and Child Development and Mental Retardation Center, University of Washington, Seattle, WA (103)

*Jacquelyn Bertrand:* Department of Psychology, Emory University, Atlanta, GA (291)

*Kayreen A. Burns:* School of Psychology, Northwestern University, Evanston, IL (199)

*William J. Burns:* School of Psychology, Nova University, 3301 College Ave., Ft. Lauderdale, FL (199)

*Norman A. Constantine:* Far West Laboratory for Educational Research and Development, San Francisco, CA (187)

*James S. Gyurke:* The Psychological Corporation, 555 Academic Court, San Antonio, TX (215)

*Louis Hainline:* Infant Study Center, Department of Psychology, Brooklyn College of the City University of New York, Brooklyn, NY (39)

*Claes von Hofsten:* Department of Psychology, Umea University, Umea, Sweden (147)

*Kathy E. Johnson:* Department of Psychology, Emory University, Atlanta, GA (291)

*Robert I. Kabacoff:* School of Psychology, Nova University, 3301 College Ave., Ft. Lauderdale, FL (199)

*Philip J. Kellman:* Department of Psychology, Swarthmore College, Swarthmore, PA (147)

*Lynn Lagasse:* Child Study Center, Brown University, Providence, RI (215)

*Dana LeTendre:* Department of Psychology, Pittsburg State University, Pittsburg, KS (187)

*Lewis P. Lipsitt:* Dept. of Psychology, Brown University, Providence, RI (215)

*Susan J. Lynch:* The Psychological Corporation, 555 Academic Court, San Antonio, TX (215)

*Carolyn B. Mervis:* Department of Psychology, Emory University, Atlanta, GA (291)

*Cynthia A. Mervis:* Department of Psychology, Emory University, Atlanta, GA (291)

*Hanuš Papoušek:* Strassbergerstrasse 43, D 8000 Munich, Germany (xix)

*Jerry W. Rudy:* Department of Psychology, University of Colorado, Boulder, CO (247)

*David T. Scott:* Department of Pediatrics, Yale University School of Medicine, New Haven, CT (187)

*Linda Siegel:* Department of Special Education, The Ontario Institute for Studies of Education, 252 Bloor St.W., Toronto, Ontario, Canada (227)

*Donna Spiker:* Department of Pediatrics, Stanford University, Stanford, CA (187)

*Benjamin R. Stephens:* Department of Psychology, Clemson University, Clemson, SC (1)

*Lynne A. Werner:* Department of Speech and Hearing Sciences, Department of Otolaryngology, and Child Development and Mental Retardation Center, University of Washington, Seattle, WA (103)

# PREFACE

The current volume of *Advances in Infancy Research* is the seventh in a continuing series devoted to the timely presentation of innovative research on human and animal infants. The scholarly articles appearing here serve as primary references of authors' programmatic studies. They may be collations of data from the authors' laboratories along with a constructively critical view of related data from the research of others.

We especially invite presentations of work that deviates from conventional research approaches or that leads to conclusions that challenge or modify traditional theoretical perspectives. It is not our intent to reiterate older, established work that has previously appeared in edited volumes and is already widely cited. Rather, we seek to provide a forum for new technical and methodological developments, or new integrations that have the potential of influencing the theoretical and research perspectives of others who study infant behavior and development. Because the emergence of imaginative research programs is unpredictable, the volumes in this series have not been designed to be topical or thematic but to reflect current work that we judge to be at the forefront of infancy research.

We occasionally invite collections of papers that have been presented in symposia, or theoretical treatises or reviews. In the first instance, these presentations reflect between-laboratory rather than within-laboratory collaborations in addressing a common, significant research question. By presenting these papers side by side in a single collection, we seek to provide a comparative overview of the different theoretical perspectives and varying research approaches that often lead to research advances on a common research problem. In this way, we hope to stimulate new discussions and research on important and often controversial issues. In the second instance, we think it important from time to time to call attention to problem areas in which critical research is lacking. We seek to stimulate such research through the inclusion of scholarly treatises and critical reviews, so that progress on significant problems in those areas might be realized through future work.

Although appearance in this series is principally by invitation, uninvited manuscripts will be considered if submitted in outline form. Whether invited or submitted, all manuscripts will be critically reviewed. We hope to guide authors to prepare *Advances* papers that will edify experts in the area and, at the same time, provide an overview of a critical topic in the field for readers whose own work is peripheral to the area covered.

The Editors wish to acknowledge with gratitude the aid of their home institutions, Rutgers University and Brown University, both of which provided time and facilities toward the preparation of this volume.

We thank also the several editorial advisors whose service and perspicacity have helped maintain the high quality of contributions to which we aspire:

Richard Aslin
Bennett Bertenthal
James L. Dannemiller
Velma Dobson
Barbara A. Morrongiello
Mary Ann Romski
Norman A. Spear
Mark Stanton
Michael Tomasello
J. Edward Walsh

From the inception of this *Advances* series, each volume has been dedicated to a major contemporary researcher whose contributions and insights in the field of infant behavior and development have been of great importance and whose work has inspired the research of others. The Editors are pleased to continue this tradition in the current volume. Although each past honoree has been best known for his or her contribution to a particular area, it is also true—and singularly appropriate for a multifaceted series such as *Advances in Infancy Research*—that each has influenced research across a broad front of diverse and important problem areas. This is also true of Hanuš Papoušek, whose seminal research in the field of infant behavior and development, especially learning processes and the nature of early communication between infants and adults, has earned the resounding applause of his peers. We are pleased to join in this tribute by dedicating the present volume to him.

*Carolyn Rovee-Collier*, Rutgers University
*Lewis P. Lipsitt*, Brown University

**Hanuš Papoušek**

# DEDICATION

We respectfully and enthusiastically dedicate this work, the seventh volume of the *Advances in Infancy Research* series, to our brilliant colleague and friend, Dr. Hanuš Papoušek.

A pediatrician and psychologist, Hanuš Papoušek first distinguished himself through his innovative studies of learning processes in very young infants. Later, he was able to show, in collaboration with Mechthild Papoušek, his wife, that the posture and seemingly meaningless vocalizations of the infant constitute a language of their own, and are important determinants of the reciprocities that characterize the mother–infant relationship. Recently, after they detected patterns of parenting behavior of which the parents themselves were unaware in didactic supportive interventions, the Papoušeks turned their attention to new aspects of integrative and communicative competencies of infants.

Hanuš Papoušek was born September 9, 1922, in Letovice, Czechoslovakia. He earned his medical degree at Purkinje (formerly Masaryk) University in Brno, Czechoslovakia (the birthplace of Gregor Mendel's modern genetics) one day before his 27th birthday. He then did four years of postdoctoral training in pediatrics at Charles University in Prague, and in the Research Institute for Mother and Child Care, where in 1953 he began his investigations of the early development of human behavior.

At the Research Institute for Mother and Child Care, Hanuš founded and led a research lying-in unit for healthy babies and their mothers, a unique facility allowing an interdisciplinary team of pediatricians, psychologists, and biologists to conduct integrated observations on behavioral development and immunological resistance during the first six to eight months of life.

Eventually Dr. Papoušek was to be a Candidate of Sciences, in Developmental Neurophysiology, at Charles University, where he carried out a dissertation on conditioned alimentary motor reflexes in infants. About 10 years later, in 1969, he received the prestigious Doctor of Sciences degree for his studies of the development of learning abilities in the first months of human life. He was acclaimed almost immediately following these achievements, particularly by North American experimental child psychologists and other developmental scientists, as the exceptionally capable young man from Czechoslovakia who showed that newborns are far more capable of assimilating information and transferring that training to later performances than had been previously imagined possible. His procedures with babies constituted a *tour de force* in methodology, essentially combining aspects of classical conditioning procedures with operant learning techniques.

Papoušek was associated with the Research Institute for Mother and Child Care in Prague for almost 20 years, 1951–1970, and became Scientific Education Advisor from 1965 to 1970 to the Czechoslovak Academy of Sciences. During this period, he was a Visiting Professor of Developmental Psychology at the University of Denver. From 1968–72 he held various positions at Harvard University, in the Center for Cognitive Studies, the Department of Psychology and Social Relations, and the Medical Center of Children's Hospital.

Dr. Papoušek began a long and productive association with the Max Planck Institute for Psychiatry in Munich, where he did his work in developmental psychobiology from 1969 to 1988. During that period, in 1975, he began an appointment which continues today as Professor of Developmental Psychobiology at the Ludwig-Maximilian University in Munich.

Other appointments which Hanuš Papoušek has held include a year as Visiting Senior Scientist in the Laboratory of Comparative Ethology of the National (U.S.) Institute of Child Health and Human Development, and at the Free University of Amsterdam, in The Netherlands, as Special Professor of Developmental Psychology.

Prof. Papoušek has served on numerous committees and participated in many symposia in the United States and abroad, for the Social Sciences Research Council, the World Health Organization, the Wenner-Gren Foundation, the Center for Advanced Studies in the Developmental Sciences in London, the National (U.S.) Institute of Child Health and Human Development, the Committee for Interdisciplinary Cooperation in European Developmental Sciences, and the Center for Interdisciplinary Research of the University of Bielefeld, Germany. He is a member of many learned and professional societies, has received numerous awards, and has been feted by professional and research associations, including the International Society for Infancy Studies. He serves very constructively on numerous editorial boards.

While the article we reprint here is one of Hanuš Papoušek's proudest achievements, for it is a classic in the study of babies' learning and cognitive abilities, he can be as well cited for his studies of self-awareness in young children, and his studies of children in naturalistic situations, particularly of infant–adult interactions and infant play, much of this conjointly with Mechthild Papousek, a psychiatrist and human-development researcher in her own right.

The article which we reproduce at the front of this volume is one of Hanuš Papoušek's earliest major integrative publications. The date of its publication is indicative of the pioneering and inventive quality manifested throughout his career. We honor world-class scientist Hanuš Papoušek, M.D., Sc.D., for his life-long devotion to the study of human development, and for his steadfast insistence that along with methodological stringency must go an overarching dedication to the goal of putting science to work in the service of the world's children.

# TEMPORA MUTANTUR, BABIES AS WELL?

*What a feeling to re-edit a chapter that you wrote a quarter-a-century ago! It is not so much a nostalgic feeling, although it might well be; Jarmila Melicharová, an outstanding nurse and research assistant, and Oldrich Janos and Jaroslav Koch, senior psychologists who facilitated my engagement, as a pediatrician in psychological research, all died years ago. The babywatcher's subjects have finished their own studies and reached adult ages. Nevertheless, these are the author's personal aspects that cannot really be meaningful to anybody else. It is the general history of infancy research of which the reprinted chapter reminds me, and which I find overwhelming.*

*The chapter was a side-product of the Russian sputnik. That little peeper made Western scientists interested in what Eastern scientists were doing, and infancy researchers were among the first to look for chances of cooperation. There were not many such researchers at that time; 25 met in 1962 and founded a Club of Correspondence on Infancy Research, the core of the later International Society for Infancy Studies. The reprinted chapter was a part of proceedings of conferences in Madison, 1963, and in Stillwater, 1965, where the Club found the first chances to meet. Edited books still enjoyed a high reputation; authors were sponsored for both conferences in order to discuss contributions and have enough time to prepare manuscripts. Already those conferences gave infancy research its attractive features: interdisciplinary cooperation and tolerance.*

*Contacts across the Iron Curtain were difficult, risky, and supervised from both sides. To me, who had to match the number of publications in the West with that in the East (where chances for publishing were minimal), it was necessary to squeeze as much data as possible into one Western publication—more than any title could subsume. The title of my chapter introduces conditioning, but the conditioning study was only one aspect of modeling the development of movements, including neonatal intentionality ("purposeful movements," in contemporary terms), emotionality, and their ability for cross-modal integration (proprioceptive, auditory, and gustatory inputs as involved in the designs). Not included are preliminary data on memory that allowed us to tolerate interruptions in conditioning for up to 5 days without serious losses in infants' learned responses. One set of data have remained uniquely relevant although insufficiently discussed; they made it evident that with age, the rate of learning increases not only due to maturation, but also due to the amount of experience in learning.*

*Recording techniques—the combination of polygraphic records with protocols—may elicit smiles. Modern audiovisual recording, online computers, word-*

*processors, or electronic referencing systems were not yet available. Our typists had to make enough copies for 25 members of the Correspondence Club without photocopying machines. From this point of view, the selected chapter is as old-fashioned as possible.*

*Ten years later, I and my wife Mechthild found that young infants were capable of processing TV pictures, and we designed sophisticated methodology for self-perception studies, became interested in preverbal vocalizations and analyzed musical elements in them with computer-aided spectrographic techniques, introduced microanalyses of nonconscious behavioral patterns in parent–infant interactions or naturalistic learning situations, and became aware of new potential for the application of nonlinear mathematics. Nevertheless, my old data have lived with us, witnessed the progress, including the disappearance of the Iron Curtain, and have never stopped helping and motivating. And I have not stopped using them in my lectures. It may have been the number of direct observations of infants and the necessity to live with them in the residential research unit in Prague that has outweighed the significance of modern equipment in my emotional relation to the present chapter. By any means, I am very grateful to Carolyn Rovee-Collier and Lew Lipsitt for having selected it to be reproduced in my honor.*

Hanuš Papoušek
Munich, F. R. Germany
August 14, 1991

Reprinted with permission from *Early Behavior: Comparative and Developmental Approaches* (Chapter 10), edited by Harold W. Stevenson, Eckhard H. Hess, & Harriet L. Rheingold, 1967, New York: John Wiley & Sons.

# EXPERIMENTAL STUDIES OF APPETITIONAL BEHAVIOR IN HUMAN NEWBORNS AND INFANTS*

*Hanuš Papoušek*

INSTITUTE FOR CARE OF MOTHER AND CHILD
PRAGUE, CZECHOSLOVAKIA

Probably every parent has a similar experience when seeing his newborn baby's behavior for the first time: The monotonous crying that is the only vocal manifestation and the diffuse mass activity that is often elicited by inadequate stimuli are so strikingly different from the behavior of adults that they seem to be completely incomprehensible. Yet most parents are soon able to find clues for understanding the basic meaning of the neonate's behavior and to learn to detect even the very early manifestations of developing integrated patterns of voluntary activity.

The author of this report sought to find a pattern of behavior that under experimental control might be used to study the learning abilities of newborns, and that would represent a model for the analysis of the development of intentional behavior. The motor components of appetitional behavior seemed particularly advantageous for this purpose because the need for food is a factor that is both effective and controllable. Inborn responses associated with feeding have therefore been repeatedly applied in studies of such basic learning processes as conditioning or conditioned discrimination.

Conditioning methods were first used for the systematic study of higher nervous functions in immature human subjects soon after Pavlov's basic experiments in dogs (Krasnogorskii, 1907). But until the last two decades the studies of infants dealt more often with the problems of the onset of conditioning or with the capacity for sensory perception than with the development of learning processes. Recent surveys by Rheingold and Stanley (1963) and by Lipsitt

---

* The author wishes to thank his research assistants Jarmila Melicharová and Svatava Sýkorová, as well as the staff of the research unit, for their devoted and skillful assistance in both nursing care and research investigation. Thanks are due also to our statistical consultant Dr. J. Vandráček, Institute of Mathematics, Czechoslavak Academy of Sciences, Prague, for his suggestions.

(1963) have called attention to the fact that most studies of learning in infants have merely described the occurrence of the phenomenon; and the authors suggest that there is a need for additional studies of the processes underlying infant learning.

In the comparative physiology of infrahuman infants, attempts to analyze the development of the conditioning process have already appeared. Comparative data recently summarized by Sedláček (1963) indicated that the form and adaptive significance of temporary connections depended on the development of the CNS in individual species, and that the three main types of connections—the summation reflex (Wedenskii in 1881), the dominant center reflex (Ukhtomskii in 1911), and Pavlov's conditioned reflex—can be considered different evolutionary degrees of the same general process of synthesis in the CNS. Orbeli (1949) explained the ontogenetic development of central nervous functions by means of a similar evolutionary view. He hypothesized a genetic relation between inherited, unconditioned responses and acquired, conditioned responses, with an intermediate continuum of various transitory forms. Sedláček (1962; 1964) made a serious attempt to prove this hypothesis through studies of prenatal conditioning in relatively mature newborns, such as chickens and guinea pigs.

In man, prenatal conditioning has been studied either directly in the human fetus during pregnancy (Ray, 1932; Sontag & Wallace, 1934; Spelt, 1938; 1948), or in premature infants (Kasatkin, 1951; Irzhanskaia & Felberbaum, 1954). These studies have shown evidence of conditioned responses before the expected date of birth, but were not concerned with the mechanisms of temporary connections or with their development.

The lack of information about the earliest development of higher nervous functions in human infants stimulated the team to which the present author belongs to undertake a developmental study of individual differences in conditioning abilities. Unlike similar studies in the Pavlovian literature on typological differences in children (Ivanov-Smolenskii, 1953; Krasnogorskii, 1958) and infants (Volokhov, 1959), individual differences were defined by us in a much broader sense than the limits imposed by typological parameters. In order to maximize the generalizability of our conclusions, the same infants were exposed to several different conditioning methods—aversive, appetitional, and orientational—and to the analysis of sleep and waking, emotional and social behaviors, and EEG patterns.

Here we shall be concerned mainly with the data on learned appetitional responses and with the models for complex patterns of intentional behavior. Although the classical conditioning method of salivary response has been used with children, it is not appropriate for infants (Krasnogorskii, 1958). Therefore the analysis of conditioned sucking movements that was recommended by Bekhterev and Stshelovanov (1925) has been preferred by most authors. The first natural conditioned sucking was reported during the third week of life by Denisova and Figurin (1929), and Ripin and Hetzer (1930). The conditioning of sucking in infants to acoustic stimuli during the second or third month and to visual stimuli during the third or fourth month was reported by Kasatkin and Levikova (1935). Conditioned discrimination with vestibular stimulation was first reported by Nemanova (1935) in her study of infants 2 to 4 months old. Marquis (1931) reported much earlier conditionability; in 8 of 10 newborns she obtained conditioned oral responses to a buzzer at the age of 4 or 5 days, but her study lacked necessary controls for pseudoconditioning. On the other hand, Wenger (1936) could not establish conditioned responses before the tenth day of age with either appetitional or aversive techniques.

The problems of early conditioning continued to engage the attention of later investigators who used newer techniques and larger samples of infants (Kasatkin, 1964). Lipsitt and Kaye (1964) confirmed appetitional conditionability in 3- to 4-day-old newborns. Sucking movements were also used for testing the influence of hunger on conditioning (Kantrow, 1937), for detecting neonatal brain injuries (Dashkovskaia, 1953), and for studying premature infants (Polikanina, 1955; Polikanina & Probatova, 1957).

Until recent years, methods using other motor components of appetitional behavior were not employed adequately; Irwin (1930) discussed general motor activity, and Kriuchkova and Ostrovskaia mentioned head-turning (1957).

For the purposes of our studies, the sucking method appeared inconvenient, particularly because of the regressive changes in sucking movements that are in contrast to the progressive development of higher nervous functions (Papoušek, 1960). With increasing age, anticipatory sucking movements gradually disappear, perhaps because they are nonfunctional or nonadaptive.

Head-turning, therefore, was chosen by the author as another conditionable motor component of infantile appetitional behavior. As an inborn response, head-turning has been studied by many neurophysiologists since the first observations published by Darwin (1886) and Preyer (1895). According to Minkowski (1928), head movements appear in the human fetus by the third postconceptional month and are fully functional at birth. They can be elicited by various stimuli and during periods of hunger, occur without any discernible stimulation (Prechtl, 1953). According to Babkin (1953), an inborn rooting reflex, probably coordinated in the diencephalon, should be differentiated from the purposive movements that develop gradually, probably under cortical control, into various learned behavioral patterns such as orientational, aversive, or appetitional movements.

Natural conditioning of head movements to a visual (bottle) stimulus by the first month of life was described by Peiper (1958). After satiation, both conditioned and unconditioned food-seeking activity was suppressed.

For several reasons, head-turning seemed advantageous for conditioning studies. The movement matures earlier than do movements of the extremities, and its intensity and latency can be more easily quantified. It can be used with different kinds of reinforcement: appetitional or aversive, incidental or intentional. Thus it is suitable for molding a simple inborn reflex movement into a complex purposive or voluntary response. Finally, because head-turning involves bilateral response, and differential reinforcement can be applied for responses to the left or right, it can be used for the simultaneous study of two symmetrical responses in a single subject.

A method was devised for appetitional conditioning with milk reinforcement (Papoušek, 1959, 1961a, 1961b). For orientation conditioning with visual reinforcement the method was modified by another member of our team (Koch, 1962) and, within an operant framework, has been successfully explored by Siqueland (1964) and Siqueland and Lipsitt (1966).

# METHOD

## Subjects

For our investigations infants up to 6 months of age were reared in a special unit under relatively standard conditions. As far as possible, we tried to keep their life conditions comparable, at the same time meeting the demands of individual infants. Between 1956 and 1965, more than 130 infants were observed. They were healthy, full term, and without any evidence of pathology in the mothers' pregnancies or deliveries. The infants were cared for by their mothers and by specially trained nurses who could substitute for the mothers if necessary. Our team included a pediatrician who watched over the infants' health, nutrition, and somatic development, and a psychologist who was concerned with their mental development and educational care. If an occasional break in experimentation exceeded five days, the procedure being investigated during the period was eliminated from consideration.

The infants were also used by other members of the team for other experimental conditioning studies, such as conditioned eye-blinking (Janoš, 1965) and orientational head-turning (Koch, 1962).

## Stimuli and Apparatus

The sounds of an electric bell ($CS_1$) or a buzzer ($CS_2$) were the conditioning stimuli. The unconditioned reinforcement (UCS) was milk presented from one side or the other through a rubber nipple connected to a thermos bottle.

Electronic equipment enabled the experimenter to program the kind and duration of both conditioning and reinforcing stimuli and to operate them and the timing mechanisms by a single button, thus freeing the experimenter to make detailed observations of the infant's behavior.

A seven-channel polygraph recorded the presentation of the stimuli and the infant's head-turning, breathing, and general motor activity. On a protocol, the experimenter recorded, by means of codes, intensity and latency of head-turning, changes in general behavior, and vocal, facial, and oral responses.

The infant lay in a stabilimeter crib, partially immobilized, in order to eliminate any disturbing activity of his upper extremities (Fig. 10–1). An elastic pad oscillated with the infant's movements; the oscillation was transmitted to the polygraph through a pneumatic system. This system also included a special calibrator allowing actograms of infants of different body weights to be compared. Breathing movements were recorded by means of a pneumatic pick-up.

The infant's head was placed in a plastic head cradle lined with plastic foam. The cradle's rotations on a horizontal axis changed the potential in a two-potentiometer circuit, and these changes were recorded as deflections from the baseline on the polygraph (Fig. 10–2). The attachment of the head cradle to the axis could be shifted vertically to balance the cradle and eliminate the influence of head weight, enabling even a newborn to turn his head or keep it in a central position without difficulty.

Thus information was gathered not only on the specific response—head-turning—but also on concomitant changes in general activity (decrease or increase in general motor activity), vocalization, facial responses, eye movements, and breathing. Records of such changes were essential for estimating the general state of wakefulness during the experiment and the inhibitory or excitatory effects of the experimental stimuli.

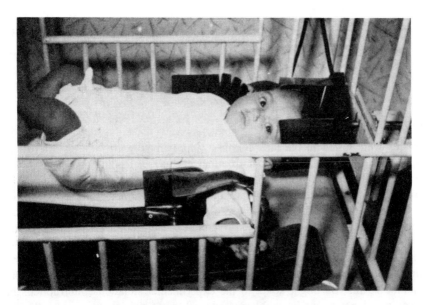

*Fig. 10–1. The stabilimeter crib.*

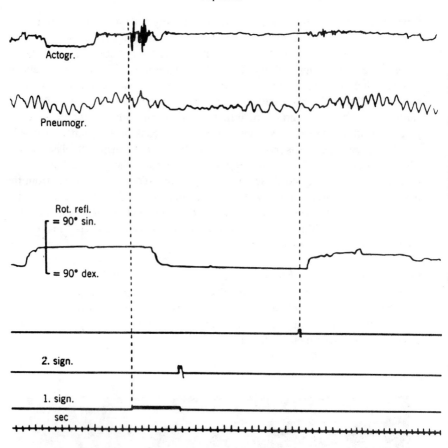

*Fig. 10–2.  Polygraph recordings from an experimental session.*

## Procedure and Measures

Infants were tested in the late morning, approximately 10 minutes after their regular sleep in the fresh air. The routine schedule of feeding and sleep in the sequence of sleep, feeding, and waking enabled us to examine the subjects in comparable states of hunger and wakefulness.

First, a baseline measure of head-turning prior to experimental stimulation was recorded. Then, all Ss received five pre-experimental trials of $CS_1$ and $CS_2$ without reinforcement. The source of the stimuli was in the midline behind the infant's head so that the sounds by themselves did not elicit head-turning. The first presentation of milk occurred prior to the conditioning trials and from the midline so that Ss might adapt to the experimental situation. Interruptions in feeding did not result in problems, particularly if the interruptions followed spontaneous breaks in the infant's sucking.

The development of the conditioned reflex to the bell (CR) was then initiated with the milk (UCS) being presented from the left side. The UCS was presented by the assistant, who sat screened behind S's head. If S responded to the bell and turned to the left, milk was offered to him immediately. The bell continued ringing until S started sucking the milk. If S did not respond to the presentation of the CS within 10 seconds, the assistant (nurse) tried eliciting the head turn by tactile stimulation, touching the left corner of his mouth with the nipple. If this stimulation was ineffective, she turned his head to the left and placed the nipple in his mouth. At the end of reinforcement the nurse turned his head back to the middle, leading it with the nipple, and then took the nipple from his mouth.

Ten such trials occurred during one session, which covered one normal feeding period of 10 to 15 minutes. The intertrial interval was one minute, on the average, but was intentionally changed to avoid temporal conditioning. A head turn of 30° or more from the central position was considered a positive response. The criterion of conditioning was five consecutive positive responses in the 10 trials of one daily session.

There was, therefore, considerable biological significance to head-turning under this procedure. The hungry infant had to rotate his head to obtain milk, and the sooner he did so, the sooner he was fed. Under these conditions, the gradual shortening of the latency of response could be considered a parameter of the process of conditioning.

Extinction was the next procedure. $CS_1$ was presented without the UCS for 10 seconds; as in the conditioning procedure, 10 trials were given in one session. After the criterion of five consecutive negative responses was reached, reconditioning took place. The process was the same as the first conditioning procedure.

Next the Ss were trained to discriminate between the two stimuli; $CS_1$ (bell) was reinforced from the left and $CS_2$ (buzzer), from the right. In any one session, five $CS_1$ and five $CS_2$ were presented in random order. Six consecutive correct responses (three bell and three buzzer CR's in random order) represented the criterion of learning for this phase of the procedure. After reaching criterion, the signals were reversed: $CS_1$ was reinforced from the right, $CS_2$ from the left. The criterion for concluding this portion of the procedure was analogous to that employed in the trials for the first discrimination.

In addition to these basic procedures, other experiments were designed for the analysis of stimulus influence and for the shaping of more complex forms of learned behavior, such as the conditioned emotional behavior or the development of intentional behavior. These experiments are discussed later.

## STUDIES OF BASIC LEARNING ABILITIES

The data given first demonstrate the early development of learning abilities in infants, their age peculiarities, and the individual differences among them. These data were gathered from the basic six conditioning procedures that were studied with three independent groups of *S*s: newborns (A), 3-month-old infants (B), and 5-month-old infants (C). The variability of initial age within each group was reduced to a minimum. The results for the 44 infants in the three groups are summarized in Table 10–1. In this table are presented the means and standard deviations for initial age, rapidity of learning as measured by the number of trials necessary to achieve criterion, and latency of CRs.

In addition to the analysis of these data, attention was also paid to the appearance of typical phases in the course of learning and to the various concomitant patterns of behavior. In these observations the group of newborns deserves more attention, particularly in comparison with group B, because a marked qualitative change in the development of higher nervous functions occurs during the first three months of life (Janoš, Papoušek, & Dittrichová, 1963).

TABLE 10.1.

Means and Standard Deviations of Responses of Three Groups of Infants
to the Six Basic Conditioning Procedures

| Groups of infants | N | Initial age in days | | Trials to criterion | | Latency in seconds | | | |
|---|---|---|---|---|---|---|---|---|---|
| | | | | | | CR 1 | | CR 2 | |
| | | Mean | S.D. | Mean | S.D. | Mean | S.D. | Mean | S.D. |
| Conditioning: | | | | | | | | | |
| A | 14 | 3.42 | 1.01 | 177.14 | 93.40 | 4.95 | 0.74 | | |
| B | 14 | 85.78 | 1.76 | 42.28 | 18.38 | 3.92 | 1.08 | | |
| C | 16 | 142.50 | 2.63 | 27.75 | 13.70 | 3.55 | 1.29 | | |
| Extinction: | | | | | | | | | |
| A | 12 | 31.83 | 13.89 | 26.83 | 12.90 | 5.49 | 1.01 | | |
| B | 14 | 94.14 | 4.58 | 25.07 | 10.39 | 3.70 | 0.94 | | |
| C | 16 | 149.06 | 4.07 | 27.31 | 15.29 | 3.25 | 0.99 | | |
| Reconditioning: | | | | | | | | | |
| A | 12 | 37.25 | 13.34 | 42.83 | 29.88 | 4.90 | 0.93 | | |
| B | 14 | 100.35 | 1.45 | 31.64 | 19.84 | 2.73 | 0.65 | | |
| C | 16 | 153.93 | 3.43 | 22.37 | 11.88 | 3.28 | 0.85 | | |
| Discrimination: | | | | | | | | | |
| A | 11 | 43.90 | 15.68 | 223.54 | 99.23 | 4.00 | 0.58 | 3.90 | 0.63 |
| B | 13 | 105.92 | 6.48 | 176.23 | 82.52 | 2.62 | 0.66 | 3.03 | 0.71 |
| C | 14 | 159.92 | 5.46 | 68.14 | 28.72 | 2.10 | 0.77 | 2.66 | 0.87 |
| Reversal 1: | | | | | | | | | |
| A | 11 | 76.36 | 18.68 | 195.18 | 86.85 | 3.43 | 0.65 | 3.47 | 0.81 |
| B | 12 | 135.58 | 11.57 | 120.00 | 66.01 | 2.58 | 0.66 | 2.48 | 0.60 |
| C | 10 | 170.00 | 4.81 | 79.40 | 79.83 | 2.83 | 1.01 | 2.56 | 0.83 |
| Reversal 2: | | | | | | | | | |
| A | 11 | 107.54 | 23.81 | 94.63 | 35.51 | 3.29 | 0.91 | 2.91 | 0.74 |
| B | 12 | 155.41 | 19.08 | 82.41 | 37.74 | 2.34 | 0.91 | 2.15 | 0.74 |
| C | 10 | 182.80 | 13.50 | 77.60 | 63.60 | 2.29 | 0.97 | 2.72 | 0.97 |

A = newborns
B = 3-month infants
C = 5-month infants

## Conditioning in Newborns

In newborns we had a rare opportunity to study experimental motor learning before spontaneous natural learning substantially interfered. Slow conditioning permitted an easier analysis of its phases that in older infants often passed too quickly and could be interpreted as accidental deviations.

In newborns the baseline before conditioning usually showed no head movements. Even tactile stimulation with the nipple elicited head-turning only in three of the 14 newborns on the first reinforcement, whereas three to 22 trials were necessary for the remaining 11 $Ss$ (mean = 6.57). In group B the tactile stimulation itself elicited head-turning more quickly, usually after one or two trials (mean = 1.23). This difference was highly significant ($p < 0.001$).[1]

The rate of conditioning, as shown in Table 10–1, was very slow in newborns. On the average, 32.21 trials preceded the first conditioned head turn in group A, whereas only 9.43 trials were necessary in group B. Such a significant decrease ($p < 0.001$) indicates a rapid development of condition-ability during the first three months of life. A similar decrease of the mean number of trials to criterion also supported this conclusion; the difference between groups A and B was highly significant ($p < 0.001$), whereas the difference between groups B and C was significant at the .05 level. The mean number of 177 trials for group A represented approximately three weeks of conditioning, and shows that during the 28 days of the neonatal period most newborns can achieve even a relatively severe criterion of conditioning. But wide individual differences in the newborns were apparent; the fastest condi-tioners needed only 7, 10, 11, or 12 days, the slowest ones, more than a month.

The latency of the CR is here considered in the behavioral sense, rather than in the physiological. Latency was defined as the interval between the onset of CS and a head turn of 30° or more. It depended, therefore, not only on the interval preceding the onset of CR, but also on the rate at which the head was turned. An analysis of variance showed significant age differences for the three groups ($p < 0.005$), indicating that newborns carry out the CRs more slowly than older infants. For newborns, there was also a significant correlation during condition-ing between latency and speed of conditioning, indicating longer reaction times in slower conditioners ($r = 0.68$, $p < 0.01$).

Several different stages could be distinguished during the course of condi-tioning. To a certain degree they were comparable to the four stages of condi-tioned sucking described by Kasatkin (1948); indifference to the CS, inhibition of general activity, unstable CR, and, finally, a stable CR.

---

[1] The following statistical procedures were employed, depending on the particular data being analyzed: the Mann-Whitney $U$ test; the Kruskal-Wallis one-way analysis of variance for $k$-sample cases; for large samples, the Snedecor $F$ test with logarithmic transformation of scores and, if necessary, with Scheffé's (1959) method of multiple comparison; and Spearman rank-order correla-tion coefficients.

During the first phase the CS usually elicited nonspecific orientational behavior (wider opening of the eyes, inhibition of other activities, changes in breathing) that was quickly extinguished. After a period of indifference to the CS, this phase was succeeded by one during which partial responses and later the first CRs were manifested. In newborns this phase was relatively long and had several features that should be noted. Its main features were gradual coordination of individual components of CR, such as head-turning and unilateral mouthing or eye turning (Fig. 10–3), increased general motor activity, and concomitant vocal and facial responses that are generally accepted as signs of distress (Fig. 10–4). Before a good coordination developed, the newborn could be seen to be upset, fussing, and grimacing, turning his eyes and contracting his mouth to the left, but not yet turning his head. Marked signs of such an insufficient coordination were present in 50% of the Ss in group A, but only in .7% of the Ss in group B.

The next phase was that of unstable conditioning. The frequency of correct responses increased, but the responses were isolated or appeared in small groups with fluctuating intensity and latency. Insufficient coordination was still evident in two characteristic features: (a) a generalized form of CR (the S responds with the whole body), and (b) an increased frequency of unilateral or bilateral intertrial head turning. The first feature, considered a sign of increased irradiation of central nervous processes in immature organisms, was more frequent in group A. The second feature, indicating central dominance, usually appeared only in the unilateral form in group A and was less frequent (50%) than in group B (71%).

The gradual consolidation of the CR, that is, the increasing ability to carry out more CRs consecutively, also appears to be a function of age. The analysis of the first 10 CRs (Table 10–2) showed that in group A, 60.7% of the responses were isolated, whereas in group C, 60.6% appeared consecutively in groups of three or more. It is evident that the main development of this ability again occurs during the first three months of life.

Three main types of cumulative curves appeared to characterize the course of conditioning in the infants: (a) relatively constant increase of percentage in CRs, (b) increase of percentage with several gross waves, and (c) increase of percentage after a retarded onset. The second type may indicate a functional lability of the CNS, typical of immature organisms, and the third, a phasic maturation of the CNS (Janoš, 1965). It can be seen in Table 10–3 that the relative frequency of the three types differed in the three age groups, and that the last two types were more characteristic of the newborns.

The final phase is that of stable conditioning. The frequency of CRs approaches 100%, and the CRs are stronger, faster, well coordinated, and carried out economically with shorter and more regular latencies. They were no longer accompanied by emotional signs of distress; on the contrary, the older infants often showed vocal or facial patterns of pleasure (Fig. 10–5). In this phase the Ss

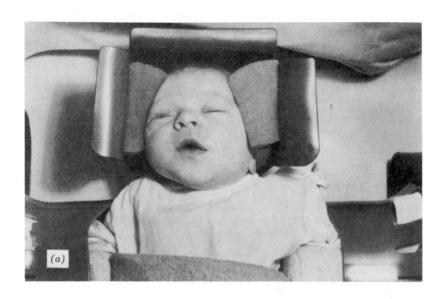

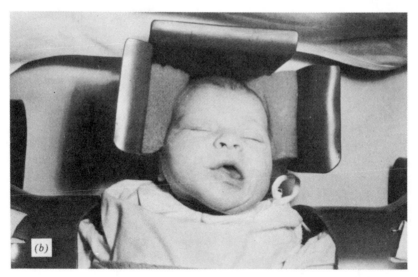

*Fig. 10–3.  Head-turning and unilateral mouthing.*

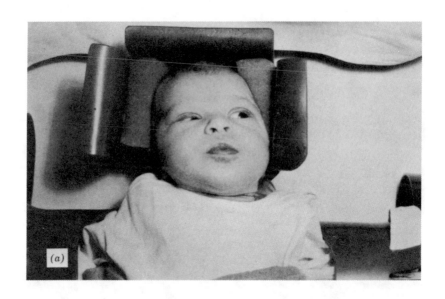

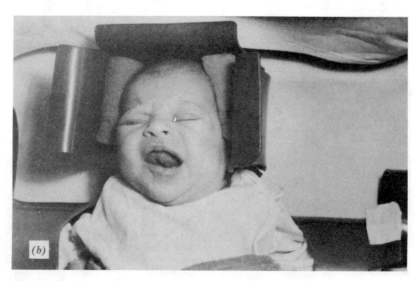

Fig. 10–4. *Facial signs of distress.*

TABLE 10.2.

Grouping of Conditioned Responses of Three Groups of Infants, in Percentages

| Group of infants | N | Isolated | The first 10 positive conditioned responses | |
| | | | In groups | |
| | | | 2 | 3 or more |
| --- | --- | --- | --- | --- |
| | | % | % | % |
| A | 14 | 60.7 | 32.9 | 6.4 |
| B | 14 | 34.9 | 17.2 | 47.9 |
| C | 16 | 18.7 | 20.6 | 60.6 |
| | | A:B $p < 0.001$ | A:B $p < 0.01$ | A:B $p < 0.001$ |
| | | B:C $p < 0.025$ | B:C $p > 0.05$ | B:C $p > 0.05$ |

A = newborns
B = 3-month infants
C = 5-month infants

reached the criterion of 5 successive correct CRs and, at the same time, the average number of CRs in three successive days usually exceeded 50%.

Even in this phase, the stability of conditioning was only relative, particularly in the younger groups in which a sudden decrease sometimes appeared after a period of consistent responses. Alternation between increased excitation and inhibition seems typical for newborns and probably caused the limited occurrence of consecutive CRs. Polygraphic records of breathing and general motor activity provided more sensitive indications of increased excitation or inhibition than the apparent state of wakefulness.

No relation was found in newborns between the occurrence of the first CR and the number of trials to criterion, but there was a significant correlation between the occurrence of the first group of two CRs and the criterion ($r = 0.71$, $p < 0.01$) or between the first group of three consecutive CRs and the criterion ($r = 0.86$, $p < 0.01$).

All these indices of age characteristics in the higher nervous functions of newborns confirm the hypothesis that the immaturity of the CNS manifests itself

TABLE 10.3.

Frequency of Occurrence of Different Types of Conditioning Curves in Individual Age Groups

| Types of acquisition curves | Age groups | | |
| | A | B | C |
| --- | --- | --- | --- |
| Relatively constant percentage increase | ·6 | 12 | 16 |
| Several gross waves | 6 | 2 | — |
| Retarded onset | 2 | — | — |
| *Total:* | 14 | 14 | 16 |

in the functional lability of higher centers and in the weakness of the basic central nervous system processes of excitation and inhibition. A similar conclusion was drawn from the analysis of developmental changes of sleeping and waking states in these infants (Dittrichová, 1962; Dittrichová, Janoš & Papoušek, 1962). Even under conditions involving relative immaturity of the CNS, it is apparent that a basic pyramidal response can be learned which, in later weeks and months, develops into a more complicated pattern of behavior. Our data suggest, in fact, that learning does occur in humans within the first days of life.

## Further Development of Conditioning Capacity

In the older infants, as compared with the newborns, developmental changes were observed of both a quantitative and a qualitative nature. The significant increase with age in the speed of conditioning was discussed in the preceding section on newborns. This finding is important for developmental studies since experimental evidence, in spite of many ontogenetic studies, is still equivocal. As shown recently (Janoš et al., 1963), during the first half-year of infancy an age difference of one month may produce significant differences in both aversive and appetitional conditioning.

With increased speed of conditioning, the individual phases in the conditioning process that are characteristic of newborns become shorter, and often such phases are detected only fleetingly, particularly in fast conditioners. Nevertheless, several qualitative differences could still be observed in groups B and C. Incoordination of partial components of the CR, associated with the appearance of the first CRs in newborns, was absent or appeared in a slight form only in a few trials. The generalization of the CR, observed in the phase of unstable conditioning, was also different. In newborns the CR was preceded or accompanied by increased movements of the whole trunk and extremities, and by changes in breathing and vasomotor responses, etc. These changes can be considered the result of nonspecific diffuse irradiation of the central excitatory process. It was observed that older infants showed more specific generalization, which was expressed in the specific vocal or facial signs of emotional arousal frequently shown by older children or adults in solving difficult problems.

An increase in the number of head turns during the intertrial intervals was more frequently found in older infants during the phase of unstable conditioning, and, unlike what is found in newborns, here the bilateral form of the intertrial head turns prevailed. It is difficult to estimate the proportion of maturation and extraexperimental learning in the qualitative differences found between newborns and older infants.

## Extinction and Reconditioning

The main purpose of our extinction and reconditioning procedures was to confirm the critical feature of the CR—its temporary character—and thus to differentiate it from pseudoconditioning. According to previous experience (Pa-

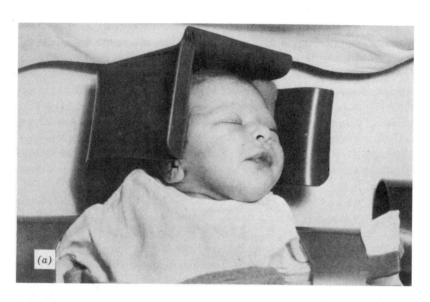

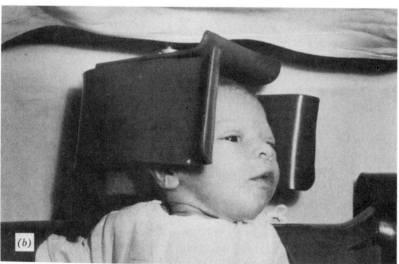

Fig. 10–5. Facial signs of pleasure.

poušek, 1961a, 1961b) and to analogous findings in aversive conditioning (Janoš, 1965), we did not expect to gain as much information about the development of learning abilities from the study of extinction and reconditioning as we found in the use of other procedures.

Table 10-1 shows that extinction occurs more quickly than conditioning but no significant difference in the speed of extinction was found among the three groups. This finding is difficult to explain. The experiments dealing with extinction may have involved an age span different from that in which the main development of extinction ability occurs; or the role of age may have been obliterated by the level of conditioning necessary to achieve the relatively severe criterion of conditioning employed. It is interesting that in group A, a negative correlation between trials to conditioning and trials to extinction was found ($r = -0.66$, $p < 0.05$), indicating faster extinguishing in slower conditioners. Moreover, the newborns had a significantly longer latency of the CR ($p < 0.001$) than did groups B and C.

To a certain extent, the course of extinction is a mirror image of conditioning. The CRs gradually cease to be made and their latencies become longer. The negative responses appear first as isolated events and later in consecutively larger numbers. The individual components of the CR do not extinguish simultaneously, particularly in younger $S$s. For example, in response to the $CS_1$, the $S$ may stop turning his head to the left but may continue to turn his eyes to the left or contract the left corner of his mouth for some time. A negative response to the CS still does not mean that the CS is totally indifferent to the $S$. Particularly during the phase of unstable extinction, the CS obviously exerts an inhibitory influence upon $S$'s behavior, sometimes to such an extent that it can elicit a catatoniclike state in the $S$ for several seconds.

Reconditioning may be considered a repetition of the first conditioning process. Here, however, the differences between individual age groups were at the limit of significance, according to a Kruskal-Wallis analysis of variance ($p > 0.05$).

Only in younger groups is reconditioning significantly faster than conditioning. The difference in speed between conditioning and reconditioning can be the effect of either maturation or relearning. The first seems more plausible since the difference was highly significant in group A ($p < 0.001$), in which the $S$s were 34 days older during reconditioning than they were during conditioning, but was at the limit of significance in group B ($p < 0.05$), and nonsignificant in group C ($p < 0.05$), in which the $S$s were only 15 and 11 days older. Within the total sample (but not within individual age groups), the correlation between trials to conditioning and trials to reconditioning was significant ($r = 0.38$, $p < 0.01$).

## Discrimination

There is a lack of data in the literature on the development of discriminative abilities in man. It was not the goal of this study to answer the question of the age at which human infants begin to discriminate different acoustic stimuli. The Ss had to proceed through several other procedures before the discrimination tests were begun. But even under these conditions evidence was found that in the fastest conditioners the ability to discriminate was functional as early as the second month of life. In group A, the mean age at which the Ss reached the criterion of discrimination between bell and buzzer was 2½ months.

During the following months of the first half year of life the ability to discriminate improves substantially and the speed of differentiation increases. An analysis of variance among groups A, B, and C, showed significant differences dependent on age ( $p < 0.005$ ). Furthermore, the latencies of response to both $CS_1$ and $CS_2$ were significantly lower ( $p < 0.005$ ) for group A than for groups B and C.

Individual variability in the speed of acquisition of prior procedures results in a gradual increase of the variability in the age at which Ss begin subsequent procedures. Ranking according to age is in this case identical with ranking in order of decreasing speed in the preceding procedures; within individual groups the slower the Ss were in preceding tests the older they were in succeeding tests. Therefore, the correlation between age and speed of discrimination or its reversals was not significant within individual groups, although in some procedures the span of the initial age exceeded one month. It has been reported by Janoš et al. (1963) that such an age difference may be associated with significant differences in the speed of conditioning.

Several main phases may be distinguished in the course of discrimination and particularly in the reversal of discrimination. There is first a disintegration of the previously learned ability that is followed by a gradual adaptation leading to successful acquisition of the new discrimination. Secondary phases were also present, such as alternating dominance of left or right CRs in Ss' responses to both kinds of CSs. The frequency, sequence, and expressiveness of these secondary phases were, however, less constant.

Developmental differences were evident in the course of discrimination. In group A, a marked decline in both CRs was observed in 6 of the 11 Ss soon after $CS_2$ was introduced. After the period of decline, a gradual increase in both CRs occurred simultaneously, with gross waves as the dominant type of acquisition curve. In groups B and C, such a general decline was never observed. A gradual increase in responses to $CS_2$ usually occurred with a stable or only a transitory decrease in the level of responses to $CS_1$. The periods of alternating dominance of left or right responses were less frequent in groups B and C. In all groups the stability of discrimination was only relative even after reaching criterion; a marked decline could be easily produced by various interfering factors.

## Reversals of Discrimination

In the last two procedures included in Table 10-1, the variability of the age at which the procedures were introduced increased to such an extent that the group limits overlapped, but the differences between mean ages still remained highly significant.

The speed of learning significantly increased from discrimination to the second reversal in groups A and B, but not in group C. It appears that by 6 months of age further improvement based upon age alone was not in evidence. For the first reversal, a one-way analysis of variance showed a reliable age trend reflecting a decrease in the number of trials to criterion ($p < 0.005$). In the second reversal, however, this trend was no longer significant. Similar relations were observed in the latency data. Within individual age groups there was no significant correlation between age and speed of the reversals. A possible interpretation was discussed in the previous section on discrimination. The speed with which the first reversal was acquired was positively related to the speed of discrimination ($r = 0.37$, $p < 0.025$).

The first reversal was established, on the average, in group A by the third month of life, and the second reversal by 31/2 months. We may conclude, therefore, that during the first trimester there has developed not only the capacity to discriminate but also the capacity to reverse a discrimination.

## DETERMINANTS OF INDIVIDUAL DIFFERENCES

Individual differences in addition to those based upon age were found in all groups and in all of the quantitative and qualitative indices. The literature contains different opinions on the detectability of differences in higher nervous function during early infancy. Chesnokova (1951) and Krasuskii (1953) assumed that differences in higher nervous activity continued to develop until adulthood and could not be assessed definitely at earlier ages. Troshikhin (1952) and Volokhov (1953), on the other hand, recommended that they be studied as early as possible. Kriuchkova and Ostrovskaia (1957) and, in a project similar to ours, Kaplan (1963) reported stable individual differences in higher nervous function from the first months of life through later infancy.

In the present study, marked individual differences were found to be present in newborns according to all indices. As an illustrative example, acquisition curves of conditioning for groups A and B are presented in Fig. 10–6. Whether or not the observed differences represent permanent characteristics of individual *S*s cannot be answered because our studies have not yet been oriented toward this problem. It should be noted, however, that studies on aversive conditioning in the same infants have also shown marked individual differences in learning abilities at early ages (Janoš, 1965).

In Table 10–1, the standard deviations for the trials-to-criterion measures of conditioning and discrimination decreased from group A to group C, indicating a developmental change in the variability of these functions. The $F$ tests comparing groups A and C indicated that the decrease in variability was significant in both instances ($p < 0.001$).

Group A
(newborn)

Group B
(3–month infants)

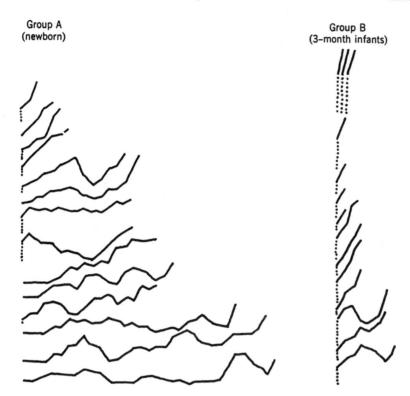

*Fig. 10–6. Acquisition curves of conditioning for groups A and B.*

Other determinants of the individual differences found in learning abilities were also investigated, for example, sex differences, nutrition, somatic differences, seasonal influences, etc. A preliminary analysis of our data showed no significant sex differences in any procedure between 19 girls and 25 boys of the present sample. Seasonal difference was not significant either when performances were compared for the first and second halves of the calendar year, or for the spring through the summer with the autumn through the winter.

It did not appear that the individual differences in learning ability that were found could be attributable to somatic or constitutional factors studied, such as birth weight and birth length, head and chest circumference, or gain in weight or length during the first trimester. Only in newborns did some parameters of learning abilities seem to be related to some of the mentioned determinants. A significant correlation was found, for example, between the CR latency and chest circumference $(r = -0.67, p < 0.05)$, indicating that a conditioned head turn was carried out more quickly in stouter newborns.

Since appetitional behavior can be substantially influenced by nutritional factors, the mean caloric quotient (daily intake in calories per kilogram of body weight) was calculated during each experimental procedure and was correlated with the conditioning parameters. In groups A and B, significant correlations of .59 ($p < 0.05$) and .63 ($p < 0.02$), respectively, indicated that conditioning proceeded more quickly in infants with a lower daily intake of milk, that is, they indicated an excitatory effect of a mild degree of hunger that can appear in younger infants during, for example, the period of additional feeding when a supplementary formula is kept slightly reduced in order to maintain adequate sucking at the mother's breast.

Similarly, a breast-to-cow-milk ratio was calculated during conditioning to test the influence of breast feeding and, indirectly, also of mother's presence, since mothers usually stayed at our unit as long as they could nurse. No significant correlation was evident between this ratio and the parameters of conditioning. It was the practice, however, to compensate for the mother's absence by providing substitute mothering and adequate emotional stimulation.

Thus, in general, we can conclude that this preliminary analysis of the potential determinants of individual differences in performance during the procedures employed did not contradict the hypothesis that with the conditioning procedures considered here, we were testing differences in higher nervous functions.

## ROLE OF ENVIRONMENTAL STIMULATION

In the preceding sections it has been shown that various indifferent external stimuli may play an important role if they become conditioned stimuli, particularly in connection with a significant form of reinforcement such as that used in these studies of appetitional conditioning. Acoustic signals can elicit striking changes in general motor activity, in the general state of excitation or inhibition, and in emotional and other forms of behavior. Although the effect sometimes can be too slight to be observed in general behavior, it can still be detected during the process of conditioning.

Such an example is illustrated in Fig. 10–7. In a 5-month-old infant with an established discrimination between the bell, reinforced with milk from the left, and the buzzer, reinforced from the right, the reinforcement associated with the buzzer was stopped in order to reverse the buzzer to an inhibitory stimulus. After a period of training, the buzzer ceased to elicit the CR, but an inhibitor aftereffect appeared in an increased latency in succeeding CRs to the bell. The more inhibitory stimuli were applied consecutively, the greater was the increase in latency.

In infants of the second trimester, further observation illustrated the effectiveness of the CSs, and, in addition, an interesting interrelation between learned and unlearned behavior. For instance, in several Ss, after completing a normal conditioning session with 10 trials and after a normal amount of milk had been

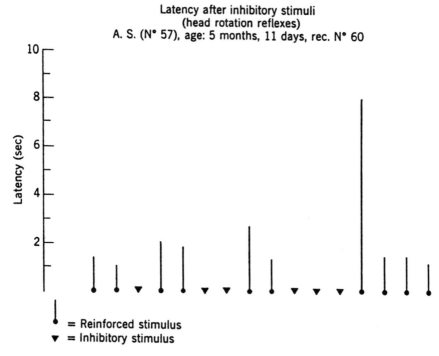

Fig. 10–7. *Latencies of responses after presentation of inhibitory stimuli.*

presented as reinforcement, another 10 or 20 CSs were applied to test the influence of satiation upon the emission of CRs. Under these conditions the Ss did not stop responding to the CSs, even when they were fully satiated. At every sound of the bell they turned to the left, even though they refused the milk presented. Any attempts to feed them elicited avoiding head turns.

Other experimental situations for studying the interrelations between learned and nonlearned behavior were undertaken by using different tasting fluids. These situations used 15 Ss, aged 88 to 201 days, in whom a left-right discrimination in head-turning had already been established. For instance, sweet milk was used as the UCS presented from the left in $CS_1$, and a weak solution of the quinine tincture was presented from the right in $CS_2$. Soon the concomitant emotional responses appropriate to the kind of UCS became differentiated, so that the Ss responded to the $CS_1$ with quiet sucking and head-turning, but to the $CS_2$ with arousal, grimacing, increased salivation, and aversive tongue movements. When in this situation the discrimination was reversed, the Ss sucked the bitter solution from the left with $CS_1$ without any signs of displeasure, and refused the sweet milk from the right with $CS_2$. For some period, this maladaptive behavior indicated that the effectiveness of conditioning stimuli was stronger than the effects of unconditioned reinforcement. Finally, a readaptation appeared and led to a new, adequate differentiation. These studies indicate that even emotional behavior, like other kinds of behavior, can be conditioned and thus put under experimental control.

Natural conditioning procedures, similar to those described above, can normally occur in the infant's life. Various environmental stimuli can in this way become conditioned stimuli of great effectiveness. It is not difficult to realize that under unfavorable conditions, for example, in various frustration situations in which many CSs remain unreinforced and become inhibitory stimuli, a cumulative inhibitory influence can produce undesirable effects in the infant's behavior.

## MODELS OF VOLUNTARY BEHAVIOR

We attempted to mold a simple example of voluntary behavior in 12 infants of whom four were newborns aged 4-5 days on the average, and eight were in the second trimester, with an average age of 130.1 days. The Ss were trained in a discrimination and one or two reversals of it with only one kind of CS. The CS was reinforced with either sweetened milk from the left or unsweetened milk from the right. If he did not carry out a head turn himself, tactile stimulation with a rubber nipple was applied with the restriction that equal numbers of tactile stimulations were applied to both sides. Otherwise, the S was allowed to choose the kind of milk himself.

An exact quantitative analysis was not possible since different kinds of stimulation were used, but several general conclusions seem warranted. All Ss preferred the sweetened milk, and this preference gradually developed in a manner similar to the discrimination described in the basic conditioning procedures. The criterion of five consecutive CRs to the same side was reached in an average of 290 trials (ranging from 246 to 390) in the newborns and in 38 trials (9 to 109) in the older infants.

After achieving the criterion, the UCSs were reversed—the sweetened milk was presented from the right side and the unsweetened milk from the left. A gradual reversal in CRs occurred, consequently, and its course was analogous to that of the reversal described earlier. During the disintegration phase of a previously learned ability, accidental head turns to the side of sweetened milk helped the Ss to find the source of the preferred UCS. Concomitant emotional responses, gradual grouping of CRs to the preferred side, and other signs indicated that this simple model of voluntary behavior was learned in the same way as in the basic conditioning procedures. In the younger infants 108 trials (15 to 185) were necessary for achieving the criterion, whereas only 70 (10 to 162) were necessary in the older infants. In a schematic form, one typical case is illustrated in Fig. 10–8.

Z.C. (no 51), age: 5 months 22 days, rec. no: 1-8

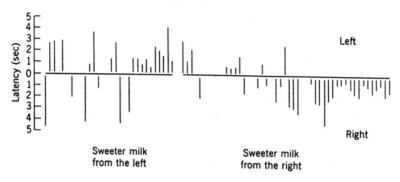

Fig. 10–8.   *Latencies of responses in initial learning and following reversal of the UCSs.*

When I speak of voluntary behavior in infants of prelingual age, I do not assume that I am thereby simplifying a difficult problem. I wish only to emphasize that the chosen pyramidal movement, brought under experimental control at a very early stage of postnatal development, can be molded to patterns resembling voluntary behavior. Perhaps it would be better to say that through conditioning processes, the organism can be brought to the beginning of a long and complicated pathway of structuring, at the end of which there are patterns of behavior as highly coordinated as those generally designated as voluntary behavior.

## SUMMARY

Head movements were chosen as a conditionable motor complex of infantile appetitional behavior to study the early development of learning abilities and the molding of a simple response to a pattern of intentional behavior.

A method was developed for appetitional conditioning with milk reinforcement in newborns and infants. The basic conditioning procedures—condtioning, extinction, reconditioning, discrimination and its double reversal—were studied as early forms of learning in three independent age groups of healthy full-term infants (newborns, 3-month infants, and 5-month infants).

Quantitative and qualitative differences among these groups were analyzed with particular attention to the peculiarities of the learning processes in newborns, and evidence was found that learning occurs during the first days of life. In the course of investigating various procedures in the study of conditioning in newborns, different phases of learning became apparent. The immaturity of the central nervous system manifests itself in the functional lability and in the infirmity of the basic central nervous processes of excitation and inhibition. The evidence for this appears in the slow grouping of consecutive CRs, gross waves in the acquisition curves, and instability in the percentage, intensity, and latency of CRs.

In several indices the comparison among individual groups indicated that major developmental changes occur during the first three months of life. During this period there develops not only the capacity to discriminate between various acoustic stimuli but also the capacity to reverse such a discrimination.

Marked individual differences are present from the neonatal period on in all parameters of conditioning employed. An analysis of the correlation between these differences and various potential determinants such as sex, somatic development, nutrition, mother–infant interaction, or seasonal influence support the hypothesis of independent variability in higher nervous function as a cause of the observed individual differences.

Further studies helped to eludicate the interrelation between learned and nonlearned behavior, indicating increasing effectiveness of conditioning stimuli in comparison to unconditioned ones. A left-right differentiation of head-turning reinforced by two as different and as emotionally effective taste stimuli as sweet and bitter solutions indicated that even emotional behavior can be put under experimental control and can be conditioned in young infants.

Finally, there is reported the attempt to design experimental conditions under which the learned response can be considered as the earliest precursor of later intentional or voluntary behavior. Here, head-turning was conditioned to one CS, and that CS was reinforced either with sweetened or unsweetened milk, depending on the side to which $S$ turned his head. All $S$s appeared to prefer the sweetened milk and to be able to find its source on the opposite side when the two variants of UCS were reversed. Learning of such a response proceeded on the same principles as conditioned discrimination or its reversal.

## REFERENCES

Babkin, P. S. (1953). Head-turning reflexes in infants. (Rus.) *Zh. Nevropat. Psikhiat.* **53**, 692–696.

Bekhterev, V. M., & Stshelovanov, N. M. (1925). The principles of genetic reflexology. (Rus.) In *Novoie refleksologii i fiziologii nervnoi sistemy.* USSR: Leningrad-Moscow.

Chesnokova, A. P. (1951). Dynamism of higher nervous activity in puppies during their individual development. (Rus.) *Zh. vys. nerv. Deiat.* **1**, 555–565.

Darwin, C. (1886). Biographische Skizze eines kleinen Kindes. (Germ). *Kleinere Schriften* (Leipzig) 2.B., 134.

Dashkovskaia, V. S. (1953). The first conditioned responses in newborns under normal and pathologic conditions. (Rus.) *Zh. vys. nerv. Deiat.* **3**, 247–259.

Denisova, M. P., & Figurin, N. L. (1929). The question of the first associated appetitional reflexes in infants. (Rus.) *Vopr. genet. Refleksol. Pedol. Mladen.* **1**, 81–88.

Dittrichová J. (1962). Nature of sleep in young infants. *J. appl. Physiol.* **17**, 543–546.

Dittrichová, J., Janoš, O., & Papoušek, H. (1962). Characteristics of higher nervous activity in newborns. (Czech.) *Sb. čsl. lékař. kongresu.* Prague. Pp. 254–255.

Irwin, O. C. (1930). The amount and nature of activities of newborn infants under constant external stimulating conditions during the first ten days of life. *Genet. Psychol. Monogr.* **8**, 1–92.

Irzhanskaia, K. N., & Felberbaum, R. A. (1954). Some data on conditioned activity in premature infants (Rus.) *Fiziol. Zh. SSSR* **40**, 668–672.

Ivanov-Smolenskii, A. G. (1953). Studies on the types of higher nervous activity in animals and in man. (Rus.) *Zh. vys. nerv. Deiat.* **3**, 36–54.

Janoš, O. (1965). (Czech.) *Age and individual differences in higher nervous activity in infants.* Prague: SzdN.

Janoš, O., Papoušek, H., & Dittrichová, J. (1963). The influence of age upon various aspects of higher nervous activity in the first months of life. (Czech.) *Activ. nerv. super.* **4**, 407–410.

Kantrow, R. W. (1937). Studies in infant behavior. IV. An investigation of conditioned feeding responses and concomitant adaptive behavior in young infants. *Univer. Iowa Stud. Child Welf.* **13**, No. 3, 1–64.

Kaplan, L. I. (1963). To the question of the development of individual typologic differences of higher nervous activity in infants. (Rus.) *Mater. 6th scient. conf. devel. morphol., physiol., biochem.* Moscow: Izd. APN. P. 354.

Kasatkin, N. I. (1948). (Rus.) *Early conditioned reflexes in the ontogenesis of man.* Moscow: Medgiz.

Kasatkin, N. I. (1951). (Rus.) *An outline of the development of the higher nervous activity during early infancy.* Moscow: Medgiz.

Kasatkin, N. I. (Ed.). (1964). (Rus.) *From the simple to the complex.* Moscow-Leningrad: Izd. Nauka.

Kasatkin, N. I., & Levikova, A. M. (1935). On the development of early conditioned reflexes and differentiation of auditory stimuli in infants. *J. exp. Psychol.* **18**, 1–9.

Koch, J. (1962). Die Veränderung des Exzitations Prozesses nach der Nahrungsein-nahme und nach dem Schlafe bei Säuglingen in Alter von 5 Monaten. (Germ.) *Z. arztl. Fortb.* **55**, 219–223.

Krasnogorskii, N. I. (1907). An experience with establishing experimental conditioned reflexes in infants. (Rus.) *Russkii vrach* 36. In (Rus.) *Studies in the research of higher nervous activity in man and animals.* (1954). Moscow: Medgiz.

Krasnogorskii, N. I. (1958). (Rus.) *The higher nervous activity in the child.* Leningrad: Medgiz.

Krasuskii, V. K. (1953). Methods of studying the types of nervous system in animals. (Rus.) *Trudy Inst. Fiziol. Pavlov* 2, 111–119.

Kriuchkova, A. P., & Ostrovskaia, I. M. (1957). Developmental and individual differences of higher nervous activity in infants. (Rus.) *Zh. vys. nerv. Deiat.* **7**, 63–74.

Lipsitt, L. P. (1963). Learning in the first year of life. In L. P. Lipsitt & C. C. Spiker (Eds.) *Advances in child development and behavior.* Vol 1. New York: Academic Press, Pp. 147–195.

Lipsitt, L. P., & Kaye, H. (1964). Conditioned sucking in the human newborn. *Pyschon. Sci.* **1**, 29–30.

Marquis, D. P. (1931). Can conditioned responses be established in the newborn infant? *J. genet. Psychol.* **39**, 479–492.

Minkowski, H. (1928). Neurobiologische Studien an menschlichen Früchten. *Abderhalden's Handb. biolog. Arbeitsmeth* (Berlin) **5, 5b**, 511–618.

Nemanova, C. P. (1935). The earliest positive and negative aversive and nutritive conditioned responses to vestibular stimuli in infants. (Rus.) *Vopr. Pediat. Okhran.* **7**, 278.

Orbeli, L. A. (1949). On the mechanism of the development of cerebrospinal coordinations. (Rus.) In *The problems of higher nervous activity*. Moscow-Leningrad: Izd. AN SSSR. Pp. 7–20.

Papoušek, H. (1959). A method of studying conditioned food reflexes in young children up to the age of six months. (Rus.) *Zh. vys. nerv. Deiat*. **9**, 136–140.

Papoušek, H. (1960). Conditioned motor alimentary reflexes in infants. I. Experimental conditioned sucking reflexes. (Czech.) *Cesk. Pediat*. **15**, 861–872.

Papoušek, H. (1961). Conditioned head rotation reflexes in infants in the first months of life. *Acta Paediatr*. **50**, 565–576. (a)

Papoušek, H. (1961). (Czech.) *Conditioned motor nutritive reflexes in infants*. Thomayer, Sb., Prague: SzdN. P. 409. (b)

Peiper, A. (1958). Unbedingte und bedingte Reflexe der Nahrungsaufnahme. (Germ.) *Kinderäerzt. Prax*. **26**, 507–515.

Polikanina, R. I. (1955). Origin and development of a nutritive conditioned response to sound in premature infants. (Rus.) *Zh. vys. nerv. Deiat*. **5**, 237–246.

Polikanina, R. I., & Probatova, L. J. (1957). Development of an orienting response and a conditioned motor nutritive response to color in premature infants. (Rus.) *Zh. vys. nerv. Deiat*. **7**, 673–682.

Prechtl, H. F. R. (1953). Die Kletterbewegungen beim Säugling. (Germ.) *Mnschr Kinderhk*, **101**, 519–521.

Preyer, W. (1895). *Die Seele des Kindes*. (4th ed.) (Germ.) Leipzig.

Ray, W. S. (1932). A preliminary report on a study of fetal conditioning. *Child Developm*. **3**, 175–177.

Rheingold, Harriet L., & Stanley, W. C. (1963). Developmental psychology. *Ann. Rev. Psychol*. **14**, 1–28.

Ripin, R., & Hetzer, H. (1930). Frühestes Lernen des Säuglings in der Ernährungssituation. (Germ.) *Z. Psyhcol*. **118**, 82–127.

Scheffé, H. (1959). *The analysis of variance*. New York: Wiley.

Sedláček, J. (1962). Functional characteristics of the center of the unconditioned reflex in elaboration of a temporary connection in chick embryos. (Czech.) *Physiol. Bohemoslov*. **11**, 313–318.

Sedláček, J. (1963). Problems of the ontogenetic formation of the mechanism of temporary connections. (Rus.) *Acta Univer. Carol. Medica* **4**, 265–317.

Sedláček, J. Hlaváčková, V., & Švenlová, M. (1964). New findings on the formation of the temporary connections in the prenatal and perinatal period in the guinea pig. (Czech.) *Physiol. Bohemoslov*. **13**, 268–273.

Siqueland, E. R. (1964). Operant conditioning of head turning in four-month infants. *Pyschon. Sci*. **1**, 223–224.

Siqueland, E. R., & Lipsitt, L. P. (1966). Conditioned head-turning behavior in newborns. *J. exp. child Psychol. 3*, 356–376.

Sontag, L. W., & Wallace, R. F. (1934). Study of fetal activity. (Preliminary report on the Fels Fund) *Amer. J. Dis. Child*. **49**, 1050.

Spelt, D. K. (1938). Conditioned responses in the human fetus in utero. *Psychol. Bull*. **35**, 712–713.

Spelt, D. K. (1948). The conditioning of the human fetus in utero. *J. exp. Psychol*. **38**, 338–346.

Troshikhin, V. A. (1952). Some tasks in the research of higher nervous activity in ontogenesis. (Rus.) *Zh. vys. nerv. Deiat*. **2**, 561–571.

Ukhtomskii, A. A. (1952). The principle of dominant center. (Rus.) In I. M. Sechenov, I. P. Pavlov, & N. E. Wedenskii (Eds.), *Physiology of the nervous system*. Vol. 1. (3rd ed.) Moscow: Medgiz. Pp. 262–266.

Volokhov, A. A. (1953). Typologic differences of nervous system in infants (Rus.) *Med. Rabot.* **16**, 2–3.

Volokhov, A. A. (1959). Typologic differences in higher nervous activity in infants and their reflection in some autonomic functions. (Rus.) *Mater. 7th Congr. Soviet. Pediat.* 77–80.

Wedenskii, N. E. (1952). Relationship between rhythmical processes and functional activity of an excitated neuromuscular apparatus. (Rus.) In I. M. Sechenov. I. P. Pavlov, & N. E. Wedenskii (Eds.), *Physiology of the nervous system.* Vol. 2. (3rd ed.) Moscow: Medgiz.

Wenger, M. A. (1936). An investigation of conditioned responses in human infants. *Univer. Iowa Stud. Child Welf.* **12**, 9–90.

# LIST OF PUBLICATIONS BY PAPOUŠEK

1. Papoušek, H. (1954). Hemorrhagic diathesis in toxic diarrhoea in infants. *Pediat. Listy, 9*, 95–96. (in Czech)
2. Papoušek, H. (1955). The Pavlovian concept of disease in pediatrics. *Čs. Pediatrie, 10*, 641–649. (in Czech)
3. Papoušek, H. (1955). The Pavlovian concept of disease and its application in pediatrics. In *The Textbooks of the Medical Institute for Postdoctoral Training* (pp. 1–34). Prague. (in Czech)
4. Trapl, J., Vojta, M., et al. (1955). *The textbook of obstetrics* (3rd ed.). Prague, SZdN. (in Czech)
5. Papoušek, H. (1956). Activity recording in small infants. *Cs. Pediatrie, 11*, 850–854. (in Czech)
6. Papoušek, H., Brachfeld, K., Svatý, J., & Roušarová, J. (1956). The care for injured newborns. In *Neonatal Birth Injury* (Sb. věd. prací, No. 8, pp. 335–353). Prague, SZdN. (in Czech)
7. Papoušek, H., and Janele, J. (1956). The factors of hemocoagulation in the pathogenesis of birth injury of the central nervous system in fullterm newborns. In *Neonatal Birth Injury* (Sb. věd. prací, No. 8, pp. 379–392). Prague, SZdN. (in Czech)
8. Papoušek, H. (1957). The conference on the problems of the physiology of the human and animal infancy. *Čs. Pediatrie, 12*, 375–392. (in Czech)
9. Papoušek, H., & Janovský, M. Infant nutrition. In K. Kubát (Ed.), *The principles of the care for newborns* (pp. 93–122). Prague, SZdN. (in Czech)
10. Papoušek, H. (1959). Method of studying conditioned food reflexes in infants during the first six months of their life. *Zh. vyssh. nerv. Deyat., 9*, 143–148. (in Russian)
11. Papoušek, H. (1959). New methods for studying the higher nervous functions in early human infancy. *Activ. nerv. super., 1*, 130–131. (in Czech)
12. Papoušek, H. (1959). The group rearing of children below three years in the USSR. *Čs. Pediatrie, 14*, 183–186. (in Czech)
13. Papoušek, H. (1959). Studies of the higher nervous activity in the early childhood in the USSR. *Čs. Pediatrie, 14*, 275–280. (in Czech)
14. Papoušek, H. (1959). Research in human neonatology in the USSR. *Čs. Pediatrie, 14*, 471–476. (in Czech)
15. Papoušek, H. (1959). *Conditioned alimentary motor reflexes in infants.* Dissertation for the degree of Canditate of Siences. The Charles' University in Prague. 183 pp. (in Czech)
16. Papoušek, H. (1960). Conditioned motor alimentary reflexes in infants. I. Experimental conditioned sucking reflexes. *Čs. Pediatrie, 15*, 861–872. (in Czech)
17. Papoušek, H. (1960). Conditioned motor alimentary reflexes in infants. II. A new experimental method of investigation. *Čs. Pediatrie, 15*, 981–988. (in Czech)

18.   Papoušek, H. (1960). Conditioned alimentary motor reflexes in infants. III. Experimental
      conditioned rotation reflexes of the head. *Čs. Pediatrie, 15*, 1057–1065. (in Czech)
19.   Papoušek, H. (1960, September). Physiological aspects of the early ontogenesis of the so-
      called voluntary activity. In *Proceedings of the I. International Symposium on Development
      of Functions and Metabolism in the Higher Sections of the Central Nervous System*. Pilsen.
20.   Papoušek, H. (1961). *Conditioned alimentary motor responses in infants*. Prague, Thomayer.
      Sb. Předen. Vol. 409, SZdN, 92 pp. (Czech)
21.   Papoušek, H. (1961). Über die Beziehungen einiger Formen des Hospitalismus bei Säu-
      glingen zur Ontogenesis der Nahrungsreflexe. In H. Schwarz (Ed.), *Das milieugeschädigte
      Kind. Samml. zwangl. Abhandl. aus dem Gebiete der Neurol* (H. 21, pp. 37–39). Jena, G.
      Fischer. (in German)
22.   Papoušek, H. (1961). Conditioned head rotation reflexes in infants in the first month of life.
      *Acta Paediat.* (Uppsala), *50*, 565–576.
23.   Papoušek, H. (1961). A physiological view of early ontogenesis of so-called voluntary
      movements. *Plzeň. lék. Sbor., Suppl. 3*, 195–198.
24.   Janoš, O., Dittrichová, J., Koch, J., & Papoušek, H. (1961). The higher nervous functions in
      early infancy. In M. Vojta (Ed.), *10 years of the care for the health of the youngest
      generation* (pp. 20–23). Prague: UPMD. (in Czech)
25.   Cibulec, A., & Papoušek, H. (1961). Electro-acoustical metronom. *Activ. nerv. super., 3*,
      448–452. (in Czech)
26.   Papoušek, H. (1962). On the development of the so-called voluntary movements in the
      earliest stages of the child's development. *Čs. Pediatrie, 17*, 588–591. (in Czech)
27.   Papoušek, H. (1962). Physiological aspects of "voluntary movements" in early ontogeny.
      *Acta Univ. Carol. Med.* (Prague), *8*, 665–680. (in Russian)
28.   Dittrichová, J., Janoš, O., & Papoušek, H. (1962). Higher nervous activity in newborn
      infants. In *100 years of the Czechoslovak Medical Society of J. E. Purkinje* (p. 243). Prague.
      (in Czech)
29.   Janoš, O., Papoušek, H., & Dittrichová, J. (1962). The influence of age upon some
      manifestations of higher nervous activity in infants in the first months of life. In *100 Years of
      the Czechoslovak Medical Society of J. E. Purkinje* (pp. 306–307). Prague. (in Czech)
30.   Papoušek, H. (1963). A pediatrician looks at some ideological problems in brining up
      children. *Čs. Pediatrie*, 1963, 18, 636–639. (in Czech)
31.   Papoušek, H. (1963). Paediatric care in Great Britain. *Čs. Pediatrie, 18*, 568–571. (in Czech)
32.   Papoušek, H. (1963). The education of pre-school children in Great Britain. *Čs. Pediatrie,
      18*, 757-760. (in Czech)
33.   Papoušek, H., Janoš, O., & Dittrichová, J. (1963). Development of higher nervous activity
      of infant in the first months of life. *Proceedings of the 6th Congr. of develop. Morphol.,
      Physiol., Biochem.* (pp. 435–436). Moscow, Acad. Pedag. Nauk. (in Russian)
34.   Dittrichová, J., Janoš, O., & Papoušek, H. (1963). Methods and criteria in research work
      concerning the development of infants during the first year of life. In *Handbook of efficiency
      criteria. Proceed. of The Conference of the Czechoslovac Academy of Science at Liblice 1963*
      (pp. 199–204). Prague, CSAV.
35.   Janoš, O., Papoušek, H., & Dittrichová, J. (1963). The influence of age upon some
      manifestations of higher nervous activity in the first months of life. *Activ. nerv. super., 5*,
      407–410. (in Czech)
36.   Kubát, K., Papoušek, H., & Stolová, O . (1963). On some comments to the problems of child
      rearing in family and in institutions. *Čs. Pediatrie, 18*, 468-/. (in Czech)
37.   Papoušek, H. (1964). Some problems of child care institutions. *Čs. Pediatrie, 19*, 1117-/. (in
      Czech)
38.   Papoušek, H. (1964). Conditioned reflectory movements of the head in the human newborn.
      *Activ. nerv. super., 6*, 83–84.
39.   Papoušek, H. (1965). The development of higher nervous activity in children in the first half-

year of life. In *European Research in Cognitive Development. Monogr. Soc. Res. Child Development* (Ser. 100, Vol. 30, 2, pp. 102–111).

40. Papoušek, H. (1965). Manifestations of genetic differences in the behavior of man. Wenner-Gren Foundation Symposium in Wartenstein 1964. *Activ. nerv. super.*, 7, 92–94. (in Czech)
41. Papoušek, H. (1965). Individual differences in conditioned food-seeking reflexes in newborns. *Activ. nerv. super.*, 7, 140–141.
42. Janoš, O., Dittrichová, J., Koch, J., Papoušek, H., Tautermannová, M., & Melichar, V. (1966). Early development of higher nervous activity in premature infants with respiratory distress syndrome. *Activ. nerv. super.*, 8, 201-/.
43. Janoš, O., & Papoušek, H. (1966). Comparison of appetitional and aversive conditioning in the same infants. *Activ. nerv. super*, 8, 203–204.
44. Papoušek, H. (1967). Experimental studies of appetitional behavior in human newborns and infants. In H. W. Stevenson, E. H. Hess, & H. L. Rheingold (Eds.), *Early behavior: Comparative and developmental approaches*, (pp. 277). New York: Wiley.
45. Papoušek, H. (1967). Conditioning during early post-natal development. In Y. Brackbill & G. G. Thompson (Eds.), *Behavior in infancy and early childhood*, (pp. 259–274). New York: The Free Press.
46. Papoušek, H. (1967). Genetics and child development. In J. N. Spuhler (Ed.), *Genetic diversity and human behavior* (pp. 171–186). Chicago: Aldine Publ. Co.
47. Papoušek, H. (1967). When longitudinal inquiry is essential. In J. L. Fearing & G. T. Kowitz (Eds.), *Some views of longitudinal inquiry* (pp. 108–120). Houston, Research and Services Series No. 321.
48. Papoušek, H. (1967). Experimental studies of the development of learning abilities in human infants during the first months of life. *Pediatria internazionale (Roma)*, 17, 199–206.
49. Papoušek, H. (1967). Studies on early mental development, their social importance, and needs of international cooperation. *Material i Prace antropol.*, No. 75, 26–27. Wroclaw, Polska Akademia Nauk.
50. Papoušek, H., Jungmannová, C. (1967). Nutrition. In K. Kubát (Ed.), *Care of the newborn infant* (pp. 50–83). Prague, SZdN. (in Czech)
51. Papoušek, H. et al. (1967). Symposium on nurseries. Prague, 24–26 Oct., 1966. *Čs. Pediatrie*, 22, 1036–1042. (in Czech)
52. Kubát, K., Štolová, O., Syrovátka, A., & Papoušek, H. (1969). Sociologic aspects of modern pediatrics. *Demografie*, 11, 30–36. (in Czech)
53. Papoušek, H., Bernstein, P. (1969). Basic cognitive functions in the pre-verbal period of infancy. *Activ. nerv. super.*, 11, 285–286.
54. Papoušek, H., & Bernstein, P. (1969). The functions of conditioning stimulation in human neonates and infants. In A. Ambrose (Ed.), *Stimulation in early infancy* (pp. 229–252). London: Academic Press.
55. Papoušek, H. (1969). Individual variability in learned responses in human infants. In R. J. Robinson (Ed.) *Brain and early behavior* (pp. 251–266). London: Academic Press.
56. Martinius, J. W., & Papoušek, H. (1970). Responses to optic and exteroceptive stimuli in relation to state in the human newborn: Habituation of the blink reflex. *Neuropädiatrie*, 1, 452–460.
57. Papoušek, H. (1970). Effects of group rearing conditions during the preschool years of life. In V. H. Denenberg (Ed.), *Education of the infant and young child* (pp. 51–59). New York: Academic Press.
58. Papoušek, H. (1973). Grouper rearing in day care centers and mental health: Potential advantages and risks. In J. I. Nurnberger (Ed.), *Biological and environmental determinants of early development* (Res. Publ. Ass. nerv. ment. Dis., Vol. 51, (pp. 398–411). Baltimore: Williams & Wilkins Co.
59. Papoušek, H., & Papoušek, M. (1974). Mirror image and self-recognition in young human infants: I. A new method of experimental analysis. *Dev. Psychobiol.*, 7, 149–157.

60. Papoušek, H., & Papoušek, M. (1974). Die Mutter-Kind-Beziehung und die kognitive Entwicklung des Kindes. In R. Nissen & P. Strunck (Eds.), *Seelische Fehlentwicklung im Kindesalter und Gesellschaftsstruktur*, (pp. 83–100). Neuwied: Luchterhand Verlag.

61. Papoušek, H. (1975). Soziale Interaktion als Grundlage der kognitiven Frühentwicklung. In T. Hellbrügge (Ed.), *Kindliche Sozialisation und Sozialentwicklung. Fortschritte der Sozialpädiatrie* (Vol. 2, pp. 117–141). München/Berlin/Wien: Urban & Schwarzenberg.

62. Papoušek, H. (1975). Der Säugling und seine soziale Umwelt: Heutige Forschung und gesellschaftliche Trends. In H. Heinemann & H. Wichterich (Eds.), *Kind und Gesellschaft* (pp. 28–41). Neuburgweier: Schindele.

63. Papoušek, H. (1975). Early human ontogeny of the regulation of behavioral states in relation to information processing and adaptation organizing. In P. Levin & W. P. Koella (Eds.), *Sleep 1974. 2nd Europ. Congr. Sleep Res., Rome 174* (pp. 384–387). Basel: Karger.

64. Papoušek, H. & Papoušek, M. (1975). Cognitive aspects of preverbal social interaction between human infants and adults. In *Parent–Infant Interaction. Ciba Foundation Symposium 33 (New Series)* (pp. 241–260). Amsterdam: Elsevier.

65. Papoušek, H. (1975). Die Entwicklung früher Lernprozesse im Säuglingsalter. *Der Kinderarzt, 1975* 6: (10) 1077–1081, (11) 1205–1207, (12) 1331–1334.

66. Papoušek, H. (1976). Food and psychological development. In D. N. Walcher, N. Kretchmer, & H. L. Barnett (Eds.), *Food, man, and society* (pp. 244–254). New York/London: Plenum Press.

67. Papoušek, H., & Papoušek, M. (1977). Das Spiel in der Frühentwicklung des Kindes. *Suppl. pädiat. prax., 18*, 17–32.

68. Papoušek, H., & Papoušek, M. (1977). Mothering and cognitive head-start: Psychobiological considerations. In H. R. Schaffer (Ed.), *Studies in mother-infant interaction* (pp. 63–85). London/New York: Academic Press.

69. Papoušek, H. (1977). Entwicklung der Lernfähigkeit im Säuglingsalter. In G. Nissen (Ed.), *Intelligenz, Lernen und Lernstörungen*, (pp. 89–107). Berlin/Heidelberg/New York: Springer.

70. Papoušek, H., & Papoušek, M. (1977). Die ersten sozialen Beziehungen: Entwicklungschance oder pathogene Situation? *Praxis der Psychotherapie, 22*, 97–108.

71. Janoš, O., & Papoušek, H. (1977). Acquisition of appetitional and palpebral conditioned reflexes by same infants. *Early Human Development, 1*, 91–97.

72. Papoušek H. (1977). Individual differences in adaptive processes of infants. In A. Oliverio (Ed.), *Genetics, environment and intelligence* (pp. 269–283). Amsterdam: Elsevier.

73. Schoetzau, A., & Papoušek, H. (1977). Mütterliches Verhalten bei der Aufnahme von Blickkontakt mit dem Neugeborenen. *Zeitschrift für Entwicklungpsychologie und pädagogische Psychologie, 9*, 231–239.

74. Papoušek, H., & Papoušek, M. (1977). Die Entwicklung kognitiver Prozesse im Säuglingsalter. *Der Kinderarzt, 8* (8), 1071–1077, (9) 1088–1089.

75. Papoušek, H. (1977). Entwicklung der Lernfähigkeit im Säuglingsalter. In G. Nissen (Ed.), *Intelligenz, Lernen und Lernstörungen: Theorie, Praxis und Therapie* (pp. 75–93). Berlin/Heidelberg/New York: Springer-Verlag.

76. Simons, G., & Papoušek, H. (1978). Methoden der Kleinkindforschung: Beobachtung und Experiment. In R. Dollase (Ed.), *Handbuch der Früh- und Vorschhulpädagogik, Band 2.* (pp. 93–110). Düsseldorf: Pädagogischer Verlag Schwann.

77. Papoušek, H., & Papoušek, M. (1978). Interdisciplinary parallels in studies of early human behavior: From physical to congitive needs, from attachment to dyadic education. *International Journal of Behavioral Development, 1*, 37–49.

78. Papoušek, H. (1979). From adaptive responses to social cognition: The learning view of development. In M. H. Bornstein & W. Kessen (Eds.), *Psychological development from infancy: Image to intention* (pp. 251–267). Hillsdale, NJ: Erlbaum.

79. Papoušek, H. (1979). Verhaltensweisen der Mutter und des Neugeborenen unmittelbar nach der Geburt. *Archives of Gynecology, 228* (42. Gynäkologen-Bericht), 26–32.

80. Papoušek, H., & Papoušek, M. (1979). Lernen im ersten Lebensjahr. In L. Montada (Ed.), *Brennpunkte der Entwicklungpsychologie* (pp. 194–212). Stuttgart: Kohlhammer.

81. Papoušek, H., & Papoušek, M. (1979).The infant's fundamental adaptive response system in social interaction. In E. B. Thoman (Ed.), *Origins of the infant's social responsiveness* (pp. 175–208). Hillsdale, NJ: Erlbaum.

82. Papoušek, H., & Papoušek, M. (1979). Early ontogeny of human social interaction: Its biological roots and social dimensions. In M. von Cranach, K. Foppa, W. Lepenies, & D. Ploog (Eds.), *Human ethology: Claims and limits of a new discipline* (pp. 456–478). Cambridge, UK: Cambridge University Press.

83. Papoušek, H., & Papoušek, M. (1979). Care of the normal and high risk newborn: A psychobiological view of parental behavior. In S. Harel (Ed.), *The at risk infant. International Congress Series No. 492* (pp. 368–371).

84. Papoušek, H. (1980). Diskussionsbeitrag zur Frage von Kontinuität und Diskontinuität in der Verhaltensbiologie von Depression. In H. Heimann & H. Giedke (Eds.), *Neue Perspektiven in der Depressionsforschung* (pp. 48–52). Bern/Stuttgart/Wien: Huber.

85. Papoušek, H. (1980). Diskussionsbeitrag zur Bedeutung der Kontingenz in der Verhaltensbiologie von Depression. In H. Heimann & H. Giedke (Eds.), *Neue Perspektiven in der Depressionsforschung* (pp. 188–190). Bern/Stuttgart/Wien: Huber.

86. Papoušek, H., & Mangione, P. (1980). A comment to Keogh, B. K. & Glover, A. T., "Research needs in the study of early identification of children with learning disabilities." *Thalamus, 1*, 21–22.

87. Papoušek, H., & Papoušek, M. (1981). Die frühe Eltern-Kind-Beziehung und ihre Störungen aus psychobiologischer Sicht. In O. Hövels, E. Halberstadt, V. V. Loewenich, & I. Eckert (Eds.), *Geburtshilfe und Kinderheilkunde: Gemeinsame aktuelle, praktische Probleme. Symposium in Bad Kreuznach 1979* (pp. 72–79). Stuttgart/New York: Thieme.

88. Papoušek, H. (1981). The common in the uncommon child: Comments on the child's integrative capacities and on intuitive parenting. In M. Lewis & L. A. Rosenblum (Eds.), *The uncommon child* (pp. 317–328). New York: Plenum Publishing.

89. Papoušek, H. (1981). Audiovisuelle Verhaltensregistrierung mit Hilfe von Film- und Fernsehtechnik. In H. Remschmidt & M. Schmidt (Eds.), *Neuropsychologie des Kindesalters* (pp. 49–57). Stuttgart: Enke.

90. Papoušek, H., & Papoušek, M. (1981). Frühentwicklung des Sozialverhaltens und der Kommunikation. In H. Remschmidt & M. Schmidt (Eds.), *Neuropsychologie des Kindesalters* (pp. 182–190). Stuttgart: Enke.

91. Papoušek, M., & Papoušek, H. (1981). Neue Wege der Verhaltensbeobachtung und Verhaltensmikroanalyse. *Sozialpädiatrie in Praxis und Klinik, 3*, 20–22.

92. Papoušek, M., & Papoušek, H. (1981). Verhaltensmikroanalyse mit Hilfe der Filmtechnik. *Sozialpädiatrie in Praxis und Klinik, 3*, 60–64.

93. Papoušek, M., & Papoušek, H. (1981). Verhaltensmikroanalyse mit Hilfe der Fernsehtechnik. *Sozialpädiatrie in Praxis und Klinik, 3*, 137–141.

94. Papoušek, M., & Papoušek, H. (1981). Intuitives elterliches Verhalten im Zwiegespräch mit dem Neugeborenen. *Sozialpädiatrie in Praxis und Klinik, 3*, 229–238.

95. Papoušek, M., & Papoušek, H. (1981). Musikalische Ausdruckselemente der Sprache und ihre Modifikation in der "Ammensprache". *Sozialpädiatrie in Praxis und Klinik, 3*, 294–296.

96. Papoušek, H., & Papoušek, M. (1981). How human is the newborn, and what else is to be done? In K. Bloom (Ed.), *Prospective issues in infancy research* (pp. 137–155). Hillsdale, NJ: Erlbaum.

97. Papoušek, H., & Papoušek, M. (1981). Lernpsychologische Grundlagen der normalen psychischen Entwicklung. *Der Kassenarzt, 21*, 1832–1838.

98. Papoušek, M., & Papoušek, H. (1981). Musical elements: Their significance for communication, cognition, and creativity. In L. P. Lipsitt (Ed.), *Advances in infancy research* (Vol. 1, pp. 163–224). Norwood, NJ: Ablex.

99. Papoušek, H., & Papoušek, M. (1982). Vocal imitations in mother-infant dialogues. *Infant behavior and Development* (Special ICIS Issue), *5*, 176.

100. Papoušek, H., & Papoušek, M. (1982). Integration into the social world: Survey of research. In P. M. Stratton (Ed.), *Psychobiology of the human newborn* (pp. 367–390). London: Wiley & Sons.

101. Papoušek, H., & Papoušek, M. (1982). Infant-adult social interactions, their origins, dimensions, and failures. In T. M. Field, A. Huston, H. C. Quay, L. Troll, & G. A. Finley (Eds.), *Review of developmental psychology* (pp. 148–163). New York: Wiley & Sons.

102. Papoušek, H., & Papoušek, M. (1982). Zur Frühentwicklung der Kommunikation. In K. R. Scherer (Ed.), *Vokale Kommunikation* (pp. 78–84). Weinheim/Basel: Beltz.

103. Papoušek, H., & Papoušek, M. (1982). Die Rolle der sozialen Interaktionen in der psychischen Entwicklung und Pathogenese von Entwicklungsstörungen im Säuglingsalter. In G. Nissen (Ed.), *Psychiatrie des Säuglings- und des frühen Kleinkindalters* (pp. 69–74). Bern/Stuttgart/Wien: Huber.

104. Papoušek, H., & Papoušek, M. (1983). Interactional failures: Their origins and significance in infant psychiatry. In J. D. Call, E. Galenson, & R. L. Tyson (Eds.), *Frontiers of infant psychiatry* (pp. 31–37). New York: Basic Books.

105. Papoušek, H., & Papoušek, M. (1983). Biological basis of social interactions: Implications of research for an understanding of behavioural deviance. *Journal of Child Psychology and Psychiatry* (Special Issue No. 1), *24*, 117–129.

106. Papoušek, H., & Papoušek, M. (1983). The psychobiology of the first didactic programs and toys in human infants. In A. Oliverio, & M. Zappella (Eds.), *The behavior of human infants* (pp. 219–239). New York/London: Plenum Press.

107. Papoušek, H., & Papoušek, M. (1984). Learning and cognition in the everyday life of human infants. In J. S. Rosenblatt (Ed.), *Advances in the study of behavior* (Vol. 14, pp. 127–163). New York: Academic Press.

108. Papoušek, H., Papoušek, M., & Giese, R. (1984). Die Anfänge der Eltern-Kind-Beziehung. In V. Frick-Bruder & P. Platz (Eds.), *Psychosomatische Probleme in der Gynäkologie und Geburtshilfe* (pp. 187–204). Berlin/Heidelberg/New York/Tokyo: Springer.

109. Papoušek, H., & Papoušek, M. (1984). Qualitative transitions in integrative processes during the first trimester of human postpartum life. In H. F. R. Prechtl (Ed.), *Continuity of neural functions from prenatal to postnatal life* (Spastics International Medical Publications) (pp. 220–244). Oxford: Blackwell Scientific Publications Ltd./Philadelphia: Lippincott.

110. Papoušek, M., & Papoušek, H. (1984). Categorical vocal cues in parental communication with presyllabic infants (Abstract). *Infant Behavior and Development* (Special ICIS Issue), *7*, 283.

111. Papoušek, H., & Papoušek, M. (1984). The evolution of parent-infant attachment: New psychobiological perspectives. In J. D. Call, E. Galenson, & R. L. Tyson (Eds.), *Frontiers of infant psychiatry* (Vol. 2, pp. 276–283). New York: Basic Books.

112. Papoušek, H., Papoušek, M., & Bornstein, M. H. (1985). The naturalistic vocal environment of young infants: On the significance of homogeneity and variability in parental speech. In T. Field & N. Fox (Eds.), *Social perception in infants* (pp. 269–297). Norwood, NJ: Ablex.

113. Papoušek, H., & Papoušek, M. (1985). Der Beginn der sozialen Integration nach der Geburt: Krisen oder Kontinuitäten? *Monatsschrift der Kinderheilkunde, 133*, 425–429. Berlin: Springer.

114. Koester, L. S., Papoušek, H., & Papoušek, M. (1985). Patterns of rhythmic stimulation by mothers with young infants: A comparison of multiple modalities (Abstract). *Cahiers de Psychologie Cognitive, 5*, 270–271.

115. Papoušek, H., Papoušek, M., & Haekel, M. (1985). Der Vater und sein Säugling: Anfänge einer Beziehung. In C. Mühlfeld, H. Oppl, H. Weber, & W. R. Wendt (Eds.), *Brennpunkte sozialer Arbeit* (pp. 48–63). Frankfurt: Diesterweg.

116. Papoušek, H. (1985). Biologische Wurzein der ersten Kommunikation im menschilichen Leben. In W. Böhme (Ed.), *Evolution der Sprache: Über Entstehung und Wesen der Sprache*

(Herrenalber Texte, No. 66, pp. 33–47). Karlsruhe: Evangelische Akademie. (Also published in W. Böhme, H. Greifenstein, E. Lohse, G. Ruhbach, K. Schmidt-Clausen, & M. Seitz (Eds.), *Zeitwende, 57,* 1–16. Karlsruhe: Zeitwende Verlagsgesellschaft, 1985.)

117. Papoušek, M., & Papoušek, H. (1986). Didactic adjustment in parental speech to three-month old infants: Age-specificity, and universality across sex of parent (Abstract). *Infant behavior and Development* (Special Issue), *9,* 285.

118. Papoušek, H., Papoušek, M., & Giese, R., (1986). Neue wissenschaftliche Ansätze zum Verständnis der Mutter-Kind-Beziehung. In J. Stork (Ed.), *Zur Psychologie und Psychopathologie des Säuglings: Neue Ergebnisse in der psychoanalytischen Reflektion.* Problemata 112, 53–71. Stuttgart/Bad Cannstatt: Frommata-Holzboog, 1986.

119. Papoušek, H., Papoušek M., & Koester, L. S. (1986). Sharing emotionality and sharing knowledge: A microanalytic approach to parent-infant communication. In C. E. Izard, & P. Read (Eds.), *Measuring emotions in infants and children* (Vol. 2, pp. 93–123). Cambridge, UK: Cambridge University Press.

120. Papoušek, H., & Papoušek, M. (1986). Structure and dynamics of human communication at the beginning of life. *European Archives of Psychiatry and Neurological Sciences, 236,* 21–25.

121. Papoušek, M., & Papoušek, H., & Harris, B. J. (1987). The emergence of play in parent-infant interactions. In D. Görlitz, & J. F. Wholwill (Eds.), *Curiosity, imagination, and play: On the development of spontaneous cognitive and motivational processes* (pp. 214–246). Hillsdale, NJ/London: Erlbaum.

122. Papoušek, H., & Papoušek, M. (1987). Intuitive parenting: A dialectic counterpart to the infant's integrative competence. In J. D. Osofsky (Ed.), *Handbook of infant development* (2nd ed. 669–720). New York: Wiley & Sons.

123. Papoušek, H., Papoušek, M., & Harris, B. J. (1987). Intuitive parenting behaviors: An early support for the infant's mental health development. In H. Galjaard, H. F. R. Prechtl, & M. Veličkovič (Eds.), *Early detection and management of cerebral palsy* (pp. 121–136). Dordrecht: Martinus Nijhoff Publishers.

124. Koester, L. S., Papoušek, H., & Papoušek, M. (1987). Psychobiological models of infant development: Influences on the concept of intuitive parenting. In H. Rauh & H.-C. Steinhausen (Eds.), *Psychobiology and early development. Advances in Psychology, 46* (pp. 275–287). North Holland: Elsevier.

125. Papoušek, H., & Papoušek, M. (1987). *The structure and dynamics of early parental interventions: A potential contribution to evolution and ontogeny of speech.* (ERIC Document 276 528). Resources in Education. Urbana: Clearing House on Early Childhood Education.

126. Papoušek, M., Papoušek, H., & Haekel, M. (1987). Didactic adjustments in fathers' and mothers' speech to their three-month-old infants. *Journal of Psycholinguistic Research, 16,* 491–516.

127. Papoušek, H., & Papoušek, M. (1988). Musikalität am Anfang des Lebens. *Uben und Musizieren, 5* (H. 1), 25–30.

128. Papoušek, H. (1988, March). The Middle European contribution to infancy research. *Research and Clinical Center for Child Development Annual Report No. 10* (pp. 9–20). Hokkaido University, Sapporo Japan.

129. Papoušek, H., & Papoušek, M. (1989). Frühe Kommunikations-entwicklung und körperliche Beeinträchtigung. In A. Fröhlich (Ed.), *Kommunikation und Sprache körperbehinderter Kinder* (pp. 29–44). Dortmund: Verlag Modernes Lernen.

130. Papoušek, H. (1989). Coevolution of supportive counterparts in caretakers: A potential contribution to the hemispheric specialization during early infancy. Cahiers de Psychologie Cognitive. *European Bulletin of Cognitive Psychology, 9,* 113–117.

131. Koester, L. S., Papoušek, H., & Papoušek, M. (1989). Patterns of rhythmic stimulation by mothers with three-month-olds: A cross-modal comparison. *International Journal of Behavioural Development, 12,* 143–154.

132. Papoušek, H., & Papoušek, M. (1989). Intuitive parenting: Aspects related to educational

psychology. In B. Hopkins, M.-G. Pecheux, & H. Papousek (Eds.), *Infancy and education: Psychological cc•siderations. European Journal of Psychology of Education, 4*, (2, Special Issue), 201–210.

133.   Papoušek, M., & Papoušek, H. (1989). Stimmliche Kommunikation im frühen Säglingsalter als Wegbereiter der Sprachentwicklung. In H. Keller (Ed.), *Handbuch der Kleinkindforschung* (pp. 465–489). Berlin/Heidelberg: Springer-Verlag.

134.   Papoušek, H., & Papoušek, M. (1989). Ontogeny of social interactions in newborn infants. In C. von Euler, H. Forssberg, & H. Lagercrantz (Eds.), *Neurobiology of early infant behaviour. Proceedings of an International Wallenberg Symposium at the Wenner-Gren Centre* (Stockholm, August 28–September 1, 1988, Vol. 55, pp. 217–225). London: Mac-Millan Press.

135.   Papoušek, H. (1989). A remedy for Stendhal's syndrome. /Review of J. B. Lancaster, J. Altmann, A. S. Rossi, and L. R. Sherrod (Eds.), Parenting across the life span: Biosocial dimensions. (New York: A. de Gruyter, 1987). *Contemporary Psychology, 34*, 688–689.

136.   Papoušek, M., & Papoušek, H. (1989). Wie wird die unbekannte Welt vertraut? Ein Blick in die frühe Erfahrungswelt des Kindes. *Welt des Kindes, 5*, 31–36.

137.   Papoušek, M., & Papoušek, H. (1989). Forms and functions of vocal matching in interactions between mothers and their precanonical infants. *First Language, 9*, 137–158. (Special Issue on "Precursors to speech").

138.   Papoušek, H. (1989). Kinderärzte und Früherziehung. *Der Kinderarzt, 20*, 1605–1610.

139.   Papoušek, H. (1990). Frühe Eltern-Kind-Interaktion in ihrer Bedeutung für die kindliche Entwicklung. *Der Kinderarzt, 21* (2), 191–194.

140.   Papoušek, H., &. Papoušek, M. (1990). Frühe Kommunikation, soziale Integration. *Beschäftigungstherapie und Rehabilitation, 29*, 189–194.

141.   Papoušek, M., & Papoušek, H. (1990). Intuitive elterliche Früherziehung in der vorsprachlichen Kommunikation I: Grundlagen und Verhaltensrepertoire. *Sozialpädiatrie in Praxis und Klinik, 12*(7), 521–527.

142.   Papoušek, M., & Papoušek, H. (1990). Intuitive elterliche Früherziehung in der vorsprachlichen Kommunikation II: Früherkennung von Störungen und therapeutische Ansätze. *Sozialpädiatrie in Praxis und Klinik, 12*(8), 579–583.

143.   Papoušek, H., & Papoušek, M. (1990). Die Kunst der Mutterliebe. In Foundation Scientific Europe (Ed.), *Wissenschaft und Technik in Europa* (pp. 382–387). Heidelberg: Spektrum der Wissenschaften.

144.   Papoušek, M., Bornstein, M. H., Nuzzo, C., Papoušek, H., & Symmes, D. (1990). Infant responses to prototypical melodic contours in parental speech. *Infant Behavior and Development, 13*, 539–545.

145.   Papoušek, M., & Papoušek, H. (1990). Excessive infant crying and intuitive parental care: Buffering support and its failures in parent-infant interaction. *Early Child Development and Care* (Ed. R. Evans), *65*, 117–126. (Special Issue on Infant crying, Ed. J. Kirkland.)

146.   Papoušek, H., & Papoušek, M. (1990). The art of motherhood. In N. Calder (Ed.), *Scientific Europe: Research and technology in 20 countries* (pp. 382–387). Maastricht, Holland: Scientific Publishers Ltd.

147.   Papoušek, H., & Papoušek, M. (1991). Innate and cultural guidance of infants' integrative competencies: China, the United States, and Germany. In M. H. Bornstein (Ed.), *Cultural approaches to parenting* (pp. 23–44). Hillsdale, NJ: Erlbaum.

148.   Papoušek, H. (1991). Frühe menschliche Kommunikation: Biologisches Erbe und Entwicklungspotential. In H. Viebrock & U . Holste (Eds.), *Therapie. Anspruch und Widerspruch* (pp. 70–83). Bremen: Bremische Evangelische Kirche.

149.   Papoušek, H., Papoušek, M., Suomi, S., & Rahn, C. (1991). Preverbal communication and attachment: Comparative views. In J. L. Gewirtz & W. M. Kurtines (Eds.), *Intersections with attachment* (pp. 97–122). Hillsdale, NJ: Erlbaum.

150.   Papoušek, H. (1991). Toward hemispheric specialization during infancy: Manual skills

versus acquisition of speech. In H. E. Fitzgerald, B. M. Lester, & M. W. Yogman (Eds.), *Theory and research in behavioral pediatrics* (Vol. 5, pp. 209–215). New York: Plenum.

151. Papoušek, M., & Papoušek, H. (1991). Early verbalizations as precursors of language development. In M. E. Lamb & H. Keller (Eds.), *Infant development: Perspectives from German-speaking countries* (pp. 299–328). Hillsdale, NJ: Erlbaum.

152. Papoušek, M., Papoušek, H., & Symmes, D. (1991). The meanings of melodies in motherese in tone and stress languages. *Infant Behavior and Development, 14*, 415–440.

153. Papoušek, H., & Papoušek, M. (1992). Early integrative and communicative development: Pointers to humanity. In H. M. Emrich & M. Wiegand (Eds.), *Integrative biological psychiatry* (pp. 45–60). Berlin: Springer-Verlag.

154. Papoušek, H., Jürgens, U., & Papoušek, M. (Eds.). (1992). *Nonverbal vocal communication: Comparative and developmental aspects.* New York: Cambridge University Press.

155. Papoušek, H., & Bornstein, M. H. (1992). Didactic interactions: Intuitive parental support of vocal and verbal development in humans. In H. Papoušek, U. Jürgens, & M. Papoušek (Eds.), *Nonverbal vocal communication: Comparative and developmental aspects* (pp. 209–229). Cambridge: Cambridge University Press.

156. Papoušek, H., & Papoušek, M. (1992). Beyond emotional bonding: The role of preverbal communication in mental growth and health. *Infant Mental Health Journal, 13*, 42–52.

157. Papoušek, H. (1992). Láska rodiče pod mikroskopem. (Microscopic view of parental love. In Czech.) *Efeta, 2*(1), 11–14. Bratislava, ČSFR: Slovak Pedagocical Publishers, Ed. V. Lechta.

158. Beek, Y. van, Papoušek, H., & Hopkins, B. (1962). Beweging en vroege communicatie bij prematuren. (Movement and early communication in prematures. In Dutch.) In B. Hopkins & A. Vermeer (Eds.), *Kinderen in beweging (Children in movement.* in Dutch) (pp. 63–77). Amsterdam: Free University Press.

# USES OF LINEAR SYSTEMS MODELS OF INFANT PATTERN VISION*

*Benjamin R. Stephens*

DEPARTMENT OF PSYCHOLOGY
CLEMSON UNIVERSITY

I. INTRODUCTION ............................................. 1
II. PATTERN DETECTION AND CSF-BASED MODELS ............ 3
   A. Adult Pattern Detection .................................... 3
   B. Infant Pattern Detection .................................... 5
III. SUPRATHRESHOLD PATTERN VISION ...................... 7
   A. Apparent Contrast ......................................... 7
      1. Adult apparent contrast ................................. 7
      2. Infant apparent contrast ................................ 9
   B. Contrast Discrimination ................................... 12
      1. Adult contrast discrimination ........................... 12
      2. Infant contrast discrimination .......................... 14
   C. Implications for Adult Models ............................ 18
IV. APPLICATIONS: FACE PREFERENCE AND SELF-PERCEPTION .. 27
V. CONCLUSIONS ............................................. 33
VI. REFERENCES ............................................. 34

## I. INTRODUCTION

For many developmental psychologists, the primary value of research on pattern vision in infancy is gauged in terms of applications to cognitive, social, and clinical issues (e.g., object identification and recognition, social interactions,

* Preparation of this chapter was supported by National Science Foundation Grant BNS-8819964 to BRS. I thank Martin S. Banks and James L. Dannemiller for the discussions that helped me to improve my ideas. I also thank Dannemiller and Reviewer B for their comments on the manuscript.

1

neurological screening, etc.). Consider an infant's ability to respond to a complex stimulus, such as a face. Estimates of infant acuity suggest that some of the features of the face may not be visible to the infant. If research on infant visual development could specify which features are available to the infant for further cognitive processing, those findings may help inform models of cognitive development. To speculate, it may be possible that developmental differences in attention or schema formation for faces may be due in part to the inability of the very young infant to detect critical features in the face. In a similar vein, parent–infant interactions may be influenced by poor infant vision to the extent that the infant responds to features in the face that are visible, thereby influencing parental behaviors that are designed to attract infant attention. Although the above examples are speculative, they do illustrate the point that developmental differences in infant vision constrain the infant's access to information about objects in the environment. To the extent this missing object information is required for cognitive and social tasks, research on visual development may aid our understanding of development in these domains.

To comprehend this research in visual development, a little background will be described in the next section. For example, it turns out that the acuity estimates mentioned above do not specify which features are detectable and which are not detectable developmentally, because the stimuli used in estimating acuity do not clearly generalize to all features. One approach that does provide a way of specifying which features are detectable is the so-called *linear systems approach*. The application of linear systems models of form perception, based on measurements of the infant *contrast sensitivity function* (CSF), have led researchers to a deeper understanding of the development of infants' ability to detect information in their environment. The success of this approach derives in part from the general nature of the model. Any stimulus can be described in the Fourier domain. The CSF can be used to describe the responses of the infant's visual system to the stimulus, and simulate the information in the stimulus that is available to the infant. The CSF-based model has been used in this fashion to simulate the pattern information in a human face that is detectable for infants at different ages (Banks & Ginsburg, 1985; Souther & Banks, 1979).

This CSF-based model of infant pattern vision may be limited in two ways. First, the models are based on threshold functions. Our research indicates that the threshold-based models should be modified to apply to suprathreshold conditions. This modification is nontrivial, since most objects in the environment are high in contrast and hence fall within the suprathreshold range of pattern vision (Switkes, Mayer, & Sloan, 1978). Second, the models do not deal with "meaningfulness" and other more complex variables. Thus, caution is required in applying these models to domains such as face- and self-perception. In the section describing suprathreshold pattern vision I will review this recent research and try to explain how these modifications and limitations of CSF-based models are both interesting and important.

In addition to describing our recent findings, there are two points of general interest to developmental psychologists that are illustrated by our research. The first point is that infancy research should not be isolated from adult research. The bulk of our developmental research is based on the adult literature. That literature contains much of the research identifying pattern processing mechanisms and models, and so I describe that research below when appropriate, to highlight the background that guides our studies. What is interesting about the application of these models to developmental populations is that the results sometimes aid our evaluation of the adult models per se. Furthermore, a developmental perspective may suggest that some new adult studies are needed. I describe these implications and research to illustrate our belief that interactions between the infant and adult literature can lead to a deeper understanding of pattern vision.

The second point of interest to developmental psychologists was described at the beginning of this section, concerning the possibility that research on the development of pattern vision can lead to data and models that are useful in areas beyond pattern vision per se. The last section of this chapter describes some research that illustrates this idea. In some cases, these models may make quite specific predictions regarding socially important capabilities, such as infant face preferences. In other cases, these models provide a heuristic and suggest how limitations in pattern vision may constrain the development of complex skills, such as self-perception.

## II.  PATTERN DETECTION AND CSF-BASED MODELS

### A.  Adult Pattern Detection

Recent research on the development of form perception has been heavily influenced by the application of models based on linear systems techniques. These types of models were initially developed in the adult literature. One aspect of this approach involves Fourier's theorem. Fourier's theorem states that any pattern can be exactly described by a set of sinewave gratings of various spatial frequencies, contrasts, orientations, and phases. A sinewave grating is an alternating pattern of light and dark bars whose luminance varies sinusoidally over space. *Spatial frequency* is defined as the number of times the sinusoidal cycle repeats per degree of visual angle (cycles/degree). *Contrast* is defined as the difference between the peak and the trough of the luminance profile, divided by twice the mean luminance. *Orientation* is the extent to which the grating deviates from horizontal (measured by the angle of deviation in degrees). *Phase* is the relative location of the grating in space, usually referred to some common arbitrary reference point. Fourier's theorem is useful for generating the predictions of a linear system. For example, linear systems analysis describes the input–output functions for a linear visual system: The output of the visual system is simply a weighted sum of the input, with the weights given by the visual systems' contrast sensitivity function (CSF). (It is important to note that the visual system violates the assumptions of a linear system, so these violations must be taken into account for linear systems techniques to be useful. This point will become important in applications to suprathreshold pattern processing.)

A key ingredient to models employing linear systems techniques is the CSF, which represents the contrast threshold for sinewave gratings of different spatial frequencies. One can estimate contrast threshold for a sinewave grating by presenting two stimuli; one is the grating, and the other is a uniform field that is equal to the grating in all respects save that there is no pattern. The subject's task is to indicate which stimulus is the grating. The contrast threshold is defined as the contrast associated with some arbitrary level of performance, usually 75% correct performance.

The CSF can be used to test models that attempt to predict the detectability of pattern information. The derivation and testing of these models is usually based on the techniques of linear systems analysis (Gaskill, 1978; Cornsweet, 1970). Using this approach, several investigators have shown that the CSF provides a reasonable description of pattern detection under some conditions. For example, visual acuity and the ability to detect complex patterns can be predicted from an observer's CSF (Campbell, Carpenter, & Levinson, 1969), and the discriminability of different waveforms can be predicted based on the detectability of their Fourier components (Campbell, Howell, & Johnstone, 1978; Ginsburg, 1978).

Contrast detection thresholds can also reflect the behavior of basic visual mechanisms. Two mechanisms are particularly germane to subsequent discussion. First, the high-frequency loss in contrast sensitivity is generally thought to result from optical imperfections and peripheral neural summation (Campbell & Green, 1965; Campbell & Gubisch, 1966). These optical and neural limitations degrade pattern information and pose an interesting problem for object perception in everyday situations, a topic discussed in more detail in the section on suprathreshold applications.

Second, psychophysical and physiological evidence indicates that the CSF represents the envelope of sensitivities of several parallel mechanisms, each responsive to a limited range of spatial frequencies. These spatial-frequency-selective mechanisms have been demonstrated psychophysically in masking, adaptation, and detection experiments (Blakemore & Campbell, 1969; Campbell & Robson, 1968; Graham & Nachmias, 1971; Stromeyer & Julesz, 1972). Masking experiments, for example, show that contrast threshold for a target is increased in the presence of a masking stimulus if the spatial frequencies are within about a factor of two of one another (Stromeyer & Julesz, 1972), and are similar in orientation (Campbell & Kulikowski, 1966). Adaptation experiments show that contrast threshold for a grating is increased following prolonged exposure to a grating of similar spatial frequency, and that these effects transfer interocularly. These adult data suggest that these spatial-frequency-selective mechanisms are located beyond the primary visual cortex (Blakemore, Muncey, & Ridley, 1973).

Consider briefly some interesting perceptual functions of spatial frequency channels. Georgeson and Sullivan (1975) have argued that channels may be an important component of contrast constancy (the stable apparent contrast of high-contrast objects across changes in viewing distance). Also, Ginsburg (1978, 1984) has provided a number of simulations employing linear systems techniques and spatial frequency channels. The results suggest that different properties of objects (e.g., existence, general form, classification, identification, texture, and edges) may be encoded by different channels. That is, relative to object size, very low-frequency channels may encode pattern information corresponding to the existence of an object. High-frequency channels may encode pattern information allowing the identification of an object.

The visibility of the frequency components of an object may determine one's ability to identify various object properties. In addition, the relative phases of these components are also important for normal object perception. This point has been demonstrated by exchanging only the phase relationships of two different images. The effect of such a switch is a clear tendency to identify the images with the phase of their components, and not their contrasts (Piotrowski & Campbell, 1982). However, this result does not imply that relative contrast is not important as well for accurate pattern perception. In fact, in the section below on contrast discrimination, I demonstrate how simple distortions of the amplitudes of the components may also disrupt pattern perception.

## B. Infant Pattern Detection

Investigators have applied the linear systems approach to the study of infant pattern vision with general success. The refinement of different experimental techniques is mainly responsible for the surge in the study of infant visual · development. Perhaps the most popular behavioral technique employs a version of the preferential-looking procedure (Fantz, 1961; Teller, 1979). In this procedure, infants are given a choice between viewing a patterned or an unpatterned field. Preferential behavior toward one of the two fields is evidence that the infant detected the pattern. Contrast threshold is defined as the minimum contrast for which the infant demonstrates reliable discriminative behavior.

Using infant preferential looking, investigators have provided reasonably consistent descriptions of CSF development in early infancy (Atkinson, Braddick, & Moar, 1977; Banks & Salapatek, 1978). At 1 month of age, the range of spatial frequencies infants can detect is quite restricted relative to the adult, and they require much more contrast to detect the frequencies that are within their range. By 3 months of age, the infant CSF has improved, showing sensitivity to higher spatial frequencies and lower contrasts. As in adults, estimates of infant CSFs have been useful in predicting performance in a variety of threshold tasks, including acuity (Banks & Salapatek, 1981) and contrast sensitivity for complex waveforms (Atkinson et al., 1977; Banks & Stephens, 1982).

Two studies have reported data concerning the development of spatial frequency channels in human infants. Fiorentini, Pirchio, and Spinelli (1983) examined infant visually evoked potentials in a modified spatial-frequency-masking task. They reported adultlike masking functions in one 6-week-old and one 14-week-old. Based on this limited evidence, they concluded that multiple channels are present with mature, narrowband selectivity at 6 weeks of age.

Banks, Stephens, and Hartmann (1985) employed a forced-choice preferential-looking technique in two experiments designed to identify the presence of spatial-frequency-selective mechanisms in 6- and 12-week-old infants. In the first experiment, a masking paradigm similar to the adult technique described above was employed. Infant contrast sensitivity was estimated for three spatial frequencies with and without the presence of narrowband noise. The results for 6- and 12-week-olds are represented in Figure 1. Notice that the effect of the noise masker is different in the two age groups. For the 6-week-olds, the presence of the noise masker reduces sensitivity in a similar fashion for all three test frequencies, whereas, for the 12-week-olds, the masker reduces sensitivity primarily for test frequencies similar to the frequency content of the masker, but not for the test frequency that is a factor of four higher in frequency. This result suggests adultlike selectivity is present in 12-week-olds, but not 6-week-olds. This interpretation was confirmed in a second experiment employing a different paradigm and type of stimulus. Thus, the 6-week-old results of Banks et al. are

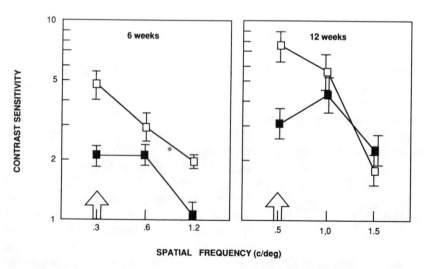

Fig. 1. Masking functions at six and 12 weeks of age. Contrast sensitivity is plotted as a function of spatial frequency both without noise (open symbols) and in the presence of a low-frequency, narrowband noise masker.

inconsistent with Fiorentini et al. Since Banks et al. employed a much larger sample of infants and provided consistent data from two different paradigms, their conclusions seem more convincing that those of Fiorentini et al. This suggests that there is a fundamental change in the way pattern information is processed between 6 and 12 weeks of age.

## III. SUPRATHRESHOLD PATTERN VISION

What are the implications of contrast sensitivity and spatial frequency channel development during the first few months of life? Consider the development of the ability to recognize and identify objects based on pattern information. The structure of an object, for example, boundaries, shading, texture, and so on, is partially defined by the relative physical contrasts of pattern components (i.e., spatial frequency components). Certainly it is important to be able to detect the contrast of these components. However, recognition and discrimination require more than just contrast detection. Most objects in the environment are high in contrast; thus, the representation of these objects involves suprathreshold pattern processing, and the visual system must represent these suprathreshold contrasts in a consistent fashion. We can refer to the visual system's representation of contrast as *apparent contrast*. The apparent contrast of pattern information helps define the structure of an object. The discriminability of the contrast of an object's pattern components helps differentiate one object from another. Clearly, apparent contrast and contrast discrimination are crucial for accurate object identification and recognition. By modifying paradigms developed in adult research for use in infant tasks, we have identified important developmental changes in both apparent contrast and contrast discrimination. These developmental data, in turn, aid our evaluation of the adult models.

### A. Apparent Contrast

#### 1. Adult Apparent Contrast

In the adult literature, contrast-matching tasks have been used to determine the relationship between apparent contrast and stimulus parameters such as physical contrast and spatial frequency. In this task, the observer is presented with a standard stimulus whose spatial frequency and contrast are fixed. The observer adjusts the contrast of a comparison stimulus until its contrast appears to match the perceived contrast of the standard. To obtain a full description of how apparent contrast varies with contrast and spatial frequency, several different contrasts of the standard are employed and are matched to comparison gratings of different spatial frequencies.

Several investigators have examined adult's contrast matching under near-threshold and suprathreshold conditions (e.g., Blakemore et al., 1973; Cannon,

1979; Davidson, 1968; Georgeson & Sullivan, 1975; Ginsburg, Cannon, & Nelson, 1980; Kulikowski, 1976). The results are generally consistent. Consider Georgeson and Sullivan's (1975) main experiment. The standard was a grating of 5 c/deg, a value near the peak of the adult CSF. The results are illustrated in the right panel of Figure 2. When the contrast of the standard was near threshold, adults set the contrast of the comparison gratings to relatively higher values. These values were predictable from the CSF (left panel). For example, a 20 c/deg comparison grating was set to a value eightfold higher than the contrast of the 5 c/deg standard, and this ratio was equal to the ratio of contrast thresholds for 5 and 20 c/deg. The most interesting result in this experiment occurred when the contrast of the standard was set to a value well above threshold. Adults in this situation adjusted the contrast of the comparison to the same physical value as the contrast of the standard. This is a surprising result because two gratings of equal contrast, but different spatial frequencies, will produce different retinal image contrasts. This differential retinal contrast is due to the blur function of the optics of the eye, which indicates that the higher the spatial frequency, the greater the reduction in retinal contrast due to the eye's optical imperfections. Specifically, when the adults set 5 and 20 c/deg gratings to equal physical contrasts, they were accepting as equal in apparent contrast two gratings whose retinal image contrasts differed substantially. Clearly, the CSF cannot predict this result, so models of adult pattern vision should employ flatter functions than the CSF at suprathreshold stimulus contrasts.

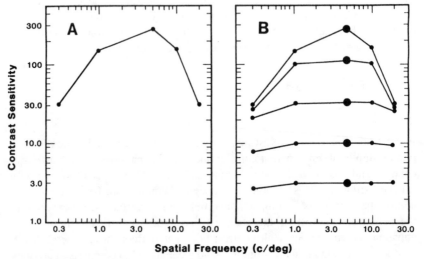

Fig. 2.   *Adult contrast-sensitivity and contrast-matching data. Contrast sensitivity is plotted as a function of spatial frequency and contrast of the 5 cy/deg standard (large symbols).*

This phenomenon has been called *contrast constancy*. Like other constancies, contrast constancy aids veridical object perception. As an object moves away from an observer, its spatial frequency content shifts to progressively higher values. For low-contrast objects, apparent contrast would change according to the CSF; so for medium-sized (mid-frequency) objects, apparent contrast would decrease with greater viewing distances because contrast sensitivity decreases monotonically for higher frequencies. Georgeson and Sullivan's observations imply, however, that the apparent contrast of high-contrast objects would not change with viewing distance. Thus, contrast constancy confers a useful property on the perception of real objects: so long as the contrast that defines an object and its features is suprathreshold, apparent contrast remains invariant across a wide range of viewing distances.

Georgeson and Sullivan's model of contrast constancy employs multiple spatial frequency channels. Compensation for threshold deficits is accomplished by setting the gains of different spatial frequency channels to different values. Channels tuned to high frequencies are assumed to have higher gains (that is, their response grows more rapidly with increases in contrast) than channels tuned to intermediate frequencies. Near threshold, the response of channels tuned to intermediate frequencies would be greater than that of high-frequency channels, due to the effects of optical defocus and neural summation. As the contrast of the gratings is raised, however, the contrast response of high-frequency channels grows more rapidly and eventually catches up with the contrast response of intermediate channels. In this fashion the visual system is able to undo differences in detectability caused by optical defocus and neural summation.

## 2.   Infant Apparent Contrast

If Georgeson and Sullivan's model of contrast constancy is correct, contrast constancy should not be observed at 6 weeks (assuming that 12-week-olds, but not 6-week-olds, possess multiple spatial frequency channels with narrow tuning). One is tempted to predict that contrast constancy should be observed at 12 weeks, but this is not a logical implication. Georgeson and Sullivan's model claims that multiple channels are necessary, but not sufficient, for the realization of contrast constancy. Sufficiency requires the additional assumption that the various channels have different contrast response functions.

To examine the development of contrast constancy, we examined 6- and 12-week-old infants' responses to near-threshold and suprathreshold pattern information (Stephens & Banks, 1985). Infants were tested using a standard pattern preference procedure to examine the effects of spatial frequency and contrast on their pattern preferences and, by inference, on their apparent contrast matches. Two sine wave gratings, differing by a factor of three in spatial frequency, were presented side by side to each infant. An observer recorded visual fixations during 20-sec presentations of the stimulus pairs. All infants were presented three contrasts of 3F paired in all possible combinations with six contrasts of F.

The data for each stimulus pairing were represented as preferences for F over 3F. For each contrast of 3F, the equal preference point (the contrast of F associated with 50% preference) was estimated by fitting least-squares regression lines to the preference functions. Figure 3 displays the estimates of F for the different contrasts of 3F. The error bars represent $+/-$ 1 standard error of the mean. Adult data (squares) are included for comparison. The diagonal dashed line represents the functions that would be obtained if equal preference occurred when the physical contrasts of F and 3F were equal. Consider the 12-week estimates first (circles). When the contrast of 3F was 0.14, the estimate of F was

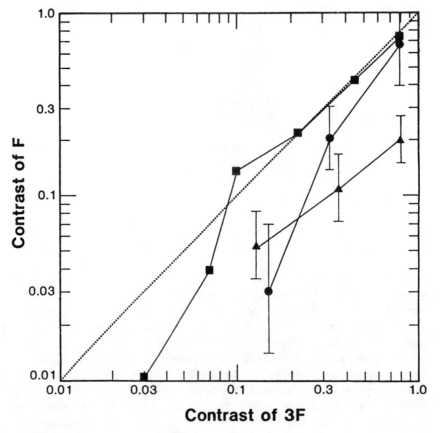

Fig. 3. *Infant contrast-matching data. Contrast of F estimated to be equally preferred to three contrasts of 3F is plotted for 6-week-olds (triangles) and 12-week-olds (circles). Adult data (squares) are included for comparison.*

a factor of 4.5 lower (similar to the ratio of contrast thresholds obtained for these stimuli under similar conditions (Banks et al., 1985)). When the contrast of 3F was 0.79, F was a factor of 1.2 lower. These data show quite clearly that the contrasts of F and 3F at the equal preference point became more similar as contrast was increased. Assuming that equal preference corresponds to equal apparent contrast, the 12-week data are very similar to adult contrast matching data.

The 6-week data (triangles) were not similar to adult data. When 3F was 0.14, F was a factor of 3.2 lower (again, similar to the ratio of contrast thresholds obtained for these stimuli under similar conditions (Banks et al., 1985)). When 3F was 0.79, F was a factor of 3.9 lower. Thus, the ratios of contrasts of F and 3F at the equal preference point were similar for high and low contrasts. Assuming equal preference is analogous to equal apparent contrast, these data do not provide evidence of contrast constancy at 6 weeks of age.

These data suggest that models of infant pattern vision should be modified for 12-week-olds, but not 6-week-olds. Like adults, models of 12-week-old pattern vision should employ functions flatter than the CSF for high contrast pattern components. Six-week-old models, however, seem well served by the CSF at low and high contrasts.

These data also suggest that contrast constancy emerges between 6 and 12 weeks of age, if we assume that equal preference in infants is analogous to equal apparent contrast in adults. If we accept this assumption, the following picture of development emerges. At 12 weeks, the visual system compensates above threshold for differences in detectability that result from optical defocus, spatial summation, and receptor immaturities (immaturities such as shorter and fatter cones, density of foveal cone distribution, etc.). Thus, contrast constancy is present much like it is in adults. At 6 weeks, however, no such compensation occurs. Contrast constancy then does not seem to be present at that age. Current models of contrast constancy are based on the operation of spatial frequency channels. Banks et al. (1985) showed that multiple channels develop between 6 and 12 weeks after birth. Those data then are consistent with current models of contrast constancy, because the age at which multiple channels emerge is similar to the age at which contrast constancy is observed. In summary, acceptance of the assumption that equal preference corresponds to an apparent contrast match leads to a simple developmental picture that is quite consistent with Georgeson and Sullivan's model of contrast processing.

The perceptual consequences of contrast constancy should be advantageous to infants. When contrast constancy is observed, the contrast that defines an object and its features would be perceived as roughly invariant despite changes in the object's distance. Thus, contrast constancy may allow a more stable representation of pattern information, and may allow the infant to more easily represent cues associated with important objects in its environment, such as faces.

## B.  Contrast Discrimination

### 1.  Adult Contrast Discrimination

Contrast constancy should prove useful in pattern recognition tasks: The apparent structure of an object will remain relatively stable across changes in viewing distance. It seems reasonable that, if such relative contrast information is an important characteristic of objects, then it will prove useful to represent a variety of pattern contrasts differentially. It follows that contrast discrimination is an important component of pattern recognition and discrimination.

Researchers have employed standard psychophysical tasks to assess adult contrast discrimination capabilities. For example, adults may be presented with two patterns that differ only in contrast; one contains a fixed level of contrast (C), and the other pattern contains the background plus the contrast increment ($\Delta$C). The observer's task is to indicate which stimulus contains the greater contrast. Notice that this type of task is more similar to a detection task than to matching tasks. That is, any "perceptual" cue can be used to identify the target.

The contrast increment threshold is generally taken as the value of $\Delta$C that corresponds to 75% correct performance. Typically, the contrast increment threshold is expressed relative to the background contrast, $\Delta$C/C, which is termed the *Weber fraction*. A complete description of contrast discrimination requires estimates of the Weber fraction for a number of different background contrasts. Figure 4 shows an example of an adult contrast discrimination function. Notice that the function is dipper shaped. At low levels of background contrast, the contrast increment decreases as the background contrast increases. This has been referred to as the *pedestal* or *facilitation effect* (Legge, 1981; Foley & Legge, 1981; Nachmias & Sansbury, 1974). As the contrast of the background increases from threshold levels, the log contrast increment generally rises as a linear function of log background contrast.

The shape of the discrimination function over its rising portion conforms to a power law. That is,

$$\Delta C = kC^n$$

where $\Delta$C is the increment threshold, C is the background contrast, k is a sensitivity parameter, and n is the slope of the function. Note that for $n = 1.0$, the function would reflect Weber's law

$$\Delta C = k\,C^{1.0}$$

which reduces to

$$\Delta C = kC$$

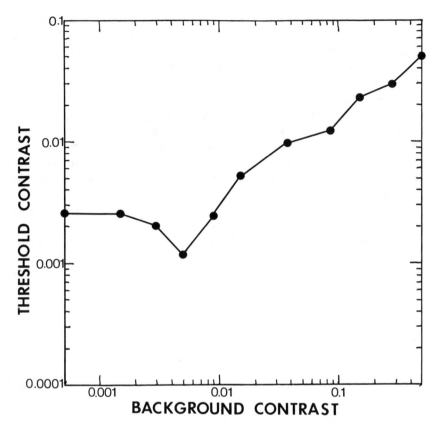

Fig. 4. *Adult contrast-discrimination function. Contrast increment threshold is plotted as a function of background contrast.*

If Weber's law held, the contrast increment would be a constant proportion of the background contrast. However, most researchers find that, under a variety of testing conditions and spatial frequencies, the value of the exponent of the power function is between 0.5 and 1.0, which means that the Weber fraction is not constant, but decreases as the background contrast increases (Peli, 1980; Legge, 1979, 1981; Legge & Foley, 1980).

Measures of the contrast increment threshold function can be useful as an index of the physiological mechanisms involved in pattern vision under both threshold and suprathreshold conditions. This index is accomplished within the context of models that link physiological activity to behavior in the discrimination task. Most models posit three processes to account for the shape of the contrast discrimination function: (a) a transducer, that is, contrast-response function, which describes how the physiological response grows with increasing contrast; (b) one or more sources of noise; and (c) a decision rule (Legge & Foley, 1980; Nachmias & Sansbury, 1974). Under the assumptions of these models, the shape, or slope, of the contrast discrimination function depends directly on the shape of the transducer function. The dipper of the adult function implies that the transducer function is S-shaped: accelerative at low contrasts and decelerative at high contrasts.

Contrast discrimination may be an important component of several different processes in pattern perception, such as pattern recognition (Burton, 1981), accommodation (Banks, 1980), and hyperacuity (Carlson & Klopfenstein, 1985; Wilson, 1986). Consider pattern discrimination. To discriminate different patterns, one needs to be able to represent pattern information differentially. In other words, the nature of neural activity associated with two images must differ. How can we quantify this skill for contrast differences? One approach is to determine the number of discriminable contrast levels available to the visual system for different types of pattern information. Burton (1981) has used estimates of contrast discrimination at different spatial frequencies to determine the number of contrast ''steps,'' or grey levels, contained within the dynamic range of the adult visual system. To illustrate his approach, consider the obvious example of a frequency near the acuity cutoff. In this case, only one contrast step is represented, since a contrast of 1.0 is required to detect the pattern. At intermediate spatial frequencies, Burton shows that the number of contrast steps increases to approximately 60. Obviously, this number of contrast steps represents a reduction from the infinite number of contrast steps available in a complex scene. One consequence of this reduction is that two scenes that differ physically in the number of contrast steps may be represented by the visual system in an identical fashion if the physical differences are too slight to be encoded.

## 2. Infant Contrast Discrimination

Despite the importance of contrast discrimination for understanding pattern perception and physiological mechanisms in vision, until recently there have been no direct measurements of contrast discrimination in infants. If contrast discrimination is poor in infants, then the infant's ability to discriminate and recognize patterns may be seriously constrained. Indeed, limitations on the development of pattern recognition in the face of poor contrast discrimination may be analogous to the limitations imposed by poor contrast sensitivity. How might infants encode the characteristics of a pattern based on relative contrast information if their contrast discrimination is poor? Consider the extreme case of poor contrast discrimination resulting in only one contrast step. Within the linear systems approach, one can simulate one step contrast discrimination by taking the spatial frequency components of a pattern and assigning the values of the amplitude spectrum to equal relative values if the physical amplitude is above a fixed criterion, and 0.0 if the physical amplitude is below criterion. This approach is illustrated in Figures 5 and 6 for two different waveforms (Stephens, 1985). In the top panel of Figure 5, the normal amplitude spectra for a ramp wave form and a square wave form are presented. (Note that the x-axis in the two panels is different in scale, due to the different harmonic structure of the waveforms.) The middle panels represent the intensity profile for two cycles of the pattern resulting from synthesizing the first 20 components of the amplitude spectra, and the bottom panels show the actual appearance of the waveforms. In Figure 6, the two top panels represent the modified amplitude spectra for these images, where the amplitudes have been assigned to equal relative values. These amplitude spectra in Figure 6 mimic the representation of a visual system that cannot discriminate contrast levels above threshold. The middle panels represent the intensity profiles for the two synthesized amplitude spectra. (The y-axis is an order of magnitude greater in scale than the corresponding y-axis in Figure 5 due to the relatively greater amount of energy in the amplitude spectra.) The images were scaled down in contrast to fit the response of the monitor and are presented in the bottom panel of Figure 6. Comparing the differences in the middle and bottom panels of Figures 5 and 6, three effects of the reduced number of contrast steps are apparent. First, edge transitions are overemphasized. Second, there is a loss of gradual intensity changes in the ramp grating, and a reduction in the intensity differences of the peak and trough of the square wave relative to the edge. Third, the harmonic structure of the pattern (the ripples that appear in the intensity profile) is pronounced in both waveforms. It is clear from this demonstration that some level of contrast discrimination is important for determining the structure of patterns. Therefore, if very young infants were unable to discriminate contrasts above threshold, their representation of pattern information may be quite different from adults. This demonstration also suggests that veridical pattern perception relies on veridical representation of the relative amplitudes of the spatial-frequency components. This implication makes it difficult to claim that phase information is somehow more important than contrast information in pattern recognition tasks.

We examined contrast discrimination in 6- and 12-week-old infants using a modified version of the forced-choice preferential-looking technique (Stephens & Banks, 1987). Between trials, the display was filled with a background grating. An observer pressed a button to begin a trial. A high-contrast increment was presented suddenly on one side of the display, while the other side of the display remained at the background level. The observer scored a trial by judging the location of the increment using any cue from the infant. He or she was provided feedback as to the correctness of that judgment. For each of four background contrasts (0.0, 0.14, 0.28, and 0.55), three different increment contrasts were presented using the method of constant stimuli. Contrast increment threshold estimates were defined as the contrast increment associated with 70% correct performance.

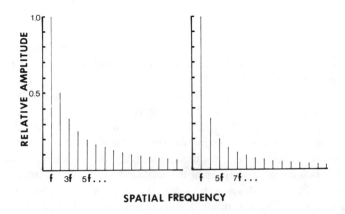

SPATIAL FREQUENCY

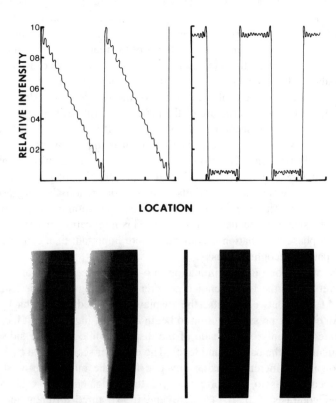

LOCATION

Fig. 5. Ramp and square-wave gratings. Amplitude spectra (top row), intensity profiles (middle row), and appearance (bottom row) for a ramp grating (left column) and square-wave grating (right column).

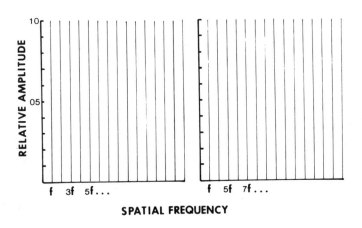

SPATIAL FREQUENCY

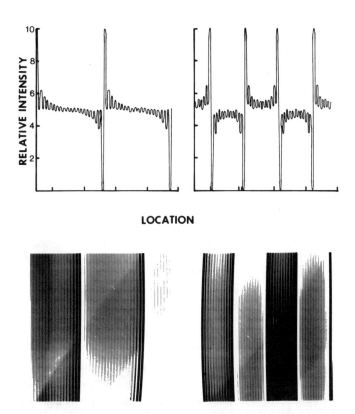

LOCATION

*Fig. 6. Modified ramp and square gratings. Identical presentation as Figure 5, except sine-wave components have been assigned equal relative amplitudes.*

In Figure 7, the infant and adult contrast increment thresholds are plotted as a function of background contrast. Both infant groups exhibited high increment thresholds and shallow slopes relative to the adult. High increment thresholds translate into high Weber fractions. Since the data of the 6- and 12-week-olds are quite similar, the infant data are combined in Figure 8, where the average Weber fractions (circles) are plotted as a function of background contrast. The adult Weber fractions (squares) are included for comparison. As the background contrast increased, the average infant Weber fractions decreased dramatically compared to the adult. To estimate the exponent of the infant power function (n), the data of each infant were fit with least-squares regression. In Figure 9, slope estimates are provided based on the results of those infants who provided complete data sets (C), partial data sets (P), and all infants (C + P). Clearly, the infants exhibit a lower slope estimate relative to the adult.

These findings may have implications for both physiological processes and pattern perception in infants. According to the adult models described above, noise and/or the rate of growth of the infant contrast response function could differ in infants and account for the high Weber fractions. The lower slope of the infant functions could result from a less compressive contrast response function. Alternatively, noise may grow more slowly with contrast in infants relative to adults. At present there are no data that favor one factor over the other. Nonetheless, the results are important in that they indicate that infant and adult contrast discrimination differs dramatically under threshold and suprathreshold conditions.

Consider the impact of high infant Weber fractions on pattern recognition and discrimination. If one assumes that the value of the infant Weber fractions reflects mostly sensory factors, then the number of contrast steps available to infants for pattern representation and discrimination is small relative to the adult. Following Burton (1981), there are four contrast steps available to the infant from near threshold to a contrast of 1.0. This is a factor of approximately 9.0 less than the adult over the same dynamic range. Thus the infant's ability to represent pattern contrast is quite poor (although it is better than the one-step images presented above). This constraint implies that infants would be unable to discriminate among classes of patterns that differ only in terms of the amplitudes of their Fourier components, even though these images may be easily discriminated by adults.

## C.  Implications for Adult Models

Taken together, the infant data on suprathreshold pattern perception can provide interesting implications for the adult models that guided the research. For example, the development of contrast constancy may be partly contingent on the development of spatial frequency channels. This interpretation indirectly supports Georgeson and Sullivan's (1975) model of contrast constancy. Thus developmental data aid our understanding of the adult system by confirming the importance of posited mechanisms in adult models.

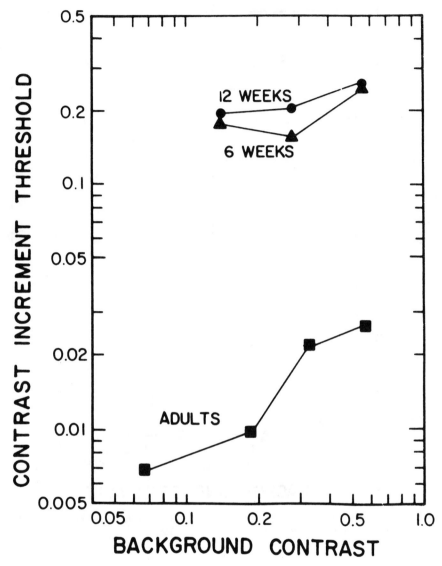

Fig. 7. *Infant contrast-increment thresholds. Mean contrast-increment threshold is plotted as a function of background contrast for 6-week-olds (circles) and 12-week-olds (triangles). Adult data (squares) are included for comparison.*

There are two additional implications of the infant data for adult models that illustrate the interaction of infant and adult research. The development of contrast constancy by 12 weeks of age suggests that experience plays a role in maintaining contrast constancy. This inference is based on the observation that the shape of the infant CSF changes dramatically from 12 weeks to adulthood. At 12 weeks, contrast sensitivity is better at 0.5 cy/deg relative to 1.5 cy/deg. In

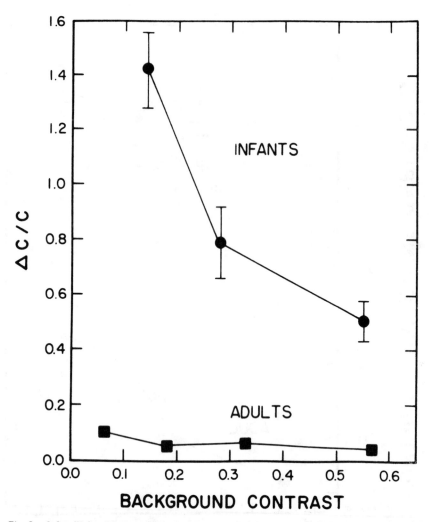

*Fig. 8. Infant Weber fractions. The infant data of Figure 7 are combined and replotted as Weber fractions. Error bars represent +/− 1 S.E.M.*

adults, sensitivity is higher at 1.5 cy/deg relative to 0.5 cy/deg. Thus, the compensation required to achieve contrast constancy at 12 weeks for 0.5 and 1.5 cy/deg is quite different from the compensation required for those frequencies in adulthood. This difference in infant and adult CSFs implies that experience is employed to recalibrate the gain of the contrast-response functions in the face of developments in sensitivity. However, as described above, the contrast response function is also a central mechanism of models of contrast discrimination. Changing the gain of the CRF to maintain contrast constancy would imply that

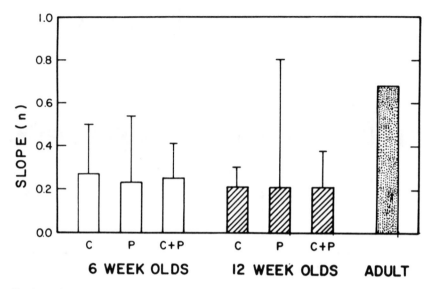

*Fig. 9.   Infant slope estimates. Estimates of the slope of the infant power functions are provided for 6- and 12-week-olds based on those infants who provided complete data sets (C), partial data sets (P), and all infants (C + P).*

the shape of the contrast discrimination function would change as well. Yet the adult data indicate little difference in the shape of the contrast discrimination function for different spatial frequencies (Legge & Foley, 1980). Is it possible that contrast discrimination and contrast constancy tasks tap different pattern processing mechanism?

With this possibility in mind, we revisited the adult literature and discovered indirect evidence that there may be a dissociation of the processes involved in contrast perception and contrast discrimination. Consider the missing fundamental grating. Figure 10 presents the intensity profile and amplitude spectra for a sine, square, and missing fundamental grating. The missing fundamental grating is simply a square-wave grating with the fundamental (F) removed. The missing fundamental grating is nonetheless perceived as a square-wave grating under low-contrast, low-spatial-frequency conditions. One popular explanation of this missing fundamental illusion is that F is not normally detectable under these conditions, so its removal does not alter the appearance or detectability of the square wave (Campbell et al., 1978). This account is inconsistent with Ginsburg et al.'s (1980) explanation of apparent contrast in square-wave gratings. Their contrast matching data show that adults require roughly 27% more contrast in a sine-wave grating to be equal in apparent contrast to a square-wave grating of the same fundamental frequency. Since the fundamental of a square wave is 27% higher in contrast than the physical contrast of the grating, they interpreted their

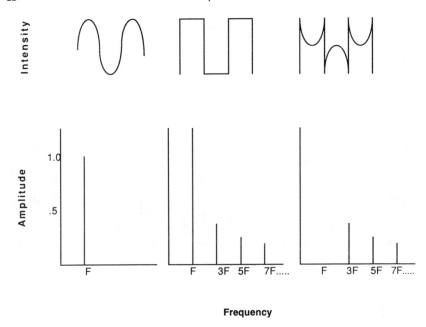

Fig. 10.  *Intensity profiles (top row) and amplitude spectra (bottom row) for sine, square, and missing fundamental gratings.*

results as indicating that the fundamental mediates apparent contrast, even under low-contrast, low-frequency conditions.

This inconsistency in the adult literature could be due to the higher harmonics of the square wave, which might mediate both detection and apparent contrast under low-frequency conditions. Alternatively, our developmental work suggests that judgments concerning the quality of a pattern (e.g., apparent contrast) may not involve identical mechanisms as those involving detection or discrimination. Thus our developmental data led us to conduct matching, adaptation and discrimination experiments with adults to resolve the inconsistency in the adult literature (Stephens, Niles, Thomas, & Gonzalas, 1989). The contrast-matching experiment employed a two-interval method of adjustment procedure. Naive subjects ($N + 21$) matched the apparent contrast of a 0.5 cy/deg sinewave grating (F) to 6 different contrasts of a 0.5 cy/deg square-wave and MF grating. The sine/square contrast ratios at match-point were 1.27 or greater, which indicates that subjects required more contrast in the sine wave to equal the apparent contrast of a square wave. This result replicates Ginsburg et al. The sine/MF ratios were lower than the sine/square ratios at all contrast levels by a factor of 1.3. Since the only difference between the square and missing fundamental gratings is the presence of the fundamental, these results suggest that the fundamental does influence square-wave apparent contrast, even at low contrast levels where the illusion exists. This interpretation was confirmed in an adaptation experiment, where subjects adjusted the contrast of a 0.5 c/deg square wave to match the apparent contrast of an low-contrast, illusory missing fundamental grating. The ratio of square and missing fundamental contrasts at the match point without adaptation were reliably higher than the square/missing–fundamental ratios after adaptation to a 0.4 contrast fundamental. This difference in adapted and unadapted ratios suggests that the fundamental does influence the apparent contrast of a square-wave grating since adaptation to the fundamental has a greater effect on apparent contrast of a square-wave grating than a missing fundamental grating. These two experiments suggest that Campbell et al.'s explanation of the missing fundamental illusion is incorrect.

On the other hand, we have replicated and extended Campbell et al.'s data in a third experiment, using a contrast discrimination task employing identical stimuli and a two-interval, forced-choice procedure. Trained subjects provided contrast detection and discrimination functions, for 0.5 cy/deg square and MF gratings, defined over eight background contrasts. The square and MF functions were nearly identical for all three subjects, providing no evidence that F influences detection or discrimination.

This adult research supports Ginsburg et al.'s notion that the fundamental influences apparent contrast. We also replicated and extended Campbell et al.'s observation that the fundamental does not influence detection or discrimination. This difference in adult matching and detection/discrimination data may reflect differences in pattern processes associated with the two tasks. Judgments of the quality of a stimulus (matching task) may reflect processes that are independent of, or subsequent to, processes that mediate detection/discrimination judgments.

The interpretation that there is a dissociation of mechanisms involved in matching and detection/discrimination tasks increases the plausibility that apparent contrast could be influenced by experience during development without influencing detection/discrimination performance. In other words, it is possible that recalibration occurs at some point subsequent to the CRF (which is presumably involved in contrast detection and discrimination tasks).

One simple account of the maintenance of contrast constancy through development is that the visual system in some fashion "knows" its optical blur function and recalibrates its interpretation of the neural contrast response function to compensate for blur (or other deficits) under suprathreshold viewing conditions. Evidence consistent with this view was reported by Georgeson and Sullivan (1975) for astigmats who either used or did not use optical correction for their astigmatism. (*Astigmatism* is a change in optical blur as a function of orientation.) Frequent users of correction exhibited contrast constancy in the astigmatic orientation with correction, and undercompensation without correction. Infrequent users of optical correction exhibited contrast constancy in the astigmatic orientation without correction, and overcompensation with correction.

Georgeson and Sullivan's results lead to the same implication as our developmental data, namely, that the visual system may use experience to correctly compensate above threshold for differences in detectability. If this implication is correct, then consider myopes (near-sighted individuals). The conditions for which contrast constancy is observed in myopes should depend on whether or not they experience optical correction. This prediction is illustrated in Figure 11. The effect of blur should be spatial-frequency-dependent under low contrast (threshold) conditions (Campbell & Green, 1965). Under suprathreshold conditions, myopes who frequently use optical correction should show contrast constancy with correction and undercompensation without correction, since their visual systems are calibrated to their corrected blur functions. Myopes who infrequently use corrective lenses may show contrast constancy *without* correction and *overcompensation* with correction, if their visual systems are calibrated for their uncorrected blur functions.

To evaluate these predictions, we conducted a retrospective study of adult myopes who either used corrective lenses infrequently or frequently (Stephens, Mead, & Molitor, 1990). Subjects were tested in a two-interval method of adjustment contrast matching task. At a 350 cm viewing distance, estimates of equal apparent contrast were provided, with and without optical correction, for 1, 2, 4 and 8 cy/deg sinewave gratings under both threshold and suprathreshold viewing conditions. Figures 12 and 13 represent the mean contrast settings, as a

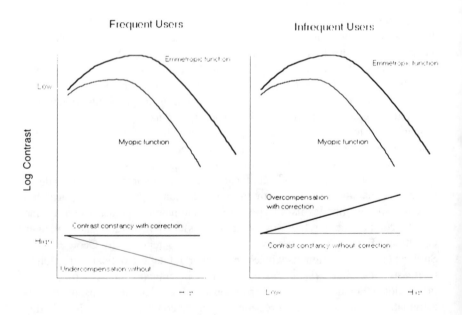

Fig. 11.   Predictions for frequent and infrequent users of optical correction as a function of viewing condition (corrected vs. uncorrected) and contrast level.

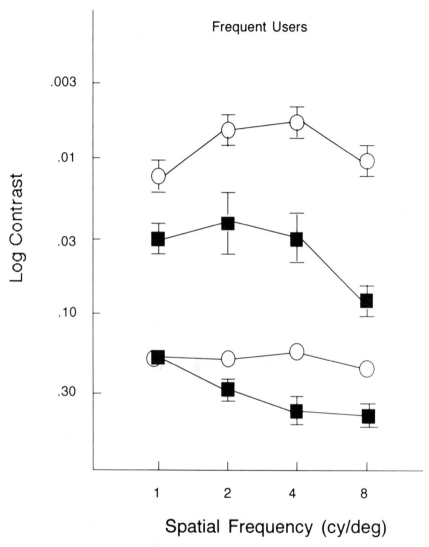

*Fig. 12. Mean contrast settings, as a function of spatial frequency, for frequent users of optical correction. The corrected and uncorrected viewing conditions are represented by open circles and filled squares, respectively. The error bars represent +/− 1 S.E.M.*

function of spatial frequency, for frequent and infrequent users of optical correction, respectively. The corrected and uncorrected viewing conditions are represented by open circles and filled squares, respectively. The error bars represent +/− 1 S.E.M. Under low-contrast conditions, the data for the two groups are qualitatively similar. Estimates provided without optical correction suffer from blur, and the effect of the blur is spatial-frequency dependent. Contrary to

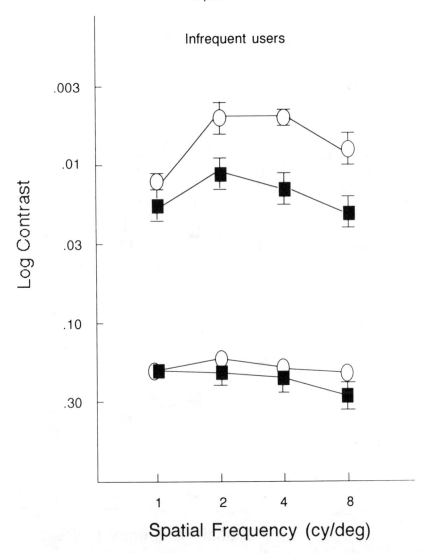

Fig. 13.   *Mean contrast settings, as a function of spatial frequency, for infrequent users of optical correction. Conventions identical to Figure 12.*

expectations, both infrequent and frequent users of corrective lenses showed contrast constancy with correction and undercompensation without. This observation is more clearly illustrated in Figure 14, which plots the ratio of variable to fixed contrast as a function of spatial frequency under corrected (open circles) and uncorrected (closed squares) viewing conditions for both groups. In this format, a ratio of 1.0 corresponds to contrast constancy (represented by the dashed horizontal line). Although the effects are stronger in the frequent users

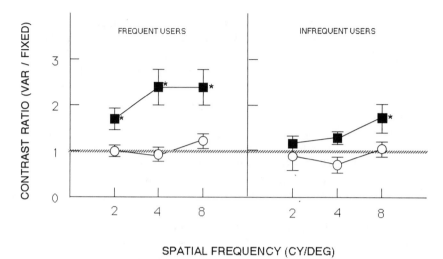

Fig. 14. Ratio of fixed to variable contrast as a function of spatial frequency under corrected (open circles) and uncorrected (closed squares) viewing conditions for both groups. The horizontal dashed line represents the ratio (1.0) that would be evidence for contrast constancy. The asterisks indicate data values that are reliably different from 1.0.

group, both patterns are similar. The ratios are not reliably different from 1.0 under corrected viewing conditions. The ratios are reliably greater than 1.0 only for uncorrected viewing conditions.

These results indicate that infrequent users of optical correction for myopia exhibit contrast constancy under optically corrected viewing conditions. Therefore a simple view of the role of experience in contrast constancy may not be tenable. The visual system may use experience to calibrate its blur function, but it compensates for the "best" (least optical and neural attenuation) blur function. Myopes' "best" blur function exists under corrected and/or near viewing conditions. Our results imply that myopes who do not regularly use correction are calibrated for near viewing conditions. According to this interpretation, Georgeson and Sullivan observed overcompensation in uncorrected astigmats because the astigmatic optical blur is chronic.

## IV.  APPLICATIONS: FACE PREFERENCE AND SELF-PERCEPTION

One popular application of CSF-based models of infant pattern vision to aid understanding of more complex topics such as perception of ecologically valid stimuli. Consider how one can apply these models to the development of face preferences. Some theorists attribute special significance to the human face and argue that young infants should prefer the human face per se, with this preference due either to the advantage such an innate preference might confer on the formation of early social attachments (Bowlby, 1958), or to the infant's familiarity with faces (Kagan, 1967). Most reports indicate that, by 2 to 4 months of age, infants prefer and discriminate a normal from a scrambled version of a schematic face (Haaf & Bell, 1967; Maurer & Barrerra, 1981). Most researchers interpret this finding as indicating infants' appetitive response to some dimension of faceness  However, an alternative explanation is possible. Models of infant pattern preferences, based on the CSF and linear systems techniques, predict that young infants will prefer the stimulus that contains the greatest contrast once filtered by their CSF (Banks & Ginsburg, 1985). When one scrambles a schematic face, one changes, not only faceness, but also the spatial-frequency components of that face. Thus demonstrations of a face preference are confounded. It is not clear whether the preference is due to faceness or visibility.

We attempted to disambiguate the development of infant face preferences by presenting 6- and 12-week-old infants with normal and abnormal versions of a schematic face without the confound described above (Dannemiller & Stephens, 1988). The stimuli we designed are presented in Figure 15. In each pair of stimuli, the member on the right is a reversed contrast version of the one on the left. (We termed the contrast-reversed face *abnormal* because the stimulus rarely corresponds to the measured intensity relationships of facial features in any adult face.) The members of each pair are identical on all stimulus dimensions, yet they vary in faceness. Thus, any preference between the pairs would be evidence for a response on the basis of faceness, as opposed to some stimulus confound.

Using a standard preferential looking procedure, we found that 12-week-olds, but not 6-week-olds, exhibited a preference for the normal version of the schematic face. This result represents the first unambiguous demonstration of a face preference in infants. Although CSF-based models of infant pattern preferences do not predict face preferences per se, it is interesting to examine how these models might inform our understanding of the development of these more complex responses. For example, the ability to detect contrast during the first month of life may constrain the emergence of face preferences. Linear systems techniques, and measurements of infant CSFs have been employed to simulate the pattern information available in the face for infants at different points in development (Banks & Ginsburg, 1985; Souther & Banks, 1979). These demonstrations show that the available facial information changes dramatically from 1 to 3 months of age. At 1 month, the pattern information suggests that an oval-shaped object exists. However, no internal features are represented. At 2 months of age, there is a rough hint of internal facial features (e.g., faint patches corresponding to the eyes and mouth). By 3 months of age, facial features (eyes, mouth, hair) are defined somewhat, suggesting that the infant has access to features that could allow some discrimination of faces and facial expressions.

One is tempted to argue from these demonstrations that the absence of a face preference in very young infants is due to poor contrast sensitivity; the infant

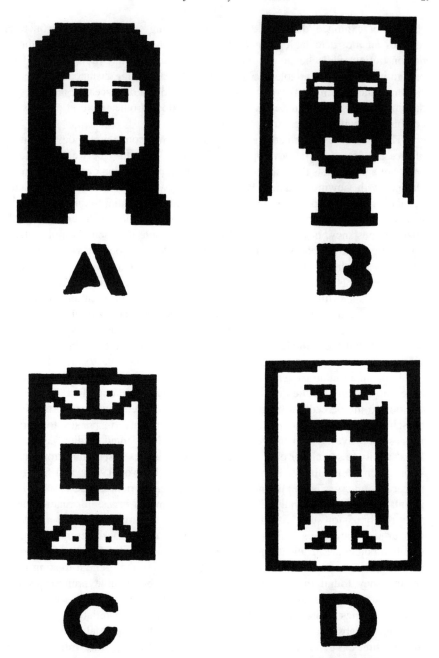

*Fig. 15. Face and control stimuli. Each stimulus is composed of equal light and dark areas. The image on the right of each pair is simply a contrast-reversed version of the left image.*

should not exhibit a differential preference among stimuli whose distinctive features are not detectable. However, reducing the viewing distance in these demonstrations will change the information provided to the young infant. The pattern information available to a 12-week-old at a viewing distance of 4 feet is similar to the information available to a 6-week-old at a distance of 2 feet. So the development of face preferences may be a function of other factors, perhaps in combination with poor contrast sensitivity.

There are several such additional factors that may constrain the development of face preferences. The development of contrast constancy between 6 and 12 weeks of age suggests that a 1- to 2-month-olds' representation of facial structure changes with viewing distance. Perhaps the very young infant cannot represent facial characteristics per se (e.g., distinctive features or spatial frequency components), since these features are unstable in everyday situations. The emergence of contrast constancy, however, may allow a more stable representation of pattern information, and may allow the infant to represent cues associated with faceness. Alternatively, the ability to encode phase differences may not be sufficiently mature in infants younger that 8 weeks of age (Braddick, Atkinson, & Wattam-Bell, 1986), and this immaturity may prevent preferential attention to normal versus phase-abnormal facial stimuli (Kleiner, 1987; Kleiner & Banks, 1987). In any case, the CSF-based models do not explain why infant's exhibit a face preference, but these models may help us understand why they do not exhibit such preferences by indicating what information is available to the infant.

Poor infant contrast sensitivity and the absence of contrast constancy may have implications for the development of other perceptual/cognitive abilities in addition to the perception of faceness. Consider self-perception. Investigations of self-perception development typically assess infants' responses to mirror images, or "live" video images. More cognitively oriented studies assess infants' ability to search for objects or detect discrepancies based on mirror-image information (Bertenthal & Fisher, 1978; Lewis & Brooks, 1975), and find that this ability emerges late in infancy. More perceptually oriented studies ask when infants respond differentially to mirror versus nonmirror image information, and what the basis for such discrimination might be. Bahrick and Watson (1985) have argued that infants' sensitivity to isomorphic visual-proprioceptive information is a potential sufficient basis for self-perception, and that this information mediates infants' responses to mirror images. Using a preferential-looking procedure, they found that 5-month-old infants exhibit reliable preferences for other-child and prerecorded-self video segments when paired with live mirror-image segments. Three-month-olds did not demonstrate a reliable preference, although the absence of a preference could be due to a bimodal distribution of looking times; i.e., some infants prefer live self-images, other infants prefer prerecorded-self or other-child segments.

Although it is logically correct to argue that isomorphic visual proprioceptive information is sufficient to mediate self-perception, infants may not use such logic. Pattern information may also play a role in infant self-perception. Some studies of self-perception have employed static pictures and have found only much older infants (18 months of age) can identify a static self-image (e.g., Bigelow, 1982). Does the quality of pattern information play any role in young infants' response to mirror images?

The CSF-based models of pattern vision indicate that very young infants do not have access to pattern information that would allow the identification of features important in static self-identification. It is also possible that pattern information is necessary, but not sufficient, for infants to respond to the dynamic information present in a mirror-image. To investigate this possibility, we blurred video images presented to infants so that details were attenuated (Stephens & Hart, 1989). Although blur reduces the visibility of details, gross features (and hence visual-proprioceptive isomorphism) are still present. Thus, infants should treat the focused and blurred images in a similar fashion if isomorphic visual-proprioceptive information is the basis of infants' responses to live self-images. Alternatively, if the quality of pattern information present in a mirror-image influences the richness of the isomorphic information, then the absence of the higher frequency pattern information in the blurred image may influence the infant's ability to respond to the isomorphic information.

We measured visual fixation to video images successively presented to 18 6-month-old infants in a pretest–familiarization–posttest design illustrated in Table 1. In pretest and posttest, infants were presented with two sets of counterbalanced, 20-sec segments of live contingent video images of self, prerecorded noncontingent images of self; and recorded images of another child. In familiarization, infants viewed six 20-sec segments of live contingent images. For half of the infants, all images were normal and in-focus. The other infants viewed images that were blurred by increasing the camera focal distance by 2 Diopters.

Figure 16 presents mean looking times during pretest, familiarization, and posttest for the focus (open symbols) and blur (closed symbols) conditions. Although the looking time was greater for focus versus blurred stimuli during

TABLE 1

Experimental Design

| Viewing condition | Pretest | Test session | Posttest |
|---|---|---|---|
| | | Familiarization | |
| Focus | Self | Self | Self |
| | Prerecord Self | | Prerecord Self |
| | Other Child | | Other Child |
| Blur | Self | Self | Self |
| | Prerecord Self | | Prerecord Self |
| | Other Child | | Other Child |

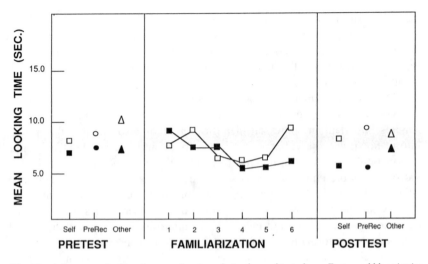

*Fig. 16.   Infant mean looking time as a function of stimulus and test phase. Focus and blur viewing conditions are represented by open and closed symbols, respectively. The live self-image, pre-recorded self-image, and other-child images are represented by squares, circles, and triangles, respectively.*

pretest, this difference was not reliable. During familiarization, looking time decreased reliably across trials in both focus and blur conditions. In addition, there was an increase (albeit nonsignificant) in looking time during the last familiarization trial in the focus condition only.

Familiarization led to a pattern of change in pretest–posttest looking times that were reliably different in the focus and blur conditions. These change scores are presented in Figure 17 for the focus and blur conditions. In the focus condition, there was a reliable increase in looking time to the live self-image (preceded by the increase during the last familiarization trial), but no change in looking time to the prerecorded self or other-child stimuli. The increase in attention to the live self-image is unlikely to be a result of general arousal since attention to the other two stimuli remained stable. In the blur condition, familiarization led to a reliable decrease in looking time to both the live and prerecorded self-images, but no change for the other-child image. Again, the decrease in attention to the two self-images is unlikely to be a result of general boredom or fatigue, since attention to the other-child stimulus remained stable.

These results indicate that the effect of proprioceptive-visual isomorphism may be qualitatively different depending on the quality of the pattern information. As a result of familiarization, infants presented with focused pattern information responded differentially to isomorphic versus nonisomorphic information. Infants presented with blurred pattern information did not respond differentially on the basis of isomorphic information. We suspect that for degraded images, infants do not respond differentially to self and prerecorded

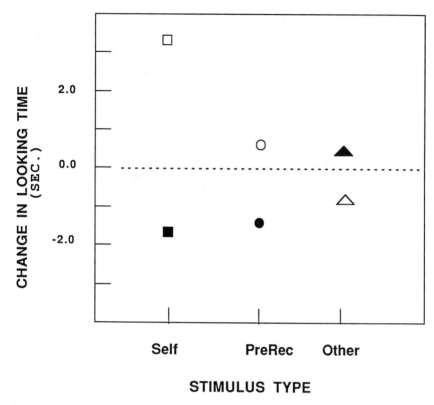

*Fig. 17. Mean change in looking time from pretest to posttest is presented for focus (open symbols) and blur (closed symbols) conditions for each of the three stimuli.*

images, because the isomorphic information is also degraded and more difficult to identify. Interestingly, Bahrick and Watson (1985) report that younger infants (< 3 mos) do not demonstrate preferences for self versus prerecorded images. It is possible that the poor spatial vision of younger infants makes it difficult for them to identify this degraded isomorphic information.

## V. CONCLUSIONS

One point of our research that should be stated clearly is that the initial linear systems models of infant pattern vision, such as those employing a simple CSF filter, are clearly useful for a number of research questions. They do provide a rough guide as to the nature of the infant's visible "window to the world" and how that window changes with age. They are particularly impressive predictors of early pattern preferences for abstract stimuli (Banks & Ginsburg, 1985). When these models fail, the failure should not be taken as an indictment of linear systems approach per se. Sometimes the failure is due to the oversimplified model that attempts to characterize the way the system processes pattern information. As we learn more about those processes, for example, spatial frequency channels and the contrast response function, we learn more about the appropriate model for the infant's system.

Consider such a "failure." Freedland and Dannemiller (1990) have recently reported that 3-month-old infants respond to the global orientation in the herringbone pattern despite the fact that, within the Fourier domain, there is no component represented in that global orientation. Their interpretation that this ability to respond to herringbone pattern is a nonlinear process seems correct. However, that interpretation does not imply that a linear systems approach is inherently inadequate. The nonlinearity may be modeled by a pattern processing mechanism (as Freedland and Dannemiller suggest) to develop a more accurate representation of the infant's system.

In other cases, the linear systems model is not useful in explaining the presence of certain perceptual skills, but may help account for the absence of such skills. The emergence of infant face preferences may be a good example of this point. Although there is currently some debate concerning the age at which a reliable face preference emerges (see Morton, Johnson, & Maurer, 1990; and Kliener, 1990, for an interesting discussion), the presence of a face preference tells us that a new ability is present in the infant's perceptual repertoire. Linear systems models do not indicate when such an ability should be observed because the approach is blind to variables such as "meaningfulness" or "appetitive value." The approach may be useful, however, in helping to explain the absence of a face preference, to the extent that the absence of pattern information degrades the ability to identify critical features in a face.

## VI.   REFERENCES

Atkinson, J., Braddick, O., & Moar, K. (1977). Infants' detection of image defocus. *Vision Research, 17,* 1045–1047.

Bahrick, L. E., & Watson, J. S. (1985). Detection of intermodal proprioceptive-visual contingency as a potential basis for self-perception in infancy. *Developmental Psychology, 21,* 963–973.

Banks, M. S. (1980). The development of visual accommodation during early infancy. *Child Development, 51,* 646–666.

Banks, M. S., & Ginsburg, A. P. (1985). Early visual preferences: A review and new theoretical treatment. In H. W. Reese (Ed.), *Advances in child development and behavior.* New York: Academic Press.

Banks, M. S., & Salapatek, P. (1978) Acuity and contrast sensitivity in 1-, 2-, and 3-month-old human infants. *Investigative Opthalmology and Visual Science, 17,* 361–365.

Banks, M. S., & Salapatek, P. (1981). Infant pattern vision: A new approach based on the contrast sensitivity function. *Journal of Experimental Child Psychology, 31,* 1–45.

Banks, M. S., & Stephens, B. R. (1982). The contrast sensitivity of human infants to gratings differing in duty cycle. *Vision Research, 22,* 739–744.

Banks, M. S., Stephens, B. R., & Hartmann, E. E. (1985). The development of basic mechanisms of pattern vision: Spatial frequency channels. *Journal of Experimental Child Psychology, 40,* 501–527.

Bertenthal, B., & Fisher, K. (1978). Development of self-recognition in the infant. *Developmental Psychology, 14,* 44–55.

Bigelow, A. (1981). The correspondance between self and image movements as a cue to self-recognition for young children. *The Journal of Genetic Psychology, 139,* 11–26.

Blakemore, C., & Campbell, F. W. (1969). On the existence of neurons in the human visual cortex selectively sensitive to the orientation and size of retinal images. *Journal of Physiology, 203,* 237–260.

Blakemore, C., Muncey, J. P. J., & Ridley, R. M. (1973). Stimulus specificity in the human visual system. *Vision Research, 13,* 1915–1931.

Bowlby, J. (1958). The nature of the child's tie to his mother. *International Journal of Psychoanalysis, 49,* 315–318.

Braddick, O. J., Atkinson, J., & Wattam-Bell, J. R. (1986). Development of the discrimination of spatial phase in infancy. *Vision Research, 26,* 1223–1239.

Burton, G. J. (1981). Contrast discrimination by the human visual system. *Biological Cybernetics, 40,* 27–38.

Campbell, F. W., Carpenter, R. H. S., & Levinson, J. Z. (1969). Visibility of aperiodic patterns compared with that of sinusoidal gratings. *Journal of Physiology, 204,* 283–298.

Campbell, F. W., & Green, D. G. (1965). Optical and retinal factors affecting visual resolution. *Journal of Physiology, 181,* 576–593.

Campbell, F. W., & Gubish, R. W. (1966). Optical quality of the human eye. *Journal of Physiology, 186,* 558–578.

Campbell, F. W., Howell, E. R., & Johnstone, J. R. (1978). A comparison of threshold and suprathreshold appearance of gratings with components in the low and high spatial frequency range. *Journal of Physiology, 284,* 193–210.

Campbell, F. W., & Kulikowski, J. J. (1966). Orientational selectivity of the human visual system. *Journal of Physiology, 187,* 437–445.

Campbell, F. W., & Robson, J. G. (1968). Application of Fourier analysis to the visibility of gratings. *Journal of Physiology, 197,* 551–566.

Cannon, M. W. (1979). Contrast sensation: A linear function of stimulus contrast. *Vision Research, 24,* 1049–1055.

Carlson, C. R., & Klopfenstein, R. W. (1985). Spatial-frequency model for hyperacuity. *Journal of the Optical Society of America, 2,* 1747–1751.

Cornsweet, T. N. (1970). *Visual perception.* New York: Academic Press.

Dannemiller, J. L., & Stephens, B. R. (1988). A critical test of infant pattern preference models. *Child Development, 59,* 210–216.

Davidson, M. (1968). Perturbation approach to spatial brightness interaction in human vision. *Journal of the Optical Society of America, 318,* 413–427.

Fantz, R. L. (1961). The origin of form perception. *Scientific American, 204,* 66–72.

Fiorentini, A., Pirchio, M., & Spinelli, D. (1983). Electrophysiological evidence for spatial frequency selective mechanisms in adults and infants. *Vision Research, 23,* 119–127.

Foley, J. M., & Legge, G. E. (1981). Contrast detection and near-threshold discrimination in human vision. *Vision Research, 21,* 1041–1053.

Freedland, R. L., & Dannemiller, J. L. (1990). Evidence for a nonlinear pattern vision process in 12-week-old human infants. *Investigative Opthalmology and Visual Science (Suppl.)., 31*(4), 7.

Gaskill, J. D. (1978). *Linear systems, Fourier transforms, and optics.* New York: Wiley.

Georgeson, M. A., & Sullivan G. D. (1975). Contrast constancy: Deblurring in human vision by spatial frequency channels. *Journal of Physiology, 252,* 627–656.

Ginsburg, A. P. (1978). *Visual information processing based on spatial filters constrained by biological data.* Unpublished doctoral dissertation, Cambridge University.

Ginsburg, A. P. (1984). Visual form perception based on biological filtering. In L. Spillmann & B. Wooten (Eds.), *Sensory experience, adaptation, and perception.* Hillsdale, NJ: Erlbaum.

Ginsburg, A. P., Cannon, M. W., & Nelson, M. A. (1980). Suprathreshold processing of complex stimuli: Evidence for linearity in contrast perception. *Science, 208,* 619–621.

Graham, N., & Nachmias, J. (1971). Detection of grating patterns containing two spatial frequencies: A comparison of single-channel and multiple-channel models. *Vision Research, 11,* 251–259.

Haaf, R. A., & Bell, R. Q. (1973). The facial dimension in visual discrimination by human infants. *Child Development, 38,* 893–899.

Kagan, J. (1967). The growth of the "face" schema: Theoretical significance and methodological issues. In J. Hellmuth (Ed.), *The exceptional infant: Vol. 1. The normal infant* (pp. 337–348). New York: Brunner/Mazel.

Kleiner, K. A. (1987). Amplitude and phase spectra as indices of infants' pattern preferences. *Infant Behavior and Development, 10,* 45–55.

Kleiner, K. A. (1990). Models of neonates' preferences for facelike patterns: A response to Morton, Johnson, and Maurer. *Infant Behavior and Development, 13,* 105–108.

Kleiner, K. A., & Banks, M. S. (1987). Stimulus energy does not account for 2-month-olds' face preference. *Journal of Experimental Psychology, 13,* 594–600.

Kulikowski, J. J. (1976). Effective contrast constancy and linearity of contrast sensation. *Vision Research, 16,* 1419–1431.

Legge, G. E. (1979). Spatial frequency masking in human vision: binocular interactions. *Journal of the Optical Society of America, 69,* 838–847.

Legge, G. E. (1981). A power law for contrast discrimination. *Vision Research, 21,* 457–467.

Legge, G. E., & Foley, J. M. (1980). Contrast masking in human vision. *Journal of the Optical Society of America, 70,* 1458–1471.

Lewis, M., & Brooks, J. (1975). Infant's social perception: A constructivist view. In L. Cohen & P. Salapatek (Eds.), *Infant perception: From sensation to cognition* (Vol. II). New York: Academic Press.

Maurer, D., & Barrerra, M. E. (1981). Infants' perception of natural and distorted arrangements of a schematic face. *Child Development, 52,* 196–202.

Morton, J., Johnson, M. H., & Maurer, D. (1990). On the reasons for newborns' responses to faces. *Infant Behavior and Development, 13,* 99–103.

Nachmias, J., & Sansbury, R. (1974). Grating contrast: Discrimination may be better than detection. *Vision Research, 14,* 1039–1042.

Peli, D. G. (1980). *The effects of visual noise.* Unpublished doctoral dissertation, Cambridge University.

Piotrowski, L. N., & Campbell, F. W. (1982). A demonstration of the visual importance and flexibility of spatial-frequency amplitude and phase. *Perception, 11,* 377–346.

Souther, A., & Banks, M. S. (1979, April). *The human face: A view from the infant's eye.* Paper presented Society for Research in Child Development, San Francisco.

Stephens, B. R. (1985). *Infant pattern vision: Apparent contrast and contrast discrimination.* Unpublished doctoral dissertation, University of Texas.

Stephens, B. R., & Banks, M. S. (1985). The development of contrast constancy. *Journal of Experimental Child Psychology, 40,* 528–547.

Stephens, B. R., & Banks, M. S. (1987). Contrast discrimination in human infants. *Journal of Experimental Psychology: Human Perception and Performance, 13,* 558–565.

Stephens, B. R., & Hart, S. (1989, April). *Infant self perception: Isomorphism and image quality.* Paper presented at the meeting of the Society for Research in Child Development, Kansas City.

Stephens, B. R., Niles, A., Thomas, N., & Gonzalas, L. (1989). The missing fundamental illusion. *Investigative Opthalmology and Visual Science (Suppl.), 30*(3), 504.

Stephens, B. R., Mead, S., & Molitor, C. (1990). Contrast constancy in myopia. *Investigative Opthalmology and Visual Science (Suppl.), 31*(4), 323.

Stromeyer, C. F., & Julesz, B. (1972). Spatial frequency masking in human vision: Critical bands and spread of masking. *Journal of the Optical Society of America, 62,* 1221–1232.

Switkes, E., Mayer, M. I., & Sloan, J. A. (1978). Spatial frequency analysis of the visual environment: Anisotrophy and the carpentered environment hypothesis. *Vision Research, 10,* 1393–1399.

Teller, D. Y. (1979). The forced-choice preferential looking procedure: A psychophysical technique for use with human infants. *Infant Behavior and Development, 2,* 135–153.

Wilson, H. R. (1986). Responses of spatial mechanisms can explain hyperacuity. *Vision Research, 26,* 453–469.

# ASSESSING VISUAL DEVELOPMENT: IS INFANT VISION GOOD ENOUGH*

*Louise Hainline and Israel Abramov*

INFANT STUDY CENTER
BROOKLYN COLLEGE OF CUNY

I. INTRODUCTION ............................................. 40
  A. A Context for Assessing Infant Vision ....................... 41
  B. The Need for Assessment of Infant Vision ................... 42
II. DEVELOPMENT OF VISUAL STRUCTURES ................... 43
  A. Infant Retina ............................................. 44
III. DEVELOPMENT OF SPATIAL VISION ...................... 47
  A. Spatial Contrast Sensitivity ............................... 47
  B. Infant Spatial CSF ........................................ 49
  C. Spatiotemporal Interactions ................................ 54
  D. Functional Consequences of the Infant CSF ................. 58
IV. DEVELOPMENT OF ACCOMMODATION AND VERGENCE ..... 62
  A. Accommodation .......................................... 62
  B. Vergence ................................................. 63
  C. Measures of Accommodation and Vergence .................. 64
  D. Developmental Studies of Accommodation and Vergence ........ 67
    1. Accommodation ........................................ 67
    2. Vergence .............................................. 69
    3. Simultaneous measures of accommodation and vergence ....... 69
V. OCULOMOTOR DEVELOPMENT ............................ 71
  A. Measuring Infants' Eye Movements ......................... 73
    1. Observation ........................................... 73
    2. Electro-oculogram (EOG) ............................... 74
    3. Corneal reflection eye trackers .......................... 75

* The research reported here was supported in part by grant NIH-EY03957, and PSC-CUNY Faculty Research award program grants 666183, 667435, 668461, 668454, and 669455. The number of people who have helped in the research reported here is too large to credit individually, but we thank all of them collectively for their assistance. We also thank Seth Bonder for this assistance in preparing the figures for this chapter.

39

B. Pointing the Fovea: Saccades and Fixations ................... 78
    1. Infants' saccades ...................................... 78
    2. Infants' fixations ..................................... 82
C. Stabilizing Moving Images: Smooth Pursuit, Optokinetic
   Nystagmus, and the Vestibulo-ocular Reflex ................... 85
    1. Smooth pursuit (SP) .................................... 85
    2. Optokinetic nystagmus (OKN) and vestibulo-ocular reflex
       (VOR) ................................................ 87
VI. CLINICAL APPLICATIONS OF INFANT VISION RESEARCH ..... 91
VII. CONCLUSION ............................................. 94
VIII. REFERENCES ............................................ 95

## I. INTRODUCTION

Infants do not see as well as adults do. The extent to which human infants' vision is deficient compared with that of adults is well documented. For example, one recent and representative review of infants' visual abilities contends that young humans "see poorly. Contrast sensitivity, grating acuity and vernier acuity in the first months of life are all at least an order of magnitude worse than in adulthood. Chromatic discrimination is much reduced too" (Banks & Bennett, 1988). Another contends that "vision improves significantly during the first year. . . .It is well known that vision is quite poor in human neonates" (Van Sluyters, Atkinson, Banks, Held, Hoffman, & Shatz 1990). Numerous studies over the last two decades have described the limitations in young infants' acuity, spatial vision, color vision, stereopsis, and other basic sensory visual processes. All these sensory functions continue to develop at different rates through the first year, and in some cases beyond. On the basis of these research findings, it might be legitimate to consider the young infant as significantly visually handicapped.

It is thus surprising to watch infants interact with people, objects, and events in their natural environments. These interactions are often complex and impressively nuanced, as if infants are not manifestly handicapped by their purported primitive visual abilities. The limitations in their behaviors seem more obviously related to attentional and cognitive factors than to the lack of well-developed visual abilities. Indeed, one has the impression (bolstered by studies in the Gibsonian tradition; e.g., Spelke, 1988; Kellman, 1988) that infants actually are fairly competent when faced with visual stimuli that are more complex and regular than the isolated patches of light or sine wave gratings favored by researchers working in the tradition of experimental sensory psychophysics. This paradox is one of the more interesting issues in the study of infant vision. While infants may not, indeed, see as well as adults do, they normally see well enough to function effectively in their roles as infants. Vision doesn't limit an infant's development, although for an infant with abnormal vision, it may be another matter.

## A. A Context for Assessing Infant Vision

This chapter is not intended to be another comprehensive review of all aspects of infants' vision; in particular, our choice of citations is designed to be representative rather than comprehensive. Excellent recent reviews of infant vision research can be found in Aslin (1987), Atkinson and Braddick (1989), and Van Sluyters et al. (1990). A common organization in many reviews has been to treat each visual ability separately, and to summarize the research on these basic visual abilities, one by one (e.g., acuity, stereopsis, pattern vision, etc.). This focus on separate visual abilities can be misleading, since effective use of visual information requires coordination among different functions and abilities. The image of the visually deficient infant may in part be the result of the failure to consider infant vision as an ensemble of mutually supportive functions. Rather than discussing developments in isolated visual functions, this chapter is a preliminary attempt at such an integration, exploring the implications that developments in one basic attribute of vision, spatial resolution, have for other visual abilities such as the control of eye movements and the ability to change the eye's plane of focus. We will also examine how spatial resolution itself depends on these other abilities.

Another point of discussion will be whether we should accept uncritically reports of reduced vision in young infants. While there is no question that infants see more poorly than adults, the situation may not be as bad as it has been portrayed. Inherent in many of the methods in the tool kit used to test infants is the tendency to under- rather than overestimate infants' capacities. Most of the paradigms that are currently used to study vision in infants depend on some level of interest and attentiveness toward the test stimuli. A legitimate concern with maintaining a desirable level of experimental control has meant that stimuli have been physically well specified but rather simple, varied along one dimension of interest at a time. Despite the merit of this rationale for designing stimuli, certain of the early "deficiencies" in vision may actually be reflections of infants' disinterest in the austere stimuli chosen by researchers.

Even if we acknowledge that current methods yield underestimates, infant vision is still obviously inferior compared with adult vision. But which adults? In many aspects, everyday adult vision may also be far less acute and precise than we imagine, probably because many of the daily tasks requiring vision can be done with less than full attention and the recruitment of the highest levels of performance. Indeed, in our own studies, we regularly find that adults, if they are naive and uninstructed, also perform at a level considerably below that commonly reported in the literature for the practiced adult subjects who are measured in most psychophysical experiments. While an interesting observation about vision in its own right, this fact must change our perspective on the visual performance of infants, who necessarily are unpracticed and uninstructed. Comparing infant performance to that of "world class" adult subjects can give a misleading impression of infant vision; not all adults are equal.

Further, infants might not have much use for better, more adultlike vision, were it available to them. To put infant vision in some perspective, it is useful to ask what infants use their vision for. Adopting a functionalist stance, it could be said that the sensory "deficits" of early infancy may not really make much difference in the infant's daily life. The most acute levels of adult vision depend on anatomical structures that are immature in young infants, but these structures support visual functions that are not of great use early in life (for example, extremely fine acuity for detecting and hunting distant prey, and its modern analogue, reading, or exquisitely fine stereoscopic discriminations of depth). Young babies simply do not need to be good hunters or be able to read the fine print in a contract. What this amounts to is the suggestion that visually normal infants have the level of visual functioning that is required for the things that infants need to do. Despite documented immaturities, infants' vision is good enough to derive an accurate impression of the world in their immediate vicinity and to stimulate further visual, cognitive, and social developments. Even with their poor vision, it would be a mistake to see infants as "handicapped" functionally, given the functions appropriate for their age. We might even posit that higher levels of visual functioning could actually interfere with these tasks, if they add to the visual "noise" that needs to be filtered out in order for infants to attend to the most relevant information.

## B.  The Need for Assessment of Infant Vision

The observation that infants might not benefit from more acute vision does not detract from the need to study the development of visual abilities. To the contrary, it is important to understand visual development in early infancy and to evaluate infants' vision earlier and on a much wider basis than has been customary. Visual development does not follow a fixed blueprint, and irregularities in the normal developmental sequence can have permanent effects on the final level of visual functioning. A well documented fact about mammalian vision is that the development of the visual system depends greatly on the nature of the visual stimulation early in life; in other words, visual development is characterized by a series of sensitive periods for different visual functions, with the developmental process shaped by the nature of the inputs the system receives. Animals that are visually deprived when young often fail to develop a full range of visual abilities as they age (Atkinson & Braddick, 1988; Mitchell, 1988; Movshon & Van Sluyters, 1981).

Time-limited visual plasticity is a characteristic of primates, including humans. Within the normal range, development of vision is similar from individual to individual, despite minor differences across individuals in the visual stimulation that is experienced. The development of vision is, in the terminology of Greenough, Black, and Wallace (1987), a good example of *experience expectant* development; in such forms of neural development, the outlines are genetically prespecified, so that the function develops normally with the range of inputs typically encountered. However, when the organism receives a restricted or skewed range of inputs, neural and functional development do not proceed in the usual fashion.

Besides describing the results of a large body of animal research, this characterization agrees with the available data on long-term visual development of visually impaired humans. Certain optical conditions can make it impossible for the eye to create clear retinal images at all viewing distances (refractive errors such as myopia—short-sightedness, or hyperopia—far-sightedness) or for all orientations of lines (astigmatism—where lines of specific orientation are distorted or blurred). Further difficulties arise when there is a problem of pointing the two eyes at the same point in space (i.e., problems of eye alignment such as strabismus). Probably the best human analogues of the animal experiments on early visual experience are individuals who develop functional amblyopia (a permanent, presumptively neural, loss of vision not caused by disease). Individuals with different refractive power in the two eyes may develop anisometropic amblyopia, while those with large amounts of astigmatism can develop meridional amblyopia. Uncorrected strabismus may lead to strabismic amblyopia. While direct experiments on humans are obviously impossible, clinical data (see reviews in Aslin, 1981b; Held, 1981; Mitchell, 1981) support the view that humans too have some critical period for proper visual development on a neural level.

The problem now is to delineate the normal sequence of visual milestones. Such research yields a useful normative basis for early clinical assessment and a set of validated methods for that assessment. The need for such screening is beginning to be acknowledged. Recently, for example, the Committee on Practice and Ambulatory Medicine of the American Academy of Pediatrics called for regular vision screening of all infants during the first 6 months of life or "as early as practicable" (American Academy of Pediatrics, 1986).

## II. DEVELOPMENT OF VISUAL STRUCTURES

The visual system consists of a sequence of stages for the translation of light energy in the world into neural impulses, which are processed at a series of higher and increasingly more complex levels in the nervous system. At the earliest stage, the relevant parts of the visual system are optical (cornea, lens, etc); these structures form an adjustable optical system to bring images into focus on the retina at the back of the eye. Actually, since we have two eyes, at this stage the system consists of two separate optical systems, independently forming images on each of the eyes' retinas. Thus, the quality of vision depends, first of all, on the ability to change the lens's focus appropriately (accommodation), and to rotate the eyes to point at a specific target location (convergence). Failure of accommodation results in blurred images. Failure of convergence results in the perception of double images (diplopia), or the suppression of information from one of the eyes. The brain is responsible for fusing the two retinal images into one coherent image; in most cases, the brain also uses the information from the two eyes to allow fine depth discriminations through stereopsis.

Since humans' eyes move to allow inspection of the details of the world, visual functioning also depends on how well an individual is able to control movements of the eyes during periods of stable viewing (fixations), fast reorienting movements (saccades), and movements that follow moving targets (smooth pursuit). In normal life, the head is not stabilized by laboratory artifices, such as chin rests or bite bars; rather, some form of compensation is needed for movements of both head and body in order for vision to remain stable. The vestibulo-ocular reflex serves to stabilize vision in the face of self-produced motion, while smooth pursuit and optokinetic nystagmus assist in nulling the motion of the retinal image that results both from self-produced motion and from movement of objects past a stationary viewer. Problems or immaturities in any of these abilities can significantly compromise basic sensory as well as "higher" aspects of vision and visual information processing.

The image formed on the retina by the eye's optics consists of a pattern of energy that contains information about the colors and spatial arrangements of objects in the world. It is the job, first, of the cells in the retina, and, later, of cells as subsequent neural processing sites in the visual pathway to transduce and encode this pattern of energy into one which the brain can interpret. The visual system, in other words, is also a complex neural network for coding the spatial, temporal, and chromatic characteristics of successive visual images; it serves as an important "front end" for higher mental processing. In turn, both perceptual and higher cognitive processes modify the way in which basic optical, oculomotor, and sensory functioning proceeds (e.g., see Neisser, 1976). In the final analysis, seeing is both a sensory and a cognitive process.

## A.  Infant Retina

The visual system of the human infant is structurally immature compared to the level of development seen in older children and adults. This immaturity begins at the retina, particularly in its area of highest acuity, the fovea (Abramov, Gordon, Hendrickson, Hainline, Dobson, & La Bossiere, 1982; Hendrickson & Yuodelis,

1984; Yuodelis & Hendrickson, 1986). Figure 1a is a photograph through a light microscope of a section from a region just outside the fovea of an adult retina; Figure 1b is a stylized drawing (based partly on electron-microscopy) of the cell types and interconnections shown in panel (a). In these figures, the front of the eye is in the direction of the top of the page, so that light passes, as indicated, through three layers of cells before reaching the outer segments of the receptors; the outer segments contain the photopigments that absorb and transduce the incident light in the image formed by the eye's optics. It is clear from Figure 1b that there is considerable neural interaction and processing of the responses of the receptors before the information is transmitted to the brain by the axons of the ganglion cells, which together form the optic nerve. Figure 1c is a section through an adult fovea, which shows some of the features that are unique to the fovea: first, the receptors are more slender and more densely packed together. Second, the inner nuclear and ganglion cell layers are much *less* dense and even absent from the very center, which creates the pit-like appearance of the fovea. However, this apparent reduction in cell density is misleading: The relevant cells associated with the foveal receptors are in fact more numerous than in peripheral regions—the bodies of these cells have simply migrated to the edges of the fovea so that light does not have to pass through them, which might reduce the sharpness of the image on the fovea.

Figures 1d and 1e show sections from the retina of a human neonate. Figure 1d is from a region just outside the fovea, which is just beyond the range of this photograph on the right. The left-hand portion of this section appears to be much like the adult peripheral retina in Figure 1a, and only on the right, as the fovea is approached, are any marked immaturities encountered: The density of receptor cells decreases, the available space for the outer segments of the receptors becomes progressively narrower, and the inner nuclear layer is divided into two sublayer; this gap in the inner nuclear layer (the transient layer of Chievitz) occurs everywhere in the retina at an early stage of embryogenesis, but only in the fovea does it persist postnatally. Figure 1e shows the neonate's fovea, in which the above abnormalities are even more pronounced. In addition, the cells in the inner nuclear and ganglion cell layers have not yet migrated to the edges of the foveal pit. At this point we know that these neonatal immaturities have mostly disappeared by the end of the first year, but we still lack detailed information of the time course of many of the changes, especially during the first two to three months when visual performance is changing very rapidly. The structural immaturity of the fovea is mirrored at successive levels in the visual pathway (e.g., Garey & De Courten, 1983; Hickey, 1977; Huttenlocher, 1979).

Given the striking state of the anatomy at birth, it has not been difficult to assimilate data purportedly showing that young infants are unskilled or inept at behaviors such as accommodation and convergence (e.g., Aslin, 1977; Banks, 1980; Haynes, White, & Held, 1965), eye movements (Aslin, 1981a; Aslin & Salapatek, 1975), or the detection of spatially distributed patterns (Atkinson,

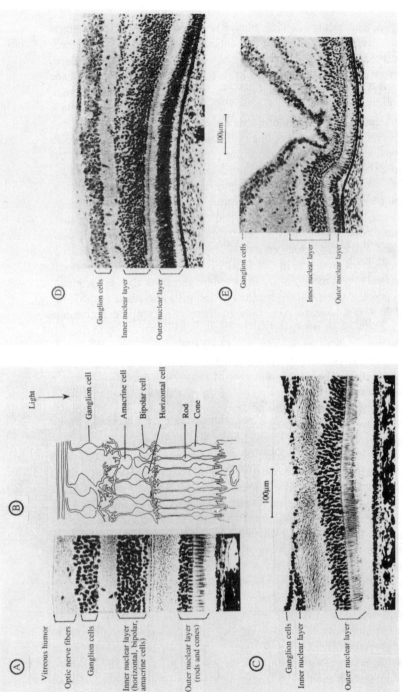

Fig. 1. Anatomy of the human retina. (a) Photomicrograph of a section through an adult primate's retina, near the fovea. (b) Schematic representation of the cells and connections in the previous photograph. (c) Photomicrograph of an adult retina in the foveal region. (d) Section through a newborn human infant's peripheral retina, near the fovea which is off to the right of this view. (e) Section through the fovea of the same infant as in the previous panel. Note the decrease in number of receptors in the fovea. (Panels a, b, c modified from Abramov & Gordon, 1973a. Panels d, e modified from Abramov, Gordon, Hendrickson, Hainline, Dobson, & La Bossiere, 1982).

46

Braddick & Moar, 1977; Banks & Salapatek, 1981). But attribution of functional immaturities to anatomical immaturities must be done cautiously. We rarely know how much of a structural change it takes to produce a functional change. However, there have been some detailed attempts to relate structure and function, based largely on the still incomplete data on changes in retinal anatomy during the first year (Banks & Bennett, 1988; Brown, Dobson, & Maier, 1987; Wilson, 1988); clearly there is much that remains to be learned about the relationship between structural development and functional vision in infancy, but with ready access to structural immaturity as an explanation of infants' assessed incompetence, it is easy to lose sight of other characteristics of infants that can be as influential for performance on standard laboratory tasks, namely, vagaries of infant attentional state, inherent attentional preferences, and habituation.

## III.   DEVELOPMENT OF SPATIAL VISION

### A.   Spatial Contrast Sensitivity

Discrimination among objects in the world depends on spatial vision, that is, the ability to resolve the components of the image on the retina. According to linear systems analysis, based on Fourier's theorem, any such image can be analyzed into a linear summation of a specific set of basic functions (see Levine & Shefner, 1990, for an introductory treatment; also, De Valois & De Valois, 1988, and Graham, 1989). It is common to use sine waves as the basis functions; each sinusoidal component of the particular set is described by its spatial frequency (measured as cycles per degree of visual angle), phase (starting point relative to the other sinusoids), and amplitude (power); in most cases the results of the analysis are given as a power spectrum, which plots the amplitude of each sinusoidal component versus spatial frequency.

Like all optical systems, the visual system selectively filters different spatial frequencies due to imperfections in its optical structures. These factors are most obvious at the acuity limit, which is a measure of the finest pattern (i.e., highest spatial frequency) that the eye can resolve when the pattern consists of extreme dark/light transitions (i.e., high contrast). However, since the retinal image also contains many lower frequency components, measures of only acuity provide incomplete descriptions of visual performance. A more complete measure of spatial vision is the spatial contrast sensitivity function (CSF), on which acuity is only one high-frequency point.

The stimuli typically used to measure the spatial CSF are gratings with alternating lighter and darker bars, each pair of light and dark bars constituting one cycle of the grating. Starting with the edge of a light bar, the luminance of the pattern gradually increases, then gradually decreases, and so on across the grating, to produce a luminance profile that varies sinusoidally across the grating (Figure 2a). In an experiment, the spatial frequency of the grating (number of

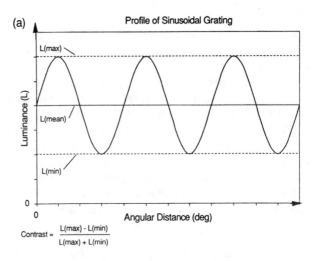

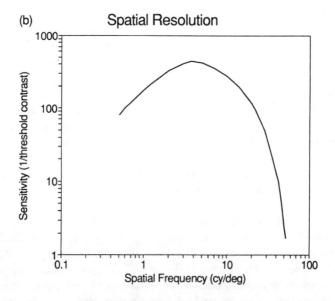

Fig. 2. (a) Contrast sensitivity is typically measured by presenting patterns whose luminance profile across the stimulus increases and decreases according to a sine function, as illustrated in this example. Contrast is a measure describing the difference between the highest and lowest luminances compared to the mean. (b) An example of an adult spatial contrast sensitivity function (CSF), based on data presented by Van Nes and Bouman (1967). Spatial frequency, on the abscissa, is a measure of the fineness of the pattern; high spatial frequencies have many cycles of light to dark transitions in the same spatial extent for which a low frequency grating has only a few such transitions. Contrast sensitivity is the reciprocal of the contrast at threshold, that is, the minimum contrast required for the detection of that spatial frequency; high-contrast sensitivity implies that a low contrast is enough for detection, while low-contrast sensitivity implies that a high level of contrast is needed to detect the pattern.

grating cycles per degree of visual angle) is varied parametrically, and for each grating, the contrast needed for threshold detection is found. The normal CSF has a characteristic inverted U-shape when contrast sensitivity (i.e., reciprocal of threshold contrast) is plotted as a function of spatial frequency (see Figure 2b). At higher spatial frequencies, as the acuity limit is approached, optical factors impose a fundamental limit: the eye's optics simply cannot form an image of an extremely fine grating—the light and dark bars are so blurred that the image is a spatially uniform field. However, the drop in sensitivity at lower spatial frequencies cannot be optical in origin in a human eye and is caused, in all likelihood, by neural factors such as lateral inhibition, that is, a type of neural interaction in which stimulation of one area reduces responses to stimulation of a neighboring area (e.g., Ratliff, 1965). The exact location of the spatial CSF with respect to the spatial frequency and contrast sensitivity axes depends greatly on the conditions under which the function is measured. For example, changes in the mean luminance shift the absolute location of the curve, with higher luminances increasing sensitivity particularly at high spatial frequencies. The method used to measure the function also influences the form and location of the curve (Graham, 1989).

Psychophysical experiments have shown that adapting to a grating of a particular frequency reduces sensitivity to that frequency and to a narrow band of frequencies around that frequency (Blakemore & Campbell, 1969). Such masking studies have led to the model that the spatial CSF is the envelope representing the contribution of a number of separate channels, each tuned to a particular region of the spatial frequency spectrum. The channels are often identified with neurons whose receptive field sizes and antagonistic center–surround organizations determine the particular spatial frequencies to which they are most sensitive; because of other properties of the channels, such as orientation specificity, the neurons in question are most probably located in the visual cortex (De Valois & De Valois, 1988; Graham, 1989). In crude terms, the visual system consists of a family of receptive channels whose sensitivities range from those sensitive to fine details through to those most sensitive to the coarser components of an image. While sine waves are not per se "ecologically valid" stimuli, quantitative approaches to vision argue that detection and recognition of objects (at least while stationary) can be predicted from the functions measured with such stimuli; this is discussed further, below.

## B. Infant Spatial CSF

The early studies of spatial resolution in infants concentrated on acuity (see Dobson & Teller, 1978). While very important, these studies cannot provide all the information inherent in measures of complete spatial CSFs; for example, systematic changes in the CSF could provide information about the rate of maturation of channels tuned to particular frequency ranges that would not be recoverable from acuity estimates.

The methods that have been used to obtain CSFs from infants include *forced-choice preferential looking* (FPL), *visual evoked potentials* (VEP), and a method we have developed that is based on recordings of subjects' eye movements, that we term *eye-movement-voting* (EMV). FPL is derived from Fantz's (1956) preferential-looking paradigm, with the variant that the dependent measure is not seconds of looking but a judgment by a person observing the infant about the position of a stimulus being viewed by the infant (Teller, 1979). Visibility and position of the stimuli are manipulated across trials. VEP methods use electrodes attached to the scalp to record the EEG during presentation of the stimulus. Since the visually evoked response is very small and the record very noisy, stimuli are presented in some repetitive fashion, and successive responses are averaged. Usually this is done by alternating between two versions of the grating stimulus such that a pattern is always present, but the bright bars of one replace the dark bars of the other; this counterphase reversal of the pattern is at some fixed temporal rate, and the responses to each cycle of the temporal alternation are averaged. The studies we will describe below use a specific form of VEP, the *sweep-VEP*. In this variant, one of the stimulus parameters is "swept" through a series of values to find the value at which some criterion response level is reached; for the spatial CSF, the contrast of each grating is varied, in a series of small steps from high to low to find the contrast at which the averaged response falls within the EEG signal's noise (Norcia, Clarke, & Tyler, 1985; Tyler, Apkarian, Levi, & Nakayama, 1979).

Our EMV method (Hainline, de Bie, Abramov, & Camenzuli, 1987) is a direct analogue of the typical FPL method, with a more fine-grained response measure. In EMV, the stimulus for any trial is a grating of fixed spatial frequency and contrast, but the stimulus screen is not simply filled with the bars of a static grating: The bars drift across the screen at some fixed velocity, either to the left or to the right for that trial. If the grating is above threshold, it entrains following eye movements on the part of the subject. We use the output of a TV-based infra-red eye tracking system (Hainline, 1981) to obtain a continuous record of the position of the subject's eye at each instant during a trial. This record is presented to an observer who is "blind" to the direction of stimulus drift and who must vote which way the stimulus was moving, based solely on the eye movements; the contrast of the grating is then either reduced on successive trials until the observer makes an error or, if the initial response is an error, increased until the voter is correct. The contrast at that point is defined as the subject's threshold. The specific psychophysical algorithm is somewhat unorthodox, but has the virtue of being very quick and appears to yield reasonable functions for adults, children and infants (Abramov, Hainline, Turkel, Lemerise, Smith, Gordon, & Petry, 1984; Hainline, Camenzuli, Abramov, Rawlick, & Lemerise, 1986; Hainline et al., 1987).

Since, as discussed below, the different methods do not yield the same absolute contrast sensitivities from infants of a given age, it would be useful to identify some of the reasons for the variations. Most basically, it would be useful to show that a method does not systematically distort adults' CSFs, which represent "known" cases. We have validated the EMV method with adult subjects by comparing CSFs from such indirect observer's votes with CSFs obtained from the direct votes of the subjects themselves (Hainline et al., 1987). The two versions of the CSF agree well with each other in shape, although the absolute sensitivity of the function from direct subject voting is higher, probably because of the loss of information necessarily entailed by having a "vote" made by a second party rather than directly by the observer. Similar within-adult validations also exist for the VEP; while it is not free of statistical assumptions, VEP at least has the advantage of not needing a blind observer's vote to determine threshold; consequently it is not surprising that there is good agreement between swept parameter VEP estimates of adult spatial CSFs and traditional psychophysical methods (Norcia, Tyler, & Hamer, 1990). There are no such adult comparison data using the FPL technique, so we do not have a direct measure of the sensitivity of that method itself. Because FPL uses the vote of an observer, there is reason to believe that like EMV, its sensitivity will be reduced compared to direct psychophysical measures of the adult CSF.

There are several sets of data on the development of the spatial CSF for human infants, including but not limited to: Atkinson et al. (1977), Banks & Salapatek (1978), Hainline, Camenzuli, et al. (1986), Norcia, Tyler, & Allen (1986), and Norcia et al. (1990); some of these are shown in Figure 3a. While these studies differ in the absolute sensitivities that are found, they agree in finding a gradual improvement in both absolute contrast sensitivity and in the range of spatial frequencies to which the system is sensitive; that is, with increasing age over the first year, the CSF (plotted as in Figure 2b) shifts laterally to higher frequencies and upward to higher sensitivities. There is also evidence that sensitivity to low and middle frequencies approaches the adult asymptote at an earlier age than does the sensitivity to high spatial frequencies close to the acuity limit (Norcia et al., 1990). Examples of these changes can be seen in Figure 3b.

Many of the studies on spatial CSF during infancy have been done with FPL, and these are the studies usually cited as evidence for the poor spatial resolution of the infant visual system. However, other methods yield different estimates of how sensitive the infant visual system is to the contrast of sine wave gratings. For example, there is a factor of roughly 10 in contrast sensitivity at the peak of the CSF for the most sensitive methods using the sweep VEP as compared with the lowest estimates from FPL. Our data from EM are intermediate in sensitivity between VEP and FPL (see, e.g., data for 2- and 3-month-olds in Figure 3a). The reasons for these variations are not entirely clear. All of these methods are necessarily indirect as psychophysical measures of contrast sensitivity. Also, the various methods often use different psychophysical algorithms and different criterion responses to define thresholds. For example, VEP thresh-

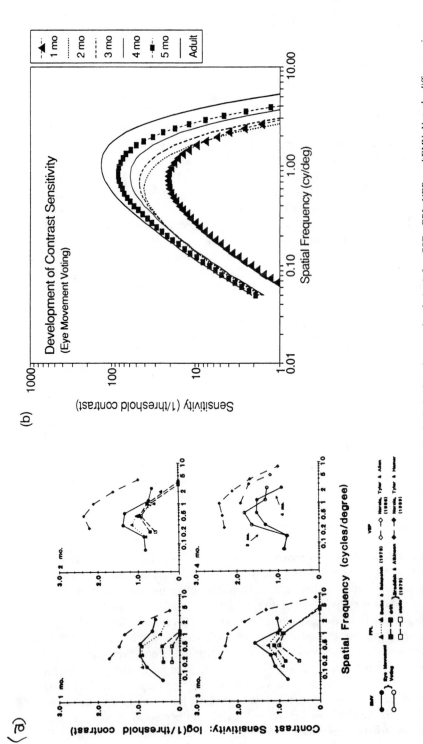

*Fig. 3.* (a) Examples of infant spatial CSFs obtained from the three methods that have been used to derive infant CSFs: *FPL, VEP, and EMV. Note the differences in absolute sensitivities, but the general similarity of the shapes of the curves, in most cases.* (b) *Illustration of age-related changes; the curves represent the best fits of a standard model (Kelly, 1979b) fitted to our EMV data (Hainline, Abramov, Camenzuli, & Moore, 1991). Stimuli were sinusoidal gratings drifting at 7 deg/sec. The data were collected at lower luminances than used for the adult CSF presented in Figure 2b, which accounts for the reduced sensitivities for the adult curve, especially*

olds are usually defined by extrapolating to find contrast for zero response, whereas FPL thresholds are usually defined as the contrast required for 75% correct responses (for further discussion, see Teller, 1985). Moreover, there is no commonly accepted set of stimuli for measuring CSFs: with adults, increasing the mean luminance of the gratings increases sensitivity and shifts the entire CSF towards higher spatial frequencies (Kelly, 1961; Van Nes & Bouman, 1967); also, increasing the number of cycles of the grating present in the stimulus improves sensitivity especially at low spatial frequencies (Robson & Graham, 1981). All these factors undoubtedly influence the outcome and need to be investigated systematically in the research on infants.

There have been suggestions that the results from the various methods diverge because they are tapping different levels of the visual system and/or the sensitivities of different regions of the retina. FPL has been seen as the most "cognitive" method. FPL is, of course, dependent on detecting infants' relatively gross attentional discriminations between more and less visible stimuli; it has been assumed that these attentionally driven responses are voluntary and thus dependent on "higher" neural centers. At the same time, because the stimuli for FPL are presented on the left and on the right, it is possible that the shifts in attention seen in FPL are due to a reflexive orienting to salient peripheral stimuli. A VEP depicts an average of the composite neural activity to repeated presentations of a stimulus, after processing at many different levels in the visual system. Except for the need for a minimal level of alertness, it does not depend on voluntary behaviors from the infant. VEP is generally believed to reflect the spatial sensitivity of central retina. Our EMV method is based on following eye movements elicited by moving gratings. Such eye movements are a behavorial response to moving stimuli; some kinds of following eye movements have been described as reflexive, although in practice it is not easy to discriminate between reflexive and voluntary following eye movements. Although it is a behavioral method, EMV may be more similar to VEP than FPL; in both cases, stimuli are presented directly in front of the subject, and so the thresholds are more likely to represent those of central, rather than peripheral, retina.

Another major difference among methods is how long it takes to get an estimate of the CSF. The methods clearly demand different degrees of cooperation from the infant. FPL is time-consuming. With FPL, derivation of a full CSF extends over several lengthy sessions, with the risk of significant habituation to the stimuli and to the testing situation itself, as well as the possibility of centrally caused reductions in alertness. Compared with FPL, VEP is a rapid method; in some sweep-VEP procedures, a complete spatial CSF can be obtained in 10–15 minutes. The EMV method takes about the same time as the sweep-VEP to derive a CSF.

There are thus many reasons why one would not expect identical spatial CSFs from the different methods—indeed, the similarities in results are all the more striking in the face of these methodological variations.

## C. Spatiotemporal Interactions

Visual stimuli vary simultaneously in both space and time, and the visual system's sensitivities to these dimensions are inextricably linked. Despite this, it is common for reference chapters on the visual system to treat them separately; the spatial CSF, plotting spatial frequency versus contrast, and the temporal CSF, plotting temporal frequency versus contrast of a large uniformly flickering field, are presented as distinct functions (e.g., Abramov & Gordon, 1973b; Woodhouse & Barlow, 1982). In fact, however, the visibility (i.e., contrast at threshold) of a grating of any given spatial frequency depends on the temporal parameters of the stimulus; that is, a CSF is best expressed as a particular section through a three-dimensional spatiotemporal solid (Kelly, 1979a, b). Kelly used a very precise eye tracker to eliminate completely the effects of the subject's own eye movements on the retinal image. It was then possible for him to vary independently both the spatial and temporal characteristics of the stimulus on the retina. The results clearly indicate that there is no such thing as *the* CSF, but rather an infinite family of spatiotemporal CSFs that describe an entire spatiotemporal contrast sensitivity surface. Moreover, the details of any such surface also depend on a host of other stimulus parameters such as luminance, spatial extent, and so on.

An example of a spatiotemporal surface we have obtained is shown in Figure 4. The data were collected from naive adult subjects using EMV; spatial CSFs were derived by drifting gratings of spatial frequencies ranging from 0.5 to 4.7 cy/deg at each of five constant velocities. Because temporal frequency results from the interaction of spatial frequency and velocity, the temporal frequency of the gratings differed across trials. For example, a 1 cy/deg grating drifting at 10 deg/sec has a temporal frequency of 10 cy/sec. The figure shows the smooth surface fitted over the separate CSFs thus obtained. The exact ordinate values for such a surface will depend, of course, on stimulus details. For example, Figure 4 shows that we did not use gratings of a very high spatial frequencies, and hence the front corner of the solid is truncated; the reason was simply that the mean luminance of our display was relatively low, and, under these conditions, very high frequencies were not visible. Spatiotemporal surfaces have, however, general properties that hold over a range of experimental conditions. Consider the changes in the shape of the spatial CSF that would result from changes in the temporal rate. Such curves can be obtained by slicing the solid parallel to the spatial frequency abscissa. At very low temporal rates, overall sensitivity of the spatial CSF is depressed and the peak is shifted towards higher spatial frequencies. As temporal rate is increased, the peak shifts to lower spatial frequencies, and sensitivity to those frequencies increases. However, because of the shift of the function towards lower spatial frequencies, there is a *loss* in sensitivity at the highest frequencies (i.e., the acuity limit is shifted to lower values), and a *gain* in sensitivity at low frequencies; indeed, the usual drop in sensitivity at low spatial frequencies may no longer be evident at very high temporal rates. This is the

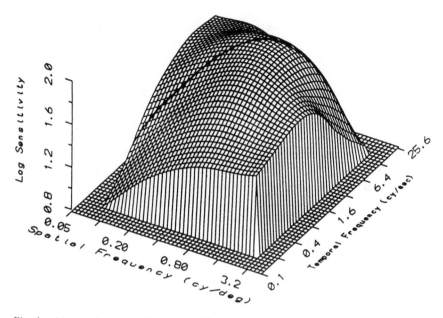

*Fig. 4. An example of a spatiotemporal CSF. The smooth surface was fitted to EMV data from adults (data from Hainline, de Bie, Abramov, & Camenzuli, 1987). Stimuli were sinusoidal gratings at the same low photopic luminance as in Figure 3b, but the gratings were drifting at various velocities. The smooth surface was fitted across the data points, but following the usual convention, we have plotted contrast sensitivity vs. spatial and temporal frequency, rather than velocity. The dark line traces as single CSF at a retinal velocity of 7 deg/sec.*

reason why the infant VEP CSFs in Figure 3a fail to "turn down" at lower spatial frequencies; in order to obtain a VEP, it is necessary to use a time-varying stimulus, which increases sensitivity at lower spatial frequencies compared to a static stimulus. Similarly, temporal CSFs are represented by the planes parallel to that axis. The heavy line in the figure represents a CSF whose plane is at 45 deg to each abscissa and was obtained not with a fixed temporal rate, but with gratings drifting at a constant velocity of 7 deg/sec.

Results such as those in Figure 4 require the consideration of another variable that is usually uncontrolled in studies of spatial vision. Temporal variation for the visual system results jointly from the experimenter's deliberate temporal variation of the stimulus (through movement or flashing) and from the effects of the subject's eye movements (which are only rarely controlled for). Except in the few cases when the effects of eye movements have been nullified (e.g., Kelly, 1979b), unknown temporal variations influence measures of the spatial CSF, even for stimuli that the experimenter intends to be "static." How much this affects the resulting CSF is an empirical question and depends on many factors; one of particular interest in considering infant data is the precision of the subjects' eye movement control. It is worth noting that the eyes of even highly motivated adult observers fixating static targets can drift at rates of the order of ½ to 1 deg/sec, unless subjects' heads are rigidly stabilized (Skavenski, Hansen, Steinman, & Winterson, 1979). When these drifts are orthogonal to the bars of a static grating, they necessarily introduce a temporal flicker whose rate depends on the grating's spatial frequency; in general, these rates are sufficient to produce marked changes in threshold (see Kelly, 1979b; also, Figure 4).

Eye movements cannot simply be ignored in studies of spatial sensitivity, although the role that poor eye movement control could play in limiting infants' spatial vision has not been investigated systematically. FPL studies have typically used static gratings, which emulate the conventional stimuli in the adult literature. In FPL, the actual temporal value will depend on how well the infant is able to stabilize the stimulus on the retina by means of the joint action of the vestibulo-ocular reflex and fixational mechanisms, and possibly of optokinetic nystagmus. In some FPL laboratories, it is the practice to swing the infant from side to side during the first phase of stimulus presentation to insure that the infant has "sampled" both of the stimulus choices; this practice may introduce unintended temporal variations to the stimulus. Both VEP and our EMV studies use stimuli that are deliberately varied in time and/or space. In order to record a VEP, the stimulus varies in time, usually by alternating between two versions of the relevant pattern. However, the temporal properties of the proximal stimulus (i.e., on the retina) have not been precisely controlled, and indeed, are unknown. Eye movements could also contaminate the temporal rate selected for the VEP, but because the measure represents an average across many brief stimulus presentations, the problem is minimized.

In EMV, since we depend on following eye movements to judge stimulus visibility, retinal velocity must be less than stimulus velocity when the stimuli are above threshold. At threshold, however, there are no systematic following eye movements, and the retinal velocity of the stimulus should be determined solely by stimulus velocity; that is, we should be estimating the slice through the spatiotemporal surface for the nominal stimulus velocity. We have applied Kelly's (1979b) model for spatiotemporal responses to our EMV results and the fits are good both for our infant and adult subjects (Hainline, Abramov, Camenzuli, & Moore, 1992). Figure 3b shows these fitted curves for the different ages; in all cases, the gratings were drifting at 7 deg/sec (see heavy line in Figure 4).

Besides this sensory effect of spatiotemporal interactions, motion of the stimulus has attentional implications for infants. A fact established fairly early about infant preferences is that, even for simple stimuli, infants prefer moving and time-varying stimuli over the equivalent static stimulus (e.g., Carpenter, 1974; Volkman & Dobson, 1976), possibly because movement is an important characteristic of the stimuli infants naturally attend to; it is likely that infants find the stimuli in VEP studies and in our EMV studies more interesting than in many FPL versions and this may influence measured thresholds. Gibsonians and neo-Gibsonians would of course argue that motion is not interesting because of its influence on sensory thresholds, but because much information about objects and our relationship to objects is revealed by motion (e.g., Gibson, 1979). Indeed, it can be argued that, for very young infants, the components of the world that are perceived as relating to ''objects'' are those components that move as a coherent unit (Kellman & Spelke, 1983); this motion could either be due to real motion of the object relative to the background or to motion of the infant (Kellman, Gleitman, & Spelke, 1987).

At low to moderate temporal frequencies, the spatial CSF has a reduction in sensitivity at lower spatial frequencies. This low-frequency attenuation is generally believed to stem from a neural phenomenon, lateral inhibition. Its absence in young infants would be of major significance. Initial studies of the FPL-derived spatial CSF of 1-month-olds reported that, as a group, they showed no low-frequency attenuation, suggesting a fundamental neural difference between older and younger infants (see Figure 3a). Our data from younger infants do not agree, showing CSFs from even 1-month infants that have low frequency attenuation, provided that one measures at low enough spatial frequencies. Spatiotemporal differences in the effective retinal stimulus might account for some of this discrepancy in findings about low-frequency sensitivity across methods. The FPL studies (Atkinson et al., 1977; Banks & Salapatek, 1978) include data from individual infants at 1 month, and some of them show the expected attenuation, although the group functions do not. If for some reason (reduced attention and/or low arousal?) 1-month-olds have trouble maintaining stable fixation, the resulting retinal slip could increase sensitivity to low spatial frequencies (see Figure 4); this is not implausible, because attention problems are certainly much greater with 1-month-olds than with older infants. Similar arguments can be used to account for some of the higher sensitivities obtained with EMV as compared with FPL: if we assume that, at threshold, the retinal stimulus in EMV has a higher temporal component than would a static grating in an FPL study, then the EMV-derived CSF will have higher sensitivities, at least for middle and low frequencies. But this cannot be the entire explanation. Spatial resolution generally improves as luminance increases. The luminances of the displays in the FPL studies were at least an order of magnitude greater than those for EMV, which should have compensated for the temporal effects, so there is still some problem reconciling the results.

These observations are not intended to argue for or against any particular method. We must distinguish, however, between relative and absolute estimates of infant visual capacities. While all of our methods are necessarily indirect, some may underestimate actual abilities more than others. An advantage of FPL is that it is relatively inexpensive in personnel and equipment compared with the other two methods we have discussed and thus may be a practical choice for widespread clinical application. For example, if the normative developmental sequence of the full CSF can be established with the most sensitive measure, VEP at this point, it may be possible to use FPL diagnostically as a probe for selected points on the spatial CSF, although it is likely also to underestimate infants' spatial vision. Although it suffers from the loss in sensitivity that follows from the use of an observer-voter, EMV is well suited to studying the temporal aspect of spatial vision because of its ability to measure the relationship between stimulus and eye velocity for moving stimuli, thus allowing an estimate of the retinal velocity of spatial patterns.

## D.  Functional Consequences of the Infant CSF

A subject's CSF can be regarded as a selective filter for the spatial frequencies represented by the Fourier power spectrum of a given stimulus; this is the central assumption of "linear systems" approaches in vision (see, e.g., Ginsburg, 1986; De Valois & De Valois, 1988). While it is clear that, above threshold, vision is in many respects nonlinear, the linear systems approach has been successful in describing many aspects of visual performance. Some studies, for example, suggest that object recognition depends heavily on information at lower spatial frequencies (Ginsburg, Evans, Sekuler, & Harp, 1982); low frequencies communicate information about an object's broad features. Discrimination among similar objects may depend, however, much more on high frequency information; this is clearly seen in letter discrimination tasks like the traditional Snellen test, in which reductions in high spatial frequency vision (i.e., acuity), often due to optical blur, severely impair visual performance (e.g., Thorn & Schwartz, 1990). At this point we must add that it is a serious oversimplification to consider only the power spectrum of a stimulus: the phase spectrum (i.e., the starting point on its cycle of each sinusoidal component of the stimulus) is also very important; if a stimulus is recreated using its original power spectrum but with a random phase spectrum, the object may no longer be recognized (Piotrowski & Campbell, 1982).

The ability of the visual system to recognize and discriminate among patterns will depend both on the individual viewer's CSF and on the Fourier spectra of the particular stimuli involved. The assumptions of linear systems analysis allow us to simulate what various objects might look like to a young infant, in essence, to substitute their visual system for our own in a limited way. Since faces are such an important part of the infant's visual world, we have used them to illustrate some of these points. In Figure 5a we start with a sharply focused image of a face, that of one of the editors of this volume, which we will filter so that, when it is viewed by an adult with normal vision, it will appear as if the adult's visual system had been replaced by that of a 2-month infant. In Figure 5b we show the CSFs for a normal adult and a typical 6–8-week infant that will be used in the filtering process. These particular curves are in fact examples of Kelly's (1979b) model of spatial CSFs that we have generated for a specific set of viewing conditions, as follows: a moderate photopic luminance level (e.g., equivalent to viewing the figure under a good reading light), and a temporal parameter value approximating a normal, casual, nonlaboratory degree of fixational stability (1 deg/sec). The original image of Dr. Lipsitt's face was analyzed to obtain its two-dimensional Fourier spectrum; the power at each spatial frequency was then rescaled according to the infant's sensitivity to each frequency to produce an *effective* (or filtered) power spectrum of the image. (Strictly speaking, the CSF, or filter, in Figure 5b is for a one-dimensional stimulus, and a two-dimensional filter had to be derived from it for the filtering operation.) This filtered spectrum could have been used to resynthesize a filtered image of the face. But had we done so, the resulting image would have been quite misleading. The reason is that, when adults look at such a filtered image, they are imposing a second stage of filtering—that due to their own visual systems. The problems raised by this are best appreciated by considering some low spatial frequency to which the adult and the infant are approximately equally sensitive; at that frequency the double filtering would be equivalent to squaring the infant's filter, which would lead to overfiltering at these frequencies. To compensate for this, we have rescaled the infant-filtered power spectrum by the inverse of the adult's CSF before resynthesizing the image. Thus, assuming that the viewer's CSF is like the adult CSF in Figure 5b, the inverse filtering according to that function is negated by the filtering imposed by the viewer's own CSF, and the viewer should see the face as if the viewer's visual system had been replaced by that of the infant. Because the spatial frequency content of a face necessarily changes with viewing distance, we have repeated the operations for two viewing distances of 30 and 150 cm. The resulting images are shown in Figure 5c,d. At the near distance, the stimulus is clearly still recognizable as a face, although at the further distance, this becomes a questionable identification. In all of these manipulations, the original phase relationships have been maintained; otherwise the image would have been "scrambled." In short, at the distances at which infants are called on to recognize faces (arm's length), even the visual system of a young infant is probably adequate to discern a face's critical features.

The linear systems approach to visual discrimination has already been applied to normal infant preference data with some success: simply by using an age-appropriate CSF to filter stimuli, it is possible to predict infants' visual preferences (Atkinson, 1977; Banks & Salapatek, 1981; Gayl, Roberts, & Werner, 1983; Slater, Earle, Morison, & Rose, 1985). A lot of the work on stimulus recognition and discrimination has dealt with faces, probably because of the high "ecological validity" of such stimuli. There have recently been some attempts to examine the relative importance of phase and power spectra for recognition of faces by infants. As already noted, for adults, the phase spectrum of a stimulus is a much more important determinant of recognition than is the

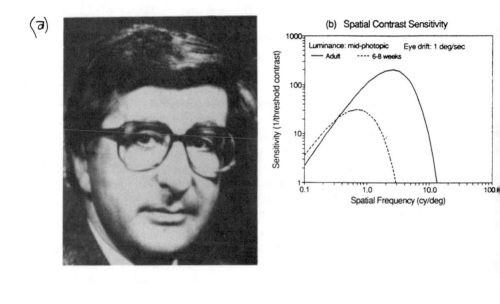

(a)

(b) Spatial Contrast Sensitivity

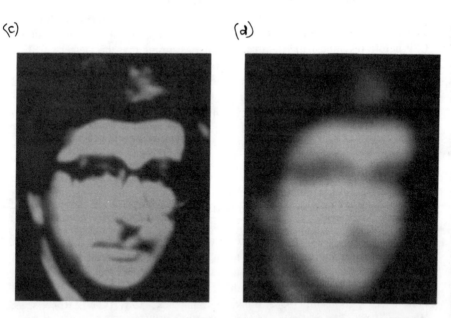

(c)

(d)

Fig. 5. The effect of the infant CSF on visibility of an "ecologically valid" stimulus. (a) A photograph of a prominent developmental psychologist. (b) Hypothetical CSFs for a normal 6–8-week infant and an adult under conditions of good photopic luminance and moderate fixational stability. These are used to filter the image in (a), as described in the text. (c) Dr. Lipsitt's face as it might be seen by a 2-month old viewing him from a distance of 30 cm. More correctly, when the figure is viewed by an adult with a normal CSF, it will be seen as if the adult's visual system had been replaced by one with the CSF of the infant in (b). (d) A similarly filtered view of Dr. Lipsitt, but at a distance of 150 cm. Image processing was done by M. M. Aguisky.

power spectrum. Thus, in the recent developmental studies, "facelike" stimuli were analyzed into their Fourier components and then recombined using different phase relations, but preserving the original power spectra (Dannemiller & Stephens, 1988; Kleiner, 1987; Kleiner & Banks, 1987). The results have been interpreted as showing that infants younger than 2 months are responding in their preferences on the basis of total power, irrespective of the phase relations among the components. That is, they do not always prefer the stimuli seen as facelike by adults. However, these interpretations must be treated cautiously: for example, Kleiner (1987) compared newborns' preferences for a schematic face versus a lattice made up of squares on a blank background; comparisons also pitted preferences for stimuli created from the phase spectrum of one and the power spectrum of the other. Kleiner's conclusions focus on the fact that newborns, unlike 2-month-olds (Kleiner & Banks, 1987), do not prefer the lattice stimulus with the face's phase relations (which looks like a slightly distorted face to adults). However, the data also show that newborns, like 2-month-olds, prefer the original schematic face over the stimulus with the face's power spectrum but the lattice's phase spectrum, which shows that they are not phase insensitive and that the face's phase structure may be inherently attractive, even to newborns (Morton, Johnson, & Maurer, 1990).

Beyond the above problems, there is a more general question of whether such studies are indeed examining the perception of "faceness." The designation of these schematic and simplified stimuli as "facelike" is based on adult's categorizations. It is not clear that infants categorize such stimuli equivalently (Cohen, 1988). Before concluding that young infants respond to faces primarily on the basis of some low-level sensory signal (such as the total effective power in a stimulus as derived from a linear systems analysis), the studies need to be repeated using real faces.

While powerful quantitatively, linear systems analysis may not tell us all that we need to know about stimulus appearance. Strictly, linear systems approaches to stimulus discriminations can predict performance only when responses vary linearly with intensity. When contrasts are close to threshold, it is probably safe to assume that the visual system is behaving linearly. However, when contrasts are well above threshold, as in normal viewing conditions, the system may become nonlinear. Furthermore, the nonlinearities may be associated more strongly with certain regions of the spatial frequency spectrum. Finally, different tasks may be biased towards particular frequency ranges; but example, reading may depend more on higher spatial frequencies, but categorizing something as this or that object may be more affected by sensitivity to lower frequencies. These factors make it difficult to predict exactly how a given CSF will affect visibility of real objects above threshold.

Most of the studies of the effects of the CSF on perception have dealt with static "snapshots" of the stimulus. Gibsonian theory reminds us, however, that stimulus recognition may be more crucially dependent on invariant features of *dynamic* displays extended in time (e.g., Bertenthal, Proffitt, Spetner, &

Thomas, 1985; Kellman & Spelke, 1983; Ruff, 1982). Until recently, motion of the stimulus or of the subject with respect to the stimulus have been regarded as nuisance variables rather than as a necessary dimension of study. As we saw in the discussion of spatiotemporal interactions, it is far from trivial to deal with both spatial and temporal dimensions in a controlled fashion. These problems notwithstanding, linear systems analysis of the capacities of the developing visual system offers a powerful means to understand the implications of neural immaturity, to predict what visual information is available to the infant for other developmental functions, and to evaluate early visual system dysfunction. Comparisons among results from different methods can serve as the source of converging information to give a perspective on the development of spatial vision not accessible from any single method of data collection.

## IV.  DEVELOPMENT OF ACCOMMODATION AND VERGENCE

In our discussions of spatial resolution and the CSF, we assumed implicitly that changes in the eyes' optical properties had been controlled or optimized. However, in order to produce a good image on the retina, one that preserves high spatial frequencies, the eye must be appropriately focused; also, to see a single image of an object, both eyes must rotate correctly to point at the object. The abilities to do all these things change with age and must be considered when evaluating infants' visual performance.

### A.  Accommodation

*Accommodation* refers to the process of changing the curvature of the crystalline lens to change the eye's refractive power. Refraction is a measure of the bending of light rays by an optical system, expressed in diopters (D), a unit defined as the reciprocal of the focal length of the lens in meters (and also of viewing distance, given correct accommodation). For example, 1 D corresponds to 1 meter, 2 D to a ½-meter distance, 4 D to ¼ meter, and so on. Less accommodation is needed to focus far objects, more to focus near objects. Emmetropia refers to the condition when an individual completely relaxes accommodation and the resulting plane of focus is very far (optical infinity, effectively about 6 meters); by increasing accommodation, it is possible to focus nearer objects. In myopia, when accommodation is relaxed, the eye is focused at a relatively close distance and therefore distant objects will appear blurred. In contrast in hyperopia, the plane of focus when accommodation is relaxed is beyond optical infinity and all objects appear blurred. If they start with completely relaxed accommodation, all three of the above types of individual can, in principle, focus nearer objects. Hyperopes must accommodate to some degree for all distances, including very distant ones. Myopes must accommodate for objects closer than their relaxed plane of focus. Note, however, that myopes cannot use accommodation to focus on objects beyond their plane of relaxed accommodation; also, since the ability to accommodate declines steadily with age, the range of focusable distances ultimately declines for all individuals, particularly after age 40 (e.g., Millodot, 1982).

Although the accommodative system has been studied for centuries, there is still dispute about what controls the accommodative response, even though there is agreement that it is important to consider the spatial frequencies present in the stimulus (Owens, 1980). One theory proposes that a primary factor controlling accommodation is contrast at the retina, and that the goal of the system is to maximize retinal contrast (e.g., Adams & Johnson, 1987); this theory predicts that accommodative responses will be most accurate in the midrange of spatial frequencies (i.e., near the peak of the spatial CSF) where visual sensitivity to contrast is maximal. Another position believes that the goal of the accommodative system is to reduce defocus or blur, which is defined by high spatial frequencies (e.g., Kruger & Pola, 1986). Actually both ranges of spatial frequencies may be important, with low to intermediate spatial frequencies responsible for reflexive accommodation to abrupt changes of target position (e.g., Bour, 1981), and higher frequencies useful for fine-tuning the accommodative response (Ciuffreda & Rumpf, 1985). It is also clear that low and intermediate spatial frequencies provide useful visual information over larger degrees of defocus than do higher spatial frequencies; inaccurate focus has relatively little effect on performance when relevant contrast information is contained in lower spatial frequency regions, while contrast information at high spatial frequencies is severely degraded with only minimal blur.

## B. Vergence

Functional vision depends not only on the clarity of the image for each eye, but also on how the eyes are jointly positioned. Vergence refers to the rotation of the eyes so that their viewing axes intersect, ideally on a plane for which the eyes are accommodated. The angle of rotation is measured in prism diopters (a prism of one diopter shifts the image by 1 cm at a distance of 1 m). The primary function of vergence is to reduce the disparity of the two retinal images and to bring the target into single binocular registration. In most adults, the accommodative and vergence systems are synergistically linked so that each system influences the other's performance (see Schor & Ciuffreda, 1983). Thus, there is another component of vergence caused by a change in accommodation (*accommodative vergence*); similarly, an important component of the accommodative response is accommodation caused by a change in vergence (*vergence accommodation*). Since each eye looks at objects from slightly different angles, there is a disparity between the images in the two eyes that is inversely related to viewing distance.

The images of an object on the plane to which the eyes are converged fall on corresponding retinal regions and are normally fused and seen as a single object. There is also a region, known as *Panum's fusion area,* which extends in front and back of the binocular fixation plane, within which all points are fused and seen as single objects, even though they do not fall on strictly corresponding points. For adults, vergence driven by disparity is much more precise than accommodative vergence, and so *fusional vergence* is more likely to be seen under normal conditions (Schor, 1979). As fixation disparity increases, a point is reached in which Panum's region is exceeded and the fusion breaks down, resulting in double vision or diplopia. Stereoscopic information about an object's depth also depends on disparity, although it appears to be a higher function than fusion; one can have single vision, that is, fusion, without achieving stereoscopic depth perception. It is likely that these skills depend on the development of different cortical centers.

As with accommodation, the spatial frequency content of the stimulus and the observer's spatial contrast sensitivity (or, more correctly, spatiotemporal contrast sensitivity) interact with the vergence response. Low spatial frequency information is fused sooner than high spatial frequency information, since Panum's area is broader for low spatial frequencies than for higher (Schor, Wood, & Ogawa, 1984); it would actually be more correct to speak of a series of Panum's areas, since the area defined by fine detail is only one of many possible regions. As with accommodation, accommodative (i.e., blur-driven) vergence results in a fine-tuning of the vergence response initially driven by lower spatial frequencies. From a developmental standpoint, we would expect to see some correspondence between developments of the spatial CSF and the accommodation/vergence system.

## C. Measures of Accommodation and Vergence

With cooperative, instructable subjects, the most common method to measure refractive status is retinoscopy, in which a practitioner evaluates the refractive error by determining the power of lenses that need to be substituted externally to null the amount of refraction of a test light by the various optical elements of the eye. In static retinoscopy, the adjustable refractive power of the subject's lens is disabled, usually by drugs (cycloplegics) that temporarily paralyze accommodation; while this makes assessment of the eye as an optical instrument both quicker and more interpretable, it is not appropriate for the study of the accommodative response, since accommodation is frozen by the cycloplegic agent. In dynamic retinoscopy, the subject is instructed or induced to fixate points at known distances while the evaluation of the refractive power of the optics is performed. The validity of the method is critically dependent on whether the subject maintains focus on the specified plane during the evaluation. Retinoscopy with infants, particularly dynamic retinoscopy, requires considerable practice.

In order to facilitate the evaluation of infant refractive status, several photographic methods have been devised; among these are orthogonal, isotropic, and paraxial photorefraction (Atkinson, Braddick, Ayling, Pimm-Smith, Howland, & Ingram, 1981; Bobier & Braddick, 1985; Howland & Howland, 1974; Norcia, Zadnik, & Day, 1986). The methods differ in the exact optical principles employed, but all provide an instantaneous photographic sample of refractive state from an uninstructed subject, with or without cycloplegia. (A specific method, which we use, is described in greater detail, below.) Vergence is measured by monitoring changes in the eyes' angle of rotation. A common method is to measure changes in the position within each pupil of the image of a fixed reference light source reflected from the eye's cornea. The position of this corneal reflection and its shift with a given degree of eye rotation depend on a number of physical features of the eye, including corneal curvature, the location of the fovea and the separation of the eyes, all of which are known to change developmentally. There is a similar clinical measure of strabismus, the *Hirschberg ratio,* which is the extent of movement of the corneal reflection for a given angle of eye rotation (Jones & Eskridge, 1970).

In our studies of infants, we use a form of *paraxial photorefraction,* also called *eccentric photorefraction, photoretinoscopy,* and *static photographic skiascopy.* First developed by Kaakinen (1979), the optical details of paraxial photorefraction are fully described elsewhere (Abramov, Hainline, & Duckman, 1990; Bobier & Braddick, 1985; Howland, 1985). Essentially, the method takes advantage of a problem encountered by amateur photographers: snapshots of people taken with inexpensive cameras often show an effect known as *red-eye,* caused by the reflection of light from the flash back from the retina into the lens of the camera. The effect is caused by the close flash-to-camera distance, and can be eliminated by moving the flash further from the lens. In our case, we use to our advantage the same reflected light from the retina in a camera/flash system specifically designed to place the flash as close as possible to the lens. Our system is shown schematically in Figure 6a.

In a paraxial photorefraction system, an emmetrope fixating at the distant camera (ours is 4.5 m from the subject for maximum resolution) will show no red-eye; because of the optical arrangement, none of the reflected light from the retina will reach the camera's lens. But, if the subject is misaccommodated for the plane of the camera, a crescent of light will appear in the pupil. Because of the placement of the optical elements in our system (with the flash above the lens), for a myope, the crescent is at the top of the pupil, while a hyperope has a crescent at the bottom of the pupil. The degree of misaccommodation is gauged by the size of the crescent. We have already alluded to the major problem in using such a system with infants: namely, that it is unlikely that infants will attend reliably to a target 4.5 m distant. We deal with this problem by using highly attractive targets, small lighted dolls presented in a darkened room. The targets are realistic, three-dimensional, colorful and roughly of equal angular

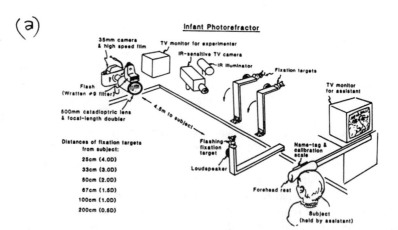

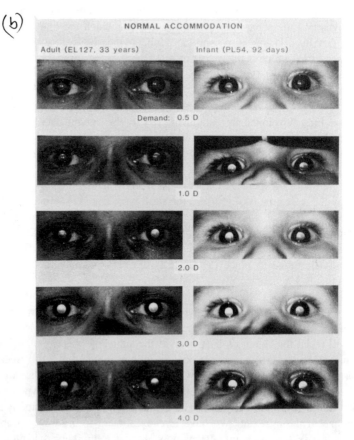

Fig. 6. *Paraxial photorefraction of infants (from Abramov, Hainline, & Duckman, 1990) (a) Schematic view of photorefractor and stimuli, showing the relationship between the camera, the flash unit and the series of accommodation targets to the subject. The infrared television equipment is used to position the subject correctly for each photograph. (b) Paraxial photorefraction pictures of a visually-normal adult and infant viewing targets at different distances (demands to accommodation). The critical aspects of the photograph are the size and the position of the bright "crescent" in each eye.*

subtense. They are internally illuminated and can be flashed to increase their attractiveness. In addition, each target has directly underneath a small speaker that plays a song when the target is presented, again to attract attention. For the more distant targets, if the infants appear not to have noticed them, we bring them close to the target and then gradually move them back to the required distance where the picture is taken.

Figure 6b presents a series of pictures from an adult and an infant, both with normal refractive status. As the subject accommodates on the progressively closer targets, the crescents that are photographed through the eyes' pupils grow in size. The crescents are all across the top of the pupil, which indicates myopia in our system, because the targets are all closer than the camera distance: a subject who accommodates correctly for any of these targets will appear myopic with respect to the camera. To relate the size of a crescent to accommodation, in diopters, requires calibration. To calibrate the crescents, we used a group of visually normal adult subjects and measured the crescents associated with different target distances and pupil sizes; to insure that they are indeed accommodating accurately, the targets are replaced by short lengths of text, printed in small type, which the subjects must read during the refraction (Abramov et al., 1990). The findings from our system are described below.

## D. Developmental Studies of Accommodation and Vergence

### 1. Accommodation

Young infants have been reported to accommodate poorly, if at all. The earliest study of infant accommodation by Haynes et al. (1965) used dynamic retinoscopy. They reported that infants under 1 month had essentially frozen accommodation even without cycloplegia; however, refractive power changed when the subjects fell asleep, and thus the findings from the subjects when awake could not have been caused by factors such as inherent inelasticity of the lens. Not until 4 months did infants accommodate competently to targets at different distances. Subsequent research (e.g., Banks, 1980; Braddick, Atkinson, French, & Howland, 1979; Brookman, 1983), using different methods and stimuli, lowered the age of acceptable accommodation closer to 2 months but still concluded that, before 2 months, infants were poor accommodators. Assuming that accommodation was driven primarily by the need to keep high spatial frequencies in focus (i.e., to reduce retinal blur), Banks (1980) proposed that young infants did not accommodate better because the small sizes of their pupils together with their low acuity created an optical system with a large depth of focus, making accommodation unnecessary and irrelevant. With small viewing apertures, a wide range of focal planes is in focus simultaneously, reducing the need to accommodate.

Accepting for the moment that infants younger than 2 months cannot accommodate well (although later we will present some of our data in disagreement with this conclusion), let us examine the proposed explanation for this poor performance and its subsequent improvement after the second month. The prevailing explanation is that very young infants cannot accommodate well because they have small pupils, resulting in large depths of focus, and that, coupled with their low acuities, they lack the information to drive accommodation. In other words, targets over a wide range of distances are equally well (or perhaps, more accurately, poorly) focussed. This argument overlooks another critical factor in determining depth of focus of an optical system. Decreasing pupil diameter, like reducing the aperture in a camera, increases depth of focus, but only if the focal length of the optical system is constant. That is not the case in infants' eyes, which not only have smaller pupils but also are shorter in axial length. The small size of the infant eye is compensated for by the greater optical power of the infant lens and cornea (Bennett & Francis, 1962; Lotmar, 1976). Relative depth of focus can be measured by the ratio of an optical system's focal length to the diameter of its pupil. When both factors are taken into account, there is no great difference in depth of focus between infant and adult eyes (Banks & Bennett, 1988), so this cannot be an explanation to account for developmental differences in accommodation.

There may also be problems with the assumption that 1-month-old infants' poor accommodation is related to their reduced acuities, and the role that high spatial frequencies play in accommodation. Acuity develops continuously over the first year (see, e.g., Dobson & Teller, 1978), with no sudden increase being reported between 1 and 2 months. Consequently, an explanation of poor accommodation as the result of reduced acuity would seem to require the additional assumption that good accommodation requires some as yet unspecified threshold level of acuity. Alternatively, acuity may not be the most relevant ability here. High frequency sensitivity develops over a longer time course than sensitivity to low and middle spatial frequencies (see above; Figure 3). If intermediate spatial frequencies are more important for infants' accommodation, the time course for the development of acuity would not be immediately relevant in predicting accommodative development. The time course for development of sensitivity to intermediate sensitivities is a closer match to the accommodation data; in the data described above for spatial CSF development, sensitivity to intermediate spatial frequencies changed significantly between 1 and 2 months, and then stabilized.

It is also possible that accommodative performance improves for reasons other than a change in visual ability. In order to assess accommodation without cycloplegia, studies have typically used infants' response to targets at different distances and have found that they accommodate more accurately to near than to far targets (Braddick & Atkinson, 1979; Banks, 1980). There are also findings that an infant's attention to stationary objects is inversely related to their distance from the infant, even when retinal size is kept invariant (de Schonen, McKenzie, Maury, & Bresson, 1978; McKenzie & Day, 1972). This preferential attention to near objects is not seen if the objects move, flash, or rotate, presumptively because these manipulations enhance infants' attention (McKenzie & Day,

1976). If young infants' accommodative performance were to improve with the addition of attention enhancing features, we might not need to seek optical factors as an explanation of earlier results.

## 2. Vergence

There is a small number of studies of binocular convergence in infancy. They agree that convergence is relatively poor, particularly for closer targets, until around 2 months, not surprisingly the age at which accommodation is also reported to be markedly improved (Aslin, 1977; Aslin & Jackson, 1979; Slater & Findlay, 1975b). Unfortunately, these studies did not simultaneously measure accommodation, so that the direct link between accommodation and vergence was not explored developmentally. Aslin and Jackson (1979) made an initial attempt to study the relationship between accommodation and convergence by assuming that infants were accommodating targets presented at varying target distances and measuring the angle of convergence. They compared convergence when the targets were seen by both eyes with convergence when only one eye could see the target. If there were no link between accommodation and convergence, there should have been no evidence of convergence under monocular viewing because there would then be no disparity to drive convergence. In fact, in the youngest age studied (2 months), they found evidence of consistent convergence to different target distances for both monocular and binocular viewing. Unfortunately, their study did not include infants under 2 months, so that we know little of the link between the two systems at a time when accommodation has been reported to be generally poor.

## 3. Simultaneous Measures of Accommodation and Vergence

We have been measuring accommodation and convergence simultaneously in infants from age 1 month. Since earlier studies suggested that significant developments occurred early in infancy, we looked carefully at infants 4 months and younger (Hainline, Gheorghiu, & Abramov, 1988). We found that infants around 1 month showed, as a group, poorer evidence of accommodation compared with the other age groups, who looked surprisingly adultlike from 2 months on; this result was thus in agreement with the earlier studies. There were occasional older infants, however, who did not change focus across the targets, despite the fact that most of their age group did. When we examined the simultaneous vergence behavior of the 1-month-olds and these aberrant older infants, we discovered that, in both cases, the infants who did not vary accommodation also, in almost all cases, did not vary vergence. There was little evidence in either behavior that they were trying to attend to the targets. We then divided the subjects into those who showed some evidence of distance-appropriate response on accommodation and convergence, those who did nei-

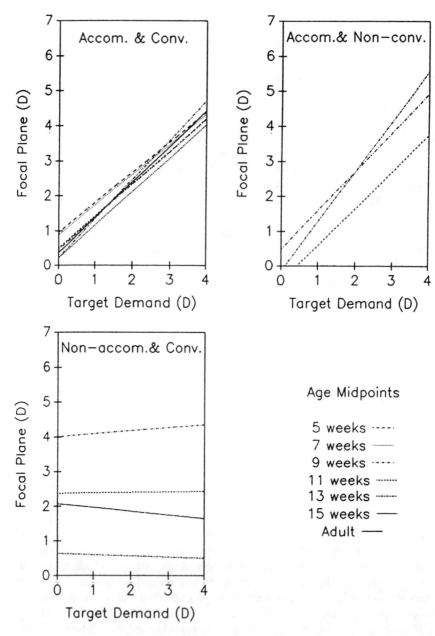

Fig. 7. Mean accommodative response as a function of target demand (distance) for infants of different ages and adults (from Hainline, Gheorghiu, & Abramov, 1988). Infants were classified into those who both accommodated and converged (i.e., those who clearly were attending the targets at the different distances, the classification observed most frequently across all ages), those who converged but did not accommodate (the next most frequent category), and those who accommodated but did not converge (fairly uncommon). A very small proportion of infants did neither across target distance, and their mean data have not been plotted here.

ther, and those who showed a change in one behavior but not the other (for example, accommodated but did not converge). The majority of subjects in all age groups fell into the accommodating/converging category, although the youngest subjects had the lowest proportion of this behavior. Further, the behavior of the 1-month-olds who both accommodated and converged was indistinguishable from that of older infants and adults. There is thus no need to recruit factors such as the large depth of focus of the infant eye or low acuities to explain why young infants do not accommodate. Under the right circumstances, it seems that they can. What we do not know, at this point, is how young infants do it. Is there a relationship within individual infants between peak CSF sensitivity and accommodation, so that younger accommodators would be found to have "precocious" spatial vision? Or are we observing vergence-driven accommodation, executed to maintain fusion? Evidence is beginning to accumulate (Hainline et al., 1988; Currie & Manny, 1990) that binocular fusional mechanisms are important in determining correct accommodation in young infants. More within-subject measures are needed to address these questions.

Although we do not have an independent measure of behavioral state, our best guess is that the infants who showed no response in our system were in the open-eyed, trancelike state often seen in young infants; Banks (1980) also reported cases of flat accommodation in drowsy infants. Such results point up a common problem in work on sensory development; if we use the kinds of stimuli that allow maximal experimental control and which are scientifically justifiable, and indeed, required in adult studies, we may at the same time be stripping the stimulus of many of the dimensions that rouse infants' interest. Sensory psychophysics typically calls for static, silent stimuli that are hard to see because they are close to threshold. Yet research on infant attentional preferences tells us that infants would rather look at moving, flashing, or otherwise changing stimuli, well above threshold contrast and rich in contours. The Gibsonian tradition demands that stimuli have *ecological validity,* usually meaning that a preference is given to real objects or events. When real objects are used as stimuli, however, it is easy to make the mistake that the infant is responding to the stimuli as an adult would and end up attributing too much cognitive competence to an infant who is, in actuality, responding to differences across displays on only a sensory level. The obvious answer is to test the same ability with both well controlled and more complex realistic stimuli, but this is rarely done.

## V. OCULOMOTOR DEVELOPMENT

Human infants are obviously motorically immature compared with other primates. Because poor control of eye movements could adversely influence functional vision, it is thus interesting to ask how mature their oculomotor systems are, since poor control of eye movements could adversely influence functional vision. The field of eye movement research is a large one, with an interesting sociology. Many eye movement researchers come from an engineering background and devote their efforts to modeling the oculomotor neurocontrol systems. There are also clinical researchers who are interested in understanding disorders of eye movement control in patients; their interest is less in vision than in how eye movements are compromised by different pathological conditions. Another large group of eye movement researchers do physiological studies to understand the specific neural sites responsible for various types of eye movements. An odd thing to an outsider is how often studies of eye movements are dissociated from studies of other aspects of vision. Often, there is little acknowledgement in the work of many of these researchers that parameters of the visual stimulus, apart from mere visibility, affect how eye movements are executed. Conversely, in most vision research, every effort is made to eliminate eye movements so that the "visual system" can be studied apart from oculomotor interference; frequently, subjects are given fixation targets or presentation times are made too brief to allow eye movements. Most commonly, eye movements that may be made by the subject are simply ignored or trials on which eye movements occurred are excluded and rerun.

This is probably a mistake on both sides. The quality of the visual signal must influence the ability to execute different kinds of eye movements. At the same time, the quality of the eye movements will influence how well a sensory capacity functions. As previously discussed, the ability of the visual system to respond to spatial patterns is inseparable from its ability to respond to temporal change. Interestingly, in his work on spatiotemporal interactions in vision, Kelly (1979a,b) found that contrast sensitivity is not maximal for the lowest rate of slippage of the image on the retina; zero retinal velocity actually leads to stabilized retinal images and Troxler fading, the disappearance of objects whose retinal image motion is completely eliminated. The retina apparently requires change in visual stimulation in order to maintain visual responsiveness. Movements of the eyes in the head provide the needed retinal variation.

The human oculomotor system has to deal with several different problems. A central portion of the primate retina (fovea) has evolved into a region of high spatial resolution. The oculomotor system has to point this region at any interesting object so that it can be examined with greater precision than is possible with the peripheral retina. That object, however, may be moving, as may the observer, so that the eyes must also be capable of tracking the object so as to maintain its image on the fovea. A further complication is that the oculomotor "system" may not be a single, uniform entity: the human system may contain elements of phylogenetically earlier mechanisms. The earlier mechanisms are often thought of as associated with lateral-eyed species (e.g., many rodents and ruminants); these are usually prey species and placement of the eyes on the sides of the head increases the extent of the field that can be kept under surveillance. Frontal eyes are associated with predatory species, presumably because this evolutionary migration conferred an additional measure of precision in depth perception, a necessary attribute for a predator (Walls, 1963).

## A. Measuring Infants' Eye Movements

Only a few of the many different forms of eye-tracking devices developed for studying eye movements in adults or animals have been used with infants. Some devices were rejected as being too intrusive (e.g., subjects had to wear special contact lenses), while others required very rigid head restraints, such as bite-bars. The systems that have been used vary considerably in technological sophistication: since the nature of each system constrains the sorts of data that can be obtained, a brief review is necessary (see also Aslin, 1985, and Maurer, 1975).

### 1. Observation

The simplest method is for an experimenter to observe the infant's eyes directly. Usually the experimenter is screened from the infant's view and may even see the infants' eyes indirectly through a simple, unobtrusive TV camera and monitor. Such observation is good enough to detect relatively large eye movements and can specify grossly the direction in which the eyes are pointed. Clearly, however, observation cannot provide quantitative information about the fine structure of any movement.

The method is, of course, at the heart of the FPL technique, where it works very well. In FPL the stimuli are usually well-separated and interobserver reliability, when tested, is quite high (Teller, 1979). But in studies for which reaction time of an eye movement or direction of first look is recorded, it is unclear how the technique can be validated easily. If the initial, critical eye movement is small or very rapid, it may be missed by all observers— interobserver reliability can be high even though critical events are missed. What is required is yet another boring but necessary study of a method's validity. An entire FPL study would have to be run in conjunction with a system that accurately and continuously recorded the infants' eye movements, and the two sets of data compared. However, the comparison is not trivial: We do not know to which aspects of the infant's eye movements the FPL observer was attending—was the judgment based on a particularly large and salient eye movement, or was it some sort of perceived overall pattern from many smaller eye movements?

Direct observation has also been used to specify the features of a stimulus to which infants attend, as for example, in some of the classic studies of how infants look at forms or faces (e.g., Salapatek, 1975; Maurer & Salapatek, 1976). In some cases, the estimation has been a judgment by an observer about where the infant was looking based on a magnified image of the eye. While this sort of scoring will probably yield greater precision than when judgments are made from a life-sized eye, there has been little systematic attention paid to issues of either reliability or validity of such scoring techniques. In fact, in one case in which observational and more precise quantitative scoring methods have been compared (Salapatek, 1975), the results often look rather different. Simple observation of eye movements has also been used to investigate the properties of certain classes of eye movements, such as optokinetic nystagmus (discussed below). In this case the eye movements are repetitive and often quite large, and so their presence or absence is readily observable.

## 2.  Electro-oculogram (EOG)

There is a standing voltage difference between the front and the back of the eye. It is as if the eye contained a battery, oriented front to rear, which rotates together with the eye. Recording electrodes placed on the face next to each canthus (corner) of an eye can be used to measure eye movements: as the eye rotates, the difference in the voltage recorded by the pair of electrodes changes. This single pair of electrodes can only record the horizontal component of any movement; at least one more electrode, placed above or below the eye, is needed to record the vertical component as well.

The EOG procedure is relatively noninvasive and is not very complicated. Since it provides a time-varying signal whose amplitude is continuously graded with the eye's angle of rotation, it can be used to study fine details such as velocities and accelerations of movements. However, it, too, must be used carefully. One set of problems stems from head movements. Any contraction of the muscles of the face or head generates electrical potentials that could be recorded by the EOG electrodes and could mask the voltages due to relatively small eye movements. Also, if the subject's head moves, the eyes often compensate by rotating to maintain fixation on the stimulus. In the EOG this eye movement could be misinterpreted as a look away from the stimulus, unless head movements are also recorded. Other problems are related to the source of the voltage recorded in the EOG. The absolute magnitude of this potential varies with the eye's state of light or dark adaptation. Thus, as adaptation changes, the signals recorded for movements of the same amplitude will change. To avoid such errors, subjects would have to be preadapted to the average luminance of the stimuli, which would also have to be controlled to prevent changes in adaptation during a session.

Finally, there is the problem of calibration, of relating a particular voltage to a particular direction-of-regard, and a particular voltage change to a movement of a particular amplitude. With adults, this is accomplished by instructing them to move their eyes to look at each of a series of locations on the stimulus plane; the separations of these known locations can then be related to the EOG's voltages. With infants, the only recourse is to present calibration targets, one at a time, and to measure the responses when the infant appears to be attending to the target. This is to some extent circular: the device is intended to tell us when the infant looks at a certain target, but we must know when the infant looks at that target in order to calibrate the device. Finocchio, Preston, and Fuchs (1990a) have recently described a quick and effective means of calibrating infant EOG records that may lead to an increase in infant EOG studies. The problem of calibration is general to all forms of measuring eye position, and we discuss it further when we describe our device, below.

3. Corneal reflection eye trackers

"Optical" eye trackers typically focus on some landmarks on the eye and record their changing positions as the eye moves (see Young & Sheena, 1975, for a review). These systems have one principal advantage over the EOG: They usually do not require that anything be attached to the subject. Our particular system (Hainline, 1981) is based on analysis of an enlarged TV image of the eye (Figure 8). The eye is illuminated by an infrared source, which is invisible to the subject even in the dark, and an image of the eye is acquired by an infrared-sensitive camera. The landmarks of interest are the *corneal reflection* and the *bright pupil*. The corneal reflection is the image of the infrared light source formed by reflection from the cornea; the pupil is seen rear-illuminated by light reflected back out of the eye by the retina, and hence the pupil appears bright. As illustrated in Figure 8a, whenever the eye rotates, the position of the corneal reflection moves with respect to the center of the pupil. The images are obtained at the frame-rate of the TV camera (60 Hz), and each frame is analyzed in real-time to derive the differential motion of the image landmarks and so specify where the eye was pointed during that TV frame. Note that only one eye is recorded, the assumption being that the other eye is pointed at the same target; it would be technically more than twice as difficult to record from both eyes simultaneously and as yet no one has achieved such a system for infants.

Our system can tolerate minor head movements, provided that the recorded eye remains within a small volume of space bounded by the limited field of view of the telephoto lens on the tracker's TV camera; one serious drawback of all corneal reflection systems for infants is that they necessarily restrict head movements. The system can specify eye position anywhere on a frontal field subtending about 40 x 40 deg, but the price for such wide tolerances is that the system's resolution is only about ½ deg. This is not enough for exact studies of eye movements with highly practiced adults, but is sufficient for most studies with infants and naive adults (to whom we typically compare our infants). The entire system is shown schematically in Figure 8b. The infant is held over the shoulder of an experimenter, who gently stabilizes the infant's head. To minimize biases, the experimenter cannot see the stimuli, but does see an image of the infant's face, which he or she must keep within a delimited portion of the face-camera's

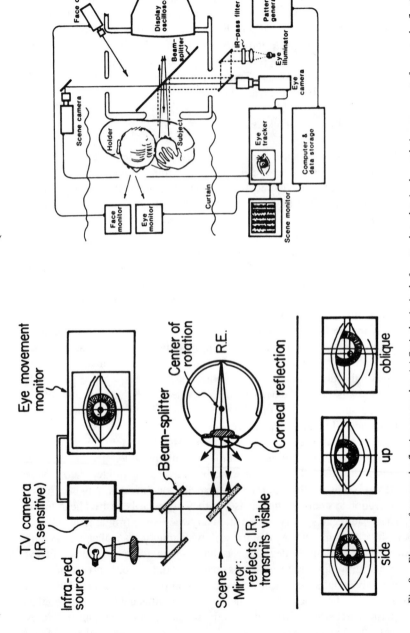

Fig. 8. Elements of a corneal reflection eye tracker. (a) Optical principal of eye tracker, showing how relative movement of a fixed light source in the image of the pupil is interpreted to yield information on changes in eye position over time. (b) Schematic representation of eye tracking system designed for use with infants (from Hainline & Abramov, 1985). Besides the equipment associated with imaging the eye, there is other TV equipment in the system; the face camera and monitor are used to position the infant correctly. The scene camera and monitor allow a crosshair

field. The subject views the stimulus through a beam-splitter that transmits visible light while reflecting the infrared light of the eye tracker.

As with EOGs, the system must be calibrated. The differential motion of the two landmarks (corneal reflection and pupil) is determined by the curvature of the cornea, the location of the plane of the pupil as seen through the cornea, and the location of the eye's center of rotation. Infants' eyes are smaller than adults', but the maturational growth rates of the relevant structures are such that a given rotation of the eye produces approximately the same differential motion of the landmarks at all ages (Abramov & Harris, 1984; Bronson, 1982; Hainline, Harris, & Krinsky, 1990). Thus, one can use a calibration appropriate for the *average* adult, and the system will also be set for the *average* infant, though not for any individual who differs markedly from the mean. This "group" calibration is primarily useful for correction of the eye tracker's gain (measured change/ actual change). Additional calibration is needed if one also wants to specify where on the stimulus plane the eye is actually pointed. Part of the problem is that the fovea is not on the optic axis of the eye, so that, when the subject looks at a stimulus, the angle of convergence of the optic axis is less than the angle of convergence of the visual axes; the angle between the optic and visual axes in each of an adult's eyes is about 5 deg and is known as angle $\alpha$. Angle $\alpha$ is much larger in young infants (Hainline et al., 1988; London & Wick, 1982; Slater & Findlay, 1972, 1975a), decreasing from about 10 deg to the adult value over the first 6 months.

Another set of problems stems from using TV technology: with standard TV systems, eye position can only be sampled 60 times per second, which means that, in principle, very rapid eye movements will not be well specified. Nonetheless, we have used our specific instrument to measure accurately the velocity profiles even of fast eye movements such as saccades. We took advantage of nonlinearities in our device to extend its bandwidth; using a model eye rotated at known velocities and recording the output of the tracker, we created nomograms for deriving the true velocities of saccadic movements (Harris, Abramov, & Hainline, 1984). It should be noted that some of the earlier versions of corneal reflection devices sampled eye position at even slower rates, from 1 to 4 Hz (see Hainline & Lemerise, 1985). At these rates many brief eye movements will necessarily be lost.

Ideally, each subject is calibrated individually by presenting small targets at various locations across the stimulus plane; a calibration equation is then obtained by asking how the set of measured eye positions must be transformed in order to make it coincide with the set of known locations of the targets; some of the circularity alluded to in the discussion of EOGs is avoided if a single transformation is enough to achieve this coincidence for all stimuli viewed by an individual (Harris, Hainline, & Abramov, 1981). Since calibration is a tedious procedure, we typically begin by studying each infant using an average calibration. The design of some studies allows calibration data to be collected in the course of the experiment, but in other cases, a calibration procedure follows the experiment if the subject is still alert and cooperative.

## B.  Pointing the Fovea: Saccades and Fixations

Saccadic eye movements, among the most rapid of all muscular responses, serve to point the fovea at targets that must be examined in some detail during a fixation. They are fast, presumably to minimize visual "downtime" as the eye moves from fixation to fixation. What are the consequences for saccades and fixations if the fovea is still quite immature at birth, as in humans? If the system were preprogrammed to orient a nonfunctional *fovea*, as soon as a small stimulus fell on the fovea it would become invisible (at least in the foveal region), thereby triggering a look-away, which would again make the target visible in the periphery, triggering a look-back, and so on—the eye would oscillate back and forth, never reaching a steady position. Alternatively, the infant might use areas of the retina close to the fovea, areas which are more mature at birth and which presumably have higher acuity than the peripheral retina—fixations could be stable, but refixations of the same target might either be scattered about an annular zone surrounding the fovea, or a consistent extrafoveal area might be used.

We shall begin by examining the development of saccades, first as a class of eye movement, and second as a movement intended to aim the eye in a particular direction. The first step is to identify the different types of eye movement that can be observed in a continuous record of eye position. An example, from an infant, is shown in Figure 9; the horizontal and vertical components are shown separately, and it is their joint values that specify direction-of-regard at any instant. Such records are partitioned (parsed) offline by an experimenter, who assigns each episode to one of a predetermined set of possible movements (Harris, Hainline, Abramov, Lemerise, & Camenzuli, 1988). In our more recent work we have chosen to parse all records in this exhaustive fashion; abstracting episodes of only the type of movement that is important for the specific study can hide interesting phenomena associated with the other movement types.

### 1.  Infants' saccades

Saccades are the prototypical movements for placing images of interest on the foveas, and their precise, quantitative properties have been studied in great detail in adults. These properties have also been related to responses of specific neuronal control centers in subhuman primates. We have examined the properties of saccades made by infants (1–6 mos) and uninstructed adults when freely scanning stimuli such as simple geometric forms or more complex textured fields (Hainline, Turkel, Abramov, Lemerise, & Harris, 1984). Under these conditions the general shapes of infant and adult saccades appeared the same: smooth

**Parsing an Eye Movement Record**

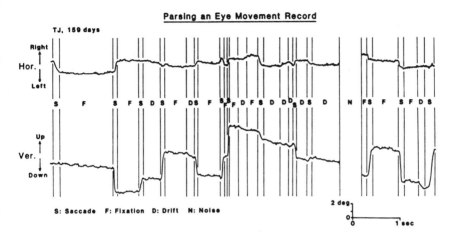

Fig. 9.  *Parsing a typical eye movement record. Upper trace shows the horizontal component of the eye's position in time, and lower trace shows the vertical component. Vertical lines are experimenter-determined boundaries between different types of movement. (From Harris, Hainline, Abramov, Lemerise, & Camenzuli, 1988.)*

acceleration from the starting point, and a symmetrical deceleration to the final resting point (Figures 10a,b). Also, both groups produced the same proportions of saccades of different amplitudes (Hainline & Abramov, 1985). For a more quantitative appraisal, we examined the relationships between peak velocities of the saccades, attained at approximately the midpoints of the movements, and the amplitudes of the saccades (a relationship referred to as the *main sequence* function; Bahill, Clark, & Stark, 1975); an example of an infant's main sequence is shown in Figure 10c. In many cases, the main sequences of infants and adults were indistinguishable, as indicated by the group mean sequences in Figure 10d.

Given the general motoric immaturity of infants, it is surprising that their saccadic system is capable of producing saccades that are as well-controlled as those of adults, at least in terms of their velocity properties; it is worth emphasizing that these movements can attain peak velocities of several hundred deg/sec. However adultlike saccades are not produced under all conditions. We observed them when the stimuli were visually rich textures. But, infants' saccades are much slower and the associated main sequences have considerably lower slopes (Figure 10d) when the infants view the austere geometrical forms (e.g., a single circle) often used to study their visual behavior. We interpret this stimulus-related difference as being due to a difference in arousal/attentiveness/motivation, and it raises an interesting problem: had we used only geometrical forms, we would have accepted infants' saccades as always being slower than those of adults simply because infants are immature. The neurons that constitute the first stages of saccadic control are located in the brainstem and presumably are

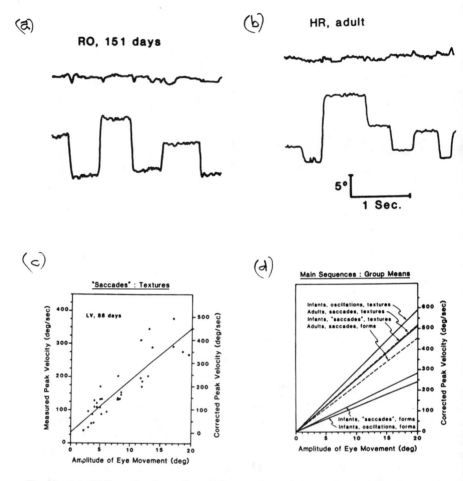

Fig. 10. (a), (b) Examples of saccades and fixations from an infant and an adult (from Harris et al., 1988). Each upper trace shows the horizontal component of the eye's position in time, and the lower trace shows the vertical component. (c) Typical main sequence for peak saccadic velocity versus amplitude, with best fitting linear regression; right ordinate shows the peak velocities corrected for the bandwidth limitations of our tracker. (d) Average main sequences for infants and adults scanning two types of stimuli. (Redrawn from Hainline, Turkel, Abramov, Lemerise, & Harris, 1984.)

sensitive to influences from brainstem arousal mechanisms; the attentional value of the stimulus may be even more salient for infants, whose brain stem arousal mechanisms are relatively less influenced by higher cortical centers. In the case of saccades, and for many of the other forms of eye movements discussed below, infants generally come equipped with well-developed oculomotor systems—the problem is to ''persuade'' them to entrain these systems. This is a continually recurring theme in all our attempts to assess the visual abilities of infants.

Infants also produce another class of unusual saccadic movements: oscillations, or back-to-back saccades with minimal intersaccadic times; these are more prevalent in younger infants, but even they produce them only occasionally. We have tentatively explained these movements on the basis of slight mismatch or noisiness in the relative timing of the groups of neurons that control the initial accelerative burst of a saccade and those controlling the final pause (Hainline et al., 1984). Alternatively, these oscillations could be a result of foveal immaturities, as already discussed, but oscillations have also been recorded from adults when they are fatigued or their arousal is low (Abel, Traccis, Troost, & Dell'Osso, 1983), which is indirect support for the effects of brainstem arousal mechanisms. As a general conclusion from these studies, we can say that the perceptual abilities of infants are probably not limited by immaturities in the basic saccadic generator, although how saccades are executed varies across situations.

Since saccades are designed to place specific images onto the fovea, we can ask how well infants do this by comparison with adults. The saccadic accuracy of adults is usually studied in a demand-saccade situation: Subjects begin by fixating a small, stationary target, which then jumps to a new location; subjects are instructed to refixate the target as quickly as possible. Typically their first saccade reaches the new location with about 90% accuracy, with only a small "corrective" saccade sometimes needed to foveate the image. When infants are tested in a similar situation, there have been reports that their initial saccades grossly undershoot the new location, which they then approach with a series of saccadic steps of roughly equal amplitude; this pattern is especially marked in younger infants (Aslin & Salapatek, 1975; Salapatek, Aslin, Simonson, & Pulos, 1980). Interestingly, adults, when tired, inattentive, or unaroused, also sometimes produce series of saccadic steps (Bahill & Stark, 1975), suggesting that arousal could also be a factor in infants' saccadic steps. One of the unusual things about infants' saccadic steps is that they occur primarily for longer excursions of the target. Thus, it is possible that these steps result from the infants' inability to correctly localize the target in the absence of good information about stimulus position. At the same time, the successive steps are all the same size, which is probably not what would be expected of any system that had to deal with positional uncertainty.

Saccadic steps are not commonly observed when infants have more to look at than single spots on a blank background. We have examined saccades made by large numbers of subjects freely scanning visual scenes. It was extremely rare to find a sequence of saccadic steps, all in the same direction, that might be interpreted as an attempt to reach a particular peripheral element in the scene. Perhaps subjects were more accurate in our situation because of the good spatial frame of reference provided by our relatively rich visual fields. The problem is that we do not know the intended target of each saccade. It has been suggested, therefore, that our infants were as inaccurate as those studied by Aslin and colleagues, but that after executing the first of a series of steps their foveas landed on some intervening contour, which then "captured" the fovea and blocked the rest of the steps to the originally intended target. Certain aspects of our data make this an unlikely explanation; infants and uninstructed adults (whom we presume not to produce saccadic steps) produced the same frequency distributions of saccadic amplitudes. Furthermore, the shapes of the distributions changed in similar fashion for both groups when the stimulus scenes were changed (Hainline & Abramov, 1985). If these infant saccades were truncated-step saccades, their amplitude distributions should have reflected this fact, but this is not what was seen. Thus, the phenomenon of saccadic steps is probably not an essential characteristic of the infant saccadic system, but the result of low arousal and/or the infant's difficulty in localizing small targets in an otherwise featureless scene.

## 2.  Infants' fixations

A saccade is usually followed by a fixation, during which the eyes are held more or less stationary and the new target is examined (Figures 9, 10a, 10b). Even young infants can maintain reasonably stable fixations, although it is not always easy to distinguish long fixations (presumed periods of attentiveness to the target) from periods when the subject is in a state of low arousal and is simply staring into space without any eye movements.

The first issue is how long it takes to "examine" a target, that is, when and why a fixation is terminated during uninstructed free-scanning of a stimulus (these analyses do not necessarily apply to situations in which specific search instructions are given or to overpracticed skills like reading). There have been claims that young infants are visually "captured" by stimuli (Stechler & Latz, 1966), which could lead to very long fixations. We have examined a very large number of fixations in infants and uninstructed adults viewing a variety of stimuli ranging from simple geometric forms to color slides of complex natural scenes; the stimuli and procedures are described in Harris et al. (1988). In contrast to the notion that infants are visually "captured," we find that infant fixations are, on average, shorter than those of adults; the exact durations vary with the type of stimulus. The frequency distributions of the durations of these fixations are all positively skewed toward longer durations. From the statistical properties of the distributions, Harris (Harris et al., 1988; Harris, 1989) established the precise form of the underlying distribution, and based on that he has proposed a model that the duration of a free-scanning fixation is divided into two components. There is an early refractory period during which a terminating saccade does not occur; this may be related to processing of the visual information encountered during the fixation, which differs from task to task and across age from infancy to adulthood. After the initial period, the system is "ready" to make a saccade, but when a saccade will occur is determined by the occurrence of a random event with some fixed probability at any instant. For both infants and adults, the duration of each fixation was shorter for larger and visually richer stimuli, suggesting that fixation duration depends in part on stimulation of the peripheral retina: In other words, the end of a fixation during free scanning ultimately depends on the probability that some visual element in the retinal periphery will elicit a saccade to it. This in turn depends on the spatial CSFs of the periphery and also, possibly, on cognitive factors such as recognition of a feature by peripheral vision.

The next issue is the stability of the eye during a fixation. We have also measured the velocity of ocular drift during each of the fixations whose durations we considered above. It might also be argued that ideally, a fixation should have no drift, but in practice, this is never the case, especially in nonlaboratory situations, when the eye actually drifts quite a bit (e.g., Skavenski et al., 1979; Murphy, 1978). Also a rigorous lack of drift would create a stabilized retinal image, which would reduce visibility (see the earlier discussion of spatiotemporal factors in spatial vision). Our free-scanning data show that, on average, fixational drift is inversely related to duration: shorter fixations are associated with higher drift velocities, and on average, infants have shorter fixations than adults. A simple explanation of this finding would be that fixations simply vary in stability, for any number of reasons, and that the duration of a fixation is then limited by the tolerance for slippage of the image away from the fovea. Obviously, this criterion amount of retinal slippage will occur sooner for a fixation with a higher drift velocity. This cannot be the whole story, however. We have already noted that the type of stimulus being viewed affects fixation durations, which are shorter when infants are viewing visually rich, complex scenes and textures than when they are looking at relatively simple forms, suggesting that drift of contours in the peripheral retina maybe more important than drift of the foveal image itself. There are no clear age trends over the first year in the data on fixational drift. As Figure 11 illustrates, when infants' fixations are long, their fixational stability is only marginally worse than that of adults, but this will depend on what they are looking at. The infants' spatiotemporal sensitivity is relevant here, because whether slippage of a peripheral target elicits a saccade will depend on whether the change is above threshold or not.

A final point about fixations is the precision of "foveation." When a target is looked at several times (i.e., refixated), how widely scattered about the target are the successive fixations? Even highly trained adults refixating small targets show some scatter (with an SD of about 0.1 deg; de Bie, 1986; Snodderly, 1987). We have presented to infants and uninstructed adults small, bright square targets (1.5 deg on a side); the targets moved at a fixed velocity from a central starting position to one of several peripheral locations and, after a pause, back again (Hainline et al., 1990). This sequence was repeated several times for each target presentation. Each pause of the target permitted the subject to refixate it, and we compared the fixation position data from each of these episodes. The distributions of the standard deviations of the refixations from infants were

# Fixation Drift Velocities

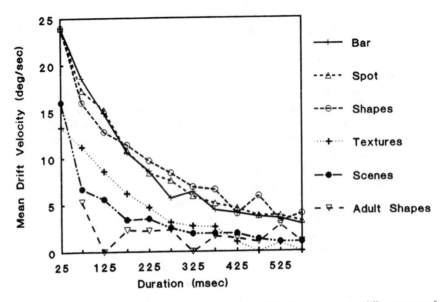

Fig. 11. Mean drift velocity of fixations as a function of fixation duration, for different types of stimuli. The adults viewed only simple shapes and textures. The infants viewed either single long bars or small spots on a plain background; geometric shapes (squares, circles, triangles); patterns of black and white textures filling the scene; or realistic, complex visual scenes. The stimuli are described more fully in Harris et al. (1988).

roughly constant over the first year and had a mean of about 0.8 deg. The corresponding adult value was about 0.4 deg. Some of this scatter probably came from the fact that the subjects were looking at slightly different parts of the square targets across trials. In such situations, small eye movements (less than about 1–2 deg) may not actually be "aiming" the fovea at a new target but simply shifting the image to an equivalent alternative retinal area. Such "casual" inspection may not require the ultimate high acuity of the central fovea.

The results of these studies imply that, despite the fact that infants lack high acuity in the early months, they appear to be using some small consistent retinal area to direct fixations; it is not possible with present methods to establish where this region is located. We do not at this point know anything about what spatial and temporal frequencies are needed to provide the visual feedback for fixational stability, but presumably infant spatial vision is sufficiently good relatively early in life. Fixational stability during infancy is related jointly to attentional factors, to the richness of the visual scene in contours in the peripheral retina, and to the spatiotemporal spatial sensitivity of the infant visual system. After a certain period of time for the acquisition of information (which needs considerably more study in infants), fixation durations fit a model that posits that fixations are terminated by the presence of perceptually salient contours in peripheral vision that stimulate a saccade towards them. The velocity of fixational drift is also related to the termination of fixations; we do not see long fixations with high drift velocities in infants, suggesting at a minimum that there is some corrective feedback mechanism at this age, probably visual but also possibly proprioceptive, that keeps the eye reasonably stable during fixations. Further research needs to be done to determine which if any of these factors is the primary causal one in fixational control, and how the various factors interact. However, the present data on saccades and fixations support the contention that infants possess sufficient sensory and oculomotor function to allow deliberate inspection of visual scenes.

## C. Stabilizing Moving Images: Smooth Pursuit, Optokinetic Nystagmus, and the Vestibulo-ocular Reflex

We have discussed the abilities of infants to foveate and fixate images of items of interest. The retina, however, is mounted in a moving eye in a moving head on a locomoting body. Moreover, the images on the retina are often of moving objects. The highest spatial frequencies are those most readily lost due to the temporal factors associated with image motion, but, as we have seen for accommodation and convergence and for object recognition, many aspects of functional vision may continue uninterrupted based on intermediate spatial frequencies. Nonetheless, a reasonable degree of image stabilization is useful and several of the ways in which the oculomotor system does this have been studied developmentally.

### 1. Smooth pursuit (SP)

Smooth pursuit is the ability to rotate the eye smoothly so as to keep the image of a moving target stable on the fovea. When a fixated target begins to move, there is some latency before an eye movement is entrained, and if the stimulus movement is rapid, the first movement may be a catch-up saccade followed by SP. To stabilize a moving target, the gain of the SP (ratio of eye velocity to target velocity) must be close to unity. Well-trained adults can maintain such gains for velocities as high as 30–40 deg/sec (Howard, 1982). It has been argued that very young infants, whose foveas are quite immature (see earlier), will have poorly developed SP. (But, SP does not logically require a fully functioning fovea—it could be used to stabilize the image on any retinal region that was pointed at an interesting target by the saccadic system; with a bit of practice, adults can pursue objects with their peripheral retinas (Robinson, 1981).) Some studies have, indeed, failed to find SP in infants younger than about 2–3 months; instead targets were tracked by a series of saccades (Aslin, 1981a; Atkinson & Braddick,

1981; Dayton, Jones, Steele, & Rose, 1964; Shea & Aslin, 1984). Others, using targets that may have been more salient to the infant, have shown some evidence for SP at slow target speeds even in neonates (Hainline, 1985; Kremenitzer, Vaughan, Kurtzberg, & Dowling, 1979; Roucoux, Culee, & Roucoux, 1983; Shea & Aslin, 1988).

There are two aspects to the issue of how infants pursue moving targets. First is the question of whether infants have the capability to pursue a target *smoothly* and under what conditions this is done. Second is the question of how well an infant keeps up with a moving target, regardless of the types of eye movements used. Shea and Aslin (1990) report some relevant findings for 2-month-old infants. Targets moved at a range of fixed velocities from 3 to 12 deg/sec. The eye movement records were processed to remove any saccades that occurred during periods when the target was moving. Their overall measure of pursuit gain was then based on the mean eye velocity from the processed records, that is, with only the saccades removed. Infants had pursuit gains considerably less than 1.0, ranging from 0.5 for slow targets down to 0.1 for the fastest. The systematic drop in gain was such that the average eye velocity was the same for all stimulus velocities. This finding suggests that moving targets triggered some sort of following response, but one that was not matched to the movement of the stimulus. The problem is that filtering out "pursuit" saccades necessarily reduces pursuit gain, in the sense of keeping up with the target. Fixations that occurred after the stimulus began to move but before following began, as well as pauses between pursuit or saccadic episodes, were averaged with actual SP, thus necessarily lowering the estimate of gain. In the limiting case, a subject could pursue with a series of saccades separated by fixations, and with this analysis, the filtered eye velocity would reflect only the near-zero velocities of the fixations. It is noteworthy that Shea and Aslin also report that most infants showed episodes of SP whose gains were indeed close to 1.0, but because of the form of data analysis they employed, these episodes could not be evaluated as a separate class.

We have used our eye tracking system to study SP in a group of infants (1–7 mos) and naive adults, all of whom were individually calibrated; the eye movements were to small, bright targets moved 15 deg across a screen at constant velocities (2.5–15 deg/sec) in horizontal, vertical, and oblique directions (a preliminary report appeared in Krinsky, Hainline, & Scanlon, 1990). We parsed our data into individual segments representing episodes of saccades, pursuit, fixations, etc. prior to analysis. We were thus able to isolate eye movements that occurred when the stimulus was moving and to measure latencies of SP or saccades from the onset of stimulus movement. None of the subjects pursued all targets accurately or smoothly for the entire duration of a trial. For the adults this was presumably because they did not know what was expected of them, because we assume that they all had well-functioning SP systems and these targets were not particularly difficult to pursue. Infants spent less time in smooth pursuit for any moving stimulus than did adults but the incidence of SP declined as velocity increased, for both infants and adults; for the slowest velocity, 2.5 deg/sec, the proportion of SP was around 25% for infants and 57% for adults, whereas corresponding figures for the 15 deg/sec target were 12% for infants and 13% for adults. The average duration of each "bout" of SP also decreased in a very similar way for both infants and adults as target velocity increased: the mean for both age groups was about 2 sec for the slowest target, declining to around half a second for the fastest. For the episodes when they showed SP, both infants and adults stabilized the retinal images rather well; gains for both groups were between 0.9 and 1.0 even at stimulus speeds of 15 deg/sec. To examine the point at which a moving stimulus elicited pursuit (either SP, or a catch-up saccade), we measured the latency to the first following movement. While somewhat longer, infants' latencies compared favorably with those of adults at a given velocity. For both groups, latencies decreased as stimulus velocity increased (Figure 12a), suggesting that following movements were elicited when retinal displacement of the stimulus exceeded some criterion value: for SP, the value ranged from 3 to 5 deg across velocities; if the response was delayed until the stimulus was displaced more than this, the first movement was usually a catch-up saccade (Figure 12b). Unlike some of the previous studies, we found few significant age trends, except that the proportion of time spent in SP increased with age for the higher velocities. In short, infants did not pursue moving targets as long as adults did, but when they did, their SP was very similar to that of adults—even young infants are apparently equipped with a pursuit system capable of maintaining a target in central vision under some circumstances of stimulus movement and infant attention.

## 2. Optokinetic nystagmus (OKN) and vestibulo-ocular reflex (VOR)

OKN and the VOR are two oculomotor systems that are closely linked to the vestibular system and are important in compensating for movement of the organism through the world and some of the associated movements of the retinal image (e.g., Cohen, 1974; Cohen, Henn, Raphan, & Dennett, 1981). OKN is the repetitive series of eye movements produced when a large portion of the visual field's retinal image drifts across the retina. In response, the two eyes move as a unit with alternating phases of smooth tracking (with a gain close to 1.0) and return saccades. As a result, the slippage of the image on the retina is minimized. In the laboratory, OKN is typically elicited by surrounding the subject with a large cylinder on whose sides are painted vertical stripes. The cylinder is rotated around the subject so that all parts of the visual field drift with the same velocity. In the real world, such massive unidirectional movement of the entire field is rare. (It could occur if one were riding in a car and looking sideways out of the window at the passing scenery, but on an evolutionary scale, such locomotion is very recent.) One relevant type of movement that does occur

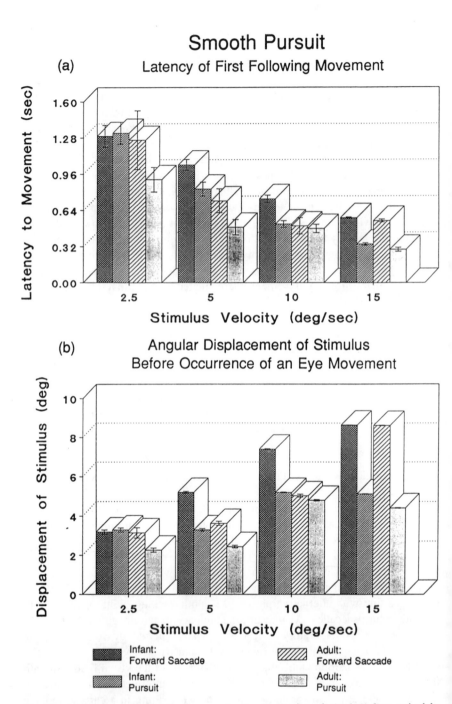

Fig. 12. (a) Latency to begin following as a function of stimulus velocity for infants and adults reported separately for cases in which the first movement was SP and for when the first movement was a catch-up saccade. Latencies for both types of movement decrease with stimulus velocity. (b) Angular displacement of the stimulus before an eye movement, for different velocities of target movement. Note that the frequency of saccades increases for greater angular displacements.

is head rotation. Twisting the head from side to side provides, in principle, the right sort of stimulus to entrain OKN, although it is not clear that the duration of the average head rotation is sufficiently long actually to produce OKN for one rotation.

OKN is a phylogenetically "old" oculomotor system which developed in lateral-eyed animals. Most of these species do not possess specialized retinal areas of high acuity and do not show SP of a small target. A good example is the rabbit, whose OKN has been studied extensively (e.g., Collewijn, 1981a). Interestingly, in such animals there is one natural condition under which OKN is *not* elicited: when a rabbit moves forward through the world, the visual field seen by each eye streams from a nasal to a temporal direction and no OKN is triggered. Inasmuch as OKN is supposed to stabilize retinal slippage and such locomotion is common, the lack of OKN under these circumstances might seem bizarre. However, the real situation is somewhat more complex than just described. If the rabbits' eyes gazed strictly out to the sides and had no overlapping (binocular) region in the visual field, then each eye could show OKN driven only by the stimulus on its retina; in many lower vertebrates, the eyes can move in this independent fashion. However, the fields of view of the rabbits' two eyes, as in all mammals, overlap considerably in the central binocular region, and rabbits do look ahead to where they are going. Although they do not have a punctuate fovea, rabbits have a retinal region, the visual streak, with higher spatial resolution. If the corresponding retinal regions in each eye are aimed at some point on the field in front of the animals as it moves forward, the visual images stream symmetrically in all directions radiating from that "fixation" point (see Gibson, 1950, 1966). There is no one predominant direction of stimulus movement to trigger OKN in order to stabilize retinal slippage and still maintain the correct overlap of the binocular visual fields as the animal moves forward.

For the frontal-eyed foveate animals, the argument could be made that OKN is largely unnecessary: most of the time, slippage of large portions of the image occur only when moving forward, in which case the elements of the scene stream radially from the point of regard. Moreover, the emergence of fixational and SP mechanisms, and their use in holding images of particular objects on the fovea, implies that there must actually be a mechanism for blocking OKN: when the eyes track a target moving from right to left, the image of all the rest of the background moves from left to right. If this movement of most of the field were to trigger OKN, the target's image could not be held on the fovea during SP. Indeed this ability to block OKN is the basis of a technique (arrestovisography; Voipio & Hyvarinen, 1966) for measuring acuity in uninstructed subjects: A large portion of the visual field drifts constantly in one direction, eliciting OKN; a test pattern is presented in a central region and its visibility is increased until the subject fixates it, thus arresting the OKN.

While OKN in humans may be less important for image stabilization than the foveational systems, it still may be quite important in its intricate interactions with the mechanisms for vestibular stabilization (see below). Certainly, in the laboratory, OKN is easily elicited in both horizontal and vertical directions and is a very useful tool for assessing the intactness of many parts of the oculomotor system and evaluating the status of neurological development. In infants, OKN exists at birth. Most studies have used horizontally moving stimuli. At this point, there is relatively little information about the quantitative details when large stimulus areas are moved. Typically, researchers have simply observed infants' eyes and noted only gross properties such as presence or absence of OKN.

There clearly are gross developmental changes in OKN. The most interesting finding is that young infants exhibit some of the properties of the OKN associated with animals such as rabbits. When one eye is covered, OKN in young infants is elicited only when stimuli stream in temporal-to-nasal direction across the visual field; movement in the nasal-to-temporal direction does not entrain good OKN (e.g., Atkinson & Braddick, 1981; Naegele & Held, 1982). This monocular asymmetry in horizontal OKN disappears over the early months; the time course depends somewhat on the characteristics of the OKN stimulus. The asymmetry is not seen in normal adults, although it does occur in some cases of visual system anomaly (e.g., Schor & Levi, 1980; van Hof-van Duin & Mohn, 1983). This monocular OKN asymmetry is interesting from the perspective of neural control. There are two neural pathways that support monocular OKN control, one involving a subcortical system and the other a cortical pathway (Hoffman, 1979). The cortical pathway is immature in early infancy and presumably is needed to support symmetrical monocular OKN. Thus the gradual appearance with time of symmetrical monocular OKN can be used diagnostically as a marker for proper visual neural development.

We have examined quantitatively some of the developmental aspects of OKN using binocular viewing and studying both horizontal and vertical OKN (Hainline, Lemerise, Abramov, & Turkel, 1984). Since our stimulus field was only 30 x 22 deg, it may have been eliciting "small-field" OKN which may be driven by both the full-field OKN and small-target SP systems jointly (e.g., Collewijn, 1981b). In our infants, the fast phases of horizontal and vertical OKN were saccadic, in that they fell on the same main sequence as other saccadic movements (see discussion of saccades, above). The slow phases of horizontal OKN were of smaller amplitude and frequency than vertical. In general, infants' slow phases in all directions had lower gains but higher amplitudes and longer durations than did those of adults. Since viewing was binocular, there were not directional asymmetries in horizontal OKN; a stimulus that drifts in the nasal-to-temporal direction for one eye drifts in the opposite direction for the other eye, so even subjects with marked monocular asymmetry will show OKN in both directions. We did, however, find a binocular asymmetry in vertical OKN which lasted through about 4 months of age: downward moving stimuli elicited OKN with slow phases of much lower gain and greater variability. This asymmetry may be the vertical analogue of the horizontal asymmetry seen in lateral-eyed animals in which the image streaming due to self-motion does not elicit OKN.

An infant necessarily locomotes close to the ground, so that most of the visual field streams in a downward direction as the infant moves forward. A similar vertical OKN asymmetry has been reported for "short" primates like the squirrel monkey, but is less likely to be seen in frontal-eyed animals that locomote with their eyes further from the ground (Takahashi & Igarashi, 1977; Takahashi, Sakurai, & Kanzaki, 1978).

The VOR and OKN systems share many neuronal elements, but the VOR is designed to maintain the eye's direction of gaze in spite of head rotation. Since the head can rotate very rapidly, the VOR has a very short time constant—it can respond very rapidly but, correspondingly, cannot respond for a prolonged period to compensate for lengthy accelerations. It is possible that in humans, the major role of these systems in natural conditions is to compensate for head turns; the VOR provides the initial ocular stabilization response, and OKN adds any necessary longer duration components. However, both responses can be overridden when voluntarily fixating a target, and it may be that they are of much less importance once good foveational mechanisms of fixational control and SP appear. Some very suggestive evidence comes from recent studies of the development of the VOR. In adults, the gain of the VOR is much less than one (often about 0.5), so that it functions poorly as an overall image-stabilizing system. In contrast, the gain of the VOR in infants and even in young children, is close to 1.0 and so compensates quite accurately for image slippage caused by head rotations or other bodily movements through space (Finocchio, Preston, & Fuchs, 1990b). But if adults' VOR gain is low because other systems are more suitable for keeping the fovea pointed at interesting targets, one might expect to find some correspondence between the developmental time courses of, for example, VOR and SP gain. In fact there is a fairly large mismatch between the time courses of the changes in VOR gain and SP; SP is well developed within the first year, whereas VOR gain continues to drop to adult levels over at least the first 5 to 6 years, if not longer. Clearly, there is much which still needs to be understood about the developmental relationships among these eye movement systems.

## VI.  CLINICAL APPLICATIONS OF INFANT VISION RESEARCH

Like all developmental phenomena, different visual abilities have a natural range of variability, although for some functions we still need to establish what is the normal variability for each age. From the animal literature and corroborating human data (e.g., Mitchell, 1988; Atkinson & Braddick, 1988), there is reason to suppose that the human visual system is susceptible to disruption if developments do not proceed appropriately early in life (see the previous discussion in the Introduction, above). The problem is that we do not at this point know enough to allow us to predict when an early developmental delay is significant and severe enough to cause a permanent disruption in the visual system.

Assume one checks an infant's vision and detects a correctable optical problem that might predispose to a poor developmental outcome. The issue is whether or not to treat or correct this error during infancy. Some early visual problems may resolve themselves naturally with time, as many pediatricians advise concerned parents. There is evidence from animal work for a normal process of emmetropization (Medina, 1987; Schaeffel & Howland, 1988), which naturally compensates for some early refractive errors as the eye grows in size to adult levels. This emmetropization process is not fully understood, but appears to be a complex set of muscular, neural, and biochemical processes to adjust the different facets of eye growth to achieve a total system that is optically correct. If such an emmetropization process were uniformly found in humans, the best strategy, at least optically, would probably be to ignore many kinds of optical problems detected in infancy. However the relevance of these animal models to the human case is undemonstrated. Animal models of development must be used carefully; even different species of macaque monkey differ in their optical responses to early visual deprivation (e.g., Raviola & Wiesel, 1985), suggesting that care must be taken in generalizing the animal models to humans.

The significance of early astigmatism provides a good example of the problem. Animal studies have demonstrated that severe and optically uncorrected astigmatism early in life can lead to meridional amblyopia in the adult; this loss of acuity for the more blurred contours is not reversed by optical correction at the older age, a finding that also applies to humans (e.g., Mitchell, Freeman, Millodot, & Haegerstrom, 1973). Infants are reported to have a relatively high incidence of astigmatism (Atkinson, Braddick, & French, 1980; Gwiazda, Scheiman, Mohindra, & Held, 1984; Howland & Sayles, 1984). But why, then, do we not find more meridional amblyopia in adults, given this incidence of astigmatism in young infants. Infants' astigmatism is of a type referred to as *against-the-rule,* because the axis of the astigmatism is at right angles to that most commonly found in adults *(with-the-rule).* Against-the-rule astigmatism declines during the first months of life, while the prevalence of with-the-rule astigmatism increases to adult levels by early school age (Dobson, Fulton, & Sebris, 1984; Gwiazda et al., 1984). However, the studies are mostly cross-sectional, sampling infants at different ages rather than following individuals longitudinally. What is not generally known is the outcome for any one infant with severe against-the-rule astigmatism: does this simply reduce with age, or does its axis rotate towards the typical adult axis—does the astigmatism associated with adult meridional amblyopia start as against-the-rule astigmatism?

Gwiazda, Thorn, Bauer, and Held (1990) recently reported some longitudinal data from humans that suggests that the process of emmetropization observed in early childhood may not be permanent. They report a high correlation between optical disorders measured at 6 months and those seen at 7 years, despite the fact that many of the children with eventual visual problems appeared to improve or *emmetropize* during the preschool years. If this very interesting finding is supported by further research, it would suggest that early assessment may be extremely important for predicting subsequent visual problems. Whatever the general process of emmetropization in humans, it is clear that some deviations from the expected developmental sequence are *not* outgrown and cause permanent visual losses, and thus should not be ignored; this is especially true of imbalances between the eyes, such as marked anisometropia (i.e., each eye focussed at a different distance) and strabismus.

While we have made great progress in developing methods that can be used to evaluate infant vision, progress in having these methods adopted in clinical settings has been disappointing. There has been some success in getting clinicians to test infant acuity with systems such as the Teller Acuity Cards (e.g., Teller, McDonald, Preston, Sebris, & Dobson, 1986), derived directly from laboratory work with FPL measures of acuity. However, as indicated above, acuity may be insufficient for detecting many forms of functional deficits of spatial vision, and FPL appears to be one of the less sensitive techniques for measuring acuity, although properly normed it can be quite effective in diagnostic usage.

Since many visual functions depend on spatial sensitivity away from the acuity limit, and sensitivities to different spatial frequencies apparently have different time courses, it would be beneficial to have clinicians see the relevance of measuring the full infant spatial CSF. The spatial CSF is being used more and more with adults as part of a complete clinical evaluation of vision (e.g., Regan, 1986). Differences in the shape or absolute sensitivity of the CSF can aid in the diagnosis of many visual disorders (e.g., Bodis-Wollner, 1980). For example, persons with early onset amblyopia have been shown to have changes in spatial CSFs at both high and low frequencies (e.g., Hess & Howell, 1977); presumptively, these deficiencies in spatial vision also had an early onset.

In our own laboratory, we have a few serendipitous observations of CSFs from infants who have some refractive error of a magnitude that could lead to the development of amblyopia. In these cases, the CSFs were depressed at all spatial frequencies compared with those obtained from age-matched, visually normal infants. There is reason to be worried about other aspects of these infants' development apart from basic visual functions. Clearly, even if their visual problems do not ultimately result in amblyopia, infants with problems of spatial vision from either optical or neural factors will not be able to make many visual discriminations that visually normal infants can. The extent to which this restricted experience might hamper normal cognitive and social development can only be surmised. The unfortunate fact is that many of the same children who are at risk for developmental delay from prematurity and other perinatal insults also have been reported to have a higher than normal incidence of visual and optical disorders (e.g., Fledelius, 1976; Orel-Bixler, Haegerstrom-Portnoy, & Hall,

1989). There is continuing interest in being able to test infants, particularly those thought to be at risk for developmental delay, to predict later intelligence. An area of concern for us at the moment is to understand the impact that moderate and severe visual disorders can have on performance on one of the emerging class of infant tests based on visual information processing, such as the Fagan Test of Infant Intelligence (Fagan, Singer, Montie, & Shepard, 1986). The assumption on these tests is that poor performance is related to some central information-processing problem, but since the items are all visual and require some reasonably fine visual discriminations, it is important to establish how variations in visual abilities alone influence test performance.

## VII. CONCLUSION

The study of infant visual development has seen significant advances in the last 20 years. Real progress has been made in describing the developmental course of many visual subsystems, only some of which we have dealt with here. The major hindrance to faster progress in understanding infant vision is methodological. There is a continuing tension between making the research hew closely to the model of "good science" found in numerous elegant adult studies and adjusting the methodologies to be sensitive to the characteristics of the organism we are studying, the human infant. Speaking for ourselves, we have frequently been frustrated by having our studies criticized by members of the adult-vision community as faulty science because, for example, our psychophysical procedures do not include the expected hundreds of trials, and being criticized by members of the developmental community for using rigorously controlled stimuli that are not seen as "ecologically valid."

We continue to be intrigued by the contrast between how poorly infants often perform in laboratory studies and how well integrated they appear to be in their natural environments. In part, this paradox may stem from the kinds of stimuli that have been used in the laboratory; greater attention needs to be paid to using a wider and more natural range of stimuli, particularly with the addition of coherent motion. We have probably not given sufficient attention to how the various components of vision combine to yield a reasonably competent ensemble of visual functions. There is also the continuing problem that many of our most reliable methods are likely to underestimate infants' visual abilities. In the normal situation, whatever the laboratory results may say, it is difficult to muster data to argue that normal infants are limited in their daily lives and in their development by visual immaturities. In the main, when exercised in the rich stimulus context of the infant's everyday world, infant vision is a highly functional sense. While single abilities may be less than fully mature, the ensemble of visual functions allows the infant to respond appropriately to relevant aspects of the environment, including the distinctive features and affordances described by

Gibson (1966, 1979). In answer to the question raised in the title of this chapter then, when it adheres to the normal developmental sequence, infant vision does, in fact, seem good enough for appropriate adaptive responses to environmental objects and events, even though we still need to reorient some of our basic research to allow more systematic examination of vision under these conditions that approximate the real world.

A different conclusion may be drawn, however, for infants with early visual and optical problems. We now have enough basic data on normal visual development and methods that we are in a position to begin to study directly in individuals the influence of early visual problems on vision and on other psychological entities. While there are still many things to be learned about normal visual development, the field of infant vision is poised to enter the arena of applied developmental research to study the development of infants whose vision is not "good enough."

## VIII. REFERENCES

Abel, L., Traccis, S., Troost, B. T., & Dell'Osso, L. F. (1983). Saccadic variability: Contributions from fatigue, inattention and amplitude. *Investigative Ophthalmology and Visual Science, Supplement, 24,* 272.

Abramov, I., & Gordon, J. (1973a). Vision. In E. Carterette & M. Friedman (Eds.), *Handbook of perception* (Vol. 3). New York: Academic Press.

Abramov, I., & Gordon, J. (1973b). Seeing. In E. Carterette & M. Friedman (Eds.), *Handbook of perception* (Vol. 3). New York: Academic Press.

Abramov, I., Gordon, J., Hendrickson, A., Hainline, L., Dobson, V., & LaBossiere, I. (1982). The retina of the newborn human infant. *Science, 217,* 265–267.

Abramov, I., Hainline, L., & Duckman, R. (1990). Screening infant visual with paraxial photo-refraction. *Optometry and Vision Science, 67,* 538–545.

Abramov, I., Hainline, L., Turkel, J., Lemerise, E., Smith, H., Gordon, J., & Petry. S. (1984). Rocket-ship psychophysics: Assessing visual functioning in young children. *Investigative Ophthalmology and Visual Science, 25,* 1307–1315.

Abramov, I., & Harris, C. M. (1984). Artificial eye for assessing corneal-reflection eye trackers. *Behavior Research Methods, Instruments and Computers, 16,* 437–438.

Adams, C. W., & Johnson, C. A. (1987). Accommodation to spatially filtered images. *Investigative Ophthalmology and Visual Science, Supplement, 28,* 317.

American Academy of Pediatrics, Committee on Practice and Ambulatory Medicine. (1986). Vision screening and eye examination in children. *Pediatrics, 77,* 918–919.

Aslin, R. N. (1977). Development of binocular fixation in human infants. *Journal of Experimental Child Psychology, 23,* 133–150.

Aslin, R. N. (1981a). Development of smooth pursuit in human infants. In D. F. Fisher, R. A. Monty, & J. W. Senders (Eds.), *Eye movements: Cognition and visual perception.* Hillsdale, NJ: Erlbaum.

Aslin, R. N. (1981b). Experiential influences and sensitive periods in perceptual development: A unified model. In R. N. Aslin, J. R. Alberts, & M. R. Peterson (Eds.), *Development of perception: Psychobiological perspectives, Vol. 2: The visual system.* New York: Academic Press.

Aslin, R. N. (1985). Oculomotor measures of visual development. In G. Gottlieb & N. A. Krasnegor (Eds.), *Measurement of audition and vision in the first year of postnatal life*. Norwood, NJ: Ablex Publishing Corp.

Aslin, R. N. (1987). Visual and auditory development in infancy. In J. Osofsky (Ed.), *Handbook of infant development* (2nd ed.). Hillsdale, NJ: Erlbaum.

Aslin, R. N., & Jackson, R. W. (1979). Accommodative-convergence in young infants: Development of a synergistic sensory-motor system. *Canadian Journal of Psychology, 33,* 222–231.

Aslin, R. N., & Salapatek, P. (1975). Saccadic localization of visual targets by the very young human infant. *Perception and Psychophysics, 17,* 293–302.

Atkinson, J. (1977). Contrast sensitivity in infants. In H. Spekreise & L. H. van der Tweel (Eds.), *Spatial contrast*. Amsterdam: North Holland.

Atkinson, J., & Braddick, O. (1981). Development of optokinetic nystagmus in infants: An indicator of cortical binocularity? In D. F. Fisher, R. A. Monty, & J. W. Senders (Eds.), *Eye movements: Cognition and visual perception*. Hillsdale, NJ: Erlbaum.

Atkinson, J., & Braddick, O. (1988). Infant precursors of later visual disorders: correlation or causality. In A. Yonas (Ed.), *Perceptual development in infancy: The Minnesota Symposium on Child Psychology* (Vol. 20). Hillsdale, NJ: Erlbaum.

Atkinson, J., & Braddick, O. (1989). Development of basic visual functions. In A. Slater & G. Bremner (Eds.), *Infant development*. Hillsdale, NJ: Erlbaum.

Atkinson, J., Braddick, O., Ayling, L., Pimm-Smith, E., Howland, H. D., & Ingram, R. M. (1981). Isotropic photorefraction: A new method for photorefractive testing of infants. *Documenta Ophthalmologica, 30,* 217–223.

Atkinson, J., Braddick, O., & French, J. (1980). Infant astigmatism: Its disappearance with age. *Vision Research, 20,* 891–893.

Atkinson, J., Braddick, O., & Moar, K. (1977). Development of contrast sensitivity over the first three months of life in the human infant. *Vision Research, 17,* 1037–1044.

Bahill, A. T., Clark, M. R., & Stark, L. (1975). The main sequence: a tool for studying human eye movements. *Mathematical Biosciences, 24,* 191–204.

Bahill, A. T., & Stark, L. (1975). Overlapping saccades and glissades are produced by fatigue in the saccadic eye movement system. *Experimental Neurology, 48,* 95–106.

Banks, M. S. (1980). The development of visual accommodation during early infancy. *Child Development, 51,* 646–666.

Banks, M. S., & Bennett, P. J. (1988). Optical and photoreceptor immaturities limit the spatial and chromatic vision of human neonates. *Journal of the Optical Society of America A, 5,* 2059–2079.

Banks, M. S., & Salapatek, P. (1978). Acuity and contrast sensitivity in 1-, 2-, and 3-month-old human infants. *Investigative Ophthalmology and Visual Science, 17,* 361–365.

Banks, M. S., & Salapatek, P. (1981). Infant pattern vision: A new approach based on the contrast sensitivity function. *Journal of Experimental Child Psychology, 40,* 1–45.

Bennett, A. G., & Francis, J. L. (1962). The eye as an optical system. In H. Davson (Ed.), *The eye: Vol. 4. Visual optics and the optical space sense*. New York: Academic Press.

Bertenthal, B. I., Proffitt, D. R., Spetner, N. B., & Thomas, M. A. (1985). The development of infant sensitivity to biomechanical motions. *Child Development, 56,* 531–543.

Blakemore, C., & Campbell, F. W. (1969). On the existence of neurones in the human visual system selectively sensitive to the orientation and the size of retinal images. *Journal of Physiology, 203,* 237–260.

Bobier, W. R., & Braddick, O. (1985). Eccentric photorefraction: Optical analysis and empirical measures. *American Journal of Optometry and Physiological Optics, 62,* 614–620.

Bodis-Wollner, I. (1980). Detection of visual defects using the contrast sensitivity function. *International Ophthalmology Clinics, 20,* 135–153.

Bour, L. J. (1981). The influence of the spatial distribution of a target on the dynamic response and fluctuations of the accommodation of the human eye. *Vision Research, 21,* 1287–1296.

Braddick, O., & Atkinson, J. (1979). Accommodation and acuity in the human infant. In R. D. Freeman (Ed.), *Developmental neurobiology of Vision*. New York: Plenum.

Braddick, O., Atkinson, J., French, J., & Howland, H. C. (1979). A photorefraction study of infant accommodation. *Vision Research, 19*, 1319–1330.

Bronson, G. (1982). The scanning patterns of human infants: Implications for visual learning. *Monographs on infancy* (Vol. 2). Norwood, NJ: Ablex Publishing Corp.

Brookman, K. E. (1983). Ocular accommodation in human infants. *American Journal of Optometry and Physiological Optics, 60*, 91–99.

Brown, A. M., Dobson, V., & Maier, J. (1987). Visual acuity of human infants at scotopic, mesopic and photopic luminances. *Vision Research, 27*, 1845–1858.

Carpenter, G. C. (1974). Visual regard of moving and stationary faces in early infancy. *Merrill-Palmer Quarterly, 11*, 182–193.

Ciuffreda, K. J., & Rumpf, D. (1985). Contrast and accommodation in amblyopia. *Vision Research, 25*, 1445–1457.

Cohen, B. (1974). The vestibular-ocular reflex arc. In H. H. Kornhuber (Ed.), *Handbook of sensory physiology, VI/1, vestibular systems, Part I: Basic mechanisms*. Berlin: Springer-Verlag.

Cohen, B., Henn, V., Raphan, T., & Dennett, D. (1981). Velocity storage, nystagmus, and visual-vestibular interactions in humans. In B. Cohen (Ed.), *Vestibular and oculomotor physiology*. New York: New York Academy of Sciences.

Cohen, L. B. (1988). An information processing approach to infant cognitive development. In L. Weiskrantz (Ed.), *Thought without language*. New York: Oxford University Press.

Collewijn, H. (1981a). *The oculomotor system of the rabbit and its plasticity*. Berlin: Springer-Verlag.

Collewijn, H. (1981b). The optokinetic system. In B. L. Zuber (Ed.), *Models of oculomotor behavior and control*. Boca Raton, FL: CRC Press.

Currie, D. C., & Manny, R. E. (1990). Proximity as a cue for accommodation in infants. *Investigative Ophthalmology and Visual Science, Supplement, 31*, 82.

Dannemiller, J. L., & Stephens, B. R. (1988). A critical test of infant preference models. *Child Development, 59*, 210–216.

Dayton, G. O., Jones, M. H., Steele, B., & Rose, M. (1964). Developmental study of coordinated eye movements in the human infant. II. Electrooculographic study of the fixation reflex in the newborn. *Archives of Ophthalmology, 71*, 871–875.

de Bie, J. (1986). *The control properties of small eye movements*. Unpublished dissertation. Technische Universiteit, Delft, The Netherlands.

de Schonen, S., McKenzie, B., Maury, L., & Bresson, F. (1978). Central and peripheral object distances as determinants of the effective visual field in early infancy. *Perception, 7*, 499–506.

De Valois, R. L., & De Valois, K. K. (1988). *Spatial vision*. New York: Oxford University Press.

Dobson, V., Fulton, A. B., & Sebris, S. L. (1984). Cycloplegic refractions of infants and young children: The axis of astigmatism. *Investigative Ophthalmology and Visual Science, 25*, 83–87.

Dobson, V., & Teller, D. Y. (1978). Assessment of visual acuity in infants. In J. C. Armington, J. Krauskopf, & B. R. Wooten (Eds.), *Visual psychophysics and physiology*. New York: Academic Press.

Fagan, J. F., Singer, L. T., Montie, J. E., & Shepard, P. A. (1986). Selective screening device for the early detection of normal or delayed cognitive development in infants at risk for later mental retardation. *Pediatrics, 78*, 1021–1026.

Fantz, R. L. (1956). A method for studying early visual development. *Perceptual Motor Skills, 6*, 13–15.

Fledelius, J. (1976). Prematurity and the eye: ophthalmic 10-year follow-up of children of low and normal birthweight. *Acta Ophthalmologica Supplementum*, Whole No. 128.

Finocchio, D. V., Preston, K. L., & Fuchs, A. F. (1990a). Obtaining a quantitative measure of eye movements in human infants: A method of calibrating the electroculogram. *Vision Research,* *30,* 1119–1128.

Finocchio, D. V., Preston, K. L., & Fuchs, A. F. (1990b). A quantitative analysis of the development of the vestibulo-ocular reflex and visual-vestibular interactions in human infants. *Investigative Ophthalmology and Visual Science, Supplement, 31,* 83.

Gayl, I. E., Roberts, J. O., & Werner, J. S. (1983). Linear systems analysis of infant visual pattern preferences. *Journal of Experimental Child Psychology, 35,* 159–170.

Garey, L., & De Courten, C. (1983). Structural development of the lateral geniculate nucleus and visual cortex in money and man. *Behavioural Brain Research, 10,* 3–15.

Gibson, J. J. (1950). *The perception of the visual world.* Boston: Houghton Mifflin.

Gibson, J. J. (1966). *The senses considered as perceptual systems.* Boston: Houghton Mifflin.

Gibson, J. J. (1979). *The ecological approach to visual perception.* Boston: Houghton Mifflin.

Ginsburg, A. (1986). Spatial filtering and visual form perception. In K. R. Boff, L. Kaufman, & J. P. Thomas (Eds.), *Handbook of perception and human performance.* New York: Wiley.

Ginsburg, A., Evans, R., Sekuler, R., & Harp, S. (1982). Contrast sensitivity predicts pilots' performance in aircraft simulators. *American Journal of Optometry and Physiological Optics, 59,* 105–109.

Graham, N. V. (1989). *Visual pattern analyzers.* New York: Oxford University Press.

Greenough, W. T., Black, J. E., & Wallace, C. S. (1987). Experience and brain development. *Child Development, 58,* 539–559.

Gwiazda, J., Scheiman, M., Mohindra, I., & Held, R. (1984). Astigmatism in children: Changes in axis and amount from birth to six years. *Investigative Ophthalmology and Visual Science, 25,* 88–92.

Gwiazda, J., Thorn, F., Bauer, J., & Held, R. (1990). Prediction of school-age myopia from infantile refractive errors. *Investigative Ophthalmology and Visual Science, Supplement, 31,* 255.

Hainline, L. (1981). An automated eye movement recording system for use with human infants. *Behavior Research Methods and Instrumentation, 13,* 20–24.

Hainline, L. (1985). Oculomotor control in human infants. In R. Groner, G. W. McConkie, & C. Menz (Eds.), *Eye movements and human information processing.* Amsterdam: Elsevier-North-Holland.

Hainline, L., & Abramov, I. (1985). Saccades and small-field optokinetic nystagmus in infants. *Journal of the American Optometric Association, 56,* F:620–626.

*Hainline, L., Abramov, I., Camenzuli, C., & Moore, L. (1992). Development of spatial contrast sensitivity in infants.* Manuscript submitted for publication.

Hainline, L., Camenzuli, C., Abramov, I., Rawlick, L., & Lemerise, E. (1986). A forced-choice method for deriving infant spatial contrast sensitivity functions from optokinetic nystagmus. *Investigative Ophthalmology and Visual Science, Supplement, 27,* 266.

Hainline, L., de Bie, J., Abramov, I., & Camenzuli, C. (1987). Eye movement voting: A new technique for deriving spatial contrast sensitivity. *Clinical Vision Sciences, 2,* 4–9.

Hainline, L., Gheorghiu, B., & Abramov, I. (1988). Accommodation and convergence in young infants. *Investigative Ophthalmology and Visual Science, Supplement, 29,* 75.

Hainline, L., Harris, C. M., & Krinsky, S. (1990). Variability of refixations in infants. *Infant Behavior and Development, 13,* 321–342.

Hainline, L., & Lemerise, E. (1985). Corneal reflection eye movement recording as a measure of infant pattern perception: What do we really know? *British Journal of Developmental Psychology, 3,* 229–242.

Hainline, L., Lemerise, E., Abramov, I., & Turkel, J. (1984). Orientational asymmetries in small-field optokinetic nystagmus in human infants. *Behavioural Brain Research, 13,* 217–230.

Hainline, L., Turkel, J., Abramov, I., Lemerise, E., & Harris, C. (1984). Characteristics of saccades in human infants. *Vision Research, 24,* 1771–1780.

Harris, C. M. (1989). The ethology of saccades: A non-cognitive model. *Biological Cybernetics, 60*, 401–410.

Harris, C. M., Abramov, I., & Hainline, L. (1984). Instrument considerations in measuring fast eye movements. *Behavior Research Methods, Instruments and Computers, 16*, 341–350.

Harris, C. M., Hainline, L., & Abramov, I. (1981). A method for calibrating an eye-monitoring system for use with human infants. *Behavior Research Methods and Instrumentation, 13*, 11–20.

Harris, C. M., Hainline, L., Abramov, I., Lemerise, E., & Camenzuli, C. (1988). The distribution of fixation durations in the human infant. *Vision Research, 28*, 419–432.

Haynes, H., White, B. L., & Held, R. (1965). Visual accommodation in human infants. *Science, 148*, 528–530.

Held, R. (1981). Development of acuity in infants with normal and anomalous visual experience. In R. N. Aslin, J. R. Alberts, & M. R. Peterson (Eds.), *Development of perception: Psychobiological perspectives, Vol. 2: The visual system*. New York: Academic Press.

Hendrickson, A., & Yuodelis, C. (1984). The morphological development of the human fovea. *Ophthalmologica, 91*, 603–612.

Hess, R. F., & Howell, F. R. (1977). The threshold contrast sensitivity in strabismus amblyopia: Evidence for a two type classification. *Vision Research, 17*, 1049–1055.

Hickey, T. L. (1977). Postnatal development of the human lateral geniculate nucleus: Relationship to a critical period for the visual system. *Science, 198*, 836–838.

Hoffman, K. P. (1979). Optokinetic nystagmus and single-cell responses in the nucleus tractus opticus after early monocular deprivation in the cat. In R. D. Freeman (Ed.), *Developmental neurobiology of vision*. New York: Plenum Press.

Howard, I. P. (1982). *Human visual orientation*. New York: Wiley.

Howland, H. C. (1985). Optics of photoretinoscopy: Results from ray-tracing. *American Journal of Optometry and Physiological Optics, 62*, 621–625.

Howland, H. C., & Howland, B. (1974). Photorefraction: a technique for study of refractive state at a distance. *Journal of the Optical Society of America, 64*, 240–249.

Howland, H. C., & Sayles, N. (1984). Photorefractive measurements of astigmatism in infants and young children. *Investigative Ophthalmology and Visual Science, 25*, 93–102.

Huttenlocher, P. (1979). Synaptic density in human frontal cortex: Developmental changes and effects of aging. *Brain Research, 163*, 195–205.

Jones, R., & Eskridge, J. B. (1970). The Hirschberg test: A re-evaluation. *American Journal of Optometry and Archives of American Academy of Optometry, 47*, 105–114.

Kaakinen, K. (1979). A simple method for screening children with strabismus, anisometropia, or ametropia by simultaneous photography of the corneal and fundus reflexes. *Acta Ophthalmologica (Kbh), 57*, 161–171.

Kelly, D. H. (1961). Visual responses to time-dependent stimuli: I. Amplitude sensitivity measurements. *Journal of the Optical Society of America, 31*, 422–429.

Kelly, D. H. (1979a). Motion and vision: I. Stabilized images of stationary gratings. *Journal of the Optical Society of America, 69*, 1266–1274.

Kelly, D. H. (1979b). Motion and vision. II. Stabilized spatiotemporal threshold surface. *Journal of the Optical Society of America, 69*, 1340–1349.

Kellman, P. J. (1988). Theories of perception and research in perceptual development. In A. Yonas (Ed.), *Perceptual development in infancy. The Minnesota Symposium on Child Psychology, Vol. 20*. Hillsdale, NJ: Erlbaum.

Kellman, P. J., Gleitman, J., & Spelke, E. (1987). Object and observer motion in the perception of objects by infants. *Journal of Experimental Psychology: Human Perception and Performance, 13*, 586–593.

Kellman, P. J., & Spelke, E. (1983). Perception of partly occluded objects in infancy. *Cognitive Psychology, 15*, 483–524.

Kleiner, K. A. (1987). Amplitude and phase spectra as indices of infants' pattern preferences. *Infant Behavior and Development, 10,* 45–55.

Kleiner, K. A., & Banks, M. S. (1987). Stimulus energy does not account for 2-month-olds' face preferences. *Journal of Experimental Psychology: Human Performance and Perception, 13,* 594–600.

Kremenitzer, J. P., Vaughan, H. G., Kurtzberg, D., & Dowling, K. (1979). Smooth-pursuit eye movements in the newborn infant. *Child Development, 50,* 442–448.

Krinsky, S. J., Hainline, L., & Scanlon, M. (1990). In pursuit of smooth pursuit: A repeated excursion approach. *Infant Behavior and Development, 13,* 462a.

Kruger, P. B., & Pola, J. (1986). Stimuli for accommodation: Blur, chromatic aberration and size. *Vision Research, 26,* 957–971.

Levine, M. W., & Shefner, J. M. (1990). *Fundamentals of sensation and perception.* Pacific Grove, CA: Brooks/Cole.

London, R., & Wick, B. C. (1982). Changes in angle lambda during growth: Theory and clinical applications. *American Journal of Optometry and Physiological Optics, 59,* 568–572.

Lotmar, W. (1976). A theoretical model for the eye of new-born infants. *Albrecht von Graefes Archiv für Klinische und Experimentelle Ophthalmologie, 198,* 179–185.

Maurer, D. (1975). Infant visual perception: Methods of study. In L. B. Cohen & P. Salapatek (Eds.), *Infant perception: From sensation to cognition, Vol 1.,* New York: Academic Press.

Maurer, D., & Salapatek, P. (1976). Developmental changes in scanning of faces by young infants. *Child Development, 47,* 523–527.

McKenzie, B. E., & Day, R. H. (1972). Distance as a determinant of visual fixation in early infancy. *Science, 178,* 1108–1110.

McKenzie, B. E., & Day, R. H. (1976). Infants' attention to stationary and moving objects at different distances. *Australian Journal of Psychology, 28,* 45–51.

Medina, A. (1987). A model for emmetropization. *Acta Ophthalmologica, 65,* 565–571.

Millodot, M. (1982). Accommodation and refraction of the eye. In H. B. Barlow & J. D. Mollon (Eds.), *The senses.* Cambridge, UK: Cambridge University Press.

Mitchell, D. E. (1981). Sensitive periods in visual development. In R. N. Aslin, J. R. Alberts, & M. R. Peterson (Eds.), *Development of perception: Psychobiological perspectives, Vol 2: The visual system.* New York: Academic Press.

Mitchell, D. E. (1988). The recovery from monocular visual deprivation in kittens. In A. Yonas (Ed.), *Perceptual development in infancy. The Minnesota Symposium on Child Psychology, Vol. 20.* Hillsdale, NJ: Erlbaum.

Mitchell, D. E., Freeman, R. D., Millodot, M., & Haegerstrom, G. (1973). Meridional amblyopia: Evidence for modification of the human visual system by early experience. *Vision Research, 13,* 535–558.

Morton, J., Johnson, M. H., & Maurer, D. (1990). On the reasons for newborn's response to faces. *Infant Behavior and Development, 13,* 99–103.

Movshon, J. A., & Van Sluyters, R. C. (1981). Visual neural development. *Annual Review of Psychology, 32,* 477–522.

Murphy, B. J. (1978). Pattern thresholds for moving and stationary gratings during smooth eye movements. *Vision Research, 18,* 521–530.

Naegele, J. R., & Held, R. (1982). The postnatal development of monocular optokinetic nystagmus in infants. *Vision Research, 22,* 341–346.

Neisser, U. (1976). *Cognition and reality.* San Francisco: W. H. Freeman.

Norcia, A. M., Clarke, M., & Tyler, C. W. (1985). Digital filtering and robust regression techniques for estimating sensory thresholds from the evoked potential. *IEEE Engineering in Medicine and Biology, 4,* 26–32.

Norcia, A. M., Tyler, C. W., & Allen, D. (1986). Electrophysiological assessment of contrast sensitivity in human infants. *American Journal of Optometry and Physiological Optics, 63,* 12–15.

Norcia, A. M., Tyler, C. W., & Hamer, R. (1990). Development of contrast sensitivity in the human infant. *Vision Research, 30,* 1475–1486.

Norcia, A. M., Zadnik, K., & Day, S. H. (1986). Photorefraction with a catadioptric lens: improvement on the method of Kaakinen. *Acta Ophthalmologica (Kbh), 14,* 379–385.

Orel-Bixler, D., Haegerstrom-Portnoy, G., & Hall, A. (1989). Visual assessment of the multiply handicapped patient. *Optometry and Visual Science, 66,* 530–536.

Owens, D. A. (1980). A comparison of accommodative responsiveness and contrast sensitivity for sinusoidal gratings. *Vision Research, 20,* 159–167.

Piotrowski, L. N., & Campbell, F. W. (1982). A demonstration of the visual importance and flexibility of spatial-frequency amplitude and phase. *Perception, 11,* 337–346.

Raviola, E., & Wiesel, T. (1985). An animal model for myopia. *New England Journal of Medicine, 312,* 1609–1615.

Ratliff, F. (1965). *Mach bands: Quantitative studies on neural networks in the retina.* San Francisco: Holden-Day.

Regan, D. (1986). *Manual for the Regan Contrast Sensitivity Letter Charts.* Lower Sackville, Nova Scotia: Paragon Services.

Robinson, D. (1981). Control of eye movements. In V. B. Brooks (Ed.), *Handbook of physiology: The nervous system* (Vol. II). Baltimore: Williams and Wilkins.

Robson, J. G., & Graham, N. (1981). Probability summation and regional variation in contrast sensitivity across the visual field. *Vision Research, 21,* 409–418.

Roucoux, A., Culee, C., & Roucoux, M. (1983). Development of fixation and pursuit eye movements in human infants. *Behavioural Brain Research, 10,* 133–139.

Ruff, H. A. (1982). The effect of object movement on infants' detection of object structure. *Developmental Psychology, 18,* 462–472.

Salapatek, P. (1975). Pattern perception in early infancy. In L. B. Cohen & P. Salapatek (Eds.), *Infant perception: From sensation to cognition* (Vol. 1). New York: Academic Press.

Salapatek, P., Aslin, R. N., Simonson, J., & Pulos, E. (1980). Infant saccadic eye movements to visible and previously visible targets. *Child Development, 51,* 1090–1094.

Schaeffel, F., & Howland, H. C. (1988). Mathematical model of emmetropization in the chicken, *Journal of the Optical Society of America, A., 5,* 2080–2086.

Schor, C. M. (1979). The relationship between fusional vergence eye movements and fixational disparity. *Vision Research, 19,* 1359–1367.

Schor, C. M., & Ciuffreda, K. J. (1983). *Vergence eye movements: Basic and clinical aspects.* Boston: Butterworths.

Schor, C. M., & Levi, D. M. (1980). Disturbances of small-field horizontal and vertical nystagmus in amblyopia. *Investigative Ophthalmology and Vision Science, 19,* 668–683.

Schor, C. M., Wood, I., & Ogawa, J. (1984). Binocular sensory fusion is limited by spatial resolution. *Vision Research, 24,* 661–665.

Shea, S. L., & Aslin, R. N. (1984). Development of horizontal and vertical pursuit in human infants. *Investigative Ophthalmology and Visual Science, Supplement, 25,* 263.

Shea, S. L., & Aslin, R. N. (1988). Oculomotor responses to step-ramp targets by young human infants. *Investigative Ophthalmology and Visual Science, Supplement, 29,* 165.

Shea, S. L., & Aslin, R. N. (1990). Oculomotor responses to step-ramp targets by young human infants. *Vision Research, 30,* 1077–1092.

Skavenski, A. A., Hansen, R. M., Steinman, R. M., & Winterson, B. J. (1979). Quality of retinal image stabilization during small natural and artificial body rotations in man. *Vision Research, 19,* 675–683.

Slater, A., Earle, D. C., Morison, V., & Rose, D. (1985). Pattern preferences at birth and their interaction with habituation-induced novelty preferences. *Journal of Experimental Child Psychology, 39,* 37–54.

Slater, A. M., & Findlay, J. M. (1972). The measurement of fixation position in the newborn baby. *Journal of Experimental Child Psychology, 14,* 349–364.

Slater, A. M., & Findlay, J. M. (1975a). The corneal reflection technique and the visual preference method: Sources of error. *Journal of Experimental Child Psychology, 20,* 240–247.

Slater, A. M., & Findlay, J. M. (1975b). Binocular fixation in the newborn baby. *Journal of Experimental Child Psychology, 20,* 248–273.

Snodderly, M. (1987). Effects of light and dark environments on macaque and human fixational movements. *Vision Research, 27,* 401–415.

Spelke, E. (1988). Where perceiving ends and thinking begins: The apprehension of objects in infancy. In A. Yonas (Ed.), *Perceptual development in infancy: The Minnesota Symposium on Child Psychology* (Vol. 20). Hillsdale, NJ: Erlbaum.

Stechler, G., & Latz, E. (1966). Some observations on attention and arousal in the human infant. *Journal of American Academy of Child Psychiatry, 5,* 517–525.

Takahashi, M., & Igarashi, M. (1977). Comparison of vertical and horizontal optokinetic nystagmus in the squirrel monkey. *Oto-rhino-laryngology, 39,* 321–329.

Takahashi, M., Sakurai, S., & Kanzaki, J. (1978). Horizontal and vertical optokinetic nystagmus in man. *Oto-rhino-laryngology, 40,* 43–52.

Teller, D. Y. (1979). The forced-choice preferential looking procedure: A psychophysical technique for use with human infants. *Infant Behavior and Development, 2,* 135–153.

Teller, D. Y. (1985). Psychophysics of infant vision: definitions and limitations. In G. Gottlieb & N. A. Krasnegor (Eds.), *Measurement of audition and vision in the first year of postnatal life.* Norwood, NJ: Ablex Publishing Corp.

Teller, D. Y., McDonald, M. A., Preston, K., Sebris, S. L., & Dobson, V. (1986). Assessment of visual acuity in infants and children: The acuity card procedure. *Developmental Medicine and Child Neurology, 28,* 779–789.

Thorn, F., & Schwartz, F. (1990). Effects of dioptric blur on Snellen and grating acuity. *Optometry and Vision Science, 67,* 3–7.

Tyler, C. W., Apkarian, P. A., Levi, D. M., & Nakayama, K. (1979). Rapid assessment of visual function: An electronic sweep technique for the pattern VEP. *Investigative Ophthalmology and Visual Science, 18,* 703–713.

van Hof-van Duin, J., & Mohn, G. (1983). Optokinetic and spontaneous nystagmus in children with neurological disorders. *Behavioural Brain Research, 10,* 163–175.

Van Nes, F. L., & Bouman, M. A. (1967). Variation of contrast sensitivity with luminance. *Journal of the Optical Society of America, 57,* 401–406.

Van Sluyters, R. C., Atkinson, J., Banks, M. S., Held, R. M., Hoffman, K. P., & Shatz, C. J. (1990). The development of vision and visual perception. In L. Spillman & J. S. Werner (Eds.), *Visual perception: The neurological foundations.* New York: Academic Press.

Volkman, F. C., & Dobson, M. V. (1976). Infant responses of ocular fixation to moving visual stimuli. *Journal of Experimental Child Psychology, 22,* 86–99.

Voipio, H., & Hyvarinen, L. (1966). Objective measurement of visual acuity by arrestovisography. *Archives of Ophthalmology, 55,* 799–802.

Walls, G. L. (1963). *The vertebrate eye and its adaptive radiation.* New York: Hafner.

Wilson, H. R. (1988). Development of spatiotemporal mechanisms in infant vision. *Vision Research, 28,* 611–628.

Woodhouse, J. M., & Barlow, H. B. (1982). Spatial and temporal resolution and analysis. In H. B. Barlow & J. D. Mollon (Eds.), *The senses.* Cambridge, UK: Cambridge University Press.

Young, L. R., & Sheena, D. (1975). Survey of eye movement recording methods. *Behavior Research Methods and Instrumentation, 7,* 397–429.

Yuodelis, C., & Hendrickson, A. (1986). A qualitative and quantitative analysis of the human fovea during development. *Vision Research, 26,* 847–855.

# PSYCHOACOUSTIC DEVELOPMENT OF HUMAN INFANTS*

*Lynne A. Werner*
*Jill Y. Bargones*

DEPARTMENT OF SPEECH AND HEARING SCIENCES
DEPARTMENT OF OTOLARYNGOLOGY—HEAD & NECK SURGERY
AND
CHILD DEVELOPMENT AND MENTAL RETARDATION CENTER
UNIVERSITY OF WASHINGTON
SEATTLE, WA

I. INTRODUCTION ........................................... 103
   A. Auditory System Development ........................... 105
   B. Infant Psychoacoustics: Methods and Limitations ............... 106
II. ABSOLUTE SENSITIVITY ................................... 111
III. DIFFERENTIAL SENSITIVITY ............................... 123
IV. FREQUENCY RESOLUTION ................................ 125
V. TEMPORAL RESOLUTION ................................. 131
VI. CONCLUSIONS .......................................... 135
VII. REFERENCES ........................................... 137

## I. INTRODUCTION

The auditory capacities of human infants have been the subject of numerous studies during the 20th century (e.g., see Eisenberg, 1976). However, the extent to which the infant's auditory system functions like the adult's has been a matter

* This research and the preparation of this chapter were supported by grants from NIDCD, DC00396 and DC00520, and by a grant from the March of Dimes Birth Defects Foundation, #12-176, to L. A. Werner. We wish to acknowledge the assistance of Elizabeth Carter, JoAnn Chavira-Bash, Pat Feeney, Rich Folsom, Jay Gillenwater, Chris Halpin, Elizabeth Koch Marrs, Cam Marean, and Nancy Fishette in the research described and in the preparation of the chapter. Ed Rubel, Ellen Levi, and two anonymous reviewers were kind enough to provide comments on earlier versions of the manuscript.

of debate. While some have argued that the newborn is functionally deaf, others have concluded that little if any development in basic auditory processing occurs postnatally. The last 10 years have seen the publication of the first auditory detection thresholds for infants (Moore & Wilson, 1978; Trehub, Schneider, & Endman, 1980), as well as difference thresholds for frequency and intensity (Olsho, 1984b[1]; Sinnott & Aslin, 1985), masked thresholds (Nozza & Wilson, 1984; Schneider, Trehub, Morrongiello, & Thorpe, 1989), and thresholds for changes in angular displacement of a sound source in space (Ashmead, Clifton, & Perris, 1987; Morrongiello & Rocca, 1987). In each case, infants have been found to respond to sound in a consistent way, but their average performance rarely equals that of adults (but see Olsho, 1984b, and Schneider, Trehub, & Bull, 1980).

The primary purpose of this chapter is to review our own work in infant auditory development in the context of these recent advances in the area of infant psychoacoustics. Our work has been directed toward two general goals. The first of these is to characterize infant performance in psychophysical tasks tapping basic auditory capacities. Of special interest are *absolute sensitivity,* the ability to detect a sound in an otherwise quiet environment; *differential sensitivity,* the ability to respond to a change in the frequency, intensity, or duration of a sound; *frequency resolution,* the ability to respond selectively to one frequency in a complex sound; and *temporal resolution,* the ability to follow changes in a sound over time. The second goal is to establish the extent to which infant–adult differences in performance reflect immaturity of the primary auditory pathway, as opposed to immaturity of mechanisms mediating the response to sound. In other words, we seek to understand the nature of the infant–adult psychoacoustic performance difference.

To accomplish these goals it is important, first, to view human auditory development in the general context of vertebrate auditory development. Naturally, there are cross-species differences in development that complicate this endeavor (e.g., Javel, Walsh, & McGee, 1986). However, since much more is known about the anatomical and physiological changes occurring during development in nonhuman species, observations of nonhuman development are a major source of hypotheses concerning human psychoacoustic development. A brief outline of vertebrate auditory system development precedes the review of infant psychoacoustic data. More detailed reviews of nonhuman development can be found in Rubel (1978, 1984, 1985), Sanes and Rubel (1988a), and Romand (1983). In addition, a brief introduction to infant psychophysical methods is provided, by way of explaining how earlier investigators influenced and contributed to the methods used in our work.

---

[1] L. A. Werner's papers were published under the name L. W. Olsho prior to 1990.

## A. Auditory System Development

The development of the auditory nervous system can be thought of as proceeding in three phases. During early embryonic development, receptors (auditory hair cells) and neurons proliferate, migrate to the appropriate areas of the pathway, undergo initial differentiation, and may form primitive connections with other cells (see Rubel, 1978, 1984; Whitehead, 1986, for reviews). Responses to sound cannot be recorded, although apparently functional connections between auditory nuclei may in fact be present (e.g., Jackson, Hackett, & Rubel, 1982). In the cat, this period ends around the time of birth; in the chicken, around embryonic day 10.[2] Anatomical studies suggest that the corresponding age in the human is around 18 weeks gestational age (Bredberg, 1968; Fujimoto, Yamamoto, Hayabuchi, & Yoshizuka, 1981; Igarashi & Ishii, 1980; Lavigne-Rebillard & Pujol, 1987, 1988; Pujol & Lavigne-Rebillard, 1985).

A period of very rapid change ensues, beginning with the first sound-evoked responses from the inner ear. Although very high levels of sound are initially required to elicit a response, response thresholds decline rapidly during this time (e.g., Pujol & Hilding, 1973). By the end of this period, many of the characteristics of the neural response are well established (Brugge, 1983; Moore, 1983).

After about 3 weeks in the cat, around 4 days posthatch in the chick, the rate of change slows. This defines the beginning of the final phase of development. At this point response thresholds and frequency resolution measured at the cochlear level and at least through the level of the brainstem appear to be adultlike (e.g., Brugge, Kitzes, & Javel, 1981; Rubel & Parks, 1986; Pujol, 1985). However, behaviorally measured absolute thresholds may still be elevated, particularly at high frequencies (Ehret & Romand, 1981; Gray & Rubel, 1985). Temporal aspects of coding also appear to continue developing during this final period (Brugge, Javel, & Kitzes, 1978; Kettner, Feng, & Brugge, 1985; Saunders, Coles, & Gates, 1973).

A similar "breakpoint" in auditory evoked potential development seems to occur around 45 weeks gestational age in humans (Eggermont, 1985; Javel et al., 1986; Schulman-Galambos & Galambos, 1979). Furthermore, the limited available data (Bredberg, 1968) suggest that the human cochlea is structurally mature by (full-term) birth. Thus, the prevailing view has been that observations of human infants are primarily confined to the final "late" stage of auditory development, with the concomitant assumption that any changes seen during this period are likely to reflect central nervous system development, since the cochlea is mature by most standards by the time the late period begins.

---

[2] As a rule, the rate of auditory development is correlated with the general rate of development across species. However, to our knowledge, the strength of this correlation has not been examined systematically.

This viewpoint has been the framework for our work in infant psychoacoustics. However there are several recent observations of cochlear maturation in nonhuman vertebrates which suggest that the traditional view is overly simplistic. Ryals and Rubel (1985) and Lippe and Rubel (1985) have shown that the position along the cochlear partition, at which various frequencies are coded, shifts apically as much as 15% between posthatch days 10 and 30 in the chick. In other words, the frequency map, or tonotopic organization of the system, continues to develop for some time after other processes are mature. While some contradictory evidence has been reported (Manley, Brix, & Kaiser, 1987), evidence in support of a shift in the tonotopic map has been reported in developing mammals (Harris & Dallos, 1984; Hyson & Rudy, 1987; Norton, Bargones, & Rubel, 1991; Sanes, Merickel, & Rubel, 1989; Yancey & Dallos, 1985). Moreover, Arjmand, Harris, and Dallos (1988) have shown that, in gerbils, this shift occurs in the cochlear microphonic recorded at the base of the cochlea, but not in the middle turn. Thus, the organization of the cochlea and its development may be more complex than previously believed. Although it is still too early to relate these recent findings to age-related changes in human infant psychoacoustics, one should keep in mind that the final word is not in on this issue.

## B.  Infant Psychoacoustics: Methods and Limitations

Psychophysics is one of the oldest and most powerful sets of research techniques in the behavioral scientist's arsenal. By *psychophysics* is meant the investigation of the relationship between sensation and the physical characteristics of stimuli. The sensory threshold, the weakest detectable stimulus intensity or the smallest discriminable change in the stimulus, is the most common way to express that relationship. Although most of what we know of perception in the mature human has been learned through psychophysical methods, until recently these methods were rarely applied to the study of development. In other words, while investigators frequently asked whether infants responded to various classes of sound or whether the probability of response depended on stimulus properties, they rarely attempted to estimate thresholds. For example, Hutt, Hutt, Lenard, von Bernuth, and Muntjewerff (1968) recorded limb movements of newborns stimulated with pure tones and square-wave stimuli of various frequencies and with human voice. They found that infant were most responsive to the voice, least responsive to pure tones, and more likely to respond to 125–250 Hz signals than to other frequencies.[3]

---

[3] This study has been criticized on the grounds that the characteristics of the stimuli used were not well specified, due to limitations of the stimulus delivery system (e.g., Bench, 1973). Thus, it is not clear whether the differential response was determined by stimulus sensation level, frequency, or bandwidth.

Another approach has been to repeat stimuli until the infant's response declines, or habituates. If response probability or amplitude subsequently increase following a change in the stimulus (dishabituation), this is taken as evidence that the infant discriminates between the original and novel stimuli. For example, Wormith, Moffitt, and Pankhurst (1975) reinforced infant high-amplitude sucking with the presentation of a tone at either 200 or 500 Hz. Presentations of the tone at one frequency were repeated until sucking rate fell below some criterion. The frequency of the tone was changed on the next trial (from 500 to 200 or from 200 to 500 Hz), and discrimination was inferred from an increase in average sucking rate on the change trial.

Both of these studies provide evidence that infants process and respond differentially to sounds. However, they fail to address the issue of the relative maturity of auditory processing in infancy. Even if we assume no contribution of immaturity of the response system, the response to a 75 dB SPL pure tone depends on both absolute sensitivity and the growth of loudness with signal intensity. In order to interpret the response to stimuli of equal physical intensity, it is also necessary to establish the minimum intensity eliciting a response. Similarly, given that well-trained adults can discriminate frequency changes as small as 0.1%, knowing that infants can tell that the frequency has doubled provides little information about the maturity of differential sensitivity during infancy.

Unfortunately, methods such as those just described, while taking advantage of the infant's natural tendencies to respond to stimulation, are also limited by the fact that infants are not spontaneously responsive to narrow bandwidth sounds. Moreover, infants' responses to such sounds tend to habituate quickly. As a result, the range of, say, intensities between "100% response" and "0% response" is small, making it difficult to estimate thresholds reliably. Furthermore, the tendency for responses to habituate means that too few trials are obtained to estimate a threshold for an individual infant. Finally, a demonstration of habituation and dishabituation (i.e., discrimination between two stimuli) requires too many trials to make more than a single comparison practical.

Clearly, what was needed was a technique that allows the perceptual system to be probed independently of the infant's responsiveness to the probe itself. A discrimination learning paradigm, in which the probe serves as a cue that a response will result in reinforcement, is such a technique. The first procedure to successfully apply this paradigm to the study of infant hearing was *visual reinforcement audiometry* (VRA). Based on early work by Suzuki and Ogiba (1961), VRA was developed by Moore, Thompson, and Thompson (1975). The response required of the infant is a head turn of specified magnitude and direction. The response is reinforced by the activation of a mechanical toy, such as a drumming bear. Availability of reinforcement is signaled by the acoustic stimulus. Thus, the infant might learn to turn her head when she hears a tone in order to see the mechanical toy. Logically, the important variable is the attractiveness of the mechanical toy, rather than the acoustic stimulus. Moore et al. (1975) demonstrated that infants continued to turn toward a sound source for significantly more trials if they were reinforced for turning. As a consequence, it is possible to estimate thresholds with this technique, by varying stimulus intensity, for example, over trials. The utility of the technique is evidenced by the fact that most of the infant psychoacoustic data available today was obtained using some variation of this procedure. Trehub, Schneider, and associates (see Schneider & Trehub, 1985, for a recent review) have developed an extremely powerful two-alternative, forced-choice version of VRA.

The primary limitation of VRA is that it only works well for infants once they are 5 or 6 months old. It does not work for younger infants, who do not generally make short-latency, well-defined head turns toward sound sources. As should be evident from the review of auditory system development literature above, there is good reason to believe that many important events in auditory development occur prior to 6 months postnatal age in humans. One solution to this problem would be to try to identify a response that is within the repertoire of a large proportion of younger infants; better still, a response that remains within the repertoire of infants over a long period of development.

Such a response might be found, but another approach circumvents the problem. Teller, Morse, Borton, and Regal (1974) introduced a procedure called *forced-choice preferential looking* (FPL), which they used to assess visual acuity in infants. An infant was shown two stimuli, a grating and a solid gray of equal overall luminance, side by side. An observer with no prior knowledge of the grating's position watched the infant, and on each trial judged whether the grating was to the infant's left or right. Not only were observers able to make such judgments reliably, but the percentage of correct judgments varied monotonically with grating stripe width. Thus, it was possible to calculate a threshold from such data. Although infants typically look toward the grating, the beauty of FPL is that it does not require the infant to make any particular response. The only requirement is that the observer be able to judge the grating's location. Furthermore, such a procedure is objective and potentially very sensitive: The observer is either "right" or "wrong" on every trial, and by providing feedback, the observer's ability to distinguish subtle responses to narrow stripe widths might be improved.

Olsho (1984a) and Olsho, Koch, Halpin, and Carter (1987) applied this logic in developing the *observer-based psychoacoustic procedure* (OPP) for testing infants as young as 3 months of age. The idea was to ask whether an observer would be able to tell whether an infant was being presented a specified sound. The sound to which the observer would respond "yes" was designated as the "signal;" the other sound was the "no-signal." In an absolute threshold experiment, a signal would be the sound to be detected, while a no-signal would be silence. In frequency discrimination, a signal would be a series of sounds which change in frequency, while a no-signal would be a series of sounds which were all at the same frequency.

The situation is similar to that normally used in VRA: The parent holds the infant facing an observation window and video camera; an assistant, the "toy waver," sits to the infant's left and manipulates toys to keep the infant quiet and facing forward; to the infant's right at eye level is a dark Plexiglas box containing a mechanical toy and lights. The observer watches the infant through the window or using the video monitor. The observer starts a trial when the infant is in a "ready" state. The observer knows that a trial is in progress, but does not know the type of trial being presented. The observer's job is to decide whether a "signal" or "no-signal" trial has occurred. At the conclusion of the trial the observer receives feedback. In addition, if the observer correctly identifies a signal trial (i.e., scores a hit), the lights in the Plexiglas box come on, and the mechanical toy is activated as reinforcement for whatever behavior the infant emitted that allowed the observer to make the correct decision. In a discrimination experiment, the reinforcer has the added function of defining signal and no-signal sounds for the infant, since the presentation of the reinforcer during training tells the infant which of the sounds to respond to. One of the strengths of OPP is that it allows the observer to use whatever response a particular infant makes, even if that response changes over time. These include head turns and eye movements toward the reinforcer, increases or decreases in general activity, changes in facial expression, changes in gaze (e.g., the baby looks "through" the toy held by the toy waver), and looks at the parent or toy waver.

Examples of data collected using OPP speak to the observers' ability to use a variety of behavioral responses in making their judgments. Figure 1 shows psychometric functions obtained in a frequency discrimination experiment for 3- and 6-month-old infants and for adults. It is clear from the infant functions that the observer was able to tell when the infant was hearing a frequency change: When the frequency did not change, the observer said "yes" between 5 and 20% of the time; when the frequency changed by 10%, the observer said "yes" between 85 and 95% of the time. More importantly, the observer's percentage of "yes" judgments increased regularly with increasing frequency change.

Figure 2 compares detection thresholds of 6-month-olds obtained using OPP with thresholds obtained using VRA at three frequencies. In general, thresholds obtained using the two techniques are comparable at ages where both techniques can be applied.

No discussion of infant psychoacoustics can conclude without treating the problem of interpreting such data. The procedures just described solve many of the problems that plagued nonpsychophysical approaches. However, at the most basic level, one must still ask whether we can ever be sure that a behavioral measure aimed at assessing infant sensory function is not influenced by immaturity of nonsensory processes such as attention, motivation, cognition, and response bias. There is not yet a general consensus on the answer to that question (e.g., Olsho, 1986; Schneider, Trehub, Morrongiello, & Thorpe, 1986; Trehub, Schneider, Morrongiello, & Thorpe, 1988). We consider our approach conservative in that we assume that nonsensory factors are always making some contribu-

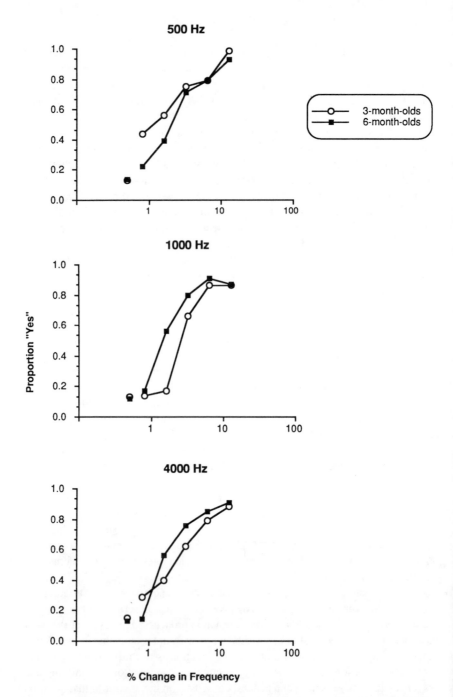

Fig. 1. Averaged psychometric functions in frequency discrimination at 500, 1000, and 4000 Hz for 3- and 6-month-olds infants, obtained using OPP. Points at left represent the average false alarm rate.

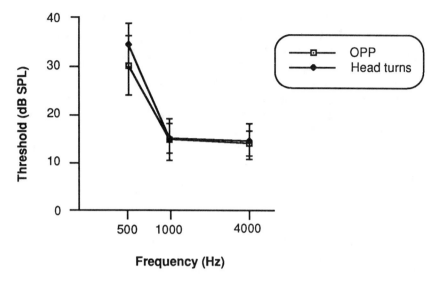

Fig. 2. Absolute threshold ( ± 1 standard error) as a function of frequency for 6-month-old infants tested with two methods, observer-based psychoacoustic procedure (OPP) and conditioned head turns, a variant of Visual Reinforcement Audiometry.

tion to an age difference in sensory thresholds. Our reasons for that assumption will become evident in the review that follows. At the same time, the admission that nonsensory factors influence infant psychoacoustic performance does not condemn the enterprise to failure. There are numerous approaches one might use to disentangle sensory and nonsensory processes (e.g., Aslin, 1987; Olsho, 1986). Banks and Dannemiller (1987) provide a cogent review of such "verification techniques;" applications of these approaches will be highlighted in this review.

## II. ABSOLUTE SENSITIVITY

Perhaps the most basic way to characterize the auditory system is to describe the audibility curve, the function relating absolute sensitivity to frequency. This function is the most commonly used metric for determining if a person has "normal" hearing. The question of whether the infant audibility curve differs from that of adults has only recently been systematically addressed.

In other vertebrates, much of the development of absolute sensitivity appears to be complete by the end of the period of rapid growth. Changes in the characteristics of the external and middle ears (Ehret & Romand, 1981; Saunders et al., 1973), as well as striking changes in the structure and electrochemistry of the inner ear (e.g., Anniko, 1985; Carlier & Pujol, 1978; Fernandez & Hinojosa,

1974; Kraus & Aulbach-Kraus, 1981; Lenoir, Schnerson, & Pujol, 1980; Pujol, 1985) occur during this period. Threshold for single-unit responses in the auditory nervous system develops along a time course closely following that of the cochlea (e.g., Brugge et al., 1978; Schnerson & Willott, 1979).

Behavioral sensitivity, moreover, develops in synchrony with these events. There is a 30-dB improvement in behavioral threshold for 100- to 4000-Hz tones between 10 and 22 days postnatal age in kittens, and responses can be elicited at progressively higher frequencies over this time period (Ehret & Romand, 1981). Whether behavioral sensitivity is completely mature in kittens at 30 days is difficult to judge: While little improvement is seen between 22 and 30 days, Ehret and Romand (1981) did not test older cats. The thresholds they report are still about 30–60 dB higher than those reported for adult cats by Neff and Hind (1955), and the difference between kittens and adult cats increases with increasing frequency. Again, caution is in order when making cross-study comparisons, but a similar pattern of development has been observed in other species. In chicks, Gray and Rubel (1985) report that absolute thresholds are apparently mature from 125 to 2000 Hz on posthatch day 4, but still elevated by about 10 dB at 4000 Hz, as the period of rapid growth in that species ends. Ehret (1976a) examined behavioral sensitivity in the mouse from postnatal day 10 to postnatal day 24. Thresholds improved by 20–30 dB, with most of that change occurring between day 11 and day 16. Thresholds approached mature values at 1000 Hz before 5000 Hz and at 5000 Hz before 15000 Hz. Ehret (1976b) reported thresholds for adult (8- to 10-week-old) mice using a different procedure. Thresholds were 10–20 dB lower than those of 24-day-old mice across the range from 1000 to 80000 Hz. Thus, there seems to be agreement that sensitivity develops along a low-to-high frequency gradient in nonhuman vertebrates, but the extent to which sensitivity, and in particular, high-frequency sensitivity, continues to develop beyond the period of rapid growth is not clear.

Early studies suggested that human neonates, like young kittens, mice, and chicks, are initially most responsive to low frequencies (Eisenberg, Griffin, Coursin, & Hunter, 1964; Hutt et al., 1968; Lenard, Bernuth, & Hutt, 1969; Turkewitz, Birch, & Cooper, 1972). This pattern is also seen in the results of early attempts to apply a psychophysical approach to neonatal sensitivity. Eisele, Berry, and Shriner (1975) allowed neonates to control sound intensity by their sucking rate, and measured the intensities at which infants tended to maintain the sound at different frequencies. Mean response levels were 50 to 60 dB above adult threshold norms, but they were closer to adult thresholds in the low frequencies than in the high frequencies. Weir (1979) analyzed neonatal body movement and respiration during presentation of 125- to 4000-Hz pure tones. Infants responded at about the same mean intensity level at each frequency. Since adult thresholds are higher at low frequencies, this finding also suggests that newborns are more adultlike in the low frequency range.

Until recently, Hoversten and Moncur (1969) had reported the only data regarding the audibility curve for infants beyond the neonatal period. Two observers recorded infants' behavioral responses to sounds presented at different intensity levels. Three-month-olds' thresholds were 40 to 70 dB worse than adults' and were closer to adults' in the low frequencies. Similar results were reported for the 8-month-olds: Infant thresholds were 30 to 60 dB above adults' and were more like adults' in the low frequencies.

Several recent studies have used VRA or modifications of VRA, to describe the shape of the audibility curve for infants 6 months of age and older (Berg & Smith, 1983; Moore & Wilson, 1978; Nozza & Wilson, 1984; Schneider et al., 1980; Sinnott, Pisoni, & Aslin, 1983; Trehub et al., 1980). The absolute values of the reported infant thresholds vary considerably across studies. While there is no obvious relationship between methodological variables and the thresholds obtained, when the thresholds from a given study are calculated relative to adult thresholds obtained in the same study (Figure 3), the interstudy variability is somewhat reduced: By 6 months of age, infant thresholds are within 10–30 dB of adult thresholds and are slightly closer to adult thresholds in the *high* frequencies.

Given the rapid rate at which thresholds attain mature values in nonhuman species, and the fact that, by 6 months, human infants' thresholds are approaching those of adults, it is somewhat surprising that reduced auditory sensitivity until about 10 *years* of age has been reported (Elliott & Katz, 1980; Maxon & Hochberg, 1982; Schneider et al., 1986; Trehub et al., 1988; Yoneshige & Elliott, 1981). As in 6-month-old infants, this effect in children tends to be frequency specific, with the biggest age difference in the low frequencies. For example, Elliott and Katz (1980) obtained thresholds at 500 and 2000 Hz in 6- and 10-year-olds. Ten-year-olds' thresholds were adultlike at both frequencies. While 6-year-olds' thresholds were not significantly different from adults' at 2000 Hz, they were elevated by about 15 dB at 500 Hz. Thresholds at very high frequencies (10000–25000 Hz) suggest that children equal or surpass adults in sensitivity in that frequency range (Schechter, Fausti, Rappaport, & Frey, 1986; Schneider et al., 1986; Trehub et al., 1988; Trehub, Schneider, Morrongiello, & Thorpe, 1989).

Examination of the psychophysical data, then, indicates that, prior to 6 months, thresholds may be closer to adults' in the low frequencies than in the high frequencies. By 6 months of age, absolute sensitivity approaches that of adults, particularly in the high frequencies, and low-frequency threshold elevation is reported as late as 8 years of age. The pattern of development seen in infants prior to 6 months is similar to that reported for other mammals in that low-frequency thresholds are initially more adultlike than high-frequency thresholds (e.g., Ehret & Romand, 1981). Since no study of nonhuman development has actually followed the course of behavioral development to adulthood using the same procedure, there are no data available with which to compare the results seen in humans after 6 months of age.

Our studies of absolute sensitivity were aimed toward a more detailed description of the infant audibility curve prior to 6 months postnatal age. A

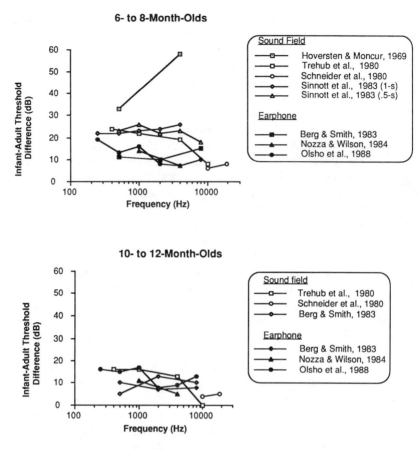

Fig. 3. Absolute threshold as a function of frequency, relative to adult thresholds obtained in the same study, for several studies. Top panel summarizes studies of 6- to 8-month-old infants; bottom panel, 10- to 12-month-olds.

second goal was to ask how much of the previously reported 10–30 dB difference in behavioral thresholds between older infants and adults can be accounted for by immaturity of the sensory system.

The youngest infants for whom we have obtained thresholds were 2 to 5 weeks old (Werner & Gillenwater, 1990). The number of infants tested were 26 at 500 Hz, 28 at 1000 Hz, and 29 at 4000 Hz. The infants were tested in an awake, alert state. The parent was permitted to hold the infant in any position that would encourage the infant to remain in that state, with the restriction that the observer have a clear view of the infant's face. Stimuli were presented using Etymotic ER-1 insert earphones. The procedure used to assess sensitivity was a variation of OPP. No reinforcer was presented to the infants in this study. The trial structure also differed from its usual configuration. A trial consisted of three

5-s intervals. During the first interval, five repetitions of a 500-ms tone were presented at a rate of 1/s. The frequency of the tone was either 500, 1000, or 4000 Hz; one of four levels between 25 and 70 dB SPL was presented. The second 5-s interval was silent. The third interval was either another five repetitions of the tone that occurred in the first interval or another 5 seconds of silence. The observer's job was to decide whether or not a sound had occurred during the third interval. The advantage of this trial configuration is that it gives the observer a current baseline for response on each trial. This proved to be necessary because of frequent fluctuations in the very young infant's level of responsiveness, despite our efforts to hold state of arousal constant. In addition, on each trial, the observer gave a confidence rating (1 = certain that no signal occurred to 4 = certain that a signal occurred). Receiver operating characteristic (ROC) curves were constructed from the confidence ratings, and the area under these curves, p(A), provided a criterion-free estimate of sensitivity.[4]

The area under the ROC curve in a yes–no experiment, like this one, is equal to the proportion of correct responses in a two-alternative, forced-choice experiment with the same stimulus (Egan, 1975; Falmagne, 1985), and, thus, should range from chance (0.50) to 1.00. Figure 4 shows p(A) as a function of stimulus

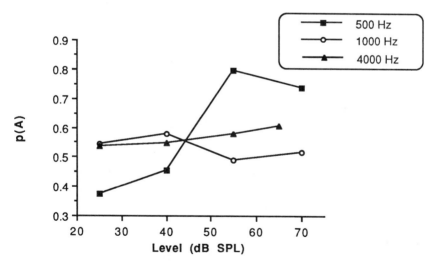

*Fig. 4. Averaged psychometric functions at three frequencies for 2- to 5-week-old infants tested using a variant of OPP. The performance measure, p(A), is the area under the confidence rating ROC curve.*

---

[4] Detailed discussion of the confidence rating procedure and ROC analysis is beyond the scope of this chapter. The interested reader is referred to Green and Swets (1966), Egan (1975), or McNicol (1972).

intensity, calculated from all of the trials obtained at each intensity and frequency for all infants. At 500 Hz, p(A) increases with intensity; performance asymptotes at 0.75–0.80 between 40 and 50 dB SPL. At 4000 Hz, on the other hand, p(A) increases with intensity, but the curve is very shallow and performance is generally poor. Even at 65 dB SPL, p(A) just exceeds 0.60. At 1000 Hz, there is little evidence for improvement of performance with increasing intensity. In fact, p(A) is higher at 40 dB SPL than at either higher or lower intensities. In a second experiment, however, a lower range of intensities of a 1000-Hz tone was presented to 2- to 4-week-olds. Performance was still not very good in this experiment, but p(A) was 0.64, better than chance, at 25 dB SPL. Reducing the range of intensities does not appear to lead to better performance at either 500 or 4000 Hz (Werner & Feeney, 1989). If threshold is defined as the intensity at some constant p(A), then the infants would be closest to adults at 1000 Hz, followed by 500 Hz, and, finally, 4000 Hz.

We have also estimated pure-tone thresholds for 3-, 6-, and 12-month-olds using OPP (Olsho, Koch, Carter, Halpin, & Spetner, 1988). Frequencies ranging from 250 to 8000 Hz were used. Stimulus duration was 500 ms; on a signal trial 10 tone bursts were presented at a rate of 1/s. The earphone used was a Sony "Walkman"-style phone, held in place with micropore tape at the entrance to the infant's ear canal.

The results are shown in Figure 5. There is an improvement in sensitivity between 3 and 6 months, which is greater at high frequencies than at low frequencies. Between 6 and 12 months, little or no improvement is seen. While 3-month-olds' thresholds are 15 to 30 dB higher than those of adults, with the greatest difference at 8000 Hz, 6- and 12-month-olds' thresholds are only 10–15 dB higher than those of adults. This infant–adult difference is within the range reported in the earlier studies of 6- to 12-month-olds (Figure 3). Moreover, we find, as Trehub et al. (1980) and Sinnott et al. (1983) did, that, by 6 months of age, infant thresholds are somewhat closer to adult thresholds at higher frequencies. Thus, our thresholds for 6- to 12-month-olds are in good agreement with those reported in other studies both qualitatively and quantitatively (see Figure 5).

It is difficult to make direct comparisons between the thresholds of 2- to 5-week-olds and older infants, since a different definition of threshold was used for the younger infants. However, we can say, at least, that the audibility curve of the 2- to 5-week-olds parallels that of 3-month-olds in the 500 to 1000 Hz range, but shows a sharp upturn at 4000 Hz. One explanation for these results, then, would be that the development of sensitivity between birth and 6 postnatal months in humans mirrors that reported in other species, with sensitivity improving at progressively higher frequencies during the early stages of development. The findings among the youngest infants are also consistent with earlier observations of responsivity in neonates (e.g., Eisele et al., 1975; Weir, 1979).

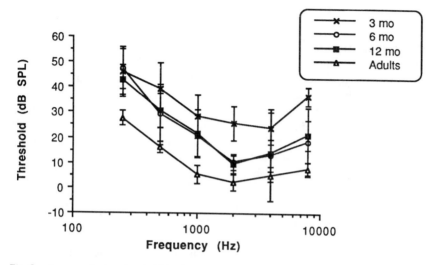

*Fig. 5. Average absolute threshold ( ± 1 standard deviation) as a function of pure-tone frequency, for 3 infant groups and for adults, obtained using OPP.*

There is only one glaring discrepancy between our results and those previously reported: Hoversten and Moncur's (1969) thresholds for 3-month-olds are higher at 4000 Hz than they are at 500 Hz, while we find that at this age the 4000 Hz threshold is lower than that at 500 Hz. We have noted a similar discrepancy between the audibility curves reported for 8-month-olds by Hoversten and Moncur (1969) and by other investigators for the same age group (see Figure 3). Hoversten and Moncur found that infant thresholds, even at 8 months, were higher at 4000 Hz than at 500 Hz, while nearly every other study found that 4000 Hz sensitivity was at least as good as at lower frequencies at that age. It is noteworthy that Hoversten and Moncur's (1969) study was the only one not to use visual reinforcement. Wilson and Gerber (1983) also commented on this effect of reinforcement, and Schneider and Trehub (1985) have argued that by conferring "significance" on the stimulus, the reinforcer makes it possible to obtain responses to sounds that are well below the infant's "attentional threshold."

This observation suggests that methodological effects can be frequency specific and that such effects may account for the differences between our results and Hoversten and Moncur's (1969). It also leads one to ask how much of the rather large elevation of Werner and Gillenwater's (1990) 2- to 5-week-olds' thresholds at 4000 Hz results from not reinforcing responses in this youngest group. In fact, we have preliminary data (Werner & Feeney, 1990) for 2- to 4-week-olds from a procedure in which the infants received auditory reinforcement (a recording of passages from children's books). Thresholds calculated from p(A) in this study are lower than thresholds obtained without reinforcement, and the effect of reinforcement is greater at 4000 Hz than at the lower frequencies. However, it still appears that the 4000 Hz threshold is relatively higher than the 500 or 1000 Hz thresholds.

A fairly consistent picture seems to be emerging then. Human neonates appear to have more adultlike sensitivity at low frequencies. In the early postnatal months, there is a progressive improvement in high-frequency sensitivity, until by 6 months, infant thresholds approach those of adults in the high-frequency range. Very high-frequency thresholds (> 8000 Hz) may reach adult values first. Thresholds at low frequencies, however, improve at a slower rate over this age range, and may not reach adult values until middle childhood. The early pattern of better low-frequency sensitivity and improving high-frequency sensitivity is consistent with that observed in other species, and one hypothesis for the age-related change in threshold prior to 6 months would be that it results from maturation at the auditory periphery.

It is difficult to reconcile observations in nonhuman species with the finding that, in humans, low-frequency thresholds continue to mature for such a long time, especially once high-frequency sensitivity matures (Sanes & Rubel, 1988a). In adults, the cochlea is the limiting factor in absolute sensitivity (reviewed by Pickles, 1988), and it appears that, in nonhuman species, cochlear development is the limiting factor in the maturation of absolute sensitivity (Sanes & Rubel, 1988a). Even if cochlear development is more complex than previously believed, few investigators would accept the idea that a cochlea as mature as a human newborn's would take 10 years to completely mature. The difference between humans and nonhumans in developmental rates of low frequency thresholds is far too great to be accounted for by species differences in general rate of maturation (e.g., Javel et al., 1986). Although changes in the resonance characteristics of the external and middle ear are probably occurring during infancy and childhood (e.g., Kruger, 1987; Kruger & Ruben, 1987), neither the magnitude nor the frequency dependence of such changes matches the pattern of threshold development observed during that period. On another level, one might ask why human sensitivity to low-frequency sounds should take so long to develop, especially if one considers that the frequencies at which infants and children are reported to be insensitive are the frequencies that are critical to speech perception.

If low-frequency sensitivity is actually developing beyond infancy, then one would expect to see similar results if one examined auditory sensitivity using methods other than behavior. This is the approach to understanding developmental psychophysical data that Banks and Dannemiller (1987) refer to as *response convergence*.

The *auditory brainstem response* (ABR) is another measure of auditory capacity that has been studied developmentally in humans, and it has been well characterized in the mature system as well. The ABR in neonates does not reveal the same sort of insensitivity observed in the psychophysical studies, although it does suggest that very young infants process low-frequencies in a more mature way than they process high frequencies. Click-evoked thresholds in newborns are within 15 to 20 dB of adult thresholds (Kaga & Tanaka, 1980; Schulman-Galambos & Galambos, 1979). However, there is evidence that evoked potential thresholds mature at a low frequency (500 Hz) by 1 month of age, while thresholds at a high frequency (4000 Hz) do not attain adult values until sometime after 3 months of age, possibly as late as 7 months (Klein, 1984; Rickard, 1988). Furthermore, masking studies demonstrate that low-frequency spectral components provide the major contribution to the 3-month-old's ABR, whereas the adult response is generated primarily by high-frequency stimulus components (Folsom, 1984, 1985; Folsom & Wynne, 1986; Hecox, 1975). In fact, when high-frequency regions of the auditory system are prevented from contributing to the response, by using maskers, responses from 3-month-olds and adults are the same (Folsom & Wynne, 1986).

ABR thresholds for very high frequencies are consistent with behavioral thresholds obtained in this frequency range for older infants and children. Auditory brainstem response thresholds for 8000–12000 Hz tone pips equal those of adults before 3 months of age (Klein, 1984; Rickard, 1988), and thresholds at 16000 Hz are on the average 10 dB better than adult thresholds at both 1 and 3 months of age (Rickard, 1988). The ABR and behavioral data, then, seem to be in agreement insofar as infant thresholds prior to 6 months appear to be most immature in the 4000 Hz region. The ABR data support the idea that infant thresholds converge with or even surpass those of adults beyond 10000 Hz.[5]

There are two notable discrepancies between ABR and behavioral studies. First, ABR low-frequency sensitivity appears to reach maturity much earlier (by 3 months) than behavioral low-frequency sensitivity (as late as 10 years). Second, our data for 3-month-olds at 8000 Hz indicate rather poor sensitivity (Olsho, Koch, Carter, Halpin, & Spetner, 1988) while ABR thresholds at 8000 Hz seem to be nearly mature by this age (Rickard, 1988). Whether these discrepancies resulted from the measures themselves or the stimuli used to elicit responses was unclear.

We have recently evaluated the contribution of stimulus variables by collect-

---

[5] Calibration issues cloud interpretation of both ABR and behavioral data at very high frequencies. Because the resonance of the external ear may be different in children than in adults (e.g., Saunders, Kaltenbach, & Relkin, 1983; Kruger, 1987; Kruger & Ruben, 1987), it is very difficult to know what sound pressure level is actually being delivered to different age groups without making ear canal measurements. Such measurements have rarely been made in developmental studies (but see Feigin, Kopun, Stelmachowicz, & Gorga, 1989). Moreover, when such measurements are made, even slight changes in the position of the microphone used to measure sound pressure levels can lead to rather large changes in the measurement (e.g., Tonndorf & Kurman, 1984). Thus, one explanation for the apparently good very high-frequency thresholds reported for children is that the sound pressure levels being delivered to the children were actually higher than the investigators believed them to be. This issue will only be resolved when more accurate calibration techniques are developed and applied to studies of sensitivity in children.

ing behavioral (OPP) and ABR thresholds for 3-month-olds and adults (Werner, Rickard, & Folsom, 1990). For both measures, the stimuli used were tone pips at 1000, 4000, and 8000 Hz, of about 5 ms duration. The interstimulus interval was also the same (70 ms) for the two measures. The same ER-1 insert earphone was used to deliver the stimuli for both measures.

The average ABR and behavioral thresholds for 3-month-olds and adults are shown in Figure 6. Adult behavioral thresholds are 15–20 dB lower than their ABR thresholds at all frequencies. This result is consistent with other reports (e.g., Kileny, 1981). Infant behavioral thresholds grow poorer with increasing frequency, as we have found with longer duration tone bursts (Olsho, Koch, Carter, Halpin, & Spetner, 1988). However, infant ABR thresholds are about the same at each frequency and about the same as adult ABR threshold in each case. This result is generally consistent with previous reports (Klein, 1984; Rickard, 1988), with the exception that Klein (1984) reported significant ABR threshold elevation in the 4000 Hz region at this age. In any case, it is clear that the reported discrepancies between behavioral and ABR studies regarding high-frequency sensitivity are not accounted for by stimulus differences. The discrepancy arises even when the same stimuli are used for both measures.

Another result of the Werner et al. (1990) study was that, for 4000 and 8000 Hz stimuli, there was a significant correlation between behavioral and ABR thresholds, on the order of 0.5. Thus, although 3-month-olds' ABR thresholds are, on average, adultlike, there is some variability in ABR threshold that is related to variability in behavioral threshold. This relationship is not found at 1000 Hz, nor is it typically found in normal-hearing adults at any frequency. The implication is that there are individual differences in rate of peripheral or brainstem development that are reflected in both ABR and behavioral measures.

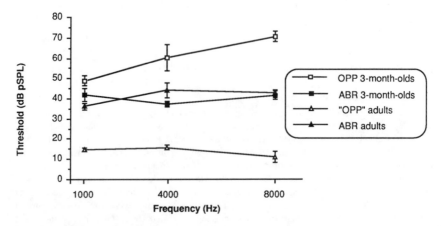

Fig. 6. *Average absolute threshold ( ± 1 standard error) as a function of frequency of 5-ms tone pips, obtained using a behavioral measure, OPP, and the auditory brainstem response (ABR) for infants and adults.*

Of course, a correlation of 0.5 implies that 75% of the variance in behavioral threshold cannot be explained by peripheral or brainstem factors. Maturation of structures central to the brainstem must be responsible.

The ABR results, both our own and those of earlier studies, imply that maturation of structures from the periphery through the brainstem cannot account for the improvement in behavioral thresholds from 3 months to adulthood. They suggest, further, that maturation of structures central to the brainstem must be responsible for the continued maturation of behavioral thresholds after 3 months. There are two classes of central factors, either or both of which might be responsible. First, maturation of neural structures in the primary auditory pathway but central to the brainstem may play a role. This explanation depends on several assumptions: (a) structures central to the brainstem contribute to behavioral sensitivity; (b) the maturation of these structures central to the brainstem lags maturation of more peripheral structures; and (c) low-frequency responses are relatively more mature than high-frequency responses at this level of the system, at 3 months, but high-frequency responses become adultlike first. Although age-related morphological changes in higher levels of the auditory system have been documented (e.g., Moore, 1985), the effect of these changes on behavioral sensitivity is unknown. Further, different mechanisms may be responsible for maturation in different frequency ranges.

The second possibility is that nonsensory factors are responsible. Certainly pronounced changes in attention and memory occur during infancy, and these processes continue to develop through childhood (e.g., Gelman, 1969; Kendler & Kendler, 1975; Pick, 1975). Given immature attention, for example, a child's threshold would be elevated relative to older listeners. Of course, it is also necessary that this effect be frequency specific, since a uniform threshold elevation across frequency is never seen during development. Frequency-specific nonsensory effects have been documented. For example, in adults practice effects are seen for detection of low-frequency signals but not high frequencies (e.g., Watson, Franks, & Hood, 1972; Zwislocki, Maire, Feldman, & Rubin, 1958).

It is all but impossible to test this hypothesis directly by giving infants extensive practice at tone detection. However, an insensitive system should be affected differently from, say, an inattentive system by certain stimulus manipulations. For example, hearing-impaired adults show less of an improvement in threshold with increases in stimulus duration than do normal hearing listeners (Watson & Gengel, 1969). Do infants show a similar effect, as might be predicted if they are really insensitive to low-frequency sounds? Banks and Dannemiller (1987) call this approach to understanding age differences the stimulus convergence approach. Figure 7 compares 1000-Hz thresholds of 3-month-olds, 6-month-olds, and adults in three experiments, one in which the stimuli were 500 ms in duration (Olsho, Koch, Carter, Halpin, & Spetner, 1988), one in which the stimuli were 16 ms in duration (Werner & Marean, 1991) one in which the stimuli were 5 ms in duration, but had short rise–fall

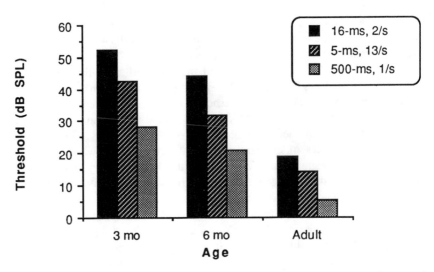

*Fig. 7.   Average threshold for 3 frequency-specific stimuli varying in duration, rise-fall time, and repetition rate (see text), for 3- and 6-month-old infants obtained using OPP, and for adults.*

times and a rapid repetition rate (Olsho, Feeney, & Folsom, 1989). Although we cannot determine which stimulus variable(s) account for the shifts in threshold, it is clear that the stimulus manipulation creates about the same effect in all three age groups. This implies that infants and adults have auditory systems that function in a qualitatively similar way with respect to duration, rise–fall time, and repetition rate. Moreover, it suggests that the factors responsible for the age differences at each frequency are not sensitive to these variables. As noted above, sensorineural hearing loss is sensitive to changes in stimulus duration (e.g., Watson & Gengel, 1969), and central auditory system deficits have been reported to be sensitive to changes in repetition rate (e.g., Stockard & Rossiter, 1977). One is forced to conclude, then, either that the form of insensitivity exhibited by infants is quite different from other forms of insensitivity, or that some nonsensory process is responsible for the low-frequency threshold elevation.

Of course, some combination of sensory and nonsensory mechanisms may be necessary to completely account for these observations. For example, age-related and noise-induced hearing losses occur first in the high frequencies and spread to the lower frequencies with time (Corso, 1963; Olsho, Harkins, & Lenhardt, 1985). Perhaps adult thresholds have declined in the high frequencies due to age or the effects of living in a noisy environment, so that infants and young children are actually more sensitive than adults are in the high frequencies. Thresholds of infants and children at frequencies higher than those typically measured (10000–25000 Hz) support this hypothesis (Schechter et al., 1986; Schneider et al., 1980; 1986; Trehub et al., 1988, 1989). The infant's audibility curve might, in addition, be elevated by a uniform amount across frequency due to general nonsensory factors. Thus, during the period from 6 months to early adulthood, thresholds may generally decline as humans become more efficient at attending to and detecting tones. At the same time, adult thresholds at high frequencies may be increasing as a result of age-related hearing loss.

In conclusion, a consistent picture of the development of absolute thresholds seems to be emerging from several laboratories. While it is clear that sensory maturation accounts for some of the age-related change in threshold, the contribution of nonsensory processes has not been adequately addressed. Final conclusions await direct evaluation of nonsensory factors in both infants and children.

## III. DIFFERENTIAL SENSITIVITY

Differential sensitivity for duration,[6] intensity and frequency have been studied in infants, typically using habituation paradigms in which gross motor behavior (e.g., Bench, 1969; Leventhal & Lipsitt, 1964), sucking or heart rate (e.g., Berg, 1972; Bronshtein & Petrova, 1967; Moffitt, 1973; Stratton, 1970; Wormith et al., 1973) were monitored during signal changes. Several of the early studies employed auditory signals but were designed to study habituation rather than sensory discrimination per se; often the auditory signals, serving primarily as tools, were poorly specified. For example, Bronshtein and Petrova (1967) studied habituation in newborn and 1- to 5-month-old infants. They used organ pipes, a harmonica, a whistle, and a pencil tap on a table, at "some distance from the infant's head." They report dishabituation; that is, infants as young as 4 hours of age discriminated among stimuli which varied in pitch or "some other aspect of their character." Such studies are important in that they demonstrated that very young infants can discriminate among sounds. However, the cues which the infant used to discriminate the sounds cannot be determined.

More recent studies attempted to control for signal variables. There is good evidence that infants discriminate between tones of different intensities. Moffitt (1973) used a heart-rate habituation paradigm and demonstrated that 5- to 6-month-old infants can discriminate a 10 dB change in intensity of a 500 Hz tone. More recently, Sinnott and Aslin (1985) applied a modification of VRA to study intensity discrimination psychoacoustically in 7- to 9-month-old infants. A trial consisted of an increment, a decrement, or no change in the intensity of 1000 Hz, 60 dB SPL tone bursts. The size of the increment or decrement was varied adaptively to determine each individual infant's threshold or difference limen for intensity (IDL). Infants discriminated intensity increments with IDLs ranging from 3 to 12 dB. Adult IDLs ranged from 1 to 2 dB. Of six infants, not

---

[6] The developmental studies of duration discrimination will be discussed below with other information on temporal processing.

one demonstrated discrimination of intensity decrements as large as 15–25 dB. The reasons for this are not known, though it is clear that infants can discriminate quite small increments in intensity, at least at 1000 Hz. It will be important to replicate this experiment over a larger frequency range as well as in younger and older infants to determine how and when intensity discrimination matures.

Despite conflicting reports, several studies provided evidence of frequency discrimination by young infants (e.g., Bench, 1969; Berg, 1972; Bronshtein & Petrova, 1967; Wormith et al., 1975). However, in most cases the frequency differences presented were large (e.g., 200–2000 Hz in Bench, 1969; or 200–500 Hz in Wormith et al., 1975). Thus, while it was clear that infants could discriminate between sounds of different frequencies, it was not clear whether they were using changes in pitch or changes in loudness or some other aspect of the sound. Moreover, we had no information about the limits of infants abilities: How small of a change in frequency can infants discriminate?

We have used both VRA and OPP to address this question. In preliminary studies, we demonstrated that 5- to 8-month-old infants could discriminate approximately a 2% change in frequency for signals between 1000 and 3000 Hz, compared to 1% by adults in the same study (Olsho, Schoon, Sakai, Turpin, & Sperduto, 1982a, b). Recently, frequency discrimination abilities have been systematically evaluated for 3- to 12-month-olds in two laboratories (Olsho, 1984b; Olsho, Koch, & Halpin, 1987; Sinnott & Aslin, 1985). In the first comprehensive study of infant frequency discrimination, we examined difference limens for frequency (FDLs) across a broad range of frequencies in 5- to 7-month-old infants (Olsho, 1984b). Infants discriminated among high-frequency tones (4000 and 8000 Hz) at least as well as adults in the same study did, but performed significantly worse than adults in the low frequencies (250–2000 Hz). Sinnott and Aslin (1985) tested infants at 1000 Hz with similar results; adults detected smaller differences in frequency than infants did.

There are several explanations for these results. First, it is possible that the physiological mechanisms underlying frequency discrimination mature first at high frequencies. Alternatively, the difference could be due to the fact that in both our studies and the Sinnott and Aslin (1985) study, the stimuli were presented at the same intensity for infants and adults. If a difference in detection thresholds between the groups exists, particularly in the low frequencies (see above), the observed differences in frequency discrimination abilities might be due to frequency specific differences in sensation level. A third possible explanation is that the differences in the low frequencies are due to nonsensory factors, such as practice effects. We have recently completed studies of infant and adult frequency discrimination abilities which attempt to address these issues as well as to examine frequency discrimination abilities in younger infants.

Using OPP, we estimated FDLs for 3-, 6-, and 12-month-old infants and for adults for pure tones at 500, 1000, and 4000 Hz (Olsho, Koch, & Halpin, 1987). Each listener was tested at 40 dB and at a higher (80 dB in most cases) sensation level (SL). Overall, infant thresholds were greater than those of adults, but this trend was frequency dependent (Figure 8). The 3-month-olds performed worse than adults at all frequencies. The older infants performed as well as adults at 4000 Hz, but as poorly as 3-month-olds in the lower frequencies. This low-frequency difference in performance between infants and adults was present in both SL conditions.

As was the case for absolute sensitivity, the development of frequency discrimination in children follows a similar frequency gradient to that observed in infants. Maxon and Hochberg (1982) reported that, at 4000 Hz, 4-year-olds performed about as well as trained and naive adults (Harris, 1952; Olsho, Koch, & Carter, 1988; Wier, Jesteadt, & Green, 1977). At lower frequencies, there was a progressive improvement in discrimination with age. By 8 years, performance was quite similar to that of untrained listeners at all but the lowest frequency (Harris, 1952). This finding together with the observation that adults benefit most from detection training in the low frequencies (e.g., Watson et al., 1972) led us to ask more specifically about training effects on frequency discrimination.

We examined the effects of practice on frequency discrimination in naive adults for 500, 1000, and 4000 Hz pure tones (Olsho, Koch, & Carter, 1988). Naive adults performed like practiced adults at 4000 Hz, but in the low frequencies, average performance of unpracticed adults was poorer than that of trained adults. In the low frequencies, the smallest (as opposed to the average) frequency changes detected by the untrained listeners in each session equaled their average performance at the end of training. Practice seems to have the effect of reducing variability and allowing the subject to maintain asymptotic performance.

Subsequently, we reanalyzed the data from the Olsho (1984b) study to evaluate 6-month-old infants' best performance relative to the best performance of adults tested in that study. As expected, little or no difference between best and average performance was seen for the 4000 and 8000 Hz FDLs for infants or adults. However, best FDLs below 4000 Hz for both infants and adults were considerably better than average FDLs. In fact, at 500 and 2000 Hz, infants' best performance equaled adults' best performance; while at 250 and 1000 Hz, infants still performed significantly worse than adults. Thus, it seems likely that at least part of the difference between infants and adults in frequency discrimination abilities in the low frequencies can be attributed to nonsensory, practice effects. Such effects may also contribute to the residual differences between infant and adult performance in the low frequencies, as it is quite likely that infants do not benefit as much as adults do from training.

## IV. FREQUENCY RESOLUTION

Frequency resolution refers to the auditory system's ability to resolve, or respond selectively to, the individual components in a complex sound. In adults, frequency resolution is established at the level of the cochlea (Yates, 1986), though

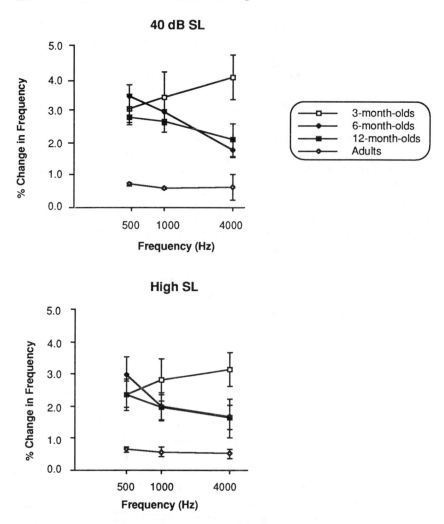

Fig. 8.  *Average frequency difference limen (± 1 standard error) in percentage of standard
frequency, as a function of standard frequency, for four age groups obtained using OPP. Top panel
shows results for 40 dB SL tone bursts, bottom panel for approximately 80 dB SL.*

during development, neural processes may limit the frequency resolution of the
system as a whole (Moore, 1983; Sanes & Rubel, 1988b). In general, by the end
of the rapid phase of development (see above), about 3 weeks in cat and 4 days
posthatch in chick, frequency resolution measured at the cochlear level and at
least through the level of the brainstem appears to be adultlike (e.g., Brugge et
al., 1981; Rubel & Parks, 1986; Pujol, 1985). Most studies, particularly those
that examine single-unit responses, find that frequency resolution matures for
high frequencies before low frequencies (e.g., Brugge et al., 1981; Dolan, Teas,

& Walton, 1985; Moore & Irvine, 1979). However, there are studies reporting the opposite frequency gradient (e.g., Rebillard & Rubel, 1981; Saunders, Dolgin, & Lowry, 1980). The reasons for these discrepancies are not clearly related to the species or the level of the auditory system studied.

The frequency resolving ability of the ear is often evaluated psychoacoustically using masking paradigms. In masking studies, a threshold for one signal is obtained in the presence of a competing stimulus, or masker. The masker may be a tone or a noise and may be presented simultaneously with the signal or precede or follow it in some prescribed relation. Fletcher (1940) demonstrated that only a *critical bandwidth* of noise within a wide band of noise contributes to the masking of a tone. He modeled the auditory system as a series of filters such that only the noise going through a given filter would mask a tone at the center frequency of that filter. Thus, if one assumes that the tone is detected at some fixed signal-to-noise ratio, the width of the auditory filter can be calculated from the masked threshold; the filter width provides a measure of the frequency resolving ability of the ear.

Several developmental masking studies have demonstrated that infants perform qualitatively like adults. For example, Bull, Schneider, and Trehub (1981) and Schneider et al. (1989) evaluated localization responses to octave-band noises in a broadband background noise as a function of age. The octave-band noise signals had center frequencies ranging from 400 Hz through 10000 Hz, and the broadband masking noise was presented at two levels. As expected (Hawkins & Stevens, 1950), when the background noise level increased 10 dB, adult thresholds increased 10 dB (Schneider et al., 1989). Although infant thresholds were about 10 to 15 dB worse than those of adults at all frequencies, their thresholds also increased about 10 dB across noise conditions. Similar findings were reported for speech detection in broadband noise; infant thresholds were elevated 10 to 12 dB relative to adults (Trehub, Bull, & Schneider, 1981). Nozza and Wilson (1984) also obtained masked thresholds for 6- and 12-month-old infants and for adults using 1000 Hz and 4000 Hz pure tones in broadband noise. Infant masked thresholds were 8 to 10 dB higher than adult masked thresholds at both frequencies.

Under conventional interpretation, these findings that infant masked thresholds are higher than adult masked thresholds would suggest that infants have relatively poor frequency resolution. However, if one considers the fact that infant *unmasked* thresholds are also higher than adult *unmasked* thresholds, a more appropriate question would be, "Does the presence of the masker influence the infant threshold more than it influences the adult threshold?" Olsho, Bargones, Marean, and Feeney (1989) compared the difference between masked and unmasked thresholds (amount of masking) for infants and adults using the thresholds obtained by Nozza and Wilson (1984). Similarly, Schneider et al. (1989) calculated the amount of masking as a function of age; they obtained masked thresholds as a function of age and subtracted unmasked thresholds that had previously been estimated in the same laboratory by Trehub et al. (1980).

Identical stimuli and procedures were used in the two studies. The results of both analyses clearly indicate that the amount of masking for infants is not more than that for adults and may even be less at some frequencies. This result suggests that filter width may be mature by 6 months of age but that infants may be less "efficient" than adults at detecting signals both in quiet and in the presence of a masker. Efficiency may include both sensory (e.g., variability of neural response) and nonsensory (e.g., response bias) processes.

A current model of frequency resolution allows processing efficiency and filter width to be estimated independently (Patterson, Nimmo-Smith, Weber, & Milroy, 1982). Recent studies have applied this approach to the study of frequency selectivity in preschool and school-aged children (Allen, Wightman, Kistler, & Dolan, 1989; Irwin, Stillman, & Schade, 1986). These studies suggest that frequency resolution as well as efficiency may be developing through about 6 years of age at all frequencies. The paradigm and measures used in these studies have not yet been applied to infants.

We have separated filter width from efficiency effects by measuring psychophysical tuning curves (PTCs) in infants and adults. A tuning curve is an isoresponse curve showing the intensity of a signal required to elicit a criterion response as a function of frequency. Narrow curves indicate fine resolution, while broader curves suggest poorer frequency resolution. In general, human tuning curves resemble single-unit tuning curves obtained from the auditory nerve in other animals (e.g., Kiang, Watanabe, Thomas, & Clark, 1965). For a psychophysical tuning curve, the response is the threshold for one tone, the probe, in the presence of another tone, the masker. Tuning curve width provides a relative measure of frequency resolution: If masked thresholds are affected equally across frequency by nonsensory factors, the tuning curve width would not be affected. This is Banks and Dannemiller's (1987) "use of thresholds as relative rather than absolute information" verification technique.

In the first study (Olsho, 1985), we obtained psychophysical tuning curves with simultaneous tonal maskers for 6-month-old infants and for adults at probe frequencies from 500 through 4000 Hz using a modified version of VRA. The probe intensity was 25 dB SL. Psychophysical tuning curve widths were similar for infants and adults at all frequencies. However, the infants needed a greater probe-to-masker ratio than the adults did in every masker condition; that is, their tuning curves, while similar in width, were shifted down about 14 dB relative to the adults' (Figure 9). This result indicates that frequency resolution is adultlike by 6 months of age. However, in this case, the infants do appear to be more susceptible to masking. The important point here is that the apparent elevation in masked thresholds, indicated by the overall position of the infant tuning curves, cannot be due to an immaturity in frequency resolution. Schneider, Morrongiello, and Trehub (1990) subsequently showed that 6-month-olds' critical bandwidths do not differ substantially from those of adults, further suggesting that frequency resolution does not contribute to the elevation observed in infant masked thresholds.

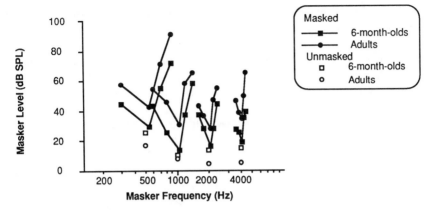

Fig. 9. *Average tuning curves obtained in simultaneous masking from 6-month-olds and adults at four frequencies, obtained using a conditioned head-turn technique.*

If 6-month-olds have adultlike frequency resolution, then their tuning curves should be sharper in a nonsimultaneous than in a simultaneous masking paradigm (e.g., Houtgast, 1972; Moore, 1978). Spetner and Olsho (1990) applied this stimulus convergence approach (Banks & Dannemiller, 1987) to infant frequency resolution. Tuning curves were obtained using a pulsation threshold response in 3- and 6-month-old infants and in adults for pure tones at 500, 1000, and 4000 Hz using OPP. In this procedure, two tones, a masker and a probe, alternate in sequence. At some masker level, the pulsation threshold, the perception changes from that of two pulsing tones to a pulsing masker and a continuous probe. The psychophysical tuning curve then shows the masker level at pulsation threshold as a function of masker frequency.

All subjects were tested with the probe at 10 dB SL. To take into account the possible effects of differences in absolute sensitivity on the tuning curves, adults were tested under three conditions: (a) probe at 10 dB SL; (b) probe at a sound pressure level (SPL) equal to that of the average 3-month-olds' 10 dB SL, and (c) probe at an SPL equal to the average 3-month-olds' 10 dB SL but with a broadband background noise present so that listeners were effectively operating at 10 dB SL. As expected (e.g., Houtgast, 1972; Moore & O'Loughlin, 1986), pulsation threshold tuning curve widths were narrower than the simultaneous tuning curve widths for both 6-month-olds and adults (Olsho, 1985). This finding strengthens the argument that frequency resolution operates in a mature fashion at 6 months. Furthermore, in the pulsation threshold task, as in simultaneous masking, 6-month-old infants' tuning curve widths were the same as adults' at all frequencies whether probe level was equated for SPL or SL. Three-month-olds performed like adults in the low frequencies under these conditions, but at 4000 Hz, 3-month-olds' tuning curves were wider than adults', indicating poorer frequency selectivity in the high frequencies.

Physiological studies of frequency resolution in human infants are consistent with these findings. Folsom and Wynne (1987) measured ABR tuning curves in 3-month-olds and adults. A 50% reduction in ABR wave-V amplitude in response to a tonal masker was defined as masked threshold. Folsom and Wynne's (1987) data indicate that tuning of the 3-month-olds' ABR is mature in the low frequencies but is slightly broader than adults' in the high frequencies (4000 and 8000 Hz).

Frequency resolution appears to be mature at a more peripheral level of the system, however. Bargones and Burns (1988) obtained tuning curves in which the response was a decrease in the level of an *otoacoustic emission* (OAE) resulting from the presence of an external tone. Otoacoustic emissions are low-level sounds which can be recorded in the ear canals of normally hearing infants, children, and adults (e.g., Kemp, 1978; Strickland, Burns, & Tubis, 1985; Zurek, 1981), and are presumably a manifestation of an active process within the cochlea (e.g., Zwicker & Lumer, 1986). Tuning of OAEs is thought to reflect basilar membrane frequency selectivity. Bargones and Burns (1988) reported that OAE tuning curves are adultlike by at least 3 months of age and probably before 3 weeks of age for frequencies between 3000 and 7000 Hz, indicating that cochlear frequency resolution matures quite early in humans. Consistent with our psychophysical studies, neither of the physiological studies found a general increase in filter width across frequency as was reported for young children (Allen et al., 1989; Irwin et al., 1986).

In summary, our psychophysical studies indicate that when thresholds are taken as relative measures, frequency resolution is adultlike by 6 months of age. The psychophysical studies indicate that in some cases, "excess" masking is observed, but the source of the excess masking is not clear. If excess masking is due to sensory processes, threshold for a signal should only be altered when masker components fall within the auditory filter centered on the signal frequency; components outside of the filter should not affect masked threshold. Alternatively, if nonsensory factors contribute to excess masking, masker components outside of the filter centered on the signal might affect performance. Werner and Bargones (1991) attempted to measure the amount of masking stemming from nonsensory factors by measuring 6-month-old infants' and adults' abilities to detect a signal in noise when the noise would not be expected to produce any sensory masking. We estimated thresholds for a 1000-Hz tone burst in quiet and in the presence of a high-frequency, band-pass noise (4000–10000 Hz) at either 40 or 50 dB SPL. Each subject was tested in quiet and in the two levels of noise. As expected, adult thresholds did not differ across conditions. However, infant thresholds were significantly higher in both noise conditions compared to their thresholds in quiet. If this result were due to sensory masking, it would suggest that the infants' auditory filters were extremely broad; this is inconsistent with what we know about infant frequency resolution. The effect could not be attributed to changes in response bias in quiet versus noise. A more likely explanation is that the presence of the external noise "distracted" the infant, and he was no longer able to respond to the tone at near threshold levels. This type of "distraction masking" might be responsible for the shifts we observed in infant psychophysical tuning curves.

Moreover, we have found excess masking among infants in a forward masking paradigm. Forward masking occurs when a masker which precedes the signal in time interferes with the detection of the signal. In brief, Olsho and Marean (1989) found that, for a given masker-signal interval, 6-month-old infants show about 15 dB more forward masking than adults do. This experiment is described in detail with other data on the development of temporal processing.

In summary, frequency resolution in 3-month-olds is mature in the low frequencies but is not yet adultlike in the high frequencies. The timing of maturation in human infants is consistent with predictions based on nonhuman auditory development (Brugge et al., 1981; Javel et al., 1986). The low-to-high-frequency gradient found both psychophysically and physiologically in human development is consistent with some (Rebillard & Rubel, 1981; Saunders et al., 1980) but not other (Brugge et al., 1981; Dolan et al., 1985; Moore & Irvine, 1979) reports on nonhuman animals. Neural immaturities probably limit frequency resolution at 3 months. This conclusion is supported by physiological data in human infants (Bargones & Burns, 1988; Folsom & Wynne, 1987) and in young gerbils (Sanes & Rubel, 1988b).

Several lines of evidence suggest that frequency resolution is mature by 6 months of age. First, reanalysis of infant masked thresholds in terms of amount of masking indicates that 6- to 24-month-old infants often do not demonstrate more masking than do adults. Furthermore, our studies indicate that when excess masking is observed, it can be completely accounted for by nonsensory factors. Finally, direct measures of tuning curve width indicate that frequency resolution is mature by 6 months of age. It is not clear at this point why poor psychophysical frequency resolution has been observed as late as 6 years of age. The paradigm and measures used in the studies of young children have not been applied to infants and such factors might be important in estimating frequency resolution.

## V. TEMPORAL RESOLUTION

Data in nonhuman species suggests that temporal coding matures relatively late. Brugge and colleagues (Brugge et al., 1978; Kettner et al., 1985) have reported that neurons in the auditory pathway become able to follow, or phase-lock to, progressively higher stimulus frequencies with increasing age in the cat. In addition, it appears that phase-locking develops later in the cochlear nucleus than in the eighth nerve (Kettner et al., 1985). Development of these processes may account for many of the age-related changes in auditory evoked potentials that have been documented in human infants as late as 1 year of age (e.g., Hecox & Burkard, 1982). Timing information is critical to speech perception, auditory localization, detection of signals in noise, and a variety of other complex perceptual processes. Thus, the development of temporal resolution may be a critical factor in the maturation of complex auditory perception.

Only one published study, however, has directly examined infant temporal processing. Morrongiello and Trehub (1987) tested the ability of 6-month-old infants, 5-year-olds, and adults to detect changes in sound duration. A train of 18 bursts was presented on each trial, and listeners learned to respond to a change in the duration of the middle six bursts. Infants exhibited a significant number of responses only to changes in duration 25 ms or longer, while 5-year-olds responded reliably to changes as small as 15 ms, and adults detected changes of 10 ms. While this might suggest that infants are still immature in temporal coding, the possibility that the result stems from age-related deficits in nonsensory performance factors cannot be eliminated.

At the same time, deficits in gap detection, the minimum detectable gap duration in an otherwise continuous sound, have also been reported among preschool children by two laboratories.[7] Irwin, Ball, Kay, Stillman, and Rosser (1985) estimated gap detection thresholds in broadband noise at two sound pressure levels, and in octave bands of noise centered at 500, 1000, and 2000 Hz. There was a progressive improvement in gap detection threshold until about 10 years. The age effect was most pronounced at lower sound pressure levels and at 500 Hz. Wightman, Allen, Dolan, Kistler, and Jamieson (1989) have also tested gap detection in 3- to 6-year-old children and reported poorer performance among the younger children, particularly at a low frequency. These investigators noted, though, that both between-subject and session-to-session variability were much greater for children than for adults. They also conducted computer simulations of performance assuming various proportions of trials on which the subject guessed, and found that thresholds as high as those obtained from children could be produced if the subject guessed on about 50% of the trials. While it is not clear that this is an accurate representation of the child's behavior in the task, this observation certainly raises the possibility of nonsensory contributions to these age differences in gap detection performance.

Having attempted to cast doubt on a purely sensory interpretation of these studies of gap detection in children, we must add that we have observed deficits in gap detection among infants. Werner, Marean, Halpin, Spetner, and Gillenwater (in press) presented continuous broadband noise at an overall level of 50 dB SPL to 3-, 6-, and 12-month-olds and equally well-trained adults. Using OPP, thresholds were estimated for gaps in this noise. On a signal trial, a series

---

[7] Davis and McCroskey (1980) measured "auditory fusion" thresholds (essentially gap detection with repeated bursts) for 3- to 12-year-olds for tones ranging from 250 to 8000 Hz at three sensation levels. Threshold was found to decline with age. However, no effect of frequency was found at any age, and the effect of intensity was the same at all ages. As Irwin et al. (1985) point out, the failure to find a frequency effect, universally reported in other studies of temporal resolution, makes the actual spectral content of the stimuli in this study suspect. It is possible that the stimuli were actually much more similar in their spectra than the nominal frequency would lead one to believe.

of 10 gaps, spaced at 500-ms intervals was presented. On no-signal trials the noise simply continued throughout the trial period. The frequency information available to the subject was manipulated by simultaneously presenting a high-pass masking noise, with a low-frequency cutoff of 500, 2000, or 8000 Hz. Thus, in a given condition, only the frequencies below this cutoff could be used to detect the gaps. This paradigm avoids the difficulties of spectral splatter associated with rapid gating of bandpass signals. The results of the experiment are shown in Figure 10. The adults have thresholds similar to those typically reported, and their thresholds improve with increasing frequency as expected. Three- and 6-month-old infants have highly elevated thresholds in all conditions, but the effect of frequency is very similar to that seen in the adults. The two younger age groups do not differ significantly in any condition. The results for 12-month-olds are puzzling. In the 2000 Hz cutoff, 8000 Hz cutoff, and un-masked conditions, the oldest infants are quite similar to the younger ones. However, when the masker cutoff is at 500 Hz (i.e., when only low-frequency information is available), 12-month-olds perform as well as adults. At first glance, this suggests that temporal coding begins to mature between 6 and 12 months, and that it matures first at low frequencies. This pattern of development is consistent with that observed in other mammals (e.g., Brugge et al., 1978). On the other hand, since the same low-frequency information is available when the

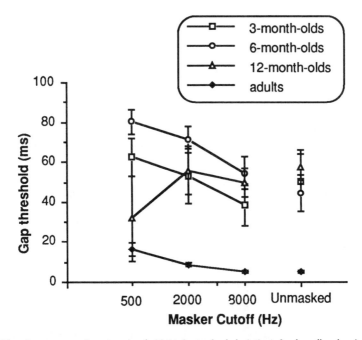

*Fig. 10. Average gap detection threshold ($\pm 1$ standard deviation) for broadband noise, un-masked, and as a function of the low frequency cutoff of a high-pass noise masker for four age groups, obtained using OPP.*

masker cutoff frequency is above 500 Hz, it is not clear why the 12-month-olds do not use that information in the other conditions. If they can detect shorter gaps in the low frequencies, one would expect them to listen at low frequencies in all conditions, producing a gap detection threshold that does not vary with masker frequency cutoff. That 12-month-olds do not appear to listen in the most benefi-cial frequency region raises questions about how infants direct attention across the sound spectrum. Such issues clearly complicate the interpretation of develop-mental psychoacoustic data and have not been adequately addressed to date.

Olsho and Marean (1989) presented forward masking data for 6-month-olds that suggest that temporal resolution is qualitatively adultlike at that age. In that experiment, OPP was used to estimate unmasked and forward masked thresholds for a 1000-Hz tone burst, or probe. The masker was a burst of white noise at 70 dB SPL. The level of the probe was fixed at either 15 or 30 dB above the unmasked threshold for each listener, and the time interval between the offset of the masker and the onset of the probe, $\Delta t$, was manipulated to define masked threshold at each probe intensity. In other words, this experiment determined the value of $\Delta t$ that produced 15 or 30 dB of forward masking. A system with good temporal resolution would be expected to exhibit less masking at a given value of $\Delta t$ than a system with poor temporal resolution. While the results indicated that, at a given value of $\Delta t$, 6-month-olds exhibited about 15 dB more masking than adults, the slope of the infants' masking function paralleled that of adults. That is, increasing $\Delta t$ by some amount led to the same improvement in performance for the two age groups. Moreover, preliminary data suggests that the 15 dB of excess forward masking exhibited by 6-month-olds can be completely accounted for by nonsensory effects: 6-month-olds show 15 dB of excess forward masking even when $\Delta t$ is as long as 200 ms (Olsho & Marean, 1989). Thus, given the apparent discrepancy between the gap detection and forward masking data, it is difficult to say when temporal resolution is mature.

Measures such as duration discrimination and gap detection address the *minimum* integration time of the auditory system. There are very limited data with respect to the *maximum* temporal integration capacity of the infant auditory system. Adult thresholds for signals of constant power improve in direct propor-tion to duration (i.e., by 3 dB per doubling of duration), up to about 200 ms (Zwislocki, 1960). Thorpe and Schneider (1987) used a conditioned head-turn paradigm to examine the effects of duration on thresholds of 6- to 7-month-olds and adults. On each trial, a single noise burst was presented to either the left or right, and the trial continued until the infant made a head turn in either direction. Thresholds calculated from group psychometric functions showed that adult performance was similar to that reported in earlier studies. Infant performance improved at a much faster rate for short durations, by about 10 dB per doubling of duration, and continued to improve with duration to 300 ms. Thorpe and Schneider (1987) concluded that infants may have longer integration times than adults do. However, the fact that a given increase in duration leads to a *greater* improvement in threshold for infants than for adults is curious: The system cannot integrate more energy than was originally present in the stimulus. Gray (1987) reported a result in chicks which was similar to Thorpe and Schneider's, in that chicks had much higher thresholds at very short durations than expected from their long duration thresholds. Gray suggests, however, that this particular difficulty with short duration stimuli among young animals is an effect of responsiveness rather than sensitivity: Infrequent short duration sounds may not elicit optimal responses.

We have recently completed a study that suggests that temporal integration is actually mature as early as 3 months. Werner and Marean (1991) measured detection thresholds for individual 3- and 6-month-olds and for adults using OPP. Sixteen 16-ms tone bursts at 1000 Hz were presented on each trial with 444 ms between bursts. The difference in threshold between infants and adults, 14 dB for 6-month-olds and about 21 dB for 3-month-olds, was about the same as that in the earlier Olsho, Koch, Carter, Halpin, and Spetner (1988) study in which thresholds for 500-ms tone bursts were measured (see Figure 6). These results are limited in that only one frequency was included and only two durations can be compared, but they suggest mature temporal integration by 3 months. However, it is difficult at this point to make any strong statement with respect to temporal integration among human infants.


## VI. CONCLUSIONS

Our goals in this review and in our own research have been, first, to characterize infant performance in traditional psychophysical measures, and, second, to determine the extent to which infant performance reflects immaturity of the primary auditory system. We have concentrated on four aspects of hearing: absolute sensitivity, differential sensitivity, frequency resolution, and temporal resolution. We believe that the data support three general conclusions with respect to auditory function during the first year of life.

First, some changes in absolute sensitivity and frequency resolving power of the sensory system, particularly at high frequencies, occur after 3 months of age in human infants. By 6 months of age, the human auditory system is nearly adultlike in these capacities, although some low-frequency threshold elevation is reported into middle childhood. The pattern of development in humans prior to 6 months of age is consistent with the time frame proposed by Javel et al. (1986) and the general developmental course described for other mammals by many investigators. Later changes in low-frequency sensitivity are not seen in other species and the source of these changes is not known. In contrast to absolute sensitivity and frequency resolution, we find that temporal resolution in infants is not qualitatively like that in adults until 6 months or later. This result also seems consistent with the relatively late development of temporal coding in other mammals (e.g., Brugge et al., 1981; Kettner et al., 1985; Sanes & Constantine-Paton, 1985).

As we noted at the outset, it is unusual to find a case where infant performance in a psychophysical task is as good as adult performance. Our second conclusion is that much of the "main effect of age" and perhaps even some interaction effects involving age, stem from immaturity in the nonsensory processes that contribute to psychophysical performance. For example, our studies of "distraction masking" demonstrate that the presence of a competing sound, irrespective of its frequency relationship to the target sound, will substantially influence the infant's performance in a masking experiment. In the case of frequency discrimination we have found that the amount of experience in the task has rather large, and more importantly, frequency specific effects on *adult* performance. While such effects do not appear to account totally for the difference between infants and adults in frequency discrimination, they undoubtedly contribute to it. Just as certainly, there are other nonsensory processes that we have yet to address that also contribute to the infant's poorer performance. Given that we usually cannot directly control these variables, the only way to be able to evaluate their impact on the infant's performance is to examine it directly.

While considerably more work will be required to fully characterize nonsensory factors influencing infant psychoacoustic performance, we believe that it will be impossible to understand age differences in thresholds without doing so. It is no news to developmental psychologists that processes such as memory and attention undergo tremendous development in humans. Moreover, that these processes influence psychophysical performance in adult observers is also well established (e.g., Green & Swets, 1966; Jesteadt & Sims, 1975; Watson, 1987). Investigators in nearly every subarea of developmental psychology have addressed the so-called "competence–performance" distinction (e.g., Banks & Dannemiller, 1987; Dale, 1976; Donaldson, 1978; Labouvie-Vief, 1985). In cognitive development, for example, apparently irrelevant changes in the wording of a question may elicit a response from a child that shows him to be capable of far more sophisticated reasoning than previously believed (e.g., McGarrigle, Grieve, & Hughes, cited in Donaldson, 1978). On the other hand, developmental studies of memory tell us that young children are not able to improve recall even with direct instruction in mnemonic strategies (e.g., Flavell, 1985). This literature holds at least two messages for those of us trying to determine how nonsensory factors affect psychophysical performance. First, it is possible that changes in procedure or paradigm may allow us to show that infants are capable of adultlike psychophysical performance under certain conditions. However, the second message is that it may be impossible to completely eliminate such factors from developmental psychophysical studies. No matter how hard the young child seems to be trying, how quietly he is sitting, how attentive he appears to be, he may simply be incapable of the type of directed cognitive effort that adults bring to bear in a psychophysical task. The best we can do in such circumstances is to use the verification techniques described earlier to attempt to understand the nature of the age difference in performance.

Our final conclusion is that much of the information that we need to make definitive statements about human auditory development and its relationship to development in other species must be obtained from infants and children both younger and older than those for whom we now have data. Whether younger or older subjects are involved, it is clear that progress in this respect will depend on methodological advances. In the case of younger infants, it appears that the techniques that have been applied to 3- to 12-month-olds may be extended, with some modifications, to younger ages. While we are not confident that thresholds we are now obtaining from 2- to 4-week-olds represent the limits of the ''nearly newborn's'' auditory capacity, our work and work in progress in other labs is convincing evidence that these techniques will be successfully applied in this age range.

In the case of preschool and school-aged children, the directions for future research are less clear-cut. Recent studies have taken procedures developed with adult listeners, and attempted to make them more fun for children. The results show that young children tend not to perform as well as adults; in some cases preschool children do not perform as well as 6-month-old infants! To complicate matters, the differences between preschool children and adults are sometimes specific to certain listening conditions, arguing that the age difference does not result from a general nonsensory deficit. At the same time, it is difficult to believe that individuals who perform so well in daily speech communication are operating with major deficits in temporal processing or frequency resolution. We know, furthermore, that deficits of the magnitude reported in some studies of children are associated with severe hearing loss in adults. Moreover, although the available data are sparse, there is no evidence from other mammals that suggests such a long time course for development of basic auditory coding. Finally, it makes little sense that natural selection would favor a strong dependence on acoustic communication and a relatively early emergence of acoustic communication in a species whose auditory system takes so long to develop. Thus, despite the recent progress, it is likely that a major effort to develop procedures that bypass immature nonsensory processes must be undertaken before we will be able to establish the age at which sensory processes actually mature in humans.

## VII.  REFERENCES

Allen, P., Wightman, F., Kistler, D. J., & Dolan, T. R. (1989). Frequency resolution in children. *Journal of Speech and Hearing Research, 32,* 317–322.

Anniko, M. (1985). Histochemical, microchemical (micropore) and organ culture approaches to the study of auditory development. *Acta Otolaryngologica (Suppl.), 421,* 10–18.

Arjmand, E., Harris, D., & Dallos, P. (1988). Developmental changes in frequency mapping of the gerbil cochlea: Comparison of two cochlear locations. *Hearing Research, 32,* 93–96.

Ashmead, D. H., Clifton, R. K., & Perris, E. E. (1987). Precision of auditory localization in human infants. *Developmental Psychology, 23,* 641–648.

Aslin, R. N. (1987). Visual and auditory development in infancy. In J. D. Osofsky (Ed.), *Handbook of infant development* (2nd ed.). New York: John Wiley & Son.

Banks, M. S., & Dannemiller, J. L. (1987). Infant visual psychophysics. In L. B. Cohen & P. Salapatek (Eds.), *Handbook of infant perception* (Vol. 1). New York: Academic Press.

Bargones, J. Y., & Burns, E. M. (1988). Suppression tuning curves for spontaneous otoacoustic emissions in infants and adults. *Journal of the Acoustical Society of America, 83,* 1809–1816.

Bench, J. (1969). Audio-frequency and audio-intensity discrimination in the human neonate. *International Audiology, 8,* 615–625.

Bench, J. (1973). Square wave stimuli and neonatal auditory behavior: Some comments on Ashton (1971), Hutt et al. (1968), and Lenard et al. (1969). *Journal of Experimental Psychology, 16,* 521–527.

Berg, W. K. (1972). Habituation and dishabituation of cardiac responses in 4-mo-old infants. *Journal of Experimental Child Psychology, 14,* 92–107.

Berg, K. M., & Smith, M. C. (1983). Behavioral thresholds for tones during infancy. *Journal of Experimental Child Psychology, 35,* 409–425.

Bredberg, G. (1968). Cellular pattern and nerve supply of the human organ of Corti. *Acta Otolaryngologica (Suppl.), 236,* 1–135.

Bronshtein, A. I., & Petrova, E. P. (1967). The auditory analyzer in young infants. In Y. Brackbill & G. G. Thompson (Eds.), *Behavior in infancy and early childhood.* New York: Free Press.

Brugge, J. F. (1983). Development of the lower brainstem auditory nuclei. In R. Romand (Ed.), *Development of the auditory and vestibular systems.* New York: Academic Press.

Brugge, J. F., Javel, E., & Kitzes, L. M. (1978). Signs of functional maturation of peripheral auditory system in discharge patterns in anteroventral cochlear nucleus of kittens. *Journal of Neurophysiology, 41,* 1557–1579.

Brugge, J. F., Kitzes, L. M., & Javel, E. (1981). Postnatal development of frequency and intensity sensitivity of neurons in the anteroventral cochlear nucleus of kittens. *Hearing Research, 5,* 217–229.

Bull, D., Schneider, B. A., & Trehub, S. E. (1981). The masking of octave-band noise by broadband spectrum noise: A comparison of infant and adult thresholds. *Perception & Psychophysics, 30,* 101–106.

Carlier, E., & Pujol, R. (1978). Role of inner and outer hair cells in coding sound intensity: An ontogenetic approach. *Brain Research, 147,* 174–176.

Corso, J. R. (1963). Age and sex differences in pure tone thresholds. *Arch. Otolaryngol., 77,* 385–405.

Dale, P. S. (1976). *Language development* (2nd ed.). New York: Holt Rinehart and Winston.

Davis, S. M., & McCroskey, R. L. (1980). Auditory fusion in children. *Child Development, 51,* 75–80.

Dolan, D. F., Teas, D. C., & Walton, J. P. (1985). Postnatal development of physiological responses in auditory nerve fibers. *Journal of the Acoustical Society of America, 78,* 544–554.

Donaldson, M. (1978). *Children's minds.* New York: Norton.

Egan, J. (1975). *Signal detection theory and ROC analysis.* New York: Academic Press.

Eggermont, J. J. (1985). Physiology of the developing auditory system. In S. E. Trehub & B. Schneider (Eds.), *Auditory development in infancy.* New York: Plenum Press.

Ehret, G. (1976a). Development of absolute auditory thresholds in the house mouse *(Mus musculus). Journal of the American Audiology Society, 1,* 173–184.

Ehret, G. (1976b). Temporal auditory summation for pure tones and white noise in the house mouse *(Mus musculus). Journal of the Acoustical Society of America, 59,* 1421–1427.

Ehret, G., & Romand, R. (1981). Postnatal development of absolute auditory thresholds in kittens. *Journal of Comparative and Physiological Psychology, 95,* 304–311.

Eisele, W. A., Berry, R. C., & Shriner, T. H. (1975). Infant sucking response patterns a conjugate function of change in the sound pressure level of auditory stimuli. *Journal of Speech and Hearing Research, 18,* 296–307.

Eisenberg, R. B. (1976). *Auditory competence in early life.* Baltimore: University Park Press.

Eisenberg, R. B., Griffin, E. J., Coursin, D. B., & Hunter, M. A. (1964). Auditory behavior in the human neonate: A preliminary report. *Journal of Speech and Hearing Research, 7,* 233–244.

Elliott, L. L., & Katz, D. R. (1980). Children's pure-tone detection. *Journal of the Acoustical Society of America, 67,* 343–344.

Falmagne, J-C. (1985). *Elements of psychophysical theory.* New York: Oxford University Press.

Feigin, J. A., Kopun, J. G., Stelmachowicz, P. G., & Gorga, M. P. (1989). Probe-tube microphone measures of ear-canal sound pressure levels in infants and children. *Ear and Hearing, 10,* 254–258.

Fernandez, C., & Hinojosa, R. (1974). Postnatal development of the endocochlear potential and stria vascularis in the cat. *Acta Otolaryngologica, 78,* 173–186.

Flavell, J. H. (1985). *Cognitive development.* Englewood Cliffs, NJ: Prentice-Hall.

Fletcher, H. (1940). Auditory patterns. *Review of Modern Physics, 12,* 47–65.

Folsom, R. C. (1984). Frequency specificity of human auditory brainstem responses as revealed by pure-tone masking profiles. *Journal of the Acoustical Society of America, 75,* 919–924.

Folsom, R. C. (1985). Auditory brain stem responses from human infants: Pure tone masking profiles for clicks and filtered clicks. *Journal of the Acoustical Society of America, 78,* 555–562.

Folsom, R. C., & Wynne, M. K. (1986). Auditory brain stem responses from human adults and infants: Restriction of frequency contribution by notched-noise masking. *Journal of the Acoustical Society of America, 80,* 1057–1064.

Folsom, R. C., & Wynne, M. K. (1987). Auditory brain stem responses from human adults and infants: Wave V tuning curves. *Journal of the Acoustical Society of America, 81,* 412–417.

Fujimoto, S., Yamamoto, K., Hayabuchi, I., & Yoshizuka, M. (1981). Scanning and transmission electron microscopic studies of the organ of Corti and stria vascularis in human fetal cochlear ducts. *Archives of Histology of Japan, 44,* 223–235.

Gelman, R. (1969). Conservation acquisition: A problem of learning to attend to relevant attributes. *Journal of Experimental Child Psychology, 7,* 167–187.

Gray, L., (1987, February). *Development of temporal integration.* Paper presented to the Mid-winter Research Meeting of the Association for Research in Otolaryngology, Clearwater Beach, FL.

Gray, L., & Rubel, E. W. (1985). Development of absolute thresholds in chickens. *Journal of the Acoustical Society of America, 77,* 1162–1172.

Green, D. M., & Swets, J. A. (1966). *Signal detection theory and psychophysics.* New York: John Wiley & Son.

Harris, D. M., & Dallos, P. (1984). Ontogenetic changes in frequency mapping of a mammalian ear. *Science, 225,* 741–742.

Harris, J. D. (1952). Pitch discrimination. *Journal of the Acoustical Society of America, 24,* 750–755.

Hawkins, J. E., & Stevens, S. S. (1950). The masking of pure tones and of speech by white noise. *Journal of the Acoustical Society of America, 22,* 6–13.

Hecox, K. (1975). Electrophysiological correlates of human auditory development. In L. B. Cohen & P. Salapatek (Eds.), *Infant perception: From sensation to cognition.* New York: Academic Press.

Hecox, K., & Burkard, R. (1982). Developmental dependencies of the human brainstem auditory evoked response. *Annals of the New York Academy of Sciences, 388,* 538–556.

Houtgast, T. (1972). Psychophysical evidence for lateral inhibition in hearing. *Journal of the Acoustical Society of America, 51,* 1885–1894.

Hoversten, G. H., & Moncur, J. P. (1969). Stimuli and intensity factors in testing infants. *Journal of Speech and Hearing Research, 12*, 677–686.

Hutt, S. J., Hutt, C., Lenard, H. G., von Bernuth, H., & Muntjewerff, W. J. (1968). Auditory responsivity in the human neonate. *Nature, 218*, 888–890.

Hyson, R. L., & Rudy, J. W. (1987). Ontogenetic change in the analysis of sound frequency in the infant rat. *Developmental Psychobiology, 20*, 189–207.

Igarashi, Y., & Ishii, T. (1980). Embryonic development of the human organ of Corti: Electron microscopic study. *International Journal of Pediatric Otorhinolaryngology, 2*, 51–62.

Irwin, R. J., Ball, A. K. R., Kay, N., Stillman, J. A., & Rosser, J. (1985). The development of auditory temporal acuity in children. *Child Development, 56*, 614–620.

Irwin, R. J., Stillman, J. A., & Schade, A. (1986). The width of the auditory filter in children. *Journal of Experimental Child Psychology, 41*, 429–442.

Jackson, H., Hackett, J. T., & Rubel, E. W. (1982). Organization and development of brain stem auditory nuclei in the chick: Ontogeny of postsynaptic responses. *Neuroscience, 16*, 80–86.

Javel, E., Walsh, E. J., & McGee, J. D. (1986). Development of auditory evoked potentials. In R. N. Aslin (Ed.), *Advances in neural and behavioral development*. Norwood, NJ: Ablex Publishing Corp.

Jesteadt, W., & Sims, S. L. (1975). Decision processes in frequency discrimination. *Journal of the Acoustical Society of America, 57*, 1161–1168.

Kaga, K., & Tanaka, Y. (1980). Auditory brainstem response and behavioral audiometry: Developmental correlates. *Archives of Otolaryngology, 106*, 564–566.

Kemp, D. T. (1978). Stimulated acoustic emissions from within the human auditory system. *Journal of the Acoustical Society of America, 64*, 1386–1391.

Kendler, H. H., & Kendler, T. S. (1975). From discrimination learning to cognitive development: A neobehavioristic odyssey. In W. K. Estes (Ed.), *Handbook of learning and cognitive processes*. Hillsdale, NJ: Erlbaum.

Kettner, R. E., Feng, J-Z., & Brugge, J. F. (1985). Postnatal development of the phase-locked response to low frequency tones of auditory nerve fibers in the cat. *Journal of Neuroscience, 5*, 275–283.

Kiang, N. Y. S., Watanabe, T., Thomas, E. C., & Clark, L. F. (1965). *Discharge patterns of single fibers in the cat's auditory nerve*. Cambridge, MA: MIT Press.

Kileny, P. (1981). The frequency specificity of tone-pip evoked auditory brain stem responses. *Ear and Hearing, 2*, 270–275.

Klein, A. J. (1984). Frequency and age-dependent auditory evoked potential thresholds in infants. *Hearing Research, 16*, 291–297.

Kraus, H. J., & Aulbach-Kraus, K. (1981). Morphological changes in the cochlea of the mouse after the onset of hearing. *Hearing Research, 4*, 89–102.

Kruger, B. (1987). An update on the external resonance in infants and young children. *Ear and Hearing, 8*, 333–336.

Kruger, B., & Ruben, R. J. (1987). The acoustic properties of the infant ear: A preliminary report. *Acta Otolaryngology (Stockh), 103*, 578–585.

Labouvie-Vief, G. (1985). Intelligence and cognition. In J. E. Birren & K. W. Schaie (Eds.), *Handbook of the psychology of aging* (2nd ed.). New York: Van Nostrand Reinhold.

Lavigne-Rebillard, M., & Pujol, R. (1987). Surface aspects of the developing human organ of Corti. *Acta Otolaryngologica (Stockh), Suppl. 436*, 43–50.

Lavigne-Rebillard, M., & Pujol, R. (1988). Hair cell innervation in the fetal human cochlea. *Acta Otolaryngology (Stockh), 105*, 398–402.

Lenard, H. G., Bernuth, H. V., & Hutt, S. J. (1969). Acoustic evoked responses in newborn infants: The influence of pitch and complexity of the stimulus. *Electroencephalography and Clinical Neurophysiology, 27*, 121–127.

Lenoir, M., Schnerson, A., & Pujol, R. (1980). Cochlear receptor development in the rat with emphasis on synaptogenesis. *Anatomy and Embryology, 160,* 253–262.

Leventhal, A., & Lipsitt, L. P. (1964). Adaptation, pitch discrimination and sound localization in the neonate. *Child Development, 35,* 759–767.

Lippe, W., & Rubel, E. W. (1985). Ontogeny of tonotopic organization of brain stem auditory nuclei in the chicken: Implications for the development of the place principle. *Journal of Comparative Neurology, 237,* 273–289.

Manley, G. A., Brix, J., & Kaiser, A. (1987). Developmental stability of the tonotopic organization of the chick's basilar papilla. *Science, 210,* 655–656.

Maxon, A. B., & Hochberg, I. (1982). Development of psychoacoustic behavior: Sensitivity and discrimination. *Ear and Hearing, 3,* 301–308.

McNicol, D. (1972). *A primer of signal detection theory.* London: George Allen & Unwin.

Moffitt, A. R. (1973). Intensity discrimination and cardiac reaction in young infants. *Developmental Psychology, 8,* 357–359.

Moore, B. C. J. (1978). Psychophysical tuning curves measured in simultaneous and forward masking. *Journal of the Acoustical Society of America, 63,* 610–619.

Moore, B. C. J., & O'Loughlin, B. J. (1986). The use of nonsimultaneous measure of frequency selectivity and suppression. In B. C. J. Moore (Ed.), *Frequency selectivity in hearing.* London: Academic Press.

Moore, D. R. (1983). Development of inferior colliculus and binaural audition. In R. Romand (Ed.), *Development of auditory and vestibular systems.* New York: Academic Press.

Moore, D. R. (1985). Postnatal development of the mammalian central auditory system and the neural consequences of auditory deprivation. *Acta Otolaryngologica (Suppl.), 421,* 19–30.

Moore, D. R., & Irvine, D. R. F. (1979). The development of some peripheral and central auditory responses from the inner ear of the chick. *Brain Research, 229,* 15–23.

Moore, J. M., Thompson, G., & Thompson, M. (1975). Auditory localization of infants as a function of reinforcement conditions. *Journal of Speech and Hearing Disorders, 40,* 29–34.

Moore, J. M., & Wilson, W. (1978). Visual Reinforcement Audiometry (VRA) with infants. In S. E. Gerber & G. T. Mencher (Eds.), *Early diagnosis of hearing loss.* New York: Grune and Stratton.

Morrongiello, B. A., & Rocca, P. T. (1987). Infant's localization of sounds in the horizontal plane: Effects of auditory and visual cues. *Child Development, 58,* 918–927.

Morrongiello, B. A., & Trehub, S. E. (1987). Age-related changes in auditory temporal perception. *Journal of Experimental Child Psychology, 44,* 413–426.

Neff, W. D., & Hind, J. E. (1955). Auditory thresholds of the cat. *Journal of the Acoustical Society of America, 27,* 480–483.

Norton, S. J., Bargones, J. Y., & Rubel, E. W. (1991). Development of otoacoustic emissions in gerbil: Evidence for micromechanical changes underlying development of the place code. *Hearing Research, 51,* 73–91.

Nozza, R. J., & Wilson, W. R. (1984). Masked and unmasked pure-tone thresholds of infants and adults: Development of auditory frequency selectivity and sensitivity. *Journal of Speech and Hearing Research, 27,* 613–622.

Olsho, L. W. (1984a, April). *Preliminary results of an observer-based method for infant auditory testing.* Paper presented at the International Conference for Infant Studies, New York.

Olsho, L. W. (1984b). Infant frequency discrimination. *Infant Behavior and Development, 7,* 27–35.

Olsho, L. W. (1985). Infant auditory perception: Tonal masking. *Infant Behavior and Development, 8,* 371–384.

Olsho, L. W. (1986). Early development of human frequency resolution. In R. J. Ruben, T. R. Van De Water, & E. W. Rubel (Eds.), *The biology of change in otolaryngology.* Amsterdam: Elsevier.

Olsho, L. W., Bargones, J. Y., Marean, G. C., & Feeney, M. P. (1989, June). *On the nature of auditory masking in human infants.* Paper presented to the first annual meeting of the American Psychological Society, Alexandria, VA.

Olsho, L. W., Feeney, M. P., & Folsom, R. C. (1989, November). *Behavioral thresholds for tonepips in 3- and 6-month-old infants and adults.* Paper presented at the 118th meeting of the Acoustical Society of America, St. Louis.

Olsho, L. W., Harkins, S. W., & Lenhardt, M. L. (1985). Aging and the auditory system. In J. E. Birren & K. W. Schaie (Eds.), *Handbook of the psychology of aging* (2nd ed.). New York: Van Nostrand Reinhold.

Olsho, L. W., Koch, E. G., & Carter, E. A. (1988). Nonsensory factors in infant frequency discrimination. *Infant Behavior and Development, 11,* 205–222.

Olsho, L. W., Koch, E. G., Carter, E. A., Halpin, C. F., & Spetner, N. B. (1988). Pure-tone sensitivity of human infants. *Journal of the Acoustical Society of America, 84,* 1316–1324.

Olsho, L. W., Koch, E. G., & Halpin, C. F. (1987). Level and age effects in infant frequency discrimination. *Journal of the Acoustical Society of America, 82,* 454–464.

Olsho, L. W., Koch, E. G., Halpin, C. F., & Carter, E. A. (1987). An observer-based psychoacoustic procedure for use with young infants. *Developmental Psychology, 23,* 627–640.

Olsho, L. W., & Marean, G. C. (1989, February). *Forward masking in 3- and 6-month-old human infants.* Paper presented to the Midwinter Research Meeting of the Association for Research in Otolaryngology, St. Petersburg, FL.

Olsho, L. W., Schoon, C., Sakai, R., Turpin, R., & Sperduto, V. (1982a). Auditory frequency discrimination in infancy. *Developmental Psychology, 18,* 721–726.

Olsho, L. W., Schoon, C., Sakai, R., Turpin, R., & Sperduto, V. (1982b). Preliminary data on frequency discrimination in infancy. *Journal of the Acoustical Society of America, 71,* 509–511.

Patterson, R. D., Nimmo-Smith, I., Weber, D. L., & Milroy, R. (1982). The deterioration of hearing with age: Frequency selectivity, the critical ratio, the audiogram, and speech threshold. *Journal of the Acoustical Society of America, 72,* 1788–1803.

Pick, A. D. (1975, April). *The development of strategies of attention.* Paper presented to the Biennial Meeting of the Society for Research in Child Development, Denver.

Pickles, J. O. (1988). *An introduction to the physiology of hearing* (2nd ed.). San Diego: Academic Press.

Pujol, R. (1985). Morphology, synaptology and electrophysiology of the developing cochlea. *Acta Otolaryngologica (Suppl.), 421,* 5–9.

Pujol, R., & Hilding, D. A. (1973). Anatomy and physiology of the onset of auditory function. *Acta Otolaryngologica, 76,* 1–10.

Pujol, R., & Lavigne-Rebillard, M. (1985). Early stages of innervation and sensory cell differentiation in the human fetal organ of Corti. *Acta Otolaryngologica (Suppl.), 423,* 43–50.

Rebillard, G., & Rubel, E. W. (1981). Electrophysiological study of the maturation of auditory responses from the inner ear of the chick. *Brain Research, 229,* 15–23.

Rickard, L. (1988). *Auditory brainstem responses from infants and adults to extended high-frequency tone pips.* Unpublished master's thesis, University of Washington, Seattle.

Romand, R. (1983). *Development of auditory and vestibular systems.* New York: Academic Press.

Rubel, E. W. (1978). Ontogeny of structure and function in the vertebrate auditory system. In M. Jacobson (Ed.), *Handbook of sensory physiology: Vol. 9. Development of sensory systems.* New York: Springer-Verlag.

Rubel, E. W. (1984). Ontogeny of auditory function. *Annual Review of Physiology, 46,* 213–229.

Rubel, E. W. (1985). Auditory system development. In G. Gottlieb & N. A. Krasnegor (Eds.), *Measurement of audition and vision in the first year of postnatal life: A methodological overview.* Norwood, NJ: Ablex Publishing Corp.

Rubel, E. W, & Parks, T. N. (1986). Organization and development of the avian brain stem auditory system. In J. Brugge, I. Hafter, & M. Merzenich (Eds.), *Functions of the auditory system.* New York: John Wiley & Son.

Ryals, B. M., & Rubel, E. W. (1985). Ontogenetic changes in the position of hair cell loss after acoustic overstimulation in avian basilar papilla. *Hearing Research, 19,* 135–142.

Sanes, D. H., & Constantine-Paton, M. (1985). The development of stimulus following in the cochlear nerve and inferior colliculus of the mouse. *Developmental Brain Research, 22,* 255–267.

Sanes, D. H., Merickel, M., & Rubel, E. W. (1989). Evidence for an alteration of the tonotopic map in the gerbil cochlea during development. *Journal of Comparative Neurology, 279,* 436–444.

Sanes, D. H., & Rubel, E. W. (1988a). The development of stimulus coding in the auditory system. In A. F. Jahn & J. R. Santos-Sacchi (Eds.), *Physiology of the ear.* New York: Raven.

Sanes, D. H., & Rubel, E. W. (1988b). The ontogeny of inhibition and excitation in gerbil lateral superior olive. *Journal of Neuroscience, 8,* 682–700.

Saunders, J. C., Coles, R. B., & Gates, G. R. (1973). The development of auditory evoked responses in the cochlea and cochlear nuclei of the chick. *Brain Research, 63,* 59–74.

Saunders, J. C., Doglin, K. G., & Lowry, L. D. (1980). The maturation of frequency selectivity in C57BL/6J mice studied with auditory evoked response tuning curves. *Brain Research, 187,* 69–79.

Saunders, J. C., Kaltenbach, J. A., & Relkin, E. M. (1983). The structural and functional development of the outer and middle ear. In R. Romand (Ed.), *Development of auditory and vestibular systems.* New York: Academic Press.

Schecter, M. A., Fausti, S. A., Rappaport, B. Z., & Frey, R. H. (1986). Age categorization of high-frequency auditory threshold data. *Journal of the Acoustical Society of America, 79,* 767–771.

Schneider, B. A., Morrongiello, B. A., & Trehub, S. E. (1990). Size of critical band in infants, children, and adults. *Journal of Experimental Psychology: Human Perception and Performance, 16,* 642–652.

Schneider, B. A., & Trehub, S. E. (1985). Infant auditory psychophysics: An overview. In G. Gottlieb & N. A. Krasnegor (Eds.), *Measurement of audition and vision in the first year of postnatal life: A methodological overview.* Norwood, NJ: Ablex Publishing Corp.

Schneider, B. A., Trehub, S. E., & Bull, D. (1980). High-frequency sensitivity in infants. *Science, 207,* 1003–1004.

Schneider, B. A., Trehub, S. E., Morrongiello, B. A., & Thorpe, L. A. (1986). Auditory sensitivity in preschool children. *Journal of the Acoustical Society of America, 79,* 447–452.

Schneider, B. A., Trehub, S. E., Morrongiello, B. A., & Thorpe, L. A. (1989). Developmental changes in masked thresholds. *Journal of the Acoustical Society of America, 86,* 1733–1742.

Schnerson, A., & Willott, J. F. (1979). Development of inferior colliculus response in C57BL/6J mouse pups. *Experimental Brain Research, 37,* 373–385.

Schulman-Galambos, C., & Galambos, R. (1979). Brainstem auditory evoked responses in newborn hearing screening. *Archives of Otolaryngology, 105,* 86–90.

Sinnott, J. M., & Aslin, R. N. (1985). Frequency and intensity discrimination in human infants and adults. *Journal of the Acoustical Society of America, 78,* 1986–1992.

Sinnott, J. M., Pisoni, D. B., & Aslin, R. N. (1983). A comparison of pure tone auditory thresholds in human infants and adults. *Infant Behavior and Development, 6,* 3–17.

Spetner, N. B., & Olsho, L. W. (1990). Auditory frequency resolution in human infancy. *Child Development, 61,* 632–652.

Stockard, J. J., & Rossiter, V. S. (1977). Clinical and pathologic correlates of brainstem auditory response abnormalities. *Neurology, 27,* 316–325.

Stratton, P. M. (1970). The use of heart rate for the study of habituation in the neonate. *Psychophysiology, 7,* 44–56.

Strickland, E. A., Burns, E. M., & Tubis, A. (1985). Incidence of spontaneous otoacoustic emissions in children and infants. *Journal of the Acoustical Society of America, 78,* 931–935.

Suzuki, T., & Ogiba, Y. (1961). Conditioned orientation reflex audiometry. *Archives Otolaryngologica, 74,* 192–198.

144 Werner and Bargones

Teller, D. Y., Morse, R., Borton, R., & Regal, D. (1974). Visual acuity for vertical and diagonal gratings in human infants. *Vision Research, 14,* 1433–1439.

Thorpe, L. A., & Schneider, B. A. (1987, April). *Temporal integration in infant audition.* Paper presented to the Biennial Meeting of the Society for Research in Child Development, Baltimore.

Tonndorf, J., & Kurman, B. (1984). High frequency audiometry. *Annals of Otorhinolaryngology, 93,* 576–582.

Trehub, S. E., Bull, D., & Schneider, B. A. (1981). Infants' detection of speech in noise. *Journal of Speech and Hearing Research, 24,* 202–206.

Trehub, S. E., Schneider, B. A., & Endman, M. (1980). Developmental changes in infants' sensitivity to octave-band noises. *Journal of Experimental Child Psychology, 29,* 283–293.

Trehub, S. E., Schneider, B. A., Morrongiello, B. A., & Thorpe, L. A. (1988). Auditory sensitivity in school-age children. *Journal of Experimental Child Psychology, 46,* 273–285.

Trehub, S. E., Schneider, B. A., Morrongiello, B. A., & Thorpe, L. A. (1989). Developmental changes in high-frequency sensitivity. *Audiology, 28,* 241–249.

Turkewitz, G., Birch, H. G., & Cooper, K. K. (1972). Responsiveness to simple and complex auditory stimuli in the human newborn. *Developmental Psychobiology, 5,* 7–19.

Watson, C. S. (1987). Uncertainty, informational masking, and the capacity of immediate auditory memory. In W. A. Yost & C. S. Watson (Eds.), *Auditory processing of complex sounds.* Hillsdale, NJ: Erlbaum.

Watson, C. S., Franks, J. R., & Hood, D. C. (1972). Detection of tones in the absence of external masking noise. I. Effects of signal intensity and signal frequency. *Journal of the Acoustical Society of America, 52,* 633–643.

Watson, C. S., & Gengel, R. W. (1969). Signal duration and signal frequency in relation to auditory sensitivity. *Journal of the Acoustical Society of America, 46,* 989–997.

Weir, C. (1979). Auditory frequency sensitivity of human newborns: Some data with improved acoustic and behavioral controls. *Perception & Psychophysics, 26,* 287–294.

Werner, L. A., & Bargones, J. Y. (1991). Sources of auditory masking in infants: Distraction effects. *Perception & Psychophysics, 50,* 405–412.

Werner, L. A., & Feeney, M. P. (1989). *Unreinforced responses to low-intensity tones by young infants.* Unpublished manuscript, Department of Otolaryngology, RL-30, University of Washington.

Werner, L. A., & Feeney, M. P. (1990, April). *Pure-tone sensitivity of 2- to 4-week-old infants assessed with auditory reinforcement.* Paper presented to the International Conference for Infant Studies, Montreal.

Werner, L. A., & Gillenwater, J. M. (1990). Pure-tone sensitivity of 2- to 5-week-old infants. *Infant Behavior and Development, 13,* 355–375.

Werner, L. A., Marean, G. C., Halpin, C. F., Spetner, N. B., & Gillenwater, J. M. (in press). Infant auditory temporal acuity: Gap detection. *Child Development.*

Werner, L. A., & Marean, G. C. (1991). Methods for estimating infant thresholds. *Journal of the Acoustical Society of America, 90,* 1867–1875.

Werner, L. A., Rickard, L. K., & Folsom, R. C. (1990, November). *Correlation between frequency-specific ABR and behavioral thresholds in three-month-old infants.* Paper presented to the 120th meeting of the Acoustical Society of America, San Diego.

Whitehead, M. C. (1986). Development of the cochlea. In R. A. Altschuler, D. W. Hoffman, & R. P. Bobbin (Eds.), *Neurobiology of hearing: The cochlea.* New York: Raven Press.

Wier, C. C., Jesteadt, W., & Green, D. M. (1977). Frequency discrimination as a function of frequency and sensation level. *Journal of the Acoustical Society of America, 61,* 178–184.

Wightman, F., Allen, P., Dolan, T., Kistler, D., & Jamieson, D. (1989). Temporal resolution in preschool children. *Child Development, 60,* 611–624.

Wilson, W. R., & Gerber, S. E. (1983). Auditory behavior in the neonatal period. In S. E. Gerber & G. T. Mencher (Eds.), *The development of auditory behavior.* New York: Grune & Stratton.

Wormith, S. J., Moffitt, A. R., & Pankhurst, D. B. (1975). Frequency discrimination by young infants. *Child Development, 46,* 272–275.

Yancey, C., & Dallos, P. (1985). Ontogenetic changes in the cochlear characteristic frequency at a basal turn location as reflected in the summating potential. *Hearing Research, 18,* 189–195.

Yates, G. K. (1986). Frequency selectivity in the auditory periphery. In B. C. J. Moore (Ed.), *Frequency selectivity in hearing.* London: Academic Press.

Yoneshige, Y., & Elliott, L. L. (1981). Pure-tone sensitivity and ear canal pressure at threshold in children and adults. *Journal of the Acoustical Society of America, 70,* 1272–1276.

Zurek, P. (1981). Spontaneous narrow-band acoustic signals emitted by human ears. *Journal of the Acoustical Society of America, 69,* 514–523.

Zwicker, E., & Lumer, G. (1986). Evaluating traveling wave characteristics in man by an active nonlinear preprocessing model. In J. B. Allen, J. L. Hall, A. Hubbard, S. T. Neely, & A. Tubis (Eds.), *Peripheral auditory mechanisms.* New York: Springer.

Zwislocki, J. (1960). Theory of temporal auditory summation. *Journal of the Acoustical Society of America, 32,* 1046–1060.

Zwislocki, J., Maire, F., Feldman, A. S., & Rubin, H. (1958). On the effect of practice and motivation on the threshold of audibility. *Journal of the Acoustical Society of America, 30,* 254–262.

# THE WORLD OF THE MOVING INFANT: PERCEPTION OF MOTION, STABILITY, AND SPACE*

*Philip J. Kellman*

SWARTHMORE COLLEGE

*Claes von Hofsten*

UMEA UNIVERSITET

I. INTRODUCTION ........................................... 148
II. DEVELOPMENT OF SENSITIVITY TO OPTICAL MOTION ....... 149
   A. Attention to Motion ..................................... 149
   B. Sensitivity to Motion ................................... 149
   C. Thresholds vs. Preferences .............................. 151
III. INFORMATION FOR MOTION AND STABILITY DURING
   OBSERVER MOTION ....................................... 152
   A. Object Motion and Observer Motion ....................... 152
   B. Analyses of Optic Flow ................................. 154
      1. Rigidity vs. nonrigidity .............................. 154
      2. Specification of self-motion .......................... 155
      3. Limitations of optic flow information ................. 155
IV. OPTICAL CHANGE, MOTION, AND DISTANCE ............... 156

* Portions of this work were presented at meetings of the Society for Research in Child Development, the International Conference on Event Perception and Action, and the International Conference on Infant Studies between 1987 and 1990.

We gratefully acknowledge support from National Science Foundation Research Grants 85-19851 and 89-13707 and several Swarthmore College Faculty Research Grants to PJK, and funding from the Swedish Research Council for Research in the Humanities and Social Sciences to CVH.

We thank Kirsten Condry, Erin Conner, John Monterosso, Louise Ronnqvist, Birgit Rosblad, Gretchen VandeWalle, and Peter Vishton for able assistance in the experiments, and Richard Aslin, Martin Banks, Carl Granrud, Sandra Shea, and an anonymous reviewer for helpful discussions. We express special gratitude to Donald R. Reynolds for his expertise, and patience in constructing the object–observer motion apparatus.

Requests for reprints should be addressed to Philip J. Kellman, Department of Psychology, Swarthmore College, Swarthmore, PA 19081.

V. THE DEVELOPMENT OF MOTION PERCEPTION AND POSITION
   CONSTANCY DURING OBSERVER MOTION ................. 158
   A. The Kellman, Gleitman, and Spelke (1987) Experiment .......... 159
   B. The Object–Observer Motion Paradigm ....................... 163
VI. DEVELOPMENT OF DEPTH PERCEPTION FROM MOTION ...... 177
VII. CONCLUSION ............................................. 181
VIII. REFERENCES ............................................. 182

# I. INTRODUCTION

When William James characterized the world of the newborn as a "blooming, buzzing confusion," one source of confusion he had in mind involved the relative motions of observers and objects. In the "primitive form of perception" available to us as neonates, he believed that:

> Any relative motion of object and retina both makes the object seem to move, and makes us feel ourselves in motion. (Vol. 2, p. 173)

Although his assessment may have shortcomings, James calls attention to a fundamental problem. Understanding how observers, while moving their eyes, heads, and bodies, can accurately perceive the motion and stability of different parts of the environment is a basic challenge for research in perceptual development. Without ways of ascertaining motion and stability, one's experience of the world would chaotically shift and slide, if not bloom and buzz. Obtaining a coherent representation of oneself and one's environment would hardly be possible.

This chapter addresses the development of visual perception of motion and stability by moving observers. How do infants obtain a representation of a stable world, while also detecting the motions of moving objects (and self-motion) in that world? Our discussion will begin with a review of what is known about motion detection in infancy. We then offer some analysis of the information available to moving observers for perceiving motion and stability, and some discussion of adult abilities. Then, we describe recent research on these problems with 8–16-week-old infants, which has begun to reveal early perceptual capacities as well as their limits. In examining both the general problem of motion and stability perception and the performance of infant perceivers, it will become obvious that perception of motion and stability is linked with other perceptual abilities, such as perception of distance. Thus, one of the insights of to be gained from work in this area is that perception of motion, stability, and distance are interdependent, and studies of each may help illuminate the others.

## II. DEVELOPMENT OF SENSITIVITY TO OPTICAL MOTION

### A. Attention to Motion

Visual motion is a powerful stimulus for young infants. Indeed, neonates are commonly known to move their eyes toward moving stimuli and track them with a combination of head and eye movements (Haith, 1983; Hofsten, 1982; Kremenitzer, Vaughan, Kurtzberg, & Dowling, 1979; Tauber & Koffler, 1966; Tronick & Clanton, 1971; White, Castle, & Held, 1964). Hofsten (1982) also found that slow and irregular motion of an object was a an effective stimulus in eliciting directed reaching movements in neonates.

Young infants seem to prefer looking at motion to most other stimuli. In an early experiment, Fantz and Nevis (1967) presented infants with a red dot on a rotating yellow disc and found that 2–6-week-old infants preferred that stimulus to a complex three-dimensional form. The attractiveness of moving visual stimuli has been utilized in measuring various aspects of early visual perception. Atkinson, Braddick, and Moar (1977) used drifting gratings in estimating visual acuity and contrast sensitivity in 1- and 3-month-olds. Shimojo, Birch, Gwiazda, and Held (1984) used a moving vernier offset in estimating vernier acuity in infants 2 to 9 months of age. Fox, Aslin, Shea, and Dumais (1980) used a moving binocular offset to study the emergence of binocular stereopsis in infants.

### B. Sensitivity to Motion

Few empirical studies have been devoted to the study of the basic sensitivity to visual motion in early development. Volkmann and Dobson (1976) reported the 1-, 2-, and 3-month-olds prefer to fixate a checkerboard pattern undergoing horizontal oscillatory motion over an identical but stationary pattern. The moving stimulus oscillated up to a peak of 2 cycles/sec across a fixed spatial distance of 4.8 cm. The patterns were viewed at a distance of 35 cm. Preferences were stronger for more rapid motions at all three ages studied. However, even at the second slowest speed of the pattern (about 2 deg/sec) preference for the moving stimulus was apparent also in the 1-month-olds, although it did not quite reach 75%.

Kaufmann, Stucki, and Kaufmann-Hayoz (1985) used a rotary motion display in determining the velocity interval, such as both the upper and the lower limits, within which reliable visual preference for motion was elicited in 1- to 3-month-olds. The slower angular velocities used ranged from 0.46 to 2.06 deg/sec. They found a clear developmental improvement in motion thresholds from 1 to 3 months of age (1.4 deg/sec and 0.93 deg/sec respectively).

Neither Kaufmann, Stucki, and Kaufmann-Hayoz (1985) nor Volkmann and

Dobson (1976) asked critical questions about the mechanisms underlying motion preference. There can at least be two reasons for infants to attend to a motion display apart from true sensitivity to smooth motion. First, the infant might be responding to positional changes without perceiving motion. Second, the visual system of the infant could be sensitive to local changes in luminance. As the checkerboard pattern of Volkmann and Dobson (1976) moved, the amount of light falling on a specific point on the retina will change from one moment to the next. This flickering might constitute the critical parameter controlling infant gaze. Thus, we need to distinguish between motion-sensitive mechanisms, position-sensitive mechanisms, and flicker-sensitive mechanisms.

Three recent studies (Freedland & Dannemiller, 1987; Dannemiller & Freedland, 1989; Aslin & Shea, 1989) provide evidence on the question of mechanisms underlying infant motion thresholds. Freedland and Dannemiller (1987) used a checkerboard pattern oscillating back and forth between two vertically separated positions. They parametrically varied both the spatial displacement and the temporal frequency and found that 20-week-olds' preference for the oscillating pattern was influenced independently by both these factors. However, apparent velocity did not affect preference for motion in any systematic way. This does not imply that young infants are unable to differentiate velocity of visual motion. When continuous and unidirectional motion of a single bar was used instead of stepwide oscillation (Dannemiller & Freedland, 1989), thresholds were found to be exclusively determined by velocity in 16- to 20-week-olds. Amount of displacement did not systematically affect the results. The minimum velocities eliciting significant preferences for motion were 5.08 deg/sec and 2.32 deg/sec at 16 and 20 weeks of age, respectively. Unfortunately, the youngest age group (8-week-olds) did not show systematic preference for motion at any of the velocities tested.

Aslin and Shea (1989) tested whether the motion sensitivity of infants 6 and 12 weeks of age could be explained in terms of a flicker-sensitive mechanism instead of a velocity-sensitive mechanism. Vertically moving gratings were used. Velocity was varied independently of local change in luminance per unit time (flicker) through appropriate combinations of spatial frequency and velocity. For instance, the local flicker will stay constant if the spatial frequency is halved when velocity is doubled. The results provide strong evidence that young infants' preference for moving stripes are based on the velocity rather than flicker. Using 75% correct as the criterion for estimating a velocity threshold, the 6-week-olds' thresholds were approximately 10 deg/sec and the 12-week-olds' thresholds were approximately 4 deg/sec.

Dannemiller and Freedland (1991) have recently made an attempt to estimate the differential velocity threshold in 20-week-old infants. Two horizontal bars, placed adjacent to each other and moving up and down with different velocities, were used as stimuli. The assumption was that infants would prefer to look at the faster of two discriminable moving stimuli. Starting position and magnitude of motion was varied randomly to ensure that discrimination was based on speed rather than frequency of oscillation. They found that 2.0 deg/sec but not 2.5 deg/sec was discriminated from 3.3 deg/sec.

## C. Thresholds vs. Preferences

The absolute and differential velocity thresholds reported above seem rather high. Are they really measuring the processing limits of the young infant's visual system for linear motion? If the results of the Dannemiller and Freedland (1989) and Aslin and Shea (1989) reflect true motion detection ability, a 3-month-old infant would not even be able to detect an object moving at 8 cm/sec at an observation distance of 1 meter (corresponding to a visual motion of 5 deg/sec). If the child is moving the head sideways with a velocity of 4 cm/sec, the resulting motion parallax would not discriminate between an object 50 cm away and one 25 cm away.

One possibility is that the threshold for preferential looking at linearly moving bars is higher than the motion detection threshold itself. The results of Kaufmann et al. (1985) support such a suggestion. It can be argued, of course, that the low threshold found by this group (0.93 deg/sec in 3-month-olds) is only valid for circular motion but not for linear motion. However, when using indicators of perceived motion other than preferential looking, Kellman, Hofsten, and Soares (1987) also found higher sensitivity for linear motion. They habituated 14 16-week-olds to a display consisting of three points moving alternately toward and away from a central point (not seen) in a dark room. The dots moved with a velocity of 1.48 deg/sec. In adults, this display evoked perceived motion in depth. All of the 14 infants tested showed evidence of having perceived the motion in depth. It could be argued, however, that the specific motion studied, concurrent motion evoking perceived motion in depth, recruited special motion detection mechanisms in the visual system not triggered by linear motion (Regan & Beverley, 1978).

Another important consideration when evaluating motion sensitivity in young infants is the context of the motion. In all the studies reported above, including Kaufmann et al. (1985) and Kellman et al. (1987), motion occurred against a homogeneous background. In an ordinary environment objects nearly always move relative to a textured background, creating accretion and deletion of background texture elements along the edges of the moving object. In such a situation, motion sensitivity might be far greater than reported above. For adults, sensitivity to such object-relative motion is better than to purely subject-relative motion by about a factor of 10 (Kaufman, 1974).

## III. INFORMATION FOR MOTION AND STABILITY DURING OBSERVER MOTION

### A. Object Motion and Observer Motion

Studies of basic motion sensitivity seek the limits of sensory capacities for registering optical change. Ecologically, however, not all optical changes are created equal. Both the optical changes arising from objects in motion and those produced by self-motion have functional importance but of different sorts. Moving objects might be tracked, intercepted, or avoided. Optic flow produced by self-motion, on the other hand, controls posture and locomotion (Lee & Aronson, 1974; Bertenthal, Dunn, & Bai, 1986) and carries information about spatial relationships in the stationary environment.

Are these distinctions important to the very young perceiver? Is there some means by which infants can distinguish the motions of objects from optical changes resulting from their own, passive or active, motion? To answer this question, we must first consider what information is available to a moving observer for distinguishing optical changes due to moving and stationary objects.

In certain respects, the information for motion of an object and motion of the observer are equivalent. Consider the optical change given when an observer translates (i.e., moves linearly) perpendicular to the line of sight. Assuming for this example that the observer's eyes do not move, the projected position of the viewed object will change by a certain visual angle (see Figure 1). This same angular change can be given if the observer is stationary and the object moves. The direction of motion in the object motion case must be opposite to that in the observer motion case. (Students of special relativity will notice that there is in fact no absolute sense in which the motion can be ascribed to the object or observer; whether the observer or the object or both are said to be moving depends on the choice of a reference frame.)

The equivalent optical consequences of object and observer motion were discussed by Helmholtz (1885/1925). He argued that the two cases cannot be distinguished without learning, and he suggested a principle by which such learning might occur. Observer motions, at least those which are actively initiated, are in general reversible, while object motions are not. Thus, an infant perceiver might cause an object's projection to slide across the retina by making a head movement to one side, and return it to the original position by making the reverse head movement. Object motions, in contrast, cannot ordinarily be undone in this manner. This account depends on information being available to an infant about self-initiated action (cf. Piaget, 1954), and it would not seem to generalize easily to passive (e.g., vehicular, motion).

The apparent equivalence of object and observer motion in the simple case we have been discussing breaks down when context is considered. Gibson (1966, 1979) argued forcefully that the available information differs in cases of object and observer motion. When an observer moves, much or all of the optic array

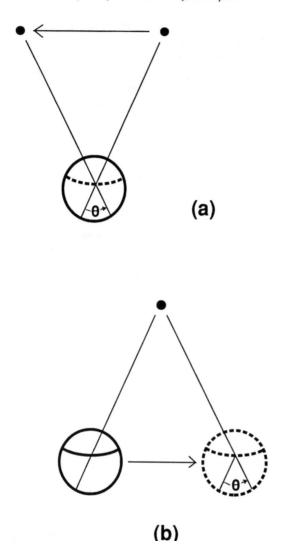

**(a)**

**(b)**

Fig. 1. *A given optical displacement, here the angular change* Θ, *can be given by a) motion of an object or b) an equal observer motion in the opposite direction. (See text.)*

changes. In fact, the nature of the optic flow depends on the type of observer motion. (Some specific cases are discussed below.) When a stationary observer views a mostly stationary environment in which one object moves, the disturbance in the optic array is confined to a local region.

If available optical information distinguishes object and observer motion, then perceivers might be able to utilize such information without learning about reversible motions or even necessarily having nonvisual information about their own active movements. In fact, the optic flow itself may inform the observer about her own movements, a possibility termed *visual kinesthesis* by Gibson.

From a ecological standpoint, the "design" of perceptual systems to discriminate observer motion from object motion would seem to be of high adaptive significance. Thus, the possibility of unlearned capabilities to perceive motion and stability is compatible with this point of view. We discuss research relevant to this issue below, following a more detailed consideration of available information that might be useful in perceiving motion and stability.

## B. Analyses of Optic Flow

What information is available to specify object and observer motion, and what characteristics of motion can be specified? These questions have been the subjects of a great deal of theoretical analysis and empirical research in the past two decades.

## 1. Rigidity vs. Nonrigidity

A number of analyses have considered the optic flow given to an observer moving on a linear path (Lee, 1974; Nakayama & Loomis, 1974) or more general paths (Longuett-Higgins & Prazdny, 1980). Such analysis indicate that optical changes could in principle specify whether the environment is at rest or whether it contains some moving objects or surface areas. Lee (1974) gives an example of an invariant of optic flow that can indicate whether the environment is entirely rigid (at rest) or whether it contains moving objects or deformations. According to Lee's Rigidity Property III:

> Along any flow line on the optic projection surface, the faster-moving optic elements temporarily "occlude" those they overtake. (p. 257)

To understand this idea, consider an example. Suppose one walks by a house with a car parked in front. If all objects are stationary, the retinal displacements of all projected elements will be opposite to the observer's direction of motion. Furthermore, their optical velocity will decrease monotonically as a function of distance from the observer. Thus, the car will have a faster optical velocity than the house. Because the car is in front of the house, and opaque, it will also progressively *occlude* parts of the house. Rigidity Property III states this fact. Now, suppose the car is in fact moving in the same direction as the moving observer. For simplicity, suppose also that its velocity is just enough to nullify any optical change from the observer's position. (That is, it keeps pace so as to remain in a constant visual direction.) In this case, the car's optical velocity is zero and less than that of the house. The fact that the slower optical elements of the car will nonetheless occlude the faster elements of the house over time constitutes a violation of Rigidity Property III. From this violation, one knows, at a minimum, that the environment is nonrigid; that is, something is moving.

Another type of information is available for detecting motion stability when objects rest on a ground surface. When an object moves along a surface, its optical elements will "shear" relative to adjacent elements projected from the ground surface. In contrast, when only the observer moves, adjacent object and ground points will remain adjacent. This latter relationship might be the more informative one, since shearing occurs between stationary objects at differing depths and even between objects and ground surfaces when the object does not rest on the ground. Thus, shear alone does not necessarily indicate object motion. The *absence* of shear during observer motion, on the other hand, is relatively specific to the case of stationary objects resting on, or attached to, a surface (ordinarily the ground surface).

## 2. Specification of Self-Motion

Optic flow patterns given to a moving observer in a stationary environment contain information about the path of the observer's motion, i.e., trajectory and heading, and there is evidence that perceivers readily use such information (Banks, Crowell, & Royden, in preparation; Lee, 1974; Warren, 1976; for a review see Andersen, 1986).

Intuitively, the simplest mappings between optic flow and particular events are those in which the entire flow field undergoes the same transformation. A horizontal scanning motion of the eye is produced by a rotation of the eye in its orbit. Roughly speaking, the optical consequences are that the same motion vector is present at every point in the field. Conversely, when every point in the field undergoes an identical optical displacement, it is reasonably good information for eye rotation, since this kind of flow field would virtually never occur from any other circumstance (outside perception laboratories). Another example is rotation of the observer around the line of sight, as when an aerobatic pilot executes a barrel roll. Every point in the flow field has an identical angular velocity. Again, the mapping works fairly well in the reverse direction. A pilot who sees this kind of flow pattern perceives herself and her craft to be rotating; it is hard to imagine any other event in ordinary environments that would present this kind of flow field.

These types of optical changes are relatively specific to particular observer movement events. Thus, the detection of the respective flow patterns can specify the event. Algorithms of modest complexity have been proposed that could carry out detection of such optical changes (Nakayama & Loomis, 1974; Koenderink, 1986; Banks, Crowell, & Royden, in preparation).

## 3. Limitations of Optic Flow Information

Despite the richness of the information available in optic flow, it has limitations in specifying concurrently the motion of the observer and parts of the environment. Part of the difficulty involves what has been called the *inverse-mapping problem*. Mathematical analyses indicate the optical consequences of various types of observer motion through certain types of environments, e.g., stationary ones. The perceptual problem, however, is always the reverse, namely, to recover from optic flow the spatial layout and the motions of observers and objects. Although we have given some examples of more or less invariant relations between optical changes and types of observer motion, the general problem of decomposing flow unambiguously into components due to observer motion and object motion is more complex. Moreover, it can be proven that certain kinds of ambiguities cannot be resolved from flow information alone (Banks, Crowell, & Royden, in preparation).

A specific limitation can be seen in the principle we considered above, Lee's (1974) Rigidity Property III. The limitation arises from the fact that ordinary environments are not necessarily densely layered in depth. Within certain limits, an object may move without producing a violation of the principle. Continuing the example given above, if there is some distance between the car and the house, the car could move parallel to the observer up to some velocity without its optical elements being slower than those of the house. Faster optical elements (given by the car) would then occlude slower ones (given by the house), yet the environment would not be rigid (because the car is moving). Similarly, if there were no optical elements from other objects between the observer and the car, the car could move in the direction opposite to that of the observer without providing any violation of Rigidity Property III.

The limitations on optic flow extend beyond the existence of normal environments in which rigidity may be inadequately specified. Determining rigidity/ nonrigidity is a relatively small part of what is needed for effective perception and action. Determination of speed, trajectory, size, etc., are important as well, and it is clear that optic flow alone does not suffice to specify these other aspects of moving objects. The problems posed for perception by moving observers, as well as their solution, depend on relations between optical change, observer motion, object motion and distance, to which we now turn.

## IV.  OPTICAL CHANGE, MOTION, AND DISTANCE

Ambiguities in optic flow arise because the optical changes for a given object are the result of the observer's motion, the object's motion, and the relative positions of the object and observer. Especially important is the effect of object distance from the observer. When an observer moves through space on a linear path, the extent of optical displacement associated with stationary points in the environment is a decreasing function of distance. Consider an observer looking out the side window of a car moving at a constant velocity. Very distant objects remain relatively fixed in the field of view, while close-by telephone poles have high optical velocities. In a stationary environment, these distance-dependent changes provide the depth information known as *motion parallax* or *motion perspective*.[1] Assuming all optical changes are the result of the observer's movement, the extent (or velocity) of displacement will be a reliable indicator of relative depth.

When objects as well as observers move, however, the situation is more complex. The optical changes given to the observer are the combined result of the object motion and the observer's. A given optical change may thus be the result of various combinations of object and observer movement. Optical changes thus cannot ordinarily specify both the position and the motion characteristics of objects.

This geometry of distance-dependent motions and their perceptual consequences has been studied by Gogel (1980, 1982). In his view, "perceived distance always is an essential component in the perception of motion" (1980, p. 155). Although this position may be a bit extreme, it is easily illustrated in some cases. Consider the observer motion in Figure 2, a lateral translation perpendicular to the line of sight. For an object at rest at point 1, the angular change is given

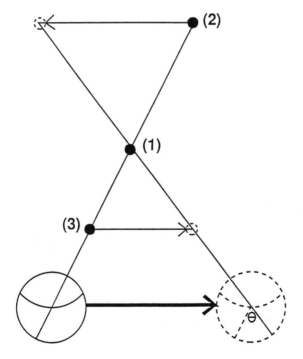

*Fig. 2. The geometry of object and observer motions on parallel paths. (See text.)*

---

[1] While the traditional notion of *motion parallax* was defined as differential optical change of two points at different depths, Gibson argued that gradients of change, comprised of many more elements, might function as information. An experiment by Gibson, Gibson, Smith, and Flock (1959) provided some evidence consistent with this view.

by $\Theta$. However, this same optical change can be given by a moving object which starts at point 3 and moves to along a path parallel to the observer. Likewise, an object starting at point 2 and moving in a direction opposite that of the observer gives identical optic flow.

There is in fact a family of possibilities for the position in space and the motion characteristics of an object giving a particular optical change. Gogel terms the point at which the object is at rest the *pivot distance*. Objects further from the observer than the pivot point must move opposite in direction from the observer's motion, while those nearer must move in the same direction. The consequence of this geometry is that a given optical change registered at the eye of a moving observer is ambiguous. It could be the result of a stationary object at one position, or a moving object further away, or an oppositely moving object closer than the pivot distance. To determine whether an object is actually moving or stationary, information about the object's distance may be required. There is experimental evidence that motion perception does in fact depend on perceived distance (Gogel, 1980; Gogel & Tietz, 1974).

In these experiments with adults, the observer's lateral back-and-forth head motion was coupled to movements of a target object. The geometry of this situation demands that, if the object is stationary, it must be at the pivot distance from the observer. An object closer to the observer should appear to move opposite to the observer's movement, and an object further than the pivot distance should appear to move in the same direction as the observer. Perceptually, if these relations are utilized, one might expect that perceived motion should depend on perceived distance. Experiments assessing subjects perceived motion and distance yield results confirming this expectation (Gogel, 1980, 1982). Moreover, when illusory distance information was provided, for example, by altering convergence with wedge prisms, illusions of motion perception were produced. When subjects were instructed to adjust the optical change of the target so that it appeared motionless, they selected values at which the object was actually in motion. Likewise, a stationary target appeared to move contingent on the observer's movement, when illusory distance information is given (Gogel & Tietz, 1974).

## V. THE DEVELOPMENT OF MOTION PERCEPTION AND POSITION CONSTANCY DURING OBSERVER MOTION

How do these relations between optical change, distance information, and perceived motion apply in early perception? More generally, what abilities do moving observers have early in development to perceive moving and stationary objects? The development of perception of motion and stability has not been the subject of experimental investigation until recently.

## A. The Kellman, Gleitman, and Spelke (1987) Experiment

Kellman, Gleitman, and Spelke (1987) explored the connections of these abilities to object perception. Earlier work indicated that infants at 16 weeks of age detected the unity of a partly occluded object when its visible parts shared a common translatory motion (Kellman & Spelke, 1983; Kellman, Spelke, & Short, 1986). The method in these studies involved habituation of visual attention to an occlusion display (a rod whose center was hidden by a rectangular block in front). After habituation, generalization of habituation was tested by presenting an unoccluded complete rod in one test display and two pieces separated by a gap in the other. Dishabituation to the "broken" display, that is, the display with the gap, but not to the complete display, was taken to indicate that the original occluded display had been perceived as containing a unitary object behind the occluder.

In these studies, specific types of motion of the occluded object were crucial for obtaining the effect. Lateral, vertical, and depth translations were all effective; rotation in the frontal plane was not, however. Infants in the first half year did not respond as if they perceived unity in displays with stationary objects, even when the visible parts were related by aligned edges or had other relations that would support unity perception in adults. (For a discussion of the bases of visual interpolation in adult perception, see Kellman & Shipley, 1991.) It was also important for the occluded object alone to move. When only the occluding object moved, or when the occluding object and the partly occluded rod moved together, infants did not dishabituate more to the broken test display.

Effective information for an object's unity, then, is given by common motion of its visible parts, separate from its occluder. Kellman et al., (1987) pointed out, however, that all of these results are consistent with two interpretations of the role of motion. One possibility is that relationships in perceived motion constitute the information for object unity. The other possibility is that relationships in *optical* displacements specify unity, regardless of whether these are produced by object motion or motion of the observer. For example, when an observer moves perpendicular to the line of sight, the visible parts of a stationary partly occluded object may share a common optical change, different from the optical changes of other objects in the scene (if other objects are at differing distances from the observer). Is a unique optical displacement sufficient to specify unity of an occluded object?

The question of whether both object-generated and observer-generated optical changes can specify object unity is especially intriguing because it raises another, more fundamental question: Can infant perceivers tell the difference between optical changes given by their own and by objects' motion?

Kellman et al. (1987) attempted to address these questions together. There were two groups in their experiment, diagrammed in Figure 3. Infants were moved back and forth in a moving infant chair while viewing arrays of objects. In both groups, infants were habituated to a partly occluded rod, whose center

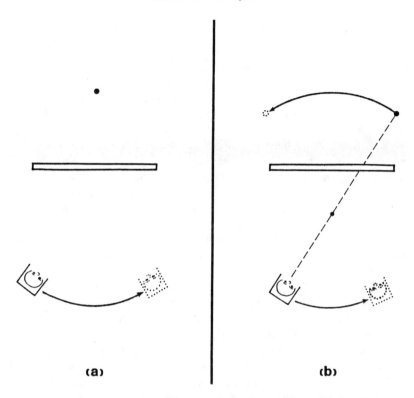

(a)                                              (b)

Fig. 3.    Habituation and test displays in the Kellman, Gleitman, and Spelke (1987) experiment. The
upper portion of the figure depicts the partly occluded rod shown during habituation; the lower
portion depicts the complete and broken rod test displays shown on alternate trials after habituation.
(Copyright 1987 by the American Psychological Association. Reprinted by permission.)

was hidden by a nearer rectangular object. After habituation, infants were tested
for generalization/dishabituation to alternating presentations of an unoccluded
complete rod and an unoccluded display with two separated rod pieces, as in
earlier studies (Kellman & Spelke, 1983; Kellman et al., 1986). (See Figure 4.)

The difference between groups involved the motion characteristics of the
rods. In the observer motion group, the rod displays were stationary throughout
the entire experiment (see Figure 3a). However, the occluding block, the rod,
and the background were separated in depth, so that, during the observer's
motion, the visible parts of the rod underwent a unique optical displacement. The
differences in optical displacement between the rod and the occluder, and also
between the rod and the background, were designed to be the same as in earlier
studies when stationary observers viewed a moving rod. Thus, if perceived
object unity depends on differences between the optical displacement of the
object's visible parts and other visible surfaces, unity should be perceived in this
case. If, however, perceived unity depends on real motion of the occluded object

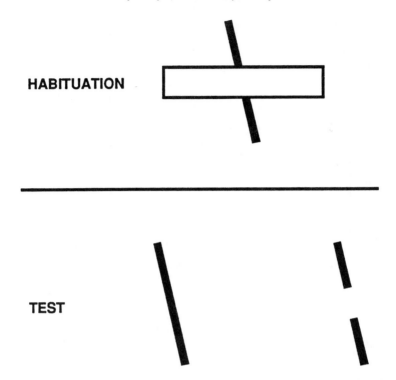

HABITUATION

TEST

Fig. 4. *Conditions in the Kellman, Gleitman, and Spelke (1987) experiment. a) Observer movement condition. b) Conjoint movement condition. (Top views of the object and observer positions at one extreme of movement are shown, with positions at the other extreme shown by dotted figures.) (Copyright 1987 by the American Psychological Association. Reprinted by permission.)*

in space, and infants can accurately perceive the object as stationary, unity would not be perceived.

The other group (conjoint motion group) was designed to be the logical converse of the first, having real motion of the occluded object in space, but no subject-relative movement. This was achieved by linking the moving infant chair and the partly occluded rod mechanically (out of sight beneath the chair and display; see Figure 3b). The object and the observer were rigidly connected so that they moved around a fixed pivot point in between. Thus, when the infant's chair moved to the left, the object moved to the right, and so forth. Because the pivot point was close to the front of the block, there was little relative displacement between the occluded object and the occluder.

The experiment sought to assess perceived unity and perceived motion in different ways. Perceived unity was assessed from dishabituation patterns to unoccluded complete and broken rod displays, as in previous studies. Motion perception was assessed by comparing the absolute levels of looking time to those in previous studies in which stationary infants viewed moving or stationary

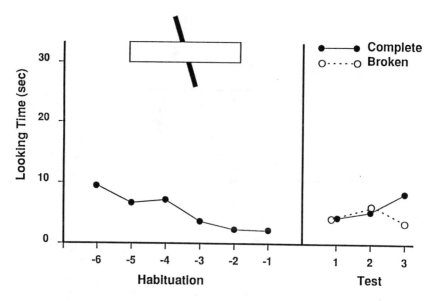

Fig. 5.   *Looking times during habituation and test periods in the observer movement condition of the Kellman, Gleitman, & Spelke (1987) experiment. (Backward habituation curves are displayed, showing looking times on the final six habituation trials. Test trials consisted of alternate presentations of broken and complete rod displays that had the same movement characteristics as the rod parts visible during habituation.) (Copyright 1987 by the American Psychological Association. Reprinted by permission.)*

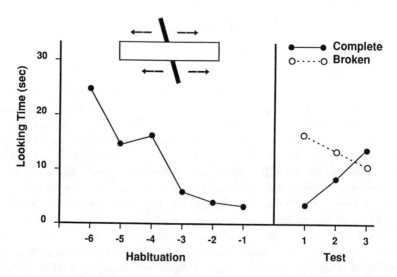

Fig. 6.   *Looking times during habituation and test periods in the conjoint movement condition of the Kellman, Gleitman, & Spelke (1987) experiment. (Copyright 1987 by the American Psychological Association. Reprinted by permission.)*

displays. In those studies, looking times were consistently two to three times higher to moving displays than to stationary ones.

The results for the observer movement group (Figure 5) suggested that infants did distinguish optical changes given by their own motion from those given by moving objects. Looking times to stationary objects were of the same order as those in earlier studies in which stationary observers viewed stationary displays. The results in the conjoint movement group, shown in Figure 6, were quite different. Looking times to the moving rods were markedly higher, resembling looking times shown by stationary observers to moving objects. Moreover, perception of unity depended on real motion. Patterns of dishabituation indicated that infants perceived the occluded display as unitary only in the conjoint movement condition.

These findings have several interesting implications for perception of motion and stability. First, it appears that young infants have position constancy, at least under some circumstances. Infants did not respond to optical displacements produced solely by their own motion as they respond to moving objects. Second, it appears that infants were able to detect the moving object in the conjoint condition during their own motion. This finding is especially noteworthy given the absence of subject-relative motion by the object.

Although the findings of Kellman et al. (1987) suggest early abilities for perceiving what is moving and what is stable during one's own motion, they do not tell much about how the task is accomplished. What information underlies these abilities? Do infants integrate information about distance with information about optical change to determine whether something is moving or not, as Gogel has suggested?

## B. The Object–Observer Motion Paradigm

To explore these questions further, we developed a new method, which we will refer to as the object–observer motion paradigm (Kellman, Hofsten, Condry, & O'Halloran, in preparation). In this paradigm, infants are passively moved laterally back and forth in a moving chair while viewing arrays of objects. On each trial, one object in the array also moves, along a path parallel to the infant's. The object and observer motion are always either in phase or in opposite phase (180 deg out of phase), so that points of acceleration/deceleration always coincide. These connections are achieved by mechanical linkage between the infant's chair and the moving object. Figure 7 shows the arrangement. On any given trial, a moving object is either on the right or left side of the array. A stationary object, at a different distance, is always placed on the other side of the display in such a position as to give the same amount of optical displacement as the moving object. When the moving object is in phase with the observer, this means that the stationary control object is placed further away, and when the object moves in opposite phase, the control object is nearer. Figures 8 and 9 illustrate.

As in the Kellman et al. (1987) study, we assumed that if infants could

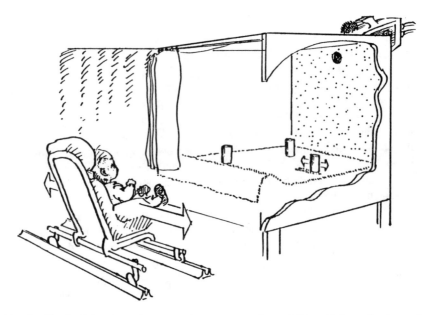

Fig. 7.  *Sketch of the object-observer motion apparatus. From Kellman, Hofsten, Condry, and O'Halloran (in preparation). (See text.)*

detect one moving object in an array of stationary ones, they would tend to fixate that object preferentially. Infants ordinarily devote greater visual attention to moving objects (Carpenter, 1974; Volkmann & Dobson, 1976). Preferential looking in the direction of the moving object is thus taken to indicate motion detection.

We began with a relatively difficult case. As noted earlier, the relative optical changes of nearby object and surface points differ when objects rest or move upon a ground surface. This information was excluded by placing a hump at the near edge of the surface which occluded the bottoms of all objects. Objects in the arrays varied somewhat in visual angle (from about 2.7 deg diameter × 5.5 deg height to 4 deg diameter × 8 deg height), but these angular differences were uncorrelated with distance.

Additionally, we were concerned with response tendencies other than a motion preference that might affect our results. The design thus incorporated several additional control features. One possibility is that infants might always prefer to fixate the closest object in an array. This possibility was controlled in opposite phase conditions, because the stationary object with equivalent optical change was always nearer than the moving object. When motion was in phase, an additional stationary object, closer than the moving one and on the opposite side, was always present. A second possibility is that subjects might attend to the locus of maximum optic flow. In its simplest form, this possibility was con-

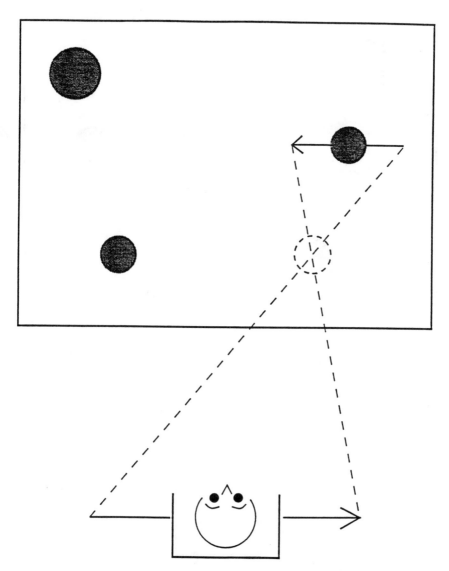

*Fig. 8. One of two object arrays for the opposite-phase condition in the object-observer motion experiments (Kellman, Hofsten, Condry, & O'Halloran, in preparation). (Top view is shown; solid circles are cylindrical objects; arrows indicate motion. The dotted object represents the position a stationary object would occupy to give identical optical change to the moving object. Such a stationary object is placed in the corresponding position on the other side of the display—here, the medium-sized stationary object on the right occupies the relevant position.)*

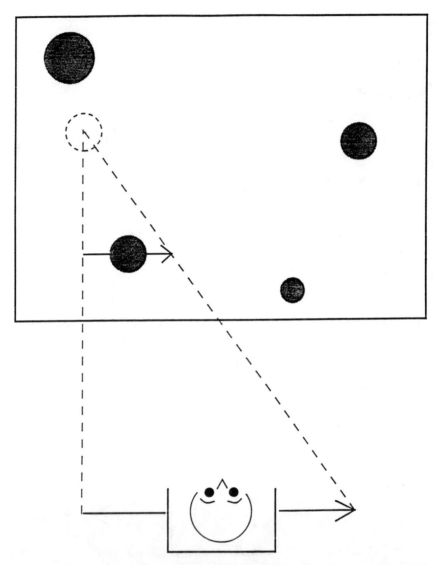

Fig. 9. *One of two object arrays for the in-phase condition in the object-observer motion experiments (Kellman, Hofsten, Condry, & O'Halloran, in preparation). (Top view is shown; solid circles are cylindrical objects; arrows indicate motion. The dotted object represents the position a stationary object would occupy to give identical optical change to the moving object. Such stationary object is placed in the corresponding position on the other side of the display—here, the medium-sized stationary object on the right occupies the relevant position.)*

trolled for by the front edge of the hump, which always had the fastest optical velocity in all conditions. However, a more complex version of this concern is that subjects might attend to the locus of greatest optical *shear*, that is, discontinuities in the optic flow (cf. Nakayama & Loomis, 1974). The use of the hump to obscure the bottoms of objects ensured that the shear relations between the moving object and other visible surfaces were equivalent for the moving and stationary control objects.

Given these design features, the experimental situation required combining registered optical change with distance information to determine the motion or stability of objects in the arrays. On any trial, the optical change given by the moving object was duplicated by a stationary object on the other side of the array; information about the location of the objects in depth was therefore needed to detect which object was moving. The dependent variable was looking time to the left or right halves of the array, as a function of presence of the moving object on the right or left. (Subjects could also be judged to be not looking at the array.) Subjects were presented with a series of 15-sec trials; the moving object was varied across trials between left and right. The session continued until a subject became fussy or a maximum of 25 trials was reached. Some criteria were established in advance for including subjects and trials in the analyses. A trial was considered valid if the infant looked at least 1.5 sec at some object. This criterion was used to weed out random, nonattentive glances. Subjects were disqualified if they did not have at least one valid trial of looking to the right and one to the left during the experiment (regardless of whether their looks to a given side occurred when the moving object was on that side). This criterion eliminated infants whose position bias was so strong that they never looked to one side. Perception of motion was assessed by comparing infants' looking times to the two sides of the display as a function of the placement of the moving object. To control for side preferences, the following comparison was used. For all trials, the measure L-R (looking time to the left minus the right) was calculated. Then for each subject, mean L-R was calculated separately for trials with the moving object on the left $(L-R)_L$ and right $(L-R)_R$ sides of the display. Finally, $(L-R)_R$ was subtracted from $(L-R)_L$. This gave a single number for each subject, ensuring that each subject counted equally in the overall analysis, regardless of differences across subjects in the number of valid trials. This measure—$(L-R)_L$ minus $(L-R)_R$—was then tested against the null hypothesis of 0. If looking times are the same regardless of the position of the moving object, then this derived measure will not differ from 0. The measure will be positive if the moving object is detected and preferentially fixated.

Our initial series of experiments involved 16-week-old infants who viewed the displays binocularly. Separate groups of 16 infants were tested with in-phase and opposite-phase motion. Figures 10 and 11 show the results.

As the figures indicate, overall looking times in this paradigm are not high. The position of the moving object, however, had a very reliable effect on infants'

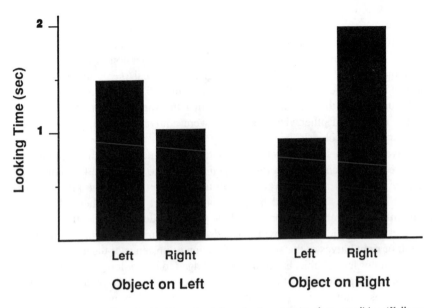

*Fig. 10. Data from 16-week-old, binocular infants in the opposite-phase condition (Kellman, Hofsten, Condry, & O'Halloran, in preparation). Looking times are shown to the left and right sides of the array when the moving object was on the left and on the right.*

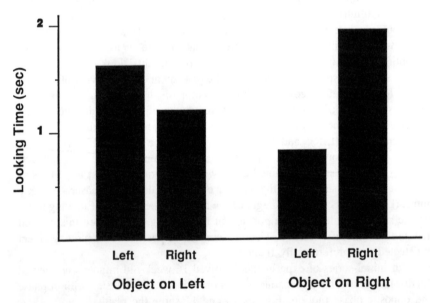

*Fig. 11. Data from 16-week-old, binocular infants in the in-phase condition (Kellman, Hofsten, Condry, & O'Halloran, in preparation). Looking times are shown to the left and right sides of the array when the moving object was on the left and on the right.*

fixation tendencies. When the moving object was on the left, subjects looked more to the left and vice versa. This pattern occurred both when the phase of the object's movement was the same as or opposite to the subject's. (Note that this complete reversal is not a necessary hallmark of motion detection; any reliable shift in preferences, e.g., a change from an extreme left looking bias to a milder one, could indicate motion detection.) The shift in looking patterns dependent on the position of the moving object was statistically robust ($p<.01$).

The results of these initial experiments suggested that moving infant observers can distinguish optical changes resulting from their own motion from those resulting from object motion. Infants seemed to detect real motion and preferentially attend to it. The results confirm and extend the findings of Kellman et al. (1987), in which the motion of the object was opposite in phase to the observer's motion.

Perception of motion and stability in this situation required use of distance information not given by optical change, since in every condition identical optical changes, (i.e., velocity and extent of displacement) were given by two objects on opposite sides of the array. One of these was always stationary at a given distance (the "pivot distance", in Gogel's, 1980, terminology), whereas the other was a moving object at a different distance. The reliable detection of the moving object indicates that subjects were able to combine optical change information with other distance information. Not only do infants at 16 weeks of age manifest perception of motion and constant position, but they do so in a situation in which distance information is necessary to determine motion.

So far, however, we have not said much about what specific distance information could be operating in this task. The question is jointly one of ecological optics—what information is available—and perceptual capacity— what information can 16-week-olds use?

Information about depth and distance may usefully be divided into four classes: kinetic, stereoscopic, oculomotor, and pictorial information (e.g., Kaufman, 1974). Pictorial cues to depth, such as interposition, relative size, and so on, do not seem to operate in the first half year of life (Yonas & Granrud, 1985). Moreover, in our experiments, cues that provide only relative depth information, for example, interposition, would be insufficient to determine whether an object is moving or at rest. Some metrical information about distance would seem to be required. Relevant pictorial cues, such as relative size, were removed by approximately equating the visual angle of relevant objects in the array and randomizing others (i.e., there was no correlation between visual angle and distance). Kinetic information may be useful early in infancy, although more research is needed (see below). However, in our arrangement, kinetic information about depth could not serve to determine object motion and stability. In terms of discontinuities in optic flow, for example, shear, the situation was designed to remove its informativeness. As for motion perspective, the differential optical change as a function of distance applies when an observer moves through a stationary environment. When both the motion/stability and the distance of an object are in question, the optical change to the perceiver cannot specify both. Two other classes of information remain. Oculomotor cues—accommodation and convergence—involve information from the adjustments of eye muscles needed to focus or converge the eyes. Stereoscopic or binocular disparity—the use of differences in the projections to the two eyes—might also operate. These sources of information are closely related. For example, proper convergence of the eyes is prerequisite for obtaining meaningful disparity information. Moreover, binocular disparity, in a mature perceiver, gives perhaps the greatest sensitivity to depth differences of any information source, but cannot by itself furnish *absolute* distance information. (This fact is due to a constancy problem: a given disparity could arise from a certain depth interval in the world at one distance from the observer, or from a larger depth interval at a further distance.) Convergence, on the other hand, may provide absolute distance information and may work in combination with stereopsis to allow perception of absolute depth intervals (Wallach & Zuckerman, 1963; Hofsten, 1976). In Gogel's studies of adults, convergence was found to be an important source of distance information; accommodation, on the other hand, was relatively unhelpful.

Not much is known about the role of convergence as a source of distance information early in life. Several studies have assessed the accuracy of convergence (Aslin, 1977; Slater & Findlay, 1975), indicating that, from birth, vergence changes are at least appropriate in direction to changes in target distance. Only one study tested the perception of distance based on convergence. Hofsten (1977) altered 20-week-olds' convergence using optical devices, and found appropriate changes in the lengths of subjects' reaches for objects. It is not known how much earlier than 20 weeks convergence might supply distance information. In our motion detection results with 16-week-olds, however, we suspected that convergence, or a combination of convergence and binocular disparity, provided the needed distance information. Similar inferences have been made in size perception by Granrud (1987).

To test this hypothesis, we repeated the experiments under monocular viewing. An eyepatch was used to cover one eye. If motion detection depended on convergence or convergence plus disparity, it should not be possible from monocular viewing.[2] Figures 12 and 13 show the results from these studies for opposite-phase and in-phase object–observer motions. As predicted, monocular

---

[2] Excluding the possibility of accommodative vergence. The signals for accommodation and convergence have some complex interactions, one of which is that the signal for accommodation given to one eye can trigger appropriate convergence in both. Although accommodative vergence has been observed in infants (Aslin & Jackson, 1979), whether it provides distance information equivalent to that of normal convergence has not been studied. As discussed below, the outcome of the monocular studies suggests a provisional negative answer to this question.

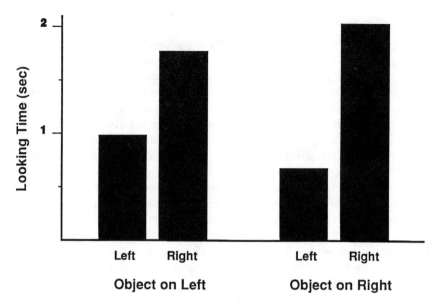

*Fig. 12. Data from 16-week-old, monocular infants in the opposite-phase condition (Kellman, Hofsten, Condry, & O'Halloran, in preparation). Looking times are shown to the left and right sides of the array when the moving object was on the left and on the right.*

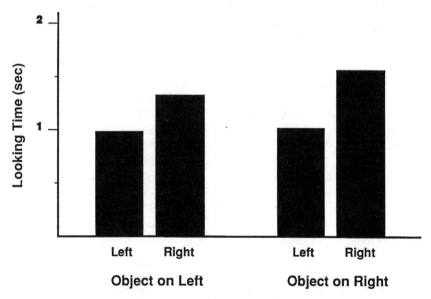

*Fig. 13. Data from 16-week-old, monocular infants in the in-phase condition (Kellman, Hofsten, Condry, & O'Halloran, in preparation). Looking times are shown to the left and right sides of the array when the moving object was on the left and on the right.*

viewing eliminated motion detection: Infants showed no reliable change in their looking patterns dependent on the position of the moving object.

Although the pattern of results in these studies seemed to indicate that moving infants' detection of motion and stability depended on binocular distance information, we were concerned about an alternative interpretation of our monocular results. Perhaps the eyepatch caused some general distress or inattention rather than an inability to detect motion.[3] An experiment carried out by Kirsten Condry tested for this possibility (Condry, 1988; Kellman et al., in preparation). Infants were equipped with an eyepatch and seated in a stationary infant seat. The moving objects appeared just as in previous studies, half of the time on the left and half on the right, but their movement was decoupled from the infant's chair (which did not move). The condition was thus a straightforward test for motion detection by stationary observers. If the negative results in the previous monocular conditions resulted from general inattention or distress caused by the eyepatch (rather than from an inability to detect motion) then these infants were predicted to fail to look preferentially at the moving object. However, if moving monocular infants in the previous studies were unable to perceive which object was moving, subjects were predicted to show motion detection in this case.

The stationary, monocular infants in this study provided robust evidence of motion detection, as shown in Figure 14. Wearing an eyepatch did not cause distraction sufficient to keep them from attending to motion. The failure of moving monocular infants to detect object motion seems more likely to stem from the lack of needed binocular distance information, rather than from some extraneous effect of wearing an eyepatch.

Taken together, these results implicate binocular distance information in infant's motion detection. As noted above, this binocular information could be supplied by convergence or a combination of convergence and binocular disparity. Can we specify further which information is at work?

In recent years, a clear picture of the emergence of stereoscopic depth perception has emerged from thorough and creative studies in several laboratories (Held, Birch, & Gwiazda, 1980; Fox et al., 1980; Braddick, Wattam-Bell, Day, & Atkinson, 1983). Stereoacuity seems virtually nonexistent from birth to about 12–14 weeks, after which it reaches near-adult levels fairly rapidly. By 16 weeks, estimates are that about half of infants have stereoscopic function (Held et al., 1980). The relatively abrupt onset and increase in acuity, along with certain electrophysiological findings, are consistent with a maturational account of stereoscopic depth perception (Held et al., 1980; Braddick & Atkinson, 1988).

In our studies of 16-week-old infants, we did not pretest for stereoscopic ability. It is thus possible that some combination of binocular disparity and convergence furnished the relevant information about distance. Although binoc-

---

[3] We thank Carl Granrud for raising this issue.

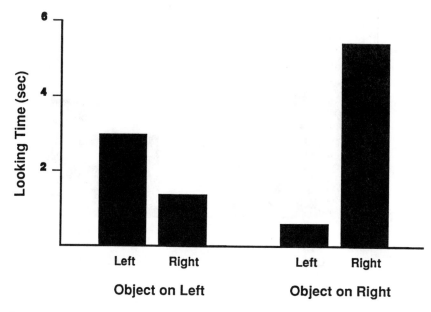

Fig. 14. Data from 16-week-old, monocular, stationary infants (Kellman, Hofsten, Condry, & O'Halloran, in preparation). Looking times are shown to the left and right sides of the array when the moving object was on the left and on the right. (See text.)

ular disparity cannot specify absolute distance by itself, it is known to give highly accurate metrical information about depth intervals when combined with some other information, such as convergence, that can specify the absolute distance of at least one visible point (Wallach, Moore, & Davidson, 1963).

To begin to untangle the relative contributions of convergence and disparity, we conducted experiments in the object–observer motion paradigm with 8-week-old infants (Kellman, Hofsten, VandeWalle, & Condry, 1990). Infants of this age in general show no stereoscopic depth perception, but they do converge. However, there are little or no data indicating whether convergence in the first 8 weeks provides usable information about distance.

The experiments were carried out in the same way as those with older infants. Object motion of the same phase and of opposite phase were tested in separate studies. Only binocular conditions were run; we assumed that, since monocular 16-week-olds had been unable to detect motion, younger infants would be also.

The results, shown in Figures 15 and 16, were interesting and perplexing. When the object moved in opposite phase to the observer, 8-week-olds showed clear evidence of motion detection (Figure 15), but when the object's motion had the same phase as the observer's, there was no reliable detection of motion (Figure 16).

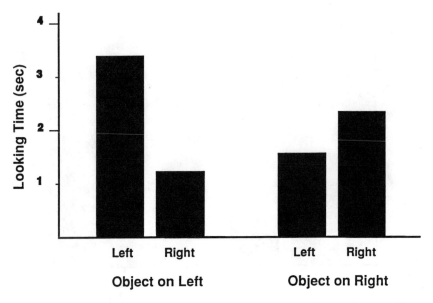

Fig. 15. Data from 8-week-old, binocular infants in the opposite-phase condition (Kellman, Hofsten, VandeWalle, & Condry, in preparation). Looking times are shown to the left and right sides of the array when the moving object was on the left and on the right.

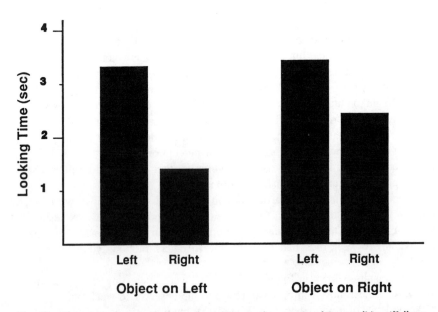

Fig. 16. Data from 8-week-old, binocular infants in the opposite-phase condition (Kellman, Hofsten, VandeWalle, & Condry, in preparation). Looking times are shown to the left and right sides of the array when the moving object was on the left and on the right.

These results suggest that motion detection is possible from convergence information alone. The pattern of motion detection in the opposite-phase group was as strong as it was for 16-week-olds in either phase condition. The failure of 8-week-olds in the in-phase condition is puzzling, however.

Why should the task of motion detection be more difficult when the object moves in phase with the moving observer? Several important aspects of the task do not differ in these two conditions. The motion tracks for the objects on the left and right were the same in both conditions. The extents of motion were likewise the same. Furthermore, in each condition, a control stationary object was placed, on the opposite side from the moving object, to duplicate its optical change, both absolute and relative to other visible surfaces. Analysis of the task does, however, reveal one interesting difference between the two conditions. The stationary object that duplicates the motion of an object moving opposite to the observer necessarily lies nearer to the observer, while the stationary control object for motion in the same direction as the observer must be placed further away. The difference in distance between a moving object and the "pivot point" (see Figure 2) is in general considerably further when the object moves in phase than when it does not. (This follows from the fact that the extent of optical change and distance are inversely proportional.) In our study, the average distance of the stationary control objects in the in-phase condition was 109 cm, compared with 58 cm for the stationary control objects in the opposite-phase condition. (The moving objects averaged 74 cm from the subject in both conditions.)

Thus, the task of discriminating a moving object on one side of the display from a stationary object on the other side may differ somewhat in the two conditions. In the in-phase condition, the discrimination involves a stationary control object considerably further away. It is possible that some acuity limitation, relevant to determining either the distance of the further object or accurately registering its optical change, makes the task more difficult in the in-phase condition. Whatever the limitation, it seems to be overcome by 16 weeks of age, where no difference between in-phase and opposite-phase motion was observed.

There are several candidates for relevant acuity limitations at 8 weeks. Accurate registration of optical change is needed to determine motion or stability. In the in-phase condition, the optical displacement averages about 6 deg/sec for the moving and stationary control objects. Although this value is well above threshold estimates for motion detection, the relevant issue is how precisely the extent or velocity of optical change can be registered. For comparison, a stationary object positioned as far from the subject as the moving objects would move about 8.8 deg/sec. Discrimination of the velocity or extent differences here may be limiting performance. A second candidate for a sensory limitation is the accuracy of convergence. It is possible that the convergence difference between moving objects and further stationary objects are near threshold for 8-week-olds. Both the geometry of convergence and its accuracy in early infancy suggest that relatively small changes in convergence angle occur beyond 50 cm (Aslin,

1988). As noted above, existing data do not indicate much about the accuracy of convergence as distance information. However, it would not be surprising if precise comparisons of distance via convergence for objects at 50–100 cm were difficult for 8-week-olds.

Although the hypothesis of an acuity limitation in the present study must remain conjectural for the time being, it is consistent with a post-hoc analysis of the data. Subjects in the in-phase sample ranged from 46 to 68 days of age (mean = 53.4 days). When the youngest 8 subjects (below the median of 53 days) were omitted from the analysis, the remaining subgroup showed a reliable tendency to fixate the moving object, $t(7) = 2.10$, $p < .05$. By comparison, a similar breakdown of the opposite-phase group, which ranged from 42 to 69 days (mean 53.9 days), showed no difference in motion detection between the younger and older subjects. Table 1 shows mean looking times and standard errors for the older and younger subjects in each phase condition. Preferential looking at the moving object is absent only for the younger infants in the in-phase condition; this condition also shows the highest variance.

From these studies with 8-week-olds, it appears that convergence alone can furnish absolute distance information that underlies motion detection. Subjects' difficulty with in-phase motion indicates that these younger infants are not so well equipped to use distance–motion relations as their older counterparts; nevertheless, the basic perceptual capacity appears to be present. The evidence of such a capacity in prestereoscopic infants suggests that depth perception from binocular disparity is not prerequisite. Nonetheless, it seems likely that the later onset of depth perception from disparity increases the specificity of detection of motion and stability.

TABLE 1

Eight-Week-Olds' Preferential Looking at Moving Object by Condition and Age Range

| Condition | Mean preference[1] (sec) | Std. error of mean | $p$[2] |
|---|---|---|---|
| In phase | | | |
| Above median[3] | 2.65 | 1.26 | $<.05$ |
| Below median | −.80 | 1.81 | n.s. |
| Opposite phase | | | |
| Above median[4] | 2.80 | .83 | $<.01$ |
| Below median | 3.22 | 1.07 | $<.01$ |

[1] Preferential looking at moving object is calculated for each subject by subtracting the difference of left and right looking when the moving object was on the right from the difference of left and right looking when the moving object was on the left $[(L-R)_L - (L-R)_R]$. Positive numbers indicate greater looking in the direction of the moving object.

[2] Significance level of difference from null hypothesis of 0 preferential looking at moving object.

[3] Median = 55 days.

[4] Median = 53.5 days.

The idea that convergence is a primary source of distance information is also consistent with recent studies of size constancy in newborns (Granrud, in press; Slater, Mattock, & Brown, 1990). In these studies, some indication has been found that newborns are sensitive to the real sizes of objects across changes in their projected size and distance. Both the logic and experimental data of size constancy implicate its dependence on distance information (e.g., Holway & Boring, 1941). Although size constancy may sometimes be achieved in other ways, such as in connection with optical texture gradients (Gibson, 1950, 1979), these recent reports include situations in which distance information, implicit or explicit, appears to be required. Hence, they suggest that some form of absolute distance perception is innate.

Although the evidence is not direct, convergence is the likely source of distance information in these experiments. Perhaps the only other candidate is motion perspective. Motion perspective is rendered less plausible by the fact that the objects in Granrud's studies underwent continuous lateral (back and forth) motion to maintain newborns' interest. The most natural head movements—lateral ones—that a seated infant might perform would thus yield ambiguous or inaccurate information in terms of distance. It is possible, but not likely given the age and seating arrangement of subjects, that some other head movement, e.g., a vertical one, could provide unconfounded motion perspective information about distance. Further research will be needed to ascertain if convergence is an innate foundation of distance perception, as now seems likely.

## VI. DEVELOPMENT OF DEPTH PERCEPTION FROM MOTION

Depth within a structure, during relative motion between it and an observer, is specified by its differential retinal velocities. Rogers and Graham (1979) have demonstrated a remarkable sensitivity to this information in adults. They used a random-dot pattern on an oscilloscope screen which was transformed by each movement of the observer (or movement of the oscilloscope) to simulate the relative motion information produced by a 3-D surface. They found that, under these conditions, the sensitivity of the visual system to motion parallax is comparable to the sensitivity to retinal disparity.

Little is known about when sensitivity to motion parallax develops. The question is of considerable interest, however. The importance of motion and change for monocular space perception in adults (see, e.g., Johansson, Hofsten, & Jansson, 1980) argues for deep biological roots of this ability. Furthermore, earlier research indicates that sensitivity to motion and change as information about depth appears very early in development and might play a crucial role in the emergence of space perception in infancy. Already at 3 to 5 months of age, infants show a variety of motion perception abilities. Yonas, Petterson, Lockman, and Eisenberg (1980) demonstrated that 3-month-olds blinked and withdrew the head when presented with an optical expansion, but only if it accelerated and filled large optical fields. Such "explosive" magnification patterns signify an approaching object whose collision with the observer is imminent. Kellman et al. (1987) found that 4-month-olds generalized the motion of three dots toward and away from a common point to the motion in depth of a triangle. Expansion and contraction is by no means the only motion information studied. For instance, Kellman (1984) found that 4-month-olds perceived the 3-D form of a rotating object whose shape was specified by kinetic information, and Granrud et al. (1984) found that 5-month-olds are sensitive to accretion and deletion of texture as information about depth at an edge.

One problem connected to the question of the emergence of motion parallax information about distance and depth has to do with the relatively high velocity thresholds found for young infants. Take, for instance, the differential velocity thresholds reported by Dannemiller and Freedland (1991). They found that 20-week-old infants discriminated 3.3 deg/sec but not 5 deg/sec from 10 deg/sec, and 2 deg/sec but not 2.5 deg/sec from 3.3 deg/sec. If these values reflect true differential motion detection ability in a motion parallax, a child moving the head sideways with a velocity of 4 cm/sec would discriminate an object at a distance of 69 cm (3.3 deg/sec) from one at 114 cm. (2 deg/sec) but not from one at 92 cm (2.5 deg/sec). These differential motion thresholds are obviously too crude to be of much use in perceiving space. If motion parallax is to supply reasonably differentiated distance information to the infant, the perceptual system needs to be more sensitive to differential motion than indicated by Dannemiller and Freedland (1991).

Dannemiller and Freedland (1991) used preferential looking as their dependent variable. It is possible that the smallest velocity differences evoking preferential looking are higher than the smallest velocity differences perceived. A habituation paradigm might be a more sensitive instrument for detecting differential velocity sensitivity as it does not require a looking preference, only detection of differences between habituation and test displays.

Hofsten, Kellman, and Putaansuu (in press) used a habituation-of-looking technique to assess the sensitivity of young infants to motion parallax information. While seated in a moving infant chair, infants were habituated to a display consisting of three vertical rods aligned in the fronto-parallel plane. The outer rods were stationary, and the middle rod moved parallel to the infant contingently with the infant's chair. The contingent motion was achieved by mechanical linkage between the infant's chair, the middle rod, and a pivot point 15 cm more distant than the moving rod.

After habituation, subjects saw two stationary displays in alternation. The first of these was spatially identical to the habituation display; that is, the three rods were aligned in the fronto-parallel plane. In the other test display, the middle rod was displaced backward 15 cm relative to the side rods, that is, to a position denoted by the motion parallax in the habituation display. The configuration of the rods was then triangular. If the infant had detected the contingent motion and perceived the middle rod to be at an altered distance, the triangular display should have been perceived as familiar and the aligned display perceived as new. If the infant had not detected the contingent motion, the aligned display should be perceived as familiar and the triangular as new.

The amplitude of differential motion chosen in the first experiment (0.32 deg/sec) was a guess based on the assumption that habituation would be a more sensitive measure of motion perception than preferential looking. This value is well below the smallest threshold previously reported of 0.93 deg/sec (Kaufmann et al., 1985). If the results indicated that infants did not detect the motion of 0.32 deg/sec, we intended to increase the amplitude in a subsequent experiment, and if the result did indicate that infants perceived this motion, we intended to decrease the amplitude to get a better idea of the threshold value. All infants in these experiments were 15 weeks old.

The experiments were performed under binocular viewing in spite of the possibility that the presence of binocular information might have confused the infants. The reasons for using binocular viewing were as follows. First, every additional manipulation done on infant subjects increases the probability of fussing. Fussing during any part of the habituation or test procedures tends to obscure trends in data and fussing infants have to be excluded. Allowing natural binocular viewing minimized this problem. Second, we expected the binocular system of our subjects to be rather crude (see, e.g., Birch, Gwiazda, & Held, 1982). Finally, if the presence of binocular information had any effect on the subjects, it would show up as an inability to detect the contingent motion. In other words, any effect of binocular vision would be in the direction of underestimating the motion detection ability of the infant.

The infants habituated to the contingent motion display showed a clear preference for the Aligned-Rods display indicating that the infants perceived this as new. A control group, who saw only the test displays, looked longer at the Triangular-Rods display. Data from both groups are shown in Figure 17.

In the second experiment, the velocity of the middle rod was decreased to half its previous value, or 0.16 deg/sec. Subjects showed no signs of having detected that motion. In other words, the threshold for detecting contingent motions in 15-week-old infants seems to be somewhere between 0.16 and 0.32 deg/sec.

The results suggest that young infants are rather sensitive to contingent motion. The contingent motion used in this experiment was substantially slower than the thresholds calculated from earlier studies. The present results raise the question of whether motion perception in young infants is functionally specific. Are infants more sensitive to the contingent motions of the motion parallax than to motion perceived as such?

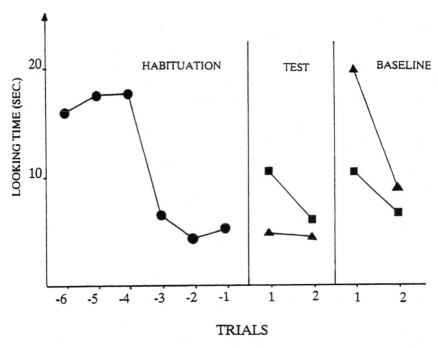

*Fig. 17. Data from Hofsten, Kellman, and Putaansuu (in press). (See text.)*

Although these experiments suggest that the sensitivity to contingent motion
is remarkably high in young infants, it does not prove that the contingent motion
was perceived in terms of space and not motion. In fact, the result of Experiment
1 does not even tell us whether the infant detected the contingency between the
object motion and the infant's motion. Therefore another experiment was performed, the purpose of which was to find out whether young infants are sensitive
to the relation between small retinal motions and their own movements. The
same habituation display was used as in the previous experiments but the test
displays were different. One of them had the same spatial configuration as the
triangular display in the first experiment; i.e., the middle rod was displaced away
from the subject as much as denoted by the motion parallax. In the other test
display, the middle rod was displaced toward the subject in such a way that is
retinal motion had the same magnitude as in the habituation display but in
opposite phase. This is illustrated in Figure 18. If infants just detected the motion
of the middle rod, both test displays would have looked equally familiar.
However, if they detected the relation between their own motion and the motion
of the middle rod, they should have found the test display with the middle rod
displaced away from them to be familiar and the test display with the middle rod
displaced toward them to be new.

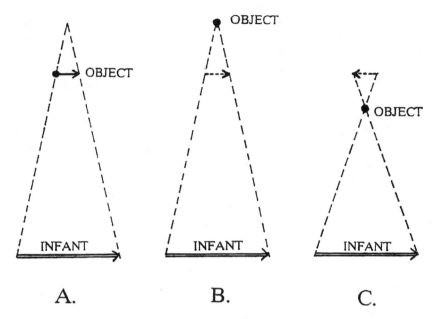

**A.** **B.** **C.**

*Fig. 18. Schematic of displays from experiment testing contingency of optical change on observer motion (Hofsten, Kellman, & Putaansuu, in press). (See text.)*

The result showed that infants increased looking to the display with the middle rod displaced toward the subject but not to the display with the middle rod displaced away from the subject. Thus, infants seem to be sensitive both to small magnitudes of retinal motions and to the contingency between these motions and their own movements. In order to finally prove that contingent motions are perceived in terms of distance, however, we need to disentangle proximal and distal variables. This would be most easily done by using different distances to the habituation display and the test displays. Then all proximal differential velocities would be changed while the spatial relations remained the same. Such an experiment remains to be done.

## VII. CONCLUSION

In recent years, accounts of perception have come to regard the mobile observer, simultaneously perceiving and acting, as paradigmatic rather than exceptional (Gibson, 1966, 1979; Johansson et al., 1980). The research described in this chapter constitutes a beginning in understanding how very young perceivers obtain a coherent representation of the environment through which both they and objects move. One might expect that a perceptual system evolved for mobile perceiver/actors would be hardwired to utilize information about motion and stability. Our findings so far are consistent with this idea. Even in relatively difficult cases, in which detection of motion requires combining optic flow information with independent distance information, infants demonstrate some ability to detect the moving and stationary parts of the environment during their own motion. Underlying this ability is binocular distance information, probably furnished by convergence initially and later by a combination of convergence and binocular disparity. Reversing the linkage, the use of motion perspective to specify depth may also be in the young perceiver's repertoire. Crucial components of this ability—sensitivity both to small optical changes and their contingency with observer motion—are present early. Determining whether these sensitivities support depth perception from motion parallax, as well as deepening our understanding generally of the interactions of distance and motion information, are important challenges for further research.

## VIII. REFERENCES

Andersen, G. J. (1986). Perception of self-motion: Psychophysical and computational approaches. *Psychological Bulletin, 99*(1), 52–65.
Aslin, R. N. (1977). Development of binocular fixation in human infants. *Journal of Experimental Child Psychology, 23,* 133–150.
Aslin, R. N. (1981). Development of smooth pursuit in infants. In D. F. Fisher, R. A. Monty, & J. W. Senders (Eds.), *Eye movements: Cognition and visual perception.* Hillsdale, NJ: Erlbaum.
Aslin, R. (1988). Anatomical constraints on oculomotor development: Implications for infant perception. In A. Yonas (Ed.), *Perceptual development in infancy: The Minnesota Symposia on Child Psychology* (Vol. 20, pp. 105–144). Hillsdale, NJ: Erlbaum.
Aslin, R. N., & Jackson, R. W. (1979). Accommodative-convergence in young infants: Development of a synergistic sensory-motor system. *Canadian Journal of Psychology, 33,* 222–231.
Aslin, R., & Shea, S. (1989). *Velocity thresholds in human infants: Implications for the perception of motion.* Manuscript submitted for publication.
Aslin, R., Shea, S., & Gallipeau, J. (1988). Motion thresholds in 3-month old infants. *Investigative Ophthalmology and Visual Science Supplement, 29,* 26.
Atkinson, J., Braddick, O. J., & Moar, K. (1977). Development of contrast sensitivity over the first three months of life in the human infant. *Vision Research, 14,* 159–162.
Banks, M., Crowell, J., & Royden, S. (in preparation). A biologically plausible model of optic flow perception.
Bertenthal, B., Dunn, S., & Bai, D. (1986). Infants' sensitivity to optical flow for specifying self motion. *Infant Behavior and Development (Abstract), 9,* 35.
Birch, E. E., Gwiazda, J., & Held, R. (1982). Stereoacuity development for crossed and uncrossed disparities in human infants. *Vision Research, 22,* 507–514.
Braddick, O., & Atkinson, J. (1988). Sensory selectivity, attentional control, and cross-channel integration in early visual development. In A. Yonas (Ed.), *Perceptual development in infancy: The 20th Minnesota Symposium on Child Development.* Hillsdale, NJ: Erlbaum.
Braddick, O., Wattam-Bell, J., Day, J., & Atkinson, J. (1983). The onset of binocular function in human infants. *Human Neurobiology, 2,* 65–69.
Carpenter, G. C. (1974). Visual regard of moving and stationary faces in early infancy. *Merrill-Palmer Quarterly, 11,* 182–193.

Condry, K. (1988). *Four-month-old infants' perception of moving objects during observer motion.* Swarthmore College Honors Thesis.

Dannemiller, J. L., & Freedland, R. L. (1989). The detection of slow stimulus movement in 2- to 5-month-olds. *Journal of Experimental Child Psychology, 47,* 335–337.

Dannemiller, J. L., & Freedland, R. L. (1991). Speed discrimination in 20-week-old infants. *Infant Behavior and Development, 14,* 163–174.

Fantz, R. L., & Nevis, S. (1967). Pattern preferences and perceptual-cognitive development in early infancy. *Merrill-Palmer Quarterly, 13,* 77–108.

Fox, R., Aslin, R. N., Shea, S. L., & Dumais, S. T. (1980). Stereopsis in human infants. *Science, 207,* 323–324.

Freedland, R. L., & Dannemiller, J. L. (1987). Detection of stimulus motion in 5-month-old infants. *Journal of Experimental Psychology: Human Perception and Performance, 13,* 566–576.

Gibson, E. J., Gibson, J. J., Smith, O. W., & Flock, H. (1959). Motion parallax as a determinant of perceived depth. *Journal of Experimental Psychology, 8*(1), 40–51.

Gibson, J. J. (1950). *The perception of the visual world.* Boston: Houghton Mifflin.

Gibson, J. J. (1966). *The senses considered as perceptual systems.* Boston: Houghton Mifflin.

Gibson, J. J. (1979). *The ecological approach to visual perception.* Boston: Houghton Mifflin.

Gogel, W. (1980). The sensing of retinal motion. *Perception & Psychophysics, 28*(2), 155–163.

Gogel, W. (1982). Analysis of the perception of motion concomitant with a lateral motion of the head. *Perception & Psychophysics, 32*(3), 241–250.

Gogel, W. C., & Tietz, J. D. (1974). The effect of perceived distance on perceived movement. *Perception & Psychophysics, 16,* 70–78.

Granrud, C. (in press). The developmental origins of visual size perception. In C. Granrud (Ed.), *The 1989 Carnegie-Mellon Symposium on Cognition.*

Haith, M. (1983). Spatially determined visual activity in early infancy. In A. Hein & M. Jeannerod (Eds.), *Spatially oriented behavior.* New York: Springer.

Held, R., Birch, E. E., & Gwiazda, J. (1980). Stereoacuity of human infants. *Proceedings of the National Academy of Sciences of the USA, 77,* 5572–5574.

Helmholtz, H. von. (1925). *Treatise on physiological optics* (J. Southall, Trans. and ed.). New York: Optical Society of America. (Original work published 1885).

Hofsten, C. von. (1976). The role of convergence in visual space perception. *Vision Research, 16,* 193–198.

Hofsten, C. von. (1977). Binocular convergence as a determinant of reaching behavior in infancy. *Perception, 6,* 139–144.

Hofsten, C. von, Kellman, P. J., & Putaansuu, J. (in press). Young infants' sensitivity to motion parallax. *Infant Behavior and Development.*

Holway, A. F., & Boring, E. G. (1941). Determinants of apparent visual size with distance variant. *American Journal of Psychology, 54,* 21–37.

Johansson, G., Hofsten, C. von., & Jansson, G. (1980). Event perception. *Annual Review of Psychology, 31,* 27–63.

Kaufman, L. (1974). *Sight and mind.* New York: Oxford University Press.

Kaufmann, F., Stucki, M., & Kaufmann-Hayoz, R. (1985). Development of infants' sensitivity for slow and rapid motions. *Infant Behavior and Development, 8,* 89–98.

Kellman, P. (1984). Perception of three dimensional form by human infants. *Perception & Psychophysics, 36*(4), 353–358.

Kellman, P. (1989, July). *Perceiving motion and stability in infancy.* Invited paper, Fifth International Conference on Event Perception and Action, Miami, OH.

Kellman, P. J., Gleitman, H., & Spelke, E. (1987). Object and observer motion in the perception of objects by infants. *Journal of Experimental Psychology: Human Perception and Performance, 13,* 586–593.

Kellman, P. J., Hofsten, C. von., Condry, K., & O'Halloran, R. (in preparation). Motion and stability in the world of the (moving) infant.

Kellman, P. J., Hofsten, C. von., & Soares, J. (1987). Concurrent motion in infant event perception. *Infant Behavior and Development, 10,* 1–10.

Kellman, P. J., Hofsten, C. von, VandeWalle, G., & Condry, K. (1990, April). *Perception of motion and stability during observer motion by pre-stereoscopic infants.* Paper presented at the 7th International Conference on Infant Studies, Montreal.

Kellman, P. J., Hofsten, C. von, VandeWalle, G., & Condry, K. (in preparation). Perception of motion and stability during observer motion by pre-stereoscopic infants.

Kellman, P. J., & Shipley, T. F. (1991). A theory of visual interpolation in object perception. *Cognitive Psychology, 23,* 141–221.

Kellman, P. J., & Spelke, E. (1983). Perception of partly occluded objects in infancy. *Cognitive Psychology, 15,* 483–524.

Kellman, P. J., Spelke, E., & Short, K. R. (1986). Infant perception of object unity from translatory motion in depth and vertical translation. *Child Development, 57,* 72–76.

Koenderink, J. J. (1986). Optic flow. *Vision Research, 26,* 161–180.

Kremenitzer, J. P., Vaughan, H. G., Kurtzberg, D., & Dowling, K. (1979). Smooth-pursuit eye movements in the newborn infant. *Child Development, 50,* 442–448.

Lee, D. N. (1974). Visual information during locomotion. In R. MacLeod & H. Pick (Eds.), *Perception: Essays in honor of J. J. Gibson.* Ithaca, NY: Cornell University Press.

Lee, D. N., & Aronson, E. (1974). Visual proprioceptive control of standing in human infants. *Perception & Psychophysics, 15,* 529–532.

Longuett-Higgins, H. C., & Prazdny, K. (1980). The interpretation of moving retinal images. *Procedings of the Royal Society of London B, 208,* 385–387.

Nakayama, K., & Loomis, J. M. (1974). Optical velocity patterns, velocity-sensitive neurons, and space perception: A hypothesis. *Perception, 3,* 63–80.

Piaget, J. (1954). *The construction of reality in the child.* New York: Basic Books.

Regan, D., & Beverley, K. I. (1978). Looming detectors in the human visual pathway. *Vision Research, 18,* 415–421.

Rogers, B., & Graham, M. (1979). Motion parallax as an independent cue for depth perception. *Perception, 8,* 125–134.

Shimojo, S., Birch, E. E., Gwiazda, J., & Held, R. (1984). Development of vernier acuity in infants. *Vision Research, 24,* 721–728.

Slater, A. M., & Findlay, J. M. (1975). Binocular fixation in the newborn baby. *Journal of Experimental Child Psychology, 20,* 248–273.

Slater, A., Mattock, A., & Brown, E. (1990). Size constancy at birth: Newborn infant's responses to retinal and real size. *Journal of Experimental Child Psychology, 49,* 314–322.

Tauber, E. S., & Koffler, S. (1966). Optomotor responses in human infants to apparent motion: Evidence of innateness. *Science, 152,* 382–383.

Tronick, E., & Clanton, C. (1971). Infant looking patterns. *Vision Research, 11,* 1479–1486.

Volkmann, F. C., & Dobson, M. V. (1976). Infants responses of ocular fixation to moving visual stimuli. *Journal of Experimental Child Psychology, 22,* 86–89.

Wallach, H., Moore, M. E., & Davidson, L. (1963). Modification of stereoscopic depth perception, *American Journal of Psychology, 76,* 191–204.

Wallach, H., & Zuckerman, C. (1963). The constancy of stereoscopic depth. *American Journal of Psychology, 76,* 404–412.

Warren, R. (1976). The perception of egomotion. *Journal of Experimental Psychology: Human Perception and Performance, 2,* 448–456.

White, B. L., Castle, P., & Held, R. (1964). Observations on the development of visually directed reaching. *Child Development, 35,* 349–364.

Yonas, A., & Granrud, C. E. (1985). Development of visual space perception in young infants. In J. Mehler & R. Fox (Eds.), *Neonate cognition: Beyond the blooming buzzing confusion.* Hillsdale, NJ: Erlbaum.

Yonas, A., Petterson, L., Lockman, J. J., & Eisenberg, P. (1980, April). *The perception of impending collision in 3-month-old infants.* Paper presented at the International Conference on Infant Studies, New Haven.

# A SYMPOSIUM ON THE BAYLEY SCALES OF INFANT DEVELOPMENT: ISSUES OF PREDICTION AND OUTCOME REVISITED

## INTRODUCTION

The Bayley Scales of Infant Development (BSID; Bayley, 1969) have long been used in both clinical and research settings. The primary focus of this work has centered on the usefulness of the Scales in predicting a child's future performance, measuring a child's progress, or measuring the effectiveness of some prescribed intervention. Questions about the reliability of items for special populations, the predictive validity of the scale for clinical populations, and the usefulness of alternative scoring procedures are just a few of the issues that have remained relatively unexplored.

Three of the four papers presented here were originally offered at a symposium at the 1989 Society for Research in Child Development in Kansas City. The symposium was assembled in order to explore the issues of reliability and validity pertaining to the BSID. Issues of the reliability and validity of a scale as important as the Bayley have previously been addressed, for the most part indirectly through studies using the scale as an outcome measure. This symposium was intended to integrate a corpus of information on the properties and the use of the scales that can be an aid to both the clinician and the researcher when faced with interpreting the meaningfulness of a child's performance on the Bayley. It is also hoped that these papers will stimulate others to investigate the important psychometric issues surrounding the use of the Bayley Scales.

The first paper, by LeTendre, Spiker, Scott, and Constantine, explores the issue of the adequacy of the Bayley Mental and Motor Scales for sampling the developmental functioning of 24-month-old children. These authors demonstrate that, for a significant percentage of the preterm infants tested, the recommended ceiling on the Mental Scale was not reached. The failure to obtain a true ceiling led the authors to conclude that the Bayley Mental Scale does not capture the 24-month-olds or older infant's full range of performance. Addressing this problem, the authors provide useful guidelines for both clinicians and researchers who must interpret a child's performance when no true ceiling is reached.

The second paper, by Burns, Burns, and Kabacoff, explores the construct validity of the Bayley Scales by examining the changing factor structure and

185

content emphasis of the scales from 3 to 24 months. Utilizing exploratory factor analytic procedures the author's results provide empirical evidence for Bayley's hypothesis that different constructs define development at different ages and that there is little evidence for accurate prediction of a child's later performance in a particular domain from his or her earlier performance. The authors discuss these findings and their significance when using the child's Bayley performance to predict his or her later performance.

The third paper, by Gyurke, Lynch, LaGasse, and Lipsitt, uses an item analysis procedure to examine the relationship between the child's speed of performance on various timed items on the BSID Mental Scale and the child's overall performance on this scale. Many infant tests rely on speed of performance as a means of establishing a child's ability to perform that task. The assumption that speed is correlated with developmental maturity is well established for school-age children, but relatively untested in preschoolers. This research finding, that speed of performance may not be as reliable an indicator for young children as for older children, can be used by clinicians who prefer to interpret the child's performance beyond the scale level.

The final paper, by Siegel, is an empirical assessment of the commonly held belief that there are continuities in development and commonalities among diverse behaviors that underlie cognitive development. Using an alternative scoring procedure for the BSID Mental Scale, Siegel attempted to predict later performance in a number of academic and cognitive areas. The results of this study point to the fact that the predictive validity of the BSID is improved when one approaches it from a domain specific perspective.

Integrative comments for these papers are provided by a distinguished developmental psychologist, Lewis P. Lipsitt, who has spent many years as the director of a large longitudinal study which used the BSID. Dr. Lipsitt's comments draw attention to the historical purposes of infant assessment as determining current level of functioning and predicting future functioning. He further points out that repeated examinations of the predictive power of the Bayley Mental or Motor Scales will continue to produce consistently unremarkable results.

Dr. Lipsitt continues his discussion by pointing out the merits of investigating the psychometric properties of the Bayley as alternative means to addressing issues relating to assessment of current functioning. His integration of the present collection of papers provides the reader with a multifaceted and yet coherent view of the methodologies currently available to answer questions about the reliability and validity of infant scales.

*James S. Gyurke*

# ESTABLISHING THE "CEILING" ON THE BAYLEY SCALES OF INFANT DEVELOPMENT AT 25 MONTHS*

*Dana LeTendre*

DEPARTMENT OF PSYCHOLOGY AND COUNSELING
PITTSBURG STATE UNIVERSITY
PITTSBURG, KS

*Donna Spiker*

DEPARTMENT OF PEDIATRICS
STANFORD UNIVERSITY

*David T. Scott*

DEPARTMENT OF PEDIATRICS
YALE UNIVERSITY SCHOOL OF MEDICINE
NEW HAVEN, CT

*Norman A. Constantine*

FAR WEST LABORATORY FOR EDUCATIONAL RESEARCH AND DEVELOPMENT
SAN FRANCISCO, CA

I. INTRODUCTION ............................................. 188
II. METHOD ................................................... 189
   A. Subjects ................................................ 189
   B. Procedures .............................................. 190
III. RESULTS ................................................. 191
IV. DISCUSSION .............................................. 194
V. APPENDIX: INFANT HEALTH AND DEVELOPMENT
   PROGRAM ............................................... 197

---

* The Infant Health and Development Program was funded by grants from the Robert Wood Johnson Foundation to the Department of Pediatrics, Stanford University; the Frank Porter Graham Child Development Center, University of North Carolina at Chapel Hill; and the eight participating Universities. Additional support for the National Study Office was provided to the Department of Pediatrics, Stanford University, from the Pew Charitable Trusts; the Bureau of Maternal and Child Health and Resources Development and the National Institute of Child Health and Human Development, HRSA, PHS, DHHS (Grant MCJ-060515); and the Stanford Center for the Study of Families, Children, and Youth. The authors thank Michael S. Shing for statistical computing, and Nancy Greenwood and Carol Oehme for processing numerous drafts of the manuscript.

# I. INTRODUCTION

The Bayley Scales of Infant Development (BSID) are used widely in clinical and research contexts to assess the developmental functioning of infants. Norms are provided by the publisher for infants and toddlers from 2 months through 30 months of age (Bayley, 1969). Longitudinal and comparative research studies of full-term and preterm infants often include the BSID as the primary assessment instrument through 24 months.

As with most individually administered developmental and intelligence tests, the BSID employs "discontinue criteria" for the examiner to use in determining the examinee's "ceiling" level, that is, determining when to stop administering items. A ceiling is defined for the BSID as the item representing the most difficult success for that examinee. The ceiling item is identified by means of a discontinue criterion. For the Mental Scale, the recommended discontinue criterion (*BSID Manual*, 1969, p. 29) is the lowest 10 consecutive failed items. That is, the item just below this series of 10 consecutive failures is, by definition, the ceiling item. For the Motor Scale, the recommended discontinue criterion is six consecutive failed items. According to the manual, "these levels must be carefully established to ensure that the infant's full range of successful functioning has been tested" (1969, p. 29). The use of this type of discontinue criterion is based on two assumptions: first, that the items are sequentially ordered by difficulty level; and second, that after the specified number of failures the infant would be unlikely to achieve any more correct responses.

Clinical experience suggests that many 24-month-olds are able to pass one or more of the last 10 items on the Mental Scale—thus effectively precluding the establishment of an empirical ceiling according to Bayley's recommended criterion for discontinuation. For at least some of these infants, it is possible that the test has not adequately sampled their behavior (that is, the infant's "full range of successful functioning" has not been tested). The extent of this problem and the functioning range of the infants most likely to be affected are not known.

This study examines the extent to which the full range of successful functioning of 24-month-olds is adequately sampled by the BSID. More specifically, the degree to which the discontinuation criteria are not met can be seen as the degree to which the BSID does not adequately sample the full range of successful functioning for 24-month-olds. This poses the possibility that the BSID may not fully delineate the full range of individual differences among 24-month-olds. To investigate this issue, the current study employs a highly standardized research administration of the BSID to a large multi-site sample of 24-month corrected-age low-birthweight (LBW) preterm infants. Because preterm and LBW infants typically function below the level of their full-term counterparts (see Pape, Buncie, Ashby, & Fitzhardinge, 1978; Field, Dempsey, & Shuman, 1979; Teberg et al., 1982; Eckerman, Sturm, & Gross, 1985; Rose & Wallace, 1985;

Ford et al., 1986), the sample assessed here should provide a conservative overall estimate of problems in meeting the ten-failure discontinue criterion on the Mental Scale.

## II. METHOD

### A. Subjects

The data reported here were collected as part of the Infant Health and Development Program (IHDP; The Infant Health and Development Program, 1990). This study was a multi-site randomized controlled trial to evaluate the efficacy of combining early child development and family support services with high quality pediatric follow-up for LBW premature infants. (See the Appendix for participating institutions and principal investigators.) One-third of the IHDP infants received the full array of services; the other two-thirds received the pediatric follow-up component only.

In the trial, a total of 4451 inborn LBW children born between January 1 and September 7, 1985 were screened for eligibility. After being screened for eligibility and giving informed consent to participate in the three-year study, 985 families were enrolled. Baseline data about neonatal health and selected sociodemographic variables were collected prior to newborn nursery discharge. Extensive data were gathered about the children's development, health, and behavior, and about family background and maternal characteristics. These data were collected through structured hospital clinic visits at 40 weeks gestation, and at 4, 8, 12, 18, 24, 30, and 36 months corrected age. Ages were corrected for weeks of prematurity based on clinical estimates of gestational age at birth using the Ballard assessment (Ballard, Novak, & Driver, 1979) as modified by Constantine et al. (1987). All subsequent references to age should be interpreted as "corrected age."

Of the 985 children in the IHDP sample, 811 were tested with the BSID within two weeks of their 24-month corrected birthday; of these, 807 were administered both the Mental and Motor Scales. These 807 constitute the sample reported here.

Approximately one-third of these infants were participating in the intensive early intervention program, and at the time of testing had been exposed to approximately two years of a home visiting program and one year of daily attendance at an IHDP Child Development Center. A structured, developmentally oriented curriculum emphasizing cognitive, language, and social development was implemented in both program components (Sparling, Lewis, & Neuwirth, in press; Sparling & Lewis, 1984).

Two features of this study are especially noteworthy. First, this is the largest sample to date to report 24-month BSID scores ($N = 807$). Second, all examiners in this multisite study participated in a highly structured training program. The examiners' abilities to maintain the standardized test administration were certified prior to testing the study children and monitored throughout the study.

## B.  Procedures

All children were administered the BSID between January and October 1987. This was the first procedure administered in the scheduled 24-month hospital clinic visit. Site staff were instructed to schedule the clinic visit within two weeks of the infant's 24-month corrected birthday. A second clinic visit was scheduled within one week of the original visit to complete any test that was terminated due to irritability, fatigue, or other behavior that interfered with obtaining optimal performance.

The coordinating center for the trial was designated the National Study Office (NSO). The NSO employed special procedures to insure that the BSID was administered in a uniform and standardized manner at all eight sites. These procedures included: careful selection of qualified examiners and site supervisors; detailed training for each BSID item; and regular surveillance of assessments, including written critiques of videotaped BSID administrations by each examiner.

At each site, a Ph.D. or Master's level psychologist with substantial experience in infant testing provided training and supervision to two or three local examiners. The BSID examiners were required to have prior infant testing experience, to participate in a highly structured training program, and to be certified on their performance by the supervisor from the NSO prior to the testing of study children.

The training was conducted in two parts. First, the supervisors participated in a two-day national training meeting conducted by the NSO. At the meeting, the BSID was reviewed item by item, and videotapes of BSID tests of 24-month-old children were critiqued. The standard BSID manuals (Bayley, 1969; Rhodes, Bayley, & Yow, 1984) and an additional manual detailing specific procedures for the IHDP also were reviewed, with special emphasis on maintaining a uniform testing protocol and standard procedures for training the examiners. This included discussion of procedures for handling different types of infant behavior (e.g., fatigue, irritability, wariness, negativistic behavior, restlessness).

In the second phase of training, the on-site supervisors trained the examiners. There were 28 examiners at eight sites. This consisted of participating in a series of prescribed instructional sessions, viewing and scoring videotapes of BSID exams (provided by the NSO), and conducting a minimum of five practice test sessions with 24-month-old children. These practice sessions were observed, co-scored, and critiqued for each examiner by the on-site supervisors. One of these practice test sessions (or an additional sixth session) was videotaped by the supervisor, and the tape was shipped to the NSO supervisor for review, written critique, and approval. A form was developed to provide written feedback to the site staff. The feedback included specific comments on the procedure for administering each item as well as comments on general testing issues, such as establishing and maintaining rapport with the child and mother, pacing, and organization of the entire test session. In this way, every effort was made to ensure that each examiner uniformly administered the BSID according to standard protocol.

During the 10 months in which study infants were tested, a monitoring system was established to ensure that the research protocol of standardized test administration was maintained. Each on-site supervisor conducted 10 periodic observations of the examiners' testing of study children at intervals mandated by the NSO. Halfway through the testing of study children, another videotape of each examiner's testing was made and sent to the NSO for review, written critique, and approval.

If an examiner's testing was judged to fall below the established standards at any time during the initial training or during the testing of study children, that examiner was temporarily prohibited from testing additional study children, and further training was instituted until a satisfactory level of performance could be reestablished. This occurred with two examiners during the initial training and with one examiner during the period of testing. All other examiners demonstrated a high level of standardized and uniform test performance during the initial training period and throughout the months during which study children were tested.

Examiners were instructed to attempt to maintain the infant in an optimal behavioral state for the test session. If the infant became restless, fatigued, or negativistic, testing was discontinued and a second test session was scheduled to occur within one week of the first session.

## III.  RESULTS

Table 1 shows baseline descriptive statistics for the sample, as well as means, standard deviations, and ranges for the 24-month Bayley Mental Developmental Indices (MDI) and Psychomotor Developmental Indices (PDI).

A tabulation of children by MDI intervals and whether they met the discontinue criterion of 10 consecutive failed items is presented in Table 2. The MDI intervals are in standard deviation increments, representing groups commonly used to define developmental ranges. Table 2 shows that 72.6% of the sample failed to meet the criteria for establishing a ceiling. In every MDI interval, except the interval of more than three standard deviations below the mean (under 52), there are some infants who did not meet the 10-failure criterion. The problem becomes more pronounced at higher MDI ranges. Of the 494 infants in mid-range (MDI 84–116), 421 (85.2%) passed at least one of the last 10 items. All but four of the 333 infants with an MDI grater than 99 passed at least one of the last 10 items.

TABLE 1

Sample Characteristics

| Variable | Mean | Standard deviation | Range |
|---|---|---|---|
| Birth weight (grams) | 1797.8 | 454.7 | 540–2500 |
| Gestational age (weeks) | 33.0 | 2.7 | 25–38 |
| Number of days in newborn nursery | 25.3 | 23.3 | 1–144 |
| Maternal age (years) | 24.9 | 6.1 | 14–43 |
| 24-Month BSID MDI[1] | 97.8 | 18.9 | 50–150 |
| 24-Month BSID PDI[2] | 96.1 | 14.7 | 50–141 |
| Variable | N | (%) | |
| Gender: | | | |
| Male | 399 | 49.4 | |
| Female | 408 | 50.6 | |
| Neonatal health indicators: | | | |
| On ventilator | 255 | 31.6 | |
| RDS[3] | 324 | 40.1 | |
| BPD[4] | 43 | 5.3 | |
| PDA[5] | 90 | 11.1 | |
| Maternal education: | | | |
| < 9th Grade | 29 | 3.6 | |
| Some high school | 286 | 35.4 | |
| High school graduate | 222 | 27.5 | |
| Some college | 159 | 19.7 | |
| College degree or more | 111 | 13.7 | |
| Maternal race: | | | |
| Black | 421 | 52.2 | |
| White | 274 | 33.9 | |
| Hispanic | 88 | 10.9 | |
| Asian | 13 | 1.6 | |
| Other | 11 | 1.4 | |
| Marital status: | | | |
| Married | 380 | 47.1 | |
| Single | 367 | 45.5 | |
| Divorced/Separated/Widowed | 60 | 7.4 | |

[1] BSID MDI = Bayley Scales of Infant Development Mental Developmental Index
[2] BSID PDI = Bayley Scales of Infant Development Psychomotor Developmental Index
[3] RDS = Respiratory Distress Syndrome
[4] BPD = Bronchopulmonary Dysplasia
[5] PDA = Patent Ductus Arteriosus

Tables 3 and 4 further illustrate the extent and nature of the criterion failure problem in our sample. Table 3 presents a cross-tabulation of MDI interval by the number of passes achieved in the last 10 items. Infants with higher MDI scores are more likely to pass more of the last 10 items, but in the mid-range (84–116), many infants passed several items out of the last 10 items. Table 4 presents a similar tabulation for the number of passes achieved in the last five items. Even

TABLE 2

Discontinue Criterion Status on Mental Scale for IHDP Sample

| MDI Score | Met criterion[1] Row % | (N) | Did not meet criterion[1] Row % | (N) | Total Column % | (N) |
|---|---|---|---|---|---|---|
| Under 52 | 100.0 | (15) | 0 | (0) | 1.9 | (15) |
| 52–67 | 94.7 | (18) | 5.3 | (1) | 2.3 | (19) |
| 68–83 | 72.3 | (115) | 27.7 | (44) | 19.7 | (159) |
| 84–99 | 24.6 | (69) | 75.4 | (212) | 34.8 | (281) |
| 100–116 | 1.9 | (4) | 98.1 | (209) | 26.4 | (213) |
| 117–132 | 0 | (0) | 100.0 | (81) | 10.0 | (81) |
| Over 132 | 0 | (0) | 100.0 | (39) | 4.8 | (39) |
| TOTAL | 27.4 | (221) | 72.6 | (586) | 100.0 | (807) |

[1] Criterion is ten consecutive failed times.

at this most upper end of the test, 50.2% of this sample passed one or more of the last five items.

Table 5 presents information on discontinue criterion status for the Motor Scale, parallel to the Mental Scale information presented in Table 2. These data indicate a much less prevalent ceiling problem. Overall, only 5% of the infants passed any of the last six items, and this only occurred with infants who obtained a PDI of at least 84. However, for infants with a PDI above 116 ($N = 68$), 33.8% ($N = 23$) passed at least one of the last six items. It appears that the criterion problem on the Motor Scale primarily affects infants performing in the higher ranges of motor functioning, and that the problem is not as pervasive as that found on the Mental Scale.

Although the BSID manual reports that the items are arranged in order of difficulty, the proportion of infants in the standardization sample who passed each item are not reported in the manual (Bayley, 1969). These data[1] were obtained and are presented in Table 6 for the last 10 Mental Scale items for the standardization sample and for the IHDP sample.

Table 6 shows that in the standardization sample these last 10 items depart slightly from sequential order of difficulty, and in the IHDP sample they depart more substantially. Each item except the last two was passed by a substantial percentage of 24-month-old infants in both samples. For the IHDP sample the most frequently passed item was item number 155 (Blue Board: Completes in 150 Seconds)—passed by 58% of the sample; for the standardization sample the most frequently passed item was item number 156 (Pegs Placed in 22 Seconds)— passed by 37% of the sample. It is notable that the IHDP sample showed relatively better performance on perceptual-motor and timed items (e.g., Blue Board; Builds Tower of Eight Cubes) compared to the standardization sample.

[1] These data were obtained from Janet Hunt, Ph.D. Institute of Human Development, University of California, Berkeley.

TABLE 3

Number of Passes in Last Ten Items by MDI Interval (Items 154–163)

| Number of passes in last ten items | MDI Scores | | | | | | | Total |
|---|---|---|---|---|---|---|---|---|
| | Under 52 | 52–67 | 68–83 | 84–99 | 100–116 | 117–132 | Over 132 | |
| 0 Passes: | | | | | | | | |
| N | 15 | 18 | 115 | 69 | 4 | 0 | 0 | 221 |
| %* | 100.0 | 94.7 | 72.3 | 24.6 | 1.9 | 0.0 | 0.0 | 27.4 |
| 1 Pass: | | | | | | | | |
| N | | 0 | 29 | 68 | 25 | 0 | 0 | 122 |
| % | | 0.0 | 18.2 | 24.2 | 11.7 | 0.0 | 0.0 | 15.1 |
| 2 Passes: | | | | | | | | |
| N | | 1 | 12 | 46 | 35 | 1 | 0 | 95 |
| % | | 5.3 | 7.5 | 16.4 | 16.4 | 1.2 | 0.0 | 11.8 |
| 3 Passes: | | | | | | | | |
| N | | | 2 | 48 | 35 | 5 | 0 | 90 |
| % | | | 1.3 | 17.1 | 16.4 | 6.2 | 0.0 | 11.1 |
| 4 Passes: | | | | | | | | |
| N | | | 1 | 39 | 47 | 19 | 0 | 106 |
| % | | | 0.6 | 13.9 | 22.1 | 23.5 | 0.0 | 13.1 |
| 5 Passes: | | | | | | | | |
| N | | | | 9 | 35 | 16 | 2 | 62 |
| % | | | | 3.2 | 16.4 | 19.7 | 5.1 | 7.7 |
| 6 Passes: | | | | | | | | |
| N | | | | 2 | 26 | 27 | 9 | 64 |
| % | | | | 0.7 | 12.2 | 33.3 | 23.1 | 7.9 |
| 7 Passes: | | | | | | | | |
| N | | | | | 6 | 12 | 12 | 30 |
| % | | | | | 2.8 | 14.8 | 30.8 | 3.7 |
| 8 Passes: | | | | | | | | |
| N | | | | | | 1 | 12 | 13 |
| % | | | | | | 1.2 | 30.8 | 1.6 |
| 9 Passes: | | | | | | | | |
| N | | | | | | | 3 | 3 |
| % | | | | | | | 7.7 | 0.4 |
| 10 Passes: | | | | | | | | |
| N | | | | | | | 1 | 1 |
| % | | | | | | | 2.6 | 0.1 |

* This is the percentage of the column N.

# IV.  DISCUSSION

Almost three-fourths of our sample (588 out of 807) did not meet the recommended discontinue criterion of 10 consecutive incorrect items on the BSID Mental Scale; and half of the sample (406 out of 807) obtained one or more passes among the last five items. The problem on the Motor Scale was less evident, with all but 5% of the sample meeting the recommended six-item criterion. Examination of the item data from the BSID standardization sample

TABLE 4

Number of Passes in Last Five Items by MDI Interval (Items 159–163)

| Number of passes in last five items | MDI Scores | | | | | | | |
|---|---|---|---|---|---|---|---|---|
| | Under 52 | 52–67 | 68–83 | 84–99 | 100–116 | 117–132 | Over 132 | Total |
| 0 Passes: | | | | | | | | |
| N | 15 | 18 | 146 | 169 | 52 | 2 | 0 | 402 |
| %* | 100.0 | 94.7 | 91.8 | 60.1 | 24.4 | 2.5 | 0.0 | 49.8 |
| 1 Pass: | | | | | | | | |
| N | | 1 | 11 | 52 | 47 | 9 | 0 | 120 |
| % | | 5.3 | 6.9 | 18.5 | 22.1 | 11.1 | 0.0 | 14.9 |
| 2 Passes: | | | | | | | | |
| N | | | 2 | 54 | 75 | 32 | 6 | 169 |
| % | | | 1.3 | 19.2 | 35.2 | 39.5 | 15.4 | 20.9 |
| 3 Passes: | | | | | | | | |
| N | | | | 6 | 35 | 33 | 17 | 91 |
| % | | | | 2.1 | 16.4 | 40.7 | 43.6 | 11.3 |
| 4 Passes: | | | | | | | | |
| N | | | | | 4 | 5 | 14 | 23 |
| % | | | | | 1.9 | 6.2 | 35.9 | 2.9 |
| 5 Passes: | | | | | | | | |
| N | | | | | | | 2 | 2 |
| % | | | | | | | 5.1 | 0.3 |

\* This is the percentage of the column N.

suggests that this problem with the discontinue criterion also occurred to some lesser degree with the standardization sample.

The findings show that the BSID Mental Scale may not capture the true range of developmental variability for 24-month-olds and older infants of even below average developmental functioning. More specifically, the BSID does not appear to adequately sample the full range of successful functioning for the

TABLE 5

Discontinue Criterion Status on Motor Scale for IHDP Sample

| PDI Scores | Met criterion[1] | | Did not meet criterion[1] | | Total | |
|---|---|---|---|---|---|---|
| | Row % | (N) | Row % | (N) | Column % | (N) |
| Under 52 | 100.0 | (21) | 0 | (0) | 2.6 | (21) |
| 52–67 | 100.0 | (36) | 0 | (0) | 4.5 | (36) |
| 68–83 | 100.0 | (99) | 0 | (0) | 12.3 | (99) |
| 84–99 | 98.4 | (370) | 1.3 | (5) | 46.7 | (376) |
| 100–116 | 94.2 | (195) | 5.8 | (12) | 25.7 | (207) |
| 117–132 | 72.6 | (45) | 27.4 | (17) | 7.7 | (62) |
| Over 132 | 0 | (0) | 100.0 | (6) | 0.7 | (6) |
| TOTAL | 95.0 | (766) | 5.0 | (40) | | (806)[2] |

[1] Criterion is six consecutive failed items.
[2] One subject is not included because ceiling status was unknown due to an assessor error.

TABLE 6

Proportion Passed for the Last 10 Items on the Mental Scale:
Comparison of Samples of 24-Month-Olds

| Item no. | Item name | Standardization[1] sample Proportion pass | IHDP[2] sample Proportion pass |
|---|---|---|---|
| 154 | Train of cubes | .36 | .26 |
| 155 | Blue board: completes in 150 seconds | .29 | .58 |
| 156 | Pegs placed in 22 seconds | .37 | .47 |
| 157 | Folds paper | .20 | .21 |
| 158 | Understands 2 prepositions | .21 | .23 |
| 159 | Blue board: completes in 90 seconds | .21 | .49 |
| 160 | Blue board: completes in 60 seconds | .14 | .37 |
| 161 | Builds tower of 8 cubes | .09 | .25 |
| 162 | Concept of one | .04 | .07 |
| 163 | Understands 3 prepositions | .07 | .09 |

[1] These data were provided by the Institute of Human Development, University of California, Berkeley. $N = 90$.
[2] IHDP = Infant Health and Development Program. $N = 807$.

overwhelming majority of 24-month-olds in our sample. Our findings also suggest that the useful upper age limit of the BSID Mental Scale may be lower than the minimal top of the test at 30 months.

It is puzzling that this discontinue criterion problem has not been reported before. It may be that many BSID examiners do not adhere to the recommended 10-successive-item discontinue criterion for the Mental Scale, and routinely discontinue testing after a smaller number of successive failed items. The nature of data collection protocols in many clinical research studies may also help explain why this problem has not been widely reported; some studies are actually reports of clinical efforts, without rigid, standardized research protocols. Developmental assessment data for preterms may be gathered as part of routine follow-up clinic visits over an extended period of time, without methodical attention to the consistency of a standardized research protocol (see review article by Kopp, 1983).

Because of the rich history and extensive previous use of the BSID and because the authors know of no better alternative at the 24-month age level, it is not recommended here that the use of the BSID at this age be limited. Instead, the authors make the following recommendations regarding the BSID Mental Scale:

1. Examiners should report whether or not the suggested discontinue criterion was employed, and if not, what criterion was used.
2. Researchers should report the proportion of their sample who do not meet the recommended discontinue criterion.

3. Readers should exercise caution in interpreting results whenever it is known that the discontinue criteria have not been met, or when it has not been reported that they have been met. This is especially true for, but not limited to, infants 24–30 months of age with MDI scores in the average range or above.

4. The next restandardization effort should consider adding more items at the upper end of the test or, as a less desirable alternative, reducing the nominal "top" of the test to a lower age.

## V. APPENDIX: INFANT HEALTH AND DEVELOPMENT PROGRAM

### National Study Office:

Ruth T. Gross, M.D., Director; Donna Spiker, Ph.D., Deputy Director; Norman A. Constantine, Ph.D., Director of Data Analysis; Wendy L. Kreitman, Director of Field Operations (The Department of Pediatrics and the Center for the Study of Families, Children, and Youth, Stanford University).

### Program Development Office:

Craig T.Ramey, Ph.D., Director; Donna Bryant, Ph.D., Associate Director; Joseph Sparling, Ph.D. and Barbara H. Wasik, Ph.D., Co-directors of Curriculum Development; Isabelle Lewis and Claudia Lyons, Curriculum Development Specialists; Kaye H. Fendt, M.S.P.H., Director of Data Management and Statistical Computing (The Frank Porter Graham Child Development Center, University of North Carolina at Chapel Hill).

### Participating Universities:

University of Arkansas for Medical Sciences (Arkansas); Albert Einstein College of Medicine (Einstein); Harvard Medical School (Harvard); University of Miami School of Medicine (Miami); University of Pennsylvania School of Medicine (Pennsylvania); University of Texas Health Science Center at Dallas (Texas); University of Washington School of Medicine (Washington); Yale University School of Medicine (Yale).

### Site Directors:

Patrick H. Casey, M.D., Arkansas; Cecelia M. McCarton, M.D., Einstein; Michael W. Yogman, M.D. and Daniel Kindlon, Ph.D., Harvard; Charles R. Bauer, M.D. and Keith G. Scott, Ph.D., Miami; Judith Bernbaum, M.D., Pennsylvania; Jon E. Tyson, M.D. and Mark Swanson, M.D., Texas; Clifford J.

Sells, M.D. and Forrest C. Bennett, M.D., Washington; David T. Scott, Ph.D., Yale.

### Educational Directors:

Joan Rorex, M.Ed., Arkansas; Katy Lutzius, Einstein; Marcia Hartley, M.S., Harvard; Mimi Graham, Ph.D., Miami; Joanne Crooms, M.Ed., Pennsylvania; Beverly A. Mulvihill, M.Ed., Texas; Randi Shapiro, M.Ed., Washington; Sandra E. Malmquist, M.A., Yale.

Bettye Caldwell, Ph.D., Educational Consultant, Arkansas; Ruth Turner, Ed.D., Dallas Independent School District Liaison, Texas; Rebecca R. Fewell, Ph.D., Educational Consultant, Washington.

### Research Steering Committee:

Helena C. Kraemer, Ph.D., Chair (Stanford University); Charles R. Bauer, M.D.; J. Brooks-Gunn, Ph.D. (Educational Testing Service, Princeton); Marie C. McCormick, M.D. (Harvard University); Craig T. Ramey, Ph.D; David T. Scott, Ph.D.; and Donna Spiker, Ph.D.

Sam Shapiro, Special Consultant to the National Study Office and Ex-Officio Member of the Research Steering Committee (The Johns Hopkins University School of Hygiene and Public Health).

# ITEM AND FACTOR ANALYSES OF THE BAYLEY SCALES OF INFANT DEVELOPMENT

*William J. Burns*

NOVA UNIVERSITY

*Kayreen A. Burns*

NORTHWESTERN UNIVERSITY

*Robert I. Kabacoff*

NOVA UNIVERSITY

I. INTRODUCTION ............................................ 199
II. METHOD .................................................. 200
   A. Subjects ................................................ 200
   B. Procedure .............................................. 201
   C. Factor Analysis ........................................ 201
   D. Correlation and Regression Analyses ..................... 210
   E. Discussion ............................................. 212

## I. INTRODUCTION

The Bayley Scales have proven to be among the most useful instruments available to study the developmental progress of infants. Despite general agreement among researchers that the Bayley Scales offer an efficient and precise measure of developmental progress, there is a lack of consensus about what it is that these scales actually measure. An analysis of the factor structure of the Bayley Scales has been attempted in the past. For instance, Nancy Bayley (1970), using a Tryon cluster analysis with an age-at-first-pass of each item as the unit of measure, computed interrelations between all items. She found no predictability across age with her clusters. Rather, she found that items on these clusters were arranged in an ascending order of difficulty. These findings led Bayley (1969) in her manual to state that the scale measured infants' ''abilities'' and that these abilities do not array themselves into neat concurrently developing ''factors'' (p.2). Further, she warned that ''any classification of abilities into parallel arrays purporting to designate different factors that develop concurrently is artificial and serves no useful purpose" (p.3).

In other words, Bayley did not believe that the content of the scales could be subcategorized any further than the original mental and motor abilities.

Stott and Ball (1965) uses Guilford's (1956) model of the intellect and included Bayley Scale results along with four other scales in a confirmatory factor analysis approach. Stott and Ball found that all of the scales including the Bayley loaded on many of Guilford's dimensions.

McCall, Eichorn, and Hogarty (1977) used Bayley Scale data from the Berkeley Growth Study and subjected individual test items to a principal components analysis for each testing at every month 1–15 months and every 3 months thereafter until 30 months. When resulting component scores were correlated across age, developmental transitions were identified at 2, 8, 13, 21, and 30 months.

These findings by Stott and Ball, and by McCall et al., provided some evidence for subcategories of abilities on the Bayley Scales. The Stott and Ball study was not exploratory but rather confirmatory. Thus, the results do not uncover the variables that contribute to test scores, as much as they fit item scoring patterns to a model or construct. The McCall et al. study had as its purpose to explore the item responses at sequential ages to identify components underlying the global measure. Both studies contributed valuable information about the structure of the Bayley Scales.

More recently several researchers have attempted to use factor methodology to investigate responses patterns of disadvantaged (Barclay & McWay, 1985) and low-birthweight (LBW), (Laskey, Tyson, Rosenfeld, Priest, Krasinski, Heartwell, & Gant, 1983) populations. Barclay and McWay supported the application of Guilford's model of the intellect to a disadvantaged population. Lasky et al. used principal component analysis and obtained results that were interpreted to evidence similarities between normal and LBW infants. Unfortunately, neither study included details that would allow evaluation of the merit and appropriateness on the analyses employed. The present study was designed to use exploratory factor analysis to investigate the factor structure of the Bayley Scales administered at four different ages: 3, 6, 12, and 24 months. The purpose in performing eight separate factor analyses, one for each scale (mental and motor) at each of the four ages, was to provide factor results for each set at each age which might be compared. A theoretical purpose was to identify any continuity of factors across age. A practical purpose was to provide clinicians with interpretable factors at each age.

## II.  METHOD

### A.  Subjects

It was our purpose to administer the Bayley Scales of Infant Development to a racially heterogeneous population of babies (48% White, 32% Black, 20%

Hispanic), whose mothers' IQs scores were average and whose mothers' educational level was on the average one year of college. The 251 infants were volunteers from a larger pool of deliveries at an inner city hospital in a large midwestern metropolitan setting. Mothers lived in the immediate vicinity of a hospital for prenatal obstetrical care. Family income on the average was middle class. It was our purpose in selecting this sample to obtain a group of urban, middle-class infants who were racially heterogenous, since it is such a sample that is most frequently administered the Bayley Scales.

## B. Procedure

Bayley Scales were administered at 3, 6, 12 and 24 months of age. Not all 251 infants were evaluated at each age level, but every completed scale was included in the current data pool. Infants born more than 4 weeks preterm were not enrolled in the study, nor were any significantly abnormal infants.

## C. Factor Analyses

We divided the data into eight separate units for the purpose of analysis: four of the mental scales and four of the psychomotor scales, with analyses at 3, 6, 12, and 24 months of age separately.

Table 1 presents the Mental Developmental Indices (MDI) and Psychomotor Developmental Indices (PDI) mean scores and standard deviations with the number of children seen at each age level. Differences in numbers for mental and psychomotor indices were due to loss of a portion of data due to lack of cooperation from the infants. These indices represent the eight separate units used in the factor analyses. The average level of these indices is consistent with the average IQ obtained by the mothers of the infants.

In Table 2 are shown the coefficients obtained from an item analysis using Cronbach's Alpha for dichotomous data (Kuder-Richardson—20). Coefficients ranging from .82 to .94 on the mental scale and .62 to .85 on the psychomotor scale indicate an acceptable level of item reliability to perform factor analyses.

An exploratory factor analysis was conducted using iterated principal axis factor analysis with squared multiple correlations as initial communality esti-

TABLE 1

Mean MDI & PDI and Standard Deviations

| | MDI | | | PDI | | |
|---|---|---|---|---|---|---|
| Age (mos.) | N | M | SD | N | M | SD |
| 3 | 222 | 93.50 | 9.61 | 224 | 99.06 | 10.57 |
| 6 | 212 | 102.80 | 13.20 | 215 | 100.52 | 12.96 |
| 12 | 216 | 102.42 | 11.27 | 218 | 98.05 | 13.92 |
| 24 | 172 | 97.19 | 14.32 | 174 | 99.27 | 18.68 |

TABLE 2
Coefficient Alphas by Age Group

| Age (months) | Mental | Psychomotor |
|---|---|---|
| 3 | .834 | .622 |
| 6 | .833 | .833 |
| 12 | .824 | .763 |
| 24 | .937 | .854 |

mates. The number of factors was chosen based upon the scree criterion (break between large factors and small ones in a plot of the total variance associated with each factor) and the logical interpretability of each factor. Varimax rotation with Kaiser normalization was used to obtain the final factor loadings. Both orthogonal and oblique rotation of the axes were attempted. However, allowing the factors to be correlated did not improve the solution, so orthogonal factors were selected. The statistical software in the analyses was the *Statistical Package for the Social Sciences* (SPSS-X, Version 3, 1988).

Only those items which contained pass-fail variance were entered into the analysis. Thus, all those items below an age level that were passed by all subjects were excluded from the analysis. Likewise, items above an age level which were failed by a particular age group were excluded from the analysis for that age group.

Initial Eigenvalues for the factors at each age level are presented in Table 3. Only factors that account for variances greater than 1 are included in the analysis, since factors with a variance less than 1 are no better than a single variable (each of which has a variance of 1) (SPSS-X, 1988).

The cumulative percentage of variance for the orthogonal factors increases with the number of factors extracted. A decision made on the basis of the screen criterion and logical interpretability of the factor resulted in the choice of the highest number of factors as seen in the cumulative percentages listed in Table 4.

The factor loadings on the 3-month mental scale are given in Table 5. Only

TABLE 3
Eigenvalues

| Age (mos.) | 1 | 2 | 3 | 4 | 5 | 6 | 7 |
|---|---|---|---|---|---|---|---|
| 3 Mental | 5.38 | 2.90 | 1.65 | 1.49 | | | |
| 3 Motor | 2.49 | 1.56 | 1.10 | | | | |
| 6 Mental | 5.53 | 2.54 | 1.68 | 1.53 | 1.38 | | |
| 6 Motor | 5.89 | 2.49 | 1.70 | 1.23 | 1.01 | | |
| 12 Mental | 5.10 | 2.83 | 1.85 | 1.69 | 1.51 | 1.38 | 1.23 |
| 12 Motor | 4.26 | 2.57 | 1.64 | 1.54 | 1.05 | | |
| 24 Mental | 12.23 | 3.15 | 2.35 | 1.77 | 1.47 | 1.39 | 1.32 |
| 24 Motor | 5.93 | 2.33 | 1.31 | 1.22 | 1.13 | 1.03 | |

### TABLE 4

Cumulative Percentage of Variance for Unrotated Orthogonal Factors

| Bayley scale | Number of factors | | | | | |
|---|---|---|---|---|---|---|
| | 2 | 3 | 4 | 5 | 6 | 7 |
| 3-month Mental | 24.5 | 28.2 | 31.8 | — | — | — |
| 3-month Motor | 24.9 | 31.6 | — | — | — | — |
| 6-month Mental | — | 27.1 | 30.5 | 33.5 | — | — |
| 6-month Motor | — | 40.1 | 43.4 | 45.7 | — | — |
| 12-month Mental | 20.2 | 23.7 | 27.6 | 30.4 | 33.2 | 35.4 |
| 12-month Motor | — | 39.4 | 44.5 | 48.1 | — | — |
| 24-month Mental | — | 36.1 | 39.3 | 41.6 | 43.7 | 45.7 |
| 24-month Motor | — | 37.5 | 40.6 | 43.7 | 47.3 | — |

items with factor loadings of .40 and greater were included. In this four-factor solution the loadings are more associated with "difficulty level" on factors 1 and 2 and more with an identifiable construct on factors 3 and 4.

Likewise, with the motor scale at 3 months of age, factors tended to be related to difficulty, with the greatest percentage variance accounted for by factors selecting items passed at older ages.

### TABLE 5

Factor Loadings 3-Month Mental Scale

| Bayley items | Factors | | | |
|---|---|---|---|---|
| | I | II | III | IV |
| 45 Inspects hands | .68 | | | |
| 48 Turns head-rattle | .64 | | | .50 |
| 46 Closes on dangling ring | .62 | | | |
| 47 Turns head-bell | .61 | | | .47 |
| 44 Carries ring to mouth | .50 | | | |
| 42 Aware strange situation | .46 | | | |
| 49 Reaches for cube | .45 | | | |
| 50 Manipulates table active | .43 | | | |
| 43 Manipulates table slight | .41 | | | |
| 37 Reaches dangling ring | .40 | | | |
| 29 Eye follows pencil | | .63 | | |
| 33 Manipulates ring | | .50 | | |
| 31 Reacts disappearance face | | .47 | | |
| 32 Regards cube | | .46 | | |
| 36 Simple play rattle | | .46 | | |
| 27 Vocalize E's voice & smile | | | .56 | |
| 21 Vocalizes 4 times | | | .55 | |
| 30 Vocalizes 2 sounds | | | .53 | |
| 25 Recognizes mother | | | | .45 |
| 28 Searches eyes-sound | | | | .42 |
| Percentage of the Variance | 16.9 | 8.3 | 3.5 | 3.1 |

TABLE 6

Factor Loadings 3-Month Motor Scale

| Bayley items | Factors | | |
|---|---|---|---|
| | I | II | III |
| 18 Head balanced | .96 | | |
| 16 Cube ulner-palmer | .50 | | |
| 19 Turns back to side | .47 | | |
| 14 Holds head steady | | .75 | |
| 13 Sits with support | | .43 | |
| 10 Turns head dorsal | | | .73 |
| 9 Head steady | | | .40 |
| Percentage of Variance | 17.6 | 9.3 | 4.7 |

These 3-month factors are primarily interpretable as a difficulty hierarchy. That is to say, the analysis identified only one factor, that of an order series of increasing difficulty across items. However, within this difficulty hierarchy the separate factors identified appear to have a common base within each factor which may be labeled. Therefore, we have provided in Table 7 a tentative list of these factor descriptors.

The factors selected for the 6-month mental (Table 8) and motor (Table 9) scale, also tended to be more related to difficulty level than content. Thus, the analysis primarily revealed a uniform factor: increasing difficulty.

However, there was a secondary trend for items to have a common base within the separate factors identified. We have expressed these content commonalities as factor descriptors in Table 10. These results seem to indicate that the BSID is primarily structured as a power hierarchy of successively more difficult age-related items, and secondarily structured within this hierarchy of groups of items with similar content. As can be seen in Tables 5, 6, 8, and 9, very few

TABLE 7

Factor Descriptors at 3 Months

Bayley scales

*Mental*
  I.   Visual guidance of head and hand
  II.  Early visual tracking and visual-motor *responses*
  III. Vocalizing response to sights voice
  IV.  Early visual and auditory reactions

*Motor*
  I.   Head, trunk and hand control
  II.  Head and trunk balance
  III. Head steadying

## TABLE 8
### Factor Loadings 6-Month Mental Scale

| Bayley items | Factors | | | | |
|---|---|---|---|---|---|
| | I | II | III | IV | V |
| 70 Picks up cube | .64 | | | | |
| 64 Reaches 2nd cube | .61 | | | | |
| 77 Retains 2 of 3 cubes | .54 | | | | |
| 69 Transfers object | .50 | | | | |
| 66 Bangs in play | .43 | | | | |
| 72 Sound production | .43 | | | | |
| 87 Fingers peg hole | | .59 | | | |
| 85 Dada or equivalent | | .55 | | | |
| 80 Pulls string adapt | | .51 | | | |
| 81 Coops in games | | .48 | | | |
| 86 Uncovers toy | | .47 | | | |
| 79 Vocalizes 4 syllables | | .46 | | | |
| 62 Turns head spoon | | | .90 | | |
| 59 Recovers rattle | | | .60 | | |
| 56 Retains 2 cubes | | | .46 | | |
| 63 Lifts inverted cup | | | | .66 | |
| 61 Likes frolic play | | | .43 | .52 | |
| 65 Smiles mirror | | | | .41 | |
| 83 Bell rings purposively | | | | | .67 |
| 78 Bell interest in detail | | | | | .59 |
| Percentage of variance | 16.9 | 6.9 | 4.2 | 3.0 | 2.7 |

## TABLE 9
### Factor Loading 6-Month Motor Scale

| Bayley items | Factors | | |
|---|---|---|---|
| | I | II | III |
| 38 Stands by furniture | .81 | | |
| 37 Raises to sit | .78 | | |
| 40 Stepping movements | .73 | | |
| 39 Midline combines | .68 | | |
| 36 Pulls to stand | .60 | | |
| 35 Inferior pincer | .58 | | |
| 34 Early step movements | .57 | .40 | |
| 31 Sits alone coordination | | .78 | |
| 29 Sits steady | | .72 | |
| 32 Thumb opposition | | .65 | |
| 27 Sits 30 seconds | | .53 | |
| 33 Prewalk progress | .44 | .52 | |
| 30 Scoops pellet | | .50 | |
| 21 Partial thumb | | | .64 |
| 24 Unilateral reaching | | | .58 |
| 26 Rotates wrist | | | .54 |
| 23 Sits alone momentarily | | | .53 |
| 20 Effort to sit | | | .42 |
| Percentage of total variance | 25.6 | 8.9 | 5.5 |

205

TABLE 10

Factor Descriptors at 6 Months

Bayley scales

*Mental*
  I.   Object manipulation
  II.  Language and adaptive behavior
  III. Visual-motor coordination
  IV.  Social interaction
  V.   Exploratory and instrumental behavior

*Motor*
  I.   Gross motor progress to stepping
  II.  Gross motor progress sitting and crawling
  III. Fine motor and early trunk control.

TABLE 11

Factor Loading 12-Month Mental Scale

| Bayley items | Factors | | | | | | |
| --- | --- | --- | --- | --- | --- | --- | --- |
| | I | II | III | IV | V | VI | VII |
| 117 Shows clothing | .72 | | | | | | |
| 115 Close round box | .62 | | | | | | |
| 111 Tower 2 cubes | .52 | | | | | | |
| 118 Pegs 70 seconds | .50 | | | | | | |
| 110 Blue board (1) | .48 | | | | | | |
| 119 Tower 3 cubes | .46 | | | | | | |
| 116 Gestures | .43 | | | | | | |
| 107 Beads in box | | .50 | | | | | |
| 100 Cubes in cup (3) | | .49 | | | | | |
| 105 Dangles ring | | .48 | | | | | |
| 102 Uncovers box | | .43 | | | | | |
| 106 Imitates words | | | .53 | | | | |
| 113 Says 2 words | | | .50 | | | | |
| 109 Removes pellet | | | .47 | | | | |
| 101 Jabbers | | | .43 | | | | |
| 88 Picks up cup & cube | | | | .85 | | | |
| 89 R to Verbal request | | | | .69 | | | |
| 93 Looks at pictures | | | | | .60 | | |
| 92 Stirs spoon | | | | | .49 | | |
| 90 1 cube in cup | | | | | .47 | | |
| 97 Repeats performance | | | | | .42 | | |
| 95 Imitates scribble | | | | | | .61 | |
| 98 Crayon adaptively | | | | | | .57 | |
| 91 Looks in box | | | | | | | .58 |
| 94 Inhibits on command | | | | | | | .55 |
| Percentage of total variance | 13.9 | 7.1 | 4.0 | 3.5 | 2.7 | 2.4 | 1.9 |

TABLE 12

Factor Loadings on 12-Month Motor Scale

| Bayley items | Factors | | | | |
|---|---|---|---|---|---|
| | I | II | III | IV | V |
| 53 Upstairs with help | .93 | | | | |
| 51 R foot with help | .87 | | | | |
| 52 L foot with help | .86 | | | | |
| 54 Downstairs with help | .73 | | | | |
| 46 Walks alone | | .88 | | | |
| 47 Stands up: I | | .69 | | | |
| 45 Stands alone | | .49 | .45 | | |
| 48 Throws ball | | .43 | | | |
| 42 Walks with help | | | .80 | | |
| 36 Pulls to stand | | | .63 | | |
| 43 Sits down | | | .48 | | |
| 40 Step movement | | | .43 | | |
| 49 Walks sideways | | | | .68 | |
| 50 Walks backwards | | | | .59 | |
| 44 Patacake midline | | | | | .62 |
| 41 Neat pincer | | | | | .56 |
| Percentage of total variance | 21.8 | 12.0 | 6.4 | 5.0 | 2.9 |

items loaded on more than one factor. This fact supports Bayley's original assumption of orthogonality of the factors and indicates a lack of correlation between these factors. Some items did not load on the factors selected or did not account for sufficient variance to be selected.

Factors for the 12-month mental (Table 11) and motor (Table 12) scales were very much structured as difficulty hierarchies in those factors that ac-

TABLE 13

Factor Descriptors at 12 Months

Bayley scale

*Mental*
    I.   Adaptive fine motor
    II.   Advanced fine motor
    III.  Expressive and receptive language
    IV.  Memory for objects and words
    V.   Response to modeling and guidance
    VI.  Scribbling
    VII. Response to command.

*Motor*
    I.   Assisted balance & stair walking
    II.   Standing and walking alone
    III.  Progress toward walking
    IV.  Walking sideways and backwards
    V.   Fine pincer and midline coordination

counted for the most significant amount of the variance. The smaller, less significant factors tended to be more content related.

The factor descriptors that we assigned tended to fall into traditional developmental categories: fine motor, gross motor, language, and adaptive behavior (Table 13).

Factors for the 24-month mental (Table 14) and motor (Table 15) scales tended to be more content related than were factors for the other age levels. However, the primary unifying factor continued to be the difficulty hierarchy.

Factor descriptors again tend to fall into traditional developmental categories (Table 16).

TABLE 14

Factor Loading 24-Month Mental Scale

| Bayley items | Factors | | | | | | |
|---|---|---|---|---|---|---|---|
| | I | II | III | IV | V | VI | VII |
| 149 Names 5 pictures | .56 | | | | | | |
| 148 Point 7 pictures | .55 | | .46 | | | | |
| 136 Sentence 2 words | .54 | | | | | | |
| 139 Points 5 pictures | .53 | | | | | | |
| 150 Names watch 2nd | .50 | | | | .41 | | |
| 152 Discriminates (3) | .50 | | | | | | |
| 130 Names one picture | .46 | | | | | | |
| 127 Uses words | | .58 | | | | | |
| 129 Blue board (4) | | .58 | | | | | |
| 137 Pink Bd completes | | .57 | | | | | |
| 124 Names one object | | .57 | | | | | |
| 142 Blue (6) board | | .51 | | | | | |
| 121 Blue (2) board | | .47 | | | | | |
| 132 Pts 3 pictures | | .47 | | | | | |
| 128 Pts parts doll | | .46 | | | | | |
| 120 Pink Bd round | | .45 | | | | | |
| 159 Blue Bd 90 seconds | | | .79 | | | | |
| 155 Blue Bd 150 seconds | | | .78 | | | | |
| 151 Pink Bd reverse | | | .63 | | | | |
| 160 Blue Bd 60 seconds | | | .63 | | | | |
| 123 Peg Bd 42 seconds | | | | .71 | | | |
| 126 Directions doll | | | | .70 | | | |
| 134 Pegs 30 seconds | | | | .58 | | | |
| 163 3 Prepositions | | | | | .77 | | |
| 162 Concept of one | | | | | .54 | | |
| 158 2 Prepositions | | | | | .47 | | |
| 156 Pegs 22 seconds | | | | | | .44 | |
| 161 Tower 8 cubes | | | | | | .40 | |
| 131 Finds hidden objects | | | | | | | .63 |
| 122 Attains toy with stick | | | | | | | .63 |
| Percentage of total variance | 26.7 | 6.0 | 4.1 | 3.1 | 2.2 | 1.9 | 1.7 |

TABLE 15

Factor Loading 24-Month Motor Scale

| Bayley items | Factors | | | | | |
|---|---|---|---|---|---|---|
| | I | II | III | IV | V | VI |
| 70 Jump 4-14 inches | .69 | | | | | |
| 72 Upstairs alternate | .63 | | | | | |
| 69 Jumps 2nd step | .60 | | | | | |
| 74 Board alternate | .59 | | | | | |
| 68 Walks backward (10) | .48 | | | | | |
| 64 Upstairs both feet | | .82 | | | | |
| 66 Downstairs both feet | | .71 | | | | |
| 60 R foot alone | | | .80 | | | |
| 58 L foot alone | | | .77 | | | |
| 55 Tries walk board | | | | .70 | | |
| 56 One foot on board | | | | .60 | | |
| 62 Both feet on board | | | | .52 | | |
| 67 Attempts step on board | | | | | .57 | |
| 63 Jumps bottom step | .42 | | | | .45 | |
| 71 Stand up: III | | | | | .43 | |
| 73 Tiptoe 10 feet | | | | | | .75 |
| Percentage of total variance | 26.2 | 8.9 | 3.7 | 3.4 | 2.7 | 2.5 |

TABLE 16

Factor Descriptors at 24 Months

| Bayley scales |
|---|

*Mental*
    I. Advanced language
    II. Early language and form board
    III. Advanced form board
    IV. Fine motor and interactive behavior
    V. Advanced receptive language
    VI. Advanced adaptive and fine motor
    VII. Instrumental and search behavior

*Motor*
    I. Advanced gross motor coordination
    II. Independent stair walking
    III. Balancing on one foot
    IV. Balancing on walking board
    V. Gross motor coordination
    VI. Balance on tiptoe

## D.  Correlation and Regression Analyses

Pearson correlation coefficients were calculated between the factors obtained for
the mental and motor scales at each age level. In most cases statistical relationships were not found among factors at other ages. Some small but significant
coefficients were obtained, but probably no more than one might expect to obtain
by chance. As an example of these coefficients we present in Table 17 a matrix
of 12-month mental factors compared with 24-month mental factors. The most
significant relationship was between factor 3 at 12 months and factor 2 at 24
months, both of which are language factors. The 24-month factor that was most
frequently related to 12-month factors was factor 7, which includes instrumental
behavior and identification of a hidden object.

Likewise, when Pearson correlation coefficients were calculated between
factors and developmental indices at each age few significant relationships were
found. Table 18 and 19 give coefficients between 12- and 24-month mental
factors and MDI and PDI at 12 and 24 months. No significant coefficients were
found between 12-month mental factors and 24-month indices. The most significant coefficient at 24 months was the relationship between factors 4 and 12-
month MDI. Factor 4 includes following directions with a doll and speeded items
on the form boards. Both MDI and PDI showed a significant but minimal
relationship to factor 2 at 24 months, which includes expressive language and
form board performance.

Tables 20 and 21 show the coefficients of correlation for PDIs at each age
and MDIs at each age. For PDI only the 3- and 24-month indices failed to show a
relationship. Although these relationships are small in terms of the amount of
variance accounted for (at most 16%), they reflect a much stronger tendency to
relate across age levels than do factors with factors or factors with indices.

TABLE 17

Pearson Correlations Coefficients

| 12-Month | 24-Month mental factors | | | | | | |
|---|---|---|---|---|---|---|---|
| mental factors | 1 | 2 | 3 | 4 | 5 | 6 | 7 |
| 1 | .06 | .08 | .13* | .07 | −.09 | −.09 | .02 |
| 2 | −.06 | −.01 | .02 | .09 | −.07 | .01 | −.06 |
| 3 | .11 | .20** | −.10 | .06 | .04 | −.12 | −.15* |
| 4 | .08 | −.02 | .05 | .07 | −.08 | −.01 | .15* |
| 5 | −.01 | .12 | .05 | .00 | −.06 | .05 | .09 |
| 6 | .05 | −.06 | −.12 | .04 | .04 | −.10 | .02 |
| 7 | .05 | .09 | −.10 | −.10 | −.09 | −.10 | −.13* |

* $p < .05$
** $p < .005$

TABLE 18

Pearson Correlation Coefficients

| 24-Month mental factors | 12 Months | |
| --- | --- | --- |
| | MDI | PDI |
| 1 | .02 | .03 |
| 2 | .15* | .15* |
| 3 | .10 | .06 |
| 4 | .19** | .00 |
| 5 | −.06 | .01 |
| 6 | .03 | .08 |
| 7 | .05 | .16* |

* $p < .02$
** $p < .009$

The relationship is even stronger when we calculated coefficients for mental versus motor indices at the same age. In Table 22 it becomes obvious that the strength of this relationship between mental and motor indices becomes less as the time between administrations becomes greater.

To perform regression analysis with the indices and factors, we used standard multiple regression, wherein variables are entered simultaneously rather than in a stepwise or hierarchical fashion. Using 3-month mental factors as predictors of 24-month MDI, we found no relationship. Nor did we find any relationship using the 12-month mental factors as predictors of the 24-month MDI. When 3- and 12-month MDIs were used as predictors of the 24-month MDI, again, no relationship was found.

Neither factors nor indices predict factors or indices at other ages. It appears that factors like indices may be useful in discussing developmental status at a given age, but we found neither to be useful in a standard multiple regression as predictors of factors or indices at other ages.

TABLE 19

Pearson Correlation Coefficients

| 12-Month mental factors | 24-Month | |
| --- | --- | --- |
| | MDI | PDI |
| 1 | −.04 | −.07 |
| 2 | −.03 | −.08 |
| 3 | .10 | .10 |
| 4 | .06 | .08 |
| 5 | .07 | .05 |
| 6 | −.03 | .02 |
| 7 | −.04 | .11 |

TABLE 20
Pearson Correlation Coefficients

| PDI months | PDI months | | |
| --- | --- | --- | --- |
| | 3 | 6 | 12 |
| 6 | .35* | | |
| 12 | .19* | .29* | |
| 24 | .13 | .21* | .40* |

\* $p < .004$

## E.  Discussion

The rationale given by Bayley (1969) for the failure to find relationships between age periods on BSID scores is that these mental and motor scale abilities increasingly differentiate with age. If we rephrase Bayley's rationale in factor analysis terms, we might say that ability factors assessed at different ages are actually separate and different factors, even if we use similar labels to describe them. Therefore, the abstract descriptors invented to label these factors may be misleading, since the underlying item functions may be dissimilar enough across factors that they do not measure the same thing.

Despite this disappointing but predictable finding of lack of continuity from age to age on BSID scores, there were encouraging signs that the data revealed some stable, orthogonal factors that account for a considerable amount of the variance in the items used. Those factor solutions with fewer factors extracted (Table 3) resulted in a tendency for items to be more logically related to a difficulty factor, whereas solutions with more factors tended to be more content oriented. One hypothesis about such an age-related phenomenon is that the homogeneity in the sample of mothers (as to environment, education and IQ) was manifested in increased similarity of scoring patterns between the infants at each age. In addition to sample homogeneity on demographic variables, it would seem

TABLE 21
Pearson Correlation Coefficients

| MDI months | MDI months | | |
| --- | --- | --- | --- |
| | 3 | 6 | 12 |
| 6 | .33** | | |
| 12 | .11 | .28** | |
| 24 | .17* | .11 | .16* |

\* $p < .02$
\*\* $p < .001$

TABLE 22

Pearson Correlation Coefficients

| PDI months | MDI months | | | |
|---|---|---|---|---|
| | 3 | 6 | 12 | 24 |
| 3 | .53** | .24** | .09 | .04 |
| 6 | .37** | .57** | .27** | .14* |
| 12 | .15* | .21* | .39** | .14* |
| 24 | .07 | .26** | .16* | .16* |

$* p < .04$
$** p < .001$

that an exploratory factor analysis on the BSID produces greater coherence of items on an age-related dimension or "difficulty factor" than on a content dimension, because of the way that the Bayley Scales were constructed and because of the nature of child development.

Bayley constructed her scale of items that were chosen to measure development in a power sequence. The items fell into a hierarchical series, so that increasing age would be required to pass each successive task. Although items were also chosen to measure a variety of content, the test construction priority was the power dimension. It is this age-dependent aspect of item selection in test construction that surfaces as the dimension of priority in our exploratory factor analysis.

Likewise, this age dependency or difficulty factor of the BSID may be a reflection of a primary dimension of the nature of a child's developmental progress. The Piagetian notion of discontinuous-continuity across age in child development may provide a rationale for our findings. If indeed children maintain continuity as they assimilate new facts, but go through a period of discontinuity as their cognitive structure accommodates to novel content, then we should expect both continuity and discontinuity when we measure developmental progress. We should expect greater continuity the closer in time are two measures of that progress and greater discontinuity the farther apart, because the closer times will be more likely to measure assimilation processes and the farther times will be more sensitive to accommodation.

Thus, the factor analysis of the BSID may have found more coherence between *different* content at the *same* age (e.g., PDI and MDI at 3 months) than between "so-labeled" *similar* content at *different* ages (e.g., language factors at 3 and 24 months). In other words, 3-month-old babies are more like other 3-month-old babies, across a variety of abilities, than like *themselves* at 24 months of age on any one specific ability. Individual patterns of abilities evidently do not remain stable over time. But individual commonalities (age factors between babies) within a given age cohort at one point in time show a measurable relationship.

In summary, we found it possible to perform exploratory factor analyses with each of the mental and motor item pools for each of the 3-, 6-, 12-, and 24-month time periods on the BSID. Factor solutions yielded between three and seven orthogonal factors, depending on age period and mental–motor dimension. At early ages, factor solutions were dominated by difficulty factors, while at later ages factor solutions were more content oriented. However, factor scores were neither predictive of factor scores at any other time period or of MDI or PDI at any other time period. Therefore, while these factors had some logical inter-pretability, they had no predictive validity within the context of the Bayley Scales themselves. This study has provided evidence for Nancy Bayley's pre-sumption that a search for factors would probably be fruitless in terms of searching for predictions across age.

# SPEEDED ITEMS: WHAT DO THEY TELL US ABOUT AN INFANT'S PERFORMANCE?*

*James S. Gyurke*
*Susan J. Lynch*

THE PSYCHOLOGICAL CORPORATION
SAN ANTONIO, TX

*Lynn Lagasse*
*Lewis P. Lipsitt*

BROWN UNIVERSITY
CHILD STUDY CENTER

I. INTRODUCTION .......................................... 215
II. METHOD ................................................ 218
  A. Subjects ............................................ 218
  B. Analyses ........................................... 218
III. RESULTS .............................................. 219
  A. 12-Month Reliability Analyses ...................... 219
  B. 18-Month Reliability Analyses ...................... 219
  C. Factor Analysis 12 Months ......................... 222
  D. Factor Analysis 18 Months ......................... 224
IV. DISCUSSION ........................................... 224

## I. INTRODUCTION

The history of intelligence and ability testing is replete with debates about what constitutes intelligence and, thus, what should be measured by an intelligence

* The authors thank Ms. Bernice Reilly, R.N., the nurse who enlisted the cooperation of the mothers and their infants in this study. We also thank Women and Infants Hospital of Rhode Island, where studies have been carried out over a 30-year period under the direction of Lewis P. Lipsitt. We especially thank William Oh, M.D., Chief of Pediatrics at Women and Infant's Hospital, who was instrumental in facilitating these studies over the last 15 years.

test (Sternberg, 1986; Eysenck & Barrett, 1985). Despite the diverse views of researchers and theoreticians on how to measure intelligence, certain mental traits consistently appear in a variety of intellectual assessments. One of those traits measured, in both traditional and contemporary intelligence assessment, is mental speed or speed of performance.

Standard practice in assessment of infant performance has involved not only measurement of whether a child can successfully complete a task, but also whether the task is completed within a prescribed time interval. Assessments such as the Bayley Scales of Infant Development (Bayley, 1969), The Cattell Infant Intelligence Scale (Cattell, 1941), and the Battelle Developmental Inventory (Newborg, Stock, Wrek, Guidibaldi, & Svinicki, 1984) impose time limits on various tasks with the intention of discriminating children of higher from those of lower mental ability. The underlying assumption is that speed of performance reflects the individuals "capacity" or "intelligence."

This assumption is backed up by research done by Chalke and Ertl (1965), Ertl and Schafer (1969), and Ertl (1971, 1973) who found significant correlations between standardized IQ test scores and physiological measures of mental speed. Using electroencephalograms to record and quantify subjects' reactions to visual and auditory stimuli, researchers studied components of averaged evoked potentials to relate to IQ measures. Chalke et al. (1965) found positive correlations between mean latency of evoked potentials and IQ scores. Several researchers (Rhodes, Dustin, & Beck, 1969) were unable to replicate these results; however, Callaway (1975) found that variability of waveforms was negatively correlated with IQ in children. He has suggested that the variability of waveforms may account for increased latency and, therefore, the significant correlations between mental speed and lower IQ. Research by Hendrickson (1982) also found significant correlations between amplitude, complexity of waveforms, variance of waveforms, and WAIS IQ scores. These results lend theoretical and physiological support to the measurement of mental speed as an index of mental ability.

Studies involving school-age children have established a relationship between speed of performance and various aspects of intelligence. Kaufman (1979) explored this issue using the WISC-R standardization sample (ages 6½–16 years). He examined children's speed of performance on three subtests: Object Assembly, Picture Arrangement, and Block Design. For each of the 20 speeded items on these three subtests, performance times for each item performed correctly were averaged across each of the 11 age groups. These mean performance times were then rank-ordered from fastest to slowest time and correlated with chronological age. All 20 correlations, ranging from 0.7 to 1.00, were significant at $p < .05$. These results indicate that a strong correlation exists between speed of performance and ability level as the age of the child increases.

Research employing experimental tasks has also shown a relationship between speed of performance and mental ability. Keating and Bobbitt (1978) examined cognitive processing efficiency among third, seventh, and eleventh graders. Half of the students in each grade were of high mental ability and half were of average mental ability. Employing a memory-search procedure in one of a series of three experiments, these investigators obtained results indicating significant differences in speed of performance depending on mental ability. High ability students consistently reacted more quickly than did average ability students. Similar results were obtained by Hunt, Frost, and Lunneborg (1973) who found that subjects with high mathematics ability performed a continuous paired associates task significantly faster than did low mathematics ability subjects.

There is considerable evidence establishing the relationship between speed of performance and ability in the school-age child; however, this relationship is much less evident in the preschool-age child. In exploring the relationship between speed of performance and ability in young children, many researchers have employed an information processing model. For example, several studies have demonstrated that younger infants take longer to habituate to a stimulus than do older infants (i.e., Lewis, Goldberg, & Campbell, 1969). This early work demonstrating differences in habituation among infants has led to the use of the habituation paradigm to discriminate infants of different ability levels. Further justification for the use of this paradigm comes from studies by Lewis and Brooks-Gunn (1981) who have found that a visual-attention task (visual fixation to novel and familiar slides) administered to a group of 3-month-old infants predicted intellectual functioning on the Bayley Scales at 24 months better than did 3-month Bayley Scale scores.

Though the information processing approach does suggest a direct relationship between speed of performance and ability, generalization of the results from this model to that employed in the traditional infant assessment model is difficult. Generalization is difficult because speeded tasks administered on traditional assessments are subject to many external influences. Outside distractions in the testing environment, the child's motor control, and the child's motivation all may affect his or her ability to perform a task quickly (Zigler & Seitz, 1982). Because the information processing research is conducted in an experimental setting, the influence of these extraneous factors is greatly reduced. A second factor affecting the generalizability of results is the task demands of traditional assessments. In traditional assessment, the examiner instructs the child to perform a task and then begins timing the performance. This introduction of a timepiece for some tasks, but not for others, may affect even the young child's perception of that task.

Information is lacking on the relationship between speed of performance and mental ability as measured by traditional assessments. The present study was undertaken to examine the relationship between children's performance on timed tasks on the Bayley Scales of Infant Development and the child's ability level. A second issue considered in this research was the general relationship of these speeded items to the construct of mental ability. Specifically, an exploratory factor analytic approach was used to investigate whether these speeded items relate more closely to mental ability as defined by the Bayley Scales or to some other facets of ability.

## II. METHOD

### A. Subjects

This research was performed in conjunction with a larger project at the Brown University Child Study Center, Providence, RI. The original sample for the study consisted of 230 mothers and their newborn infants who were recruited between the years of 1984 and 1987 at the Women and Infants Hospital of Rhode Island. Mothers were approached by a staff nurse immediately after delivery and asked to sign a consent form allowing their infant to participate in this study.

Infants in this study were seen at approximately 4, 12, and 18 months of age. At each visit the child was examined using a variety of formal and informal assessment instruments along with the *Bayley Scales of Infant Development* (Bayley, 1969). The *BSID* was administered according to standardized administration procedures by one of three trained examiners. Examiners were not permitted to perform independent evaluations for this study until they were able to reach an interrater agreement on item scores to within four points per protocol.

Not all of the children were available to be tested at the 18-month follow-up visit. Of the original 230 subjects, 166 were assessed at 18 months. Examination of those subjects who did not participate in the 18-month follow-up revealed no systematic differences between the group who participated and the attrition group.

Of the 230 infants enrolled and utilized in the present study, 223 were healthy, full-term infants (gestational age of 40 weeks ± 2 weeks). Seven infants included in the sample were preterm (mean gestational age of 34.3 weeks). Two age levels are of special concern here. The 12-month age group consisted of 117 males and 113 females. Their mean age at time of testing was 12.47 mos. (SD = .54). The 18-month age group consisted of 166 infants, 80 males and 86 females. Their mean age at time of testing was 18.79 mos. (SD = .58).

### B. Analyses

Three reliability analyses, using the reliability program from the mainframe version of SPPSx, were run on the Bayley Mental Scale data for both the 12- and 18-month age groups. Since the BSID allows the examiner to start testing a child at his or her level of competence and to stop testing when the child ceases to pass items, each age group and, indeed, each child may be administered a slightly different set of items. The range of items for the 12- and 18-month age groups used in the analyses was determined by finding the maximum number of subjects who had no missing data on the largest possible range of items given to that age group. Using this method a subsample of 74 subjects in the 12-month age group and 50 subjects in the 18-month age group remained in the reliability analyses. In the 12-month age group the item range used for the analysis was Bayley Mental Scale item #97 to item #127 (31 items), and in the 18-month age group the range of items used was Bayley Mental Scale item #117 to item #163 (46 items). Initial analysis used all items within the designated range for each age group. A second analysis for each age group was run with timed items deleted. For purposes of analysis, timed items were defined as those which require that the child complete a task within a specific time period. A third analysis deleted the timed items plus all items which, although not individually timed, are part of a series of items (i.e., completes Blue board). some of which include criteria requiring that the child complete the task within a specific time period.

To determine if the timed items all loaded on a common factor, factor analyses were completed on the item ranges for each age group using the same items as those used in the reliability analysis. The SPSSx program used to perform the analyses specified mean substitution for missing data and varimax rotation.

## III. RESULTS

### A.  12-Month Reliability Analyses

The reliability analysis on the full set of items (97 through 127) yielded a Cronbach's alpha of .62 ($N = 74$) with corrected item-to-total correlations for the items ranging from $-.14$ to .49 (see Table 1).

The two nested peg items, #118-pegs placed in 10 seconds and #123-pegs placed in 12 seconds had item-to-total correlations of .05 and .00 respectively. Exclusion of these timed items from the second reliability analysis had no effect on Cronbach's alpha. The following items, all members of a timed series, #108-Places 1 peg repeatedly, #110-Blue board: places 1 round block, #118-Pegs placed in 70 seconds, #121-Blue board: places 2 round blocks, and #123-Pegs placed in 42 seconds had corrected item-to-total correlations ranging from low to moderate (see Table 1). Deletion of all items in timed series from the third analyses resulted in Cronbach's alpha = .60.

### B.  18-Month Reliability Analyses

The reliability analysis on the full set of items (117 through 163) yielded a Cronbach's alpha of .86 ($N = 50$) with the corrected item-to-total correlations ranging from $-.16$ to .62 (see Table 2).

TABLE 1

Reliability Analysis: 12-Month Age Group; Corrected Item-to-Total Correlations (r)
and Alpha's if Item Deleted (a)

| Item # and title | r | a |
|---|---|---|
| 97 Repeats performance laughed at | .32 | .60 |
| 98 Holds crayon adaptively | .18 | .62 |
| 99 Pushes car along | .15 | .62 |
| 100 Puts 3 or more cubes in cup | .18 | .62 |
| 101 Jabbers expressively | .28 | .60 |
| 102 Uncovers blue box | .10 | .62 |
| 103 Turns pages of book | .00 | .62 |
| 104 Pats whistle doll in imitation | .05 | .62 |
| 105 Dangles ring by string | .05 | .63 |
| 106 Imitates words | .25 | .61 |
| 107 Puts beads in box | .39 | .59 |
| 108 Places 1 peg repeatedly | .15 | .62 |
| 109 Removes pellet from bottle | −.14 | .63 |
| 110 Blue board: 1 round block | .36 | .60 |
| 111 Builds tower of 2 cubes | .39 | .59 |
| 112 Spontaneous scribble | .17 | .61 |
| 113 Says 2 words | .38 | .58 |
| 114 Puts 9 cubes in cup | .11 | .62 |
| 115 Closes round box | .22 | .61 |
| 116 Uses gestures, make wants known | .33 | .59 |
| 117 Shows shoes, clothing or own toy | .08 | .63 |
| 118 Pegs placed in 70 secs. | .05 | .62 |
| 119 Builds tower of 3 cubes | −.04 | .62 |
| 120 Pink board: places round block | .15 | .62 |
| 121 Blue board: 2 round blocks | .09 | .62 |
| 122 Attains toy with stick | .18 | .61 |
| 123 Pegs placed in 42 secs. | .00 | .62 |
| 124 Names 1 object | .04 | .63 |
| 125 Imitates crayon stroke | .37 | .60 |
| 126 Follows directions, doll | .22 | .61 |
| 127 Uses words to make wants known | .14 | .62 |

Cronbach's alpha = .62

The second reliability analysis excluded: #118-Pegs placed in 70 seconds, #123-Pegs placed in 42 seconds, #134-Pegs placed in 30 seconds, #155-Blue board: completes in 150 seconds, #156-Pegs placed in 22 seconds; #159-Blue board: completes in 90 seconds; and, #160-Blue board: completes in 60 seconds. The exclusion of these 7 items from the 40-item set resulted in an increase in Cronbach's alpha from .86 to .88. The item-to-total correlations for these items were all within the lower third of the item-to-total correlations for the items in this set (see Table 2).

The final reliability analysis excluded three additional items which are part of a timed series. The additional items deleted were: #121-Blue board: places 2

# TABLE 2

Reliability Analysis: 18-Month Age Group; Corrected Item-to-Total Correlations (r)
and Alpha's if Item Deleted (a)

| Item # and title | r | a |
|---|---|---|
| 117 Shows shoes, clothing or own toy | .03 | .86 |
| 118 Pegs placed in 70 secs. | .31 | .86 |
| 119 Builds tower of 3 cubes | .23 | .86 |
| 120 Pink board: places round block | .31 | .86 |
| 121 Blue board: 2 round blocks | .44 | .85 |
| 122 Attains toy with stick | .02 | .86 |
| 123 Pegs placed in 42 secs. | −.06 | .86 |
| 124 Names 1 object | .62 | .85 |
| 125 Imitates crayon stroke | .48 | .85 |
| 126 Follows directions, doll | .26 | .86 |
| 127 Uses words to make wants known | .47 | .85 |
| 128 Points to parts of doll | .55 | .85 |
| 129 Blue board: 2 round, 2 square | .46 | .85 |
| 130 Names 1 picture | .61 | .85 |
| 131 Finds 2 objects | .37 | .85 |
| 132 Points to 3 pictures | .61 | .85 |
| 133 Broken doll: mends marginally | .46 | .85 |
| 134 Pegs placed in 30 secs. | −.04 | .86 |
| 135 Differentiates scribble, stroke | .27 | .86 |
| 136 Sentence of 2 words | .35 | .85 |
| 137 Pink board: completes | .48 | .85 |
| 138 Names 2 objects | .53 | .85 |
| 139 Points to 5 pictures | .59 | .85 |
| 140 Broken doll: mends approx. | .30 | .85 |
| 141 Names 3 pictures | .55 | .85 |
| 142 Blue board: 6 blocks | .41 | .85 |
| 143 Builds tower of 6 cubes | .11 | .86 |
| 144 Discriminates 2: cup, plate, box | .29 | .85 |
| 145 Names watch, 4th picture | .51 | .85 |
| 146 Names 3 objects | .43 | .85 |
| 147 Imitates strokes: vert., horiz. | .04 | .86 |
| 148 Points to 7 pictures | .37 | .85 |
| 149 Names 5 pictures | .24 | .86 |
| 150 Names watch, 2nd picture | .47 | .85 |
| 151 Pink board: reversed | .38 | .85 |
| 152 Discriminates 3: cup, plate, box | .17 | .86 |
| 153 Broken doll: mends exactly | .26 | .86 |
| 154 Train of cubes | .23 | .86 |
| 155 Blue board: completes 150 secs. | .27 | .86 |
| 156 Pegs placed in 22 secs. | −.03 | .86 |
| 157 Folds paper | .25 | .86 |
| 158 Understands 2 prepositions | .29 | .85 |
| 159 Blue board: completes 90 secs. | .22 | .86 |
| 160 Blue board: completes 60 secs. | .29 | .85 |
| 161 Builds tower of 8 cubes | .00 | .86 |
| 162 Concept of one | −.01 | .86 |
| 163 Understands 3 prepositions | .15 | .86 |

Cronbach's alpha = .86

round blocks; #129-Blue board: places 2 round and 2 square blocks; and, #142-Blue board: places 6 blocks. Deleting all of these 10 items from the 40-item set yielded a Cronbach's alpha of .86, unchanged from that obtained for the full set of items.

## C. Factor Analysis 12 Months

A factor analysis using the varimax rotation option was completed on items #97 through #127 to investigate the relationship of speeded items to other items in this range. The analysis yielded a five-factor solution of which only the first four factors warrant interpretation (see Table 3). The first factor, which accounted for 12.7% of the variance (eigenvalue = 3.92), appears to be a fine-motor factor.

TABLE 3

Factor Analysis: 12-Month Age Group

| Item # and title | Factors | | | | |
|---|---|---|---|---|---|
| | 1 | 2 | 3 | 4 | 5 |
| 121  Blue board: 2 round blocks | .64 | | | | |
| 108  Places 1 peg repeatedly | .63 | | | | |
| 111  Builds tower of 2 blocks | .59 | | | | |
| 115  Closes round box | .58 | | | | |
| 120  Pink board: round block | .56 | | | | |
| 118  Pegs placed in 70 seconds | .54 | | | | |
| 110  Blue board: 1 round block | .53 | | | | |
| 100  Puts 3 or more cubes in cup | | .66 | | | |
| 104  Pats whistle doll in imitation | | .53 | | | |
| 107  Puts beads in box | | .48 | | | |
| 99  Pushes car along | | .47 | | | |
| 98  Holds crayon adaptively | | .47 | | | |
| 112  Spontaneous scribble | | .45 | | | |
| 106  Imitates words | | | .70 | | |
| 101  Jabbers expressively | | | .69 | | |
| 116  Uses gestures to make wants known | | | .61 | | |
| 97  Names 1 object | | | .57 | | |
| 113  Shows shoes or other object | | | .56 | | |
| 127  Uses words to make wants known | | | | .67 | |
| 126  Follows directions, doll | | | | .66 | |
| 124  Names 1 object | | | | .64 | |
| 125  Imitates crayon stroke | | | | .60 | |
| 117  Shows shoes or other clothing, or own toy | | | | .40 | |
| 102  Uncovers blue box | | | | | .47 |
| 109  Removes pellets from bottle | | | | | .41 |

*Note:* Only factor loadings of $r \geq .40$ are reported for purposes of interpretation.

The second factor, accounting for 7% of the variance (eigenvalue = 2.17), appears to be a perceptual-motor factor. Factors 3 and 4 which account for 6.1% (eigenvalue = 1.90) and 5.6% (eigenvalue = 1.75) of the variance, respectively, appear to be language factors. The results of this analysis suggest that at age 12 months the speeded items are part of a more general fine-motor factor.

TABLE 4

Factor Analysis: 18-Month Age Group

| | | | Factors | | |
|---|---|---|---|---|---|
| Item # and title | 1 | 2 | 3 | 4 | 5 |
| 141 Names 3 pictures | .83 | | | | |
| 138 Names 2 objects | .82 | | | | |
| 146 Names 3 objects | .78 | | | | |
| 139 Points to 5 pictures | .76 | | | | |
| 149 Names 5 pictures | .70 | | | | |
| 132 Points to 3 pictures | .66 | | | | |
| 124 Names 1 object | .61 | | | | |
| 145 Names watch, 4th picture | .57 | | | | |
| 148 Points to 7 pictures | .56 | | | | |
| 150 Names watch, 2nd picture | .52 | | | | |
| 130 Names 1 picture | .51 | | | | |
| 131 Finds 2 objects | .46 | | | | |
| 142 Blue board: 6 blocks | | .68 | | | |
| 155 Blue board: completes in 150″ | | .67 | | | |
| 137 Pink board: completes | | .64 | | | |
| 129 Blue board: 2 round, 2 square blocks | | .60 | | | |
| 159 Blue board: completes in 90″ | | .56 | | | |
| 160 Blue board: completes in 60″ | | .46 | | | |
| 144 Discriminates 2: cup, plate, box | | .46 | | | |
| 121 Blue board: 2 round blocks | | .44 | | | |
| 152 Discriminates 3: cup, plate, box | | .41 | | | |
| 140 Broken doll: mends approximately | | | .67 | | |
| 133 Borken doll: mends marginally | | | .55 | | |
| 153 Broken doll: mends exactly | | | .53 | | |
| 127 Uses words to make wants known | | | .42 | | |
| 126 Follows directions, doll | | | .40 | | |
| 123 Pegs placed in 42 secs. | | | | .71 | |
| 118 Pegs placed in 70 secs. | | | | .54 | |
| 134 Pegs placed in 30 secs. | | | | .53 | |
| 120 Pink board: places round block | | | | .51 | |
| 125 Imitates crayon stroke | | | | .44 | |
| 157 Folds paper | | | | | .80 |
| 154 Train of cubes | | | | | .79 |
| 151 Pink board: reversed | | | | | .62 |
| 158 Understands 2 prepositions | | | | | .44 |
| 136 Sentence of 2 words | | | | | .40 |

*Note:* Only factor loadings of $r \geq .40$ are reported for purposes of interpretation.

## D. Factor Analysis 18 Months

A second factor analysis using the varimax rotation option was completed on items #117 through #163. This analysis also yielded a five-factor solution (see Table 4). The first factor, which accounts for 16.1% of the variance (eigenvalue = 7.42), appears to be a language factor. The second factor, which accounts for 8.4% of the variance (eigenvalue = 3.86), appears to be a fine-motor factor. The third factor, accounting for 5.5% of the variance (eigenvalue = 2.51), appears to be a problem-solving factor. Factors 4 and 5 which account for 5.1% (eigenvalue = 2.34) and 4.3% (eigenvalue = 1.97) of the variance, respectively, appear to be fine-motor/speed of performance and a problem-solving factor. Unlike the 12-month data this factor analysis did not yield a single factor containing all speeded tasks; rather, these tasks were equally divided among the second (fine-motor) and fourth (fine-motor/speed of performance) factors.

## IV.   DISCUSSION

The inclusion of speeded items on assessments of infant performance has long been standard practice. Only recently have questions been raised regarding the appropriateness of including these items.

The results of the present research indicate that speeded items as a group add very little to the reliability of the Bayley Mental Scale at either 12 or 18 months. At 12 months the exclusion of 5 of the 30 items resulted in a drop in Cronbach's alpha from .62 to .60, a negligible change. Likewise, at 18 months, 10 of 40 items were excluded with Cronbach's alpha remaining stable at .86. These findings indicate that the speeded items add little unique information about the child's performance at either 12 or 18 months.

Several explanations may account for this finding. One hypothesis is that in very young children, speed of performance is not highly related to mental ability as measured by traditional infant assessments. It is possible that regardless of ability level most children can insert the blue blocks into the form board within the prescribed time limit. The children who fail the task may do so because of factors unrelated to ability level. A prime example of this would be a child with a minor fine-motor impairment who completely understands the task requirements but, because of the impairment, fails to complete the task within the time limit. Other factors, such as motivation or persistence, may also influence the child's performance.

A competing hypothesis that may account for these results is that ability level is related to speed of performance; however, because the time limits for items are determined empirically from the standardization sample, there is insufficient variation in the normal population to allow for reliable discrimination based on speed of performance. In order for these items to provide maximum discrimination among ability levels, the criterion times chosen for these items would need to be based on a distribution of times with a wide distribution, rather than a narrow distribution of times such as that found in a normal sample. This would suggest that the distribution of time scores that should be utilized to determine time limits should include those of normal and at-risk children. The increased variability in time limits would allow the choice of time cut scores which maximally discriminate ability levels.

The results of the factor analyses at 12 months indicate that although the speeded tasks may not provide unique information about the child's performance, they do load on the factor that accounts for the largest percentage of variance at this age. This suggest that although these speeded items, individually and as a group, add little unique information, they are necessary to the extent that they provide information about the child's fine-motor performance, the facet of behavior which is most salient in development at this age.

The factor analysis at 18 months provides a less clear picture. Factor analysis on the 18-month data shows that speeded items are split between two factors: a fine-motor factor, which was the second strongest factor, and a speed of performance factor, the fourth strongest factor. These results, like those at 12 months, may be interpreted as suggestive that speeded items do provide information about the child's fine-motor performance, a salient facet of development at this age.

Overall, this research indicates that the relationship between speed of performance and intellectual ability as measured by traditional assessment instruments may not be as strong in the preschool child as in the school-age child. However, speed of performance is related to fine-motor ability, an ability that is central to the development of the young child. This finding may be limited to the Bayley Scales given the particular types of items that are speeded. Future investigations should resolve the issue of whether a variety of speeded tasks can be considered a good indicator of general mental ability or a more specific skill such as fine-motor ability.

# INFANT MOTOR, COGNITIVE, AND LANGUAGE BEHAVIORS AS PREDICTORS OF ACHIEVEMENT AT SCHOOL AGE*

*Linda S. Siegel*

DEPARTMENT OF SPECIAL EDUCATION
THE ONTARIO INSTITUTE FOR STUDIES IN EDUCATION
TORONTO, ONTARIO

I. INTRODUCTION ......................................... 227
II. METHOD ............................................... 228
  A. Subjects .............................................. 228
  B. Procedures ............................................ 229
III. RESULTS .............................................. 230
  A. Correlational Analyses ................................. 230
  B. Differences Between Average and Below Average Scores ........ 232
IV. DISCUSSION .......................................... 235

## I. INTRODUCTION

Much controversy exits about the extent to which scores on infant tests are related to later functioning. A recent review of the evidence on this issue concluded that when there is sufficient range in infant test scores, there is a significant relationship between scores on infant tests and later mental functioning (Siegel, 1989). However, the study of the relationship between infant test performance and later abilities has concentrated on global test scores. It is possible that the measurement of infant functioning might be of greater usefulness if specific abilities rather than global scores are used (Honzik, 1976). A

* This research was supported by grants from the Ontario Mental Health Foundation and the Natural Sciences and Engineering Research Council of Canada. The author wishes to thank Rita Baumgarten, Norman Himel, and Lorraine Hoult for help with the data collection and analyses. These findings were presented at a symposium at the biennial convention of the Society for Research in Child Development in Kansas City in April 1989.

227

system has been developed by Kohen-Raz (1976) in which the Bayley Mental Development Index (MDI) (Bayley, 1969) is divided into subscales measuring eye-hand coordination, manipulation, conceptual abilities, imitation and comprehension of language, and expressive language including vocalization and social responsiveness. The purpose of the present study was to determine whether the Kohen-Raz subscales of the Bayley Mental Development Index are predictors of subsequent scores on reading, arithmetic, fine-motor coordination, and language scores at school age.

There should be specificity in the relations between infant functions and later abilities. In this study, we presumed that the eye-hand coordination and manipulation scales are related to fine-motor abilities, arithmetic, and spelling. Spelling and arithmetic scores have components of fine-motor skills and are, in fact, correlated with concurrent measures of these abilities (e.g., Siegel & Feldman, 1983). The language subscales—imitation-comprehension and vocalization-social—were expected to be related to later reading and language abilities.

In addition, it has been found that with the division of the Bayley MDI into subscales a developmental pattern emerged in the prediction of subsequent development (Miller & Siegel, 1989; Siegel, 1979, 1981). This pattern is such that perceptual motor skills, as measured by the eye-hand coordination and manipulation subscales, tend to be predictive early in development at 4 and 8 months, the object relations and similar items (conceptual abilities subscale) become predictive at 12 months, and the language-related items, the imitation-comprehension and vocalization-social subscales, become most predictive at 18 and 24 months. An additional purpose of this study was to see if this developmental progression would be evident in achievement scores at school age.

In addition, the Bayley Psychomotor Scale (PDI), which measures gross and fine-motor development, has been found to be a better predictor of subsequent language and cognitive development than the mental scale, particularly in the first year (e.g., Siegel, 1979, 1981). It is possible that the items of the Bayley MDI that measure aspects of motor development are predictive early and are more highly correlated with motor, particularly fine-motor, development at a later age.

## II.  METHOD

### A.  Subjects

The subjects for this study consisted of preterm and fullterm children. The preterm infants all had birthweights below 1500 grams. The comparison group of fullterm children was demographically similar to the preterm group, and all members of that group were born after uncomplicated deliveries and had experienced a normal perinatal course. The preterm and fullterm infants were matched on socioeconomic levels, parity, sex, and age of the mother at the birth of the infant. Two cohorts were seen; Cohort 1 was followed from birth to eight years of age and Cohort 2 until six years of age. There were 35 fullterm and 36 preterm children (Cohort 1) available for testing at six, seven, and eight years, and 44 fullterm and 41 preterm available for testing at 6 years (Cohort 2).

## B. Procedures

The children were administered the Bayley Scales of Infant Development (Bayley, 1969) at 4, 8, 12, 18, and 24 months. The Bayley Mental Development Index was scored with the Kohen-Raz (1967) score system, which separates many of the Bayley MDI items into five subscales: Eye-Hand Coordination— (Eye-hand) (e.g., "reached for dangling ring," "puts three or more cubes in cup"); Manipulation—(Manip.) (e.g., "simple play with rattle," "fingers holes in pegboard"); Conceptual Relations—(Concept) (e.g., "uncovers toy," "exploitive paper play"); Imitation and Comprehension—(Imit-Comp.) (e.g., "response to verbal request," "imitates crayon strokes"); and Vocalization-Social—(Voc-Soc) (e.g., "repeats performance laughed at," "says 'da-da' or equivalent").

The children were also administered a variety of tests at 6, 7, and 8 years, including:

1. The *Wechsler Intelligence Scale for Children—Revised* (WISC-R, Wechsler, 1974). This test was used at six years as a standardized measure of intelligence. At eight years, only the Block Design and Vocabulary subtests were administered. An estimated IQ can be calculated from these two subtests (Sattler, 1982).
2. *Oral Cloze* (adapted from Siegel & Ryan, 1988). This test measures the child's understanding of syntax. For this task a sentence with one word missing is read aloud to the child. The child is required to supply the missing word.
3. *The Beery Developmental Test of Visual-Motor Integration* (VMI). For this test (Beery, 1967), the child is required to copy an increasingly difficult series of geometric forms. Performance is compared with age norms and an age equivalent score is calculated.
4. *The Wide Range Achievement Test* (WRAT). The reading and arithmetic subtests were used (Jastak & Jastak, 1978). In the Reading Subtest, at the younger age levels, the child is required to name letters and, at older ages, to read aloud on an increasingly difficult series of words. The Arithmetic Subtest requires the child to solve simple arithmetic problems presented orally at the younger ages and, at older ages, to solve increasingly difficult written computation problems.

## III.  RESULTS

### A.  Correlational Analyses

The correlations between the Kohen-Raz subscales and various outcome measures were calculated. Table 1 shows these correlations between the Kohen Raz subscales and the WISC-R Full Scale IQ at six years and the WISC-R estimated IQ at eight years. Only significant correlations are presented. As can be seen from the data presented in Table 1, the perceptual motor measures—Eye-Hand and Manipulation—correlated in the early months, although the Eye-Hand scale correlated throughout, the conceptual abilities items correlated at 8, 12, and sometimes 18 months, and the language measures were most predictive in the later months.

The IQ scores are global scores representing a variety of skills. However, the subtests measure more specific skills. Two subtests were administered at eight years. The Vocabulary subtest measures expressive language skills and the Block Design subtest measures visual spatial concepts and fine-motor coordination. The correlations of the Kohen-Raz subscales with the Vocabulary and Block Design subtests are shown in Table 2. The language items were more highly correlated with the Vocabulary scores, and the fine-motor items were more highly correlated with the Block Design subtests. The Block Design scores were predicted by the measures early in development and the Vocabulary scores were predicted by the measures at 18 and 24 months. Similar results are shown in Table 3 in terms of the correlations with the Oral Cloze task, a language task, and the Beery VMI, a measure of fine-motor coordination.

TABLE 1

Correlations of the Kohen-Raz Scale with WISC-R IQ Scores

| Kohen-Raz | Time of administration of Bayley (months) | | | | |
|---|---|---|---|---|---|
| | 4 | 8 | 12 | 18 | 24 |
| | WISC-R full scale IQ—6 years | | | | |
| Eye-hand | .18 | .25 | .40 | .34 | .40 |
| Manip. | .30 | .20 | .25 | .29 | |
| Concept. | | .31 | .32 | .35 | |
| Imit.-comp. | | .20 | .31 | .41 | .53 |
| Voc.-soc. | | .18 | .26 | .22 | .46 |
| | WISC-R estimated IQ—8 years | | | | |
| Eye-hand | .35 | .26 | .44 | | .26 |
| Manip. | .45 | .29 | | | |
| Concept. | | .33 | .40 | | |
| Imit.-comp. | | .32 | .36 | .29 | .32 |
| Voc.-soc. | | .35 | | | .31 |

TABLE 2

Correlations of the Kohen-Raz Subscales with WISC-R Subtests at 8 years

| Kohen Raz | Time of administration of Bayley (months) | | | | |
|---|---|---|---|---|---|
| | 4 | 8 | 12 | 18 | 24 |
| | Vocabulary | | | | |
| Eye-hand | | | | | .27 |
| Manip. | .34 | | | | |
| Concept. | | | | | |
| Imit.-comp. | | | | .27 | .29 |
| Voc.-soc. | | | | | .33 |
| | Block design | | | | |
| Eye-hand | .35 | | .45 | | |
| Manip. | .40 | .34 | | | |
| Concept. | | .33 | .47 | | |
| Imit.-comp. | | .34 | .42 | | |
| Voc.-soc. | | .29 | | | |

When the correlations of the Kohen-Raz subscales with the Reading and Arithmetic tests of the WRAT are examined (Table 4), similar patterns emerged. The language subscales were more highly correlated with the Reading Test, although fine-motor skills were correlated as well. The Kohen-Raz Eye-hand and Manipulation scales throughout this time period and some other scales early in development were correlated with the Arithmetic Test.

TABLE 3

Correlations of the Kohen-Raz Subscales with Language
and Beery VMI Scores at 8 Years

| | Time of administration of Bayley (months) | | | |
|---|---|---|---|---|
| | 8 | 12 | 18 | 24 |
| | Language (oral cloze) | | | |
| Eye-hand | | .27 | .35 | |
| Concept. | | | .29 | |
| Imit.-comp. | | | .37 | .32 |
| Voc.-soc. | | | | .32 |
| | Beery VMI | | | |
| Eye-hand | | .38 | | |
| Manip. | .35 | | | |
| Concept. | .29 | .35 | | |
| Imit.-comp. | .42 | .41 | | |
| Voc.-soc. | .27 | .38 | | |

TABLE 4

Correlations of the Kohen-Raz Subscales with WRAT Reading
and Arithmetic Scores at 8 Years

| Kohen-Raz | Time of Bayley administration (months) | | | | |
|---|---|---|---|---|---|
| | 4 | 8 | 12 | 18 | 24 |
| | | | Reading | | |
| Eye-hand | | .32 | .28 | .48 | |
| Manip. | .37 | | | | |
| Concept. | | .30 | | | |
| Imit.-comp. | | | .32 | .42 | .43 |
| Voc.-soc. | | | | .46 | .38 |
| | | | Arithmetic | | |
| Eye-hand | | | .28 | .48 | .32 |
| Manip. | .28 | .30 | | | |
| Concept. | | .27 | .32 | | |
| Voc.-soc. | | .31 | | | |

## B.  Differences Between Average and Below Average Scores

One way of examining the continuity issue is to determine the differences in early scores between children who are performing in the average range at school age and those whose scores are below average. These differences were examined for two IQ scores, the WISC-R Full-Scale IQ at 6 years and the WISC-R Estimated IQ at 8 years. Table 5 shows the Kohen-Raz scales on which the children with IQ scores below 90 had significantly lower scores than those who had IQ scores of 90 or higher. As can be seen from Table 5, the Eye-Hand and Manipulation Scales differentiated between these two groups at 4 and 8 months, all of the Scales did at 12 months and the language scales discriminated at 18 months, and in the case of the 6-year IQ scores, but not the 8-year IQ scores, at 24 months.

The Kohen-Raz Scale that differentiated between the 6-year-old children with Verbal and Performance IQ scores below 90 and those with IQ scores at or above 90 are shown in Table 6. It was somewhat easier to predict Performance IQ scores than Verbal IQ scores, although it should be noted that the Kohen-Raz Scales showed a significant degree of predictability for both Verbal and Performance IQ scores.

The Kohen-Raz Scales that significantly differentiated between children with low WRAT Reading or Arithmetic Scores (≤25 percentile) and those with average scores (≥30 percentile) are shown in Table 7. As can be seen from Table 7, the Eye-Hand and Manipulation Scales, both measures of fine-motor coordination skills, were better predictors of Arithmetic Scores, and the Imitation-Comprehension and Vocalization-Social Scales, both measures of language

TABLE 5

Kohen-Raz Scales Showing a Significant Difference Between Children
with IQ Scores < 90 and ≥ 90.

| | 6-Year WISC-R IQ | | | | |
| --- | --- | --- | --- | --- | --- |
| | 4 | 8 | 12 | 18 | 24 |
| Eye-hand | | x | x | | x |
| Manip. | x | | x | x | |
| Concept. | | | x | x | |
| Imit.-comp. | | x | x | x | x |
| Voc.-soc. | | | x | | x |
| | 8-Year estimated WISC-R IQ | | | | |
| Eye-hand | x | x | x | x | |
| Manip. | x | | | | |
| Concept. | | | x | x | |
| Imit.-comp. | | x | x | x | |
| Voc.-soc. | | | x | x | |

skills, were better predictors of Reading scores. Early in development, the scales were better predictors of motor and attention-mediated functions, such a arithmetic; later in development the scales were better predictors of language functions such as reading.

The same trend was apparent when specific language and fine-motor skills were evaluated. Table 8 shows the Kohen-Raz Scales that differentiated between the 8-year-old children with below average scores on the Oral Cloze, a language task, and the Beery Visual-Motor Integration Test, a measure of fine-motor

TABLE 6

Kohen-Raz Scales that Differentiated Between Children with WISC-R Verbal
or Performance 6-Year IQ Scores < 90 and ≥ 90.

| | Verbal IQ | | | | |
| --- | --- | --- | --- | --- | --- |
| | 4 | 8 | 12 | 18 | 24 |
| Eye-hand | | x | x | | x |
| Manip. | x | | x | x | |
| Concept. | | | x | x | |
| Imit.-comp. | | | x | x | x |
| Voc.-soc. | | | x | | x |
| | Performance IQ | | | | |
| Eye-hand | | x | x | x | x |
| Manip. | x | x | x | x | |
| Concept. | | x | | x | |
| Imit.-comp. | x | x | x | x | x |
| Voc.-soc. | | x | x | | x |

TABLE 7

Kohen-Raz Scales Showing a Significant Difference Between Children
with Low 8-Year WRAT Reading or Arithmetic Scores ≤25 and ≥ 30.

| | WRAT-reading | | | | |
| --- | --- | --- | --- | --- | --- |
| | 4 | 8 | 12 | 18 | 24 |
| Eye-hand | | x | | x | |
| Manip. | x | | | | |
| Concept. | | | | x | |
| Imit.-comp. | | | | x | x |
| Voc.-soc. | | | | x | |
| | WRAT-arithmetic | | | | |
| Eye-hand | x | | | x | x |
| Manip. | x | x | | | |
| Concept. | | x | x | | |
| Imit.-comp. | | x | | | |
| Voc.-soc. | | x | | | |

skills. Again, the language scales of the Kohen-Raz were related to the language
items and the motor scales were related to fine-motor skills in childhood. Early in
development the Kohen-Raz Scales were better predictors of subsequent fine-
motor development; later in development the Kohen-Raz scales were better
predictors of subsequent language development.

An alternative approach to prediction that may be useful (Siegel, 1989)
involves the use of cut-off scores to ascertain the predictability of the particular

TABLE 8

Kohen-Raz Scales Showing a Significant Difference Between Children
with Below Average and Average Scores on the Oral Cloze
and Beery VMI Tasks at 8 Years

| | Oral cloze | | | | |
| --- | --- | --- | --- | --- | --- |
| | 4 | 8 | 12 | 18 | 24 |
| Eye-hand | x | x | x | x | |
| Manip. | x | | | | |
| Concept. | | | | | |
| Imit.-comp. | | | x | x | x |
| Voc.-soc. | | | | x | |
| | Beery visual-motor integration | | | | |
| Eye-hand | x | | | x | |
| Manip. | x | | | | |
| Concept. | x | | | | |
| Imit.-comp. | | x | x | | |
| Voc.-soc. | | | | | |

TABLE 9

Ability of the Kohen-Raz Subscales to Predict IQ Score < 90 Using a Cut-off Score

| | True positives | False positives | True negatives | False negatives | % Correct prediction |
|---|---|---|---|---|---|
| | | | Full-Scale IQ | | |
| **8 months** | | | | | |
| Eye-hand | 10 | 16 | 112 | 5 | 79.7 |
| Concept. abil. | 11 | 27 | 101 | 14 | 73.2 |
| Imit.-comp. | 20 | 52 | 76 | 5 | 62.7 |
| **12 months** | | | | | |
| Concept. abil. | 10 | 21 | 113 | 15 | 77.4 |
| Imit.-comp. | 15 | 28 | 106 | 10 | 76.1 |
| Voc.-soc. | 15 | 36 | 98 | 10 | 71.1 |
| **24 months** | | | | | |
| Eye-hand | 4 | 3 | 120 | 21 | 83.8 |
| Imit.-comp. | 11 | 19 | 104 | 14 | 77.7 |
| Voc.-soc. | 16 | 23 | 100 | 9 | 78.4 |

test in question for the individual child. A selection of results using this approach is shown in Tables 9 and 10. Various cut-off scores were used. As can be seen from Tables 9 and 10, the Kohen-Raz subscales are reasonably accurate in terms of making dichotomous predictions.

# IV. DISCUSSION

The Kohen-Raz Scales are each composed of a small number of items. In spite of this, they were able to predict cognitive functioning at school ages, in some cases more than 7½ years after they were administered. This amount of continuity in intellectual functioning is quite striking and supports the predictive validity of infant tests (see Siegel, 1989, for a review).

There was a sequence in which particular developmental functions were differentially predictive at different points in time. First, the motor items, the eye-hand and manipulation scales, were the best predictors, then the conceptual abilities scale, and, finally, the language items, as measured by the Imitation-Comprehension and Vocalization Social, became predictive. This sequence is partially a function of the type of items emphasized at each age. There are not an equal number of items of each type at each age. Obviously, some methodological refinement of the Bayley scales is needed, particularly in separating the Bayley items into subscales. However, these data do indicate that some functions that are developing quickly at one point in time, as these are, provide the most sensitive indicators of the developmental level and are, therefore, predictive of the structure of subsequent cognitive functioning.

TABLE 10

Ability of the Kohen-Raz Subscales to Predict IQ Score < 90 Using a Cut-off Score

| | True positives | False positives | True negatives | False negatives | % Correct prediction |
|---|---|---|---|---|---|
| Kohen Raz | | | Verbal IQ | | |
| **8 months** | | | | | |
| Eye-hand | 10 | 16 | 113 | 15 | 80.0 |
| Imit.-comp. | 19 | 53 | 76 | 6 | 61.7 |
| **12 months** | | | | | |
| Concept. abil. | 10 | 21 | 114 | 15 | 77.5 |
| Imit.-comp. | 13 | 30 | 105 | 12 | 73.8 |
| Voc.-soc. | 13 | 38 | 97 | 12 | 68.8 |
| **24 months** | | | | | |
| Eye-hand | 4 | 3 | 121 | 21 | 83.9 |
| Imit.-comp. | 12 | 18 | 106 | 13 | 79.2 |
| Voc.-soc. | 15 | 24 | 110 | 10 | 77.2 |
| | | | Performance IQ | | |
| **8 months** | | | | | |
| Eye-hand | 8 | 19 | 122 | 6 | 83.9 |
| Manip. | 5 | 17 | 124 | 9 | 83.2 |
| Concept. abil. | 10 | 29 | 112 | 4 | 78.7 |
| Voc.-soc. | 11 | 37 | 104 | 3 | 74.2 |
| **12 months** | | | | | |
| Manip. | 6 | 17 | 130 | 8 | 84.5 |
| **18 months** | | | | | |
| Eye-hand | 4 | 7 | 126 | 8 | 89.7 |
| **24 months** | | | | | |
| Eye-hand | 3 | 4 | 134 | 9 | 91.3 |
| Voc.-soc. | 8 | 32 | 106 | 4 | 76.0 |

Even early in development there appears to be a differentiation of function, in that motor items were better predictors of subsequent fine-motor and visual spatial functions, while language items were better predictors of language skills. The actual behaviors measured at the two points in time are quite different. For example, the language behaviors measured in infancy do not remotely resemble those at 6 or 8 years. However, even if the surface structure is quite different, the underlying structure appears to be quite similar. Therefore, there is domain specificity for the predictive power of the infant tests.

The scales administered early in development were better predictors of subsequent fine-motor development than scales administered later. This relationship suggests that motor items in infant tests are, quite possibly, sensitive indicators of the level of development of the nervous system at that point in time. The scales administered later in development, of whatever type, were better predictors of cognitive and language functions. This relationship suggests that the level of development of the nervous system in the second year, as measured by Bayley scales, may be related to later language functions through a common biological substrate.

The results indicate continuity in mental function, the predictive power of infant tests, and the value of considering domain specificity in the enterprise of predicting from infant tests.

# DISCUSSION: THE BAYLEY SCALES OF INFANT DEVELOPMENT: ISSUES OF PREDICTION AND OUTCOME REVISITED

## Lewis P. Lipsitt

The two primary purposes of developmental tests are, first, to assess the developmental, cognitive, and achievement status of a child in the context of other children's comparable abilities at the same chronological age, and second, to predict what that child's later performance might be given no special interventions, grand changes in the context of the child's life, or developmentally debilitating conditions. Both of those objectives and their exceptions require a good deal of unpacking.

As to the assessment objective, we use developmental tests because they afford the opportunity to assess the child's performance under specifiable, standardized conditions and in the context of norms based on large numbers of children using comparable modes of observation. Use of developmental tests by persons "trained to the manual" ensures that anecdotal observation of the performance, and interpretation of the ability as to its rarity, will have a high probability of replication. That is, assertion of the child's proficiency with respect to this performance is more likely to be "reliable" than if no test were used and only casual observation of the child's performance were made. It is a scientific issue if I say a child can do something, or just did something, and the observer standing next to me looking at the same set of events, or "examining" this type of performance in the same child 10 minutes later, cannot verify the kind of performance I saw.

The replicability objective of test performance is on the face of it very reasonable in another respect as well. Quite apart from the prediction problem which we come to later, accurate assessment of current performance is required to make any comparison of a given child's performance with other children of the same age. If a child, for example, reaches around a translucent barrier to grasp an object seen through the barrier, one wonders whether this child is precocious in this respect or whether all children his or her chronological age will do that, given the same conditions. Thus there is a need for "norms," based upon routinized observations, clear test items or stimulating conditions, and an assemblage of statistical knowledge about the performances of other children of varying ages when stimulated in the same way.

As to the second purpose of developmental tests: If the child reaching around the barrier to grasp the coveted object is unusual in this respect, the issue arises as to whether this precocity "means" anything in terms of the child's later performance. This latter concern goes to the issue of predictive validity, or the possibility of a test given earlier in a child's life anticipating what the child's likely performance will be at later ages.

It is the second objective of standardized developmental examinations— prediction—which has attracted the most professional and public concern. This is, after all, the purpose for which Binet devised his original tests. He wanted to discover those children in classrooms in France who might be better served (i.e., presumably have their mental ages advanced) through special interventions, in the form of classes for children with what today we would call learning disabilities or performance retardation. One of Binet's objectives, besides making the teaching task in the "normal" classroom easier, was to controvert the predictions for the substandard children by providing special instruction that might yield higher performance than could be empirically anticipated on the basis of the child's tested performance! This intention of obfuscating the predictable has remained one of the ironies of scientific approaches to the study of performance, or psychometrics, since Binet's time.

The history of infant psychometrics generally, but most specifically, the experience with the Bayley Scales of Infant Development is replete with empirical demonstrations both of the usefulness and the futility of infant testing. On the one hand, the tests have been shown to be suitably reliable for "the assessment of current status." On the other hand, testing children below the age of 18 months or two years with traditional tests like the Bayley Scales has yielded little comfort for psychometricians and child developmentalists when they use these measures to anticipate the later intellectual or cognitive attributes of children. This is not the place to take up the variety of reservations that may be invoked, and have been noted, concerning the use of such tests for prediction. Suffice it to say, then, that Nancy Bayley expressed herself on the use of the tests for purely predictive purposes by suggesting that before the age of 18 months one can make better predictions by examining the mother rather than the child!

The present collection of psychometric contributions, on the use of developmental tests for understanding the mental and motor performances of infants, provides certain substantive improvements over the previous "yield" from tests of infant behavior and development. These relate to constraints and permissions with respect to the use of test items, and the collation of data about children's performances as derived from the use of the standardized Bayley Scales. These modifications to the usual style of test delivery, or deviation from the customary method of inferring quantifiable performance from the test observations, are designed to improve the utility of the tests, first, by attaining higher reliability levels than they would otherwise have and, second, by enhancing the predictive validity of the scales.

The LeTendre et al. work does this through modifying the "discontinue criterion," which necessitates that the performance ceiling of the infant be determined on the arbitrary basis of the highest attained item before 10 successively failed items for the Mental Scale, and six such items for the Motor Scale. The authors contend that such use of the tests, at least with children of 24 months as in their study, may not allow for observation and crediting of the full range of the children's abilities, and thus may obscure individual differences of developmental importance. Using a large sample of 24-month-old infants, they examined how the use of a different criterion for "failure to perform" at the upper test-item levels might alter the inferences from the child's performance, and found that children in the upper ranges of performance are more prone to variability of performance, that is, sporadic passes and failures, than children in lower performance levels.

In the Burns et al. study, item and factor analyses of the Bayley Scales revealed that subcategorizations of performance are feasible in ways that Bayley could not have envisaged. Studying children's performance at age levels 3, 6, 12, and 24 months, the authors confirm that there is relatively little continuity of performance from one of these ages to another. They further conclude that ability factors at different ages are quite different, even when similar labels are used to describe them. Difficulty is the dominant deterrent to performance at the earlier age levels, while at later ages "factor solutions were more content oriented."

Not surprisingly, Burns et al. can make the case from their data that 3-month-olds are more like other 3-month-olds across a variety of tasks than they are like themselves over a long period of time. With increasing age, behavior changes markedly, but the developmental progressions of those changes are, if one may put it this way, quite universal. Put another way, a 3-month-old normal child and the same-aged mentally retarded child are much more similar in their capacities, but when they become 3 years of age they are very different. Put yet another way, the predictive validity of the infant scales is wanting.

In yet another study of the manner in which performance may be influenced by the scoring method, Gyurke et al. suggest that intelligence assessment is a matter, in part, of discovering how quickly the subject can provide the correct response. Most infant development scales involve assessment of behavioral function in terms of time limits on various tasks in order to "discriminate" children of higher from those of lower mental ability. The assumption is that speed of performance is a relevant dimension of capacity or intelligence. While inclusion of timed items has long been standard practice in developmental testing, the Gyurke et al. study demonstrated that speeded items generally add nothing to the reliability of the Bayley Scales at either 12 or 18 months of age. Once again, the manner in which the test is administered is of importance. To the extent that speeded items can be dropped from the armamentarium of the psychometrician, the easier will it be to assess the current performance levels of the young child. By the same token, it is of great importance to determine the long-term significance of dropping timed items from the battery of items vis-à-vis prediction of later performance from earlier ones. While Gyurke et al. have shown that no loss of reliability is incurred by the dropping of timed items, the fact is that predictive validity may yet be affected. Longitudinal studies are called for with large numbers of subjects, to enable study of predictive validity with control of a variety of subject-groupings, and under different contextual circumstances. This goes to the point of what needs to be assessed early in life to anticipate the performance levels of these individuals at later ages.

The Siegel study addresses predictive validity directly, through a long-term longitudinal investigation. She found that there is "domain specificity," which is to say that to predict later developmental function one must tap some earlier manifestation of the same attribute. Prediction of language, reading, and spelling skills at 6–8 years of age, for example, was accomplished better from measures of early language skills than of perceptual-motor skills. Moreover, it was found that particular developmental functions were differentially predictive at different points in time. For example, test items administered earlier in development were better predictors of subsequent fine-motor development than scales administered later. As Siegel suggests, motor items in infants tests may be sensitive indices of nervous system maturity at successive ages.

Summarizing her results, Siegel claims that her results reveal continuity of mental function, and substantiate the predictive validity of infant tests of mental and motor performance. She also finds value in considering separately specific domains of developmental function in utilizing the Bayley Scales for predicting later performance from earlier test measures.

Nancy Bayley couldn't have been more pleased with the refinements made in infant testing by the contributions in this collection of studies. The cause of psychometric science has been well served by the authors' conscientious attention to the particulars of test-item administration and the scoring procedures. Further refinements in both of these domains will continue to improve the reliability and predictive validity of infant development tests in general and of the Bayley Infant Mental and Motor Scales which evolve as a consequent of such studies.

## REFERENCES

Ballard, J. L., Novak, K. K., & Driver, M. (1979). A simplified score for assessment of fetal maturation of newly born infants. *Journal of Pediatrics, 95,* 769–74.

Barclay, A., & McWay, J. (1985). A factor analytic study of responses to the Bayley Scales of Infant Development by a disadvantaged population. *Perceptual and Motor Skills, 60,* 713–714.

Bayley, N. (1969). *Bayley Scales of infant development.* New York: The Psychological Corporation.

Bayley, N. (1970). Development of mental abilities. In P. Mussen (Ed.), *Carmichael's manual of child psychology* (pp. 1163–1209). New York: John Wiley & Sons.

Beery, K. E. (1967). *Developmental test of visual motor integration.* Chicago: Follett.

Callaway, E. (1975). *Brain electrical Potentials and individual psychological differences.* London: Grune & Stratton.

Cattell, P. (1966). *The measurement of intelligence of infants and young children.* New York: The Psychological Corporation.

Chalke, F., & Ertl, J. (1965). Evoked potentials and intelligence. *Life Sciences, 4,* 1319–1322.

Constantine, N., Kraemer, H., Kendall-Tackett, K., Bennett, F., Tyson, J., & Gross, R. (1987). Use of physical and neurologic observations in assessment of gestational age in low birth weight infants. *Journal of Pediatrics, 110*(6), 921–928.

Eckerman, C., Sturm, L., & Gross, S. (1985). Different developmental courses for very-low-birthweight infants differing in early head growth. *Developmental Psychology, 21,* 813–827.

Ertl, J. (1971). Fourier analysis of evoked potentials and human intelligence. *Nature, 230,* 525–526.

Ertl, J. (1973). IQ, evoked responses and human intelligence. *Nature, 241,* 209–210.

Ertl, J., & Schaefer, E. W. P. (1969). Brain response correlates of psychometric intelligence. *Nature, 223,* 421–422.

Eysenck, H. J., & Barrett, P. (1985). Psychophysiology and measurement of Intelligence. In C. R. Reynolds & U. L. Wilson (Eds.), *Methodological and statistical advance in the study of individual differences* (pp. 1–49). New York: Plenum Press.

Field, T., Dempsey, J., & Shuman, H. (1979). Developmental assessments of infants surviving the respiratory distress syndrome. In T. M. Field, A. M. Sostek, S. Goldberg, & H. H. Shuman (Eds.), *Infants born at risk: Behavior and development.* Jamaica, NY: Spectrum.

Ford, G., Rickards, A., Kitchen, W., Ryan, M., & Lissenden, J. (1986). Relationship of growth and psychoneurologic status of two-year-old children of birthweight 500–999 grams. *Early Human Development, 13,* 329–337.

Guilford, J. P. (1956). The structure of intellect. *Psychological Bulletin, 53,* 267–293.

Hendrickson, D. E. (1982). The biological basis of intelligence. Part II: Measurement. In H. J. Eysenck (Ed.), *A model for intelligence.* New York: Springer-Verlag.

Honzik, M. P. (1976). Value and limitation of infant tests: An overview. In M. Lewis (Ed.), *Origins of intelligence: Infancy and early childhood.* New York: Plenum.

Hunt, E., Frost, N., & Lunneborg, C. (1973). Individual differences in cognition: A new approach to intelligence. In G. Bower (Ed.), *The psychology of learning and motivation* (Vol. 7). New York: Plenum Press.

The Infant Health and Development Program. (1990). Enhancing the outcomes of low birth weight, premature infants: A multi-site randomized trial. *Journal of the American Medical Association, 263*(22), 3035–3042.

Jastak, J. K., & Jastak, S. R. (1978). *Wide Range Achievement Test.* Wilmington, DE: Guidance Associates.

Kaufman, A. (1979). Role of speed on WISC-R performance across the age range. *Journal of Consulting and Clinical Psychology, 47*(3), 595–597.

Keating, D., & Bobbitt, B. (1978). Individual and developmental differences in cognitive processing components of mental ability. *Child Development, 49,* 155–167.

Kopp, C. B. (1983). Risk factors in development. In P. H. Mussen (Ed.), *Handbook of child psychology, Volume II: Infancy and developmental psychology.* New York: Wiley.

Kohen-Raz, R. (1967). Scalogram analysis of some developmental sequences of infant behavior as measured by the Bayley Infant Scale of Mental Development. *Genetic Psychology Monographs, 76,* 3–21.

Laskey, R. E., Tyson, J. E., Rosenfeld, C. R., Priest, M., Krasinski, D., Heartwell, S., & Gant, N. F. (1983). Principal component analyses of the Bayley Scales of Infant Development for a sample of high-risk infants and their controls. *Merrill-Palmer Quarterly, 29,* 25–31.

Lewis, M., Goldberg, S., & Campbell, H. (1969). A developmental study of learning within the first three years of life: Response document to a redundant signal. *Monographs of the Society For Research in Child Development, 34*(9, Serial No. 133).

Lewis, M., & Brooks-Gunn, J. (1981). Visual attention at three months as a predictor of cognitive functioning at two years of age. *Intelligence, 5*, 131–140.

McCall, R., Eichorn, D., & Hogarty, P. (1977). Transitions in early mental development. *Monographs of the Society for Research in Child Development, 42* (Serial No. 171).

Miller, J., & Siegel, L. S. (1989). Cognitive and social factors as predictors of normal and atypical language development. In S. von Tetzchner, L. S. Siegel, & L. Smith (Eds.), *The social and cognitive aspects of normal and atypical language development*. New York: Springer Verlag.

Newborg, J., Stock, J., Wrek, L., Guidibaldi, J., & Svinicki, J. (1984). *Battelle developmental inventory*. Allen, TX: Teaching Resource.

Pape, K., Buncie, R., Ashby, S., & Fitzhardinge, P. (1978). The status at two years of low birth weight infants born in 1974 with birthweights of less than 1000 grams. *Journal of Pediatrics, 92*, 253–260.

Rhodes, L., Bayley, N., & Yow, B. (1984). *Supplement to the Manual for the Bayley Scales of Infant Development*. San Antonio, TX: Psychological Corporation.

Rhodes, L. Dustin, R., & Beck, E. (1969). The visual evoked response: A comparison of bright and dull children. *Electroencephalography and Clinical Neurophysiology, 27*, 364–372.

Rose, S., & Wallace, I. (1985). Visual recognition memory: A predictor of later cognitive functioning in preterms. *Child Development, 56*, 843–852.

Sattler, J. W. (1982). *Assessment of children's intelligence and special abilities* (2nd ed.). Boston, MA: Allyn & Bacon.

Siegel, L. S. (1979). Infant perceptual, cognitive, and motor behaviors as predictors of subsequent cognitive and language development. *Canadian Journal of Psychology, 33*, 382–395.

Siegel, L. S. (1981). Infant tests as predictors of cognitive and language development at two years. *Child Development, 52*, 545–557.

Siegel, L. S. (1981). The use of a Piagetian analysis of infant development to predict cognitive and language development: at two years. In M. P. Friedman (Ed.), *Intelligence and learning*. New York: Plenum.

Siegel, L. S. (1982). Early cognitive and environmental correlates of language development at 4 years. *International Journal of Behavioral Development*, pp. 433–444.

Siegel, L. S. (1983). Correction for prematurity and its consequences for the assessment of very low birthweight infant. *Child Development, 54*, 1176–1188.

Siegel, L. S. (1984). Home environmental influences on cognitive development in preterm and fullterm children. In A. W. Gottfried (Ed.), *Home environment and early mental development*. New York: Academic Press.

Siegel, L. S. (1985). Biological and environmental variables as predictors of intellectual functionings at 6 years. In S. Harel & N. Anastasiow (Eds.), *The at-risk infant: Psycho/socio/medical aspects*. Baltimore, MD: Brookes.

Siegel, L. S. (1989). A reconceptualization of prediction from infant test scores. In M. Bornstein & N. Krasnegor (Eds.), *Stability and continuity in mental development*. Hillsdale, NJ: Erlbaum.

Siegel, L. S., & Feldman, W. (1983). Non-dyslexic children with combined writing and arithmetic difficulties. *Clinical Pediatrics, 22*, 241–244.

Siegel, L. S., & Ryan, E. B. (1988). Developmental of grammatical sensitivity, phonological, and short-term memory skills in normally achieving and learning disabled children. *Developmental Psychology, 24*, 28–37.

Sparling, J., & Lewis, I. (1984). *Partners for learning* (curriculum kit). Lewisville, NC: Kaplan Press.

Sparling, J., Lewis, I., & Neuwirth, S. (in press). *Early partners* (curriculum kit). Lewisville, NC: Kaplan Press.

Sternberg, R. (1986). *Intelligence applied*. New York: Harcourt Brace Jovanovich Publishers.

SPSS-X Inc. (1988). *SPSS-X User's Guide* (3rd ed.). Chicago, IL: Author.

Stott, L. H., & Ball, R. S. (1965). Infant and preschool mental tests. *Monographs of the Society for Research in Child Development, 30*(Serial No. 101).

Teberg, A., Wu, P., Hodgman, J., Mich, C., Garfinkle, J., Azen, S., & Wingert, W. (1982). Infants with birth weights under 1500 grams; Physical, neurological and developmental outcomes. *Critical Care Medicine, 10*, 10–14.

Wechsler, D. (1974). *Manual for the Wechsler Intelligence Scale for Children-Revised.* New York: The Psychological Corporation.

Woo-Sam, J., & Zimmerman, I. (1972). Speed as a variable on three WISC performance subtests. *Perceptual and Motor Skills, 34*, 451–455.

Zigler, E., & Seitz, V. (1982). Social policy and intelligence. In R. J. Steinberg (Ed.), *Handbook of human intelligence* (pp. 586–641). Cambridge, England: Cambridge University Press.

# DEVELOPMENT OF LEARNING: FROM ELEMENTAL TO CONFIGURAL ASSOCIATIVE NETWORKS*

*Jerry W. Rudy*

DEPARTMENT OF PSYCHOLOGY
UNIVERSITY OF COLORADO, BOULDER

I. INTRODUCTION ........................................... 248
II. SOME CONCEPTUAL AND METHODOLOGICAL ISSUES ....... 249
    A. Organism X Task Analysis ................................ 250
    B. Dissociations ............................................ 250
III. DEVELOPMENT OF ELEMENTAL ASSOCIATIVE SYSTEMS ..... 251
    A. Associative Learning .................................... 252
    B. Learning in the Neonate ................................. 252
    C. Learning about Gustatory Stimuli ......................... 253
    D. Learning about Auditory Stimuli ......................... 256
        1. Simple conditioning .................................. 256
        2. Differential conditioning ............................ 259
    E. Learning about Visual Stimuli ........................... 262
    F. A Generalization and Some Speculation .................... 263
    G. Stimulus Coding Changes during Early Infancy ............. 264
    H. Temporal Constraints: The Emergence of Short-Term Associative
        Memory ................................................ 265
IV. ELEMENTAL ASSOCIATIVE SYSTEMS: SUMMARY ............ 267
V. DEVELOPMENT OF THE CONFIGURAL ASSOCIATION
    SYSTEM ................................................. 268
    A. Functional Properties of Elemental and Configural Systems ....... 269
    B. The Hippocampal Formation and Configural Associations ......... 271
    C. Access to the Configural System Occurs Late In Development .... 272
        1. Place learning ....................................... 272
        2. Conditional delayed alternation ...................... 275
        3. The role of context in conditioning .................. 275

* The author's research was supported by PHS Grants DA03531 and HD23337 and NSF Grant BNS8297654.

I gratefully acknowledge the contributions that Maria Alvarado, Carl Castro, Maura Carew, Kathleen Georgen, Richard Hyson, Thomas Moye, Julian Keith, Richard Paylor, Susan Stadler-Morris, and Mark Vogt made to this research program. I thank Mark Stanton for his detailed comments on a previous version of this chapter.

D. Summary .............................................. 278
E. The Emergence of Relational Systems in Primates .............. 280
VI. DISCUSSION ........................................... 281
A. A Jacksonian Perspective ................................. 283
B. Conclusion ............................................. 284
VII. REFERENCES .......................................... 284

## I. INTRODUCTION

This chapter is concerned with the development of learning and memory systems during early infancy. Most of its empirical content comes from studies that have employed the rat as the subject. So, some comments about its relevance to human infant development may be useful. As Berntson and Boysen (1990) put it in a previous contribution to the *Advances in Infancy Research* series, at a general level,

> The study of early cognitive development is impeded by the very nature of the subject of interest—the infant. Not only does the limited sensory motor and cognitive repertoire of the neonate often preclude the application of sophisticated information-processing paradigms, but many of these paradigms would make little conceptual sense if applied to the infant. (p. 188)

Researchers in both domains encounter methodological and conceptual problems that make unambiguous statements about the relationship between learning, memory, and age hard to obtain. So, the perspective on these problems and some methodological solutions that are described here may be beneficial to human infancy research.

Yet studies of learning and memory in animals can contribute more than just methodology to our understanding of the human infant. Cross fertilization at the conceptual level in fact can be seen in several recent contributions to the *Advances in Infancy Research* series. For example, Rovee-Collier and Fagan's (1981; see also Rovee-Collier & Hayne, 1987) review of their research program reflects a rich influence of operant conditioning methodologies and memory concepts and paradigms derived from studies on infantile amnesia in animals (e.g., Campbell & Jaynes, 1966; Campbell & Spear, 1972; Spear, 1979). The research program on the determiners of the human infant's visual attention response that Kaplan, Werner, and Rudy (1990) described was guided by a conceptual framework, the *dual process model* of habituation (Groves & Thompson, 1970), derived solely from the study of nonhuman animals. So, it is hoped that the research described in this chapter can be appreciated for both its methodological and conceptual contributions to the problem of how learning and memory change during early development.

The chapter will progress through several stages. First, some conceptual and methodological issues that confront the field will be described. Next, research on the development of simple elemental associative systems will be presented. Of particular concern will be the issue of when associative processes emerge during development and if their development can be isolated from the maturation of other systems that influence behavior. Ontogenetic differences in stimulus coding processes and the temporal constraints on associative processes of the infant animal will then be considered. Next, the focus will shift to the hypothesis that *two* associative learning systems can be dissociated during development: an elemental system that emerges early in development, and a configural system that emerges later. As noted, the rat will be the subject of most of research that is considered, but it will argue that common developmental sequences can be identified in rodents, monkeys, and humans.

## II. SOME CONCEPTUAL AND METHODOLOGICAL ISSUES

It is a trivial matter to observe age-related differences in *performance* on some task that is used to study learning or memory. Yet what do such observations say about developmental changes in learning and memory? Alone they are not informative. Learning and memory are theoretical concepts inferred from the observation that an organism's behavior can be modified by experience. One can never directly observe learning and memory. Only behavior is observed, and it is the product of a functional system that is composed of a multitude of components. So before any age-related difference in performance can be attributed to maturational changes in learning and memory, one has to exclude the possibility that it is due to changes in other subsystems. This is a formidable task, because a partial listing of subsystems that must function for experience to modify behavior is long. They include sensory, attentional, motivational, and motor systems.

The task is also difficult because there is a *hierarchical* relationship among some subsystems. For example, sensory subsystems are necessarily at a lower level in the hierarchy than are learning and memory subsystems: They can function independent of learning and memory systems but the converse is difficult to imagine. There is also an asymmetrical dependency of learning and memory subsystems on motivational/arousal subsystems. A hierarchical arrangement diminishes the chances of cleanly delineating how learning and memory subsystems change during infancy, because it is difficult to eliminate maturational differences in some low level subsystem as an explanation of an effect.

To compound the problem, learning and memory may not be unitary subsystems. Multiple memory classification schemes abound in the contemporary literature. They include Tulving's (1983) ternary classification that distinguishes between procedural, semantic, and episodic memory systems; Squire and Cohen's (1984) declarative versus procedural distinction; the explicit versus implicit memory systems of Schacter and Moscovitch (1984); the taxon versus locale systems of O'Keefe and Nadel (1978); and Sutherland and Rudy's (1989) configural versus simple association systems. Arguments for multiple memory systems come from several perspectives, including evolutionary considerations (Oakley, 1983; Sherry & Schacter, 1987), experimental psychology (e.g., Tulving, 1983) and neuropsychology (e.g., Rozin, 1976; Squire, 1987; Squire & Cohen, 1984). There is no agreement about the number of learning and memory subsystems or their relationship to each other. Yet many researchers would agree there are at least two. So one must be prepared to identify the emergence during development of two or more learning and memory subsystems.

In summary, learning and memory processes influence behavior through a system composed of many components. During early infancy there is undoubtedly concurrent maturational change in most components of this system. So to study developmental changes in learning and memory requires a methodology that can discriminate between maturational variation in learning and memory and variation in other subsystems.

## A.  Organism X Task Analysis

In an important early paper, Gollin (1965) argued that a developmental analysis of learning and memory is no different from the analysis of how any organismic variable (e.g., age, brain damage, neurochemistry) influences these subsystems. In each case one wants to discriminate the influence an organismic variable has on learning and memory subsystems from its effect on other subsystems. Gollin suggested a *comparative methodology* for this purpose.

So if age influences performance on some learning task, the researcher is obliged to assess its effect on tasks that independently assess other subsystems, sensory, motor, or motivational components, essential to that performance. The pattern of results that emerges from this matrix of comparisons provides the grounds for interpreting performance on the learning task. We have called this strategy an *Organism X Task* analysis (Rudy & Castro, 1990; Castro & Rudy, 1989).

## B.  Dissociations

In essence, before anything interesting can be said about developmental differences in learning and memory, the experimenter must *dissociate* the effects of age on learning and memory subsystems from its effects on other subsystems. For some time dissociations have been recognized as essential for interpreting the effects of brain damage (Teuber, 1955). They also are critical to the developmental analysis of learning and memory. The interpretation of dissociations, however, has its limitations and recently has been the focus of intense critical discussion (see Dunn & Kirsner, 1988; Shallice, 1988). In the present context the best one can hope for is a set of strong *single dissociations*. In such cases, age will have a major effect on tasks that have a learning and memory requirement but no effect on tasks that measure the relevant sensory, motor, and motivational systems but require no learning.

Strong single dissociations, however, are rarely observed. Moreover, they do not demand the strong conclusion that it is an age-related difference in learning or memory that is responsible for the behavioral difference (cf. Dunn & Kirsner, 1988). Suppose that, compared to older animals, younger animals are impaired on the learning task but not on tasks that independently assess the relevant sensory subsystems. Such a set of dissociations does suggest that the age-related impairment on the learning task reflects a maturational difference in learning and memory subsystems. Yet it is still possible that a maturational difference in a sensory system is responsible for the impaired performance. This could happen if the resource demands the learning task placed on the sensory system are greater than the resource demands of the task used to independently assess sensory system function.

## III. DEVELOPMENT OF ELEMENTAL ASSOCIATIVE SYSTEMS

Against these considerations, I begin to describe how the capacity to learn and remember changes during early infancy. Most research that I will describe uses the rat as the subject. It is an excellent subject for developmental studies of learning and memory. Much is known about the adult rat's learning and memory abilities, and more important for present purposes, the rat is extremely altricial at birth: Much of its sensory, motor, and central nervous system development occurs during a somewhat brief postnatal period and is easily available to experimental observation. Another useful characteristic is the postnatal sequence of the rat's sensory systems development (see Gottlieb, 1971; Alberts, 1984). Roughly speaking, one can distinguish between early- and late-developing sensory systems. At birth, the rat can neither see nor hear. The external auditory canal does not open until about 12 days after birth, and the eyelids remain closed until about postnatal-day 15. So the auditory and visual systems may be termed "late-developing" systems. In contrast, the olfactory and gustatory systems develop much earlier. The olfactory system is to some degree functional at birth, and the gustatory system beings to function during the first postnatal week. This postnatal sequence of sensory system development can be exploited in several ways to reveal information about the development of learning and memory.

## A.  Associative Learning

The concept of association is central to most accounts of learning and provides a natural starting point for developmental analysis. Associations enable an organism to link otherwise independent events from its past and to anticipate the future. Associative learning is said to occur whenever a change in an organism's behavior can be attributed to its experience with a relationship of two or more environmental events. In this section I will address several questions about associative learning that occur in the context of development. When do associative processes emerge? To what extent can changes in associative processes be dissociated from changes in other subsystems upon which they depend? What attributes of the stimulus enter into association? What are the temporal constraints on associative processes, and how do they change with age?

## B.  Learning in the Neonate

About 15 years ago there was some doubt whether newborn altricial animals such as the rat were capable of associative learning. For example, Campbell and Coulter (1976), in their comprehensive review, concluded that there was little compelling evidence of such learning. A stumbling block for research then was methodological. The identification of associative learning by newborn rats is constrained by the immaturity of its sensory and motor systems. So it was not clear if failures to identify learning reflected an inability to learn, an inability to sense the to-be-learned about events, or an inability of learning to influence behavior. In the mid-1970s, methodologies were developed that enabled experimenters to overcome some of these constraints. So it is now evident that associative processes are available to the newborn (see Spear & Rudy, 1991).

An important step in this process was the import of Pavlovian conditioning procedures to developmental research with newborn animals. The Pavlovian methodology has several important advantages for studying learning by newborn (cf. Spear & Rudy, 1991). First, it allows the experimenter precise control over the events the animal is to associate, the conditioned and unconditioned stimulus (CS and US). The occurrence of these events does not depend upon the behavior of the newborn, and the experimenter controls their intensity, duration, and temporal and predictive relationship. Second, the experimenter has some flexibility in choosing a behavior (conditioned response) that can serve as an index to the association. Third, operational criteria have been established that enable the experimenter to infer when the behavioral changes produced by conditioning are due to associative learning and not to other nonassociative factors by which experience with the CS and US could influence behavior (see Rescorla, 1967, for a discussion of these rules).

Another step was recognizing that olfactory stimulation is functionally significant to the new born rat: Teicher and Blass (1976) reported that odors on the dam's teat are crucial to the newborn rat's first nipple attachment. Several reports then appeared documenting that newborn rats can condition to olfactory stimulation. Rudy and Cheatle (1977) showed that 2-day-old rats will acquire an aversion to an odor paired with an illness-inducing agent (see also Rudy & Cheatle, 1979; Cheatle & Rudy, 1979). Johanson and Teicher (1980) reported that 3-day-old rats will learn to prefer an odor paired with milk infused directly into the pups' mouths, and their observation was confirmed and extended by Johanson, Hall, and Palefone (1984). Smotherman (1982) has reported that even the fetal rat can learn an aversion to an odor paired with an illness-inducing agent.

These studies suffice to show that associative learning processes are available to alter the newborn rat's behavioral reaction to its olfactory world. Yet one should not conclude that the operating characteristics of the neonate's associative processes are similar to those of older animals nor that associative processes will be available immediately to other later developing sensory systems. This point will be illustrated in the subsequent sections in which the emergence of associative processes is described for the later developing gustatory, auditory, and visual sensory systems.

## C. Learning About Gustatory Stimuli

Several processes enable organisms to locate safe foods and avoid harmful substances. Information provided by the gustatory system plays a vital role in this matter. "It is the final point of evaluation of a potential food source and the behavioral decision it renders—ingestion or rejection—can be the difference between life and death" (Vogt & Rudy, 1984a, p. 12). Both reflexive and learned behavioral reactions are controlled by gustatory stimulation. Learning and memory control food intake at least two ways: (a) The rat is neophobic and ingests little of a novel food (Barnett, 1963; Domjan, 1977) but usually increases its intake with repeated exposure to the food; and (b) its reaction to a gustatory stimulus can be modified by ingestional consequences. If a novel gustatory sensation is followed by illness, that gustatory stimulus later will be rejected, a phenomenon commonly called *taste-aversion learning* (Garcia & Koelling, 1966).

Mark Vogt and I (Vogt & Rudy, 1984a,b) studied the development of reflexive and learned controls of taste; guided behavior to gain insight into developmental changes in learning. Our studies are built upon the work of Hall and Bryan (1981). They showed that the methodology of infusing sapid solutions directly into the pup's mouth through a small cannula (Hall & Rosenblatt, 1977) can be used to determine if rat pups can discriminate different tastes. It was also preceded by the work of Gregg, Kittrel, Domjan, and Amsel (1978), who had used this procedure to demonstrate taste aversion learning in the preweaning rat.

Figure 1 presents the results Vogt and Rudy (1984a) obtained for rat pups either 6, 9, 12, or 15 days old that had received a taste-aversion learning experience. Pups in the *paired* condition received an infusion of a 10% sucrose

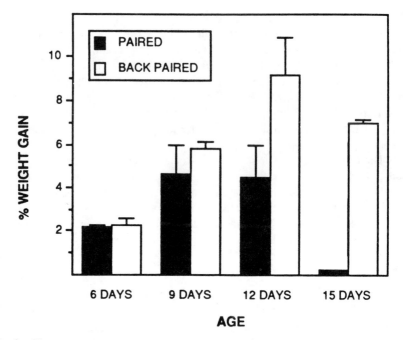

Fig. 1. Mean percentage weight gain during the taste aversion test. During the 20-min test, subjects were placed on a towel soaked in a 10% sucrose solution and allowed to ingest the sucrose. The dependent variable, %-weight-gain was obtained by weighing each pup to .01 gram both before and after the test. Each pup's %-weight-gain score was then determined by the formula: 100 X [(posttest weight-pretest weight)/pretest weight]. (From Vogt & Rudy, 1984. Copyright by John Wiley, Inc. Reprinted with permission of the publisher.)

solution directly into their mouths through a small cheek cannula. Immediately after the infusion, they were injected with an illness-inducing drug (lithium chloride) known to produce conditioned taste aversions in adult animals. Control animals received both the sucrose and LiCl events, but the LiCl injection was administered 2 hours before the sucrose infusion. When tested 48 hours later, neither 6- or 9-day-olds showed evidence of associating the taste and illness events. Yet pups 12 or 15 days old evidenced such learning, because the subjects in the paired condition ingested less sucrose than those in the backward-pairing control condition.

So pups 6 to 9 days old may not have the associative processes necessary for establishing a conditioned taste aversion. The reader should be skeptical of this conclusion. The failure to see evidence of learning could result for many reasons, including immature functioning of the subsystem that (a) detects the LiCl or enables it to reinforce the aversion, (b) enables the pup to detect the sucrose stimulus, and/or (c) enables the animal to reject the sucrose solution. As noted, before one can entertain the possibility of an age-related learning/memory impairment, the effects of age on the learning task must be *dissociated* from its effects on other tasks that independently assess other subsystems contributing to the behavior. Such data are considered below.

Many studies show that LiCl establishes robust conditioned odor aversions in rats less than 6 days old (Rudy & Cheatle, 1976, 1979; Cheatle & Rudy, 1978). Thus it is unlikely that processes that enable LiCl to function as an unconditioned stimulus are responsible for why 6- to 9-day old rats did not acquire the taste aversion.

The data presented in Figure 2 address the issue of whether rats 6- to 9-days of age can detect the sucrose stimulus. It compares pups infused with a 3% body weight, 10% sucrose solution, with animals that were infused with only distilled water. Note that pups at all ages (6- to 15-days old) ingested more of the sucrose solution than did the pups who were infused with water. Unless the pups can detect the sucrose solution and discriminate it from water there would be no basis for differential intake of the two solutions. So it appears that pups 6 days old can detect the sucrose solution.

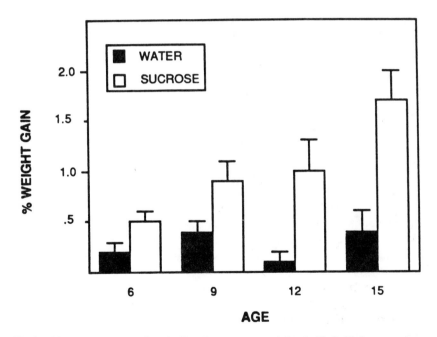

Fig. 2.    *Mean percentage weight gain. Pups in on group were infused with distilled water and pups in another group were infused with a 10% sucrose solution. The infusion volume was approximately 3% of the pup's body weight. The dependent variable, %-weight-gain was obtained by weighing each pup to .01 gram both before and after the infusion. Each pup's %-weight-gain score was then determined by the formula: 100 X [(Postinfusion weight-preinfusion weight)/preinfusion weight]. (From Vogt & Rudy, 1984. Copyright by John Wiley, Inc. Reprinted with permission of the publisher.)*

Although pups 6 to 9 days old can detect the sucrose solution, they still may lack the ability to reject it, even if it has been associated with LiCl. Other results argue against this hypothesis. Recall that a normal part of the rat's defense against harmful food sources is their tendency to be neophobic. They ingest less of a food when it is novel than when it has been previously experienced (see Domjan, 1977). If immature rats lack the ability to reject the sucrose solution, then they should not show a neophobic response. They should ingest just as much of a novel sucrose solution as they do a familiar previously experienced solution, but Vogt and Rudy (1984a) found that both 9- and 12-day-old pups display neophobia.

The 9-day-old pup can control its intake of the sucrose solution. So the inability to inhibit the ingestion of sucrose is not likely to be the source of its failure to show an acquired sucrose aversion. Parenthetically, it is worth noting that though the 9-day-old pup didn't display an acquired sucrose aversion, the results of the last experiment in some sense suggest they "remember" the sucrose experience.

Vogt and Rudy (1984a) conducted several other experiments, varying the intensity of the sucrose concentration, the interval separating the sucrose infusion and functional onset of the illness, and the retention interval. Under no conditions could we find evidence that pups 9 days old learned a sucrose aversion. So we concluded that, though other components of the system through which conditioned taste aversions influence behavior are to some extent functional, the associative processes may not be sufficiently functional in pups this age to support conditioning. Although our findings have been replicated (Hoffman, Molina, Kucharski, & Spear, 1987), it is noted that other researchers (Gemberling, Domjan, & Amsel, 1980; Hoffman et al., 1987) also have reported conditioned taste aversions in pups less than 6 days old.

## D.  Learning about Auditory Stimuli

The auditory system develops much later than either the olfactory or gustatory systems and allows one to study its ability to support associative learning just when it begins to respond to acoustic stimulation.

### 1.  Simple Conditioning

Hyson and Rudy (1984) used an appetitive Pavlovian conditioning methodology to study the development of associative learning mediated by auditory stimuli. The CS was a 10-sec, 90-dB, 2000-Hz tone, and the US was a 10% sucrose solution delivered directly into the pup's mouth by a cannula implanted in the pup's cheek. The sucrose solution evokes a vigorous unconditioned mouthing/licking response. When the tone is paired with the sucrose solution infusion, it acquires the ability to elicit this mouthing response. To quantify the mouthing conditioned response, we recorded the conditioning sessions with a video camera mounted below the transparent Plexiglas floor of the apparatus.

Figure 3 presents the results for pups either 10, 12, 14, or 16 days old at the start of training. During each daily session, animals at each age received 10 pairings of the tone and sucrose solution. Note that, independent of the pup's age at the start of training, conditioned responding did not emerge until the pups were about *16 days old.* Moreover, pups that were 14 days old at the start displayed significantly more conditioned responding when they were 16 days old than did the pups that started training when 16 days old. This pattern of results suggests that conditioning trials given to pups 10 to 13 days old did not contribute to the development of the conditioned response, whereas those administered to pups 14 days old did. This conclusion follows because if pups in the 10- to 13-day-old range were able to condition then they should have displayed conditioned responding before the animals that were 14 days old at the start.

The associative processes necessary for establishing a conditioned response to an auditory stimulus may not be functional in pups less than 14 days old. Yet again, for this conclusion to have force, one must dissociate the effects of age on the conditioning task from its effects on tasks that independently assess other subsystems that contribute to conditioned responding. There can be little doubt

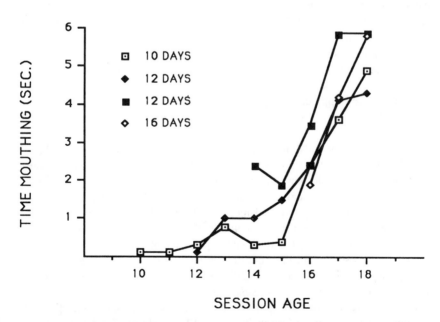

Fig. 3. *Mean time mouthing during the 10 sec of the CS that preceded US occurrence as a function of the pup's age. (From Hyson & Rudy, 1984. Copyright by John Wiley, Inc. Reprinted with permission of the publisher.)*

that the sensory processes that enable the rat to detect the 10% sucrose solution (US) are functioning in rats 10 to 13 days old. In our previous studies on the development of taste aversion learning, we showed that rats 12 days old can acquire a taste aversion to a 10% sucrose solution, and that rats only 6 days old can discriminate that taste from distilled water (Vogt & Rudy, 1984a). Besides, as noted, the sucrose solution evokes a vigorous unconditioned mouthing response in pups at each training age. So the motor subsystem for the conditioned mouthing response is functional in pups that did not condition.

The most likely developmental constraint on the 10- to 13-day-old pup's ability to condition is the maturational status of the auditory system. This age is a major transition period in the peripheral development of the auditory system. The rat's external ear canal is closed 10 days after birth and begins to open around Day 12. To the degree the ear canal is blocked, one can expect that the functional intensity of the sound vibrations arriving at the tympanic membrane will be attenuated. So the 12-day-old pup's failure to condition may be due to the inadequacy of the acoustic signal reaching the tympanic membrane.

One way to determine the functional adequacy of the acoustic signal is to evaluate its ability to evoke a reflexive startle response. To do this Hyson and I fitted pups with mercury-filled silastic tubing. This strain gauge enabled us to detect sudden inspiration (a component of the acoustic startle reflex) evoked by the phasic presentation of an acoustic stimulus. Pups were tested with five presentations of each of four stimulus frequencies (.5, 2, 5, and 10 kHz) delivered at either 80, 90, or 100 dB.

As shown in Figure 4, there were significant age-related differences in the effectiveness of these stimuli to evoke the startle response. The 10-day-old pups did not respond to any frequency x intensity combination. Only the strongest intensity evoked appreciable responding by pups 12 days old, but 14-day-old pups' responses were large in amplitude and sensitive to both intensity and frequency.

There was an interesting caveat in this study. The ear canal of half the 12-day-old subjects in this study were open at the time of the test. The response function for 12-day-old pups with closed canals was similar to that of the 10-day old. They were unresponsive to sound. In contrast, 12-day-old pups with open canals were more responsive and more similar to 14-day-old pups.

These results support the hypothesis that a reduction in the functional intensity of the stimulus arriving at the tympanic membrane could be responsible for why pups less than 14 days old did not condition. Yet a subsequent experiment made it less likely that pups 12 days old did not condition because they did not detect the CS. When the ear canals of the 12-day-old pups were open, they responded more to a 100-dB, 2000-Hz tone than 14 day olds to a 90-dB, 2000-Hz tone. So Hyson and I reasoned that, if 12-day-old pups did not condition because the 90-dB, 2000-Hz acoustic CS (the parameters used in the conditioning study) was inadequate, they should condition to a 100-dB, 2000-Hz stimulus, because it is clearly detected.

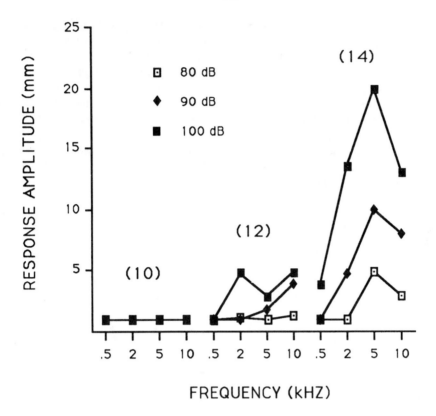

Fig. 4. *Mean amplitude of the startle responses of different-aged pups as a function of frequency and intensity (100, 90, or 80 dB) of the tones. Numbers in parenthesis designate the age of the pup. (From Hyson & Rudy, 1984. Copyright by John Wiley, Inc. Reprinted with permission of the publisher.)*

The results didn't support this idea. Pups 12 to 13 days old whose ear canals were open also did not condition to the 100-dB, 2000-Hz tone. Since pups this age respond reflexively to that stimulus, it is unlikely that they did not condition because that stimulus was not detected. So the central auditory system appears unable to support conditioning to a detectable 2000-Hz stimulus in pups less than 14 days old.

## 2. Differential Conditioning

Pups 14 days old can condition to auditory stimuli. Yet this observation does not mean that all aspects of the system involved in such learning are functional. Hyson and I also found age-related differences in the processes mediating differential conditioning to auditory stimuli (Rudy & Hyson, 1984). In these experiments, a 2000-Hz tone was paired with the sucrose US (T1 +), whereas presentations of a 900-Hz tone were never followed by the US (T2−). Eight trials of each type were administered in each daily training session.

Figure 5 shows the results for pups that were either 12, 14, or 16 days old at the start of training. The striking result was that, independent of the pups' age at the start of training, differential responding to the two tones did not emerge until the pups were about 18 days old. So it appears that the discrimination training pups received when less than 16 days old did not contribute to their learning to respond differentially to the two tones.

This conclusion was strengthened by another result. Here, two sets of 15- to 16-day-old pups and two sets of 16- to 17-day-olds received differential conditioning to the 2000 and 900 Hz tones. During the two sessions of Phase 1

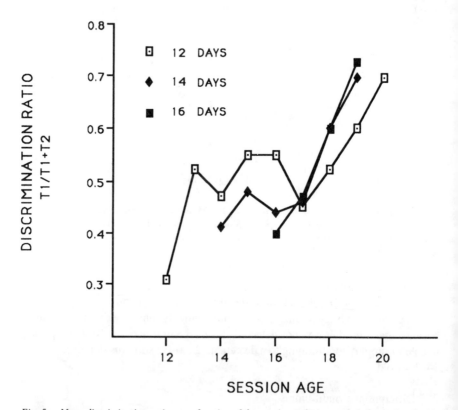

Fig. 5.   *Mean discrimination ratios as a function of the pups' age during each daily session. In this experiment a 2000-Hz tone was paired with the sucrose US (T1 + ) and a 900-Hz tone was not (T− ). To obtain the discrimination ratio, each pup's time mouthing during T1 was divided by the time it mouthed during T1 + T2 (T1/[T1 + T2)]. By this measure discrimination ratios greater than .50 indicate more responding to T1. Note that pups younger than 16 days old at the start of training did not benefit from differential conditioning to the two tones. (From Rudy & Hyson, 1984. Copyright by John Wiley, Inc. Reprinted with permission of the publisher.)*

training, the 2000 Hz tone was paired with the US and the 900 Hz tone was not for one set of animals at each age (T1 + vs. T2 −). The remaining set of pups experienced the opposite relationship (T2 + vs. T1 −). In Phase 2 the significance of T1 and T2 was *reversed* for animals trained on the T2 + vs. T1-problem, so all animals received the same problem, T1 + vs. T2 −.

The rationale for this experiment rests on the logic of the *negative transfer design*. Based on the previous experiment, we hypothesized that only rats at least 17 days old could learn to respond differentially to the two tones. If this is true, then the subjects 16 to 17 days old for whom the significance of the tones was *reversed* should be impaired in learning the Phase 2 discrimination (T1 + vs. T2), compared to pups in the nonreversal condition. This follows because what the pups this age learned in Phase 1 should be incompatible with the requirements of Phase 2. Now consider the younger 15–16-day-old pups. If they were unable to learn about the differential significance of the two tones during Phase 1, then their performance in Phase 2 should be *independent* of their Phase 1 training (T1 + vs. T2 − or T2 + vs. T1 −).

Only the older pups' Phase-2 responding was influenced by their Phase-1 training. Pups in the reversal condition were retarded in learning to respond differentially to the two tones in Phase 2. Phase 2 responding by the 15- to 16-day-olds was independent of their Phase 1 training. Thus, it appears that pups have to be about 17 days old before they condition differentially to these two stimuli.

Yet, before concluding that these results say anything interesting about the maturation of the central components of the auditory system involved in learning, another possibility must be considered. It may be that at the level of the cochlea the 2000 Hz and 900 Hz stimuli are functionally equivalent events to pups less than 17 days old. In fact there is evidence during ontogenesis of a sharpening of the sensory/perceptual processes that discriminate tone frequency in the hatchling chicken (Rubel & Rosenthal, 1975), and the rat over the age range represented in our experiments (Campbell & Haroutunian, 1983).

To evaluate this possibility, we employed the previously described methodology for measuring the rat's reflexive response to phasic acoustic stimulation. We first *habituated* 14-day-old pups to a 90-dB, 2000-Hz tone. Habituation was accomplished by exposing pups to 150 stimulus presentations separated by a 5-sec intertrial interval. By the completion of this training the response to the 2000 Hz tone decreased from an amplitude of 4.1 mm, averaged over the first 25 trials, to an amplitude of .54 mm over the last 25 trials. Subjects were then presented with each of four test frequencies (1800, 1900, 2100, or 2200 Hz). The rationale for this design was as follows. Suppose the subject cannot discriminate between the 2000-Hz training stimulus and one of the test frequencies. Then it follows that the habituated response to the 2000-Hz stimulus should generalize to the test stimulus. To the degree that the subject can discriminate the training and test stimulus, however, the test stimulus should evoke a larger reflexive response than the training stimulus (see Rubel & Rosenthal, 1975).

The surprising result of this experiment (see Rudy & Hyson, 1984) was that, by this measure, pups 14 days old could discriminate between the 2000 Hz tone and the 1800, 1900, 2100, and 2200 Hz tones. So, the inability of pups 14 to 16 days old to learn to respond differentially to a 2000 vs. 900 Hz tone is not due to some age-related constraint imposed at the periphery of the auditory system. This result likely indicates maturational differences in the centrally located components of the system more directly involved in associative learning.

## E.  Learning about Visual Stimuli

The visual system is the last sensory system to develop. The opening of the eyelids, a major landmark of visual functioning, does not occur until the pup is 14 to 15 days old. Our studies of learning mediated by the visual system suggest that associative processes enabling the rat to condition to visual stimulation develop later than those enabling the rat to sense the visual world (Moye & Rudy, 1985). This conclusion is based on a set of Pavlovian fear-conditioning experiments. Specifically, pups were exposed to a visual CS (a 6-watt light flashed on and off at a rate of 4 times/sec) that signaled the occurrence of an aversive US (an electric footshock). Evidence for associative learning was provided by comparing pups that received paired (P) presentations of the CS and US against pups in control conditions that experienced random (R) presentations of the CS and US, and pups that experienced just CS alone presentations before testing.

The dependent variable in these experiments was behavioral activity. The expected outcome was that if pups associated the CS and US they would "freeze" or become less active during a 3-min test presentation of the CS than pups in the control conditions. The test was administered 24 hours after training. A *suppression ratio* (CS/[preCS + CS]) was our index of freezing. Each subject's activity level during the 3-min. CS period was divided by its activity level during that period plus its activity during the immediate 3-min preCS period. So a suppression ratio of 0 indicates complete behavioral suppression by the CS (good conditioning) and a ratio of .50 shows no suppression.

Figure 6 presents the results of our initial experiment for pups that were 15, 17, 19, or 21 days old on the training day. The pattern of results was clear. The 15-day-old pups displayed no evidence of conditioning. Pups in the Paired condition were no more suppressed in the presence of the CS than were pups in the two control conditions. In contrast the 17- to 21-day-old pups in the Paired condition were significantly more suppressed by the CS than were control animals. So 15-day-old pups apparently did not associate the visual CS with the aversive US.

Additional experiments by Moye and Rudy (1985) supported the conclusion that no conditioned suppression by 15-day-old pups was due to immature association processes. Although pups this age didn't condition to the visual CS, they

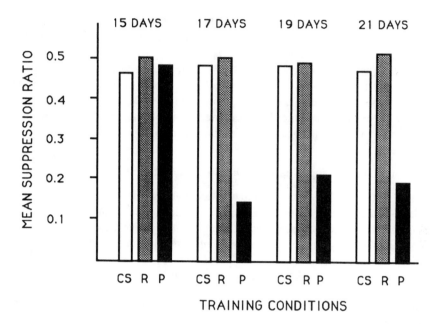

Fig. 6. *Mean suppression ratios obtained during the test from subjects trained with the visual CS when 15, 17, 19, or 21 days old. Key: P, paired, CS, CS-alone, R, random. (From Moye & Rudy, 1985. Copyright by John Wiley, Inc. Reprinted with permission of the publisher.)*

could detect its presence. This conclusion follows because pups placed in the dark conditioning chamber for 45 min were less active when 25 presentations of the flashing light were presented on a variable-time 90-sec schedule than if they remained in the dark for the entire 45-min session (Moye & Rudy, 1985, Experiment 2).

That pups 15 days old didn't condition also could not be attributed to either (a) an inability of the US to support conditioning, or (b) an inability of cues signaling shock to suppress the pups' activity. These two alternatives were precluded by our observation that 15-day-old pups strongly conditioned to an *auditory* CS paired with shock (Moye & Rudy, 1985, Experiment 3). So, simple associative processes involved in conditioning to visual stimulation also appear to develop after other components of the system are functional.

## F. A Generalization and Some Speculation

The studies just reviewed suggest a generalization: Whether a sensory system becomes functional early (e.g., gustatory system) or late (e.g., auditory or visual) during development, it goes through a similar developmental sequence: The components of the system that enable it to detect and respond reflexively to an appropriate stimulus emerge before those components that enable that system to support associative learning. This developmental sequence may have theoretical significance. As Spear and Rudy (1991) suggested, it "may be telling us that there is no unitary, localizable associative learning process, but instead there are multiple sites of associative processing that reside in each sensory system" (Spear & Rudy, 1991, p. 97). This conclusion also is compatible with recent views put forth by Squire (1987) and Crowder (1989). Both writers suggest that it may be useful to assume that memories reside in the specific information-processing systems engaged by the memory generating experience.

## G. Stimulus Coding Changes During Early Infancy

In this section I will comment on maturational changes in coding processes that select what *attributes* of the conditioned stimulus are associated with the US. Spear and his colleagues (see Spear & Molina, 1987; Spear, Kraemer, Molina, & Smoller, 1988) have made a major contribution to this domain, and some of their work will guide this discussion.

It will be useful initially to describe some attributes of the stimulus that potentially can enter into associations. The list of potential attributes can be divided into two categories. One class is designated *modality specific*. Attributes in this class depend exclusively on the sensory channel, olfactory, gustatory, tactile, auditory, or visual, that initially transduces the physical event. The other class of attributes following Spear and his colleagues is called *amodal*. Independent of modality or sensory channel, a stimulus can be described as having attributes of intensity, duration, pattern of delivery, affect, familiarity, or novelty.

The important theoretical point Spear and his colleagues have made is that the *amodal* attributes of the stimulus exert more control over behavior following conditioning early in infancy than they do later. This point has been made in a number of ways, but I will illustrate the basic principle by describing only one experiment.

One source of evidence comes from studies of *cross-modal transfer*. In one study (Spear & Molina, 1987), preweanling and adult rats were tested for cross-modal transfer of conditioning between olfactory and visual stimulation. Animals in the transfer condition were conditioned to an olfactory stimulus by pairing it with shock. Subsequently, they also received a *subthreshold* conditioning experience with a visual context: While in a black compartment they experienced a low-intensity shock that was not sufficient to produce a conditioned aversion to the black context. One set of control animals at both ages experienced the Phase-2 subthreshold conditioning treatment but only were exposed to the odor in Phase 1. Other control animals experienced the odor–shock pairings in Phase 1 but only were exposed to the black visual stimulus in Phase 2.

Adult animals did not develop an aversion to the black compartment even when they had experienced the odor–shock pairings. So, conditioning to the odor did not transfer to the visual stimulus. In contrast, the infant animals that received subthreshold conditioning displayed a reduction in the time spent in the black compartment, but only if they first were conditioned to the odor. So cross-modal transfer was evident for the infants but not for the adults.

Spear and Molina (1987) review several other cross-modal transfer studies that makes the same point. For example, they show transfer in preweanling rats between tactile stimuli and between visual and stimuli. They also review studies that show younger subjects are more likely to display transfer across other amodal attributes such as familiarity and affect than are older rats.

The developmental sequence suggested by the work from Spear's laboratory is that the stimuli attributes that acquire control over behavior change with age. The amodal features of the stimulus play a more important role early in development than they do later. So with age, learned behaviors become more tightly controlled by the modality-specific attributes of the stimulus.

## H.  Temporal Constraints: The Emergence of Short-term Associative Memory

There comes a point during development when each sensory system can support the formation of simple associations, but this does not mean that the associative processes are fully operative. Other research has revealed significant age-dependent temporal constraints on associative learning supported by each sensory system. This conclusion emerges from studies that have systematically manipulated the interval separating CS termination and US onset. In the studies of conditioning with auditory and visual stimuli that I have described, an attempt was made to insure that the CS was physically present when the US occurred. In the studies I now describe, the CS was terminated *before* the US was presented. This procedure is commonly called Pavlovian *trace conditioning*. Because the CS is not present when the US occurs, conditioning can only result if the subject can sustain a representation of the CS until the US occurs. So here the focus is on the development of short-term associative memory processes necessary for linking events separated in time.

Moye and I (Moye & Rudy, 1987) have studied age-dependent variation in temporal constraints on association formation mediated by both the auditory and visual systems. The fear conditioning procedures we used were similar to those I described for the Moye and Rudy (1985) studies of the visual system. In our study of the auditory system, the animals were either 15, 17, 21, or 25 days old at the beginning of training. The auditory CS was a 15-sec duration, 5000-Hz, 90-dB tone. For different conditions the shock US was presented either 0, 10, or 30 sec after the CS ended. The 10 trials were given in a single session and separated by an 8-min intertrial interval. All subjects were tested 24 hours after training with one 3-min presentation of the CS.

Regardless of age, pups conditioned when the trace interval was 0 sec. Yet as the interval increased the pup's age became a critical variable. Pups only 15

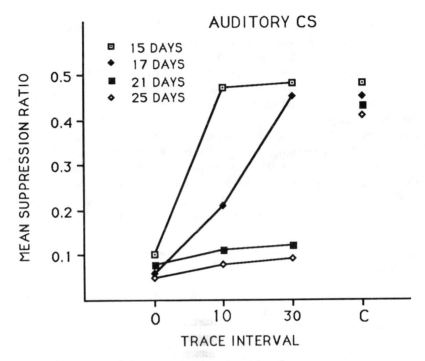

Fig. 7.   *Mean suppression ratios obtained during the test for subjects trained when 15, 17, 21 or 25 days old. Trace intervals were 0, 10, or 30 sec. Subjects in the Control condition (C) received the CS and US in an explicitly unpaired fashion. The CS was an auditory stimulus. (From Moye & Rudy, 1986. Copyright by John Wiley, Inc. Reprinted with permission of the publisher.)*

days old did not condition when the interval was either 10 or 30 sec, and 17-day olds did not condition when the interval was 30 sec. The 21 and 25 day olds, however, conditioned at all trace intervals (see Figure 10).

Our study of the visual system was like the auditory study except that the CS was a flashing light and the subjects were either 17, 21, 25, or 30 days old. In general the pattern of results (see Figure 12) was similar to that obtained with the auditory CS except that the developmental time course was much more protracted. Subjects at each age conditioned when the trace interval was 0 sec. Yet, when the trace interval was 30 sec, only the 30-day-old pups conditioned.

So during development the processes that enable the rat to associate temporal contiguous events are *dissociated* from those that enable temporally separate events to be associated. This development sequence was observed for both the auditory and visual systems. It also should be noted that work on the development of learning mediated by the gustatory system (Gregg et al., 1978; Vogt & Rudy, 1984a) has yielded results consistent with those for the auditory and visual systems. For example, Vogt and Rudy (1984a) found that both 12- and 15-day-

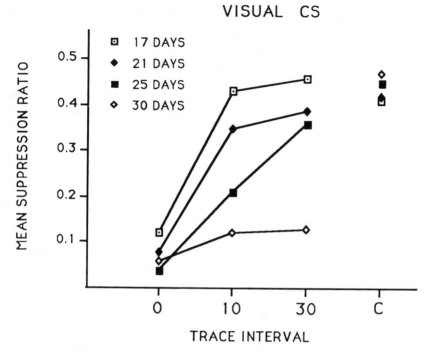

Fig. 8. *Mean suppression ratios obtained during the test for subjects trained when 17, 21, 25 or 30 days old. Trace intervals were, 0, 10, or 30 sec. Subjects in the Control condition (C) received the CS and US in an explicitly unpaired fashion. The CS was a visual stimulus. (From Moye & Rudy, 1987. Copyright by John Wiley, Inc. Reprinted with permission of the publisher.)*

old pups acquired a taste aversion when sucrose and illness were temporally contiguous. Yet only 15-day-old pups did so when the taste preceded the illness event by 60 min. These data suggest that short-term associative memory processes continue to mature for a significant period after the basic associative mechanisms are functional.

## IV.  ELEMENTAL ASSOCIATIVE SYSTEMS: SUMMARY

Research relevant to several questions about the development of learning has been reviewed. When do associative processes emerge? To what extent can changes in associative processes be dissociated from changes in other subsystems that contribute to performance on a learning task? What attributes of the stimulus enter into association? What are the temporal constraints on associative processes and how do they change during development? Now this research will be considered in relation to these questions.

Associative processes are available to the newborn rat and perhaps before birth. Yet it is important to appreciate that what can be associated is highly constrained by the functional status of the animal's sensory systems. That an early developing sensory system (e.g., olfactory or gustatory) can support associative learning does not mean that a later developing system (auditory or visual) will do so as soon as it begins to detect its relevant stimulation. One of the important lessons from this research is that each sensory system must undergo its own independent sequence of development. It can support stimulus detection and reflexive responding before it can support associative learning.

I noted that the behavioral indices by which one infers learning has occurred are a product of a system composed of several components including sensory, motivational, and motor systems that also mature significantly during early infancy. So the researcher must be able to dissociate the effects that maturational changes in learning have on performance from effects due to changes in other components of the system. The research I have reviewed suggests that even early in infancy one can make such dissociations. In studies of the gustatory, auditory, and visual systems, there was no evidence of associative learning when there was evidence that other components of the system were functional. Yet one can never prove that an animal cannot learn. So we should regard the conclusion suggested by the dissociation methodology—that associative processes emerge after other components of the system are functional—with caution.

Spear and his colleagues have identified an ontogenetic difference in the stimulus coding processes that determine what attributes of the stimulus gain control of behavior. The conceptual distinction he makes is between the *modality specific* attributes of the stimulus that depend exclusively on the sensory channel that receives the physical stimulus and the *amodal* attributes that transcend the specific sensory channels. The important empirical generalization from Spear's work is that, during early infancy, the amodal attributes play a more important role than they do later.

There are significant age-dependent temporal constraints on association processes. Sensory systems can support associative learning when the events are temporally contiguous before they can associate temporally separate events. This sequence was found for both early (gustatory) and late-developing (auditory and visual) systems. That one sensory system can associate events separated in time does not mean that a later developing system can. This observation suggests that short-term associative memory processes reside within each sensory system.

## V.  DEVELOPMENT OF THE CONFIGURAL ASSOCIATION SYSTEM

About 17 days after birth each of the rat's sensory systems can support elementary associations needed to produce conditioned responding. By this age rats also can differentially condition to stimuli from the same sensory modality. Yet the associative learning processes engaged by the auditory and visual systems still suffer significant temporal constraints that loosen as the short-term associative memory processes develop. In this section, another constraint that begins to dissolve when the pup is about 20–21 days old will be considered. Here, it will be argued that the rat does not gain access to what is called a *configural representational system* until it is about 20 days old.

An example will be useful at this point. Suppose that a subject experienced a compound stimulus composed of two components or elements *a* and *b* followed by another element *c*. There are at least two ways to conceptualize the associative linkages that are formed between the elements of the compound and the target event *c*. One might assume that each element independently associates with *c*, as represented in the left side of Figure 12, and that the subsequent capacity of the *ab* compound to activate *c* will be the sum of the associative strength of each element. This is the tactic taken by theorists such as Spence (1936) and, more recently, Rescorla and Wagner (1972). As a class, they are sometimes called elemental theories (Rudy & Wagner, 1975).

Alternatively, one might assume that the new linkage is between a representation of the *conjunction* of the *a* and *b* elements and *c*, as shown in the right side of Figure 13. This view is sometimes called configural theory (cf. Rudy & Wagner, 1975; Sutherland & Rudy, 1989). The perspective that guides the research that will be presented in the remaining sections, however, assumes that the third representation, shown in the bottom of Figure 12, is correct. It represents the assumption that a normal adult subject has access to both elemental and configural association systems.

## A. Functional Properties of Elemental and Configural Systems

I will argue that access to the configural association system occurs *late* in development in comparison to access to the elemental system. Before presenting evidence, however, it is necessary to illustrate the functional properties of the two systems. It has long been recognized that elemental-based theories such as Spence's (1936) and Rescorla and Wagner's (1972) can solve a variety of problems. For example, functional elemental systems could provide a basis for all the Pavlovian conditioning phenomena I have described to this point, including differential conditioning to two tones (cf. Rudy & Hyson, 1984). Elemental systems also would permit animals to solve other problems such as the set of concurrent simultaneous visual discriminations displayed in the right side of Figure 10.

Yet there is a set of problems that elemental systems cannot solve. Two examples should suffice to illustrate this class, the negative-patterning problem and the transverse-patterning problem. For the *negative-patterning* problem (Woodbury, 1943), the subject is rewarded ( + ) for responding when either element of a compound stimulus is presented alone, but not rewarded ( − ) when the elements occur together. The elements might be the onset of a light or tone,

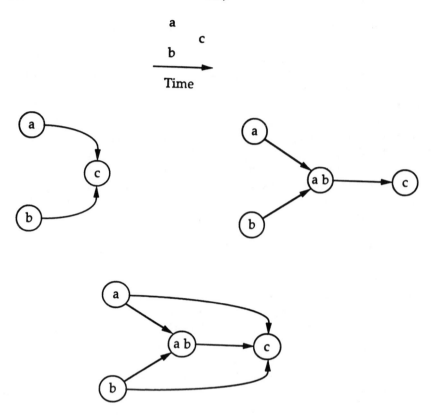

*Fig. 9. Schematic representations of associative connections that might by established when a subject experiences a presentation of a compound stimulus composed of two elements a and b followed by a third stimulus c. The representation on left notes that each element of the compound independently connects with c. The representation on the right notes that it is a representation of the conjunction of the elements (ab) that gets connected with c. The representation on the bottom notes that the elements as well as their conjunction can get associated with c.*

and the response might be a bar press (T+, L+ vs. TL−). The *transverse-patterning* problem (Spence, 1952) requires the subject to solve three concurrent visual discriminations constructed from only three independent elements. In the example displayed in Figure 14 the subject is rewarded for choosing black when it appears with white (B+ vs. W−), for choosing white when it appears with vertical stripes (W+ vs. V−), and for choosing vertical stripes when they appear with black (V+ vs. B−).

Although these problems have solutions, they cannot be solved by an elemental-based associative system. An elemental solution to the negative-patterning problem is impossible, because the combined associative strength of the elements presented in compound can never be less than the strength of an individual element. The transverse-patterning problem poses a similar problem.

## Transverse Patterning

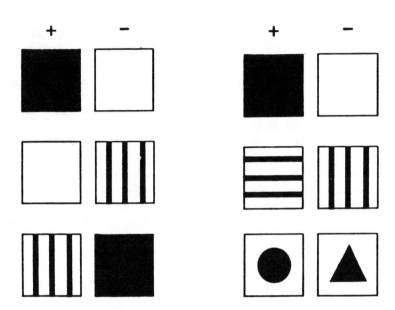

*Fig. 10. Two sets of concurrent visual discriminations. Note that the three problems in the set on the right are composed of six stimulus elements, and that each element is associated with only one outcome. So the animal is always rewarded for choosing black, horizontal stripes, or circle, and never rewarded for choosing white, vertical stripes, or triangle. These three problems can be solved by an elemental association system. Note that the three problems that compose the* transverse-patterning *problem are constructed from only three stimulus elements. So that each element can be associated with either reward ( + ) or no reward ( − ). The transverse-patterning problem cannot be solved by an elemental association system and requires a relational solution.*

Since the animal is equally often rewarded for approaching each element (B, W, and V), the individual strengths of the elements provide no basis for correct choice. In both examples the significance of each individual element is *ambiguous,* but the pattern or *configuration* of stimuli is not. Thus, these problems can be solved if the animal can construct a representation of the conjunction of two or more stimuli that can control behavior. So the critical function a *configural association system* (Sutherland & Rudy, 1989) provides is to permit subjects to solve problems when the significance of the elements is ambiguous.

## B. The Hippocampal Formation and Configural Associations

Elemental and configural association systems may depend on different neural subsystems. Although differing in some details, several theories have incorporated the hypothesis that the hippocampal formation is critical for the acquisition and retention of relational information but not for elemental-based learning (Hirsh, 1974, 1980; Mishkin & Petri, 1984; Sutherland & Rudy, 1989; Wickelgren, 1979). For example, most recently Sutherland and Rudy (1989) distinguished between simple associative systems that can operate independent of the hippocampal formation and a configural associative system that depends on the integrity of the hippocampal formation.

The empirical implication of this distinction is that animals with damage to the hippocampal formation can solve problems that permit elemental solutions but will be impaired on problems that require configural solutions. In recent years, evidence has accumulated that supports this theory of hippocampal function. For example, Rudy and Sutherland (1989) have found that hippocampal formation damage prevented rats from both acquiring and retaining the solution to the negative patterning problem. Alvarado and Rudy (1989) found that rats who solved the transverse patterning problem before surgery did not reacquire its solution after the hippocampal formation was damaged (see Ross, Orr, Holland & Berger, 1984; Sutherland, McDonald, Hill, & Rudy, 1989, for other supporting data).

## C.  Access to the Configural System Occurs Late in Development

Perhaps because the hippocampal formation and its related cortical systems show considerable postnatal maturation (see Altman & Bayer, 1975; Altman, Brunner, & Bayer, 1973), it is reasonable to suppose that the ability to solve problems that require relational solutions will develop later than those that permit elemental solutions. This hypothesis has been supported by several sources of data.

### 1.  Place Learning

One source of evidence comes from studies of two versions of the Morris (1981) water task. In both tasks the rat is placed into a large circular pool of water, and its problem is to locate an escape platform. In the *place-learning* version, the animal is started from several locations in the pool and has to find a platform that is hidden beneath the surface of the water. So to swim directly to the platform, the animal must learn its location relative to the distal cues located outside the pool. In the cued-learning version, the platform is visible and all the animal must learn is to swim directly to it. It does not require the animal learn about the spatial location of the platform. Adult rats master both problems in only a few trials (Morris, 1981).

To solve the place-learning task, an animal must have access to a representational system that enables the *relationship* among the distal cues outside the pool and its starting location to control its navigation behavior (see Sutherland & Rudy, 1989; McNaughton, 1989). Another way of stating the problem is that the significance of each distal cue, in relationship to the location of the platform, is ambiguous. Each cue's meaning is clear only in *conjunction* with other distal cues and the animal's starting location. So performance on this task should depend on a functioning configural association system. In contrast, performance on the cued version of the task does not require the use of relational processes and requires only a functioning elemental system. Animals with hippocampal damage are severely impaired on the place task but not on the cued-learning task (Morris, Garrud, Rawlins, & O'Keefe, 1982; Sutherland, Kolb, & Whishaw, 1982; Sutherland & Rudy, 1987).

We have studied developmental changes in performance on both the place- and cued-learning versions of the Morris task (Rudy, Stadler-Morris, & Albert, 1987; Rudy & Paylor, 1987). By 17 days of age, we find that rats can learn the cued version of the task. Yet it is not until the rat is about 20 days old that it learns the spatial location of the hidden platform.

This conclusion derives in part from the data presented in Figure 11. In this study, pups were either 18, 20, or 22 days old when they were trained on the task. For half the subjects at each age, the hidden platform was in the same location of the pool on each trial. For the other half, the platform location was varied from trial to trial.

A comparison of these two conditions provides a way to assess the extent to which pups can acquire place information. When platform location is fixed, then the animal's starting position in conjunction with distal cues provides a basis for navigating directly to the platform. When the platform location varies randomly, there is no information available to the animal that permits it to navigate directly to the platform. So to the degree that a subject can acquire and use this relational information, animals trained with a platform in a fixed location should have faster escape latencies than animals trained with the location of the platform randomly changing.

The left side of Figure 11 shows that the escape latencies of subjects trained when 18 to 19 day-olds were not faster when the platform was in a fixed location than when its location varied. Yet both the 20-to-21- and 22-to-23-day-olds escaped significantly faster when the platform was in a fixed location. The right side of Figure 11 provides additional evidence that the two older sets of pups learned the spatial location of the platform. After the last acquisition trial the platform was removed from the pool, and the pup was allowed to search the pool for 60 sec. During the probe trial the pool was divided into four equal quadrants, and the percentage of time the pup spent in each quadrant was recorded. Note that the two older sets of pups trained with the platform in a fixed location selectively searched the quadrant that contained the platform during training. In contrast no selective search was displayed by any other set of animals. So these and other findings reported by Rudy et al. (1987) and Rudy and Paylor (1988) indicate that pups do not acquire access to the configural association system until they are about 20 days old. Yet elemental associative processes are available at an earlier age, as suggested by the finding that pups 17 days old can learn to swim to a visible platform.

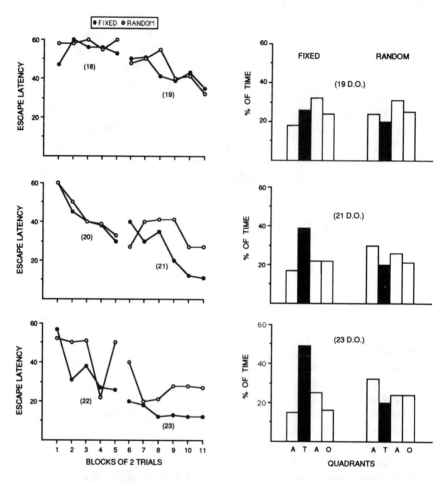

Fig. 11. Left: Mean escape latencies for the different-age subjects (open circles represent the random-platform location group, and the filled circles represent the fixed-platform location group). Subject's age is in parentheses. Right: Mean percentage of time pups in each condition spent in each of the four quadrants during the 60-sec probe trial. The probe-trial data for the random-location group are presented in the right segment of each of the lower graphs, and data for the fixed-location group are presented in the left segment. T = training quadrant; A = adjacent quadrant; O = opposite quadrant. Note that only the 21- and 23-day-old pups in the fixed-location group selectively searched the quadrant that had contained the platform during training. (From Rudy, Stadler-Morris, & Albert, 1987. Copyright by the American Psychological Association. Reprinted with permission of the publisher.)

## 2. Conditional Delayed Alternation

Additional evidence that access to the configural associative system develops late comes from studies of conditional choice problems (Castro, Paylor, & Rudy, 1987; Green & Stanton, 1989). In these studies animals were trained in a T-maze. The basic problem is presented in Figure 12. A trial consisted of two components, a forced run and a choice. On the forced run, entry to one arm of the maze is blocked, and the subject is rewarded for entering the unblocked arm. On the choice run both arms of the maze are open and the subject is required to enter one arm. Reward on the choice run trial is conditional upon the animal choosing the arm blocked on the forced run. This task requires a relational solution and is not solved by animals with hippocampal formation damage (Aggleton, Hunt, & Rawlins, 1986). It can be contrasted with a *position habit* task that permits an elemental solution. Here the subject is consistently rewarded for choosing one arm of the maze.

Although the Castro et al. (1987) and Green and Stanton (1989, Experiment 2) studies were conceptually similar, the procedures were very different. In the Castro et al. experiments, the animals were placed in a water-filled maze and rewarded for choosing the arm that contained an escape platform. In the Green and Stanton studies the subjects were food deprived and received milk as reward for making the correct response. Nevertheless, these studies yield similar outcomes. In both cases rats that were 21 days old at the start of training solved the conditional problem. Castro et al. did not train subjects at younger ages, but Green and Stanton found that animals 15 to 16 days old didn't solve this problem (see Figure 13). Green and Stanton also provided another important observation. Under the same training conditions, pups 15 to 16 days acquire a *position habit* as rapidly as the 21-day-olds. So again we see that rats less than 20 days old can solve a problem that permits an elemental solution but cannot solve a problem that requires a configural solution.

## 3. The Role of Context in Conditioning

Contemporary Pavlovian conditioning research emphasizes that the context in which conditioning occurs is a major determiner of the degree to which the CS evokes conditioned responding (cf. Balsam & Tomie, 1985; Bouton, 1990). Several proposals have been offered to explain just how the contextual stimuli can modulate responding to the CS.

One proposal is that the elements of the context directly associate with the unconditioned stimulus (Rescorla & Wagner, 1972). In this way context can provide a source of excitatory strength that can summate with the excitatory strength of the CS and *facilitate* conditioned responding. This role of context in principle requires only a functioning elemental system. There is good evidence

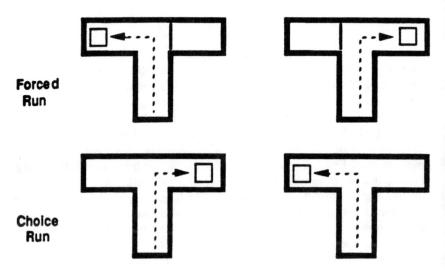

*Fig. 12. Schematic of the two components of a conditional alternation trial, the forced run and choice run. On the forced run one arm of the maze is blocked and the animal is rewarded for entering the unblocked arm. On the choice run neither arm is blocked and reward is conditional upon the animal choosing the arm that was blocked on the forced run.*

supporting this view (Balsam & Schwartz, 1981; Bouton & Bolles, 1985; Rescorla, Durlach, & Grau, 1985).

Another view emphasizes what Bouton and Bolles (1985) have called the *disambiguation function* of context. This function emerges in cases where the significance of the CS, its relationship to US occurrence is unclear, because on some trials the CS is followed by the US but on others the US does not occur.

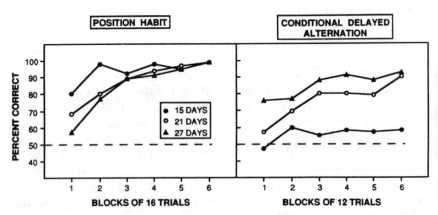

*Fig. 13. Mean percentage correct on a position habit; problem and a conditional alternation problem for pups 15, 21, and 27 days old. (Redrawn from Green & Stanton, 1989. Reprinted with permission).*

The most compelling evidence for the disambiguation function of context comes from conditional discrimination studies (see Asratyan, 1965; Rescorla et al., 1985) where the significance of two CS, A and B, depends on the context in which they occur. In one context (C1) A signals US occurrence and B signals US absence, whereas in a different context (C2), the relationship is reversed. Note that, viewed alone, the significance of A and B is ambiguous, but that in *conjunction* with C1 or C2, their significance is clear. So context here specifies the consequence that follows an otherwise ambiguous CS. It should be understood that an elemental associative system is inadequate for context to serve a disambiguation function. This function requires a relational representation system.

According to our general hypothesis, access to the configural associative system develops late in comparison to access to elemental systems. So behavioral functions of context that require only elemental systems should emerge earlier in development than those that depend upon a relational system. Maura Carew and I recently evaluated this prediction (Carew & Rudy, 1991).

One behavioral function of context that requires only an elemental system is the ability of context conditioning to *restore* responding to an extinguished CS. Suppose that an animal has been conditioned to respond to a CS in a particular context and then extinguished in that context. According to an elemental view, the loss of responding indicates a loss of excitatory strength by *both* the CS and stimulus elements that define the context. If one then places the animal back into the conditioning context and presents the US, excitatory conditioning to the context should be restored. So conditioned responding to the CS also should be restored when it is retested in that context. This "restoration" effect of context has been well documented in the adult literature (see Boulton & Bolles, 1985).

Carew and I (Carew & Rudy, 1991) also have observed the "restoration effect" of context in both young and older rats. Rat pups 17 and 20 days old were first conditioned to respond to a vibratory/auditory CS paired with a 10% sucrose solution infused directly into the pups' mouths. The resulting conditioned mouthing response was then extinguished in all animals. These two phases of training occurred in the same context. All animals then received context conditioning trials by administering several US-alone presentations. For half of the animals at each age, US presentations occurred in the original training context but for the other half they occurred in a different context. In the final phase, all subjects received test presentations of the CS in the original training context.

There were no differences among the groups in either acquisition or extinction, but when the animals were tested for responding to the extinguished CS, pups that received US presentations in the original training/extinction context responded more than animals that received them in a novel context. This "restoration" effect was, if anything, somewhat stronger in the younger animals.

In another experiment, we (Carew & Rudy, 1991) investigated a phenomenon called the "renewal" effect that Bouton and Bolles (1985) concluded required the conditioning context to serve a *disambiguation function*. One can describe a CS that has been paired with the US and presented alone (extinction) as ambiguous. It has signaled both US occurrence and absence. So, it is interesting that when a *change* in context occurs in conjunction with extinction, animals will respond more to the CS when they are later tested in the original training context than will animals that received acquisition and extinction in the same context (see Bouton, 1990; Bouton & Bolles, 1985; Bouton & King, 1983). The preserved responding to the CS that occurs when animals in the context-shift condition are tested in the original training context is sometimes called the "renewal" effect. Configural theory would account for the "renewal" effect" because the configural representation >C1cs< of the CS in conjunction with the training context (C1) is different from its representation >C2cs< in conjunction with the new context (C2) experienced during extinction. So extinction trials in the new context should leave the ability of the >C1cs< representation to evoke conditioned responding comparatively intact.

The ability of context to produce the "renewal" effect depends on the age of the rat. In our experiment, 17- and 20-day-old rats were conditioned to respond to vibratory/auditory CS paired with 10%-sucrose solution US. Half the animals then experienced extinction trials in the original training context, whereas extinction occurred in a novel context for the other half. There were no differences among the groups in either acquisition or extinction. Yet when all animals were later tested with the CS in the training context there was a difference (see Figure 14). The older animals that experienced the *context change* in conjunction with extinction responded more to the CS than did the pups who received acquisition and extinction in the same context. Test performance of the younger animals, however, was *independent* of extinction context. So the disambiguation function of context, as assessed by the "renewal" effect, is age dependent.

## D. Summary

In previous sections I distinguished between elemental and configural association systems. I argued that elemental systems are available early in development but pups don't gain access to the configural system until they are about 20 days old. Evidence was provided by reviewing studies of navigation learning (place learning versus cued learning), choice behavior (conditional-based versus position habit), and context (facilitation versus disambiguation functions). The data suggest that successful performance on the tasks that required a configural solution did not emerge until the rat was about 20 days old. Yet animals 15–17 days old were successful on the companion tasks that required only an elemental solution. Said differently, age dissociated performance on tasks that permitted an elemental solution from those tasks required a relational solution.

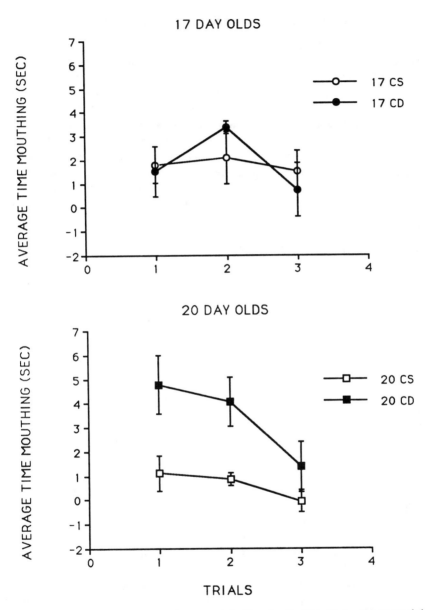

Fig. 14. Mean time mouthing on the three test trials. Note that the 20-to-23-day-olds responded more during the test when extinction had occurred in a different context (Group CD), than when it occurred in the training context (Group CS). In contrast, the test performance of the 17-to-20-day-old pups was independent of extinction context. So only the older animals showed the disambiguation function of context. (From Carew and Rudy, in press. Copyright by John Wiley, Inc. Reprinted with permission of the publisher.)

## E.  The Emergence of Relational Systems in Primates

The picture of learning and memory development portrayed to this point rests exclusively on studies of the rat. Most recently, however, we have obtained data that suggest that the generality of some of our assertions is not limited to this species. In particular, we think that the hypothesis that elemental systems emerge before the configural system also applies to humans and monkeys.

The recent data was obtained in collaboration with Julian Keith and Kathleen Georgen. We employed a version of the transverse-patterning problem suitable for use with young children. Recall that the transverse-patterning problem requires the subject to solve three concurrent visual discrimination problems created from only three stimuli. In our task the choice stimuli were small wooden boxes of different colors. Discrimination learning problems were created by asking the child to choose between two boxes. Reward for the correct choice was a yogurt covered raisin. The choice response was the removal of the lid of the box, and the reward was in the box.

In our experiment, two age groups were compared on two problems. The youngest children were 42 to 54 months old. The oldest were 55 to 62 months old. One set of children at each age was asked to solve a set of concurrent simple discriminations that permitted an elemental solution. There were three problems constructed from six different colored boxes (e.g., A+ vs. B−; C+ vs. D−; E+ vs. F−). Note that there are no ambiguous elements in this problem set. Choosing A, C, or E was always rewarded, and choosing B, D, or F was never rewarded.

Another set of children was asked to solve the *transverse-patterning* problem, three problems constructed from only three stimuli (e.g., A+ vs. B−; B+ vs. C−; C+ vs. A−). Note that each element is ambiguous. On some occasions, its choice will be rewarded, but on others no reward will occur (A±, B±, and C±). There is no elemental solution to the problems, but the pattern specifies the correct choice. For example, the conjunction [AB] signals that the A stimulus is correct. So the transverse-patterning problem can be solved but requires a configural system.

The transverse-patterning problem is difficult. So we structure the training procedure to facilitate its solution. All subjects were first trained to criterion (9/10 correct) on one problem (A+ vs. B−); then the second problem was introduced and intermixed with the first (A+ vs. B− and B+ vs. C− for the transverse problem; A+ vs. B− and C+ vs. D− for the simple discrimination problem) until criterion was achieved. Finally, the third problem was introduced to the problem set, and the children had to solve all three problems concurrently.

The young children solved the set of simple discriminations just as well as the older children, requiring no more than 20 trials to achieve criterion at each stage of training. They also did not differ from the older children over the first two phases of the transverse-patterning problem. But, only Phase 3 requires a configural solution, and the performance of the youngest subjects deteriorated in Phase 3. Only 1 of the younger children reached criterion (training terminated after 90 trials), whereas all of the older children reached criterion.

So children 42 to 54 months old easily mastered a set of simple discriminations that permitted an elemental solution but did not solve the transverse patterning problem. The older children solved both problems. Such results suggest that children also gain access to elemental processes before they are able to use the configural system.

This conclusion is strengthened by other data in the child development literature. For example, the *oddity problem* is not unlike the transverse-patterning problem. The child is presented with three stimuli, such as two red circles and one blue circle, or two blue circles and one red circle. To receive reward the child must choose the *odd* member of the set. Note that the meaning of the stimulus elements of the oddity problem is ambiguous. Sometimes the child is rewarded for choosing the red or blue stimulus, but sometimes no reward occurs (R±, G±). Yet the pattern or configuration of stimuli specifies the correct response. So it is of considerable interest that Gollin and Schadler (1972), in a systematic developmental study, reported that only about 20% of the children in the 42-to-53-month-old range solved the oddity problem. Yet about 60% of the children in the 54-to-59 month-old range, and 80% in the 60-to-65-month-old range, solved the problem. This outcome corresponds quite closely with our findings with transverse-patterning problem. Children less than about 4.5 years old are impaired on problems that require a relational solution.

To my knowledge there have been no developmental studies with monkeys on the transverse-patterning problem. But Harlow (1959), in his thorough development analysis of learning in the rhesus monkey, reports that the ability to solve the oddity problem does not emerge until the infant is about 3 years old. This is well after the monkey solves a host of other problems that permit an elemental solution, such as simple brightness discriminations and concurrent object discriminations (see Harlow, 1959, for a review; Bachevalier & Mishkin, 1984).

So the primate literature is consistent with the developmental generalization indicated from our analysis of the rat: Access to the configural association system occurs late in development compared to when the elemental associative systems become accessible.

## VI.  DISCUSSION

Harlow (1959), in an otherwise enlightening review of his work on the development of learning in the rhesus monkey, painted a bleak picture for the use of infraprimates such as the rat as a suitable animal for gaining insight into the development of learning and other cognitive capacities.

Animals below the primate order are intellectually limited compared with monkeys, so that they learn the same problems more slowly and are incapable of
solving many problems that are easily mastered by monkeys. Horses and rats, and
even cats and dogs, can solve only a limited repertoire of learning tasks, and they
learn so slowly on all but the simplest of these that they pass from infancy to
maturity before their intellectual measurement can be completed. (Harlow, 1959,
p. 46)

Harlow was right that the rat quickly passes from infancy to maturity, and
the rat may be intellectually limited. Yet research reviewed here suggests the rat
has much to offer as a model for studying learning and memory development in
higher mammals (see Spear & Campbell, 1979; Spear & Rudy, in press). The
rapid rate at which the rat matures certainly does not preclude an assessment of
developmental changes in its learning and memory systems. Nor, as this chapter
suggests, is the rat's intellectual capacity so limited as to be of little value as a
model for higher mammals.

Compared to primates, much of the rat's sensory system development is
postnatal. For example, recall that neither the auditory nor visual system is
functional until at least 10 days after the rat is born. This feature of the rat's
development permits an evaluation of the associative processes engaged by a
sensory system at the time the system begins to respond to the environment. The
research I reviewed suggests that the central components of each sensory system
that are required for associative learning are not functional when a sensory
system first responds reflexively to an appropriate stimulus. Independent of
whether a sensory system begins to function early or late, it appears to follow the
same developmental sequence: The capacity of the system to mediate reflexive
behaviors emerged before it could support associative learning.

This research also suggests that the short-term associative memory processes
that enable each sensory system to support associations between events separated
in time continue to mature well after the system permits temporally contiguous
events to be associated. For three sensory systems, gustatory, auditory, and
visual, we saw that there were significant temporal constraints on associative
learning. During ontogenesis, a sensory system could support conditioning when
the events were temporally contiguous before it could support that of temporally
separated events. The identification of two developmental sequences common to
several sensory systems has an interesting theoretical implication. It suggests that
there are sites of associative processing contained within each sensory pathway.

Perhaps the most intriguing contribution of the present research was the
suggestion of a common developmental sequence in rats, monkeys, and humans.
Across species, it appears that the organism gains access to the elemental
associative systems before they can access the configural system. Central to this
conclusion was a theoretical analysis that recognized that many behavioral tasks
permit elemental solutions, whereas other tasks require a solution that depends
on the animal being able to use a representation of the pattern or configuration of

stimuli to control behavior. The fundamental feature of tasks that require a relational solution is that the significance of the individual elements of the problem is *ambiguous* but the significance of the stimulus pattern is not. Empirical support for the conclusion was provided by showing that it was possible to obtain age-dependent *dissociation* in performance on tasks that permitted elemental solutions and those that required relational solutions. In each case, subjects were successful on tasks that permitted elemental solutions at a younger age than that at which they could solve relational problems constructed from the same elements. Some theorists argue that the hippocampal formation and its cortical inputs may be important for relational representations to control behavior but not for control by elemental systems (Hirsh, 1974, 1980; Mishkin & Petri, 1984; Sutherland & Rudy, 1989; Wickelgren, 1979). If this position is correct, it is reasonable to speculate that maturation of this system may be necessary for the relational system to control behavior (see also Rose, 1976).

## A. A Jacksonian Perspective

It may be useful to consider the overall pattern of results reviewed here with the *hierarchical* view of brain organization proposed by Hughlings Jackson (cf. Jackson, 1884/1958). Jackson's theory was based on the assumption that the mammalian brain evolved by the addition of cephalad components. He also assumed that more rostrally located brain structures provided the substrates for (a) more complex behaviors, and (b) the control of primitive behaviors that can be mediated by more caudally located components of the brain. So Jackson conceptualized the brain as organized in terms of *levels*—higher and lower brain centers. Lower centers were viewed as the simplest and most tightly organized or "hardwired," where the dimension of tightness refers to the modifiability of the organization.

Several researchers have pointed to the potential relevance of the Jacksonian view for brain/behavior relations during development (cf. Campbell, Sananes, & Gaddy, 1985; Teitelbaum, Schallert, & Whishaw, 1983; Rozin, 1976, Rudy et al., 1987). Here the view is that brain development is incomplete at birth and matures in part by the addition of more cephalad components. The behavioral implication is that, during ontogeny, behavioral capacities that depend on the lower, more tightly organized centers should emerge before those that depend upon the higher, less tightly organized (more docile) centers.

The several developmental sequences that emerged in our review of studies of the ontogeny of learning and memory systems appear to fit comfortably in the Jacksonian perspective. Indeed, research suggests that *each* sensory system, whether it begins to function early or late in development, goes through its own "Jacksonian" maturation sequence. This is implied by the observations that each system could support (a) "primitive reflexive behaviors" before it could support associative learning, and (b) associations among contiguous events before it could associate temporally separate events. This hypothesis receives additional support by the fact that in adult animals brain stem components of sensory systems are known to be able to mediate unlearned reflexive responses (cf. Davis, Gandelman, Tischler, & Gandelman, 1982; Grill & Norgren, 1978), but learned behaviors may require more rostrally located components of the system (cf. Braun, Lasiter, & Kiefer, 1982).

The elemental-to-configural association system sequence that was uncovered also fits. The configural system is conceptualized as allowing the animal to construct a representation of the joint occurrence of several stimuli and use that representation to control behavior. The functional importance of the configural system is seen when the significance of the individual elements is ambiguous but the pattern in which they occur is not. So the configural system must not only construct a representation of the stimulus pattern, in some sense it also must *control* the influence the stimulus elements of the pattern have on behavior by virtue of their individual and summed associative strengths.

The Jacksonian perspective on brain/behavior provides a convenient way to overview the data. It does not, of course, say anything about the particular maturational changes in brain that are responsible for the developmental changes in learning that have been reviewed. Such precise accounts await future research.

## B. Conclusion

Research reviewed here has focused on identifying changes in the rat's learning processes that occur primarily in the postnatal preweaning period. It reveals that associative learning processes are available at or before birth, but what the pup can learn is highly constrained by the maturational status of its sensory systems. In addition, the onset of function in a sensory system does not signify the onset of associative learning. Each sensory system can be described as going through its own "Jacksonian" caudal-to-rostral developmental sequence. So it can detect and respond reflexively to an appropriate stimulus before it can support associative learning and can support associations among temporally contiguous events before it can support associations among temporally separated events.

Even at the age in which all its sensory systems can support simple associations (about 17 days postnatally), the rat evidently cannot use relational information to guide its behavior. Several sources of evidence suggest it may be fruitful to distinguish between early developing elemental associative systems and a late developing configural system. Some research suggests this distinction also applies to infant monkeys and children.

## REFERENCES

Aggleton, J. P., Hunt, P. R., & Rawlins, J. N. P. (1986). The effects of hippocampal lesions upon spatial and non-spatial tests of working memory. *Behavioral Brain Research, 19,* 133–146.
Alberts, J. R. (1984). Sensory-perceptual development in the Norway rat: A view toward comparative studies. In R. Kail & N. E. Spear (Eds.), *Comparative perspectives on the development of memory* (pp. 65–102). Hillsdale, NJ: Erlbaum.

Altman, J., & Bayer, S. (1975). Postnatal development of the hippocampal dentate gyrus under normal and experimental conditions. In R. Isaacson & K. H. Pribram (Eds.), *The hippocampus, Part 1* (pp. 95–122). New York: Plenum.

Altman, J., Brunner, R. L., & Bayer, S. (1973). The hippocampus and behavioral maturation. *Behavioral Biology, 8,* 557–586.

Alvarado, M., & Rudy, J. W. (1989) The transverse patterning; problem, configural processes and the hippocampus. *Society for Neuroscience Abstracts, 15,* 610.

Asratyan, E. A. (1965). *Compensatory adaptations, reflex activity, and the brain.* Oxford: Pergamon.

Bachevalier, J., & Mishkin, M. (1984). An early and a late developing system for learning and retention in infant monkeys. *Behavioral Neuroscience, 98,* 770–778.

Balsam, P. D., & Schwartz, A. L. (1981). Rapid contextual conditioning in autoshaping. *Journal of Experimental Psychology Animal Behavioral Processes, 1,* 382–391.

Balsam, P. D., & Tomie, A (1985). *Context and learning.* Hillsdale, NJ: Erlbaum.

Barnett, S. A. (1963). *The rat.* Chicago: Aldine.

Bernston, G. G., & Boysen, S. T. (1990). Cardiac indices of cognition in infants, children, and chimpanzees. In C. Rovee-Collier & Lewis P. Lipsitt (Eds.), *Advances in infancy research* (Vol. 6, pp. 188–216). Norwood, NJ: Ablex Publishing Corp.

Bouton, M. E. (1990). Context and retrieval in extinction and in other examples of interference in simple associative learning. In L. W. Dachowski & C. F. Flaherty (Eds.), *Current topics in animal learning: Brain, emotion, and cognition* (pp. 25–55). Hillsdale, NJ: Erlbaum.

Bouton, M. E., & Bolles, R. C. (1985). In P. D. Balsam & A. Tomie (Eds.), *Context and learning* (pp. 133–166). Hillsdale, NJ: Erlbaum.

Braun, J. J., Lasiter, P. S., & Kiefer, S. W. (1982). The gustatory neocortex of the rat. *Physiological Psychology, 10,* 13–45.

Campbell, B. A., & Coulter, X. (1976). The ontogenesis of learning and memory. In M. R. Rosenzweig & E. L. Bennett (Eds.), *Neural mechanisms of learning and memory.* Cambridge, MA: MIT Press.

Campbell, B. A., & Haroutunian, V. (1983). Perceptual sharpening in the developing rat. *Journal of Comparative Psychology, 97,* 3–11.

Campbell, B. A., & Jaynes, J. (1966). Reinstatement. *Psychological Review, 73,* 478–480.

Campbell, B. A., Sananes, C., & Gaddy, J. R. (1985). Animal models of Jacksonian dissolution of memory in the aged. In J. Traber & W. H. Gispen (Eds.), *Senile dementia of Alzheimer type* (pp. 283–291). Berlin-Heidelberg: Springer-Verlag.

Campbell. B. A., & Spear, N. E. (1972). Ontogeny of memory. *Psychological Review, 79,* 215–236.

Carew, M. B., & Rudy, J. W. (1991). Multiple functions of context during conditioning: A developmental analysis. *Developmental Psychobiology, 24,* 191–209.

Castro, C. A., Paylor, R., & Rudy, J. W. (1987). A developmental analysis of the learning and short-term memory processes mediating performance in conditional-spatial discrimination problems. *Psychobiology, 15,* 308–316.

Castro, C. A., & Rudy, J. W. (1989). Early-life malnutrition impairs of the performance of both young and adult rats on visual discrimination learning tasks. *Developmental Psychobiology, 22,* 15–28.

Cheatle, M. D., & Rudy, J. W. (1979). The ontogeny of second odor conditioning in neonatal rats. *Journal of Experimental Psychology: Animal Behavior Processes, 5,* 142–151.

Crowder, R. G. (1989). Modularity and dissociations in memory systems. In H. L. Roediger & F. I. Craik (Eds.), *Varieties of memory and consciousness* (pp. 271–294). Hillsdale, NJ: Erlbaum.

Davis, M., Gandelman, M. D., Tischler, M. D., & Gandelman, P. M. (1982). The primary acoustic startle circuit. *Journal of Neuroscience, 2,* 791–805.

Domjan, M. (1977). Attenuation and enhancement of neophobia for edible substances. In L. M. Barker, M. Best, & M. Domjan (Eds.), *Learning mechanisms in food selection* (pp. 155–180). Waco, TX: Baylor University Press.

Dunn, J. C., & Kirsner, K. (1988). Discovering functionally independent mental processes: The principle of reversed association. *Psychological Review, 95,* 91–101.

Garcia, J., & Koelling, R. A. (1966). Relation of Cue to Consequence in avoidance learning. *Psychonomic Science, 4,* 123–124.

Gemberling, G. A., Domjan, M., & Amsel, A. (1980). Aversive learning in 5-day old rats: Taste-toxicosis and texture shock-aversive learning. *Journal of Comparative and Physiological Psychology, 96,* 105–113.

Gollin, E. S. (1965). A developmental approach to learning and cognition. In L. P. Lipsitt & C. C. Spiker (Eds.), *Advances in child development and behavior* (Vol. 2, pp. 159–186). New York: Academic.

Gollin, E. S., & Schadler, M. (1972). Relational learning and transfer by young children. *Journal of Experimental Child Psychology, 14,* 219–232.

Gottlieb, G. (1971). Ontogenesis of sensory of functioning in birds and mammals. In E. Tobach, L. R. Aronson, & E. Shaw (Eds.), *The biopsychology of development* (pp. 76–128). New York: Academic Press.

Green, R. J., & Stanton, M. E. (1989). Differential ontogeny of working memory and reference memory in the rat. *Behavioral Neuroscience, 103,* 98–105.

Gregg, B., Kittrel, E. M. W., Domjan, M., & Amsel, A. (1978). Ingestional aversion learning in preweanling rats. *Journal of Comparative and Physiological Psychology, 92,* 785–795.

Grill, H. J., & Norgren, R. (1978). The taste reactivity test: II. Mimetic responses to gustatory stimuli in chronic thalamic and chronic decerebrate rats. *Brain Research, 143,* 281–297.

Groves, P., & Thompson, R. (1970). A dual process theory of habituation: neural mechanisms. *Psychological Review, 77,* 419–450.

Hall, W. G., & Rosenblatt, J. S. (1977). Suckling behavior and intake control in the developing rat pup. *Journal of Comparative and Physiological Psychology, 91,* 1232–1247.

Hall, W. G., & Bryan, T. E. (1981). The ontogeny of feeding in rats: IV. Taste development as measured by intake and behavioral responses to oral infusions of sucrose and quinine. *Journal of Comparative and Physiological Psychology, 91,* 498–507.

Harlow, H. F. (1959). The development of learning in the rhesus monkeys. *American Scientist, 47,* 458–479.

Hirsh, R. (1974). The hippocampus and contextual retrieval of information from memory: A theory. *Behavioral Biology, 12,* 421–444

Hirsh, R. (1980). The hippocampus, conditional operations, and cognition. *Physiological Psychology, 8* (2), 175–182.

Hoffman, H., Molina. J. C., Kucharski, D., & Spear, N. E. (1987). Further examination of ontogenetic limitations on conditioned taste aversions. *Developmental Psychobiology, 20,* 455–463.

Hyson, R. L., & Rudy, J. W. (1984). Ontogenesis of learning: II. Variation in the rat's reflexive and learned responses to acoustic stimulation. *Developmental Psychobiology, 17* (3), 263–283.

Jackson, J. H. (1958). Evolution and dissolution of the nervous system. In J. Taylor (Ed.), *Selected writings of John Hughlings Jackson* (Vol. 2). New York: Basic Books. (Original work published 1884)

Johanson, I. B., Hall, W. G., & Palefone, J. M. (1984). Appetitive conditioning in neonatal rats: Conditioned ingestive responding to stimuli paired with oral infusions of milk. *Developmental Psychobiology, 15,* 357–381.

Johanson, I., & Teicher, M. H. (1980). Classical conditioning of an odor preference in 3 day old rats. *Behavioral and Neural Biology, 29,* 132–136.

Kaplan, P. S., Werner, J. W., & Rudy, J. W. (1990). Habituation, sensitization, and infant visual attention. In C. Rovee-Collier & L. P. Lipsitt (Eds.), *Advances in infancy research* (Vol. 6, pp. 61–105). Norwood, NJ: Ablex Publishing Corp.

Loy, R., Lynch, G., & Cotman, C. W. (1976). Development of afferent lamination in the fascia dentata of the rat. *Brain Research, 121,* 229–243.

McNaughton, B. L. (1989). Neuronal mechanisms for spatial computation and informational storage. In L. Nadel, L. Cooper, P. Culicover, & R. M. Harnish (Eds), *Neural connection and mental computations* (pp. 283–350). Cambridge, MA: MIT/Bradford.

Mishkin, M., & Petri, H. L. (1984). Memories and habits: Some implications for the analysis of learning and retention. In L. R. Squire & N. Butters (Eds.), *Neurobiology of learning and memory* (pp. 287–297). New York: Guilford.

Morris, R. G. M. (1981). Spatial localization does not require the presence of local cues. *Learning and Motivation, 12,* 239–260.

Morris, R. G. M., Garrud, P., Rawlins, J. N. P., & O'Keefe, J. (1982). Place navigation impaired in rats with hippocampal lesions. *Nature, 297,* 681–683.

Moye, T. B., & Rudy, J. W. (1985). Ontogenesis of learning: VI. Learned and unlearned responses to visual stimulation in the infant hooded rat. *Developmental Psychobiology, 18,* 395–409.

Moye, T. B., & Rudy, J. W. (1987). Ontogenesis of trace conditioning in young rats: Dissociation of associative and memory processes. *Developmental Psychobiology, 20,* 405–414.

Oakley, D. A. (1983). The varieties of memory: A phylogenetic approach. In A. Mayes (Ed.), *Memory in animals and humans* (pp. 20–82). Wokingham, UK: van Nostrand Reinhold.

O'Keefe, J., & Nadel, L. (1978). *The hippocampus as a cognitive map.* Oxford: Clarendon.

Rescorla, R. A. (1976). Pavlovian conditioning and its proper control procedures. *Psychological Review, 74,* 71–80.

Rescorla, R. A., Durlach, P. J., & Grau, J. W. (1985). Context learning in Pavlovian conditioning. In P. D. Balsam & A. Tomie (Eds.), *Context and learning* (pp. 23–56). Hillsdale, NJ: Erlbaum.

Rescorla, R. A., & Wagner, A. R. (1972). A theory of Pavlovian conditioning: Variation in the effectiveness of reinforcement and nonreinforcement. In A. H. Black & W. F. Prokasy (Eds.), *Classical conditioning. II: Current research and theory* (pp. 64–99). New York: Appleton-Century-Crofts.

Rose, D. H. (1976). *Dentate gyrus granule cells and cognitive development: Exploration in the substructures of behavioral change.* Unpublished doctoral dissertation, Harvard University.

Ross, R. T., Orr, W. B., Holland, P. C., & Berger, T. W. (1984). Hippocampectomy disrupts acquisition and retention of learned conditional responding. *Behavioral Neuroscience, 98,* 211–225.

Rovee-Collier, C., & Fagen, J. W. (1981). The retrieval of memory in early infancy. In L. Lipsett (Ed.), *Advances in infancy research* (Vol. 1, pp. 225–254). Norwood, NJ: Ablex Publishing Group

Rovee-Collier, C., & Hayne, H. (1987). Reactivation in infant memory: Implictions for cognitive development. In H. W. Reese (Ed.), *Advances in child development* (Vol. 20, pp. 185–238). New York: Academic.

Rozin, P. (1976). The psychobiological approach to human memory. In M. R. Rosenzweig & E. L. Bennett (Eds.), *Neural mechanisms of learning and memory* (pp. 3–46). Cambridge, MA: MIT University Press.

Rubel, E. W., & Rosenthal, M. H. (1975). The ontogeny of auditory frequency generalization in the chicken. *Journal of Experimental Psychology: Animal Behavioral Processes, 1,* 287–297.

Rudy, J. W., & Castro C. A. (1990). Undernutrition during the brain growth period of the rat significantly delays the development of processes mediating Pavlovian trace conditioning. *Behavioral and Neural Biology, 53* 307–320.

Rudy, J. W., & Cheatle, M. D. (1977). Odor-aversion learning by neonatal rats. *Science, 198,* 845–846.

Rudy, J. W., & Cheatle, M. D. (1979). Ontogeny of associative learning: Acquisition of odor aversions by neonatal rats. In N. E. Spear & B. A. Campbell (Eds.), *Ontogeny of learning and memory* (pp. 157–168). Hillsdale, NJ: Erlbaum.

Rudy, J. W., & Hyson, R. L. (1984). Ontogenesis of learning: III. Variation in the rat's differential reflexive and learned responses to sound frequencies. *Developmental Psychobiology, 17,* 285–300.

Rudy, J. W., & Paylor, R. (1988). Reducing the temporal demands of the Morris place-learning task fails to ameliorate the place learning impairment of preweanling rats. *Psychobiology, 16,* 152–156.

Rudy, J. W., Stadler-Morris, S., & Albert, P. (1987). Ontogeny of spatial navigation behaviors in the rat: Dissociation of "proximal-" and "distal-" cue-based behaviors. *Behavioral Neuro-science, 101* (5), 732–734.

Rudy, J. W., & Sutherland, R. J. (1989). The hippocampus is necessary for rats to learn and remember configural discriminations. *Behavioral Brain Research, 34*, 97–109

Rudy, J. W., & Wagner, A. R. (1975). Stimulus selection in associative learning. In. W. K. Estes (Ed.), *Handbook of learning and cognitive processes* (Vol. 2, pp. 269–304). Hillsdale, NJ: Erlbaum.

Schacter, D. L., & Moscovitch, M. (1984). Infants, amnesics, and dissociable memory systems. In M. Moscovitch (Ed.), *Infant memory* (pp. 171–216). New York: Plenum.

Shallice, T. (1988). *From neuropsychology to mental structure.* New York: Cambridge University Press.

Sherry, D. F., & Schacter, D. L. (1987). The evolution of multiple memory systems. *Psychological Review, 94*, 439–454.

Smotherman, W. P. (1982). Odor aversion learning by the rat fetus. *Physiology and Behavior, 29*, 769–360.

Spear, N. E. (1979). memory storage factors in infantile amnesia. In G. Bower (Ed.), *The psychology of learning and motivation* (Vol. 13, pp. 91–154). New York: Academic.

Spear, N. E., & Campbell, B. A. (Eds.). (1979). *Ontogeny of learning and memory.* Hillsdale, NJ: Erlbaum.

Spear, N. E., Kraemer, P. J., Molina, J. C., & Smoller, D. E. (1988). Developmental change in learning and memory: Infantile disposition for unitization. In J. Delacour & J. C. S. Levy (Eds.), *Systems with learning and memory abilities* (pp. 27–52). North-Holland: Elsevier.

Spear, N. E., & Molina, J. (1987). The role of sensory modality in ontogeny of stimulus selection. In N. Krasnegor, E. M. Blass, M. A. Hofer, & W. P. Smotherman (Eds.), *Perinatal develop-ment: A psychobiological perspective* (pp. 83–110). Orlando, FL: Academic.

Spear, N. E., & Rudy, J. W. (1991). Tests of the ontogeny of learning and memory: Issues, methods and results. In H. N. Shair, G. A. Barr, & M. A. Hofer (Eds)., *Developmental psychobiol-ogy: Current methodological and conceptual issues.* (pp. 84–113). New York: Oxford University Press.

Spence, K. W. (1936). The nature of discrimination learning. *Psychological Review, 43*, 427–449.

Spence, K. W. (1952). The nature of the response in discrimination learning. *Psychological Review, 59*, 152–160.

Squire, L. R. (1987). *Memory and brain.* New York: Oxford University Press.

Squire, L. R., & Cohen, N. J. (1984). Human memory and amnesia. In G. Lynch, J. L. McGaugh, & N. M. Weinberger (Eds.), *Neurobiology of learning and memory* (pp. 4–64). New York: Guilford.

Sutherland, R. J., Kolb, B., & Whishaw, I. (1982). Definitive disruption by hippocampal or medial frontal cortical damage in the rat. *Neuroscience Letters, 31*, 271–176.

Sutherland, R. J., McDonald, R. J., Hill, C. R., & Rudy, J. W. (1989). Damage to the Hippocampal formation in rats selectively impairs the ability to learn cue relationships. *Behavioral and Neural Biology, 52*, 331–356.

Sutherland, R. J., & Rudy, J. W. (1987). Place learning; in the Morris place navigation task is impaired by damage to the hippocampal formation even if the temporal demands are reduced. Psychobiology, 16, 157–163.

Sutherland, R. J., & Rudy, J. W. (1989). Configural association theory: The role of the hippocampal formation in learning, memory, and amnesia. *Psychobiology, 17*, 129–144.

Teicher, M. H., & Blass, E. M. (1976). Suckling in newborn rats: Elimination by nipple lavage, reinstated by pup saliva. *Science, 193*, 422–424.

Teitelbaum, P., Schallert, T., & Whishaw, I. Q. (1983). Sources of spontaneity in motivated behavior. In P. Teitelbaum & E. Satinoff (Eds.), *Handbook of behavioral neurobiology* (Vol. 6, pp 23–66). New York: Plenum.

Teuber, H. L. (1955). Physiological psychology. *Annual Review of Psychology, 9*, 267–296.

Tulving, E. (1983). How many memory systems are there? *American Psychologist, 40,* 385–398.

Vogt, M. B., & Rudy, J. W. (1984a). Ontogenesis of learning: I. Variation in the rat's reflexive and learned responses to gustatory stimulation. *Developmental Psychobiology, 17,* 11–33.

Vogt, M. B., & Rudy, J. W. (1984b). Ontogenesis of learning: IV. Dissociation of memory and perceptual-alerting processes mediating taste neophobia in the rat. *Developmental Psychobiology, 17,* 601–611.

Wickelgren, W. A. (1979). Chunking and consolidation: A theoretical synthesis of semantic networks, configuring, S-R versus cognitive learning, normal forgetting, the amnesic syndrome, and the hippocampal arousal system. *Psychological Review, 86,* 44–60.

Woodbury, C. B. (1943). The learning of stimulus patterns by dogs. *Journal of Comparative and Physiological Psychology, 35,* 20–40.

# STUDYING EARLY LEXICAL DEVELOPMENT:
# THE VALUE OF THE SYSTEMATIC DIARY METHOD

*Carolyn B. Mervis, Cynthia A. Mervis, Kathy E. Johnson,*
*and Jacquelyn Bertrand*

DEPARTMENT OF PSYCHOLOGY
EMORY UNIVERSITY

I. INTRODUCTION .............................................. 292
   A. Value of Case Study Methodology for the Study of Language
      Development ............................................. 293
   B. Characteristics of a Systematic Diary Study of Early Language
      Development ............................................. 293
II. GENERAL METHODOLOGY ................................... 295
   A. Subject ................................................. 295
   B. Procedure .............................................. 295
   C. Data Reduction and Coding ............................. 298
III. THE NATURE OF EARLY WORDS ........................... 305
   A. Introduction ............................................ 305
   B. Method ................................................. 307
   C. Results ................................................. 308
   D. Discussion ............................................. 311
IV. ANALYSIS OF A CATEGORY: THE INITIAL EXTENSION
    AND SUBSEQUENT EVOLUTION OF *DUCK* ................... 314
   A. Introduction ............................................ 314
   B. Method ................................................. 318
   C. Results ................................................. 319
   D. Discussion ............................................. 325
V. PROPORTION OF OBJECT WORDS OVEREXTENDED
   DURING EARLY LEXICAL DEVELOPMENT ................... 330
   A. Introduction ............................................ 330
   B. Method ................................................. 331
   C. Results ................................................. 332
   D. Discussion ............................................. 335
VI. ACQUISITION OF AN ATTRIBUTE DOMAIN: COLOR .......... 336
   A. Introduction ............................................ 336
   B. Method ................................................. 337
   C. Results ................................................. 339
   D. Discussion ............................................. 344

VII.  ACQUISITION OF THE PLURAL MORPHEME ................. 346
      A. Introduction .............................................. 346
      B. Method ................................................... 348
      C. Results .................................................. 349
      D. Discussion ............................................... 356

VIII. GENERAL DISCUSSION ..................................... 360
      A. The Systematic Diary Method: A Response to Previous
         Methodological Issues ................................... 360
      B. Unique Contributions of the Systematic Diary Study ............. 364
      C. Further Uses of the Diary Corpus ......................... 368
      D. Conclusion .............................................. 369

 IX.  REFERENCES ............................................... 370

  X.  APPENDIX: TWO EXAMPLES OF DIARY RECORD CARDS ..... 375

# I.  INTRODUCTION

The emergence of a child's earliest words is among the most salient developmental milestones. Decades of research have suggested that early lexical development progresses as a function of a rich interaction of factors both intrinsic and extrinsic to the language-learning child. To understand the complexity of the lexical development process, close observation of individual children is crucial. In the present chapter, we describe a systematic diary study designed to provide this type of data. The subject of the study was the first author's older son, Ari. Although data on his entire lexicon were collected, the study focused on the initial structure of Ari's object categories, as reflected by language data, and on the evolution of these object categories to conform more closely to the adult categories labeled by the same name. The study was intended to offer both theoretical and methodological contributions. Thus, the study was designed both to test certain theoretical predictions relevant to early lexical development, and to enable the methodological comparison of results obtained through the systematic diary method with results obtained through other methods of studying early lexical development. Below, we first consider the appropriateness of case study methodology for research on early lexical development. We then describe in general terms what a diary study of early lexical development involves and how problems typically associated with early diary studies may be avoided. In the subsequent sections of this chapter, we consider several aspects of early lexical development for which data were collected during the present diary study and the theoretical and methodological implications of these data.

## A.   Value of Case Study Methodology for the Study of Language Development

The case study method has been used extensively for studying phenomena in clinical psychology and educational psychology. Within experimental psychology, however, the use of this method has been relegated primarily to the generation of hypotheses for further empirical investigation. Dromi (1987), after reviewing literature concerning the application of case study methodology as a research tool, noted that case studies are designed to provide intensive investigation of domains that are constantly changing over time. More specifically, the case study method is particularly valuable for investigating psychological processes that are very complex, may be context-bound, and are highly dynamic. These three characteristics are intrinsic to the phenomenon of language development, arguing for the value of the case study method within this domain.

With regard to the first characteristic, few developmental phenomena rival the complexity inherent in the acquisition of language. Experimental studies of early language acquisition often do not provide accurate data relevant to children's linguistic abilities, because the tasks are overly simplified and too isolated from everyday experience (Clark, 1982; Dromi, 1987; Peters, 1983). Furthermore, such studies often are incapable of illuminating the rich interaction between adult input and the child's own cognitive structures in determining the meanings of early words. With regard to the second characteristic, children's early language development has the potential to be highly context-bound. Children's early verbal productions may be strongly dependent on their linguistic and/or nonlinguistic contexts (Bates, 1976; Clark, 1982; Dromi, 1987; Mervis & Johnson, 1991). Some researchers have described children's earliest words as being inseparable from the context (or script) in which they are produced (e.g., Barrett, 1986; Bloom, 1973; Nelson, 1985, 1988). With regard to the third characteristic, the process of language acquisition is highly dynamic. During the early period of production, the child's linguistic knowledge changes quickly and constantly (e.g., Dromi, 1987). In traditional longitudinal designs where relatively short visits are separated by intervals of a week or even several weeks, developmental phases that are brief may well be missed (Mervis & Johnson, 1991).

## B.   Characteristics of a Systematic Diary Study of Early Language Development

The diary method has been criticized for its literary style and reliance on anecdotal data. Early diarists often either had no rules concerning which productions should be recorded or inconsistently added or deleted rules over the course of data collection (Braunwald & Brislin, 1979). (At least some of the early diarists were aware of these problems; in 1900, Gale & Gale registered similar criticisms.) In addition, Anglin (1983) has argued that the diary method cannot detect instances of undergeneralization. These flaws may be corrected by employing the diary method as a form of *event sampling*. That is, the diarist can choose a priori to record a particular behavior (or set of behaviors) and particular types of contextual information and then simply record the occurrence and context of that behavior when it takes place. Depending on the types of rules applied for the recording of behaviors and behavioral contexts, the diary record may be as complete or as abbreviated as the diarist wishes. The use of the diary method as a form of event sampling is what characterizes the *systematic* diary method.

Although the central component of the diary record is the event sampling of previously determined behaviors and their contexts, the record may be enriched through supplemental components (cf. Braunwald & Brislin, 1979; Dromi, 1987). For example, the child and caregiver may be videotaped at regular intervals, to provide information about typical day-to-day performance. Notes may be kept concerning the child's cognitive, social, and/or motor development, as well as unusual occurrences in the child's daily life. The recording of diary data also may be enriched through the use of various quasi-experimental probes. In studying early lexical development, an important type of quasi-experimental probe involves establishing the extension of the child's earliest words. It is crucial to include a wide range of potential exemplars and nonexemplars. The probes may involve relatively unstructured activities such as placing a particular object in the child's room and waiting for the child to label it as well as systematic testing of comprehension and production of crucial potential referents.

Previous methodological criticisms of the dairy method stem largely from the early diarists' use of the diary record as an anecdotal record rather than as a form of event sampling. The present systematic diary study addresses these concerns by adhering to a priori rules for the recording of instances of comprehension or production, along with a priori rules for recording contextual information. The three supplemental components described above also were included. Furthermore, because the systematic method of diary data collection was used, certain aspects of Ari's data could be compared to those recorded in a much more limited systematic diary study of Ari's younger brother, Ethan.

In the remaining sections of this chapter, a variety of aspects of Ari's diary data are explored. We begin by describing in some detail the general methodology used. Each of the next five sections is concerned with one aspect of early lexical development. Within each of these sections, a brief introduction to the problem is provided, followed by a description of the methodology specific to the particular aspect. A description of the data is then followed by a discussion of theoretical and/or methodological implications. The first section is concerned with the initial nature of Ari's earliest words. Comparative data also are provided for Ethan. In the second section, the developmental history of Ari's first word ("duck") is discussed, including both initial extension and subsequent evolution. The third section is concerned with overextension of object words. The fourth and fifth sections concern two aspects of lexical development which occurred at the end of the one word stage for Ari: acquisition of color terms, and acquisition of plural forms for common nouns. These five topics were chosen because they are the ones for which analyses are the most complete. The diary data eventually will be used to address a large number of other questions. Many of the areas yet to be examined will be apparent based on the description provided of the general method for the study.

## II. GENERAL METHODOLOGY

### A. Subject

The subject of the systematic diary study was the first author's older son, Ari. Ari was an only child throughout the course of data collection.

### B. Procedure

The diary study had four components: systematic diary entries of instances of naturally occurring spontaneous or elicited production or comprehension; quasi-experimental probes designed to establish the extension of Ari's early object names; videotaped and audiotaped play sessions; and notes concerning Ari's overall cognitive, language, social, and motor development. Each component is described separately below.

### 1. Diary Entries

Recording of diary entries began when Ari was age 0;10.18. The earliest entries were handwritten. As Ari's vocabulary and frequency of production increased, maintaining handwritten records became difficult, and beginning when Ari was age 1;2.17, entries were audiotaped using a hand-held tape recorder. Entries were recorded by Ari's mother, father, and maternal aunt. (All three recorders have professional training in research methodology, and two have had training in phonetics and phonology, which was very helpful in interpreting early speech.) In addition, other individuals who interacted frequently with Ari (e.g., his grandparents) sometimes would report instances of comprehension or production to one of the recorders; these interactions then were added to the audiotapes. During the period of study, Ari spent relatively little time in daycare (about 3 hours per day), so that data are available for most of his waking hours. Some data from the time spent in daycare are available as well, either from maternal observation through a one-way mirror or from reports from daycare staff.

Virtually complete records of production are available until Ari was age 1;4.0, at which point his vocabulary included about 86 words. From then until Ari was approximately 1;10.0, a predetermined set of rules was followed concerning which instances were entered into the diary. Basically, all instances of underextension and overextension were recorded, as were all instances of words that appeared to be in transition. To the extent possible, the first instance of appropriate production of each relatively new word in reference to a particular object was recorded each day. Additional instances were recorded when possible. All plural forms that Ari's mother heard him produce for the first few months after he began using plurals were recorded; singular forms produced in obligatory plural contexts during this time were recorded as well. Records concerning color names were kept until all 11 basic color names consistently were used correctly. Novel instances of jokes and symbolic play were recorded. From approximately age 1;10.1 to age 2;0.1, all new words that Ari produced were recorded, as well as any overextensions that were made. Regular recording of diary entries ended at age 2;0.1. Written notes on particular topics of interest (e.g., subordinate and superordinate labels), including the same information as had been recorded for the diary entries, were kept for the next several months.

## 2.   Quasi-experimental Probes

As mentioned in the Introduction, two forms of quasi-experimental probes were used to supplement the diary record. First, to establish the extension of Ari's early words, efforts were made to provide him with a wide range of potential exemplars and nonexemplars. Most often, adults simply placed particular objects within Ari's vicinity and waited for him to label them. In other cases, Ari was taken to such places as a zoo or a farm or a specialty store so that he would have opportunities to observe particular types of objects (e.g., animals, tools). Second, systematic testing of comprehension and production for crucial potential referents occasionally was conducted. Most instances of systematic testing occurred during the first several weeks of the study.

## 3.   Play Sessions

*Videotaped play sessions.*   These sessions were designed to provide information about Ari's typical language performance, rather than his most advanced performance or his systematically elicited performance. During these sessions, Ari played with his mother with his own toys; the toys selected were chosen to reflect his current vocabulary and/or his more recently acquired cognitive skills. Additional toys in which Ari was particularly interested also were available. The sessions lasted approximately 30 minutes and occurred on a monthly basis, from age 0;11.3 to age 2;5.28.

*Audiotaped play sessions.*   A 30-minute audiotaped play session occurred monthly from age 1;1.20 to age 2;5.26. (In most months, the audiotaped and videotaped play sessions took place within 3 days of each other.) During these sessions Ari and his mother played with a standard set of toys which had been selected specifically to look at overextension of certain words (e.g., "ball," "car," "kitty"). A complete list of the toys used is presented in Table 1. These toys were very similar to those included in a previous longitudinal group design study (Mervis, 1984; Mervis & Mervis, 1988). By using the same box of toys each month, it also was possible to track Ari's labeling of a given toy over time. In addition to the audiotape of Ari's and his mother's verbal interaction, an observer audiotaped an ongoing description of the nonverbal interaction, including the referents of any object labels.

TABLE 1

Toys Used During Audiotaped Play Sessions

| Stuffed animals | Clothes[1] | Vehicles |
|---|---|---|
| siamese cat | jacket | car |
| dachshund | shirt | bus |
| cheetah | pants | dump truck |
| blackbird | socks | boat |
| seal | shoes | airplane |
| giraffe | boots | helicopter |
| horse | slippers | canoe |
| mallard | moccasins | tractor |
| swan | knit winter hat | |
| lobster | baseball cap | |
| dinosaur | | |
| zebra | | |
| tiger | | |
| lion | | |

| Food | "Balls" | Musical instruments |
|---|---|---|
| apple | ball | xylophone |
| lemon | wooden beads (spherical | drum |
| lime | and multi-sided) | drumsticks |
| carrot | spherical bell | tambourine |
| green pepper | spherical candle | |
| tomato | spherical bank | |
| cucumber | | |
| pear | | |
| bowl | | |

| People |
|---|
| doll[2] |
| helicopter pilot |
| dump truck driver |
| Fisher Price girl |
| Fisher Price boy |

[1] All clothes were actual infant clothes which fit the doll.
[2] The doll resembled a 9–12 month old infant.

## 4.  Notes Concerning Other Aspects of Ari's Development

To provide information about Ari's overall development, new cognitive, social, and motor accomplishments were noted on the audiotaped/handwritten entries as they occurred.

## C.  Data Reduction and Coding

Data reduction began with the transcription of each audiotape (or handwritten entry) onto specially printed 5″ x 8″ index cards. Each instance of comprehension or production was transcribed on a separate card. The cards included specific sections into which all of the information provided on the audiotapes was transcribed verbatim. Additional sections were provided for coding purposes. (Two sample cards, and explanations of the codes used on those cards, are presented in the Appendix.) Following transcription of the date, context, word produced or comprehended, referent, and adult response, the coding process began. At the time coding started, a detailed coding system was available only for production of common nouns that had visible referents. The purpose of the coding system was to provide sufficient information, for each instance of production of an object word, to determine what Ari said about which object, the impetus for what he said, the response to his utterance or action, and how he responded to this response. This information was necessary to address the research questions the diary study was intended to answer. (A more general coding system was used for comprehension and other instances of production; see below. More detailed versions of these coding systems currently are being designed.) Although the coding system was developed specifically for Ari's data, it would be applicable to data from any child.

The 38,925 diary entries were assigned to one of five databases, depending on the word Ari produced or comprehended and whether or not the referent of a produced word was visible at the time of production. Each database is described below, along with a description of the applicable coding system.

## 1.  Production of Common Nouns with Visible Referents

This database included 19,937 entries (51.2% of the entries in the diary study). Two basic sets of codes were used for these records: one for information contained in the context (including Ari's word) and one for information contained in the response. The description below follows the codes as they are arranged on the cards.

*Category.*  The superordinate (e.g., animal, food) and, if applicable, intermediate (e.g., mammal [nonhuman], fruit) category to which the word Ari used is assigned. (Lists indicating the category assignments of all words Ari used were given to the coders. Category assignments were determined based on consensus among the first three authors.)

*Word.* The word that Ari used. For data entry purposes, the adult form of the word is indicated. Ari's form, if it deviated significantly from the phonology of the adult form, is indicated in parentheses. (For the analyses of the development of the plural morpheme, additional codes concerning the phonology of Ari's form were developed.)

*First production.* An asterisk was placed in the upper right hand corner of the card if it was the first time Ari had produced the word.

*Date.* The date on which the interaction occurred.

*Level.* The hierarchical level of the word that Ari used. Possible levels were superordinate, intermediate, basic, and subordinate. (Lists of the hierarchical levels of all words Ari used were given to the coders. Hierarchical-level assignments were determined based on consensus among the first three authors.)

*Frequency.* The number of times this exact interaction occurred on that day. This number was almost always "1."

*Referent.* The object to which Ari was referring. This object was indicated descriptively, based on the description given on the audiotaped/handwritten diary entry. Over the course of the study, the same object sometimes was given different descriptions (e.g., Ari's Dakin mallard, Ari's Dakin duck). Therefore, to provide a standardized list of referents, a referent dictionary was developed. This dictionary contained lists of all the objects Ari ever labeled, along with a referent dictionary code for each object. The initial referent dictionary delineated the alternative descriptions for a given object and then assigned all of them the same referent dictionary code. The final version of the referent dictionary included the most accurate description of a given object and the paired referent dictionary code. This version was entered into the computer using dBASE.

The referent dictionary code consists of a prefix indicating the referent category to which the referent belongs (e.g., *dog, table, car*) and then a 3-digit suffix which indicates the specific referent within the category that is being labeled. The 3-digit code is broken down as follows: 001–199: referent is an actual object (e.g., a tiger at a zoo); 200–399: referent is a three-dimensional representation of an object (e.g., a stuffed animal tiger); 400–599; referent is a two-dimensional representation (not in a book) of an object (e.g., a postcard showing a tiger); 600–799: referent is a two-dimensional representation (in a book) of an object (e.g., a photograph of a tiger in a field guide). The referent dictionary code was indicated below the description of the referent on the card.

*Spont./elic. (spontaneous/elicited).* Whether Ari's utterance was spontaneous, or whether it was elicited by someone else (generally an adult). If elicited, the type of elicitation was coded. For example, differentiations were made between simple elicitations (e.g., "What's that?") and elicitations designed to elicit labels at other hierarchical levels (e.g., "What kind of birdie is that?" after Ari had already labeled a cardinal, "birdie"). Differentiations also were made between complex questions that required a particular answer (e.g., "What's Ari holding?") and complex questions that were open ended (e.g., "What do you want to play with?").

*Word/ref. (word/referent).* The relationship between the word Ari used and the object to which he referred. This code indicates three things. Column 1 is concerned with the semantic appropriateness of Ari's word for the object to which he referred. Codes are arranged on a six-point scale where 1 = appropriate by adult standards and 6 = completely inappropriate; essentially no similarity between appropriate referents for Ari's word and the current referent. (Lists of the word/referent codes for all situations that were not coded as "1" were given to the coders. Codes were determined based on consensus among the first three authors.) This scale is inappropriate for symbolic play, jokes, Ari's drawings, and kinship words (e.g., "mommy" used to refer to an animal); these were assigned separate codes. Column 2 indicates (for words not coded in column 1 as "1," symbolic play, joke, child drawing, or kinship) the lowest hierarchical level that subsumes both Ari's word and the correct name for the object. (In most cases, of course, there are several possible "correct names," varying in hierarchical level, for the relevant object. For this code, the "correct name" is considered to be the appropriate name that was at the same hierarchical level as Ari's incorrect name. Lists of these codes, for each type of error that occurred, were given to the coders. Codes were determined based on consensus between the first and third authors.) Column 3 indicates which, if any, other appropriate labels for that object (at other hierarchical levels) also were included in Ari's productive vocabulary. This column is coded whether or not Ari's label was itself appropriate. (This code was determined based on the dates of first production for each relevant word; these dates were available to the coders.)

*Morpheme.* Structure of Ari's word form. The initial breakdown was made according to the number of words and number of free morphemes in Ari's word (e.g., "kitty" is one word, one free morpheme; "dump truck" is two words, two free morphemes). Column 1 describes the structure of Ari's form of the word in relation to the adult form (e.g., correct, invented word, real word but with different meaning, first morpheme of a two-morpheme word). (Lists of Ari's words, indicating their various forms over time and the appropriate column 1 codes, were given to the coders. Codes were determined based on consensus among the first three authors.) Column 2 indicates any morphological markers present and their form (e.g., singular, plural: regular, plural: overregularization [-s added to mass noun], possessive).

*Link.* Additional label for same object within the same interaction. This code indicates whether Ari used more than one label for a given object within the same interaction, and if so, whether the other label(s) preceded or followed the label currently being coded.

*Context.* The situation immediately preceding Ari's utterance, as indicated on the audiotaped/handwritten diary entry. Ari's utterance itself also is included in this section.

*Response.* Includes both the response to Ari's utterance and, if applicable, the remainder of that particular interaction with the referent (including any additional times that Ari labeled the referent), as indicated on the audiotaped/handwritten diary entry. (The codes for the response are indicated under Response I, II, III below. Each response was divided into a maximum of three subinteractions, determined by whether Ari labeled the referent again, with either the same or a different label, within the response. Each response subinteraction was defined as beginning with the child's label and continuing through the last adult response prior to the child again labeling the referent. [If Ari did label the referent with a different label, that label would appear both in the response section of the current card and on its own card. The word on the second card was the new label. The entire interaction up to and including that new label constituted the context of the second card, and the remainder of the interaction constituted the response of that card.] A separate code indicates whether more than three subinteractions were present, a situation which rarely occurred. Response I, II, and III were coded for each subinteraction.)

*Response I.* Response specifically to Ari's label. Column 1 indicates the general tone of the adult response (in terms of agreeing or disagreeing with Ari's label) (character 1), whether or not the adult repeated Ari's label (character 2), and whether, and if so how, the adult response to Ari's label was qualified or hedged (e.g., "That's like a ball."; "Do you think that's a car?") (character 3). Column 2 indicates whether, and if so how, the adult requested an additional label from Ari (character 1) and the response that Ari made to that request, including, when applicable, the hierarchical level and appropriateness of any new label that Ari provided (character 2).

*Response II.* New label provided by adult. Column 1 describes the hierarchical level of any new adult label (character 1), the relationship between Ari's label and the adult label in terms of mutual exclusivity in relation to the referrant (i.e., from an adult perspective, are both Ari's and the adult's labels appropriate for the referent, or is only one label appropriate?) (character 2), and whether, and if so how, the new label was qualified or hedged (character 3). Column 2 describes the method of presentation of the new label, covering the strategies used, including any attributes mentioned (character 1) and whether or not the adult used a contrast referent (character 2).

*Response III.*    Child response to adult. This code indicates whether, and if so how, Ari indicated agreement or disagreement with any new label or, in the absence of a new label, any attribute information, provided by an adult. Ari's response to any adult disagreement with Ari's label also was indicated.

*Response continued.*    Indicates whether the response continued beyond the three subinteractions coded for in the response codes.

*Entry made by.*    The person who recorded the particular audiotaped/ handwritten diary entry.

*Card #.*    The diary audiotape number and side, and the number of the entry for that side of the tape. For the handwritten entries, the card number includes the month rather than the tape number and side. Videotaped play session entries (see below) are indicated by "VPS," followed by the play session number rather than a tape number and side. Audiotaped play session entries (see below) are indicated by "PS," followed by the play session number.

2.    Production of Proper Nouns with Visible Referents

This database included 1,664 entries (4.3% of the entries in the diary study). The coding system for these records includes all of the codes described above with the exception of the Response codes.

3.    Production of Common and Proper Nouns with Nonvisible Referents

This database included 7,615 entries (6,562 common noun entries and 1,053 proper noun entries, accounting for a total of 19.6% of the entries in the diary study). The coding system for these entries includes the category, word, first production, date, context, response, entry made by, and card # sections described above.

4.    Production of Non-nouns

This database included 8,677 entries (22.3% of the entries in the diary study). The coding system for these entries includes the word, date, context, response, entry made by, and card # sections described above. In addition, a code for part of speech (e.g., verb, adjective, adverb) was used as a preliminary criterion for subdividing Ari's non-noun vocabulary.

## 5. Comprehension

This database included 1,032 entries (2.6% of the entries in the diary study). Included in these entries are both instances of comprehension trials to which Ari did respond and those to which he did not respond. The situations where Ari did not respond to comprehension requests are particularly relevant to understanding aspects of the phenomenon of underextension.

The format used for comprehension cards was slightly different from that used for production. The major difference was that, instead of context and response sections, the diary entries were transcribed into context, action, and response sections. The context includes all information up to and including the adult request for Ari to do/get something. The action section describes how Ari responded, both nonverbally and, if applicable, verbally, to the adult request. The response section includes the adult response to Ari's action.

This format was used for all comprehension cards. The specific coding done depended on whether the adult request was a one-part or multipart request. One-part requests were defined as those where Ari was asked to do only one thing (e.g., "Where's duckie?"). Multipart requests were defined as those in which Ari was asked to do more than one thing (e.g., "Can you make duckie fly?" where Ari had to first find the duck and then make it fly). One-part requests were coded for category (for nouns) or part of speech (for non-nouns), word (used by adult), first comprehension (analogous to first production, described above), date, level (for nouns), word/referent (for nouns), context, action, response, entry made by, and card #, as described above. In addition, an "in-sight" code (for nouns) indicates whether the object Ari was asked to find was visible to Ari at the time the request was made. Multipart requests were coded for date, context, action, response, entry made by, and card #.

## 6. Conversations about Nonvisible Referents

An exception to the transcription process described above occurred for conversations about mostly nonvisible referents/events. Whenever such a conversation included three or more words referring to nonvisible referents/events, the conversation was transcribed as a whole onto a separate piece of paper instead of on individual cards. A card noting that a "conversation occurred here" was placed in the regular deck of cards for that audiotape and the card number assigned to that card was recorded on the page on which the conversation was transcribed. (Any nouns/non-nouns with visible referents which occurred within the conversation were transcribed on regular diary cards as well.) These conversations then were entered into the computer using Microsoft Word. One coder went through all the conversations and created lists of all words with nonvisible referents and applicable codes so that this information could be entered into the same computer databases as the regular diary cards (see below).

## 7. Reliability and Database Management

The second and third authors served as primary coders throughout the data reduction phase. About 75% of the entries were transcribed and coded by these primary coders. Reliability between the two primary coders was confirmed by reviewing a portion of each coder's cards. Cards for which the coder was unsure of a particular code were discussed with at least one other of the first three authors until a consensus was reached. For the remaining 25% of the entries, the second author checked the transcription against the original audiotapes. All codes were checked as well.

Toward the end of the data reduction phase, the computer hardware and software needed to enter the diary data into computer files were purchased. Databases were set up using dBASE. Four primary databases were established for production: common nouns with visible referents, proper nouns with visible referents, common and proper nouns with nonvisible referents, and non-nouns. All instances of comprehension were included in a fifth database. Screen forms were set up which were facsimiles of the actual diary cards, and all data from the cards were entered directly into the computer. To determine reliability of data entry, approximately 10% of the computer entries were checked against the diary cards. Reliability of data entry exceeded .99 for all codes.

## 8. Play Sessions

*Videotaped play sessions.* All videotaped sessions were transcribed. A subset of Ari's utterances was then coded, as described above, for entry into the appropriate diary study databases. This subset included all instances of production and comprehension from the videotaped play sessions which occurred at or before age 1; 3.0. For the remaining play sessions, the following utterances were included: (a) for every word that was overextended in a given session, all instances of that word in the session, whether overextended or not; (b) for each referent that was labeled with an overextended word, all other instances of that referent being labeled, regardless of what the label was; and (c) all instances of the first production of a word in the diary study, including all subsequent uses of that word within the session, and all instances of labels, whether correct or not, for referents which could have been labeled correctly by that word.

*Audiotaped play sessions.* Both the audiotape of Ari's and his mother's verbal interaction and the audiotaped description of the nonverbal interaction were transcribed onto a single transcript. This provided a rich description of both verbal and nonverbal interaction during the play session. All of Ari's utterances from these transcripts were coded, as described above in the Diary Entries section, and included in the appropriate databases.

## 9. Notes Concerning Various Aspects of Ari's Development

Notes relevant to Ari's cognitive, language, social, and motor development were made on the audiotapes as they occurred. During transcription of the tapes, these notes were transcribed onto paper. The coders were instructed to note all general comments recorded on the audiotapes. These comments usually were of the following types: comments that explicitly identified the first time that Ari did something (e.g., demonstrated a particular skill, saw a particular object, experienced a particular event); interpretations of Ari's behavior, comments regarding nonverbal skills or events; comments that explicitly identified the first time that an adult did any of the following: labeled a particular object for Ari, used a particular word to label a particular object for Ari, or used a particular word in talking to Ari. In addition, coders were asked to note any episodes that were especially interesting for lexical development. In particular, coders were asked to note instances in which an adult explained to Ari what something was, instances in which Ari indicated that he had noticed something unusual about a referent which might lead him to realize that the referent was a member of a different category from the one(s) to which he previously had assigned it, and any other instances that the coder considered of particular interest or likely to be of interest to other people working on the project. Coders were told to err in the direction of including too many episodes. For each notation, the date, card number, and a brief description of the comment or episode were recorded. These comments and episodes (hereafter, General Notes) later were entered into the computer using Microsoft Word.

## III. THE NATURE OF EARLY WORDS

### A. Introduction

The question of the nature of children's early words has been the focus of much debate, both theoretical and empirical. Some researchers have argued that children use words referentially from the outset of acquisition (e.g., Gopnik & Meltzoff, 1985, 1986; Harris, Barrett, Jones, & Brookes, 1988; Huttenlocher & Smiley, 1987; Mervis, 1987). That is, words are used symbolically to represent sets of referents or relations. In contrast, other researchers have contended that children's early words are not referential (e.g., Barrett, 1986; Nelson, 1985, 1988; Nelson & Lucariello, 1985). Instead, early words are linked to schematic representations of early everyday experiences. In this section, we argue that the careful comparison of different diary studies provides a point of integration across both perspectives. In particular, children may acquire both referential and nonreferential words from the onset of lexical development. The form a particular word takes depends on the interaction of adult input and child lexical operating principles.

Proponents of the view that children's first words are nonreferential typically contend that these words initially are used either in context-bound ways or in situationally based ways. Context-bound use stems from the word being inseparable from the context within which it is produced (e.g., Bloom, 1973; Nelson, 1985, 1988). Barrett (1986) provides the example of his son Adam's use of the word "chuff-chuff" (train). Adam initially produced this word only when he was engaged in the process of pushing his toy train across the floor. In a longitudinal study of 25 children between ages 9 and 13 months, Bates, Benigni, Bretherton, Camaioni, and Volterra (1979) found that nearly all of the children's earliest words were produced in the context of highly specific events. Situationally based words are used to refer to the various elements (object, action, etc.) of a particular event. Dromi (1987, in press) provides the example of her daughter Keren's uses of the word "niyar" [(a) piece of paper]. Keren used this word to indicate the elements of her writing/drawing schema. Thus, she used "niyar" to indicate pencils, pens, pieces of paper, typed pages, the action of writing/drawing, or the drawing itself. Gillis (1987) interprets this type of extension as resulting from the child's identification of familiar elements across the situations in which he or she uses a particular word. The word may be produced whenever the child encounters an element that is part of the situational context in which he or she has heard other people use the word.

Researchers who stress the existence of context-bound and/or situationally based words generally have argued that these types of words are acquired during the early stages of lexical development. Nelson and Lucariello (1985) have maintained that context-bound words emerge throughout the first half of the single-word period. In the diary study of her daughter, Dromi (1987, in press) found that all of Keren's situationally-based words were acquired during the first 17 weeks after she began to talk. McShane (1979, 1980) has argued that words can function referentially only after they have been used in a context-bound fashion for a while.

As the review above indicates, discussion of context-bound words and situationally-based words has not focused on maternal input. Recently, however, Harris and Barrett (Harris et al., 1988; Barrett, Harris, & Chasin, 1991) have considered the possibility of such a relationship. These researchers considered the first 10 words of four children who were studied longitudinally. Of these 40 words, 22 were context-bound and 18 were referential. (No mention was made of situationally based words.) When maternal uses of these words were compared with child uses, the researchers found that, in the six cases in which the mother's use of a word was context-bound, the child's use also was context-bound. Of the 34 cases in which maternal use was not context-bound, the child's use was referential in 18 cases and context-bound in 16 cases. Harris and Barrett also found that children's first use of a word was very likely to occur in the same context in which the mother's most frequent use of the word occurred (33 out of 40 cases; Harris et al., 1988), but children's later uses were less influenced by maternal input (Barrett et al., 1991). These results suggest that maternal use patterns may be an important determinant of the child's initial use of an early word.

The process of lexical acquisition also is guided by principles operating within the child. As Slobin (1985) has argued, operating principles are "necessary prerequisites for the perception, analysis, and use of language in ways that will lead to mastery of any particular input language" (p. 1159). Lexical operating principles serve as heuristics which have the effect of restricting the child's search space for word meanings by increasing the likelihood that he or she will entertain particular hypotheses over possible alternatives. One such principle is the Object Category as Referent principle (Mervis, 1990; Mervis & Long, 1987; cf. Markman's Taxonomic principle—Markman, 1989; Markman & Hutchinson, 1984). According to this principle, when a person points at or otherwise indicates an object for which the listener does not already have a name, the listener should assume that the accompanying word refers to the whole object, rather than to a part or attribute of that object or an action performed by that object. Furthermore, the name is assumed to refer to all members of the basic level category to which that object has been assigned.

For the Object Category as Referent principle to be used, it is necessary that both verbal and nonverbal input provide clear information concerning a referent object. This type of input generally has been present for many of the children whose early words have been described as referential (cf. Barrett et al., 1991; Harris et al., 1988; Mervis, 1984, 1987). If this type of input is not provided, very young children are unlikely to treat words as labels for object-based concepts. Instead, they are likely to consider these words to refer to situationally based concepts (and the major objects and/or actions which characteristically are included in the particular situational concept).

In the remainder of this section, we present diary data relevant to the initial extensions of early words by the first author's two sons. We conclude by elaborating a novel theoretical framework that integrates the effects of adult input and child principles in determining whether early words will be used to refer to object-based or situationally based categories.

## B. Method

Data were drawn from the comprehensive diary study of Ari's language and from a smaller, more circumscribed diary record for Ethan. (Ari was 4 years old when Ethan was born.) The information that generally was recorded for Ari's words was described in the General Method section. For Ari's first words, some additional types of information also were recorded. In particular, notes were made concerning available referents for these words: what potential referents for a word were available to Ari the first time he comprehended or produced a word, and what labels (if any) adults recently had used for these objects. The diary entry databases were searched using dBASE to locate all instances of Ari's use of his earliest words. The same searches provided information about adult input.

The General Notes section also was examined for information concerning adult input.

The language component of the diary study of Ethan focused almost exclusively on his earliest words. Ethan's diary was intended to provide extensive information about the types of input provided relevant to each of his earliest words, as well as information about the extension of these words. Entries were typed directly into a computer, using Microsoft Word. The search utility provided in Microsoft Word was used to locate instances of Ethan's use of his earliest words, as well as comments concerning the nature of these words and the relevant input.

## C.  Results

We begin this section by presenting detailed data concerning the initial extensions of Ari's and Ethan's first four words. We then present more general data concerning the initial extensions of their first 100 words.

### 1.  Initial Extensions: First Four Words

Ari's first three words were object labels ("duck," "cup," "dog"); his fourth word was an action word ("dance"). The initial extensions of each of these words are presented in Table 2. This table includes the age at which Ari first produced each word and all contexts (including referents) in which each word was produced during the first week it was used. As the data in Table 2 indicate, all four words were used referentially. Each word was used in more than one context, and to refer to more than one referent.

Ethan's first word was a proper name ("Mommy"), his second and third words were object labels ("cup," "pacifier"), and his fourth word was an action word ("up"). The initial extensions of each of these words is presented in Table 3. This table includes the same types of information as Table 2. The data in Table 3 indicate that Ethan also used each of his first four words referentially.

### 2.  Extensions of the First 100 Words

All of Ari's first 100 words were used referentially. An examination of the input provided to Ari by his parents indicated that Ari almost always was given clear input about the referent of any word that the speaker thought he did not comprehend. The natural style of interaction that Ari's parents followed resulted in them not talking about something with Ari unless the referent was unambiguous.

Ethan used all but 2 of his first 100 words referentially. Both words which initially were nonreferential were situationally-based; none of Ethan's words was context-bound. Both of the situationally based words were produced relatively early: "bubble" was Ethan's 24th word, and "poop" was his 60th word. This

TABLE 2

Contexts in Which Ari's First Four Words Were Used During First Week of Production

| Word | Age at first production | Context | | |
|------|------|------|------|------|
| | | First production | Second production | Examples of subsequent productions |
| Duck | 0;11.9 | Points to mantel in direction of 4 wooden water birds and black duck decoy | Sees toy mallard on mantel | Points to mechanical chicken; Picks up toy mallard on couch; Looks at toy Canada goose; Puts toy mallard on top of television; Nibbles toy swan's bill; As M unlocks front door (probably in anticipation of seeing toy mallard on mantel) (49 additional productions) |
| Cup | 0;11.29 | Touches F's mug full of hot coffee lightly with index finger, pulls finger back | Touches empty mug lightly with index finger, pulls finger back | Reaches toward juice glass with finger extended; Touches Tommee Tippee cup with index finger, pulls finger back; Points toward 6 oz. pyrex container; Touches 2 oz. plastic container lightly, withdraws finger (10 additional productions) |
| Dog | 1;0.5 | Reading with F, points to puppy in book | Looking at book alone, points to puppy | Looking at neighbor's dog while on walk with M and F; Picks up toy dog and looks at it; Looking at book with M, points at puppy (6 additional productions) |
| Dance | 1;0.12 | Bounces toy mallard up and down | Looks at toy monkey in hand | Bounces toy monkey up and down (1 additional production) |

*Note: M* = mother, *F* = father, *E* = Ethan

result is comparable to Dromi's (1987) finding for Keren. Although Keren's early vocabulary included more situationally based words than Ethan's, the last situationally based word was the 50th word that she produced.

An excellent demonstration of how dramatically the input can affect the extension that different children assign to the same word is provided by a comparison of the acquisition of "bubble" by Ari and Ethan. (Parallel data were obtained for Ethan's other situationally-based word.) The input situations in

TABLE 3

Contexts in Which Ethan's First Four Words Were Used During First Week of Production

| Word | Age at first production | Context | | |
|------|-------------------------|---------|---|---|
| | | First production | Second production | Examples of subsequent productions |
| Mommy | 0;8.10 | Looks at M working on computer | While nursing, wakes up and looks at M | While M is out, E says "mama" to F in a somewhat hesitant voice; While playing, E turns around to M; Sitting, not looking at anything in particular (M interprets E to be practicing) |
| Cup | 0;10.18 | Looking at F's mug of coffee | Looks at F's empty mug | Touches M's mug of tea with extended index finger; Looks at mug on step in family room; Points at F's mug; Watching mug in microwave; Looking at handleless cup in Chinese restaurant; Reaching for soup bowl; Looks at 2-handled baby cup; Looks at juice glass; Looks at plastic bell-shaped glass |
| Pacifier | 0;10.22 | E drops pacifier on floor and says "pacifier" while looking for it | Reaching toward pacifier | Looks down at pacifier on floor; Looks at pacifier on top of diaper box; Sucking on pacifier; Points at pacifier in crib; Touches pacifier which is wedged in space between two bolsters; Sees pacifier being rinsed in sink |
| Up | 0;10.23 | In infant seat, raises arm, then says "up" | On floor, says "up" as raises arm over head | Says "up" and immediately stands up on F's lap; Stands book up vertically; Holds reversible tray part of hammering toy up on edge; stands up in bathtub; Pulls up to a stand holding onto a closed door; Flips his sleeper up so that it lands on top of crib rail; Struggling to stand up in highchair |

*Note: M* = mother, *F* = father, *E* = Ethan

which Ari heard the word "bubble" were referentially very clear. In most cases, the referent was bubbles that formed during washing dishes or bathing Ari; reference was indicated by pointing and/or by the direction of Ari's eye gaze. Ari's use of "bubble" indicated that it referred to an object concept from the beginning. Ari most frequently used "bubble" to refer to actual bubbles. However, like almost all of Ari's early object words, "bubble" was overextended. Examples of overextensions include references to foam formed on top of boiling soup stock, a raw egg yolk projecting up above the egg white, the circular cutout housing the wheel axle of a toy telephone, "circles" forming in puddles during a light drizzle, tiny pieces of debris floating on a puddle, a small light green flower in a puddle, and a goosebump.

In contrast to the input provided for Ari, the input situations in which Ethan heard the word "bubble" were much more ambiguous. Ethan often heard Ari use the word to request that someone blow soap bubbles for him. Generally, this request occurred in the absence of bubbles or the materials needed to blow bubbles. In other cases, Ari or an adult would talk about blowing bubbles while holding the bottle of bubble soap or the bubble wand. The proportion of time that "bubble" was used when the referent clearly was a bubble was relatively small. Ethan used "bubble" to refer to the bubble-blowing event in general and to its separate components (e.g., bubble soap, bubble soap bottle, bubble wand, bubbles), rather than just to bubbles. The first time that Ethan said "bubble" occurred at supper, immediately after Ari had mentioned the bubble-making machine that Ari had seen at a children's museum. As soon as Ari said "bubble," Ethan imitated "bubble" and pointed insistently toward the family room (the only room in which bubble blowing took place at home). Later during the meal, Ethan said "bubble" spontaneously and then pointed toward the family room. At the end of the meal, Ethan's father put him down on the floor and said, "Does Ethan want to blow bubbles?" Ethan, who had been heading for the center of the living room, immediately changed course and headed for the family room. After his father began to blow bubbles, Ethan pointed at some bubbles that were falling and said "bubble." The next time Ethan used "bubble," the referent appeared to be a bottle of bubble soap. That same day, Ethan also labeled bubbles "ball." Over the next several days, Ethan also used "bubble" when looking at a differently shaped bottle of bubble soap, when looking at a cover for a bubble soap bottle, when looking at a bubble wand, when holding an empty bottle of bubble soap, and when pretending to blow bubbles. "Bubble" generally was used in this variety of aspects of the bubble-blowing situation, and almost never was used when actual bubbles were the focus of his attention. In summary, Ethan treated "bubble" as a word to be used in the context of various important elements of the bubble-blowing situation.

## D. Discussion

The results of Ari's and Ethan's diary records indicated that for both children, the input for unknown words almost always was transparent regarding the referent of the object label. For two object words, however, the input for Ari was clear, whereas the input for Ethan was not. For these two words, Ari formed object-based categories; in contrast, Ethan formed situationally based categories. Across the two children, these were the only words that were situationally based. Comparison of the input leading to object-based words with that leading to situationally based words provides the foundation, then, for the formulation of a new operating principle for early lexical acquisition. The data for Dromi's daughter Keren are consistent with this principle. Keren was given nontransparent input for more words than Ethan (E. Dromi, personal communication, September 24, 1988). In turn, Keren's early vocabulary (see Dromi, 1987) included more situationally based words. Dromi (in press) noted that the input for Keren's situationally based words did not involve ostensive definitions.

As noted earlier, Mervis (1990; Mervis & Long, 1987) has proposed the Object Category as Referent principle as one basis for the determination of reference of very young children's words. This principle assumes the provision of input from which the child can determine the intended referent of the relevant word. Another principle, however, is needed for when the input provided for the child is opaque and/or the child is not attending closely to the input. Mervis (1990) has proposed that young children also have available to them the Situation Category as Referent principle.

Children have available both prelinguistic object concepts and prelinguistic situation concepts. The choice between an object or a situation basis for a word is determined in large part by the type of input provided concerning the word and the child's level of lexical and syntactic knowledge (see also Dromi, in press), and by whether or not the child is attending closely to the input. Thus, in cases in which the input is referentially clear and fits the Object Category as Referent principle, and the child is attending to and can understand the input, the child should treat the word as a label for an object category. However, for some words, the input provided is much less specific, and does not fit with the Object Category as Referent principle. For example, potential referents belonging to different conceptual categories may be available, and/or the word may often be used in the absence of any visible referent. In these cases, if the child does not have relevant lexical, syntactic, or pragmatic knowledge that could be used to disambiguate the word, the Situation Category as Referent principle is used. This principle also may be used when the input is referentially clear and fits the Object Category as Referent principle but the child is only partially attending to the input. In these cases, the child should treat the word as a label for a situationally based category and the components of that category.

As the child's lexical, syntactic, and pragmatic knowledge increase, the input necessary for use of the Object Category as Referent principle need not be as precise. For example, as syntactic knowledge increases, the child becomes more capable of using syntactic cues to disambiguate the input. As lexical knowledge increases, the child becomes increasingly able to use information about the reference of other words in an utterance when trying to determine the referent of an unknown word. Thus, use of the Situation Category as Referent principle should be more likely early in the one-word period, and should become increasingly infrequent as language knowledge increases. This argument is consistent with the findings of other researchers that situationally based words only occur early in lexical development (e.g., Dromi, 1987; Nelson, 1985, 1988).

The diary records of Ari's and Ethan's first 100 words did not provide any examples of context-bound words. However, given the number of previous reports of this type of extension (many from other diary studies, e.g., Barrett, 1986), it is clear that operating principles concerned with early lexical development must be able to account for context-bound words as well. As discussed previously, the Situation Category as Referent principle is parallel to the Object Category as Referent principle; which principle is used depends on the input and the child's relevant linguistic knowledge. Golinkoff, Lavallee, Baduini, and Hirsh-Pasek (1985) have proposed a principle that would be foundational for the Object Category as Referent principle. This Object Scope principle states that new words refer to whole objects, rather than to parts, actions, locations, etc. Thus, the difference between the two Object principles is that Object Scope does not provide for the extension of the word beyond the initial referent. A Situation Scope principle parallel to the Object Scope principle could provide the basis for context-bound words; the Situation Scope principle would provide for the use of a word only as part of a particular event, whereas the Situation Category as Referent principle provides for the extension of a word to important components of the situation. More precise formulation of such principles should be based on data from children whose early vocabulary included some words that were context-bound.

Although children have available both the Object Category as Referent principle and the Situation Category as Referent principle, only the Object principle provides a viable route for the acquisition of conventionalized extensions. The Situation principle is a dead end lexically; language does not encode the various components of a particular situation with a single word (cf. Markman, 1989; Markman & Hutchinson, 1984, for arguments regarding thematic categories). Models of early lexical development must account for both the viable (Object) route and the dead end (Situation) route, and also for how words on the latter track eventually are rerouted to the Object track. We expect that the process of redirecting words from the Situation route to the Object route will depend on both advancing linguistic knowledge and acquisition of additional operating principles.

Our discussion has focused on accounts of both the Object route and the Situation route. These accounts have depended critically on data from diary records. The depth of information contained in these records enabled a careful analysis of both the extensions of early words and the input (both linguistic and nonlinguistic) provided regarding these words. Cross-comparison of diary records has proven to be a fruitful means for generating operating principles for early lexical acquisition. The data necessary for the formulation of these aspects of our model of early lexical development were unlikely to be discovered in cross-sectional research or even in longitudinal studies in which time-sampling techniques were combined with event-sampling. In the next section, we consider a complementary use of systematic diary data: evaluation of previously generated hypotheses concerning the initial extension and eventual evolution of early object categories.

## IV. ANALYSIS OF A CATEGORY: THE INITIAL EXTENSION AND SUBSEQUENT EVOLUTION OF *DUCK*

### A. Introduction

In the previous section, we considered the initial extensions of Ari's and Ethan's early words, as measured by production. These diary data served as the basis for the proposal of new operating principles for very early lexical development. In the present section, we use Ari's diary data to examine the initial extension and subsequent evolution of a single category, *duck,* as measured by both comprehension and production. We focus on "duck" because this was the first word that Ari comprehended and the first word that he produced. (The methods of analysis that we use could be applied to any object word.) In addition, the data from Ari's duck category serve another important purpose: These data provide an in-depth test of several previously proposed operating principles (e.g., Mervis, 1987, 1988, 1990, 1992). Some of these have been supported by the results of cross-sectional and/or longitudinal group design studies (e.g., Mervis, 1987; Mervis & Mervis, 1988); other principles have not been tested previously.

1. Initial Extension of Children's Early Categories

Children's initial categories are basic-level categories, formed and structured according to the same principles as adult basic-level categories (see Rosch, Mervis, Gray, Johnson, & Boyes-Braem, 1976; Tversky & Hemenway, 1984). Categories at the basic level are more fundamental psychologically than categories at other taxonomic levels. For example, *dog* (a basic-level category) is more fundamental than either *animal* (a superordinate-level category) or *Dalmatian* (a subordinate-level category). Basic-level categories are the most general categories whose members share similar shapes (or similar parts in particular configurations; Tversky & Hemenway, 1984) and similar functions or characteristic actions. These categories "stand out" as categories (see, e.g., the experiments reported in Rosch et al., 1976). Cross-sectional experimental studies have demonstrated that basic-level categories are much easier for 2-year-olds to acquire than categories at the subordinate or superordinate levels (Daehler, Lonardo, & Bukatko, 1979; Mervis & Crisafi, 1982).

Although the principles for the formation of basic-level categories remain constant across the lifespan, the particular exemplars included in children's initial basic-level categories may differ from those included in the adult basic-level category labeled by the same name (Mervis, 1984, 1987). Objects often afford more than one set of attribute correlations, even at the basic level. If everyone does not attend to the same set, differences in the extension of the categories formed are likely to result. Such differences are to be expected; only the principles governing the determination of basic-level categories are universal (Dougherty, 1978; Rosch, 1977; Rosch et al., 1976). In particular, the actual categories formed based on (form–function) attribute correlations may differ because different groups notice or emphasize different attributes of the same object as a function of different experiences or different degrees of expertise. Differences between child-basic and adult-basic categories are particularly likely to occur because the child's limited knowledge of culturally appropriate functions of objects and their correlated form attributes often leads him or her to emphasize different attributes than adults do, for the same object (Mervis, 1982, 1984, 1987, 1990; see Carey, 1982, for a similar position concerning verb concepts). Consider an adult's and a young child's categorization of a spherical bank. For an adult, the slot on the bank and its capacity to hold money would be most salient, leading the object to be considered a bank. For a very young child, for whom money is not a salient concept, these attributes would be overlooked in favor of the bank's sphericity and ability to roll. The child, therefore, would consider the bank to be a ball. Mothers often are aware of, and accept, these category differences. In many cases, mothers even label objects with their child-basic, rather than adult-basic, names (e.g., Mervis & Mervis, 1982). However, the child's categories are not derived simply from maternal input (Mervis, 1984).

Three types of relationships may exist between the extensions of child-basic and adult-basic categories. First, child-basic categories may be broader than the corresponding adult-basic categories. For example, the child-basic *kitty* category may correspond to the more inclusive adult *feline* category. The child's category also may be broader than the adult-basic category in the sense that it includes objects from several different adult categories. For example, the child may include spherical candles, spherical banks, beads, and balls in his or her *ball* category. Second, child-basic categories may be narrower than adult-basic categories. For example, the child's *kitty* category may not include sphynx cats (which are hairless) or other highly atypical species. Abstract representations of potential category exemplars (e.g., a two-dimensional cat-shaped sachet made of flowered cloth) also may be excluded. Finally, child-basic categories may overlap adult-basic categories; that is, the child's category may both include objects that are excluded from the adult category and exclude objects that are included in the adult category. For children's earliest categories, the difference in relevant cultural knowledge between very young children and adults makes the overlap relationship the most likely.

The results of a longitudinal study of early lexical development by normally developing children and children who have Down syndrome (e.g., Mervis, 1984, 1987) provide support for the claim that initial extensions of object words correspond to the child-basic categories predicted based on form-function attribute correlations. This study focused on the extensions of three words: "kitty," "car," and "ball." The set of potential referents for each word included one or two objects that were category members by adult standards, and three to five objects that were not members of the adult-basic category, but were predicted to be members of the child-basic category. The initial categories formed (based on comprehension data) corresponded exactly to the predicted child-basic categories in 94% of the cases for the normally developing children and in 88% of the cases for the children who had Down syndrome. This finding obtained independent of whether or not the mothers themselves labeled the objects with their child-basic names.

Stylized and/or atypical members of the adult-basic category were not added to the toy set until relatively late in the study. Thus, for most children, no measure of potential underextension was available for the initial extensions of the target categories. For the few children who had not acquired one or more of the target words prior to the addition of these objects to the toy set, the initial extensions often excluded the stylized or atypical exemplars, while including objects that were excluded from the adult-basic category. Thus, for these children, the predicted overlap relationship occurred.

## 2.  Evolution of Initial Child-Basic Categories

Child-basic categories eventually must evolve to conform to the adult standard. This evolution depends on the child becoming aware of additional attribute correlations for particular objects (or types of objects). Although the child may notice a new attribute correlation on his or her own, in most cases the new attributes are indicated by another person. The manner in which an adult provides the adult-basic label for an object already included in a child-basic category labeled by a different name has a strong influence on whether or not the child will comprehend the new label and begin to form a new category. It generally has been assumed that simple ostension, or simple correction with ostension, provides the basis for inducing very young children to learn a new category assignment for a misassigned object (e.g., Clark, 1977; Miller, 1982). However, Gruendel's (1977) data suggest that these methods often are ineffective for toddlers (e.g., if a toddler thinks that a tiger is a kitty, simply telling him or her that it is a tiger will not work).

Success in inducing a toddler to comprehend the new name and begin to form a new category is most likely if at the same time that the adult names an object, he or she provides evidence of the form–function correlation on which the adult-basic category is based. The results of three studies (Banigan & Mervis, 1988; Chapman, Leonard, & Mervis, 1986; Mervis & Mervis, 1988) indicated that, for young toddlers, the input strategy most likely to lead to formation of a new category involved an adult describing and pointing out the parts of the object that are important to the new category (i.e., form information), along with naming and demonstrating the functions that are correlated with those parts. The least effective strategy involved simply providing the adult-basic label by itself. The success of this label-only strategy probably depends on the child's acquisition of the notion of conventionality (Mervis, 1990).

Another strategy that adults are likely to use involves verbal provision of attribute information without physically indicating the attributes (e.g., without pointing to the parts or demonstrating the functions). This strategy has not been well studied. Logically, one would expect that, as toddlers become more linguistically adept, nonlinguistic support for the attribute information would become less crucial. Thus, as the toddler's linguistic abilities increase, the effectiveness of this strategy also should increase.

Experimental studies of toddlers (Banigan & Mervis, 1988; Chapman et al., 1986) have focused on form–function attribute correlations, rather than form attributes alone. Many categories, however, do not have readily discriminable function attributes (e.g., horse vs. zebra); others have functions that cannot be explained easily to a toddler, because very young children do not have the necessary background knowledge (e.g., monkey vs. gorilla) (Murphy & Medin, 1985). Form attribute information alone often provides a sufficient basis for category formation (e.g., Younger & Cohen, 1985, 1986). Therefore, category evolution, which depends on formation of a new category and acquisition of a name for that category, should be able to proceed based on form information alone. In the case of animal categories, provision of a particular type of function information (the relevant animal sound—a salient attribute from a child's perspective) along with the new category name is another likely basis for category evolution.

Comprehension of the adult-basic name for a child-basic object and formation of a new category based on that object are the first steps in the evolution of an initially overextended category (or the overextended part of an overlapped category) to conform to the adult-basic category labeled by that word. It often has been claimed that the new and old categories immediately become disjunctive (e.g., Barrett, 1978, 1982, 1986; Clark, 1973, 1983, 1987). Markman (e.g., 1987; Markman & Wachtel, 1988) has argued that the child is guided by a Mutual Exclusivity principle that precludes the assignment of an object to two categories. Thus, once the child comprehends the adult-basic name for an object, he or she should no longer consider that object to be a member of its (former) child-basic category.

In contrast, Mervis (1987, 1988, 1990) has argued that, for very young children, the complete separation of the old and new categories almost always is gradual. The child, in considering the object(s) that is changing category membership, at first finds both the attributes that make the object a member of the old category and the attributes that make the object a member of the new category relevant. For a child to exclude an object from its old category, he or she must decide that only the set of attributes that makes the object a member of the new category is important. The results of previous studies with young toddlers indicate that when they first acquire a new name for an object previously included in a category labeled by a different name, the object is considered a member of both categories. Using comprehension measures, Mervis (1984) found simultaneous assignment in 96% of the test cases for the normally developing toddlers and in 93% of the test cases for the toddlers who had Down syndrome. Banigan and Mervis (1988), in an experimental study using normally developing 24-month-olds as subjects, again found simultaneous assignment in 96% of the test cases.

In the remainder of this section, we use Ari's *duck* category to address the issues discussed above concerning the initial extension and subsequent evolution of early child-basic categories. We first present data relevant to the extension of Ari's *duck* category. Evidence for correct extension, underextension, and overextension is considered. We then discuss the processes involved in the reduction of overextension for *duck* and the concurrent evolution of new categories out of the *duck* category. In the discussion, we present a series of operating principles concerning category extension and evolution.

## B.  Method

Data were drawn from the diary study of Ari's lexical development. In addition to the information described in the General Method section, extensive notes were available concerning available referents at the time Ari first comprehended "duck." Testing of Ari's comprehension of "duck" was concentrated in the first several weeks of comprehension. A wide variety of exemplars from both within and outside the adult *duck* category was included. General descriptions of the programs written to examine particular aspects of Ari's comprehension and production of "duck" are provided below.

## 1.  Comprehension Data

Two dBASE programs were written to track complementary facets of Ari's comprehension of "duck." The first program concerned the history of the word "duck." For each instance of comprehension, the date, word comprehended, referent chosen by Ari, word/referent code, context, action, response, and card number were listed in chronological order. The second program extracted information relevant to Ari's underextension of "duck." All instances of underextension of "duck" were extracted from a printout listing all cases of Ari not responding to a comprehension request. The printout included the date, the word for which the elicitation of comprehension was attempted, the referent not chosen by Ari which was a member of the relevant referent category, context, action, response, and card number.

## 2. Production Data

Three dBASE programs were written to investigate particular aspects of Ari's production relevant to the *duck* category. The first program concerned the production history of "duck." All instances of Ari saying "duck" to label a visible referent were listed in chronological order. The printout included the word, date, referent, word/referent code, and total number of times the referent was labeled "duck" on that date. Production histories also were generated for the words corresponding to those referents that Ari incorrectly labeled "duck." The second program generated information relevant to overextensions of "duck." For each instance of overextension, the referent, word/referent code assigned to that particular word-referent combination, and card number were printed. The information generated by this program was a subset of that generated by the first program. The third program concerned underextensions in production. A chronological list was generated of all instances in which Ari used an incorrect label to name duck referents at a time when he could produce "duck" (the correct label). This program operated by first checking the first-production database to determine the date of first production of "duck" and which referent categories could be labeled correctly by that word. The program then accessed the database for common nouns with visible referents and, beginning on the date of first production of the word, printed all instances of members of the relevent referent categories being labeled incorrectly. Instances in which Ari refused to label a referent for which he knew the correct label, which were considered possible instances of underextension, were extracted from handwritten lists of such instances compiled during the data reduction phase of the study.

## C. Results

In this section, we describe Ari's extension of "duck" as measured by comprehension and then as measured by production. Finally, we consider the evolution of Ari's *duck* category, as measured by production.

## 1. Initial Extension of Duck: Comprehension

At the time Ari first comprehended "duck," the potential referents that most interested him were live mallards, which he saw several times a week at a nearby pond, and a plush mallard, which was his favorite toy. Adults often called both the live ducks and the toy duck "duck" (or "duckie") when talking with Ari. A variety of other potential referents was available. Those that often had been called "duck" for Ari included a rubber duck, a plastic duck rattle, a plush duck-head rattle, a Donald Duck head (in Disney Poppin' Pals), and a variety of pictures, ranging from very realistic to somewhat stylized, in Ari's books. Potential referents that were not named for Ari included a black-duck decoy, several miniature carved ducks, a miniature carved grebe, a porcelain snow goose, and several engravings of ducks and duck-like waterbirds. In addition, Ari had a wind-up chicken that adults consistently called "chicken" and several pictures of songbirds in his books that adults called "birdie." There also were several porcelain songbirds and engravings of songbirds that adults had not named for Ari.

A description of Ari's *duck* category, as measured by comprehension, is presented in Table 4. The items for which data are available are divided into three groups: correct extension (members of both Ari's category and the adult-basic category), overextension (members of Ari's category but not of the adult-basic category), and underextension (members of the adult-basic category but not of Ari's category). Data are provided for three discrete time intervals. The first period includes the first three days that "duck" was comprehended. The second period is from the fourth day of comprehension to the day before "duck" was first produced. The third period extends from the day on which "duck" was first produced to the end of the study.

The data in Table 4 indicate that Ari's initial *duck* category overlapped the adult-basic *duck* category. A variety of true ducks (by adult standards) were included in Ari's category. Several non-ducks were included as well (e.g., goose, swan, pelican, wind-up chicken). At the same time, Ari excluded several items from *duck* which adults would have included (e.g., pictures of ducks, duck rattles, Donald Duck head). The objects which Ari included in his *duck* category were three-dimensional and had duck-shaped torsos and heads and relatively long bills. The objects which Ari excluded (but adults would have included) were either two-dimensional or stylized.

2.  Extension of Duck: Production

Throughout the entire study, production data are available for a much wider range of exemplars than comprehension data. The major reason for this discrepancy is that formal comprehension testing was limited primarily to the period preceding or immediately following first production of "duck." During this time, Ari did not comprehend any labels in reference to two-dimensional representations. Thus, pictures could not be used in comprehension testing. We were unable to locate realistic three-dimensional representations of most types of waterbirds (e.g., shorebirds, wading birds).

The items that Ari labeled "duck" during the first week of production are listed in Table 2 in the preceding section. Consistent with the comprehension

TABLE 4

Extension of Ari's Duck Category, as Measured by Comprehension

| | Pattern of extension | | |
| --- | --- | --- | --- |
| | Correct extension | Overextension | Underextension |
| Period 1: (first 3 days of comprehension: 0;10.18–0;10.20) | toy mallard rubber duck wooden puzzle duck carved wooden common teal | carved wooden grebe mechanical toy chicken porcelain Royal Copenhagen goose | plastic duck rattle Donald Duck pop-up figure picture of duck in *I Am a Mouse* book picture of duck in *Mouse's Train Ride* book |
| Period 2: (from 0;10.21 until "duck" produced at 0;11.8) | light brown toy duck toy mallard yellow duck | rubber Big Bird toy Canada goose | picture of duck in *I Am a Mouse* book plush duck-head rattle plastic duck rattle |
| Period 3: (from first production of "duck" through end of study: 0;11.9–2;0.1[a] | toy mallard live ducks toy duck in *My Toy Animals* light brown toy duck yellow toy duck duck in puzzle hole rubber duck plush duck-head rattle ducks on poster black-duck decoy carved wooden common teal ducks on A's pajamas duck page in *Farm Animals* duck in *The Owl and the Woodpecker* *I Can Do It By Myself* book (has ducks in it) plastic duck rattle Donald Duck pop-up figure *Make Way for Ducklings* book | toy Canada goose toy swan toy pelican carved wooden grebe pelican in *Best Word Book Ever* stork in *Best Word Book Ever* Ambi musical bird | picture of duck in *I Am A Mouse* book[b] |

[a] Prior to 0;11.26, Ari never extended "duck" to two-dimensional representations. At 0;11.26, Ari comprehended "duck" in reference to toy duck in *My Toy Animals* book.

[b] Comprehension of this picture was not tested after Ari had begun to include two-dimensional representations in his category.

data, the early production data indicate overlap with the adult *duck* category. Ari's category included several representations of true ducks. In addition, several non-ducks (by adult standards; e.g., goose, swan, wind-up chicken) were included. At the same time, Ari excluded (as measured by refusal to respond to requests to provide a label) several items which adults would have considered ducks. These items, along with Ari's age at the time of refusal, are listed in the first part of Table 5. The excluded items are primarily two-dimensional or stylized representations.

During the remainder of the diary study, Ari used "duck" to refer to several hundred items which adults would agree were ducks. Overextension also continued; Ari produced "duck" in reference to a large number of birds that are not true ducks. Overextensions are listed in Table 6, according to their correct category and Ari's age at the time of first overextension to that category. Most of the overextended exemplars are of five types: duck-like waterbirds (e.g., goose, loon), shorebirds (e.g., plover, sandpiper), wading birds (e.g., egret, heron), penguin-like birds (e.g., puffin, auk), and ground-dwelling game birds (e.g., partridge, pheasant). Underextension continued as well (see the second part of Table 5). After age 14 months, Ari no longer underextended "duck" to two-dimensional and/or stylized representations. However, "duck" was underextended in reference to an extremely atypical type of duck (Muscovy duck; Ari spontaneously called it "rooster"). Underextension also occurred occasionally for items that Ari usually categorized correctly, but which had a feature that typically was found in members of a different category (e.g., white ducks twice were called "swan").

TABLE 5

Underextension of Duck: Production

| Age | Word used | Referent |
|---|---|---|
| *First week of production:* | | |
| 0;11.12 | (none) | duck on A's one-piece outfit |
| 0;11.14 | (none) | color photo of mallard in *National Wildlife* magazine |
| 0;11.15 | (none) | plastic duck rattle |
| *Remainder of study:* | | |
| 0;11.29 | (none) | picture of duck in *I Am A Mouse* book |
| 1;0.8 | (none) | picture of hooded merganser duck on coaster |
| 1;1.2 | (none) | plush duck-head rattle |
| 1;4.23 | rooster | Muscovy duck[a] |
| 1;7.0 | swan | white duck |
| 1;7.18 | swan | white duck |
| 1;11.24 | seagull | black and white drawing of flying merganser ducks in Audobon field guide |

[a] This underextension occurred in two separate episodes on the same day.

TABLE 6

Categories to Which "Duck" was Overextended at Least Twice: Production

| Category | Age at which "duck" first overextended to category |
|---|---|
| grebe | 0;11.9 |
| chicken | 0;11.11 |
| goose | 0;11.11 |
| swan | 0;11.12 |
| pelican | 1;0.29 |
| partridge | 1;1.18 |
| auk | 1;1.24 |
| heron | 1;1.25 |
| loon | 1;1.25 |
| stork | 1;2.2 |
| woodpecker | 1;2.2 |
| pheasant | 1;2.3 |
| crane | 1;2.6 |
| chick | 1;2.8 |
| crake | 1;2.11 |
| turkey | 1;2.13 |
| guillemot | 1;2.20 |
| puffin | 1;2.20 |
| egret | 1;3.4 |
| flamingo | 1;3.6 |
| ostrich | 1;3.6 |
| peacock | 1;3.6 |
| plover | 1;3.27 |
| sandpiper | 1;3.27 |
| vulture | 1;5.25 |

*Note:* "Duck" was used on only one occasion to refer to an exemplar from the following categories: anhinga, blackbird, bobcat, deer, eagle, emu, gallinule, hornbill, pegasus (as depicted on a Mobil insignia), penguin, phalarope, pigeon, road runner, robin, seagull, seal, stilt, turtle, and willet. "Duck" was used on two occasions to refer to owls seen from below.

Several stylized exemplars of birds also were referred to as "duck" on various occasions. These generally were birds with ducklike torsos and passerine-like heads, sometimes with relatively long beaks.

## 3. Evolution of Duck: Early Period

At age 13 months, Ari's *duck* category included all of the major types of birds listed above. Furthermore, none of the birds included in these types was included in any other category. At age 16 months, category evolution began. At this time, Ari first produced "turkey." Acquisition of more appropriate category names for members of his initial *duck* category continued throughout the remainder of the study. We have divided this time into an early period (prior to age 20 months) and a later period (from age 20 months to the end of the study). For both periods, we consider two aspects of the evolution of *duck:* acquisition of more appropriate

TABLE 7

New Labels Learned for Referents of *Duck*: Production

| Category | Age at which correct label for category first produced | Input used to induce acquisition of new category | Is "duck" ever used to refer to cat. after cat. label acquired? |
|---|---|---|---|
| *Early Period:* | | | |
| turkey | 1;4.23 | D + L | Yes |
| chicken | 1;5.12 | L | Yes |
| chick[a] | 1;5.24 | D + L | No |
| goose | 1;6.6 | I + D + L | Yes |
| swan | 1;6.11 | I + D + L | Yes |
| woodpecker | 1;6.29 | D + L | No |
| ostrich | 1;7.23 | I + D + L | Yes |
| *Late Period:* | | | |
| pelican | 1;8.21 | D + L | No |
| peacock | 1;8.29 | L | No |
| flamingo | 1;9.9 | D + L | Yes |
| pheasant | 1;11.2 | D + L | No |
| puffin | 1;11.12 | L | No |
| vulture | 1;11.29 | L | No |

[a] Subordinate level category

*Note:* L = label; D = description of attributes; I = illustration of attributes

category names for members of Ari's initial *duck* category and exclusion of members of the new categories from Ari's *duck* category.

During the early period of reduction of overextension, Ari acquired names for seven new categories whose exemplars previously had been included only in *duck*. The kind of input that was effective in inducing acquisition of the new category is described in Table 7. For three categories, the effective input consisted of both verbal description and nonverbal illustration of relevant attributes, accompanied by the category name. For all three of these categories, input consisting of only the new name had been provided previously but had not led to acquisition of the new category. For three other categories, the effective input consisted of relevant sounds, accompanied by the relevant category name. For these three categories, this was the first input that had been provided concerning these categories. For the remaining category, the effective input consisted of the category name by itself. Although this type of input ultimately was effective, it had been tried a large number of times previously for this category and had failed.

To address the question of whether exclusion of members of the new category from *duck* occurred immediately after acquisition of the new category, we determined whether members of the new category were called "duck" after Ari was able to produce the new category name. For five of the new categories, Ari continued to use "duck" to refer to category members even after his vocabulary included a more appropriate name. For the remaining two categories, Ari did not use *duck* in reference to members of the new category after first production of the new category name.

## 4. Evolution of Duck: Late Period

During the late period of reduction of overextension, Ari acquired names for six additional new categories whose exemplars previously were included in *duck*. For three of these categories, the input that was effective in inducing acquisition of the new category involved description of a relevant form attribute(s), accompanied by the new category name. For all three, provision of only the category name had occurred during the early period, and was not successful in inducing acquisition of the new category name. The first input provided in the late period, which was also the first description input, was successful. For the three remaining categories, provision of the label by itself was effective in inducing acquisition of the new category name. For all three, label-only input had been provided previously, but was ineffective. For two of these categories, the label-only input had occurred only in the early period. For the third category, the ineffective label-only input occurred 2 days before acqusition of the new category name.

To address the question of whether exclusion of members of the new category from *duck* occurred immediately after acquisition of the new category name, we determined whether members of the new category were called ''duck'' after Ari was able to produce the new category name. For five of the six categories, exclusion occurred immediately. For the sixth category (*flamingo*), ''duck'' was produced again only in reference to baby flamingos (who do not have the attributes included in the description provided to Ari when ''flamingo'' was introduced).

## D. Discussion

The initial extension and early evolution of Ari's child-basic *duck* category fit the pattern described in the introduction to this section. Thus, his data are consistent with those obtained in previous group-design studies (e.g., Mervis, 1984; Mervis & Canada, 1983). At the time that these studies ended, almost all of the children were still in what we have referred to as the early period of category evolution. The diary data also include information from the late period of category evolution. These data diverge from those in the early period in predictable ways. Mervis (1988, 1989, 1990) has proposed a series of operating principles to account for various aspects of children's initial category extension and subsequent evolution (during both the early and late periods). In this section, we briefly discuss three of these operating principles in relation to the data for Ari's *duck* category.

## 1. The Form–Function Principle and Child-Basic-Level Categories

By age 10 months, infants have acquired the principle that categories should be based on correlated attributes (Younger, 1990; Younger & Cohen, 1985, 1986). That is, when making categorization decisions, 10-month-olds weigh attributes that co-occur consistently more heavily than equally frequent but uncorrelated attributes. Moreover, infants' object explorations have revealed both important function attributes and their correlations with form attributes (cf. Piaget, 1954), and these correlations take precedence in categorization decisions. This operating principle may generally be expressed as the Form-Function principle:

> OP (CORRELATION): FORM-FUNCTION: The form and function of objects generally are noticeably correlated. Use this correlation as the basis for categorization.

As indicated in the introduction to this section, form attributes alone or function attributes alone may serve as the basis for categorization. When possible, however, categories will be based on form–function correlations.

The early extensions of Ari's *duck* category fit this principle. The correlation that Ari appeared to have identified was between a duck-like shape and activities such as swimming or flying (Mervis, 1987). The objects included in his category fit this correlation: They had a duck-like shape (e.g., duck-like torsos and bills) and either could be expected to carry out activities such as swimming or flying or represented something that could be expected to engage in these activities. At the same time, his child-basic *duck* category did not correspond exactly to the adult-basic *duck* category. Because Ari attended to a different attribute correlation than adults would for certain objects, he considered some things that adults would exclude from *duck* to be ducks (e.g., swan, heron [which had duck-like torsos and could—or looked like they could—swim and fly]). He also excluded some things from *duck* that adults would include (e.g., plush duck-head rattle, which did not have the characteristic duck-like torso and did not look like it represented something that could swim or fly).

## 2. Acquisition of the Initial Category Evolution Principle and the Reduction of Overextensions

The process of new categories evolving from the initial child-basic category depends on the child noticing new form attributes, function attributes, or correlations between form and function attributes on which the new category is based. The following operating principle governs this situation:

> OP (EVOLUTION): FORM-FUNCTION/ADDITIONAL CATEGORY. Assign a category member to an additional, newly formed category if you are given concrete evidence of a new attribute basis for that category.

Because this principle follows directly from the initial Form–Function principle, children should be able to use the Evolution version from the time that they can use the initial Form–Function principle.

*Identification of new form–function correlations.* Given the Category Evolution principle, one would expect that the most effective methods of introducing the adult-basic label would involve a clear indication of the new attribute basis for the category. As mentioned in the introduction to this section, the most explicit indication involves a concrete illustration of the relevant form and function attributes, accompanied by a verbal description of the attributes and the new category name. The provision of just a verbal description accompanied by the category name is somewhat less explicit. The least explicit indication is provided by use of the category name by itself.

For Ari, greater explicitness was necessary for input to be effective during the early period of category evolution than during the later period. During the early period of evolution of Ari's *duck* category, he acquired the names of seven new categories whose members previously had been assigned to *duck*. At the time he acquired the first new category name, Ari's productive vocabulary included 155 words. Thus, he should have been able to understand simple verbal descriptions. For three of the seven categories, the input effective in inducing acceptance of the new category name included description, illustration, and provision of the new name. For three more, the effective input involved description (provision of typical sound the bird made) and provision of the new name. For all six of these categories, the input described was effective the first time it was provided. For the remaining category, the effective input was the category name by itself. Although for this category label-only input finally was successful, it had been tried a large number of times previously and had failed. In summary, during the early period, in order for input to be immediately effective in inducing comprehension of a new category name, the name had to be accompanied by either a verbal description plus an illustration or by a verbal description alone.

During the late period, Ari acquired the names of six more categories whose members initially had been included in *duck*. For five of these, label-only input had been provided during the early period, but had not been successful in inducing acquisition of the new name. For three of the six categories, the effective input involved verbal description (of form attributes) accompanied by the category name. This input was effective the first time it was presented. For the other three categories, the effective input involved provision of the category name by itself. Two of these categories were acquired just before Ari's second birthday. The third (*peacock*) had a very distinctive form attribute. All three of these were acquired after either the first or the second time during the late period that an adult provided the category name. Thus, in contrast to the early period, label-only input often was successful during the late period. The principle

(Authority principle) which we think provided the basis for the success of this input during the late period is presented later in this section.

*Initial nonexclusivity of basic level categories.* The Evolution principle allows for the simultaneous assignment of an object to two or more categories that are mutually exclusive by adult standards; objects can belong to as many basic level categories as meet the requirements of the Form–Function principle (or that are formed based on salient form attributes or salient function attributes). As indicated in the introduction to this section, the simultaneous assignment provision is inconsistent with the Exclusivity principles proposed by Markman (1987; Markman & Wachtel, 1988) and by Tversky and Hemenway (1984), both of which have been proposed to be used from the time categorization begins. Once again, Ari's data indicate a difference between the early period and the late period of evolution. During the early period, simultaneous assignment was found for five of the seven new categories whose exemplars previously had been included in *duck*. In contrast, simultaneous assignment occurred for only one of the six new categories acquired during the late period. For this category, "duck" was used only in reference to juveniles of the species after the new category name was first produced. Below, we describe a principle that provides a basis for immediate mutual exclusivity of the old and new categories.

## 3.   Acquisition of the Authority Principles

For a young toddler, acquisition of the earliest categories to evolve from an initial child-basic category is dependent on the explicit provision of information relevant to the attribute bases for these categories. However, purely linguistic information gradually becomes effective in inducing the formation of new categories, as indicated above in the description of the evolution of Ari's *duck* category. Thus, during the early period, the basis for Ari's formation of a new category often involved both a verbal description and an illustration of the attribute basis for the category. At minimum, a verbal description was required for efficient formation of a new category. During the late period, however, adult use of the category name by itself provided a sufficient basis for efficient new category acquisition.

For the child to be able to treat the provision of a new category name by itself as a sufficient basis for efficient formation of a new category, another principle must be acquired. This principle depends on the child realizing that he or she is not the source of conventional names; instead, these names are provided by "authorities." The child then will realize that the authoritative use of a label for an object implies that the object is a member of the labeled category. This notion of conventionality leads to the Authority principle:

> OP (AUTHORITY): GENERAL. There exist people (authorities) who know more
> about forms, functions, and form-function correlations than you do. When these
> people label an object, they probably are referring to a valid category.

The Authority principle requires acceptance of another person's authority on categorization issues, even when the child does not understand the basis for the other person's category assignment. The data from Ari's diary indicate that this principle is not available at the beginning of lexical acquisition. For example, even as late as age 20 months, Ari considered it acceptable for him to have one name for an object and his parents to have a different name, even though the two names would be coordinate (i.e., at the same taxonomic level) for an adult (Mervis, 1987). At age 22½ months, however, Ari made it clear that he thought his mother knew the correct names for objects (generally animals) and that he expected her to use these names when labeling objects for him. Thus, he must have acquired the notion of conventionality at some time between the ages of 20 and 22½ months.

Once a child reaches this point of acceptance of another person's authority on categorization issues, the Authority principle provides a major improvement in the child's ability to acquire new categories based on very little input. In particular, the child now should be able to acquire new categories even when the only input provided by the "authority" is the new category name. The Authority principle triggers the child's search for a new attribute correlation:

OP (AUTHORITY): ADDITIONAL CATEGORY. If an authority labels an object with a name different from the one you would have used, and the category named by his or her label is not yet part of your repertoire, form a new category and assign the object to that category.

The Authority principle provides the basis for new or additional category assignments. However, as with the additional category form of the Evolution principle, application of the Authority principle does not necessarily yield mutually exclusive categories. The development of mutually exclusive categories involves another operating principle:

OP (AUTHORITY): COORDINATE DELETION. If an authority labels an object with a name different from the one you would have used, and you have reason to believe that the two categories are coordinate, delete the object from its previously assigned category.

Coordinate deletion also can occur in the absence of adult provision of a new label, if the child decides on his or her own that only the attribute correlation for the new category is relevant for categorization of the objects in question.

The data from the evolution of Ari's *duck* category indicate that during the early period, simultaneous assignment of members of the new category to *duck* and to the new category generally occurred. In contrast, during the late period, coordinate deletion was more likely to occur, both for new category names acquired during the late period and for new category names acquired during the early period (for which simultaneous assignment initially had obtained). Thus, from the time Ari was age 1;10.10 until the end of the diary study, only three overextensions of "duck" occurred.

In summary, use of the systematic diary method for an in-depth study of a single category and its evolution served two important purposes. First, although Ari's data focused on production, the results offered confirmation of previous comprehension results obtained in group-design studies of initial child-basic category formation and the evolution of these categories during the early period of category evolution. The data provided strong support for the Form–Function principle and the Category Evolution principle. Second, the data provided support for the use of the Authority operating principles during the late period of category evolution. Previous studies had yielded little or no data from this period.

# V.  PROPORTION OF OBJECT WORDS OVEREXTENDED DURING EARLY LEXICAL DEVELOPMENT

## A.  Introduction

Researchers who have studied early lexical development have consistently documented the existence of overextension of object words. Barrett (1983), in a review of the relevant literature, reported that estimates of the proportion of object words that are overextended at some point during early lexical development range from .07 to .33. These estimates suggest that most early object words are never overextended.

In contrast, as discussed in the previous section, Mervis (e.g., 1984, 1987, 1990) has argued that children's early object categories should be child-basic categories. If this position is correct, then the rate of overextension of early object words should be much higher than that previously reported; child-basic categories generally overlap the adult-basic categories labeled by the same name. That is, child-basic categories should both include some exemplars that adults would exclude (overextension) and exclude some exemplars that adults would include (underextension). This pattern should be especially characteristic of young toddlers, who are less sophisticated cognitively than older children. As the child's knowledge of objects and their culturally appropriate functions expands, the new basic-level categories that the child acquires are more likely to be based on the same (or similar) attributes as those used by adults. Basic-level categories that are based on the same (or similar) form or function attributes as adults use are much less likely to be overextended during acquisition.

In the present section, we consider two questions. First, we ask whether the relatively small proportion of overextension of object words found in previous studies may be a result of the methodologies used. In typical group designs, constraints on the type and number of objects that can be brought into someone else's home or kept in the laboratory limit the number of concepts and the number of potential exemplars of a concept that can be studied. A child cannot produce an overextension of a word unless referents appropriate for overextension of that word are available in the child's environment. It is likely that studies that were not designed to expose the child to a wide range of potential referents for each of his or her words would yield considerably lower rates of overextension than studies which were designed to include a wide range of potential referents. Previous studies (e.g., Barrett, 1982; Gruendel, 1977; Rescorla, 1980) generally have not attempted deliberately to include objects to which the child's words might be overextended. In a few studies (e.g., Mervis & Mervis, 1982, 1988; Chapman & Mervis, 1989), potential overextended referents for a few object words have been included deliberately, but such referents were not available for most of the object words. Furthermore, even for those object words for which appropriate stimuli are made available in group design studies, it is impossible to obtain complete, or nearly complete, records of comprehension and production outside of the research sessions. As a result of these factors, the previously reported rates may not accurately reflect the proportion of children's early words that would be overextended, given a thorough test. This issue is important for addressing theoretical questions concerning the likelihood of overextension. In addition, ascertaining an accurate estimate of the proportion of early words that is overextended is important because the greater this proportion, the more important the study of overextension and the means of reduction of overextension becomes in understanding early lexical development.

The second question to be addressed in this section is whether the pattern of overextension of object category names varies as a function of the child's vocabulary size at the time the name first is acquired. If the child-basic hypothesis stated above is correct, then the probability that a category name will ever be overextended should be greatest for the child's earliest words, and should decrease as the child's vocabulary size increases.

## B.  Method

1.  Materials

Four sets of data were considered. Three were derived from various components of the present diary study. The fourth set was derived from data collected in a previous longitudinal study which used a group design (see, e.g., Mervis, 1984; Mervis & Mervis, 1988). Each of the data sets contained all relevant instances of common nouns that were used to refer to visible referents between ages 1;1.20 and 1;8.28, the age range for which complete data are available for each set.

*Diary data sets.*  The first set, hereafter referred to as Play Session I, was derived from the transcripts of the monthly videotaped play sessions described above in the General Method section. This data set was designed to emulate a longitudinal study in which the child's language is examined on a regular basis, but in an unstructured setting which was not designed specifically to look at overextensions in the child's expressive language.

The second data set, hereafter referred to as Play Session II, was derived from the transcripts of the monthly audiotaped play sessions described above in the General Method section. This data set was designed to simulate a more structured longitudinal study in which the toys are selected specifically to examine the overextension of certain words.

The third set of data, hereafter referred to as Diary, includes all of the data recorded in the diary study. This set illustrates the richness of data to be found in the systematic diary method used in the present study.

*Longitudinal data set.* The fourth data set, hereafter referred to as Longitudinal, was derived from the transcripts of the audiotaped play sessions included in a previous longitudinal study. (For a detailed description of the method used in that study, see Mervis, 1984.) Six normally developing toddlers were visited at home every six weeks. The procedure used was the same as that described for the audiotaped play sessions included in the diary study. The sets of toys used in the two studies were very similar.

2.  Coding Procedure

The following coding procedure was applied to each of the first three data sets. First, all instances of Ari's use of a given word were extracted, along with the referent of the word and the word/referent code assigned to that particular word–referent combination. Each instance was coded as being correct or overextended, based on whether the word–referent code indicated that the word was correct by adult standards for the particular referent. (Instances coded as symbolic play, joke, child drawing, or kinship were excluded.) For the Longitudinal data set, word–referent codes were not used. Each instance of a word was coded as correct or overextended based on whether or not the child's use of the word for the particular referent was appropriate by adult standards. (Once again, instances of symbolic play, jokes, child drawings, and kinship words were excluded.)

After each word–referent pairing was coded as correct or incorrect, a code then was assigned to each word, indicating whether all instances of the word involved correct usage, all instances involved overextended usage, or some instances of the word were correct whereas others were overextended.

C.  Results

To determine if the proportions of words that Ari overextended during the play sessions were consistent with the proportions reported for children included in previous group design studies, we made two comparisons. For studies that were not designed to look at overextensions in expressive language, previous researchers have reported a range of .07 to .33 for the proportion of words that were ever overextended (Barrett, 1983). The comparable proportion for Ari's Play Session I data was .22, which is well within the previously reported range. To determine the range of proportions for studies in which the toys were chosen specifically to examine the possible overextension of certain words, the proportions of overextended words were computed for each of the six children included in the Longitudinal data set. The obtained proportions were: .28, .41, .44, .53, .57, and .62. The obtained proportion for the (comparable) Play Session II data for Ari was .42, once again well within the range reported for the children in the longitudinal study. In summary, Ari's data appear to fall near the middle of the range of proportions of overextension for previously studied children, for both types of play sessions.

With these findings as background, we performed two additional comparisons using Ari's data, to address the question of whether the proportions of overextensions of object words found in previous studies may be a result of the methodologies used. The first comparison included the extension patterns of the 120 object words that Ari used in Play Session I. These proportions are presented in Figure 1. The proportion of words ever overextended was .23 for the Play Session I database. In contrast, the proportion for the same 120 words for the Diary database was .79. The second comparison included the extension patterns of the 72 object words that Ari used in Play Session II. These proportions are presented in Figure 2. The proportion of words ever overextended was .42 for the Play Session II database; the proportion for the same 72 words was .76 for the Diary database. Thus, overextension was much more likely to be detected in the systematic diary study than in either type of play session.

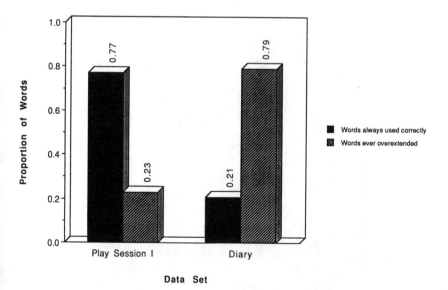

*Fig. 1. Extension patterns of words in Play Session I and Diary databases.*

*Mervis, Mervis, Johnson and Bertrand*

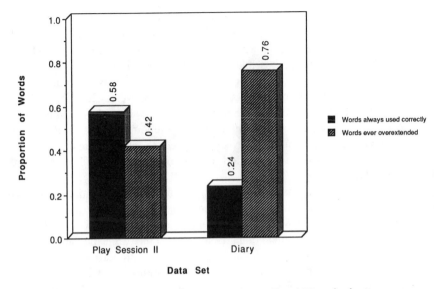

Fig. 2.  *Extension patterns of words in Play Session II and Diary databases.*

To determine if the pattern of overextension of basic-level category names varied as a function of vocabulary size (and/or cognitive level) at the time a name first was acquired, we divided Ari's basic-level object words into 13 groups, based on the month of acquisition. The extension patterns of these words, broken down by month of acquisition, are reported in Figure 3. The proportion of basic-level words that ever were overextended was 1.00 for the words acquired during

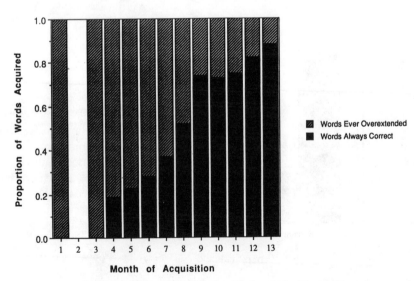

Fig. 3.  *Extension pattern of basic object words by month of acquisition.*

the first and third months (no words were acquired during the second month), and then decreased systematically to .12 for the words acquired in the last month of the study.

## D. Discussion

The results of the analyses comparing Ari's proportion of overextended words during the play sessions to those reported in previous longitudinal group designs indicated that Ari's data fell well within the ranges for previous studies. Given this background, the results of the comparisons between Ari's play session data and his diary data raise serious concerns that previously reported proportions of overextensions do not provide an accurate indication of the actual proportion of words which would be found to be overextended, given a thorough test. The difference in proportion of overextended words between the two types of play sessions (.23 vs. .42) suggests that the deliberate inclusion of objects to which certain words might be expected to be overextended will greatly increase the obtained proportion of words determined to be overextended. However, the diary data indicated that even the second type of play session resulted in a major underestimate of the proportion of overextended words. The diary data indicated that more than 75% of the object words in Ari's lexicon were overextended at some point. Furthermore, all of the basic-level words that were acquired during the first 3 months of production were overextended at some point. In contrast, the play session data suggested that less than 25% of the words were overextended in the videotaped play sessions, and even for the audiotaped play sessions, only about 40% of the words were overextended. The differing results obtained from the three databases derived from the diary data emphasize the importance of exposing the child to a wide range of potential referents for each word in his or her lexicon when attempting to measure the phenomenon of overextension. The expected extension of the child-basic category can be used to determine the minimum range to which the child should be exposed. To test for underextension, it is important to include abstract representations, as well as other types of poor exemplars of the category, from an adult perspective.

Ari's overextension patterns for basic-level object names corresponded extremely well to those predicted for child-basic categories. In particular, his earliest basic-level names were all overextended, and the proportion of overextended words decreased systematically for the rest of the period of the diary study. Thus, as Ari's vocabulary size (and/or cognitive level) increased, the proportion of his newly acquired basic-level words which showed the adult-basic extension pattern increased. Given just Ari's data, it is impossible to establish the relative importance of vocabulary size vs. cognitive level in enabling the child to form the adult-basic category from the beginning.

To complete the determination of the correspondence of Ari's early basic-level categories to the predicted child-basic categories, patterns of underextension must be determined as well as patterns of overextension. Underextension analyses have been completed only for *duck;* results indicated that, as predicted, this category showed both underextension and overextension relative to the adult category, yielding the expected overlap pattern. Preliminary analyses suggest that Ari's other very early words also showed the predicted overlap pattern.


# VI. ACQUISITION OF AN ATTRIBUTE DOMAIN: COLOR

The three previous sections have focused on Ari's acquisition of object categories, as measured by comprehension and/or production of object category names. In the present section, we change our focus to an attribute domain: color. Consideration of linguistic and nonlinguistic aspects of Ari's acquisition of color terms provides a basis for reconciling previous conflicting reports regarding the timing and difficulty of learning color names. The diary data also permit examination of the possible effect of acquisition of one type of word on acquisition of a second type. In particular, we consider the relation between Ari's acquisition of color terms and his acquisition of names for subordinate object categories for which color is an important differentiating attribute.


## A. Introduction

The acquisition of color terms often is viewed as a long and difficult task (e.g., Andrick & Tager-Flusberg, 1986; Bornstein, 1985; Johnson, 1977; Park, Tsukagoshi, & Landau, 1985). Thus, acquisition of basic color terms is likely to begin during the preschool years and perhaps continue as late as kindergarten. Explanations for the difficulty of acquisition of color terms have emphasized cognitive factors. Park et al. (1985) have suggested that, because color is a continuous dimension, children have difficulty partitioning the color space into discrete categories. Johnson (1977) has offered a different type of explanation: Children must begin the task of learning color terms by learning each color and its referent as a paired associate. The memory demands of this paired associate process prevent easy learning of color terms.

Despite the presumed difficulty of acquisition of color terms, however, there are several reports of children who began to acquire color names as toddlers. For example, in screening subjects for experimental studies, researchers have identified a number of 2-year-olds who already knew multiple color names (e.g., M. L. Rice, personal communication, June 12, 1990; Soja, 1986). Cruse (1977), in an informal diary study, found that his son Pierre had acquired seven basic color terms before his second birthday.

The social-situational context in which color terms are introduced to a child is an important variable that previous research has not examined. There are at least two ways in which context is likely to be important. First, to learn color terms, the child must hear these terms used in situations in which the referent of the color term is transparent. That is, the color term must be provided in a situation in which the child's linguistic and/or nonlinguistic knowledge allow him or her to determine that the new word must refer to the object's color. Second, assuming that the input is transparent, the activity which provides the context for the input is likely to have a strong effect on whether or not the child learns color names. Learning is most likely when the activity is a habitual one which strongly interests the child and has a pragmatic focus that relies on color.

In the remainder of this section, we describe Ari's acquisition of color terms. We first present data concerning the situational contexts in which color terms were introduced. We then consider the acquisition of color categories, based primarily on production data. Finally, we consider the possible impact of color term knowledge on acquisition of subordinate-level categories for which color is an important differentiating characteristic.

## B. Method

### 1. Materials

Three sets of data were extracted from Ari's diary study. The first consisted of the dates of first production of all color terms and all subordinate category terms. The second consisted of information included in General Notes regarding Ari's nonlinguistic knowledge of color, adult input for color terms (including situational context information), and adult input concerning subordinate-level bird names. Finally, all interactions relevant to Ari's production and comprehension of color terms were extracted from each of the diary databases. Interactions involving color terms also were extracted from the transcripts of the later videotaped play sessions and included in this set. (As indicated in the General Method section, only certain interactions from these play sessions had been included in the diary databases.) This third set included the following:

1. Productions of color terms (spontanous and elicited).
2. Instances of nonresponse to adult attempts to elicit color terms.
3. Comprehension of color terms.
4. Instances of comprehension failures for color terms.

Eight additional instances of production of color terms were excluded from the analyses because it was not clear whether the color word was used to label a color or a subordinate category (e.g., ''blue'' produced in the presence of a bluebird).

### 2. Coding

The 626 records comprising the third set of data were coded for each of the following measures:

1.  *Ari's color term.* The color term produced or comprehended by Ari during the interaction. Ari's nonresponses to a color term elicitation were coded as "not applicable."
2.  *Referent.* A description of the color of the referent object/part. Referents that could not be specifically determined or were imaginary were coded as "unknown."
3.  *Correct color term.* The basic color term that an adult would use for the referent. Referents that could not be specifically determined or were imaginary were coded as "unknown."
4.  *Adult impetus.* The communicative circumstance under which Ari produced or comprehended a color term was coded as one of the following: spontaneous (production), elicitation (production), comprehension, or unclear. When Ari did not respond to a request regarding comprehension or production of a color term, the adult impetus was coded as elicitation (production) or comprehension.
5.  *Utterance type.* Ari's color term was coded as comprehension, direct production, indirect production, or no response. Indirect productions were utterances in which Ari produced a color term in reference to a different object, or different part of an object, from the one for which the adult was attempting to elicit a color name.
6.  *Adult response.* Three aspects of the adult response were coded. The first was whether the adult agreed or disagreed with Ari's color term for a particular referent. The second was whether the adult qualified his or her response (e.g., "That looks like red."; "That's blue-ish purple."). The third was the color term (if any) the adult used in response to Ari's color term.
7.  *Appropriateness.* A five-point scale was used to assess how appropriate Ari's color term was for the referent from an adult perspective. Color terms for referents that could not be specifically determined, were imaginery, or were jokes were not coded for appropriateness.

3.  Coding Reliability

Appropriateness was coded by the first and fourth authors together; disagreements were resolved by discussion. For all other coding categories a third person coded 124 (20%) of the entries and their responses. Intercoder agreement was assessed by dividing the total number of codes agreed upon by the number of codes agreed upon plus the number of codes disagreed upon. The reliabilities for the coding categories ranged from .94 to .98.

C.  Results

We begin this section with a consideration of background information regarding Ari's initial production of color terms. Three topics are considered: the situational context and the input provided in this context, Ari's interest in these activities, and Ari's revelant nonlinguistic knowledge prior to production of his first color term. We then consider Ari's acquisition of color categories, based primarily on production data. Finally, we consider the relationship between the acquisition of color terms and the acquisition of subordinate categories for which color is an important differentiating attribute.

## 1. Background Information Regarding Initial Color Term Production

*Situational context and input.* Use of color terms in speech addressed to Ari almost always occurred in the same activity: drawing. This activity primarily involved watching an adult draw an object which Ari had requested. Occasionally the adult chose the object to be drawn. Toward the end of the pre-color term period, Ari sometimes "drew" objects himself. The adult most likely to spend time drawing with Ari was his father, who is a proficient artist. While a wide range of objects was drawn for Ari, he had particular favorites that he frequently requested. Ari asked his father to draw elephants and his mother to draw fish. Consistent colors were used for these objects. Ari's father drew elephants with a purple crayon (the closest available color to gray, when Ari had begun asking for elephants), whereas his mother drew fish with an orange crayon.

During the 2 weeks just before Ari produced his first color term, Ari's father decided to try to "help him [Ari] out with color names." To this end, his father chose the strategy of consistently selecting the natural color of the object to be drawn (e.g., green for grass, brown for monkeys) and providing both the name of the object and the name of the color (e.g., "We'll make the water blue."). The drawings almost always were single-color line drawings. In cases in which the drawings were filled in, the same color was used as for the outline. Ari's first production of a color term occurred in the drawing context, as did almost all of his color words during the period immediately following first production of color terms.

One additional context in which color terms were used in speech addressed to Ari was described in the diary record. This context occurred only once when Ari's father initially decided that Ari was ready to learn color names (about 2 weeks before first production of a color term). The activity involved a set of flat rubber flower-shaped pieces. The pieces were all the same shape but varied in color. While Ari and his father were playing with the pieces, his father would pick out the flowers of a particular color and name the color (e.g., "These are orange. See the orange flowers?"). At one point, after his father had lined up several of the orange pieces and named them and their color, he asked Ari to find another orange one. Ari picked an orange one and said "orange." When asked to find another orange one, Ari again was successful. However, when his father tried the same task with other colors, it became clear that Ari did not understand that he was being asked to select pieces based on color. Ari would repeat the requested color name as he picked up a piece, but the correct color seldom was chosen. Although Ari originally had chosen orange pieces correctly, he did not continue to do so after his father had asked for a different color and then asked for orange again. Ari's father noted that it was clear that Ari "had ended up not learning the colors at all." In fact, Ari appeared to have decided that he and his father were playing a game in which Ari was to pick up any flower piece and then repeat the [color] word that his father had just said. Ari did not consider color to be the basis for the activity.

*Ari's interest in the drawing activity.* The diary entries indicate that, throughout the month before Ari produced his first color term, he was extremely interested in drawing. During this time, Ari frequently requested that his father draw for him. A week before first production, Ari's mother noted that for the preceding few days, Ari had been requesting "almost constantly" that elephants be drawn for him. The day before first production, Ari's mother noted that "Ari's consuming interests right now [and] for the last few days have been drawing and reading. If you let him have his own way he'd spend most of his time doing one or the other of these—they've eclipsed the [toy] tool bench and the [toy] farm at this point."

*Nonlinguistic color knowledge.* During the month preceding first production of a color term, Ari began demonstrating that he had acquired some nonlinguistic knowledge of color. At age 1;5.25, he showed that he associated a particular color with a particular object. During a drawing session, Ari's father asked him to add some grass to the picture his father had been drawing. In response to this request, Ari put down the purple crayon he had been holding, picked up the green one, and made some green dots. Five days later, Ari succeeded in matching his socks. The only possible basis for matching was color. At age 1;6.15, Ari asked his father to draw a sun and then spontaneously handed him a yellow crayon.

*Changes in drawing skills.* Important advances in Ari's drawing skills occurred concurrently with the onset of color term production. When Ari was 1;6.10, his father noted that Ari's form of marking paper had changed; he had begun drawing circular squiggles, masses of lines, and zigzags. At the same time, Ari began stating what he was going to draw and then marking the paper. At age 1;6.23 (the day before first production of a color term), Ari said that he was drawing a circle and then drew a shape that resembled an oval. Although Ari had often said previously that he was drawing a circle, this was the first time that he had succeeded in stopping drawing when he had crossed the beginning point of his shape. On the day of first production of a color term, Ari made separate marks on different parts of a sheet of paper for the first time.

## 2. Acquisition of Color Terms

There were 626 diary entries regarding color terms: 568 involved production of a color term, 36 involved comprehension, 21 involved failure to respond to an adult color term elicitation, and 1 involved a noncolor term response to a color term elicitation. We consider only the production data here. The comprehension data, which are consistent with the production data, are described in Mervis and Bertrand (in press).

Between the ages of 1;6.24 and 1;8.23, Ari mastered the correct extensions of all 11 basic color terms. Two subordinate color terms (tan and silver) were acquired by age 2;5.04. A summary of the acquisition data is provided in Table 8, including for each color the age of first production and the age of last error.

*Rate of acquisition.* As is clear from Table 8, Ari learned color terms as a domain, rather than individually. Ari produced his first color term (purple) at age 1;6.24. His productive vocabulary at that time included 656 words (427 common nouns). By the end of that day, Ari had produced five other color terms (blue, brown, black, red, and green). By age 1;7.1, Ari had produced 9 of the 11 basic color terms. All 11 basic color terms had been produced by age 1;7.29.

*Errors.* Acquisition of color terms was relatively easy and straightforward for Ari. Over the course of the diary period, Ari produced an incorrect color term in only 32 instances (see Mervis & Bertrand, in press, for further description).

TABLE 8
Color Terms in Order of First Production

| Color term | Age at first production | Age at last error |
|---|---|---|
| Purple | 1;6.24 | 1;8.23[a] |
| Blue | 1;6.24 | 1;8.23 |
| Brown | 1;6.24 | 1;8.10 |
| Black | 1;6.24 | 1;8.3 |
| Green | 1;6.24 | 1;7.7 |
| Red | 1;6.24 | 1;8.21 |
| Yellow | 1;6.27 | 1;8.3 |
| White | 1;7.0 | 1;7.21 |
| Orange | 1;7.1 | 1;8.21 |
| Pink | 1;7.27 | 1;8.1 |
| Gray | 1;7.29 | no errors |
| Tan | 1;11.15 | no errors |
| Silver | 2;5.4 | no errors |

[a] After this date, Ari referred to a bluish-purple Crayola crayon as "blue" on three occasions.

Only nine errors occurred after age 1;8.0 (38 days after Ari produced his first color term).

*Adult responses.* A detailed description of the adult responses to Ari's color terms is presented in Mervis and Bertrand (in press). Here we describe only the major findings.

Adults responded to 542 (95%) of the 568 production entries. For correctly used color terms, the overwhelming majority (86%) of the responses involved unqualified agreement with Ari's color term followed by a repetition of his term. In response to 15% of Ari's errors, the adult provided the correct color name without qualifying it. In response to another 38% of Ari's errors, the adult provided the correct color name but qualified it (e.g., "It's kind of purple though."). Altogether, then, adults provided the correct color name in response to 53% of Ari's color term errors. Explicit disagreement (using the words "no" or "not") was indicated in response to only 22% of Ari's errors.

*Production of color terms in early two-word utterances.* When Ari began producing two-word utterances, color terms played an important role. When Ari was 1;9.9, his father noted that, when Ari wanted to communicate with someone, he used primarily single-word utterances, but when he was talking to himself, he usually used multiword utterances. When practicing these sequences, Ari often combined a variety of color terms with a single object name (e.g., "Brown rug. Purple rug. Red rug."). Three days later, Ari's mother noted that he was producing a variety of types of multiword utterances, but the most common were adjective–noun combinations. The most frequent type of adjective was a color term, and Ari used all of his color words in two-word utterances.

3.   Acquisition of Subordinate Category Names

Color sometimes plays an important role in differentiating among subordinate-level categories subsumed under a single basic-level category. To determine if the acquisition of subordinate categories for which color was an important attribute was related to acquisition of color terms, Ari's acquisition of subordinate labels prior to age 2;0 was divided into three periods: (a) prior to first production of a color term, (b) while basic color terms were being learned, and (c) subsequent to the mastery of basic color terms (age 1;8.23). Prior to age 2;0, Ari produced the labels for 136 subordinate categories. These were divided into categories for which color was an important differentiating attribute (color-based) and categories for which color was not important (noncolor-based). In Table 9, the number and percent of color-based and noncolor-based subordinate category labels Ari produced are listed, according to period of acquisition. These data indicate that the proportion of color-based subordinates included in Ari's productive vocabulary increased monotonically over the three periods. The proportion for the third period was more than three times that for the first period.

TABLE 9

Number (and Percentage) of Color-based and Noncolor-based Subordinates Relative
to Period of Color Term Acquisition

| | Subordinate basis | |
|---|---|---|
| Period of color term acquisition | Color | Noncolor |
| 1. Prior to color terms | 2 (6%) | 30 (94%) |
| 2. Concurrent with color terms | 5 (15%) | 27 (85%) |
| 3. Subsequent to color terms | 15 (20%) | 57 (80%) |

There are at least three (nonmutually exclusive) possible explanations for the increase in proportion of color-based subordinates. First, Ari may have been more likely to treat color as a basis for distinguishing among subordinate categories after he had learned color names. Second, adults may have been more likely to introduce color-based subordinates after it was clear that Ari understood color names. Third, adults may have been more likely to provide subordinate-relevant color information after it was clear that Ari understood color names. No data are available concerning the first possibility. To investigate the second and third possibilities, we considered Ari's acquisition of subordinate-level bird category names. (Subordinate-level bird names comprised the largest number of Ari's color-based subordinates within a single domain.) The input Ari received concerning each of the 20 subordinate types of bird whose names he acquired during the diary study is summarized in Table 10. The data are divided into two periods: before first production of a color term and after first production of a color term. The subordinate bird categories are divided into those for which color is an important differentiating attribute and those for which color is not.

The second possibility for the increase in proportion of color-based subordinate bird names was that adults were more likely to introduce subordinate bird names after Ari had acquired color terms. The data in Table 11 support this possibility. Ari acquired 5 subordinate bird names prior to color term acquisition. Of these, 1 (20%) was the name for a color-based category. The diary data

TABLE 10

Input About Subordinate Bird Labels Before and After First Production of a Color Term

| | | Input type[a] | | | |
|---|---|---|---|---|---|
| Period | Subordinate type | Color | Noncolor | None | Unknown |
| Before color terms | color-based | | 1 | | |
| | noncolor-based | | 4 | | |
| After first production of a color | color-based | 8 | 2 | 2[b] | 2 |
| term | noncolor-based | | 1 | | |

[a] Numbers indicate number of subordinate bird categories (out of 20) for which a particular type of input was provided.
[b] Ari "invented" labels for these two subordinates.

suggest that these were the only subordinate bird names that were introduced to Ari prior to color term acquisition. Ari acquired 15 subordinate bird names after first production of a color term; of these 14 (93%) were names for color-based categories.

The data in Table 10 also support the third possibility: Adults were more likely to provide subordinate-relevant color information after it was clear that Ari understood color names. Ari acquired the name for only one color-based subordinate bird (*cardinal*) prior to first acquisition of a color term. The input provided for cardinal did not include color information, even though *red* is a very salient characteristic of cardinals. Ari acquired the names of 14 color-based subordinate bird categories after his first production of a color term. Of these, he invented labels for two kinds of birds (blackbird, goldfinch). The input for two other kinds was unknown. Color information played an important role in the verbal input provided for 8 of the remaining 10 color-based subordinates. For example, Ari (age 1;11.7) was told that a meadowlark had a "yellow tummy and a black necklace."

## D. Discussion

In the introduction to this section, we argued that social-situational context should be a critical factor with regard to the age and ease of color term acquisition for a particular child. We suggested two ways in which context is likely to be important. First, the child must hear color terms in situations in which the referent of the color term is transparent. Second, the activity in which this input is embedded should be a habitual one which greatly interests the child and which has a pragmatic focus which relies on color. Ari's data provide strong evidence of the facilitative role that favorable social-situational context can play in the child's acquisition of color terms.

Throughout the month preceding Ari's first production of a color term, the diary record indicates that he had two favorite activities: drawing and reading. Starting at this time, and for at least the next year, drawing with his father was a much-anticipated daily event. Starting about 2 weeks before first production of a color term, Ari's father decided to try to help Ari learn color terms. The strategy his father chose fit naturally within the drawing activity. This strategy involved selecting the crayon of the natural color of the object to be drawn and then providing both the name of the object and the name of the color. The drawings almost always were single-color line drawings; if filled in, the same color was used as for the outline.

Ari's father's strategy yielded input in which the referent of the color word should have been transparent to Ari. In particular, because the objects drawn for Ari were ones whose names he already knew, he was able to determine which word in the input was the object name. More generally, given Ari's father's strategy, Ari should have comprehended all but one of the words in the input utterance: the color term. At this time, Ari was able to differentiate object words and attribute words (Mervis & Johnson, 1991). Ari's implicit knowledge of the characteristics of attribute words provided a basis for determining that the unknown word referred to an attribute of the named object. Because the most salient attribute of the drawing (probably the only salient attribute in most cases) was the color, Ari should have been able to use a fast-mapping strategy (cf. Carey & Bartlett, 1978, for data concerning preschoolers) to determine that the unknown word referred to the color of the object drawn, once he realized that color was a lexicizable concept. Additional input of this type for the same color should have offered Ari verification of the referent for a particular color word. This type of input was most clearly available for *purple*. Ari's most frequent request was for *elephant*, and his father consistently would search for the purple crayon, use it to draw an elephant, and then tell Ari that the elephant was purple. Interestingly, "purple" was the first color word that Ari produced.

Given the relationship between the input provided and Ari's linguistic knowledge (e.g., words included in his lexicon, realization that color was a lexicizable concept, implicit knowledge of characteristics of attribute words, availability of fast-mapping strategy), acquisition of color words should have been easy and rapid for him. The diary record confirmed this prediction. More generally, these findings offer a potential point of integration across previously divergent findings regarding age of acquisition and ease of acquisition of color terms. Social-situational context information is available for two other children for whom color term acquisition was relatively early and easy. One of these children was Ethan, for whom color terms were introduced in the same manner as for Ari. By age 22 months, Ethan was producing the names of all 11 basic color terms. The second child was the daughter of an early diarist (Pelsma, 1910). E. frequently watched her mother painting felt and china. Pelsma reported that his daughter acquired color terms considerably more rapidly than would have been expected based on the findings of Sanford (1893) and Wolfe (1890), who stated that the average 2-year-old used only one color term. E. was using five basic color terms correctly before her second birthday. Pelsma attributed this difference to "her [E's] unusual opportunity to associate almost daily with these colors. When her mother was painting she also desired to do so, and was very early given a brush and water colors." (p. 348). In contrast, Rice (1980) found that 27- to 35-month-old children who did not have a nonlinguistic concept of color did not acquire color terms even after more than 2,000 trials. This finding is not surprising. Given that these children did not have a nonlinguistic concept of color, it would have been impossible to provide them with transparent input concerning a color term.

1.   Color Terms and the Acquisition of Color-Based Subordinate Category Names

The proportion of Ari's subordinate-level category names that encoded a color-based subordinate category was 6% for the period prior to first production of a color term. In contrast, this proportion was 20% for the period after color terms were mastered, a threefold increase. This finding is consistent with Baldwin's (1989) suggestion that there should be a correlation between the acquisition of color terms and the acquisition of subordinate categories for which color is an important differentiating attribute. We offered three nonmutually exclusive explanations for this increase in proportion of color-based subordinates. First, Ari may have been more likely to treat color as a basis for distinguishing among subordinate categories after he had learned color names. Second, adults may have been more likely to introduce color-based subordinates after it was clear that Ari understood color names. Third, adults may have been more likely to provide subordinate-relevant color information after it was clear that Ari understood color names. The diary data did not allow us to address the first explanation. Consideration of the pattern of acquisition of subordinate-level bird names provided strong support for both the second and third explanations. Thus, these data provide evidence of the impact of the acquisition of one type of word (color terms) on the subsequent acquisition of a different type of word (names for color-based subordinate categories). Birdwatching was an activity that Ari and his parents all enjoyed. Ari's interest in birds preceded his acquisition of color terms, and Ari had acquired several subordinate bird names before first production of a color term. Because even color-based subordinate bird categories can also be differentiated based on details of overall shape and/or form attributes (e.g., the presence or absence of a crest), acquisition of names for these categories should have been possible prior to color terms. In fact, Ari did acquire one color-based subordinate bird category name (*cardinal*) during this period. However, his rate of acquisition of names for color-based subordinate bird categories increased dramatically after color term acquisition began.

In conclusion, previous studies of color term acquisition have ignored the social-situational context in which color terms were introduced. In many cases, potentially important information concerning cognitive (non-linguistic) knowledge of color also was unavailable. These studies, while often documenting the difficulty of acquisition of color terms, did not offer data regarding why color term acquisition was difficult. Similarly, nondiary reports of children who acquired color terms early and easily did not include information that might explain why these children did not find color term acquisition troublesome. Thus, systematically collected diary data provided the basis for the first demonstration of the interrelationships among language, cognition, and social-situational context during the acquisition of color terms and color-based subordinate category names. Understanding of these interrelations provides a solid basis for reconciling the results of previous studies of acquisition of color names.

## VII.  ACQUISITION OF THE PLURAL MORPHEME

### A.  Introduction

The four previous sections have focused on acquisition of entire words, or more precisely, free morphemes. Lexical development also involves acquisition of bound morphemes. Detailed accounts of the acquisition of this type of morpheme are an important component of descriptions of lexical development and are crucial as a basis for theorizing about the acquisition of morphology. In the present section, we consider the acquisition of the plural morpheme, the bound morpheme most frequently affixed to object names. We begin by briefly reviewing the available literature concerning acquisition of the plural morpheme. We then address two complementary aims using data from Ari's diary study. First, we provide a detailed description of the acquisition of the plural morpheme (for a more comprehensive version of this account, see Mervis & Johnson, 1991). Second, we perform a methodological comparison between the systematic diary method and the traditionally used weekly home visit method of studying early morphological development.

## 1. Stages of Acquisition

Based on data from Brown's (1973) longitudinal study of Adam, Eve, and Sarah, Cazden (1968) has argued that there are four stages in acquiring the plural morpheme. During the first stage, no plurals are produced. During the second, plurals occasionally are produced and consistently are used correctly. Cazden hypothesized that this stage begins when children start to produce unanalyzed stored fragments of previously heard speech that contained plural forms. The third stage is marked by a dramatic increase in the production of plurals accompanied by the onset of errors. Cazden argued that the transition to this stage is governed by the child's formulation of a productive rule for plural formation. In the fourth stage the plural morpheme is mastered; the child correctly produces plural forms in 90% of obligatory context.

## 2. Errors Involving the Plural Morpheme

Group studies of acquisition of the plural marker have revealed instances of both overregularization of morphological forms and nonmorphological errors. Researchers have described these errors by listing the various types that occur, rather than discussing the probability of occurrence of particular types or the circumstances under which they occur. With regard to overregularization errors, Brown (1973), Cazden (1968), and Leopold (1949) have documented examples of children adding the regular form of the plural morpheme to roots which have irregular plural forms (e.g., "mans" instead of "men"). Brown (1973) provided examples of the double marking of irregular plural forms (e.g., "feets" instead of "feet") and the addition of the plural morpheme to mass nouns (e.g., "dirts"). The addition of a regular plural ending to words which take a 0 morpheme plural (e.g., "sheeps" for "sheep") has been documented for both English (Brown, 1973) and German (Mills, 1985). Finally, Brown (1973) and Pinker and Prince (1988) have noted examples of children producing back formations, in particular, singular forms of nouns that can occur only as plurals (e.g., "pant" instead of "pants"); this type of error also has been observed in children acquiring Russian (Slobin, 1966).

Nonmorphological errors involving the plural morpheme appear to be infrequent. However, all three of the children in Brown's (1973) study overgeneralized the plural morpheme across parts of speech, attaching the plural to adjectives or quantifiers (e.g., "greens," "somes"). One child also violated the transformational rules for the plural forms of compound nouns, adding the plural ending to both nouns in a compound ("streets lights").

In the remainder of this section, we use data from the systematic diary study to provide a comprehensive account of English plural acquisition. We also compare this pattern of acquisition with that which would have been obtained if the traditional longitudinal home visit method of studying language development had been employed. Researchers using this method visit children at their homes, for at most a few hours every week or two. During this time, the speech of the children and their parents (generally their mothers) is recorded and subsequently transcribed. To mimic the home visit method, the data from one randomly chosen weekday (Wednesday) were extracted for use as the home visit method corpus. This resulted in a conservative comparison; previous studies that have used the home visit method (e.g., Brown, 1973) have collected data over a much shorter interval than an entire day and generally have visited the child at intervals more widely spaced than 1 week. Furthermore, the home visit corpus contains information concerning the meaning of words whose phonological forms deviated significantly from the standard, which an observer would have been unlikely to decipher, as well as data from any trips that occurred on Wednesdays, which an observer would have been unlikely to witness. This methodological comparison allows determination of the impact of the time gaps between visits on accounts of the process of the acquisition of the plural morpheme.

## B.  Method

All data relevant to Ari's acquisition of the plural morpheme were extracted from both the diary record and the play session transcripts. These data are referred to as the comprehensive database. To provide a simulation of the traditional home visit method, data from every Wednesday were extracted from the comprehensive database. The resulting database is referred to as the subset database. Notes also were made concerning certain aspects of Ethan's acquisition of the plural morpheme.

## 1.  Data Extraction

Ari's utterances of the types listed below that occurred from the onset of plural use were included:

1.  Plural forms of count nouns which take a marked plural morpheme (regular or irregular; e.g., *cups, geese*)

2. Duals and the singular forms of count nouns that end in /s/ or /z/ (e.g., *pliers, briefcase*)
3. Mass nouns (e.g., *rice, milk*)
4. Count nouns which take a 0 morpheme plural (e.g., *sheep, deer*)
5. Quantifiers (including the accompanying nouns, if any; e.g., *two birdies, many*)
6. Uses of the singular form of a count noun in an obligatory plural context (e.g., "cup" in reference to two cups)
7. Uses of the plural form of a count noun in an obligatory singular context (e.g., "cups" in reference to one cup)
8. Instances of the addition of the plural morpheme to non-nouns (e.g., *purples*).

2. Coding

Utterances were coded along the following five dimensions:

1. Morphological form (either correct, overregularized, or inappropriate for the referent [singular for plural referent or plural for singular referent])
2. Pronunciation (either close to the adult standard or not close to the adult standard)
3. The nature of the referent (discrete or mass, single or multiple, visible or not visible, and the semantic appropriateness of the label Ari used for the referent)
4. The nature of the adult response (in particular, whether the response indicated agreement or disagreement with the semantic and morphological aspects of Ari's label)
5. The presence or absence of a quantifier.

## C. Results

Four general areas of results are addressed. For each of these topics, results from both the comprehensive and the subset analyses are presented. Important consistencies and inconsistencies are summarized in Table 11.

1. Relation Between Onset of Syntax and Onset of Morphology

Cazden (1968) and Brown (1973) considered a child to have acquired a morpheme when it was produced in 90% of all obligatory contexts. Following this criterion, Ari acquired the plural morpheme at age 1;8.7 for the comprehensive analysis, and at age 1;8.4 for the subset analysis. Both analyses indicated that Ari also produced several other morphemes, including the past, progressive, possessive, and diminutive at the time use of the plural reached the 90% criterion.

TABLE 11

Comparison of Major Results of the Two Analyses

Important Points of Agreement

— Ari's acquisition of morphology preceded his acquisition of syntax
— New type of evidence for acquisition of a plural formation rule: Words whose pronunciations were not close to the standard (including invented word forms) were all assigned the regular plural ending
— Nonoverregularization errors included addition of plural morpheme to adjectives and use of the plural form in obligatory singular contexts

Important Points of Disagreement

— Effect of Ari's ability to produce the conventional word form on the age at which 90% obligatory use criterion was attained for the plural morpheme
  • *complete database:* considerable lag for words whose pronunciation was not close to the standard form
  • *subset:* no difference as a function of pronunciation
— Overlap between use of singular and plural forms of a word in obligatory plural contexts, after the plural form was first produced
  • *complete database:* 18 out of 87 words (21%)
  • *subset:* 1 out of 15 words (7%)
— Types of overregularizations
  • *complete database:* five: back formations, regular marking of nouns which take a 0 morpheme plural, double marking of nouns which have irregular forms, irregular nouns treated as regular, addition of plural ending to mass nouns
  • *subset:* two: regular marking of nouns which take a 0 morpheme plural; double marking of nouns which have irregular forms
— Consistency of production of a particular type of overregularization during the period in which it occurred ever occurred
  • *complete database:* varied as a function of overregularization type; length of time the relevant words had been in Ari's productive vocabulary also was an important factor for some overregularization types
  • *subset:* not enough data to evaluate
— Analysis of "people"
  • *complete database:* Ari considered "people" to be a noun which takes a 0 morpheme plural
  • *subset:* Ari considered "people" to be a count noun
— Relation between onsets of use of plural morpheme and quantifiers
  • *complete database:* simultaneous
  • *subset:* use of plural morpheme preceded referential use of quantifiers by about one month
— Presence of qualitative data indicating strength of knowledge concerning the plural morpheme
  • *complete database:* examples of correct juxtaposition of the singular and plural forms of the same stem within a single interaction, resistence to adult correction to a singular form when Ari's use of a plural form was appropriate, self-correction of overregularization upon adult request
  • *subset:* none

However, Ari's MLU in words at the time of plural acquisition was less than 1.01. Thus, both analyses reveal clearly that the onset of morphology preceded the onset of syntax. Ethan also began to use the plural, past, progressive, possessive, and diminutive morphemes at about the same age as Ari, and well before beginning to acquire syntax. This pattern is consistent with that found by Munson and Ingram (1985) and by J. Sachs (personal communication, November 29, 1988), but contrasts with Brown's (1973) finding that Adam, Eve, and Sarah began to acquire syntax before beginning to acquire morphology.

2.  Relation Between Onset of Plural Use and Use of Quantifiers

Plural use and the use of quantifiers are two important ways that the concept of quantity is expressed linguistically in English. If there is an underlying relation between these two forms of expression, one might expect that they would be manifested at about the same time (as Gopnik & Meltzoff, 1987, have found for cognitive and linguistic manifestations of the same concept; see also Bates, Benigni, Bretherton, Camaioni, & Volterra, 1977). Based on the comprehensive analysis, Ari's first production of a plural occurred on the same day as his first production of a quantifier, at age 1;6.5. On this day, "shoes" was used in reference to two shoes, and "many" was used to refer to a crowd of people. By 1;6.11, Ari had also used the quantifiers "one" and "two" correctly. It is interesting that this same pattern was demonstrated by Ethan. Ethan's first plural form was produced on the same day that he produced his first quantifiers, "many" and "two." "One" was produced a few days later. Thus for both children, the two linguistic manifestations of the concept of quantity, the plural morpheme and quantifiers, clearly were acquired synchronously. The subset analysis did not replicate this finding, however. Ari's first production of a plural occurred at 1;6.10, whereas his first referential use of the quantifiers "one" and "many" did not occur until approximately one month later.

3.  Stages in Acquiring the Plural Morpheme

The proportions of plurals used in obligatory plural contexts were compared for all count nouns, and for the subset of count nouns that was assigned a pronunciation code of "not close to the adult standard." Figure 4 illustrates the proportions of plurals used in obligatory plural contexts based on the comprehensive database; Figure 5 illustrates these same proportions based on the subset database. It is apparent that for the comprehensive analysis, the acquisition of the plural morpheme for those count nouns that Ari had difficulty pronouncing lagged considerably behind the acquisition of the plural morpheme for other count nouns. Ethan's vocabulary included only three words whose forms were not related to the adult standard; the pattern of acquisition of the plural morpheme for two of these forms was the same as for Ari[1]. Figure 5 clearly indicates that the

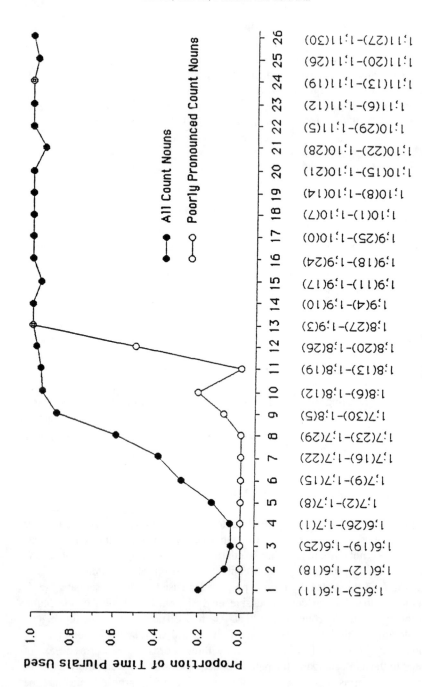

*Fig. 4.  Proportion of plurals used in obligatory contexts: Comprehensive analysis.*

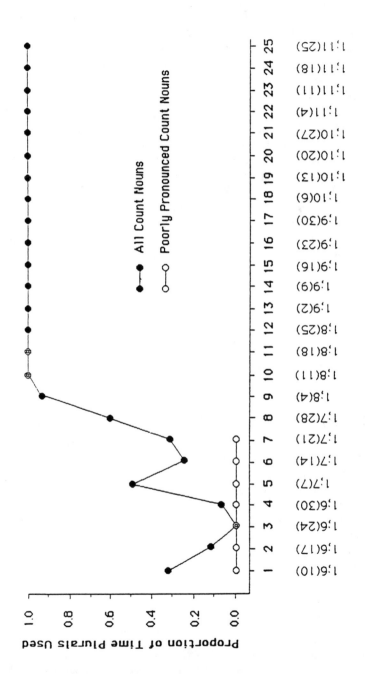

*Fig. 5.  Proportion of plurals used in obligatory contexts: Subset analysis.*

subset analysis did not replicate this finding. There are no differences in the rate at which the plural morpheme was acquired as a function of pronunciation.

Ari's plural acquisition was divided into four stages. We first discuss these stages in relation to the comprehensive database. We then describe the major stage differences between the comprehensive and the subset analyses.

In the comprehensive analysis, the *preplural* stage, during which plurals were not produced, extended through age 1;6.4. During the *transitional* stage, ranging from age 1;6.5 to 1;8.6, plurals were used in obligatory contexts some of the time. However, plural forms of words for which Ari's pronunciation was coded as "not close to the adult standard" were never produced. There were 87 words for which Ari at some point produced both the singular form in an obligatory plural context and the plural form in an obligatory plural context. For 18 of these words, Ari's use of the singular and plural forms overlapped. That is, for 21% of these words, Ari continued to vacillate back to the singular form even after the appropriate plural form had been produced.

The transitional stage was broken down into two substages; *prerule* and *postrule*. During the prerule substage, Ari produced no overregularizations. The postrule substage was characterized by the production of overregularizations which demonstrated that Ari had formulated a productive rule. Towards the end of the postrule substage, Ari was able to juxtapose appropriately the use of the singular and plural forms of the same word within the same conversation. For example, at age 1;8.1, Ari had the following conversation with his mother:

> (A is sitting on his parents' bed.) A: Geese. M: Yesterday you saw geese in the park. A: Goose. Standing up. M: That's right. One goose was standing up in the water.

The *child-plural* stage extended from age 1;8.7, the time at which plurals were produced in 90% of obligatory contexts, until age 1;11.28, when Ari no longer made errors of commission for words whose stems were established in his vocabulary. As can be seen in Figure 1, the onset of the child-plural stage for words that Ari had difficulty pronouncing lagged considerably behind the onset for other count nouns. The first plural form of any of the words for which pronunciation was coded as "not close to the adult standard" did not occur until age 1;8.11, after the onset of the child plural stage for other count nouns. Finally, the *adult-plural* stage, ranging from age 1;11.29 on, was characterized by virtually complete mastery of the plural morpheme.

---

[1] The third word was actually one of Ethan's earliest words: "pop." This word was used to refer to pacifiers; it was derived from "pip pop," which adults said when they took a pacifier out of his mouth. Shortly after Ethan first produced "pop," all of his adult caregivers, both at home and at daycare, started calling pacifiers "pop" rather than "pacifier." Thus, unlike Ethan's other two words that were not related to the adult standard and unlike Ari's invented words, "pop" became part of the adult vernacular. Not surprisingly, therefore, Ethan treated "pop" the same way as other adult words. (In fact, "pop" was the first word for which Ethan produced a plural form.)

The subset analysis stage sequence indicated three major differences from the comprehensive analysis. First, the plural morpheme is mastered much more rapidly and there are no differences as a function of Ari's pronunciation. Second, the transitional stage is not broken into two substages because no overregularization errors were produced during this stage. Ari did not provide evidence of having formulated a rule for the production of plurals until the onset of the child-plural stage, when he was producing the plural in 90% of all obligatory contexts. Finally, vacillation between the use of singular and plural forms in obligatory plural contexts once the appropriate plural form had been acquired was extremely infrequent in the subset analysis. Only 1 of the 15 words for which Ari sometimes used the singular form in an obligatory plural context and at other times used the plural form in an obligatory plural context exhibited this pattern.

4. Errors

With regard to errors, the comprehensive analysis identified five types of overregularizations, which are described below. Ethan produced the same five types. The subset analysis identified only two types of overregularizations. The comprehensive analysis also revealed three types of related errors: the use of the plural morpheme to refer to a singular referent, the pluralization of adjectives, and errors involving quantifiers. Ethan also produced all three of these types of errors. The first two of these types were identified by the subset analysis.

*Back formation.* The comprehensive analysis revealed that the first and most frequent type of overregularization Ari produced was the back formation of nouns ending in the /s/ or /z/ allomorph, which yielded a singular form through deletion of the final consonant (e.g., "plier" in reference to a single pair of pliers; "briefca" in reference to a briefcase). Back formations occurred only for the duals and count nouns ending in /s/ or /z/ that were acquired just prior to or during the period in which back formation occurred at all. Words that were well established in Ari's lexicon prior to this period (e.g., "bus," "pants") were not overregularized. For the five words that underwent back formations, overregularization occurred in 51% of their productions. Thus, even for these words, Ari did not stop producing correct forms during the overregularization period. The subset analysis did not identify any instances of back formations.

*Regular marking of nouns which take a 0 morpheme plural.* Both analyses revealed cases in which Ari added the regular plural ending to nouns that take a 0 morpheme plural. The comprehensive analysis revealed six instances of this error, all involving the words "deer" and "sheep." Interestingly, 100% of the plural uses of these words were overregularized during the 18-day period of overregularization. The subset analysis revealed one instance of "deers."

*Double marking of nouns which have irregular plural forms.* Both analyses revealed that Ari doubly marked the irregular plural form of "person" as "peoples." The comprehensive analysis provided powerful evidence that this error occurred because Ari considered "people" to be a 0 morpheme plural. Ari's caregivers at his daycare routinely referred to both individual Fisher Price human figures and groups of Fisher Price human figures as "people." Although Ari's parents used the word "people" appropriately, they produced it far less frequently than the staff at the daycare. The three instances in which Ari produced "peoples" occurred during the same period that he overregularized "sheep" and "deer." Before and after this overregularization period, Ari used "people" to refer both to singular and plural referents. Therefore, we have convincing evidence from the comprehensive analysis that Ari considered "people" to be both a singular and plural form. The subset analysis, however, did not provide sufficient evidence for this conclusion to be reached. Instead it appeared that Ari considered "people" to be a count noun.

*Mass nouns.*    The fourth type of error revealed through the comprehensive analysis involved the addition of a regular plural ending to mass nouns. This occurred in three cases, involving the words "water," "broccoli," and "macaroni." At the time of the first instance of this type of overregularization, Ari had over 80 mass nouns in his vocabulary. Overregularizations accounted for fewer than 1% of all uses of mass nouns. The subset analysis did not identify any instances of the addition of a regular plural ending to mass nouns.

*Irregular nouns treated as regular.*    Finally, the comprehensive analysis revealed that, in two instances, Ari regularized the plurals of the irregular nouns, "goose," and "mouse." These errors represented 50% of the cases in which the plural forms of these words were recorded during the interval between these two errors. Interestingly, Ari corrected his own production of "gooses" at 1;11.20, as can be seen in the following example.

> (The family is eating dinner.) A (suddenly): Gooses. F: What are gooses called? A (after hesitating): Geese. F: They're called geese.

The subset analysis did not identify any regularizations of irregular nouns.

In sum, the comprehensive analysis revealed more types of overregularizations than did the subset analysis. Furthermore, the types of overregularizations included in the comprehensive analysis demonstrated probabilities of occurrence ranging from less than 1% to 100% during the period in which that type of overregularization occurred. The subset analysis did not permit the determination of probabilities of error occurrence since too few errors were produced to accurately delineate periods of overregularization.

## D.  Discussion

The discussion addresses two areas in which these findings have important implications. The first involves methodological concerns for results obtained through the traditional longitudinal home visit method. The second involves implications for theories and models of morphological acquisition. Some of these implications are clear from both the subset analyses and the complete database analyses; others emerge only from the latter.

## 1. Methodological Concerns

One methodological concern with the home visit method is that, because of the relatively long intervals between visits, the observed patterns of morphological development might not be described accurately, and developmental phases that were relatively brief might be missed. A comparison of the subset analysis results with the complete database analysis results indicates that this concern is well founded. For example, three types of overregularizations were not detected through the subset analysis. Furthermore, no effect of the phonological form of a word on acquisition of its plural form was revealed; in contrast, the complete database analysis indicated that plural forms for words whose phonological forms differed significantly from the standard forms were acquired considerably later than for words whose phonological forms approximated the standard. The subset analysis did not yield enough data even to raise the question of how consistent the use of overregularized forms was during the period in which a particular form was overregularized. In contrast, the complete database analysis indicated a complex pattern. While use of the singular form of a word in an obligatory plural context following acquisition of the plural form of the word virtually never occurred in the subset, it occurred for more than 20% of the relevant words in the complete database. The two analyses of Ari's beliefs concerning "people" yielded very different conclusions: for the subset, that "people" was the singular form of a count noun; for the complete database, that "people" was a noun that took a 0 morpheme plural. The synchrony between the onset of use of plural forms and quantifiers was missed in the subset analysis, probably because quantifiers occurred infrequently for the first month or so of use. Finally, the subset database did not yield any good qualitative examples to support the extent of Ari's understanding of either the plural morpheme or the concept of plurality. In contrast, the complete database yielded several, as indicated in Table 15.

Another concern with the home visit method is that researchers may have difficulty understanding the child's speech. Instances of production may well be missed or misinterpreted in cases in which the child's pronunciation is poor, the meaning a child ascribes to a word does not overlap with the adult meaning (e.g., the child uses *hot* to mean *cup;* see examples in Anglin, 1983, and Mervis, 1987), or the child invents his or her own word forms (e.g., Ari's use of *sassy* for *butterfly*). In the present study, this concern was not addressed directly, because the input from every seventh day was transferred intact into the subset database. Thus, information from the complete database was used to provide glosses for all words, regardless of pronunciation. However, as pointed out above, the complete database analysis indicated an effect of the accuracy of pronunciation of a word on the acquisition of the plural form of that word. The subset analysis did not indicate such a result. If the meanings of the words whose phonological forms were not close to the standard were unknown to the researcher, as often happens in home visit studies, then these words would have been treated as unintelligible, and an analysis for the effect of accuracy of phonological form would not have been conducted at all.

A third concern with the home visit method is that relatively rare events such as particular types of excursions or activities, which often yield valuable information concerning semantics or morphology, are unlikely to take place when an observer is present. A comparison of the two databases confirms the importance of collecting data in non-everyday contexts. For example, all uses of "geese" or "gooses" were related to visits to the park. Most uses of "deers" occurred during a visit to a zoo, and "sheeps" was related to a visit to a farm. Most instances of back formation occurred while trimming or preparing to trim bushes. Finally, the correct interpretation of Ari's beliefs concerning "people" required knowledge of the language used by the daycare staff.

## 2. Theoretical Implications

The results of the comprehensive analysis have important implications for current theories and models of morphology. Two issues will be addressed: the acquisition of morphology prior to syntax, and the nature of lexical entries in models of morphological acquisition.

*Acquisition of morphology prior to syntax.* The tenet that syntax acquisition precedes the onset of morphology has been pervasive in theories of early language acquisition. Brown (1973) reported this result for Adam, Eve, and Sarah and subsequently argued that children's language must acquire considerable structure before morphology can be acquired. More recent theories, such as Pinker's (1982, 1984) model of language acquisition, also include the assumption that syntax is used as a bootstrap for the acquisition of morphology. Ari's pattern of acquiring morphology before syntax also has been demonstrated by several other English-speaking children, including his younger brother Ethan, Jacqueline Sachs's daughter (personal communication, November 29, 1988), one of Susan Braunwald's daughters (personal communication, April 18, 1991), and the child studied by Munson and Ingram (1985). These data suggest two alternative possibilities to current models of language acquisition. First, whereas some children may use syntax as a bootstrap for morphology, other children may use morphology as a bootstrap for syntax acquisition. Second, it is possible that syntax and morphology are acquired along routes that are completely independent. These alternatives are consistent with suggestions by Pinker (1987) and Bates and MacWhinney (1987) that new types of models are needed to take individual differences into account. Models of language acquisition should adopt flexible starting points, rather than continuing to assume that syntax must precede morphology.

*Nature of lexical entries.* The results are relevant to the nature of lexical entries in models of morphological acquisition. The connectionist model for the acquisition of past tense verb inflections proposed by Rumelhart and McClelland (1987), and the alternative rule-governed model proposed originally by Pinker (1984) and elaborated upon by Pinker and Prince (1988), have been based on data produced by a relatively small number of children. Ari's data indicate the need for modifications of particular elements of both models.

There was a considerable lag in Ari's inflection of nouns that he had difficulty pronouncing. This pattern was replicated by Ethan. These findings suggest that for particular lexical entries, the plural formation rule must be blocked. This blockage would be extremely difficult to represent through a connectionist model in which (as for McClelland & Rumelhart, 1987) lexical representations consist solely of phonetic strings. This is due to the fact that Ari's forms which deviated significantly from the adult standard in many cases rhymed with the phonetic string for a different word which was correctly pluralized. For example, Ari referred to both singular and multiple owls as "hoo" (derived from "hoot"), whereas one shoe was referred to as "shoe" and two shoes were referred to as "shoes." Further information about the lexical entry, beyond a phonetic string, needs to be incorporated into connectionist models. In Pinker's (1984) rule-governed model, such a blockage of the application of the plural rule could be incorporated more easily.

Other evidence that nonphonetic information is crucial in the representation of lexical entries stems from differences in probabilities of overregularizations exhibited by Ari for different types of nouns, for the period during which that type of overregularization occurred at all. For 0 morpheme plurals, overregularizations occurred in 100% of cases, whereas for mass nouns, overregularizations occurred in fewer than 1% of cases. The occurrence of back formations was affected by the length of time that a word which had the phonological features necessary to undergo back formation had been present in Ari's productive vocabulary. Only words that were acquired just prior to or during the period in which back formations occurred underwent this form of overregularization, and for these words, back formations were produced in about half of the possible instances. Connectionist models would have difficulty accounting for these overregularization patterns, and Pinker's rule-governed model would need to be modified extensively.

In conclusion, although studies conducted cross-sectionally and through the traditional longitudinal home visit method have revealed very important information about children's morphological development, these methods should not be the sole ones used when developing theories and models of acquisition. The results of the comprehensive analysis provide the outlines of fundamental modifications that would serve to enrich theories and models of early language acquisition. First, whereas current work assumes that syntax is used as a bootstrap for the acquisition of morphology, the present data indicate two clear additional possibilities: Either morphology may be used as a bootstrap for the acquisition of syntax, or morphology and syntax may be acquired along completely independent routes. Thus, theories and models must provide flexible starting points for the acquisition of language. Second, the results from the present study indicate that information related to specific lexical entries may have an important effect on the acquisition of morphology. Two such types of information are the relation between the child's phonological form for a word and the standard phonological form and how well established a word is in the child's lexicon at the time he or she begins to produce a particular type of overregularization. These findings provide a demonstration of the important role that systematic diary studies can play in the study of the acquisition of morphology and syntax.

## VIII.   GENERAL DISCUSSION

In this chapter, we have used data generated by the systematic diary method to address five different aspects of Ari's early lexical development. In the present section, we consider the ways in which our analyses depended critically on the nature of the methodology used for data collection. This discussion is divided into two subsections. In the first, we consider how the systematicity afforded by this diary study allowed us to address the methodological concerns raised earlier in the chapter. In the second, we summarize the theoretical and methodological contributions this study offered. We then briefly describe other types of phenomena that can be examined based on Ari's diary corpus. We conclude with a consideration of the role of the systematic diary method in future research on lexical development.

### A.   The Systematic Diary Method: A Response to Previous Methodological Issues

We have raised two general types of methodological concerns for the study of early lexical development. The first involved the use of the diary method as an anecdotal record. The second involved the use of group-design studies (whether cross-sectional or longitudinal, laboratory or home-visit) as the sole basis for generation of information concerning lexical development. Below we present three general properties of the systematic diary study of Ari's early lexical development and discuss how their incorporation into the research design allowed us to address the specifics of these methodological concerns. We first consider the advantages of the systematic use of event sampling. We then address the benefits of including two types of information: (a) social-situational contextual information concerning Ari's utterances and the activities in which he engaged, and (b) specific information regarding the adult input (both linguistic and nonlinguistic) that preceded and followed Ari's utterances. Finally, we consider the advantages of supplementing the diary study with quasi-experimental probes. At the end of this section, we summarize the major quantitative and qualitative differences between results obtained from the present systematic diary study and previous results obtained through studies which used traditional group design methods.

## 1. Diary Method as a Form of Event Sampling.

The use of the diary method as a form of event sampling, rather than as an anecdotal record, offers a solution to many of the problems associated with the early diary studies. When the diary method is treated as a form of event sampling, data collection is guided by a preestablished set of rules. If the set of rules provides for the recording of all of the child's utterances, as in Ari's diary prior to age 16 months, the diary record by definition provides an accurate representation of the child's typical day-to-day performance. When recording of every utterance is impossible, event sampling still can provide an accurate representation of the child's typical performance, as long as the rules which specify which utterances are to be recorded are designed to be representative, rather than just to record novel utterances. Such rules were used in Ari's diary beginning at age 16 months. This description of everyday performance proved crucial in analyzing all five aspects of early lexical development considered in the present chapter. For example, knowledge of Ari's everyday performance was invaluable for understanding the rich interaction among cognitive, linguistic, and social factors that was the basis for Ari's acquisition of color terms. Description of everyday performance also was important in documenting the process of Ari's acquisition of the plural morpheme. Because all of Ari's and Ethan's early productions of their first words were recorded, it was possible to determine the type of conceptual basis for these words.

The systematicity afforded by use of the diary method as a form of event sampling offered other important advantages as well. Because event sampling was used as the basis for data collection, specific comparisons of the diary data collected for Ari, Ethan, and Keren were possible. These comparisons were the basis for the development of operating principles concerning the nature of children's early words. The rules used as the basis for data collection for Ari's diary yielded a much more complete record of production than would have been possible using traditional group designs. The comprehensiveness of this record was important in understanding both the basis for the initial extension and subsequent evolution of Ari's categories, and the proportion of Ari's categories that were overextended sometime during the diary study. Finally, since data collection was performed by Ari's closest caregivers, problems in recording and interpreting his poorly pronounced or idiosyncratic words were minimized. These words likely would have been recorded as unintelligible by a researcher who was not familiar with Ari's phonological patterns. The analysis of such words proved crucial in the examination of Ari's acquisition of the plural morpheme and the proposal of specific modifications for current theories and models of morphological and syntactic acquisition.

2.   Importance of Contextual Information.

Ari's diary corpus included two crucial types of contextual information: a description of the social-situational context in which his utterance took place, and a record of any relevant linguistic interaction which surrounded Ari's utterance. These types of information also were included in Ethan's diary. Contextual information was essential to determining whether the basis for Ari's and Ethan's early words was referential, situational, or context-bound. A comparison of the contextual information for situationally based words and referentially based words provided the foundation for the formulation of operating principles concerning the conceptual basis for children's earliest words. The linguistic interaction portion of the contextual information made is possible to determine the effects of adult input on the extension of an initial child-basic category and on its evolution, particularly the acquisition of new names and the establishment of new categories for referents previously included in the initial category. This information regarding Ari's *duck* category provided an in-depth test of several previously proposed operating principles for category formation and evolution. Information regarding the social-situational context in which Ari was exposed to color terms proved invaluable in offering an explanation for why acquisition of color terms was relatively easy and straightforward for him.

3.   Quasi-experimental Probes.

The inclusion of quasi-experimental probes, especially in the form of deliberate naturalistic exposure to a wide range of potential referents for particular words, provided a major opportunity for in-depth studies of words in Ari's early lexicon. New objects were introduced to Ari both at home and on excursions to places where collections of novel referents would be available (e.g., for tool words, to hardware stores; for animal words, to zoos, farms, or aquariums). Information from such trips proved critical for understanding the process of Ari's acquisition of the plural morpheme. New objects, whether introduced to the home or seen during outings, were a major source of data concerning the evolution of Ari's *duck* category. The determination that overextension is characteristic of most early categories at some point in development was possible only because of the availability of a wide variety of potential referents from both within and outside the adult-basic category labeled by the same name as the child's category. The same set of referents also can provide a convincing basis for determining how characteristic underextension is for early categories. (So far, such an analysis has been completed only for *duck*.) The inclusion of comprehension trials, especially during the first several weeks of the diary study, provided the basis for determination of the initial extension of Ari's earliest words. These trials, using a wide variety of potential referents, provided evidence of both overextension and underextension. The pattern of responses to the comprehension probes (described only for *duck* in the present chapter) provided important support for operating principles relevant to the initial extension of a category, as measured by comprehension.

## 4. Major Differences in Results between Ari's Diary Study and Group-Design Studies.

There are both quantitative and qualitative differences between the results obtained in the present systematic diary study and results obtained in previous group-design studies. Before considering these differences, however, it is important to document that the differences did not occur simply because Ari was different from the children included in previous studies. This question can be addressed by examining the data from the methodological comparisons presented for proportion of object words that were overextended and for acquisition of the plural morpheme. For both these comparisons, Ari's data in typical group-design format (i.e., for overextension: play session data; for plural, subset database) are well within the range found for children previously included in longitudinal or cross-sectional group-design studies. With regard to overextension, the proportion of words that Ari overextended during the videotaped play sessions fell towards the middle of the range reported in Barrett's (1983) review of the literature. The proportion of words that Ari overextended during the audiotaped play sessions was at the low end of the middle of the range for the children included in Mervis's (e.g., 1984) longitudinal study; both studies used similar sets of toys. With regard to acquisition of the plural morpheme, Ari's developmental pattern fit well with the patterns reported for Adam, Eve, and Sarah (Brown, 1973; Cazden, 1968). The same types of overregularization and non-overregularization errors were recorded. Furthermore, the same overall pattern of acquisition (production of correct regular and irregular forms, followed by overregularization, and then by approximation to the adult standard) emerged from both studies. Finally, comparison of the initial extension and early evolution of Ari's *duck* category to that reported for *ball, car,* and *kitty* in Mervis's (1984) longitudinal study suggested that all of the children were guided by the same set of operating principles.

Despite these similarities, comparison of the complete diary record to the results of previous group-design studies indicated a number of quantitative differences. The proportion of object words that Ari overextended (as determined by the complete database) was dramatically greater than that reported in previous studies. Similarly, underextension was detected more frequently than in previous longitudinal studies. Ari produced more types of overregularizations for the plural morpheme than any single child previously studied. In fact, Ari produced all of the types that had been found (across children) in previous studies.

Two important qualitative differences were identified. First, whereas researchers concerned with the nature of children's early words generally have argued either that these words are referentially based or that they are situationally (contextually) based, the comparison of Ari's, Ethan's, and Keren's data indicated that a single child may well use both types of bases (cf. Harris et al., 1988, for a similar conclusion based largely on maternal diary records). The diary data indicate that the basis that a particular child will use for a particular word depends heavily on the input that the child hears in reference to that word, and the situational context in which the word is provided (e.g., whether or not referents for the word generally are transparent to the child). Thus, systematic diary data provided a basis for integration of the different theoretical positions that have been offered concerning the nature of children's early words (e.g., Huttenlocher & Smiley, 1987; Markman, 1989; Nelson, 1985, 1988). Second, whereas the results of the longitudinal group-design study of Adam, Eve, and Sarah had indicated that the acquisition of syntax preceded the acquisition of morphology, the diary data for Ari and Ethan and for Munson's son (Munson & Ingram, 1985) indicated that the acquisition of morphology preceded the acquisition of syntax. Thus, there does not seem to be an invariant order for the acquisition of morphology and syntax for children acquiring English. The fact that both patterns occur necessitates the reformulation of theoretical approaches to the early acquisition of morphology and syntax.

## B.   Unique Contributions of the Systematic Diary Study

Because data for Ari's diary study were collected systematically, the corpus provided much more than simply a basis for the generation of hypotheses for future empirical research. Below we consider four areas in which the diary study offered unique contributions.

### 1.   Operating Principles.

Most contemporary approaches to early language development assume that this process is guided by operating principles, biases, or constraints operating within the child (e.g., Clark, 1983, 1988; Golinkoff, Mervis, & Hirsh-Pasek, 1992; Markman, 1989; Mervis, 1990, 1992; Peters, 1985; Slobin, 1985). The general position has been that, in the absence of principles/biases/constraints, lexical acquisition would be impossible; the number of possible meanings that a word could express is infinite. Earlier in this chapter, we argued that lexical operating principles serve as heuristics that have the effect of restricting the child's search space for word meanings by increasing the likelihood that he or she will entertain particular hypotheses over possible alternatives. The data from the diary studies of Ari, Ethan, and Keren's early lexical development provided the foundation for the development of operating principles relevant to the nature of children's early words. In particular, operating principles were proposed for determining the conceptual basis for individual words. These principles rely on both the child's cognitive and linguistic skills and the linguistic input provided for a particular word. The delineation of these new principles was critically dependent on a comparison of the contexts in which a particular word was introduced to a particular child and the basis that child used for the word. Without the detailed contextual information the systematic diary method provided about the input for each of the three children's early words and the initial extensions of these words, the relationship between input context and word basis would have been much less likely to have been discovered.

The data from Ari's diary study also provided tests of previously proposed operating principles (Mervis, 1990, 1992). The principles that are available during what we described as the early period of category evolution were tested earlier using data from Mervis's longitudinal study (e.g., Mervis, 1984, 1987; Mervis & Mervis, 1988). For these principles, Ari's data provided further corroboration, based on a much more in-depth study of a single category (*duck*). For the principles proposed for the late period of category evolution, Ari's data provided the only test; few data on that period were obtained in the longitudinal study. Ari's data provided preliminary support for these principles. The availability of systematic data regarding both linguistic input concerning new category names and Ari's extension for these new names, collected across a variety of situational contexts, was crucial in documenting the acquisition of these late-period principles.

2.  Individual Differences.

The diary data provide new information regarding the importance of individual differences for theories of development. Individual differences may arise from factors either internal or external to the child. The main contribution of the present diary study concerns external factors: the individuals who interact with the child and the social-situational context in which input is provided. The richness of the contextual information regarding both linguistic input and social-situational context allowed for the identification of particularly powerful effects of context on the course of Ari's lexical development.

As noted earlier in the General Discussion, individual differences in input have a strong impact on the nature of children's earliest words. In particular, the type of input provided about a specific word had an important effect on the type of basis the child chose for that word. A comparison of the input that Ari and Ethan received for the two words for which the children differed in choice of basis indicated that Ari received transparent input for these words, whereas the input for Ethan was opaque. Ari treated these words as referentially based; Ethan treated them as situationally based. Dromi (in press) notes that, for all of Keren's situationally based words, the input had not identified a clear referent. More generally, children who receive transparent input for most of their words will have early vocabularies composed primarily of referentially based words. The general input style that Ari and Ethan heard was transparent. Accordingly, virtually all of their early words were referentially based. The general input style that Keren heard was mixed; adults were less concerned with transparency (Dromi, personal communication, September 24, 1988). Keren's early vocabulary included many more situationally based words than either Ari's or Ethan's.

The impact of these types of individual differences in input is most apparent at the beginning of lexical development, when the child's linguistic knowledge is extremely limited. At that point, the child must depend primarily on nonlinguistic information (e.g., pointing, eye gaze) to provide the transparency needed to identify the correct referent. As the child's lexical, syntactic, and pragmatic knowledge increase, the likelihood that the child will find a given input utterance transparent also increases, reducing the impact of individual differences in input form on the basis children choose for a word.

Individual differences in the social-situational context and the input provided in that context also appear to play an important role in acquisition of basic color terms. For both Ari and Ethan, color terms were introduced in the context of drawing with their father, a daily activity for them. Within this context, color terms were used to label realistic line drawings. Objects were drawn in the most natural color available. The input provided concerning color names was transparent for the children. For both children, drawing was a favorite activity. Within this context, color names were learned easily and rapidly. Pelsma's (1910) daughter E., who enjoyed daily painting sessions with her mother, was exposed to color names in that context and also learned them rapidly. The performance of these three children contrasts with previous studies of color name knowledge, which have found that most children do not learn color terms until the preschool years, and that, even then, learning color names often is difficult. While no information is available on the input provided to these children outside of the laboratory, it is likely that they had not had the opportunity to participate in the type of daily drawing or painting session in which Ari, Ethan, and E. were involved.

Individual differences in acquisition of color terms also may lead to individual differences in other aspects of lexical development for which color is important. One such aspect is color-based subordinate level categories. Once a child acquires color terms, adults can use color words to explain how to identify members of color-based subordinate categories and/or how to differentiate among color-based subordinates of a single basic-level category. Ari's diary record demonstrated this type of pattern for acquisition of subordinate-level bird names. The combination of color name knowledge and family interest in birdwatching, as well as transparent input, led Ari to be able to identify and name more subordinate bird types by age 24 months than many people who are not interested in birds are able to even as adults.

As these data make clear, an important way in which context is manifested is through the particular individuals with whom the child interacts and their corresponding interests. Different people are likely to share in different activities with the child because of these differences in interest. As a result, mothers, fathers, and other adult caregivers (and also the child's siblings) may play different kinds of roles with respect to the child's lexical development (cf. Mannle &

Tomasello, 1987). In the present study, the daily routines and shared activities which Ari experienced with his caregivers greatly influenced particular facets of his lexical development. The enjoyment that Ari and his father derived from drawing greatly facilitated Ari's acquisition of color terms. Once color terms were acquired, the interests of the entire family in birdwatching facilitated the rapid acquisition of a large number of names for color-based subordinate bird categories. Other types of shared activities also had large effects on particular aspects of lexical development. For example, Ari and his mother frequently baked cookies together. In the context of this situation, Ari acquired a large number of ingredient names and names of baking techniques, as well as a detailed "cookie baking script" prior to age 24 months (Myers & Mervis, 1989). In general, the results of Ari's diary study suggest that certain contexts are particularly suited for acquisition of particular types of words or morphemes and for demonstration of knowledge of them. This finding indicates the importance of examining a variety of contexts (or at least a context well suited to the phenomenon of interest) when studying early lexical development.

3.   Complexities in Early Lexical Development.

The present systematic diary study was particularly valuable for identifying important complexities in early lexical development that may impact greatly on the development of theories or models. These types of complexities are extremely difficult to discover using group-design methods, due to the relative sparseness of the data which can be collected. In particular, a given phenomenon is likely to be found to involve many more factors when examined based on a systematic diary study which uses rules such as those in the present study rather than based on a typical group-design study. Incorporation of these additional factors and their interactions is important for the development of more realistic theories and models of development. For example, the analysis of Ari's acquisition of the plural morpheme indicated the clear necessity for theories of language acquisition to adopt flexible starting points to account for the developmental patterns of both children who begin by acquiring syntax (as did Adam, Eve, and Sarah) and children who begin by acquiring morphology (as did Ari, Ethan, Munson's son, Sachs's daughter, and one of Braunwald's daughters). The diary data also indicated that, during the early stages of acquisition of the plural morpheme, the accuracy of the child's phonological form plays an important role in determining whether or not the child will produce the plural form of a particular word. Plural forms never were produced for words whose pronunciations were not close to the adult standard until after Ari already had entered the child-plural stage (defined as using plural forms in 90% of the obligatory contexts). How well established a word was in Ari's lexicon at the time that he was producing a type of overregularization that might apply to that word was found to affect whether or not the word actually was overregularized. These effects indicate clearly that the lexical entries in models of plural acquisition are too simplistic. Additional types of information which need to be included in the lexical entries are the accuracy of pronunciation compared to the adult standard and the length of time a word has been in the child's lexicon. It is likely that neither of these factors would have been identified in group-design studies. Poorly pronounced words probably would have been transcribed as unintelligible, obscuring the effect of phonology on the onset of use of the plural form of a word, and the necessary information concerning how well established a word was in the child's lexicon is unlikely to have been available.

### 4.   Choice of Stimuli.

The particular stimuli used in studies of early lexical development, whether conducted at the child's home or in the laboratory, will have a major impact on the outcome of the study with regard to lexical extension. This finding was demonstrated dramatically in the comparison of the proportion of Ari's words that were overextended in the videotaped play sessions (Ari's own toys), the audiotaped play sessions (toys selected to examine potential overextension of certain words), and the complete diary study. For the object labels produced in the videotaped play sessions, examination of the complete diary record indicated that the proportion of these words ever overextended (.79) was more than three times greater than that found in the videotaped sessions (.23). For the object labels produced in the audiotaped play sessions, examination of the complete diary record indicated that the proportion of these words ever overextended was nearly double (.76) that found in the audiotaped sessions (.42). Comparisons of underextension, which we have not yet conducted, are expected to show differences at least as dramatic. Thus, the particular stimuli used by a researcher will play a major role in determining how pervasive the phenomenon of overextension (or any other extension pattern of interest) is found to be. The obtained pervasiveness of a particular extension pattern in turn will be important in determining the centrality of that phenomenon from a theoretical perspective. The choice of stimuli, then, is critical for research on early lexical development and ultimately will contribute to the shaping of theories of early lexical development.

## C.   Further Uses of the Diary Corpus

In this chapter, we have examined only a few of the possible topics that can be studied using the data from the diary study of Ari's early lexical development. The wealth of data in that study allow for investigations of a wide variety of topics at linguistic levels ranging from the phonological to the pragmatic. Many such analyses are currently in progress or in the planning stages. We mention just a few of these here. Analyses of the nature of the phonological form of Ari's words (e.g., correct, invented word, real word but with a different meaning) are planned, considering both the initial form and (for words whose initial form was not correct) the subsequent evolution to the correct adult form (e.g., "sassy" to "sassyfly" to "butterfly"). The composition of Ari's object–word lexicon will be examined to determine the relative proportions of words at different hierarchical levels of abstraction and how these proportions change over time, as well as the factors influencing such changes. The composition of Ari's object–word lexicon also will be examined to determine the pattern of acquisition of words within particular domains (e.g., animals, vehicles). For example, we will consider whether Ari had a spurt of acquiring words within a particular domain (as occurred for color terms), or whether the rate of word acquisition within a domain was fairly constant over time. We also will consider whether these phenomena vary as a function of Ari's age and/or cognitive level at the time he began to acquire the domain, as well as whether variation occurred as a function of Ari's interest in the domain. Further semantic investigation will include expanding the analyses of *duck* presented in this chapter to other words in Ari's lexicon to comprehensively study the initial extension and evolution of Ari's words. At the pragmatic level, analyses using the diary record to chronicle Ari's development of a sense of humor are almost complete. Plans are being made for cross-diary comparisons of acquisition of nonnominals (e.g., action words) for Ari and for Tomasello's daughter Travis (Tomasello, 1992). Cross-language and cross-diary comparisons of Ari's pattern of rate of acquisition of words in English and Keren's (Dromi, 1987, in press) pattern of rate of acquisition of words in Hebrew are in progress.

## D. Conclusion

To reach the goal of a complete description of lexical development and a complete theory and/or model of this phenomenon, both group-design studies and systematic diary studies are crucial. The advantages of the two types of studies are complementary. We have indicated many of the strong points of systematic diary studies throughout this chapter. A large number of these advantages involve being able to offer a more accurate, realistic picture of a particular aspect of lexical development for a particular child, due to the in-depth nature of the data collected. Group-design cross-sectional studies have the obvious advantages of collecting data on a number of children in a relatively short period of time. Group-design longitudinal studies offer the advantages of collecting data on a number of children over time, yielding information concerning the processes of development. Group-design cross-lag studies combine the advantages of cross-sectional and longitudinal studies. Experiments, using any of these designs, offer the advantages of control and provide the researcher an opportunity to examine the impact on lexical development of "rare events" (Nelson, 1987) that have been identified by other types of research.

Analyses of Ari's diary data offer several suggestions for increasing the effectiveness of group-design studies in informing researchers about early lexical development. For example, the stimuli to be used should be chosen carefully, so that the child's actual pattern of extension for the words being studied can be determined. The child's extension pattern should not be artificially constrained by the researcher's failure to include particular types of potential exemplars. Researchers can vary the caregivers and/or the social-contextual situations studied to determine the impact of these factors on early lexical development.

A particularly promising research technique involves combining the systematic diary method with group-design methods. In this technique, the parent is given explicit, detailed instructions concerning the systematic recording of particular types of events (e.g., all uses of a given word; all novel uses of a given word). The scope of the diary is carefully limited so that it is realistic to expect parents to be able to follow the instructions. The child also participates in regularly scheduled research sessions (using observational and/or experimental techniques, depending on the purpose of the research). The data from a child's diary can be combined with those from the research sessions to obtain a detailed picture of the aspect of lexical development that is of interest. Data can be combined across the different children who participated in the study to obtain a more general picture of the phenomenon of interest, as well as information about individual differences. Recently, this method was used by Harris et al. (1988) in a study of the nature of children's earliest words. We are beginning a longitudinal study of early lexical development of both normally developing children and children who have Down syndrome, which will combine systematic diary techniques, regularly scheduled observation sessions, experimental tests of lexical operating principles, and assessment measures in an attempt to provide as broad a basis for theory testing and refining as possible.

In conclusion, the present study provides strong support for the value of the systematic diary study. This method was able to provide detailed descriptions of early lexical development, offering suggestions for important variables to be taken into account in future group-design studies as well as in the development of theories and models of early lexical development. The usefulness of the systematic diary method extends well beyond offering suggestions, however. In the present study, the use of the systematic diary method provided the basis for generating new lexical operating principles and also for testing and refining previously proposed principles. The systematic diary method has earned a respected position as a research tool both for generating descriptive data and for development and refinement of theories.

## IX. REFERENCES

Andrick, G. R., & Tager-Flusberg, H. (1986). The acquisition of colour terms. *Journal of Child Language, 13*, 119–134.

Anglin, J. M. (1983). Extensional aspects of the preschool child's word concepts. In T. B. Seiler & W. Wannenmacher (Eds.), *Concept development and the development of word meaning* (pp. 247–266). Berlin: Springer-Verlag.

Baldwin, D. A. (1989). Priorities in children's expectations about object label reference: Form and color. *Child Development, 60,* 1291–1306.

Banigan, R. L., & Mervis, C. B. (1988). Role of adult input in young children's category evolution. II. An experimental study. *Journal of Child Language, 15,* 493–504.

Barrett, M. D. (1978). Lexical development and overextension in child language. *Journal of Child Language, 5,* 205–219.

Barrett, M. D. (1982). Distinguishing between prototypes: The early acquisition of the meaning of object names. In S. A. Kuczaj, II (Ed.), *Language development: Vol. 1. Syntax and semantics* (pp. 313–334). Hillsdale, NJ: Erlbaum.

Barrett, M. D. (1983). The course of early lexical development: A review and an interpretation. *Early Child Development and Care, 11,* 19–32.

Barrett, M. D. (1986). Early semantic representation and early word-usage. In S. A. Kuczaj, II & M. D. Barrett (Eds.), *The development of word meaning: Progress in cognitive development research* (pp. 39–67). New York: Springer-Verlag.

Barrett, M. D., Harris, M., & Chasin, J. (1991). Early lexical development and maternal speech: A comparison of children's initial and subsequent uses of words. *Journal of Child Language, 18,* 21–40.

Bates, E. (1976). Pragmatics and sociolinguistics in child language. In D. Morehead & A. Morehead (Eds.), *Normal and deficient child language* (pp. 411–463). Baltimore: University Park Press.

Bates, E., Benigni, L., Bretherton, I., Camaioni, L., & Volterra, V. (1977). From gesture to the first word: On cognitive and social prerequisites. In M. Lewis & L. A. Rosenblum (Eds.), *Interactions, conversation, and the development of language* (pp. 247–307). New York: Wiley.

Bates, E., Benigni, L., Bretherton, I., Camaioni, L., & Volterra, V. (1979). *The emergence of symbols: Cognition and communication in infancy.* New York: Academic Press.

Bates, E., & MacWhinney, B. (1987). Competition, variation, and language learning. In B. MacWhinney (Ed.), *Mechanisms of language acquisition* (pp. 157–193). Hillsdale, NJ: Erlbaum.

Bloom, L. (1973). *One word at a time: The use of single word utterances before syntax.* The Hague: Mouton.

Bornstein, M. H. (1985). Colour-name versus shape-name learning in young children. *Journal of Child Language, 12,* 387–393.

Braunwald, S. R., & Brislin, R. W. (1979). The diary method updated. In E. Ochs & B. B. Schieffelin (Eds.), *Developmental pragmatics* (pp. 21–42). New York: Academic Press.

Brown, R. (1973). *A first language: The early stages.* Cambridge, MA: Harvard University Press.

Carey, S. (1982). Semantic development: The state of the art. In E. Wanner & L. R. Gleitman (Eds.), *Language acquisition: The state of the art* (pp. 347–389). New York: Cambridge University Press.

Carey, S., & Bartlett, E. (1978). Acquiring a single new word. *Papers and Reports on Child Language Development, 15,* 17–29.

Cazden, C. B. (1968). The acquisition of noun and verb inflections. *Child Development, 39,* 433–448.

Chapman, K. L., Leonard, L. B., & Mervis, C. B. (1986). The effects of feedback on young children's inappropriate word usage. *Journal of Child Language, 13,* 101–117.

Chapman, K. L., & Mervis, C. B. (1989). Patterns of object-name extension in production. *Journal of Child Language, 16,* 561–571.

Clark, E. V. (1973). What's in a word? On the child's acquisition of semantics in his first language. In T. E. Moore (Ed.), *Cognitive development and the acquisition of language* (pp. 65–110). New York: Academic Press.

Clark, E. V. (1977). First language acquisition. In J. Morton & J. C. Marshall (Eds.), *Psycholinguistics: Developmental and pathological* (pp. 1–72). Ithaca, NY: Cornell University Press.

Clark, E. V. (1983). Meaning and concepts. In J. H. Flavell & E. M. Markman (Eds.), *Handbook of child psychology: Vol. 3. Cognitive development* (pp. 787–840) (Gen. Ed. P. H. Mussen). New York: Wiley.

Clark, E. V. (1987). The principle of contrast: A constraint on language acquisition. In B. MacWhinney (Ed.), Mechanisms of language acquisition (pp. 1–33). Hillsdale, NJ: Erlbaum.

Clark, E. V. (1988). On the logic of contrast. Journal of Child Language, 15, 317–335.

Clark, R. (1982). Theory and method in child-language research: Are we assuming too much? In S. A. Kuczaj (Ed.), Language development: Vol. 1. Syntax and semantics (pp. 1–36). Hillsdale, NJ: Erlbaum.

Cruse, D. A. (1977). A note on learning of colour names. Journal of Child Language, 4, 305–311.

Daehler, M. W., Lonardo, R., & Bukatko, D. (1979). Matching and equivalence judgments in very young children. Child Development, 50, 170–179.

Dougherty, J. W. D. (1978). Salience and relativity in classification. American Ethnologist, 5, 66–80.

Dromi, E. (1987). Early lexical development. New York: Cambridge University Press.

Dromi, E. (in press). The mysteries of early lexical development: Underlying cognitive and linguistic processes in meaning acquisition. In E. Dromi (Ed.), Language and cognition: A developmental perspective. Norwood, NJ: Ablex Publishing Corp.

Gale, M. C., & Gale, H. (1900). The vocabularies of three children of one family to two and a half years of age. In H. Gale (Ed.), Psychological studies (No. 1) (pp. 70–117). Minneapolis: Gale.

Gillis, S. (1987). Words and categories at the onset of language acquisition: Product versus process. Belgian Journal of Linguistics, 2, 37–53.

Golinkoff, R. M., Lavallee, A., Baduini, C., & Hirsh-Pasek, K. (1985, October). What's in a word? The young child's predisposition to use lexical contrast. Paper presented at the annual Boston University Conference on Language Development, Boston, MA.

Golinkoff, R. M., Mervis, C. B., & Hirsh-Pasek, K. (1992). Early object labels: The case for lexical principles. Manuscript submitted for publication.

Gopnik, A., & Meltzoff, A. N. (1985). From people, to plans, to objects. Journal of Pragmatics, 9, 495–512.

Gopnik, A., & Meltzoff, A. N. (1986). Words, plans, things and locations: Interactions between semantic and cognitive development in the one-word stage. In S. A. Kuczaj & M. D. Barrett (Eds.), The development of word meaning: Progress in cognitive development research (pp. 199–223). New York: Springer-Verlag.

Gopnik, A., & Meltzoff, A. N. (1987). The development of categorization in the second year and its relation to other cognitive and linguistic developments. Child Development, 58, 1523–1531.

Gruendel, J. M. (1977). Referential extension in early language development. Child Development, 48, 1567–1576.

Harris, M. B., Barrett, M., Jones, D., & Brookes, S. (1988). Linguistic input and early word meanings. Journal of Child Language, 15, 77–94.

Huttenlocher, J., & Smiley, P. (1987). Early word meanings: The case of object names. Cognitive Psychology, 19, 63–89.

Johnson, E. G. (1977). The development of color knowledge in preschool children. Child Development, 48, 308–311.

Leopold, W. F. (1949). Speech development of a bilingual child: A linguist's record (Vol. 4). New York: Academic Press.

Mannle, S., & Tomasello, M. (1987). Fathers, siblings, and the bridge hypothesis. In K. E. Nelson & A. van Kleek (Eds.), Children's language (Vol. 6, pp. 23–41). Hillsdale, NJ: Erlbaum.

Markman, E. M. (1987). How children constrain the possible meanings of words. In U. Neisser (Ed.), Concepts and conceptual development: Ecological and intellectual factors in categorization (pp. 255–287). New York: Cambridge University Press.

Markman, E. M. (1989). Categorization and naming in children: Problems of induction. Cambridge, MA: Bradford/MIT Press.

Markman, E. M., & Hutchinson, J. (1984). Children's sensitivity to constraints on word meaning: Taxonomic versus thematic relations. Cognitive Psychology, 16, 1–27.

Markman, E. M., & Wachtel, G. F. (1988). Children's use of mutual exclusivity to constrain the meanings of words. *Cognitive Psychology, 20,* 121–157.

McClelland, J. L., & Rumelhart, D. E. (1987). A distributed model of human learning and memory. In J. L. McClelland & D. E. Rumelhart (Eds.), *Parallel distributed processing: Explorations in the microstructure of cognition: Vol. 2. Psychological and biological models* (pp. 170–215). Cambridge, MA: MIT Press.

McShane, J. (1979). The development of naming. *Linguistics, 17,* 879–905.

McShane, J. (1980). *Learning to talk.* Cambridge, UK: Cambridge University Press.

Mervis, C. B. (1982, May). *Mother–child interaction and early lexical development.* Paper presented at the annual meeting of the Midwestern Psychological Association, Minneapolis, MN.

Mervis, C. B. (1984). Early lexical development: The contributions of mother and child. In C. Sophian (Ed.), *Origins of cognitive skills* (pp. 339–370). Hillsdale, NJ: Erlbaum.

Mervis, C. B. (1987). Child-basic object categories and early lexical development. In U. Neisser (Ed.), *Concepts and conceptual development: Ecological and intellectual factors in categorization* (pp. 255–287). New York: Cambridge University Press.

Mervis, C. B. (1988). Early lexical development: Theory and application. In L. Nadel (Ed.), *The psychobiology of Down syndrome* (pp. 101–145). Cambridge, MA: Bradford/MIT Press.

Mervis, C. B. (1989, April). *Operating principles and early lexical development.* Paper presented at the biennial meeting of the Society for Research in Child Development, Kansas City, MO.

Mervis, C. B. (1992). *Early lexical development: The role of operating principles.* Manuscript in preparation.

Mervis, C. B. (1990). Operating principles, input, and early lexical development. *Communicazioni Scientifiche di Psicologia Generala* (Special issue on Categorization and Recognition), *4,* 7–25.

Mervis, C. B., & Bertrand, J. (in press). Transaction of cognitive-linguistic abilities and adult input: A case study of the acquisition of color terms. *Journal of Child Language.*

Mervis, C. B., & Canada, K. (1983). On the existence of competence errors in early comprehension: A reply to Fremgen & Fay and Chapman & Thomson. *Journal of Child Language, 10,* 431–440.

Mervis, C. B., & Crisafi, M. A. (1982). Order of acquisition of subordinate, basic, and superordinate level categories. *Child Development, 53,* 258–266.

Mervis, C. B., & Johnson, K. E. (1991). Acquisition of the plural morpheme: A case study. *Developmental Psychology, 27,* 222–235.

Mervis, C. B., & Long, L. M. (1987, April). *Words refer to whole objects: Young children's interpretation of the referent of a novel word.* Paper presented at the biennial meeting of the Society for Research in Child Development, Baltimore, MD.

Mervis, C. B., & Mervis, C. A. (1982). Leopards are kitty-cats: Object labeling by mothers for their 13-month olds. *Child Development, 53,* 267–273.

Mervis, C. B., & Mervis, C. A. (1988). Role of adult input in young children's category evolution. I. An observational study. *Journal of Child Language, 15,* 257–272.

Miller, J. F. (1982). Early language intervention: When and how. In M. Lewis & L. T. Taft (Eds.), *Developmental disabilities: Theory, assessment, and intervention* (pp. 331–349). New York: SP Medical and Scientific Books.

Mills, A. E. (1985). The acquisition of German. In D. I. Slobin (Ed.), *The crosslinguistic study of language acquisition: Vol. 1. The data* (pp. 141–254). Hillsdale, NJ: Erlbaum.

Munson, J., & Ingram, D. (1985). Morphology before syntax: A case study from language acquisition. *Journal of Child Language, 12,* 681–684.

Murphy, G. L., & Medin, D. L. (1985). The role of theories in conceptual coherence. *Psychological Review, 92,* 289–316.

Myers, N. A., & Mervis, C. B. (1989). A case study of early event representation development. *Cognitive Development, 4,* 31–48.

Nelson, K. (1985). *Making sense: The acquisition of shared meaning.* Orlando, FL: Academic Press.

Nelson, K. (1988). Constraints on word learning? *Cognitive Development, 3,* 221–246.

Nelson, K., & Lucariello, J. (1985). The development of meaning in first words. In M. D. Barrett (Ed.), *Children's single-word speech* (pp. 59–86). Chichester, UK: Wiley.

Nelson, K. E. (1987). Some observations from the perspective of the rare event cognitive comparison theory of language acquisition. In K. E. Nelson & A. van Kleek (Eds.), *Children's language* (Vol. 6, pp. 289–331). Hillsdale, NJ: Erlbaum.

Park, S., Tsukagoshi, K., & Landau, B. (1985, April). *Young children's mis-naming of colors.* Paper presented at the biennial meeting of the Society for Research in Child Development, Toronto, Ontario.

Pelsma, J. R. (1910). A child's vocabulary and its development. *Pedagogical Seminary, 17,* 328–369.

Peters, A. M. (1983). *The units of language acquisition.* Cambridge, UK: Cambridge University Press.

Peters, A. M. (1985). Language segmentation: Operating principles for the perception and analysis of language. In D. I. Slobin (Ed.), *The crosslinguistic study of language acquisition: Vol. 2. Theoretical issues* (pp. 1029–1067). Hillsdale, NJ: Erlbaum.

Piaget, J. (1954). *The construction of reality in the child.* New York: Basic.

Pinker, S. (1982). A theory of the acquisition of lexical-interpretive grammars. In J. Bresnan (Ed.), *The mental representation of grammatical relations* (pp. 655–726). Cambridge, MA: MIT Press.

Pinker, S. (1984). *Language learnability and language development.* Cambridge, MA: Harvard University Press.

Pinker, S. (1987). The bootstrapping problem in language acquisition. In B. MacWhinney (Ed.), *Mechanisms of language acquisition* (pp. 399–441). Hillsdale, NJ: Erlbaum.

Pinker, S., & Prince, A. (1988). On language and connectionism: Analysis of a parallel distributed processing model of language acquisition. *Cognition, 28,* 73–193.

Rescorla, R. A. (1980). Overextension in early language development. *Journal of Child Language, 7,* 321–335.

Rice, M. L. (1980). *Cognition to language: Categories, word meanings, and training.* Baltimore: University Park Press.

Rosch, E. (1977). Human categorization. In N. Warren (Ed.), *Studies in cross-cultural psychology* (Vol. 1, pp. 3–49). London: Academic.

Rosch, E., Mervis, C. B., Gray, W. D., Johnson, D. M., & Boyes-Braem, P. (1976). Basic objects in natural categories. *Cognitive Psychology, 8,* 382–439.

Rumelhart, D., & McClelland, J. (1987). Learning the past tense of English verbs: Implicit rules or parallel distributed processing? In B. MacWhinney (Ed.), *Mechanisms of language acquisition* (pp. 195–248). Cambridge, MA: MIT Press.

Sanford, E. C. (1893). Notes on studies of the language of children. *Pedagogical Seminary, 1,* 257–260.

Slobin, D. I. (1966). The acquisition of Russian as a native language. In F. Smith & G. A. Miller (Eds.), *The genesis of language: A psycholinguistic approach* (pp. 129–148). Cambridge, MA: MIT Press.

Slobin, D. I. (1985). Crosslinguistic evidence for the language making capacity. In D. I. Slobin (Ed.), *The crosslinguistic study of language acquisition: Vol. 2. Theoretical issues* (pp. 1157–1256). Hillsdale, NJ: Erlbaum.

Soja, N. N. (1986). Color word acquisition: Conceptual or linguistic challenge? *Papers and Reports on Child Language Development, 25,* 104–113.

Tomasello, M. (1992). *Verbs and early grammatical development: A case study in cognitive linguistics.* New York: Cambridge University Press.

Tversky, B., & Hemenway, K. (1984). Objects, parts, and categories. *Journal of Experimental Psychology: General, 113,* 169–193.

Wolfe, H. K. (1890, July). On the color vocabulary of children. *Nebraska University Studies,* pp. 205–234.

Younger, B. A. (1990). Infants' detection of correlations among feature categories. *Child Development, 61,* 614–620.

Younger, B. A., & Cohen, L. B. (1985). How infants form categories. In G. H. Bower (Ed.), *The psychology of learning and motivation: Advances in research and theory* (Vol. 19, pp. 211–247). Orlando, FL: Academic Press.

Younger, B. A., & Cohen, L. B. (1986). Developmental change in infants' perception of correlations among attributes. *Child Development, 57,* 803–815.

# X. APPENDIX: TWO EXAMPLES OF DIARY RECORD CARDS

Explanation of symbols on Card 1:

*Category:* 003: "00" indicates the superordinate level category *animal.* "3" indicates the intermediate category *bird.*

*Word:* duck (ə dəʔ) : The adult form of Ari's word is "duck." The actual pronunciation used by Ari was "ə dəʔ".

(*FP*: There is no asterisk in the upper right-hand corner of the card because this is not the first production of "duck.")

*Referent:* mallard200: Referent dictionary code. The "2" indicates that the referent is a three-dimensional representation of a real mallard, in this case a stuffed animal. "00" indicates that the referent was the first three-dimensional representation of a mallard to be assigned a referent code.

*Level:* 3: basic

*Spont./elic.:* S: Ari's label was spontaneous (not elicited).

*Word/ref.:* 111: The first "11" indicates that Ari's word is appropriate for the referent. The last "1" indicates that Ari's productive vocabulary includes an appropriate label for this referent only at the basic level ("duck").

*Morpheme:* 11: The first "1" indicates that the word was of the form "one word (one free morpheme)," and that Ari pronounced it correctly (nondiminutive). The second "1" indicates that it is a singular form.

*Link:* 1: Ari did not label the referent with any other word during this interaction.

*Context:* M, A, X: "M" stands for mother. "A" stands for Ari. "X" stands for what Ari actually said, as indicated in the word code.

(*Response codes*: The response codes are divided by vertical lines into the three possible subinteractions. Ari did label the referent again during the response, so this response is divided into two subinteractions. The first consists of: M: "Do you want your duckie?" As M carries A closer to mantel, so A can reach mallard. The second consists of: A picks up mallard and says "ə dəʔʔ" (duck). Ari did not label the mallard again after this point; dashes ("-") are used to indicate that subinteraction C does not exist.)

*Subinteraction A:*

- *Response I*: AA1 16: The first "A" indicates that the adult agreed with Ari's label. The second "A" indicates that the adult repeated Ari's form of the word, allowing for minor pronunciation differences. The first "1" indicates that the adult did not use laughing intonation and did not hedge or qualify the response. "16" indicates that the adult did not request that Ari provide a new label for the referent and Ari did not provide a new label on his own initiative.

- *Response II*: 11E 53: Adult response did not include a new label for the referent. (These are the default codes for when no new label is provided; had a new label been used, these codes would have been used to describe the new label and the manner in which it was provided.)
- *Response III*: 5: Adult response did not include a new label, did not provide any critical attribute information and did not disagree with Ari's label. (Again, this is the default code; if a new label had been used, critical attribute information had been provided, or the adult had disagreed with Ari, this code would have been used to indicate his response to the adult's new label, the adult's provision of attribute information, or the adult's disagreement with his label.)

*Subinteraction B:*

- *Response I*: XME 16: The "X" indicates that no adult response to Ari's label was recorded. The "16" is the default code when no adult response was recorded.
- *Response II*: 11E 53: These are the default codes when no adult response was recorded.
- *Response III*: 5: This is the default code when no adult response was recorded.

*Response continued*: N: Indicates that the entire response consists of three or fewer subinteractions.

*Entry made by*: paper records: This entry is transcribed from the handwritten (paper) records that were used prior to audiotaping of diary entries.

Explanation of new symbols on Card 2:

*Category*: 001: "00" indicates the superordinate level category *animal*. "1" indicates the intermediate category *mammal* (nonhuman).

Word: hippopotamus (huppo): The adult form of Ari's word is "hippopotamus." The actual pronunciation used by Ari was "huppo."

Referent: rhinoceros607: Referent dictionary code. "6" indicates that the referent is a picture in a book. "07" indicates that the referent was the seventh picture of a rhinoceros in a book to be assigned a referent dictionary code.

*Spont./elic.*: E: Ari's label was elicited by an adult using the form "What's that?".

*Word/ref.*: 395: "3" indicates that the referent is not a hippopotamus and that a typical adult would know that it was not, but the referent nevertheless is very similar to a hippopotamus. "9" indicates that the next highest hierarchical level that includes both *hippopotamus* and *rhinoceros* is the

```
-----------------------------------------------------------------------
| PRODUCTION          category: 003              word: duck (ə də?)    |
|                                                                       |
| date: 12/23/83                level: 3              frequency: 1      |
|                               spont.elic.: S       word/ref.: 11X     |
| referent: Dakin mallard                            morpheme: 11       |
|           (mallard200)                             link: 1            |
|                                                                       |
| context:   M brings A downstairs to put on his outerwear.  A sees mallard |
|            on mantel and says X.                                      |
|                                                                       |
| response: M: "Do you want your duckie?" as M carries A closer to mantel, so|
|            A can reach mallard.  A picks up mallard and says "ə də?" (duck).|
|                                                                       |
| response I:    AA1 16   |  XME 16  |  -  |  N                         |
| response II:   11E 53   |  11E 53  |  -  |                            |
| response III:  5        |  5       |  -  |                            |
|                                                                       |
|                      entry made by: paper records      card #: DEC:79 |
| [Note: Age = 0;11.15]                                                 |
-----------------------------------------------------------------------
-----------------------------------------------------------------------
| PRODUCTION          category: 001              word: hippopotamus (huppo) |
|                                                                       |
| date: 10/21/84                level: 3              frequency: 1      |
|                               spont.elic.: E       word/ref.: 395     |
| referent: rhinoceros (Chubby                       morpheme: 11       |
|           Book of Zoo Animals)                     link: 1            |
|           (rhinoceros607)                                             |
|                                                                       |
| context:   M, F, and A looking at book again.  When they get to the   |
|            rhinoceros, F touches it and says "What is that Ari?"  A: X.|
|                                                                       |
| response:  F: You know what Ari?  That's a rhino.  Look, it has a point on |
|            its nose there and a point on its nose there (as F touches the |
|            two points).  And look.  The hippo has a smooth nose.  A round |
|            nose.  But the rhino has points (as F touches the points again.)|
|            This is a rhino.  A watches F carefully.  When F is done, A says|
|            "rhino."  F: Yeah, that's a rhino.  And this is a hippo (as F |
|            touches the hippo again).  A: Huppo (hippopotamus).  F: Yeah, |
|            that's a hippo.  (Note: The hippo is on the opposite page from |
|            the rhino in this book, so both are visible at the same time.) |
|                                                                       |
| response I:    DH1 16   |  -  |  -  |  N                              |
| response II:   221 12   |  -  |  -  |                                 |
| response III:  1        |  -  |  -  |                                 |
|                                                                       |
|                      entry made by: CBM              card #: 81A:149| |
| [Note: Age = 1;9.13]                                                  |
-----------------------------------------------------------------------
```

intermediate level (=mammal) and the two do not share a common subintermediate level. "5" indicates that Ari's productive vocabulary includes an appropriate label for this referent at the basic (*rhinoceros*) and superordinate (*animal*) levels.

*Context*: F: "F" stands for father.

*(Response codes*: Ari did not label the referent again during the response, so the response is coded as one subinteraction. The response codes are divided by vertical lines into the three possible subinteractions. Dashes ("-") are used to indicate that subinteractions B and C do not exist.)

*Response I*: DH1 16: "D" indicates that the adult disagreed with Ari's label. "H" indicates that the adult repeated Ari's label (using same/similar pronunciation), but only for a different referent (i.e., hippopotamus in book) than the referent labeled by Ari (i.e., rhinoceros in book).

*Response II*: 221 12: The first "2" indicates that the adult did use a new label (i.e., rhino) for the referent labeled by Ari, and that the new label was correct and at the basic level. The second "2" indicates that the adult's label is mutually exclusive, from an adult perspective, with Ari's label and the adult did not juxtapose the two labels (i.e., from an adult perspective, it is not correct to label a rhinoceros both "rhino" and "hippopotamus," and the adult did not use the format "hippo-rhino"). The first "1" indicates that the adult did not use laughing intonation and did not hedge or qualify the adult new label. The second "1" indicates that the adult both mentioned a critical form attribute (i.e., "point on its nose") and physically demonstrated that attribute (i.e., by pointing to the horns). The final "2" indicates that the adult used a visible contrast object (i.e., hippopotamus in book) in the adult response to Ari's label.

*Response III*: 1: Indicates that Ari indicated agreement with the adult new label by imitating it.

*Entry made by*: CBM: This entry was recorded by the first author, whose initials are CBM.

# AUTHOR INDEX

**A**

Abel, L., 81, *95*

Abramov, I., 44, 50, 51, 54, 56, 65, 67, 69, 71, 77, 78, 79, 81, 82, 90, *95*, *98*, *99*

Adams, C.W., 63, *95*

Aggleton, J.P., 275, *284*

Albert, P., 273, 283, *287*

Alberts, J.R., 251, *284*

Allen, D., 51, *100*

Allen, P., 128, 130, 132, *137*, *144*

Altman, J., 272, *285*

Alvarado, M., 272, *285*

Amsel, A., 253, 256, 266, *286*

Andersen, G.J., 155, *182*

Andrick, G.R., 336, *370*

Anglin, J.M., 294, 357, *370*

Anniko, M., 111, *137*

Apkarian, P.A., 50, 102

Arjmand, E., 106, *138*

Aronson, E., 152, *184*

Ashby, S., 188, *244*

Ashmead, D.H., 104, *138*

Aslin, R.N., 41, 43, 45, 69, 73, 81, 85, 86, *95*, *96*, *101*, 111, 113, 116, 123, 124, *138*, *143*, 149, 150, 151, 170, 172, 175–176, *182*, *183*

Asratyan, E.A., 277, *285*

Atkinson, J., 5, 6, 30, *34*, *35*, 40, 41, 45, 47, 51, 57, 59, 65, 67, 68, 85, 90, 91, 92, *96*, *97*, *102*, 149, 172, *182*

Aulbach-Kraus, K., 112, *140*

Ayling, L., 65, *96*

Azen, S., 188, *245*


**B**

Babkin, P.S., xix, *xl*

Bachevalier, J., 281, *285*

Baduini, C., 313, *372*

Bahill, A.T., 79, 81, *96*

Bahrick, L.E., 30, 33, *34*

Bai, D., 152, *182*

Baldwin, D.A., 346, *371*

Ball, A.K.R., 132, *140*

Ball, R.S., 200, *245*

Ballard, J.L., 189, *242*

Balsam, P.D., 275, 276, *285*

Banigan, R.L., 317, 318, *371*

Banks, M.S., 2, 5, 6, 9, 11, 14, 15, 28, 30, 33, *34*, *35*, *36*, 40, 41, 45, 47, 51, 57, 59, 61, 67, 68, 71, *96*, *100*, 102, 111, 118, 121, 128, 129, 136, *138*, 155, 156, *182*

Barclay, A., 200, *242*

Bargones, J.Y., 106, 127, 130, 131, *138*, *141*, *142*, *144*

Barlow, H.B., 54, *102*

Barnett, S.A., 253, *285*

Barrerra, M.E., 28, *36*

Barrett, M.D., 293, 305, 306, 307, 313, 317, 330, 331,, 363, 364, 370, *371*, *372*

Barrett, P., 216, *243*

Bartlett, E., 345, *371*

Bates, E., 293, 306, 351, 358, *371*

Bauer, J., 92, *98*

Bayer, S., 272, *285*

Bayley, N., 185, 188, 190, 193, 199, 212, 216, 218, 228, 229, *242*, *243*, *244*

Beck, E., 216, *244*

Beery, K.E., 229, *243*

Bekhterev, V.M., xciii, *xl*

Bell, R.Q., 28, *36*

Bench, J., 106n, 123, 124, *138*

Benigni, L., 306, 351, *371*

Bennett, A.G., 68, *96*

Bennett, F., 189, *243*

Bennett, P.J., 40, 47, 68, *96*

Berenthal, B., 30, *35*, 61, *96*, 152, *182*

Berg, K.M., 113, *138*

Berg, W.K., 123, 124, *138*

Berger, T.W., 272, *287*

Bernston, G.G., 248, *285*

Bernuth, H.V., 112, *140*

Berry, R.C., 112, 116, *139*

Bertrand, J., 341, 342, *373*

Beverley, K.I., 151, *184*

Bigelow, A., 31, *35*

Birch, E.E., 149, 172, 179, *182*, *183*, *184*

Birch, H.G., 112, *144*

Black, J.E., 43, *98*

Blakemore, C., 4, 5, 7, *35*, 49, *96*

Blass, E.M., 252, *288*

Bloom, L., 293, 306, *371*
Bobier, W.R., 65, *96*
Bobbitt, B., 216, *243*
Bodis-Wollner, I., 93, *96*
Bolles, R.C., 276, 277, 278, *285*
Boring, E.G., 177, *183*
Bornstein, M.H., 336, *371*
Borton, R., 108, *144*
Bouman, M.A., 53, *102*
Bour, L.J., *96*
Bouton, M.E., 275, 276, 277, 278, *285*
Bowlby, J., 28, *35*
Boyes-Braem, P., 314, 315, *374*
Boysen, S.T., 248, *285*
Braddick, O.J., 5, 6, 30, *34, 35*, 41, 42, 47, 51, 57, 65, 67, 68, 85, 90, 91, 92, *96, 97*, 149, 172, *182*
Braun, J.J., 284, *285*
Braunwald, S.R., 293, 294, *371*
Bredberg, G., 105, *138*
Bresson, F., 68, *97*
Bretherton, I., 306, 351, *371*
Brislin, R.W., 293, 294, *371*
Brix, J., 106, *141*
Bronshtein, A.I., 123, 124, *138*
Bronson, G., 77, *97*
Brookes, S., 305, 306, 307, 364, 370, *372*
Brookman, K.E., 67, *97*
Brooks, J., 30, *36*
Brooks-Gunn, J., 217, *244*
Brown, A.M., 47, *97*
Brown, E., 177, *184*
Brown, R., 347, 348, 349, 351, 358, 363, *371*
Brugge, J.F., 105, 112, 126, 131, 133, 136, *138, 140*
Brunner, R.L., 272, *285*
Bryan, T.E., 253, *286*
Bukatko, D., 315, 372
Bull, D., 104, 113, 122, 127, 138, *143, 144*
Buncie, R., 188, *244*
Burkard, R., 131, *139*
Burns, E.M., 130, 131, *138, 143*
Burton, G.J., 14, 18, *35*

**C**
Callaway, E., 216, *243*
Camaioni, L., 306, 351, *371*
Camenzuli, C., 50, 51, 56, 78, 82, *98, 99*
Campbell, B.A., 248, 252, 261, 282, 283, *285*, 288

Campbell, F.W., 4, 5, 21, 24, *35, 36*, 49, 58, *96, 101*
Campbell, H., 217, *244*
Canada, K., 325, *373*
Cannon, M.W., 7–8, 21, *35, 36*
Carew, M.B., 277, *285*
Carey, S., 315, 345, *371*
Carlier, E., 111, *138*
Carlson, C.R., 14, *35*
Carpenter, G.C., 56, *97*, 164, *182*
Carpenter, R.H.S., 4, *35*
Carter, E.A., 108, 116, 119, 120, 121, 125, 135, *142*
Castle, P., 149, *184*
Castro, C.A., 250, 275, *285*, 287
Cattell, P., 216, *243*
Cazden, C.B., 347, 349, 363, *371*
Chalke, F., 216, *243*
Chapman, K.L., 317, 331, *371*
Chasin, J., 306, 307, *371*
Cheatle, M.D., 253, 255, *285, 287*
Chesnokova, A.P., xxxiv, *xl*
Ciufreda, K.J., 63, *97, 101*
Clanton, C., 149, *184*
Clark, E.V., 316, 317, 364, *371, 372*
Clark, L.F., 128, *140*
Clark, M.R., 79, *96*
Clark, R., 293, *372*
Clarke, M., 50, *100*
Clifton, R.K., 104, *138*
Cohen, B., 87, *97*
Cohen, L.B., 61, *97*, 317, 326, *375*
Cohen, N.J., 250, *288*
Coles, R.B., 105, 111, *143*
Collewijn, H., 89, *97*
Condry, K., 163, 165, 166, 168, 169, 171, 172, 173, 174, *183, 184*
Constantine, N., 189, *243*
Constantine-Paton, M., 135, *143*
Cooper, K.K., 112, *144*
Cornsweet, T.N., 4, *35*
Corso, J.R., 122, *138*
Cotman, C.W., *286*
Coulter, X., 252, *285*
Coursin, D.B., 112, *139*
Crisafi, M.A., 315, *373*
Crowder, R.G., *285*
Crowell, J., 155, 156, *182*
Cruse, D.A., 336, *372*
Culee, C., 86, *101*
Currie, D.C., 71, *97*

**D**

Daehler, M.W., 315, *372*
Dale, P.S., 136, *138*
Dallos, P., 106, *138*, *145*
Dannemiller, J.L., 28, 34, *35*, 61, 97, 111, 118, 121, 128, 129, 136, *138*, 150, 151, 178, *183*
Darwin, C., xix, *xl*
Dashkovskaia, V.S., xix, *xl*
Davidson, L., 173, *184*
Davidson, M., 8, *35*
Davis, M., 284, *285*
Davis, S.M., 132n, *138*
Day, J., 172, *182*
Day, R.H., 68, *100*
Day, S.H., 65, *101*
Dayton, G.O., 86, *97*
de Bie, J., 50, 51, *97*, *98*
De Courten, C., 45, *98*
Dell'Osso, L.F., 81, *95*
Dempsey, J., 188, *243*
Denisova, M.P., xviii, *xl*
Dennett, D., 87, *97*
de Schonen, S., 68, *97*
De Valois, K.K., 47, 49, 58, *97*
De Valois, R.L., 47, 49, 58, *97*
Dittrichová, J., xxiv, xxx, xxxiii, *xl*, *xli*
Dobson, V., 44, 47, 49, 56, 68, 92 , 93, *95*, *97*, *102*, 149, 150, 164, *184*
Doglin, K.G., 127, 131, *143*
Dolan, T.R., 126–127, 128, 130, 131, 132, *137*, *138*, *144*
Domjan, M., 253, 256, 266, *285*, *286*
Donaldson, M., 136, *138*
Dougherty, J.W.D., 315, *372*
Dowling, K., 86, *100*, 149, *184*
Driver, M., 189, *242*
Dromi, E., 293, 294, 306, 309, 312, 313, 365, 369, *372*
Duckman, R., 65, 67, *95*
Dumais, S.T., 149, 172, *183*
Dunn, J.C., 251, *286*
Dunn, S., 152, *182*
Durlach, P.J., 276, 277, *287*
Dustin, R., 216, *244*

**E**

Earle, D.C., 59, *101*
Eckerman, C., 188, *243*
Egan, J., 115, *138*
Eggermont, J.J., 105, *138*

Ehret, G., 105, 111, 112, 113, *138*, *139*
Eichorn, D., 200, *244*
Eisele, W.A., 112, 116, *139*
Eisenberg, R.B., 103, 112, *139*, 178, *184*
Elliott, L.L., 113, *139*
Endman, M., 104, 113, 116, 127, *144*
Ertl, J., 216, *243*
Eskridge, J.B., 65, *99*
Evans, R., 58, *98*
Eysenck, H.J., 216, *243*

**F**

Fagan, J.F., 94, *97*
Fagen, J.W., 248, *287*
Falmagne, J.-C., 115, *139*
Fantz, R.L., 5, *35*, 50, *97*, 149, *183*
Fausti, S.A., 113, 122, *143*
Feeney, M.P., 116, 117, 122, 127, *142*, *144*
Feigin, J.A., 119n, *139*
Felberbaum, R.A., xviii, *xli*
Feldman, A.S., 121, *145*
Feldman, W., 228, *244*
Fang, J.-Z., 105, 131, 136, *140*
Fernandez, C., 111, *139*
Field, T., 188, *243*
Figurin, N.L., xviii, *xl*
Findlay, J.M., 69, 77, *101*, *102*, 170, *184*
Finocchio, D.V., 75, 91, *97*, *98*
Fiorentini, A., 6, *35*
Fisher, K., 30, *35*
Fitzhardinge, P., 188, *244*
Flavell, J.H., 136, *139*
Fledelius, J., 93, *97*
Fletcher, H., 127, *139*
Flock, H., 157n, *183*
Foley, J.M., 12, 13, 14, 21, *35*, *36*
Folsom, R.C., 119, 120, 122, 130, 131, *139*, *142*, *144*
Ford, G., 189, *243*
Fox, R., 149, 172, *183*
Francis, J.L., 68, *96*
Franks, J.R., 121, 125, *143*
Freedland, R.L., 34, *35*, 150, 151, 178, *183*
Freeman, R.D., 92, *100*
French, J., 67, 92, *96*
Frey, R.H., 113, 122, *143*
Frost, N., 217, *243*
Fuchs, A.F., 75, 91, *97*, *98*
Fujimoto, S., 105, *139*
Fulton, A.B., 92, *97*

**G**

Gaddy, J.R., 283, *285*
Galambos, R., 105, 119, *143*
Gale, H., 294, *372*
Gale, M.C., 294, *372*
Gallipeau, J., *182*
Gandelman, M.D., 284, *285*
Gandelman, P.M., 284, *285*
Gant, N.F., 200, *243*
Garcia, J., 253, *286*
Garey, L., 45, *98*
Garfinkle, J., 188, *245*
Garrud, P., 273, *287*
Gaskill, J.D., 4, *35*
Gates, G.R., 105, 111, *143*
Gayl, I.E., 59, *98*
Gelman, R., 121, *139*
Gemberling, G.A., 256, *286*
Gengel, R.W., 121, 122, *143*
Georgeson, M.A., 5, 8, 18, 23, *35*
Gerber, S.E., 117, *144*
Gheorghin, B., 69, 71, 77, *98*
Gibson, E.J., 157n, 181, *183*
Gibson, J.J., 57, 89, 95, *98*, 152, 157n, 177, *183*
Gillenwater, J.M., 114, 117, 132, *144*
Gillis, S., 306, *372*
Ginsburg, A.P., 2, 4, 5, 8, 21, 28, 33, *34*, *35*, *36*, 58, *98*
Gleitman, H., 159, 160n, 161, 162, 163, 178, *183*
Gleitman, J., 57, *99*
Gogel, W.C., 157, 158, 169, *183*
Goldberg, S., 217, *244*
Golinkoff, R.M., 313, 364, *372*
Gollin, E.S., 250, 281, *286*
Gonzalas, L., 22, *36*
Gopnik, A., 305, 351, *372*
Gordon, J., 44, 50, 54, *95*
Gorga, M.P., 119n, *139*
Gottlieb, G., 251, *286*
Graham, M., 177, *184*
Graham, N., 4, *36*, 47, 49, 53, *98*, *101*
Granrud, C., 169, 170, 177, 178, *183*, *184*
Grau, J.W., 276, 277, *287*
Gray, L., 105, 112, 135, *139*
Gray, W.D., 314, 315, *374*
Green, D.G., 4, 24, *35*
Green, D.M., 125, 136, *139*
Green, R.J., 275, 276, *286*
Greenough, W.T., 43, *98*

Gregg, B., 253, 266, *286*
Griffin, E.J., 112, *139*
Grill, H.J., 284, *286*
Gross, R., 189, *243*
Gross, S., 188, *243*
Groves, P., 248, *286*
Gruendel, J.M., 316, 331, *372*
Gubish, R.W., 4, *35*
Guidibaldi, J., 216, *244*
Guilford, J.P., 200, *243*
Gwiazda, J., 92, *98*, 149, 172, 179, *182*, *183*, *184*

**H**

Haaf, R.A., 28, *36*
Hackett, J.T., 105, *140*
Haegerstrom, G., 92, *100*
Haegerstrom-Portney, G., 93, *101*
Hainline, L., 44, 50, 51, 56, 65, 67, 69, 71, 75, 77, 78, 79, 81, 82, 83, 86, 90, *95*, *98*, *99*, *100*
Haith, M., 149, *183*
Hall, A., 93, *101*
Hall, W.G., 253, *286*
Halpin, C.F., 108, 116, 119, 120, 121, 124, 132, 135, *142*, *144*
Hamer, R., 51, *101*
Hansen, R.M., 56, 83, *101*
Harkins, S.W., 122, *142*
Harlow, H.F., 281, 282, *286*
Haroutunian, V., 261, *285*
Harp, S., 58, *98*
Harris, C.M., 77, 78, 82, 83, *95*, *98*, *99*
Harris, D.M., 106, *138*, *139*
Harris, J.D., 125, *139*
Harris, M., 305, 306, 307, 364, 370, *371*, *372*
Hart, S., 31, *36*
Hartmann, E.E., 6, 9, *35*
Hawkins, J.E., *139*
Hayabuchi, I., 105, *139*
Hayne, H., 248, *287*
Haynes, H., 45, 67, *99*
Heartwell, S., 200, *243*
Hecox, K., 119, 131, *139*
Held, R., 40, 41, 43, 45, 67, 90, 92, *98*, *99*, *100*, *102*, 149, 172, 179, *182*, *183*, *184*
Hemenway, K., 314, 328, *374*
Hemholtz, H. von, 152, *183*
Hendrickson, A., 44, 45, *95*, *99*, *102*
Hendrickson, D.E., 216, *243*
Henn, V., 87, *97*

Hess, R.F., 93, *99*
Hetzer, H., xviii, *xlii*
Hickey, T.L., 45, *99*
Hilding, D.A., 105, *142*
Hill, C.R., 272, *288*
Hind, J.E., 112, *141*
Hinojosa, R., 111, *139*
Hirsh, R., 272, 283, *286*
Hirsh-Pasek, K., 313, 364, *372*
Hlaváčková, V., *xlii*
Hochberg, I., 113, 125, *141*
Hodgman, J., 188, *245*
Hoffman, H., 256, *286*
Hoffman, K.P., 40, 41, 90, *99*, *102*
Hofsten, C. von, 149, 151, 159, 163, 165, 166, 168, 169, 170, 171, 172, 173, 174, 177, 178, 180, 181, *183*, *184*
Hogarty, P., 200, *244*
Holland, P.C., 272, *287*
Holway, A.F., 177, *183*
Honzik, M.P., 227, *243*
Hood, D.C., 121, 125, *143*
Houtgast, T., 129, *139*
Hoversten, G.H., 112, 117, *140*
Howard, I.P., 85, *99*
Howell, E.R., 4, 21, *35*, 93, *99*
Howland, B., 65, *99*
Howland, H.C., 65, 67, 92, *97*, *99*, *101*
Hunt, E., 217, *243*
Hunt, P.R., 275, *284*
Hunter, M.A., 112, *139*
Hutchinson, J., 307, 313, *372*
Hutt, C., 106, 112, *140*
Hutt, S.J., 106, 112, *140*
Huttenlocher, J., 305, 364, *372*
Huttenlocher, P., 45, *99*
Hyson, R.L., 106, *140*, 256, 259, 262, 269, *286*, *287*
Hyvarinen, L., 89, *102*

**I**

Igarashi, M., 91, *102*
Igarashi, Y., 105, *140*
Ingram, D., 351, 358, 364, *373*
Ingram, R.M., 65, *96*
Irvine, D.R.F., 127, 131, *141*
Irwin, O.C., xix, *xli*
Irwin, R.J., 128, 130, 132, *140*
Irzhanskaia, K.N., xviii, *xli*
Ishii, T., 105, *140*
Ivanov-Smolenskii, A.G., xviii, *xli*

**J**

Jackson, H., 105, *140*
Jackson, J.H., 283, *286*
Jackson, R.W., 69, *96*, 170n, *182*
Jamieson, D., 132, *144*
Janoš, O., xxiv, xxvi, xxx, xxxii, xxxiii, xxxiv, *xli*
Jansson, G., 177, 181, *183*
Jastak, J.K., 229, *243*
Jastak, S.R., 229, *243*
Javel, E., 104, 105, 112, 118, 126, 131, 133, 135, 136, *138*, *140*
Jaynes, J., 248, *285*
Jesteadt, W., 125, 136, *140*
Johanson, I.B., 253, *286*
Johansson, G., 177, 181, *183*
Johnson, C.A., 63, *95*
Johnson, D.M., 314, 315, *374*
Johnson, E.G., 336, *372*
Johnson, K.E., 293, 345, 347, *373*
Johnson, M.H., 34, *36*, 61, *100*
Johnstone, J.R., 4, 21, *35*
Jones, D., 305, 306, 307, 364, 370, *372*
Jones, M.H., 86, *97*
Jones, R., 65, *99*
Julesz, B., 4, *37*

**K**

Kaakinen, K., 65, *99*
Kaga, K., 119, *140*
Kagan, J., 28, *36*
Kaiser, A., 106, *141*
Kaltenbach, J.A., 119n, *143*
Kantrow, R.W., xix, *xli*
Kanzaki, J., 91, *102*
Kaplan, L.I., xxxiv, *xli*
Kaplan, P.S., 248, *286*
Kasatkin, N.I., xviii, xix, xxv, *xli*
Katz, D.R., 113, *139*
Kaufman, A., 216, *243*
Kaufman, L., 151, 169, *183*
Kaufman, F., 149, 151, 179, *183*
Kaufmann-Hayoz, R., 149, 151, 179, *183*
Kay, N., 132, *140*
Kaye, H., xix, *xli*
Keating, D., 216, *243*
Kellman, P.J., 40, 57, 62, *99*, 151, 159, 160, 161, 162, 163, 165, 166, 168, 169, 171, 172, 173, 174, 178, 180, 181, *183*, *184*
Kelly, D.H., 53, 54, 55, 56, 59, 72, *99*

Kemp, D.T., 130, *140*
Kendall-Tackett, K., 189, *243*
Kendler, H.H., 121, *140*
Kendler, T.S., 121, *140*
Kettner, R.E., 105, 131, 136, *140*
Kiang, N.Y.S., 128, *140*
Kiefer, S.W., 284, *285*
Kileny, P., 120, *140*
Kirsner, K., 251, *286*
Kristler, D.J., 128, 130, 132, *137, 144*
Kitchen, W., 189, *243*
Kittrel, E.M.W., 253, 266, *286*
Kitzes, L.M., 105, 112, 126, 131, 133, 136, *138*
Klein, A.J., 119, 120, *140*
Kleiner, K.A., 30, 34, *36*, 61, *100*
Klopfenstein, R.W., 14, *35*
Koch, E.G., 108, 116, 119, 120, 121, 124, 125, 135, *142*
Koch, J., xx, *xli*
Koelling, R.A., 253, *286*
Koenderink, J.J., 155, *184*
Koffler, S., 149, *184*
Kohen-Raz, R., 228, 229, *243*
Kolb, B., 273, *288*
Kopp, C.B., 196, *243*
Kopun, J.G., 119n, *139*
Kraemer, H., 189, *243*
Kraemer, P.J., 264, *288*
Krasinski, D., 200, *243*
Krasnogorskii, N.I., xvii, xviii, *xli*
Krasuskii, V.K., xxxiv, *xli*
Kraus, H.J., 112, *140*
Kremenitzer, J.P., 86, *100*, 149, *184*
Krinsky, S., 77, 83, 86, 98, *100*
Kriuchkova, A.P., xix, xxxiii, *xli*
Kruger, B., 118, 119n, *140*
Kruger, P.B., 63, *100*
Kucharski, D., 256, *286*
Kulikowski, J.J., 4, 8, *35, 36*
Kurman, B., 119n, *144*
Kurtzberg, D., 86, *100*, 149, *184*

**L**

La Bossiere, I., 44, *95*
Labouvie-Vief, G., 136, *140*
Landau, B., 336, *374*
Lasiter, P.S., 284, *285*
Laskey, R.E., 200, *243*
Latz, E., 82, *102*
Lavallee, A., 313, *372*
Lavigne-Rebillard, M., 105, *140, 142*

Lee, D.N., 152, 154, 155, 156, *184*
Legge, G.E., 12, 13, 14, 21, *35, 36*
Lemerise, E., 50, 51, 77, 78, 81, 82, 90, *95, 98, 99*
Lenard, H.G., 106, 112, *140*
Lenhardt, M.L., 122, *142*
Lenoir, M., 112, *141*
Leonard, L.B., 317, *371*
Leopold, W.F., 347, *372*
Leventhal, A., 123, *141*
Levi, D.M., 50, 90, *101, 102*
Levikova, A.M., xix, *xli*
Levine, M.W., 47, *100*
Levinson, J.Z., 4, *35*
Lewis, I., 189, *244*
Lewis, M., 30, *36*, 217, *244*
Lippe, W., 106, *141*
Lipsitt, L.P., xvii-xviii, xix, xx, *xli, xlii*, 123, *141*
Lissenden, J., 189, *243*
Lockman, J.J., 178, *184*
Lonardo, R., 315, *372*
London, R., 77, *100*
Long, L.M., 307, 312, *373*
Longuett-Higgins, H.C., 154, *184*
Loomis, J.M., 154, 155, 167, *184*
Lotmar, W., 68, *100*
Lowry, L.D., 127, 131, *143*
Loy, R., *286*
Lucariello, J., 305, 306, *374*
Lumer, G., 130, *145*
Lunneborg, C., 217, *243*
Lynch, G., *286*

**M**

MacWhinney, B., 358, *371*
Maier, J., 47, *97*
Maire, F., 121, *145*
Manley, G.A., 106, *141*
Mannle, S., 366-367, *372*
Manny, R.E., 71, *97*
Marean, G.D., 121, 127, 131, 132, 134, 135, *142, 144*
Markman, E.M., 307, 313, 317, 328, 364, *372, 373*
Marquis, D.P., xix, *xli*
Mattock, A., 177, *184*
Maurer, D., 28, 34, *36*, 61, 73, *100*
Maury, L., 68, *97*
Maxon, A.B., 113, 125, *141*
Mayer, M.I., 2, *36*
McCall, R., 200, *244*

McClelland, J.L., 359, *373, 374*
McCroskey, R.L., 132n, *138*
McDonald, M.A., 93, *102*
McDonald, R.J., 272, *288*
McGee, J.D., 104, 105, 118, 131, 135, *140*
McKenzie, B., 68, 97, *100*
McNaughton, B.L., 272, *286*
McNicol, D., *141*
McShane, J., 306, *373*
McWay, J., 200, *242*
Mead, S., 24, *36*
Medin, D.L., 317, *373*
Medina, A., 92, *100*
Merickel, M., 106, *143*
Meltzoff, A.N., 305, 351, *372*
Mervis, C.A., 297, 314, 315, 317, 331, 365, *373*
Mervis, C.B., 293, 305, 307, 312, 314, 315, 316, 317, 318, 325, 329, 330, 331, 332, 341, 342, 345, 347, 363, 364, 365, 367, *371, 372, 373, 374*
Mich, C., 188, *245*
Miller, J.F., 228, *244*, 316, *373*
Millodot, M., 63, 92, *100*
Mills, A.E., 347, *373*
Milroy, R., 128, *142*
Minkowski, H., xix, *xli*
Mishkin, M., 272, 281, 283, *285, 287*
Mitchell, D.E., 42, 43, 91, 92, *100*
Moar, K., 5, 6, *34*, 47, 51, 57, *96*, 149, *182*
Moffitt, A.R., 107, 123, 124, *141, 144*
Mohindra, I., 92, *98*
Mohn, G., 90, *102*
Molina, J.C., 256, 264, 265, *286, 288*
Molitor, C., 24, *36*
Moncur, J.P., 112, 117, *140*
Montie, J.E., 94, *97*
Moore, B.C.J., 129, *141*
Moore, D.R., 105, 121, 126, 127, 131, *141*
Moore, J.M., 104, 107, 108, 113, *141*
Moore, L., 56, *98*
Moore, M.E., 173, *184*
Morison, V., 59, *101*
Morris, R.G.M., 272, 273, *287*
Morrongiello, B.A., 104, 109, 113, 122, 127, 128, 132, *141, 143, 144*
Morse, R., 108, *144*
Morton, J., 34, *36*, 61, *100*
Moscovitch, M., 250, *288*
Movshon, J.A., 42, *100*
Moye, T.B., 262, 263, 265, 267, *287*
Muncey, J.P.J., 5, 7, *35*

Munson, J., 351, 358, 364, *373*
Muntjewerff, W.J., 106, 112, *140*
Murphy, B.J., 83, *100*
Murphy, G.L., 317, *373*
Myers, N.A., 367, *373*

**N**

Nachmias, J., 4, 12, 14, *36*
Nadel, L., 250, *287*
Naegele, J.R., 90, *100*
Nakayama, K., 50, *102*, 154, 155, 167, *184*
Neff, W.D., 112, *141*
Neisser, U., 44, *100*
Nelson, K., 293, 305, 306, 313, 364, 369, *373, 374*
Nelson, M.A., 8, 21, *36*
Nemanova, C.P., xix, *xli*
Neuwirth, S., 189, *244*
Nevis, S., 149, *183*
Newborg, J., 216, *244*
Niles, A., 22, *36*
Nimmo-Smith, I., 128, *142*
Norgren, R., 284, *286*
Norcia, M., 50, 51, 65, *100, 101*
Norton, S.J., 106, *141*
Novak, K.K., 189, *242*
Nozza, R.J., 104, 113, 127, *141*

**O**

Oakley, D.A., *287*
Ogawa, J., 64, *101*
Ogiba, Y., 107, *143*
O'Halloran, R., 163, 165, 166, 168, 169, 171, 172, 173, *183*
O'Keefe, J., 250, 273, *287*
O'Loughlin, B.J., 129, *141*
Olsho, L.W., 104, 108, 109, 111, 116, 119, 120, 121, 122, 124, 125, 127, 128, 129, 131, 134, 135, *141, 142, 143*
Orbeli, L.A., xviii, *xli*
Orel-Bixler, D., 93, *101*
Orr, W.B., 272, *287*
Ostrovskaia, I.M., xix, xxxiv, *xli*
Ownes, D.A., 63, *101*

**P**

Palefone, J.M., 253, *286*
Pankhurst, D.B., 107, 123, 124, *145*
Pape, K., 188, *244*
Papoušek, H., xix, xx, xxiv, xxx, xxxii, xxxiii, *xli, xlii*

Park, S., 336, *374*
Parks, T.N., 105, 126, *142*
Patterson, R.D., 128, *142*
Paylor, R., 273, 275, *285, 287*
Peiper, A., *xlii*
Peli, D.G., 13, *36*
Pelsma, J.R., 345, 366, *374*
Perris, E.E., 104, *138*
Peters, A.M., 293, 364, *374*
Petri, H.L., 272, 283, *287*
Petrova, E.P., 123, 124, *138*
Petry, S., 50, *95*
Petterson, L., 178, *184*
Piaget, J., 152, *184*, 326, *374*
Pick, A.D., 121, *142*
Pickles, J.O., 118, *142*
Pimm-Smith, E., 65, *96*
Pinker, S., 347, 358, 359, *374*
Piotrowski, L.N., 5, *36*, 58, *101*
Pirchio, M., 6, *35*
Pisoni, D.B., 113, 116, *143*
Pola, J., 63, *100*
Polikanina, R.I., xix, *xlii*
Prazdny, K., 154, *184*
Prechtl, H.F.R., xix, *xlii*
Preston, K.L., 75, 91, 93, *97, 98, 102*
Preyer, W., xix, *xlii*
Priest, M., 200, *243*
Prince, A., 347, 359, *374*
Probatova, L.J., xix, *xlii*
Proffitt, D.R., 61, *96*
Pujol, R., 105, 111, 112, 126, *138, 140, 141, 142*
Pulos, E., 81, *101*
Putaansuu, J., 178, 180, 181, *183*

**R**

Raphan, T., 87, *97*
Rappaport, B.Z., 113, 122, *143*
Ratliff, F., 49, *101*
Raviola, E., 92, *101*
Rawlick, L., 50, 51, *98*
Rawlins, J.N.P., 273, 275, *284, 287*
Ray, W.S., xviii, *xlii*
Rebillard, G., 127, 131, *142*
Regal, D., 108, *144*
Regan, D., 93, *101*, 151, *184*
Relkin, E.M., 119n, *143*
Rescorla, R.A., 252, 269, 275, 276, 277, *287*, 331, *374*
Rheingold, H.L., xvii, *xlii*

Rhodes, L., 190, 216, *244*
Rice, M.L., 336, 345, *374*
Rickard, L., 119, 120, *142, 144*
Rickards, A., 189, *243*
Ridley, R.M., 5, 7, *35*
Ripin, R., xviii, *xlii*
Roberts, J.O., 59, *98*
Robinson, D., 85, *101*
Robson, J.G., 4, *35*, 53, *101*
Rocca, P.T., 104, *141*
Rogers, B., 177, *184*
Romand, R., 104, 105, 111, 112, 113, *142*
Rosch, E., 314, 315, *374*
Rose, D.H., 59, 101, 283, *287*
Rose, M., 86, *97*
Rose, S., 188, *244*
Rosenblatt, J.S., 253, *286*
Rosenfeld, C.R., 200, *243*
Rosenthal, M.H., 261, *287*
Ross, R.T., 272, *287*
Rosser, J., 132, *140*
Rossiter, V.S., 122, *143*
Roucoux, A., 86, *101*
Roucoux, M., 86, *101*
Rovee-Collier, C., 248, *287*
Royden, S., 155, 156, *182*
Rozin, P., 250, 283, *287*
Rubel, E.W., 104, 105, 106, 112, 118, 126, 127, 131, *139, 140, 141, 142, 143*, 261, *287*
Ruben, R.J., 118, 119n, *140*
Rubin, H., 121, *145*
Rudy, J.W., 106, *140*, 248, 250, 251, 253, 254, 255, 256, 258, 259, 262, 263, 264, 265, 266, 267, 269, 271, 272, 273, 275, 277, 282, 283, *285, 286, 287, 288, 289*
Ruff, H.A., 62, *101*
Rumelhart, D.E., 359, *373, 374*
Rumpf, D., 63, *97*
Ryals, B.M., 106, *143*
Ryan, E.B., 189, *244*
Ryan, M., 229, *243*

**S**

Sakai, R., 124, *142*
Sakurai, S., 91, *102*
Salapatek, P., 5, 6, *34*, 45, 47, 51, 57, 59, 73, 74, 81, *96, 100*, 101
Sananes, C., 283, *285*
Sanes, D.H., 104, 106, 118, 126, 131, 136, *143*
Sanford, E.C., 345, *374*

Sansbury, R., 12, 14, *36*
Sattler, J.W., 229, *244*
Saunders, J.C., 105, 111, 119n, 127, 131, *143*
Sayles, N., 92, *99*
Scanlon, M., 86, *100*
Schacter, D.L., 250, *288*
Schade, A., 128, 130, *140*
Schadler, M., 281, *286*
Schaeffel, F., 92, *101*
Schaefer, E.W.P., 216, *243*
Schallert, T., 283, *288*
Schecter, M.A., 113, 122, *143*
Scheffé, H., xxv, *xlii*
Scheiman, M., 92, *98*
Schneider, B.A., 104, 108, 109, 113, 116, 117, 127, 128, 134, *138, 143, 144*
Schnerson, A., 112, *141, 143*
Schoon, C., 124, *142, 143*
Schor, S.M., 63, 64, 90, *101*
Schulman-Galambos, C., 105, 119, *143*
Schwartz, A.L., 276, *285*
Schwartz, F., 58, *102*
Sebris, S.L., 92, 93, 97, *102*
Sedláček, J., xviii, *xlii*
Seitz, V., 217, *245*
Sekuler, R., 58, *98*
Shallice, T., 251, *288*
Shatz, C.J., 40, 41, *102*
Shea, S.L., 86, *101*, 149, 150, 151, 172, *182, 183*
Sheena, D., 75, *102*
Shefner, J.M., 47, *100*
Shepard, P.A., 94, *97*
Sherry, D.F., 250, *288*
Shimojo, S., 149, *184*
Shipley, T.F., 159, *184*
Short, K.R., 159, 160, *184*
Shriner, T.H., 112, 116, *139*
Shuman, H., 188, *243*
Siegel, L.S., 227, 228, 229, 234, 235, *244*
Simonson, J., 81, *101*
Sims, S.L., 136, *140*
Singer, L.T., 94, *97*
Sinnott, J.M., 104, 113, 116, 123, 124, *143*
Siqueland, E.R., xx, *xlii*
Skavenski, A.A., 56, 83, *101*
Slater, A.M., 59, 69, 77, *101, 102*, 170, 177, *184*
Sloan, J.A., 2, *37*
Slobin, D.I., 307, 347, 364, *374*

Smiley, P., 305, 364, *372*
Smith, H., 50, *95*
Smith, M.C., 113, *138*
Smith, O.W., 157n, *183*
Smoller, D.E., 264, *288*
Smotherman, W.P., 253, *288*
Snodderly, M., *102*
Soja, N.N., 336, *374*
Soares, J., 151, 159, *184*
Sontag, L.W., xviii, *xlii*
Souther, A., 2, 28, *36*
Sparling, J., 189, *244*
Spear, N.E., 248, 252, 256, 261, 264, 265, 282, *285, 286, 288*
Spelke, E., 40, 57, 62, *99, 102*, 159, 160, 161, 162, 163, 178, *183, 184*
Spelt, D.K., xviii, *xlii*
Spence, K.W., 269, 270, *288*
Sperduto, V., 124, *142*
Spetner, N.B., 61, *96*, 116, 119, 120, 121, 129, 132, 135, *142, 143, 144*
Spinelli, D., 6, *35*
Squire, L.R., 250, *288*
Stadler-Morris, S., 273, 283, *287*
Stanley, W.C., xvii, *xlii*
Stanton, M.E., 275, 276, *286*
Stark, L., 79, 81, *96*
Stechler, G., 82, *102*
Steele, B., 86, *97*
Steinman, R.M., 56, 83, *101*
Stelmachowicz, P.G., 119n, *139*
Stephens, B.R., 6, 9, 11, 15, 22, 24, 28, 31, *34, 35, 36*, 61, *97*
Sternberg, R., 216, *244*
Stevens, S.S., *139*
Stillman, J.A., 128, 130, 132, *140*
Stock, J., 216, *244*
Stockard, J.J., 122, *143*
Stott, L.H., 200, *245*
Stratton, P.M., 123, *143*
Strickland, E.A., 130, *143*
Stromeyer, C.F., 4, *37*
Stshelovanov, N.M., xviii, *xl*
Stucki, M., 149, 151, 179, *183*
Sturm, L., 188, *243*
Sullivan, G.D., 5, 8, 18, 23, *35*
Sutherland, R.J., 250, 269, 271, 272, 273, 283, *288*
Suzuki, T., 107, *143*
Švenlová, M., *xlii*
Svinicki, J., 216, *244*

Swets, J.A., 136, *139*
Switkes, E., 2, *37*

**T**

Tager-Flusberg, H., 336, *370*
Takahashi, M., 91, *102*
Tanaka, Y., 119, *140*
Tauber, E.S., 149, *184*
Teas, D.C., 126–127, 131, *138*
Teberg, A., 188, *245*
Teller, D.Y., 5, *37*, 49, 50, 53, 68, 73, 93, 97, *102*, 108, *144*
Teicher, M.H., 252, *286*, *288*
Teitelbaum, P., 283, *288*
Teuber, H.L., 250, *288*
Thomas, E.C., 128, *140*
Thomas, M.A., 62, *96*
Thomas, N., 22, *36*
Thompson, G., 107, 108, *141*
Thompson, M., 107, 108, *141*
Thompson, R., 248, *286*
Thorn, F., 58, 92, *98*, *102*
Thorpe, L.A., 104, 109, 113, 122, 127, 134, *143*, *144*
Tietz, J.D., 158, *183*
Tischler, M.D., 284, *285*
Tomasello, M., 366–367, 369, *372*, *374*
Tomie, A., 275, *285*
Tonndorf, J., 119n, *144*
Traccis, S., 81, *95*
Trehub, S.E., 104, 108, 109, 113, 116, 117, 127, 128, 132, *138*, *141*, *143*, *144*
Tronick, E., 149, *184*
Troost, B.T., 81, *95*
Troshikhin, V.A., xxxiii, *xlii*
Tsukagoshi, K., 336, *374*
Tubis, A., 130, *143*
Tversky, B., 314, 328, *374*
Tulving, E., 250, *289*
Turkel, J., 50, 78, 81, 90, *95*, *98*
Turkewitz, G., 112, *144*
Turpin, R., 124, *142*
Tyler, C.W., 50, 51, *100*, *101*, *102*
Tyson, J.E., 189, 200, *243*

**U**

Ukhtomskii, A.A., xviii, *xlii*

**V**

VandeWalle, G., 173, 174, *184*
van Hof-van Duin, J., 90, *102*
Van Nes, F.L., 53, *102*

Van Sluyters, R.C., 40, 41, 42, *100*, *102*
Vaughan, H.G., 86, *100*, 149, *184*
Vogt, M.B., 253, 254, 255, 256, 258, 266, *289*
Voipio, H., 89, *102*
Volkmann, F.C., 56, *102*, 149, 150, 164, *184*
Volokhov, A.A., xviii, xxxiv, *xlii*, *xliii*
Volterra, V., 306, 351, *371*
von Bernuth, H., 106, 112, *140*

**W**

Wachtel, G.F., 317, 328, *373*
Wagner, A.R., 269, 275, *287*, *288*
Wallace, C.S., 43, *98*
Wallace, I., 188, *244*
Wallace, R.F., xviii, *xlii*
Wallach, H., 170, 173, *184*
Walls, G.L., 73, *102*
Walsh, E.J., 104, 105, 118, 131, 135, *140*
Walton, J.P., 126–127, 131, *138*
Warren, R., 155, *184*
Watanabe, T., 128, *140*
Watson, C.S., 121, 122, 125, 136, *143*
Watson, J.S., 30, 33, *34*
Wattam-Bell, J.R., 30, *35*, 172, *182*
Weber, D.L., 128, *142*
Wechsler, D., 229, *245*
Wedenskii, N.E., xviii, *xliii*
Weir, C., 112, 116, *144*
Wenger, M.A., xix, *xliii*
Werner, L.A., 114, 116, 117, 120, 121, 130, 132, 135, *144*
Werner, J.S., 59, *98*
Werner, J.W., 248, *286*
Whishaw, I., 273, 283, *288*
White, B.L., 45, 67, *99*, 149, *184*
Whitehead, M.C., 105, *143*
Wick, B.C., 77, *100*
Wickelgren, W.A., 272, 283, *289*
Wier, C.C., 125, *144*
Wiesel, T., 92, *101*
Wightman, F., 128, 130, 132, *137*, *144*
Willott, J.F., 112, *143*
Wilson, H.R., 14, *37*, 47, *102*
Wilson, W., 104, 113, 117, 127, *141*, *144*
Wingert, W., 188, *245*
Winterson, B.J., 56, 83, *101*
Wood, I., 64, *101*
Woodbury, C.B., 269, *289*
Woodhouse, J.M., 54, *102*
Wolfe, H.K., 345, *374*
Woo-Sam, J., *245*
Wormith, S.J., 107, 123, 124, *145*

Wrek, L., *244*
Wu, P., 188, *245*
Wynne, M.K., 119, 130, 131, *139*

## Y

Yamamoto, K., 105, *139*
Yancey, C., 106, *145*
Yates, G.K., 125, *145*
Yonas, A., 169, 178, *184*
Yoneshige, Y., 113, *145*
Yoshizuka, M., 105, *139*
Young, L.R., 75, *102*

Younger, B.A., 317, 326 , *375*
Yow, B., 190, *244*
Yuodelis, C., 44, 45, 99, *102*

## Z

Zadnik, K., 65, *101*
Zigler, E., 217, *245*
Zimmerman, I., *245*
Zuckerman, C., 170, *184*
Zurek, P., 130, *145*
Zwicker, E., 130, *145*
Zwislocki, J., 121, 134, *145*

# SUBJECT INDEX

## A

Absolute auditory sensitivity, 104
  audibility curve, 111
  development of, 111–112
    evoked potential measures, 119
    in human neonates, 112
    in infants, 112–113
    in nonhuman vertebrates, 112
Accommodation, 44, 62–63, 170
  measures of, 64–67
    photo refraction, 65
    refractive error, 64–65
    retinoscopy, 64, 65
    studies of, 67–68, 69–71
Accretion/deletion, 151
Amodal attributes, 264, 268
Associative
  learning, 252, 265–267
  systems
    configural, 268–278
    elemental, 251–267
Auditory brainstem response (ABR), 118–121
Auditory nervous system development, 105
  frequency resolution, 104
  in humans, 105
  in nonhuman species, 105
  late aspects of, 105
  phases of, 105
  response thresholds, 105
  temporal resolution, 104
  tonotopic map, 106
Auditory stimuli, 256–262

## B

Basic-level categories, 315, 316–317; see also
  Child-basic categories
  form-function correlations, 315, 316–317
Batelle Development Inventory, 216
Bayley Scales of Infant Development (BSID), 188ff, 199ff
  mental, see Mental Developmental Indices

motor, see Psychomotor Developmental
  Indices
Beery Developmental Test of Visual-Motor
  Integration, 229, 233–234
Behavioral state, 30

## C

Case study methodology, 293
Catell Infant Intelligence Scale, 216
Child-basic categories
  early period of evolution, 323–325
  late period of evolution, 325
  relationship to adult-basic categories, 316–317, 320
  simultaneous assignment of category members, 317–318, 328
  strategies for evolution of, 317
Coding of lexical acquisition, 298–305, 332
  color terms, 337–338
  plural morphemes, 348–349
Cognitive functioning, 227
Color terms
  factors relevant to acquisition, 339–340
  nonlinguistic information, 340
  relation to subordinate object name acquisition, 337, 342–344
    color-based, 345–346
    social-situational context, 336–337, 339–340
Comparative methodology, 250
Competence vs. performance, 136
Comprehension, 303, 318–320
  measurement of initial extension of child-basic categories, 319–320
Conceptual abilities, 229
Configural
  associative system, 268–278
  representational system, 269
Connectionist models, 359
Contextual factors
  individual differences, 365
  social-situational context for introducing color terms, 336–337

Contrast
  apparent, 7–11
  -based models, 3–4
  constancy, 5, 9–11
  definition, 3
  discrimination, 12–18
  matching, 7
  response function, 9
  sensitivity function, 2, 19–20, 47, 62, 93
  threshold, 4–5
Convergence, 44, 170, 175–176; *see also*
  Vergence
Corrected birthday, 189, 190
Cronbach's Alpha, 201, 219
Cross-modal transfer, 264–265
Cycloplegia, 64–65

**D**

Declarative vs. procedural distinction, 250
Diary method
  anecdotal, 294, 360
  cross-comparison of diary records, 314
  database management, 304; *see also* Coding
    of lexical acquisition
  other uses of, 368–369
  systematic, *see* Systematic diary method
Difference limen
  for frequency (FDL), 124–125
  for intensity (IDL), 123–124
Differential sensitivity, 123–125
Disambiguation function, 276–278
Discontinuous-continuity, 213
Dissociation, 250–251, 255
Dual process theory, 248

**E**

Emmetropia (emmetropization), 62, 92–93
Eye-hand coordination, 228, 229, 231, 232
Eye movements
  control of, 56, 71–72
  fixation, 44, 82–85
  optokinetic nystagmus (OKN), 44, 56,
    87–91
  saccades, 44, 78–82
  smooth pursuit, 44, 85–87
  vestibulo-ocular reflex (VOR), 44, 56, 91
Eye movement recording, 73–78
  calibration, 77–78
  corneal reflection, 75–78
  electro-oculogram (EOG), 74–75

**F**

Face perception, 2, 27–33, 58–61
Facilitation, 275
  effect, *see* Pedastal effect
Factor analysis, 222–224
Fine motor
  abilities, 228
  coordination, 228
  development, 228, 236
  factor, 223
Fourier's theorum, 3
  spectrum, 58–59
Frequency discrimination, 124–125
Frequency resolution, 125–131
  auditory filter, 127
  critical band, 127
  development of in nonhumans, 126
  masking, 127–131; *see also* Masking
  psychophysical tuning curves, 128
  otoacoustic emission, 130
Frequency selectivity, *see* Frequency
  resolution

**G**

Gibsonian theory, 61, 67
Gross motor ability, 228
Group-design method
  comparison with systematic diary method,
    363–364
Gustatory stimuli, 253–256

**H**

Habituation, 107, 178, 217, 248, 261
Hierarchical subsystems of behavior, 248
Hippocampal formation, 271–272
Hirschberg ratio, 65
Home visit method, 357–360

**I**

Imitation–comprehension, 229, 235
Individual differences, 365
Infant examiners, training of, 190
Infant Health and Development Program, 189
Information processing model, 217
Intensity discrimination, *see* Differential
  sensitivity

**J**

Jackson, Hughlings, 283
Jacksonian perspective, 283–284

**K**
Kohen-Raz scales, 228–237

**L**
Language
  comprehension, 228, 229
  imitation, 228, 229
  scores, 228, 232
Learning tasks
  conditional delayed alternation, 275
  place learning, 272–273
  position habit, 275
  transverse patterning, 272
Lexical acquisition, *see* Lexical development
Lexical conventionality, 329
Lexical development
  complexities in, 293, 367–368
  context-bound words, 293, 306
  extensions of early words, 308–311,
    314–319, 320–325
  methodological concerns, 293
  normally developing vs. Down syndrome
    children, 316, 318
  referential basis for early words, 306, 308
  role of maternal input, 306–307, 315
  role of nonlinguistic information, 340
  situationally-based words, 306
Lexical principles, *see* Operating principles
Linear systems analysis, 2, 47
Linguistic input
  referentially ambiguous, 311
  referentially clear, 308
Low birthweight infants, 188, 189, 200, 228

**M**
Manipulation, 229, 231
Masking
  distraction, 130–131
  excess, 131
  forward, 134
  susceptibility to, 128
Mental Developmental Indices (MDI), 188,
    189, 191–193, 201, 210–211, 228
Mental speed, 216
  relationship to ability, 216–217
  relationship to age, 217
  relationship to performance, 216; *see also*
    Speed of performance
Missing fundamental illusion, 21–23
Modality-specific attributes, 264, 268

Morphology
  models of acquisition, 359–360
  nature of lexical entries, 359–360
  onset relative to onset of syntax, 349–351,
    359–360
Motion
  attention to, 149
  contingent, 179–180
  in depth, 151
  parallax, 157, 177, 178
  self-produced (observer), 44, 152–154, 155
  sensitivity to, 149–151, 179–180
  of stimulus (object), 56–57, 149–151,
    152–154
Motor skills
  fine, 228
  gross, 228
  perceptual, 228
Multiple memory systems, 250
Myopia, 24–27

**N**
Negative patterning, 269
Negative transfer, 261
Neonate learning, 252–253
Neophobia, 256
Nonsensory contributions to auditory
  responses, 109–111, 121, 124, 132

**O**
Object-observer motion paradigm, 163
Observer-based psychoacoustic procedure,
  108–109
Oddity problem, 281
Olfactory system, 251, 252–253
Operating principles, 307
  Authority, 328–330
  Form-Function, 315, 316, 326
  Initial Category Evolution, 326–328
  Mutual Exclusivity, 317
  Object Category as Referent, 307, 312
  Situation Category as Referent, 312, 313
Optic flow, 154–156
  limitations of, 155–156
Oral Cloze, 229, 233
Organism X task analysis, 250
Orientation, 3
Overextension, 297
  comprehension, 320
  factors contributing to estimates of, 331

measurement of initial extension of child-basic categories, 314–316
production, 319, 320–322
rates (proportion of words overextended), 330–331, 332–336
relationship of patterns of predictions for child-basic categories, 316, 335
Overregularization, 347, 354
back formation, 355
double marking irregular nouns, 355–356
irregular nouns treated as regular, 356
mass nouns, 356
regular marking 0 morpheme nouns, 355

**P**
Pattern
detection, 3–7
preference, 10–11
recognition, 14
Pavlovian conditioning procedures, 252, 256, 275
trace conditioning, 265
Pedestal effect, 12
Perception
of depth, 169, 173, 177–181
of distance, 156–158, 169–174
of illusions of motion, 158
of size, 177
of stability, 163, 169
Perceptual motor skills, 228
Phase, 3
sensitivity, 30
Pivot distance, 158, 169
Play sessions
audiotaped, 296–297, 304
videotaped, 296, 304
Plural morpheme, 346–360
errors, 347–348, 355–356; *see also* Overregularization
relation to onset of syntax, 349–351, 359–360
relation to quantifier use, 351, 354–355
stages of acquisition, 347, 351–355
and use of other morphemes, 349, 351
Position constancy, 158
Power law, 12
Predictive validity, 228
Preferential looking, 6, 15, 176, 178
forced choice, 50–53, 73, 108

Premature infants, *see* Low birthweight infants
Psychoacoustic development, *see* Auditory nervous system development; Psychophysical methods
Psychomotor Developmental Indices (PDI), 189, 193, 201, 210–211, 228
Psychophysical methods, 106–111
limitations to, 107
p(A), 115–116

**R**
Red-eye, 65
Reliability analysis, 218–222
Retina, 44–47
fovea, 44–45, 78
Rigidity, 154–155
ROC curve, 115

**S**
Self-motion, *see* Motion, self-produced (observer)
Sensory systems
auditory, 256–262
gustatory, 253–256
olfactory, 251, 252–253
taste, 253–256
visual, 262–263
Shearing, 155
Short-term memory, 265–267
Spatial frequency
channels, 5
definition, 3
masking, 4
Spatial vision
acuity, 42, 47, 54, 67–68
contrast sensitivity function (CSF), 2, 19–20, 47, 62, 93
face perception, 2, 27, 33, 58–61
linear systems (Fourier) analysis, 2, 47
spatiotemporal interactions, 54–58
Speed of performance, 216–218, 224
Speeded items, 210, 217–218, 224
Statistical Package for the Social Sciences (SSPSx), 202, 218–219
Stimulus coding, 264–265
Subordinate object categories
relation to acquisition of color terms, 337, 342–344, 345–346
Supression ratio, 262

Systematic diary method
  advantages, 360–364
  comparison with group design, 363–364
  contributions of, 364–368
  cross-comparison of diary records, 314
  data reduction and coding, 298–305, 332;
    *see also* Coding of lexical
    acquisition
  event sampling, 294, 361
  importance of contextual information, 362
  methodology, 295–296
  quasi-experimental probes, 296, 362–363

**T**

Taste aversion, 253–256, 267
Teller Acuity Cards, 93
Temporal constraints, 265–267
Temporal resolution
  development of, 104
    in children, 132
    in infants, 133
    forward masking, 134
    gap detection, 132
Ternary classification, 250
Thresholds
  vs. preferences, 151
  velocity, 150, 178
Timed
  items, 219
  series, 220
Training infant examiners, 190
Transducer, 13
Transverse-patterning, 269, 270, 280–281

**U**

Underextension, 335–336
  and comprehension, 303, 320

**V**

Vergence, 63–71
  measures of, 64–67
  studies of, 69–71
Visual assessment methods
  eye movement voting (EMV), 50–53
  forced-choice preferential looking (FPL),
    50–53, 73, 108
  visual evoked potentials (VEP), 50–53
    sweep-VEP, 50
Visual attention tasks, 217
Visual kinesthesis, 154
Visual plasticity, 43
Visual problems
  amblyopia, 43, 92, 93
  astigmation, 43, 92
  hyperopia, 43, 62
  myopia, 24–27, 43, 62–63
  strabismus, 43
Visual-proprioceptive sensitivity, 32
Visual reinforcement audiometry, 107–108,
    109
  limitation of, 108
Visual stimuli, 262–263
Vocalization-social, 229, 235

**W**

Weber fraction, 12, 18
Wechsler Intelligence Scales for Children—
    Revised, 229, 232
  block design, 229, 230
  vocabulary, 229
Wide Range Achievement Test, 229, 231
  arithmetic scores, 229
  reading scores, 229